THE O'LEARY SERIES

Microsoft® PowerPoint 2013: A Case Approach

Timothy J. O'Leary
Professor Emeritus,
Arizona State University

Linda I. O'Leary

McGraw-Hill Irwin

THE O'LEARY SERIES MICROSOFT® OFFICE POWERPOINT 2013: A CASE APPROACH
Published by McGraw-Hill/Irwin, a business unit of The McGraw-Hill Companies, Inc., 1221 Avenue of the Americas, New York, NY, 10020.

This book is printed on acid-free paper.

1 2 3 4 5 6 7 8 9 0 RMN/RMN 1 0 9 8 7 6 5 4 3

ISBN 978-0-07-740024-8
MHID 0-07-740024-0

Senior Vice President, Products & Markets: *Kurt L. Strand*
Vice President, Content Production & Technology Services: *Kimberly Meriwether David*
Director: *Scott Davidson*
Senior Brand Manager: *Wyatt Morris*
Executive Director of Development: *Ann Torbert*
Development Editor II: *Alaina G. Tucker*
Digital Development Editor: *Kevin White*
Marketing Manager: *Tiffany Russell*
Project Manager: *Marlena Pechan*
Senior Buyer: *Michael R. McCormick*
Designer: *Jana Singer*
Senior Content Licensing Specialist: *Jeremy Cheshareck*
Media Project Manager: *Brent dela Cruz*
Media Project Manager: *Cathy L. Tepper*
Typeface: *11/13 Times LT Std Roman*
Compositor: *Laserwords Private Limited*
Printer: *R. R. Donnelley*

All credits appearing at the end of the book are considered to be an extension of the copyright page.

Library of Congress Cataloging-in-Publication Data

O'Leary, Timothy J., 1947-
Microsoft Office PowerPoint 2013: a case approach / Timothy J. O'Leary, Professor Emeritus, Arizona State University ; Linda I. O'Leary.
pages cm.—(The O'Leary Series)
Includes index.
ISBN-13: 978-0-07-740024-8 (acid-free paper)
ISBN-10: 0-07-740024-0 (acid-free paper)
1. Presentation graphics software. 2. Microsoft PowerPoint (Computer file) I. O'Leary, Linda I. II. Title.
P93.52.O44 2014
005.5'8—dc23

2013004393

LAB 2 MODIFYING AND REFINING A PRESENTATION *PP2.1*

WORKING TOGETHER: COPYING, EMBEDDING, AND LINKING BETWEEN APPLICATIONS *PPWT.1*

Acknowledgments

We would like to extend our thanks to the instructors who took time out of their busy schedules to provide us with the feedback necessary to develop the 2013 edition of this text. The following professors offered valuable suggestions on revising the text:

Anne Acker
Jacksonville University

Jack Alanen
California State University–Northridge

Ken Araujo
Francis Marion University

Tahir Aziz
J. Sargeant Reynolds Community College

Lois Blais
Walters State Community College

Bob Clary
Patrick Henry Community College

Robert Doyle
Dona Ana Community College

Michael Dunklebarger
Alamance Community College

Jeffrey Finch
Kanawha Valley Community & Technology College

Kimberly Fish
Butler County Community College

Bob Forward
Texarkana College

Terry Griffin
Midwestern State University

Dexter Harlee
York Technical College

Tina Johnson
Midwestern State University

Dee Joseph
San Antonio College

Philip Kim
Walsh University

Ben Martz
Northern Kentucky University

Theresa McDonald
Texarkana College

David McNair
Jefferson College

Barb Norstrom
Kaskaskia College

Terry Rooker
Germanna Community College

Victor Suich
Walters State Community College

Lakeisha Vance
Alamance Community College

Barbara Wells
Central Carolina Technical College

Jensen Zhao
Ball State University

We would like to thank those who took the time to help us develop the manuscript and ensure accuracy through painstaking edits: Barbara Norstrom of Kaskaskia College, Robert Doyle of Dona Ana Community College, Candice Spangler of Columbus State Community College, and Kate Scalzi.

Finally, we would like to thank team members from McGraw-Hill, whose renewed commitment, direction, and support have infused the team with the excitement of a new project. Leading the team from McGraw-Hill are Wyatt Morris, Senior Brand Manager; Tiffany Russell, Marketing Manager; and Alaina Tucker, Developmental Editor III.

The production staff is headed by Marlena Pechan, Project Manager, whose planning and attention to detail have made it possible for us to successfully meet a very challenging schedule; Jana Singer, Designer; Michael McCormick, Senior Buyer; Kevin White, Digital Developmental Editor; Jeremy Cheshareck, Senior Content Licensing Specialist; Betsy Blumenthal and Chet Gottfried, copy editors; Sharon O'Donnell and Peter DeLissovoy; proofreaders—team members on whom we can depend to do a great job.

Preface

The 20th century brought us the dawn of the digital information age and unprecedented changes in information technology. There is no indication that this rapid rate of change will be slowing—it may even be increasing. As we begin the 21st century, computer literacy is undoubtedly becoming a prerequisite in whatever career you choose.

The goal of the O'Leary Series is to provide you with the necessary skills to efficiently use these applications. Equally important is the goal to provide a foundation for students to readily and easily learn to use future versions of this software. This series accomplishes this by providing detailed step-by-step instructions combined with careful selection and presentation of essential concepts.

Times are changing, technology is changing, and this text is changing too. As students of today, you are different from those of yesterday. You put much effort toward the things that interest you and the things that are relevant to you. Your efforts directed at learning application programs and exploring the web seem, at times, limitless.

On the other hand, it's easy to be shortsighted, thinking that learning the skills to use the application is the only objective. The mission of the series is to build upon and extend this interest by not only teaching the specific application skills but by introducing the concepts that are common to all applications, providing students with the confidence, knowledge, and ability to easily learn the next generation of applications.

Instructor's Resource Center

The online **Instructor's Resource Center** contains access to a Computerized Test Bank, an Instructor's Manual, Solutions, and PowerPoint Presentation Slides. Features of the Instructor's Resource are described below.

- **Instructor's Manual** The Instructor's Manual, authored by the primary contributor, contains lab objectives, concepts, outlines, lecture notes, and command summaries. Also included are answers to all end-of-chapter material, tips for covering difficult materials, additional exercises, and a schedule showing how much time is required to cover text material.
- **Computerized Test Bank** The test bank, authored by the primary contributor, contains hundreds of multiple choice, true/false, and discussion questions. Each question will be accompanied by the correct answer, the level of learning difficulty, and corresponding page references. Our flexible EZ Test software allows you to easily generate custom exams.
- **PowerPoint Presentation Slides** The presentation slides, authored by the primary contributor, include lab objectives, concepts, outlines, text figures, and speaker's notes. Also included are bullets to illustrate key terms and FAQs.

Online Learning Center/Website

Found at **www.mhhe.com/oleary,** this site provides additional learning and instructional tools to enhance the comprehension of the text. The OLC/website is divided into these three areas:

- **Information Center** Contains core information about the text, supplements, and the authors.
- **Instructor Center** Offers the aforementioned instructional materials, downloads, and other relevant links for professors.
- **Student Center** Contains data files, chapter competencies, chapter concepts, self-quizzes, additional web links, and more.

SimNet Assessment for Office Applications

SimNet Assessment for Office Applications provides a way for you to test students' software skills in a simulated environment. SimNet is available for Microsoft Office 2013 and provides flexibility for you in your applications course by offering:

Pretesting options
Posttesting options
Course placement testing
Diagnostic capabilities to reinforce skills
Web delivery of tests
Certification preparation exams
Learning verification reports

For more information on skills assessment software, please contact your local sales representative, or visit us at **www.mhhe.com.**

Computing Concepts

Computing Essentials 2014 offers a unique, visual orientation that gives students a basic understanding of computing concepts. *Computing Essentials* encourages "active" learning with exercises, explorations, visual illustrations, and screen shots. While combining the "active" learning style with current topics and technology, this text provides an accurate snapshot of computing trends. When bundled with software application lab manuals, students are given a complete representation of the fundamental issues surrounding the personal computing environment.

About the Authors

Tim and Linda O'Leary live in the American Southwest and spend much of their time engaging instructors and students in conversation about learning. In fact, they have been talking about learning for over 25 years. Something in those early conversations convinced them to write a book, to bring their interest in the learning process to the printed page. Today, they are as concerned as ever about learning, about technology, and about the challenges of presenting material in new ways, in terms of both content and method of delivery.

A powerful and creative team, Tim combines his 30 years of classroom teaching experience with Linda's background as a consultant and corporate trainer. Tim has taught courses at Stark Technical College in Canton, Ohio, and at Rochester Institute of Technology in upstate New York, and is currently a professor emeritus at Arizona State University in Tempe, Arizona. Linda offered her expertise at ASU for several years as an academic advisor. She also presented and developed materials for major corporations such as Motorola, Intel, Honeywell, and AT&T, as well as various community colleges in the Phoenix area.

Tim and Linda have talked to and taught numerous students, all of them with a desire to learn something about computers and applications that make their lives easier, more interesting, and more productive.

Each new edition of an O'Leary text, supplement, or learning aid has benefited from these students and their instructors who daily stand in front of them (or over their shoulders). The O'Leary Series is no exception.

About the Contributor

Bonnie Gundlach is employed as an independent technical writer, instructor, and voice messaging consultant. Possessing many years' experience in developing and delivering comprehensive technical training, system design, and voice messaging solutions to clients, Ms. Gundlach holds a BA in Elementary Education from the University of South Florida, as well as a post-baccalaureate certificate in Information Systems from Virginia Commonwealth University. As an instructor with Asheville-Buncombe Technical Community College, she has worked teaching computer skills to new and returning adult students. Residing in Asheville, North Carolina, she enjoys life with her husband and treasured feline companions.

Dedication

We dedicate this edition to our parents—Irene Perley Coats, Jean L. O'Leary, and Charles D. O'Leary—for all their support and love. We miss you.

Introduction to Microsoft Office 2013

Objectives

After completing the Introduction to Microsoft Office 2013, you should be able to:

1. Describe the Office 2013 applications.
2. Start an Office 2013 application.
3. Use the Ribbon, dialog boxes, and task panes.
4. Use menus, context menus, and shortcut keys.
5. Use the Backstage.
6. Open, close, and save files.
7. Navigate a document.
8. Enter, edit, and format text.
9. Select, copy, and move text.
10. Undo and redo changes.
11. Specify document properties.
12. Print a document.
13. Use Office 2013 Help.
14. Exit an Office 2013 application.

What Is Microsoft Office 2013?

Microsoft's Office 2013 is a comprehensive, integrated system of programs designed to solve a wide array of business needs. Although the programs can be used individually, they are designed to work together seamlessly, making it easy to connect people and organizations to information, business processes, and each other. The applications include tools used to create, discuss, communicate, and manage projects. If you share a lot of documents with other people, these features facilitate access to common documents. Additionally, Office 2013 allows you to store and share files in the cloud on SkyDrive or SharePoint. The **cloud** refers to any applications and services that are hosted and run on servers connected to the Internet. This version is designed to work with all types of devices, including desktops, laptops, tablets and hybrid tablet/laptops.

Microsoft Office 2013 is packaged in several different combinations of programs or suites. The major programs and a brief description are provided in the following table.

Program	Description
Word 2013	Word processor program used to create text-based documents
Excel 2013	Spreadsheet program used to analyze numerical data
Access 2013	Database manager used to organize, manage, and display a database
PowerPoint 2013	Graphics presentation program used to create presentation materials
Outlook 2013	Desktop information manager and messaging client
OneNote 2013	Note-taking and information organization tools

The four main components of Microsoft Office 2013—Word, Excel, Access, and PowerPoint—are the applications you will learn about in this series of labs. They are described in more detail in the following sections.

Word 2013

Word 2013 is a word processing software application whose purpose is to help you create text-based documents such as letters, memos, reports, e-mail messages, or any other type of correspondence. Word processors are one of the most flexible and widely used application software programs.

WORD 2013 FEATURES

The beauty of a word processor is that you can make changes or corrections as you are typing. Want to change a report from single spacing to double spacing? Alter the width of the margins? Delete some paragraphs and add others from yet another document? A word processor allows you to do all these things with ease.

Edit Content

Word 2013 excels in its ability to change or **edit** a document. Basic document editing involves correcting spelling, grammar, and sentence-structure errors and revising or updating existing text by inserting, deleting, and rearranging areas of text. For example, a document that lists prices can easily be updated to reflect new prices. A document that details procedures can be revised by deleting old procedures and inserting new ones. Many of these changes are made easily by cutting (removing) or copying (duplicating) selected text and then pasting (inserting) the cut or copied text in another location in the same or another document. Editing allows you to quickly revise a document, by changing only the parts that need to be modified.

To help you produce a perfect document, Word 2013 includes many additional editing support features. The AutoCorrect feature checks the spelling and grammar in a document as text is entered. Many common errors are corrected automatically for you. Others are identified and a correction suggested. A thesaurus can be used to display alternative words that have a meaning similar or opposite to a word you entered. The Find and Replace feature can be used to quickly locate specified text and replace it with other text throughout a document. In addition, Word 2013 includes a variety of tools that automate the process of many common tasks, such as creating tables, form letters, and columns.

Format Content

You also can easily control the appearance or **format** of the document. Perhaps the most noticeable formatting feature is the ability to apply different fonts (type styles and sizes) and text appearance changes such as bold, italics, and color to all or selected portions of the document. Additionally, you can add color shading behind individual pieces of text or entire paragraphs and pages to add emphasis. Other formatting features include changes to entire paragraphs, such as the line spacing and alignment of text between the margins. You also can format entire pages by displaying page numbers, changing margin settings, and applying backgrounds.

To make formatting even easier, Word 2013 includes Document Themes and Styles. Document Themes apply a consistent font, color, and line effect to an entire document. Styles apply the selected style design to a selection of text. Further, Word 2013 includes a variety of built-in preformatted content that helps you quickly produce modern-looking, professional documents. Among these are galleries of cover page designs, pull quotes, and header and footer designs. While selecting many of these design choices, a visual live preview is displayed, making it easy to see how the design would look in your document. In addition, you can select from a wide variety of templates to help you get started on creating many common types of documents such as flyers, calendars, faxes, newsletters, and memos.

Insert Illustrations and Videos

To further enhance your documents, you can insert many different types of graphic elements. These include drawing objects, SmartArt, charts, pictures, clip art, screenshots, and videos. The drawing tools supplied with Word 2013 can be used to create your own drawings, or you can select from over 100 adjustable shapes and modify them to your needs. All drawings can be further enhanced with 3-D effects, shadows, colors, and textures. SmartArt graphics allow you to create a visual representation of your information. They include many different layouts such as a process or cycle that are designed to help you communicate an idea. Charts can be inserted to illustrate and compare data. Complex pictures can be inserted in documents by scanning your own, using supplied or purchased clip art, or downloading images from the web. Additionally, you can quickly capture and insert a picture, called a screenshot, from another application running on your computer into the current document. Finally, you can easily find and insert videos from different online sources to enhance your document.

Additional Information

Excel and PowerPoint also include these collaboration features.

Collaborate with Others

Group collaboration on projects is common in industry today. Word 2013 includes many features to help streamline how documents are developed and changed by group members. A comment feature allows multiple people to insert remarks in the same document without having to route the document to each person or reconcile multiple reviewers' comments. You can easily consolidate all changes and comments from different reviewers in one simple step and accept or reject changes as needed. Finally, if you save your documents online, you can review and edit simultaneously with others. The changes are accessible to the entire group. If someone does not have Office installed on his or her computer, you can send the individual a link to your document allowing him or her to follow along in a browser.

Two documents you will produce in the first two Word 2013 labs, a letter and flyer, are shown here.

January 9, 2015

Dear Adventure Traveler:

Imagine camping under the stars in A
Costa Rica, or following in the footsteps of the
Picchu. Turn these thoughts of an adventure i
Tours on one of our four new adventure tours

To tell you more about these exciting
These presentations will focus on the features
places you will visit and activities you can part
attend one of the following presentations:

Date	Time
February 5 ------	7:00 p.m.-----
February 18-----	7:30 p.m.-----
March 7----------	1:00 p.m.-----

In appreciation of your past patronag
the new tour packages. You must book the tri
letter to qualify for the discount.

Our vacation tours are professionally
everything in the price of your tour while givi
these features:

- **All accommodations and meals**
- **All entrance fees, excursions, transfe**
- **Professional tour manager and local g**

We hope you will join us this year on
Travel Tours each day is an adventure. For res
Travel Tours directly at 1-800-555-0004.

A letter containing a tabbed table, indented paragraphs, and text enhancements is quickly created using basic Word features

Adventure Travel Tours

NEW ADVENTURES

Attention adventure travelers! Attend an Adventure Travel presentation to learn about some of the earth's greatest unspoiled habitats and learn how you can experience the adventure of a lifetime. This year Adventure Travel Tours is introducing four new tours that offer you a unique opportunity to combine many different outdoor activities while exploring the world.

Safari in Tanzania

India Wildlife Adventure

Costa Rica Rivers and Rainforests

Inca Trail to Machu Picchu

Presentation dates and times are January 5 at 7:00 p.m., February 3 at 7:30 p.m., and March 8 at 7:00 p.m. All presentations are at convenient hotel locations. The hotels are located in downtown Los Angeles, in Santa Clara, and at the LAX airport.

Call Adventure Travel Tours at 1-800-555-0004 for presentation locations, a full color brochure, and itinerary information, costs, and trip dates. Student Name will gladly help with all of your questions.

Visit our Web site at www.adventuretraveltours.com

A flyer incorporating many visual enhancements such as colored text, varied text styles, and graphic elements is both eye-catching and informative

Excel 2013

Excel 2013 is an electronic spreadsheet, or **worksheet**, that is used to organize, manipulate, and graph numeric data. Once used almost exclusively by accountants, worksheets are now widely used by nearly every profession. Nearly any job that uses rows and columns of numbers can be performed using an electronic spreadsheet. Once requiring hours of labor and/or costly accountants' fees, data analysis is now available almost instantly using electronic spreadsheets and has become a routine business procedure. This powerful business tool has revolutionized the business world. Typical uses include the creation of budgets and financial planning for both business and personal situations. Marketing professionals record and evaluate sales trends. Teachers record grades and calculate final grades. Personal trainers record the progress of their clients.

EXCEL 2013 FEATURES

Excel 2013 includes many features that not only help you create a well-designed worksheet, but one that produces accurate results. The features include the ability to quickly edit and format data, perform calculations, create charts, and print the worksheet. Using Excel 2013, you can quickly analyze and manage data and communicate your findings to others. The program not only makes it faster to create worksheets, but it also produces professional-appearing results.

Enter and Edit Data

The Microsoft Excel 2013 spreadsheet program uses a workbook file that contains one or more worksheets. Each worksheet can be used to organize different types of related information. The worksheet consists of rows and columns that create a grid of cells. You enter numeric data or descriptive text into a cell. These entries can then be erased, moved, copied, or edited.

Format Data

Like text in a Word document, the design and appearance of entries in a worksheet can be enhanced in many ways. For instance, you can change the font style and size and add special effects such as bold, italic, borders, boxes, drop shadows, and shading to selected cells. You also can use cell styles to quickly apply predefined combinations of these formats to selections. Additionally, you can select from different document themes, predefined combinations of colors, fonts, and effects, to give your workbooks a consistent, professional appearance.

Unlike the Word application, Excel includes many formatting features that are designed specifically for numeric data. For example, numeric entries can be displayed with commas, dollar signs, or a set number of decimal places. Special formatting, such as color bars, can be applied automatically to ranges of cells to emphasize data based on a set of criteria you establish and to highlight trends.

Analyze Data

The power of a spreadsheet application is its ability to perform calculations from very simple sums to the most complex financial and mathematical formulas. Formulas can be entered that perform calculations using data contained in specified cells. The results of the calculations are displayed in the cell containing the formula. Predefined formulas, called functions, can be used to quickly perform complex calculations such as calculating loan payments or performing a statistical analysis of data.

Analysis of data in a spreadsheet once was too expensive and time-consuming. Now, using electronic worksheets, you can use what-if or sensitivity analysis by changing the values in selected cells and immediately observing the effect on related cells in the worksheet. Other analysis tools such as Solver and Scenarios allow you to see the effects of possible alternative courses of action to help forecast future outcomes.

Chart Data

Using Excel, you also can produce a visual display of numeric data in the form of graphs or charts. As the values in the worksheet change, charts referencing those values automatically adjust to reflect the changes. You also can enhance the appearance of a chart by using different type styles and sizes, adding three-dimensional effects, and including text and objects such as lines and arrows.

Two worksheets you will produce using Excel 2013 are shown below.

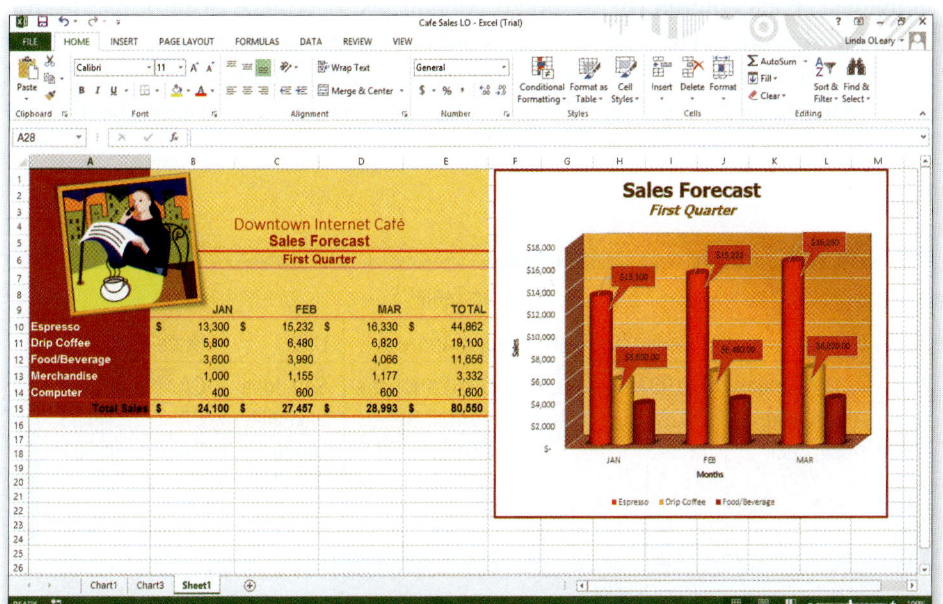

	JAN	FEB	MAR	TOTAL
Espresso	$ 13,300	$ 15,232	$ 16,330	$ 44,862
Drip Coffee	5,800	6,480	6,820	19,100
Food/Beverage	3,600	3,990	4,066	11,656
Merchandise	1,000	1,155	1,177	3,332
Computer	400	600	600	1,600
Total Sales	$ 24,100	$ 27,457	$ 28,993	$ 80,550

A worksheet showing the quarterly sales forecast containing a graphic, text enhancements, and a chart of the data is quickly created using basic Excel 2013 features

Annual Forecast - Excel (Trial)

Downtown Internet Café
Annual Forecast

	JAN	FEB	MAR	APR	MAY	JUN	JUL	AUG	SEP	OCT	NOV	DEC	ANNUAL
Sales													
Espresso	$13,300	$13,600	$14,200	$14,400	$15,200	$15,500	$15,200	$15,300	$15,800	$17,900	$18,500	$19,900	$188,800
Drip Coffee	$5,800	$6,000	$6,200	$6,200	$6,200	$6,200	$6,000	$6,000	$6,500	$6,900	$6,900	$6,900	$75,800
Food/Beverage	$3,600	$3,800	$3,800	$3,600	$3,800	$3,800	$4,000	$4,000	$4,000	$4,200	$4,400	$4,600	$47,600
Merchandise	$1,000	$1,100	$1,100	$1,500	$1,500	$1,500	$2,000	$2,000	$2,000	$2,000	$2,500	$3,500	$21,700
Computer	$400	$400	$400	$600	$600	$800	$800	$800	$600	$600	$600	$600	$7,200
Total Sales	**$24,100**	**$24,900**	**$25,700**	**$26,300**	**$27,300**	**$27,800**	**$28,000**	**$28,100**	**$28,900**	**$31,600**	**$32,900**	**$35,500**	**$341,100**
Expenses													
Cost of Goods	$7,225	$7,480	$7,690	$7,620	$7,940	$8,015	$8,000	$8,025	$8,300	$9,065	$9,335	$9,805	$98,500
Cost of Merchandise	$700	$770	$770	$1,050	$1,050	$1,050	$1,400	$1,400	$1,400	$1,400	$1,750	$2,450	$15,190
Payroll	$9,000	$9,000	$9,000	$7,860	$8,390	$8,740	$9,000	$9,000	$9,000	$9,000	$9,000	$9,000	$105,990
Internet	$325	$325	$325	$325	$325	$325	$325	$325	$325	$325	$325	$325	$3,900
Building	$2,100	$2,100	$2,100	$2,100	$2,100	$2,100	$2,100	$2,100	$2,100	$2,100	$2,100	$2,100	$25,200
Advertising	$600	$600	$600	$600	$600	$600	$600	$600	$600	$600	$600	$600	$7,200
Capital Assets	$1,500	$1,500	$1,500	$1,500	$1,500	$1,500	$1,500	$1,500	$1,500	$1,500	$1,500	$1,500	$18,000
Miscellaneous	$1,300	$1,300	$1,300	$1,300	$1,300	$1,300	$1,300	$1,300	$1,300	$1,300	$1,300	$1,300	$15,600
Total Expenses	**$22,750**	**$23,075**	**$23,285**	**$22,355**	**$23,205**	**$23,630**	**$24,225**	**$24,250**	**$24,525**	**$25,290**	**$25,910**	**$27,080**	**$289,580**
Net Income	$1,350	$1,825	$2,415	$3,945	$4,095	$4,170	$3,775	$3,850	$4,375	$6,310	$6,990	$8,420	$51,520
Profit Margin	5.60%	7.33%	9.40%	15.00%	15.00%	15.00%	13.48%	13.70%	15.14%	19.97%	21.25%	23.72%	15.10% Monthly
	Quarter Profit Margin		7.48%			15.00%			14.12%			21.72%	

Year | First Quarter | Second Quarter | Third Quarter | Fourth Quarter

A large worksheet incorporating more complex formulas, conditional formatting, and linked worksheets is both informative and attractive

Access 2013

Access 2013 is a relational database management application that is used to create and analyze a database. A **database** is a collection of related data. **Tables** consist of columns (called **fields**) and rows (called **records**). Each row contains a record, which is all the information about one person, thing, or place. Each field is the smallest unit of information about a record.

In a relational database, the most widely used database structure, data is organized in linked tables. The tables are related or linked to one another by a common field. Relational databases allow you to create smaller and more manageable database tables, since you can combine and extract data between tables.

For example, a state's motor vehicle department database might have an address table. Each row (record) in the table would contain address information about one individual. Each column (field) would contain just one piece of information, for example, zip codes. The address table would be linked to other tables in the database by common fields. For example, the address table might be linked to a vehicle owner's table by name and linked to an outstanding citation table by license number (see example below).

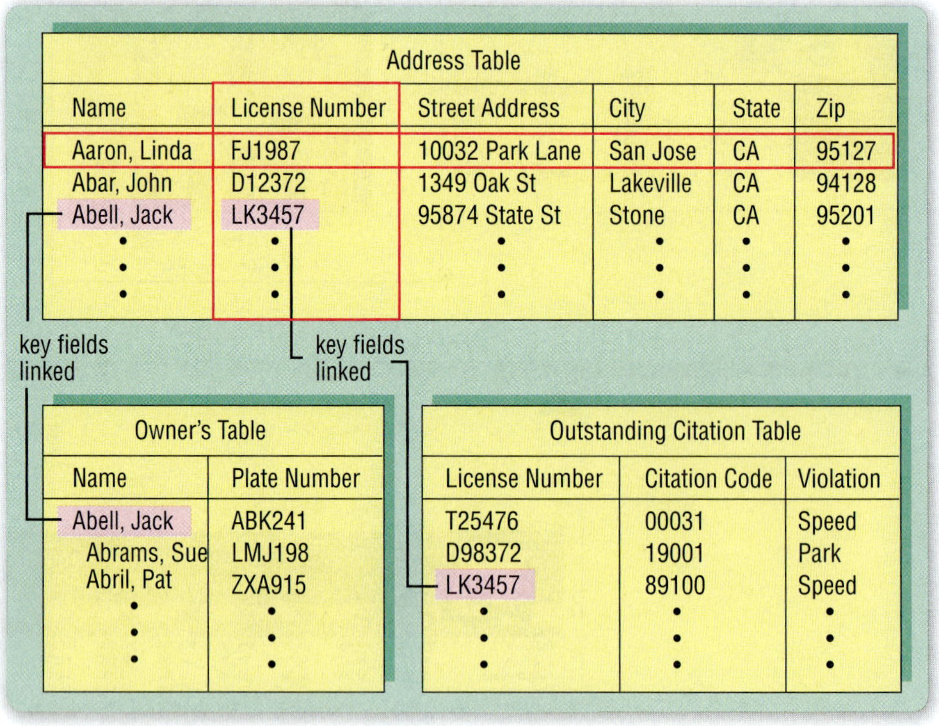

Address Table

Name	License Number	Street Address	City	State	Zip
Aaron, Linda	FJ1987	10032 Park Lane	San Jose	CA	95127
Abar, John	D12372	1349 Oak St	Lakeville	CA	94128
Abell, Jack	LK3457	95874 State St	Stone	CA	95201
•	•	•	•	•	•
•	•	•	•	•	•
•	•	•	•	•	•

key fields linked

key fields linked

Owner's Table

Name	Plate Number
Abell, Jack	ABK241
Abrams, Sue	LMJ198
Abril, Pat	ZXA915
•	•
•	•
•	•

Outstanding Citation Table

License Number	Citation Code	Violation
T25476	00031	Speed
D98372	19001	Park
LK3457	89100	Speed
•	•	•
•	•	•
•	•	•

ACCESS 2013 FEATURES

Access 2013 is a powerful program with numerous easy-to-use features including the ability to quickly locate information; add, delete, modify, and sort records; analyze data; and produce professional-looking reports. Some of the basic Access 2013 features are described next.

Find Information

Once you enter data into the database table, you can quickly search the table to locate a specific record based on the data in a field. In a manual system, you can usually locate a record by knowing one key piece of information. For example, if the records are stored in a file cabinet alphabetically by last name, to quickly find a record, you must know the last name. In a computerized database, even if the records are sorted or organized by last name, you can still quickly locate a record using information in another field.

Add, Delete, and Modify Records

Using Access, it is also easy to add and delete records from the table. Once you locate a record, you can edit the contents of the fields to update the record or delete the record entirely from the table. You also can add new records to a table. When you enter a new record, it is automatically placed in the correct organizational location within the table. Creation of forms makes it easier to enter and edit data as well.

Sort and Filter Records

The capability to arrange or sort records in the table according to different fields can provide more meaningful information. You can organize records by name, department, pay, class, or any other category you need at a particular time. Sorting the records in different ways can provide information to different departments for different purposes.

Additionally, you can isolate and display a subset of records by specifying filter criteria. The criteria specify which records to display based on data in selected fields.

Analyze Data

Using Access, you can analyze the data in a table and perform calculations on different fields of data. Instead of pulling each record from a filing cabinet, recording the piece of data you want to use, and then performing the calculation on the recorded data, you can simply have the database program perform the calculation on all the values in the specified field. Additionally, you can ask questions or query the table to find only certain records that meet specific conditions to be used in the analysis. Information that was once costly and time-consuming to get is now quickly and readily available.

Generate Reports

Access includes many features that help you quickly produce reports ranging from simple listings to complex, professional-looking reports. You can create a simple report by asking for a listing of specified fields of data and restricting the listing to records meeting designated conditions. You can create a more complex professional report using the same restrictions or conditions as the simple report, but you can display the data in different layout styles, or with titles, headings, subtotals, or totals.

A database and a report that you will produce using Access 2013 are shown on the next page.

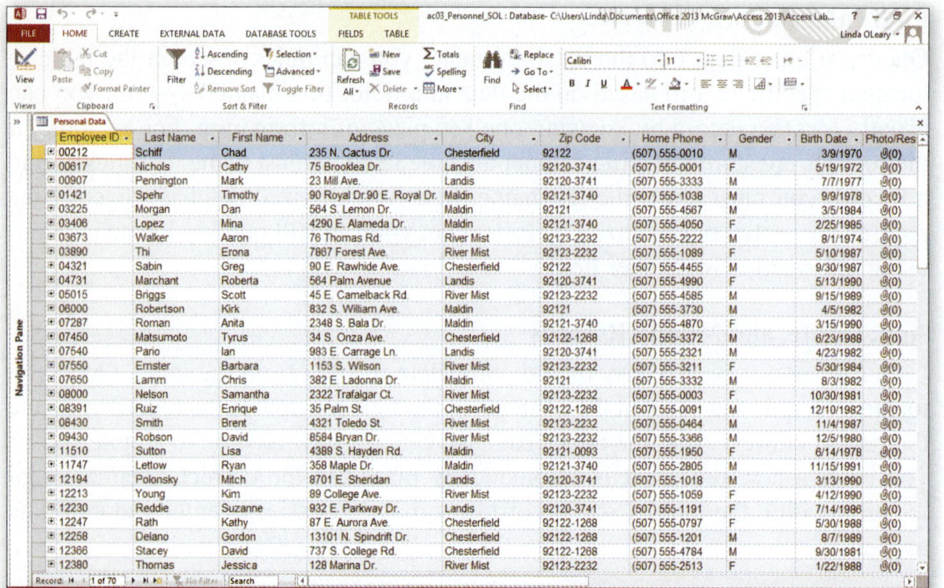

Employee ID	Last Name	First Name	Address	City	Zip Code	Home Phone	Gender	Birth Date	Photo/Res
00212	Schiff	Chad	235 N. Cactus Dr.	Chesterfield	92122	(507) 555-0010	M	3/9/1970	(0)
00617	Nichols	Cathy	75 Brooklea Dr.	Landis	92120-3741	(507) 555-0001	F	5/19/1972	(0)
00907	Pennington	Mark	23 Mill Ave.	Landis	92120-3741	(507) 555-3333	M	7/7/1977	(0)
01421	Spehr	Timothy	90 Royal Dr.90 E. Royal Dr.	Maldin	92121-3740	(507) 555-1038	M	9/9/1978	(0)
03225	Morgan	Dan	564 S. Lemon Dr.	Maldin	92121	(507) 555-4567	M	3/5/1984	(0)
03406	Lopez	Mina	4290 E. Alameda Dr.	Maldin	92121-3740	(507) 555-4050	F	2/25/1985	(0)
03673	Walker	Aaron	76 Thomas Rd.	River Mist	92123-2232	(507) 555-2222	M	8/1/1974	(0)
03890	Thi	Erona	7867 Forest Ave.	River Mist	92123-2232	(507) 555-1089	F	5/10/1987	(0)
04321	Sabin	Greg	90 E. Rawhide Ave.	Chesterfield	92122	(507) 555-4455	M	9/30/1987	(0)
04731	Marchant	Roberta	564 Palm Avenue	Landis	92120-3741	(507) 555-4990	F	5/13/1990	(0)
05015	Briggs	Scott	45 E. Camelback Rd.	River Mist	92123-2232	(507) 555-4585	M	9/15/1989	(0)
06000	Robertson	Kirk	832 S. William Ave.	Maldin	92121	(507) 555-3730	M	4/5/1982	(0)
07287	Roman	Anita	2348 S. Bala Dr.	Maldin	92121-3740	(507) 555-4870	F	3/15/1990	(0)
07450	Matsumoto	Tyrus	34 S. Onza Ave.	Chesterfield	92122-1268	(507) 555-3372	M	6/23/1988	(0)
07540	Pario	Ian	983 E. Carrage Ln.	Landis	92120-3741	(507) 555-2321	M	4/23/1982	(0)
07550	Ernster	Barbara	1153 S. Wilson	River Mist	92123-2232	(507) 555-3211	F	5/30/1984	(0)
07650	Lamm	Chris	382 E. Ladonna Dr.	Maldin	92121	(507) 555-3332	M	8/3/1982	(0)
08000	Nelson	Samantha	2322 Trafalgar Ct.	River Mist	92123-2232	(507) 555-0003	F	10/30/1981	(0)
08391	Ruiz	Enrique	35 Palm St.	Chesterfield	92122-1268	(507) 555-0091	M	12/10/1982	(0)
08430	Smith	Brent	4321 Toledo St.	River Mist	92123-2232	(507) 555-0464	M	11/4/1987	(0)
09430	Robson	David	8584 Bryan Dr.	River Mist	92123-2232	(507) 555-3366	M	12/5/1980	(0)
11510	Sutton	Lisa	4389 S. Hayden Rd.	Maldin	92121-0093	(507) 555-1950	F	6/14/1978	(0)
11747	Lettow	Ryan	358 Maple Dr.	Maldin	92121-3740	(507) 555-2805	M	11/15/1991	(0)
12194	Polonsky	Mitch	8701 E. Sheridan	Landis	92120-3741	(507) 555-1018	M	3/13/1990	(0)
12213	Young	Kim	89 College Ave.	River Mist	92123-2232	(507) 555-1059	F	4/12/1990	(0)
12230	Reddie	Suzanne	932 E. Parkway Dr.	Landis	92120-3741	(507) 555-1191	F	7/14/1986	(0)
12247	Rath	Kathy	87 E. Aurora Ave.	Chesterfield	92122-1268	(507) 555-0797	F	5/30/1988	(0)
12258	Delano	Gordon	13101 N. Spindrift Dr.	Chesterfield	92122-1268	(507) 555-1201	M	8/7/1989	(0)
12366	Stacey	David	737 S. College Rd.	Chesterfield	92122-1268	(507) 555-4784	M	9/30/1981	(0)
12380	Thomas	Jessica	128 Marina Dr.	River Mist	92123-2232	(507) 555-2513	F	1/22/1988	(0)

Record: 1 of 70

Unique 5-digit number assigned to each employee.

A relational database can be created and modified easily using basic Access 2013 features

Job Position Report

For **Landis**

Employee ID	First Name	Last Name	Position
12703	Jeff	Bader	Fitness Instructor
12389	Jennifer	Blackman	Sales Associate
05015	Scott	Briggs	Personal Trainer Director
12501	Elizabeth	DeLuca	Personal Trainer
12855	Kimberly	Fachet	Sales Associate
13484	Stephanie	Franklin	Food Service Server
12914	Alfonso	Gomez	Cleaning
22469	Ryan	Hogan	Personal Trainer
13303	Chris	Jensen	Greeter
13027	Kimberly	Kieken	Food Service Server
07650	Chris	Lamm	Sales Director
22085	Kristina	Lindau	Child Care Provider
13635	Juan	Martinez	Fitness Instructor
03225	Dan	Morgan	Food Service Director
99999	Student	Name	Human Resources Administrator
12420	Allison	Player	Maintenance
13005	Emily	Reilly	Assistant Manager
22297	Patricia	Rogondino	Greeter
07287	Anita	Roman	Child Care Director
12918	Carlos	Ruiz	Assistant Manager
00212	Chad	Schiff	Club Director
12583	Marie	Sullivan	Greeter

Page 1 of 2

A professional-looking report can be quickly generated from information contained in a database

PowerPoint 2013

PowerPoint 2013 is a graphics presentation program designed to help you produce a high-quality presentation that is both interesting to the audience and effective in its ability to convey your message. A presentation can be as simple as overhead transparencies or as sophisticated as an on-screen electronic display. Graphics presentation programs can produce black-and-white or color overhead transparencies, 35 mm slides, onscreen electronic presentations called **slide shows**, web pages for web use, and support materials for both the speaker and the audience.

POWERPOINT 2013 FEATURES

Although creating an effective presentation is a complicated process, PowerPoint 2013 helps simplify this process by providing assistance in the content development phase, as well as in the layout and design phase. PowerPoint includes features such as text handling, outlining, graphing, drawing, animation, clip art, and multimedia support. In addition, the programs suggest layouts for different types of presentations and offer professionally designed templates to help you produce a presentation that is sure to keep your audience's attention. In addition, you can quickly produce the support materials to be used when making a presentation to an audience.

Develop, Enter, and Edit Content

The content development phase includes deciding on the topic of your presentation, the organization of the content, and the ultimate message you want to convey to the audience. As an aid in this phase, PowerPoint 2013 helps you organize your thoughts based on the type of presentation you are making by providing both content and design templates. Based on the type of presentation, such as selling a product or suggesting a strategy, the template provides guidance by suggesting content ideas and organizational tips. For example, if you are making a presentation on the progress of a sales campaign, the program would suggest that you enter text on the background of the sales campaign as the first page, called a **slide**; the current status of the campaign as the next slide; and accomplishments, schedule, issues and problems, and where you are heading on subsequent slides.

Design Layouts

The layout for each slide is the next important decision. Again, PowerPoint 2013 helps you by suggesting text layout features such as title placement, bullets, and columns. You also can incorporate graphs of data, tables, organizational charts, clip art, and other special text effects in the slides.

PowerPoint 2013 also includes professionally designed themes to further enhance the appearance of your slides. These themes include features that standardize the appearance of all the slides in your presentation. Professionally selected combinations of text and background colors, common typefaces and sizes, borders, and other art designs take the worry out of much of the design layout.

Deliver Presentations

After you have written and designed the slides, you can use the slides in an onscreen electronic presentation or a web page for use on the web. An onscreen presentation uses the computer to display the slides on an overhead projection screen. As you prepare this type of presentation, you can use the rehearsal feature that allows you to practice and time your presentation. The length of time to display each slide can be set and your entire presentation can be completed within the allotted time. A presentation also can be modified to display on a website and run using a web browser. Finally, you can package the presentation to a CD for distribution.

A presentation that you will produce using PowerPoint 2013 is shown below.

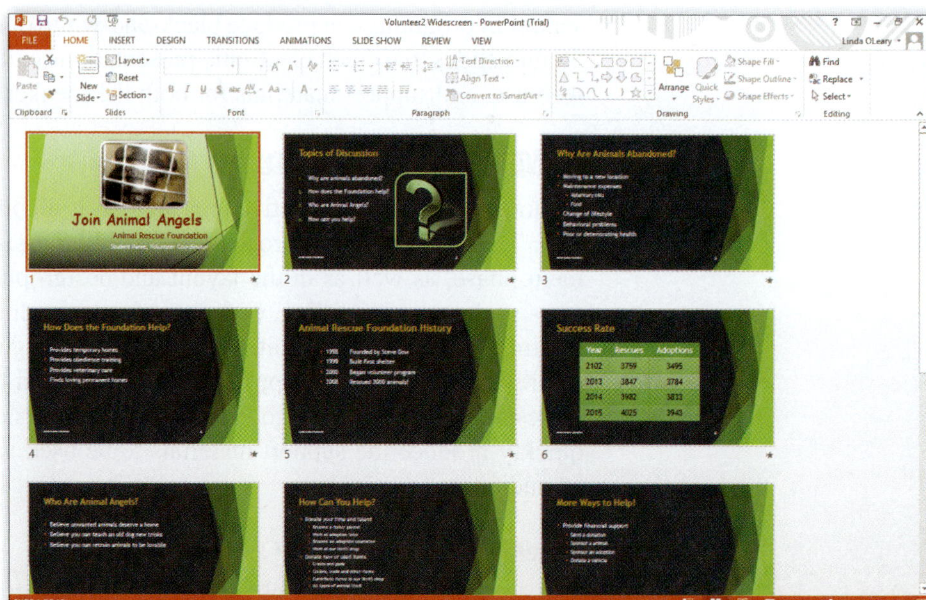

A presentation consists of a series of pages or "slides" presenting the information you want to convey in an organized and attractive manner

When running an on-screen presentation, each slide of the presentation is displayed full-screen on your computer monitor or projected onto a screen

Instructional Conventions

As you follow the directions in the upcoming hands-on section and in the application labs, you need to know the instructional conventions that are used. Hands-on instructions you are to perform appear as a sequence of numbered steps. Within each step, a series of bullets identifies the specific actions that must be performed. Step numbering begins over within each topic heading throughout the lab.

COMMANDS

Commands that are initiated using a command button and the mouse appear following the word "Click." The icon (and the icon name if the icon does not include text) is displayed following "Click." If there is another way to perform the same action, it appears in an Another Method margin note when the action is first introduced as shown in Example A.

Example A

1

- **Select the list of four tours.**
- **Open the Home tab.**
- **Click B Bold in the Font group.**

Another Method

The keyboard shortcut is Ctrl + B.

Sometimes, clicking on an icon opens a drop-down list or a menu of commands. Commands that are to be selected follow the word "Select" and appear in black text. You can select an item by pointing to it using the mouse or by moving to it using the directional keys. When an option is selected, it appears highlighted; however, the action is not carried out. Commands that appear following the word "Choose" perform the associated action. You can choose a command by clicking on it using the mouse or by pressing the Enter key once it is selected. (See Example B.)

Example B

- **Click A Font Color in the Font group of the Home tab.**
- **Select Green.**
- **Choose Dark Blue.**

FILE NAMES AND INFORMATION TO TYPE

Plain green text identifies file names you need to select or enter. Information you are asked to type appears in blue and bold. (See Example C.)

Example C

1

- **Open the document** wd01_Flyer.
- **Type** **Adventure Travel presents four new trips**

Common Office 2013 Features

Now that you know a little about each of the applications in Microsoft Office 2013, you will take a look at some of the features that are common to all Office 2013 applications. In this hands-on section you will learn to use the common user interface and application features to allow you to get a feel for how Office 2013 works. Although Word 2013 will be used to demonstrate how the features work, only features that are common to all the Office applications will be addressed.

COMMON INTERFACE FEATURES

All the Office 2013 applications have a common **user interface**, a set of graphical elements that are designed to help you interact with the program and provide instructions as to the actions you want to perform. These features include the use of the Ribbon, Quick Access Toolbar, task panes, menus, dialog boxes, and the File tab.

Starting an Office 2013 Application

To demonstrate the common features, you will start the Word 2013 application. There are several ways to start an Office 2013 application. The most common method is to click a tile on the Windows 8 Start screen for the program if it is available.

Additional Information

The procedure to start Excel, Access, and PowerPoint is the same as starting Word, except that you must select the appropriate application tile.

Having Trouble?

If you are using Windows 7, click Start and choose Word 2013. If you do not see the program name on the Start menu, select All Programs, choose Microsoft Office 2013, and then choose Word 2013.

1 **Click the** W **tile on the Start screen.**

Having Trouble?

If a tile for the application you want to open is not on the Start Screen, right-click the Start screen, click All apps, then click on the appropriate application tile.

Touch Tip

On a touch device, tap on the Word 2013 tile to start the application.

Your screen should be similar to Figure 1

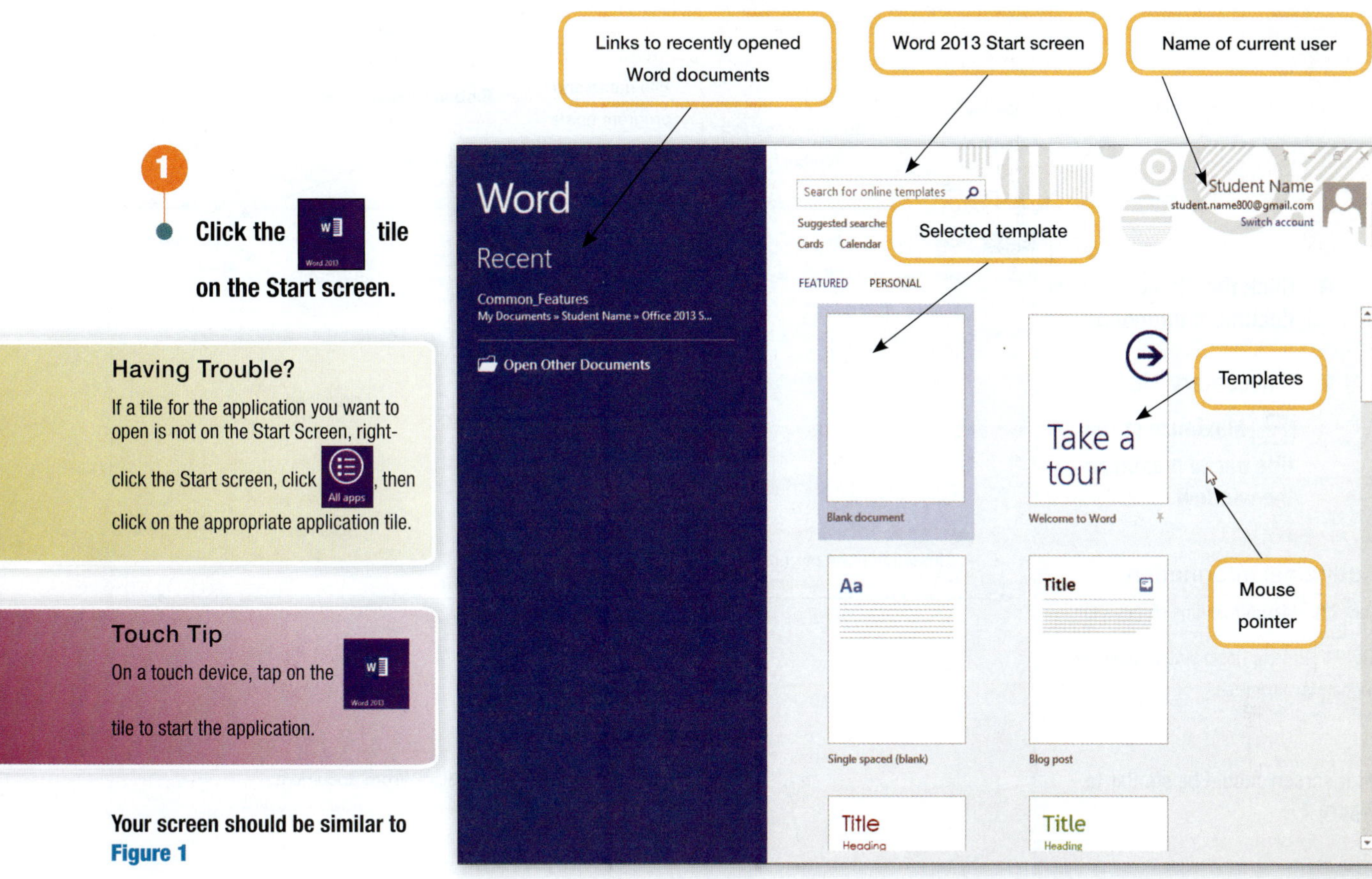

Figure 1

The Word 2013 program is started and the Start screen is displayed in a window on the desktop. A list of links to recently opened Word documents is displayed in the left column. A gallery of thumbnail images of available templates is displayed in the main window area. A **template** is a professionally designed document that is used as the basis for a new document. The Blank document thumbnail is selected by default and is used to create a new Word document from scratch.

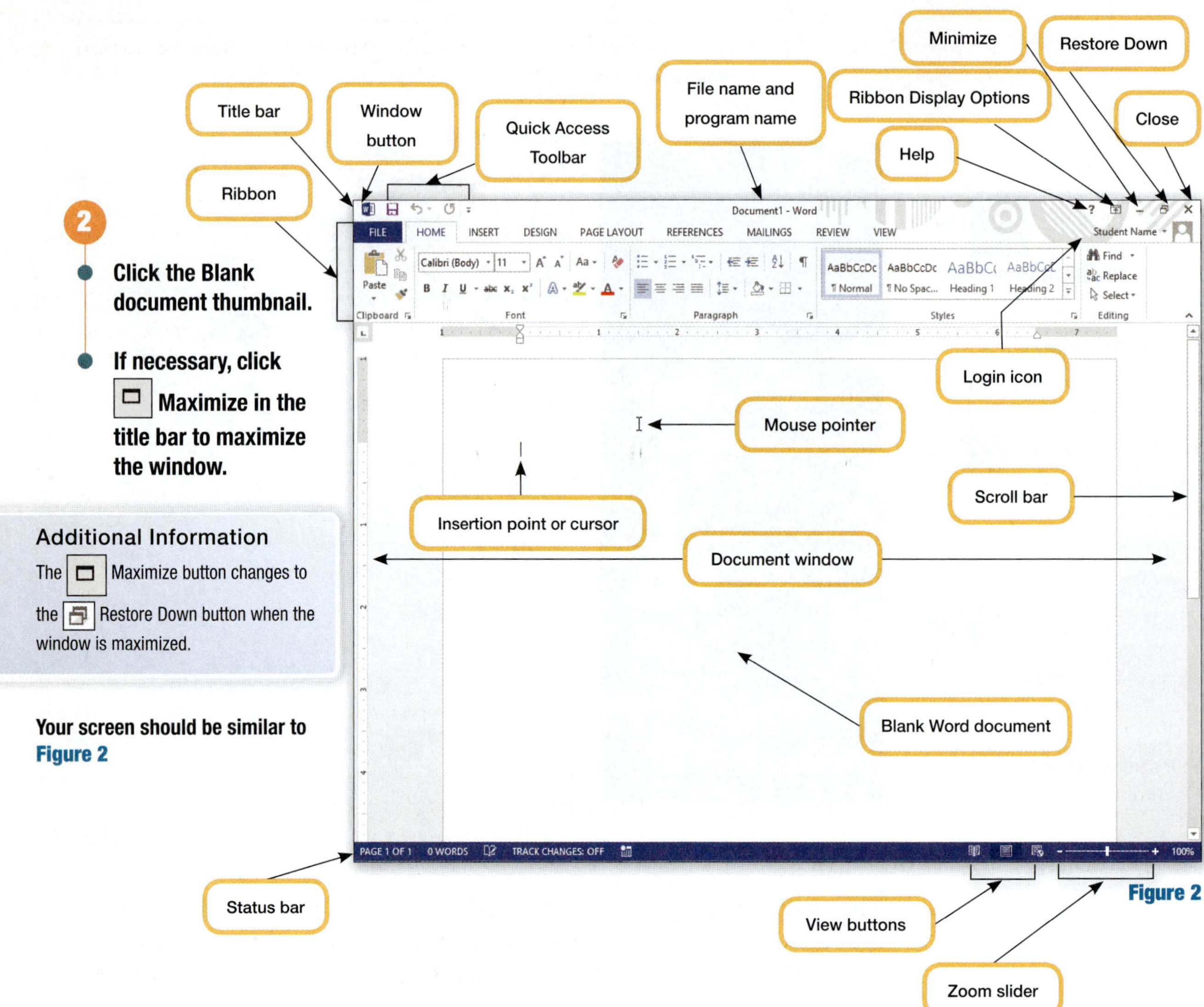

2

- **Click the Blank document thumbnail.**
- **If necessary, click ▭ Maximize in the title bar to maximize the window.**

Additional Information

The ▭ Maximize button changes to the 🗗 Restore Down button when the window is maximized.

Your screen should be similar to Figure 2

Figure 2

Additional Information

Application windows can be sized, moved, and otherwise manipulated like any other windows on the desktop.

The blank document template is open and displays in the Word 2013 application window. The center of the title bar at the top of the window displays the file name followed by the program name, in this case Word. Both ends of the title bar contain **buttons**, graphical elements that perform the associated action when you click on them using the mouse. At the left end of the title bar is the Window button. Clicking this button opens a menu of commands that allow you to size, move, and close the window. To the right of the Window button is the **Quick Access Toolbar** (QAT), which provides quick access to frequently used commands. By default, it includes the Save, Undo, and Repeat buttons, commands that Microsoft considers to be crucial. It is always available and is a customizable toolbar to which you can add your own favorite buttons. The right end of the title bar displays five buttons. The ? Help button accesses the program's Help system. The Ribbon Display Options button controls the display of the tabs and ribbon, allowing more content to be displayed in the application window. The last three buttons are shortcuts to the Window button menu commands that are used to size, move, and close the application window. The buttons on the title bar are the same in all the Office 2013 programs: Minimize, Restore Down/ Maximize, and Close.

Below the title bar is the **Ribbon**, which provides a centralized location of commands that are used to work in your document. The Ribbon has the same basic structure and is found in all Office 2013 applications. However, many of the commands found in the Ribbon vary with the specific applications. You will learn how to use the Ribbon shortly. At the right end of the Ribbon is the login icon that indicates if you are logged into Microsoft's online services for file storage and collaboration. It consists of your user name and Microsoft account photo. You can click the photo to adjust your account settings, swap in a new picture, or even switch accounts.

> **Additional Information**
>
> You will learn about opening existing files shortly.

The large center area of the application window is the **document window** where open application files are displayed. In this case, because you selected the Blank document template, a new blank Word document named Document1 (shown in the title bar) is open, ready for you to start creating a new document. In Excel, a new, blank workbook named Book1 would be opened and in PowerPoint a new, blank presentation file named Presentation1 would be opened. In Access, however, a new blank database file is not opened automatically. Instead, you must create and name a new database file or open an existing database file.

> **Additional Information**
>
> You will learn about other mouse pointer shapes and what they mean as you use the specific application programs.

The **cursor**, also called the **insertion point**, is the blinking vertical bar that marks your location in the document and indicates where text you type will appear. Across all Office applications, the mouse pointer appears as an I-beam when it is used to position the insertion point when entering text and as a when it can be used to select items. There are many other mouse pointer shapes that are both common to and specific to the different applications.

On the right of the document window is a vertical scroll bar. A **scroll bar** is used with a mouse to bring additional information into view in a window. The vertical scroll bar is used to move up or down. A horizontal scroll bar is also displayed when needed and moves side to side in the window. The scroll bar is a common feature to all Windows and Office 2013 applications; however, it may not appear in all applications until needed.

At the bottom of the application window is another common feature called the **status bar**. It displays information about the open file and features that help you view the file. It displays different information depending upon the application you are using. For example, the Word status bar displays information about the number of pages and words in the document, whereas the Excel status bar displays the mode of operation and the count, average, and sum of values in selected cells. All Office 2013 applications include **View buttons** that are used to change how the information in the document window is displayed. The View buttons are different for each application. Finally, a **Zoom Slider**, located at the far right end of the status bar, is used to change the amount of information displayed in the document window by "zooming in" to get a close-up view or "zooming out" to see more of the document at a reduced view.

Displaying ScreenTips

You are probably wondering how you would know what action the different buttons perform. To help you identify buttons, the Office applications display ScreenTips when you point to them.

1

- **Point to the [Save icon] Save button in the Quick Access Toolbar.**

Touch Tip

Hover over a button to see the ScreenTip.

Your screen should be similar to Figure 3

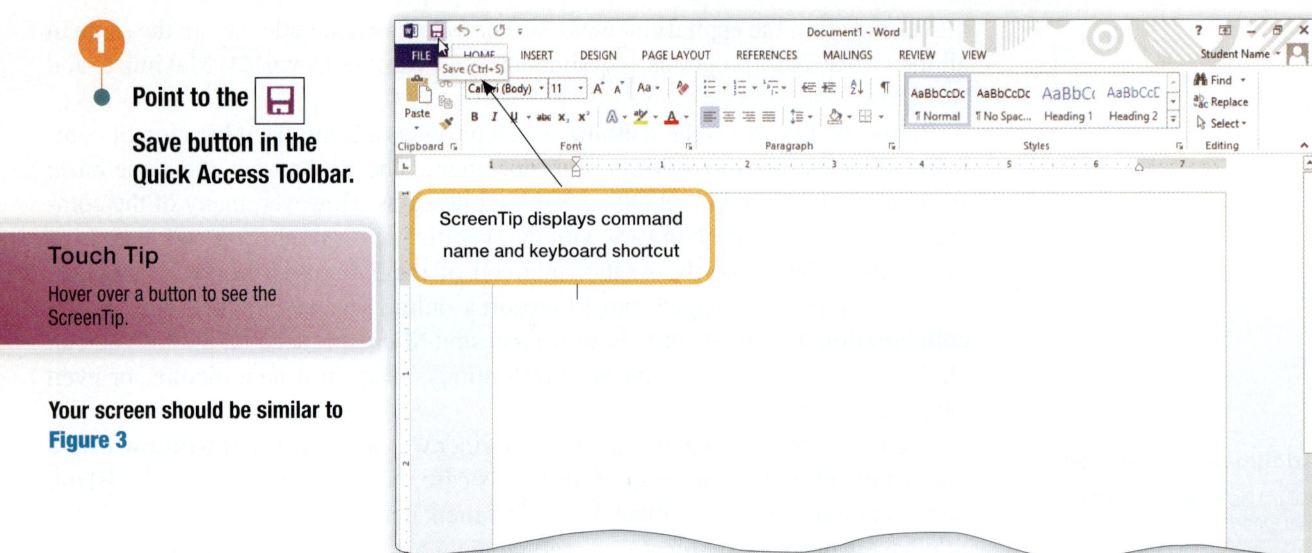

Figure 3

A **ScreenTip**, also called a **tooltip**, appears displaying the command name and the keyboard shortcut, Ctrl + S. A **keyboard shortcut** is a combination of keys that can be used to execute a command in place of clicking the button. In this case, if you hold down the Ctrl key while typing the letter S, you will access the command to save a file. ScreenTips also often include a brief description of the action a command performs.

Using Menus

Notice the small button [▾] at the end of the Quick Access Toolbar. Clicking this button opens a menu of commands that perform tasks associated with the Quick Access Toolbar.

1

- **Point to the [▾] button at the end of the Quick Access Toolbar to display the ScreenTip.**
- **Click [▾] to open the menu.**

Touch Tip

Tap the tab, command, or buttons to activate features.

Your screen should be similar to Figure 4

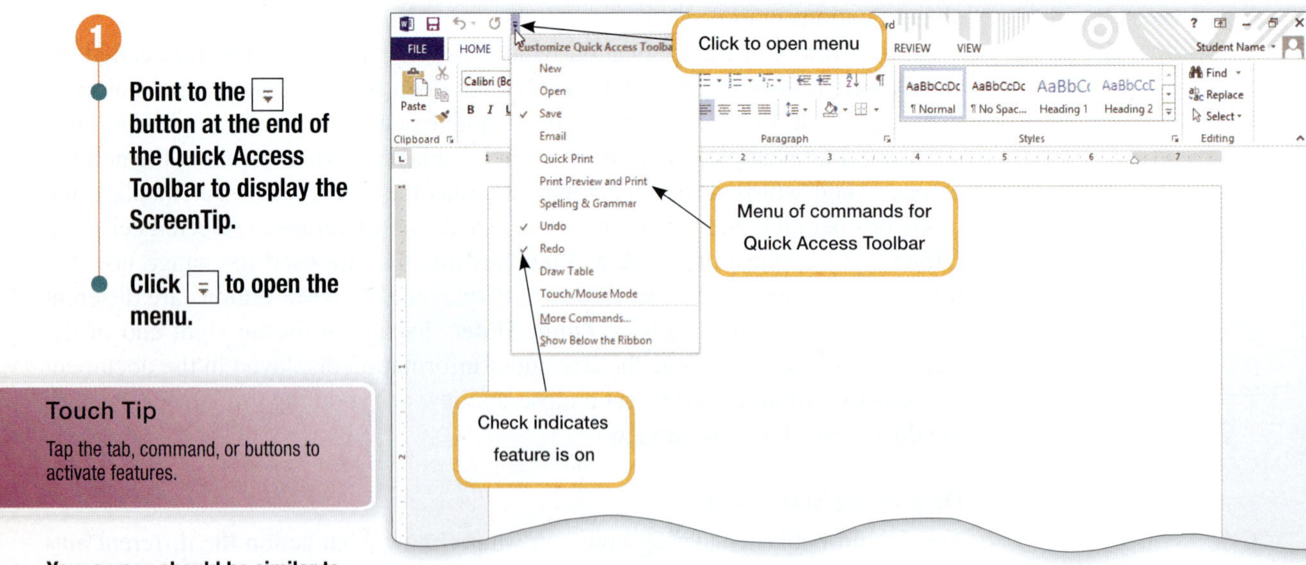

Figure 4

The first 11 items in the menu allow you to quickly add a command button to or remove a command button from the Quick Access Toolbar. Those commands that are already displayed in the Quick Access Toolbar are preceded with a checkmark.

The last two commands allow you to access other command features to customize the Quick Access Toolbar or change its location.

Once a menu is open, you can select a command from the menu by pointing to it. As you do the selected command appears highlighted. Like buttons, resting the mouse pointer over the menu command options will display a ScreenTip. Then to choose a selected command, you click on it. Choosing a command performs the action associated with the command or button. You will use several of these features next.

2

- **Point to the commands in the Quick Access Toolbar menu to select (highlight) them and see the ScreenTips.**
- **Click on the Open command to choose it and add it to the Quick Access Toolbar.**
- **Point to the Open button on the Quick Access Toolbar to display the ScreenTip.**

Your screen should be similar to Figure 5

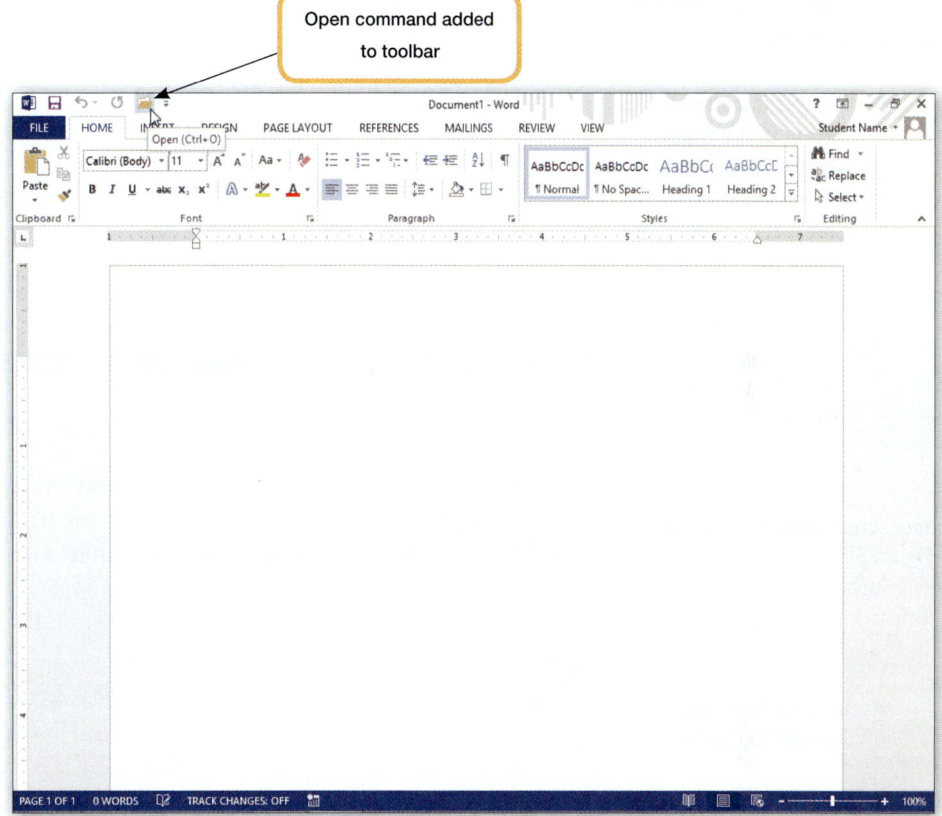

Figure 5

The command button to open a document has been added to the Quick Access Toolbar. Next, you will remove this button and then you will change the location of the Quick Access Toolbar. Another way to access some commands is to use a context menu. A **context menu**, also called a **shortcut menu**, is opened by right-clicking on an item on the screen. This menu is context sensitive, meaning it displays only those commands relevant to the item or screen location. For example, right-clicking on the Quick Access Toolbar will display the commands associated with using the Quick Access Toolbar and the Ribbon. You will use this method to remove the Open button and move the Quick Access Toolbar.

3

- Right-click on the Open button on the Quick Access Toolbar to display the context menu.
- Click on the Remove from Quick Access Toolbar command to choose it.
- Right-click on any button in the Quick Access Toolbar again and choose Show Quick Access Toolbar Below the Ribbon.

Another Method

You also can type the underlined letter of a command to choose it or press Enter to choose a selected command.

Your screen should be similar to Figure 6

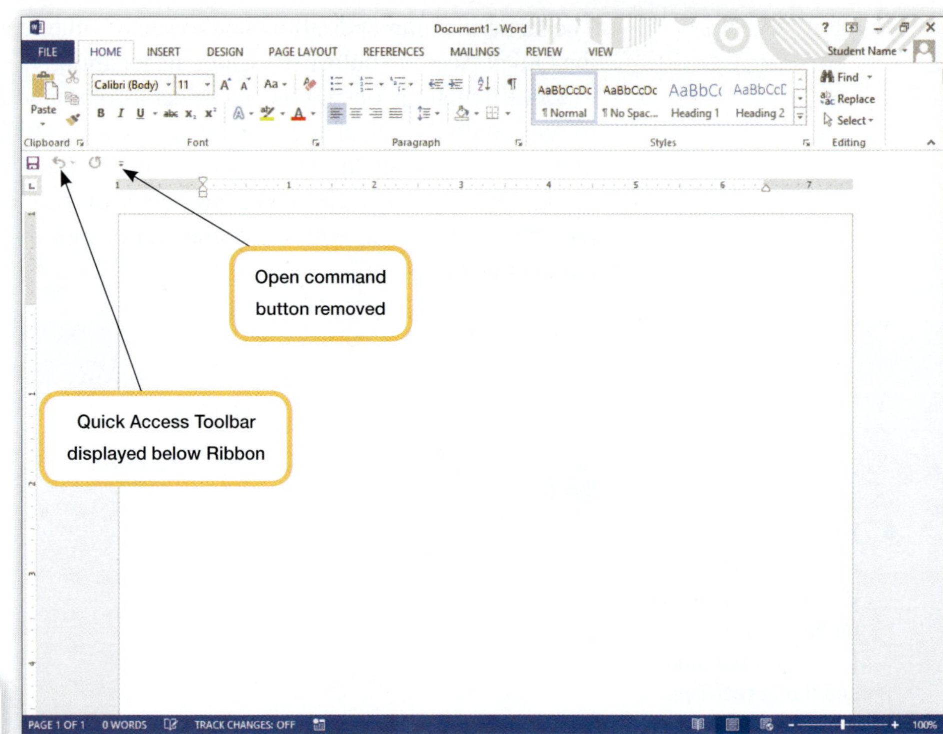

Figure 6

The Quick Access Toolbar is now displayed full size below the Ribbon. This is useful if you have many buttons on the toolbar; however, it takes up document viewing space. You will return it to its compact size.

4

- Display the Quick Access Toolbar menu.
- Choose Show Above the Ribbon.

Your screen should be similar to Figure 7

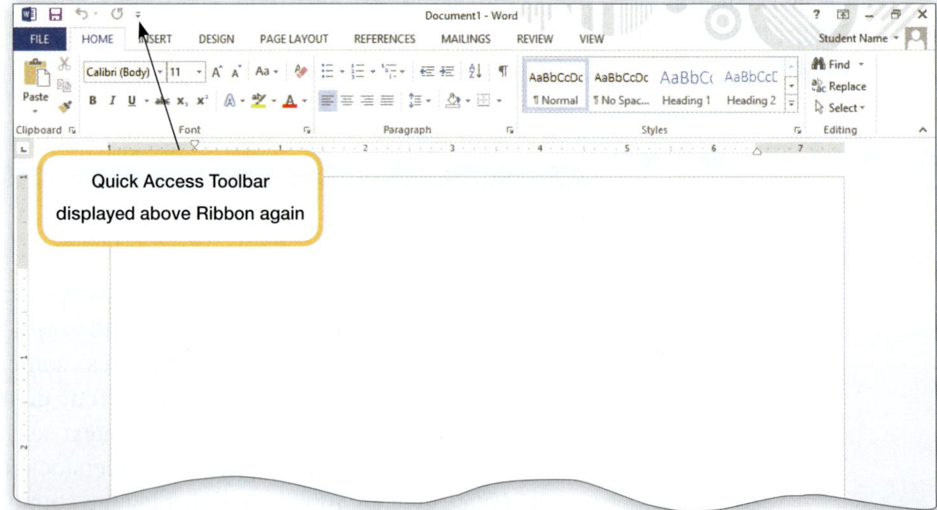

Figure 7

The Quick Access Toolbar is displayed above the Ribbon again.

Using the Ribbon

The Ribbon has three basic parts: tabs, groups, and commands (see Figure 8). **Tabs** are used to divide the Ribbon into major activity areas. Each tab is then organized into **groups** that contain related items. The related items are **commands** that consist of command buttons, a box to enter information, or a menu. Clicking on a command button performs the associated action or displays a list of additional options.

The Ribbon tabs, commands, and features vary with the different Office applications. For example, the Word Ribbon displays tabs and commands used to create a text document, whereas the Excel Ribbon displays tabs and commands used to create an electronic worksheet. Although the Ribbon commands are application specific, many are also common to all Office 2013 applications. In all applications, the Ribbon also can be customized by changing the built-in tabs or creating your own tabs and groups to personalize your workspace and provide faster access to the commands you use most.

> **Additional Information**
>
> Because the Ribbon can adapt to the screen resolution and orientation, your Ribbon may look slightly different. Additionally, the Ribbon may display an Add-Ins tab if your application setup specifies that add-in applications be made available in the Add-Ins tab.

Opening Tabs

> **Additional Information**
>
> The File tab is not a Ribbon tab. You will learn about the File tab shortly.

The Word application displays the File tab and eight Ribbon tabs. The Home tab (shown in Figure 7), consists of five groups. The tab name appears in blue and is outlined, indicating it is the open or active tab. This tab is available in all the Office 2013 applications and because it contains commands that are most frequently used when you first start an application or open a file, it is initially the open tab. In Word, the commands in the Home tab help you perform actions related to creating the text content of your document. In the other Office 2013 applications, the Home tab contains commands related to creating the associated type of document, such as a worksheet, presentation, or database. To open another tab you click on the tab name.

1 **Click on the Insert tab.**

Your screen should be similar to Figure 8

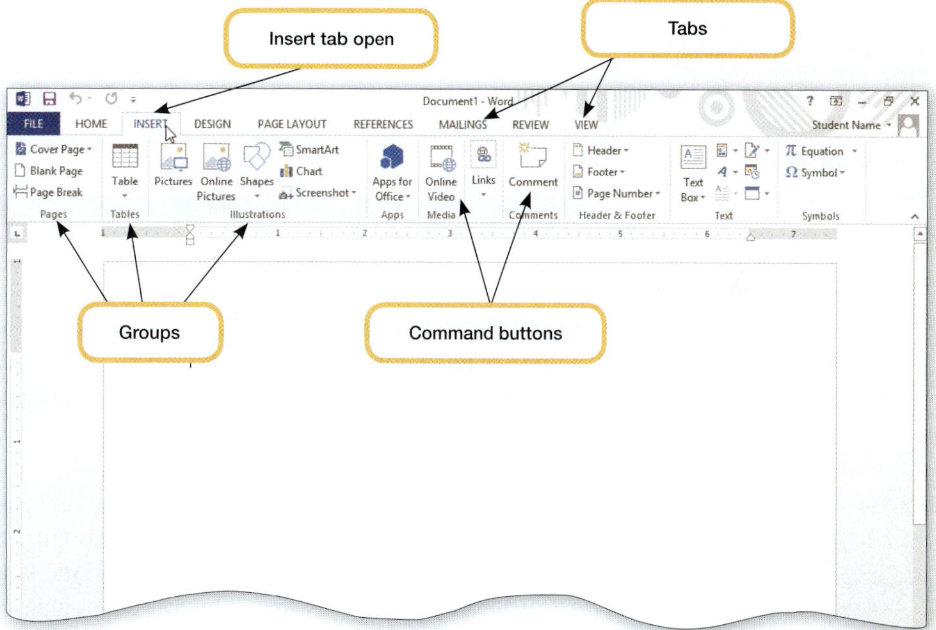

Figure 8

This Insert tab is now open and is the active tab. It contains 10 groups whose commands have to do with inserting items into a document. As you use the Office applications, you will see that the Ribbon contains many of the same tabs, groups, and commands across the applications. For example, the Insert tab is available in all applications except Access. Others, such as the References tab in Word, are specific to the application. You also will see that many of the groups and commands in the common tabs, such as the Clipboard group of commands in the Home tab, contain all or many of the same commands across applications. Other groups in the common tabs contain commands that are specific to the application.

To save space, some tabs, called **contextual tabs** or **on-demand tabs**, are displayed only as needed. For example, when you are working with a picture, the Picture Tools tab appears. The contextual nature of this feature keeps the work area uncluttered when the feature is not needed and provides ready access to it when it is needed.

2

- **Click on each of the other tabs, ending with the View tab, to see their groups and commands.**

Additional Information

If you have a mouse with a scroll wheel, pointing to the tab area of the Ribbon and using the scroll wheel will scroll the tabs.

Touch Tip

On a touch device you can swipe the Ribbon tab to scroll the tabs.

Your screen should be similar to Figure 9

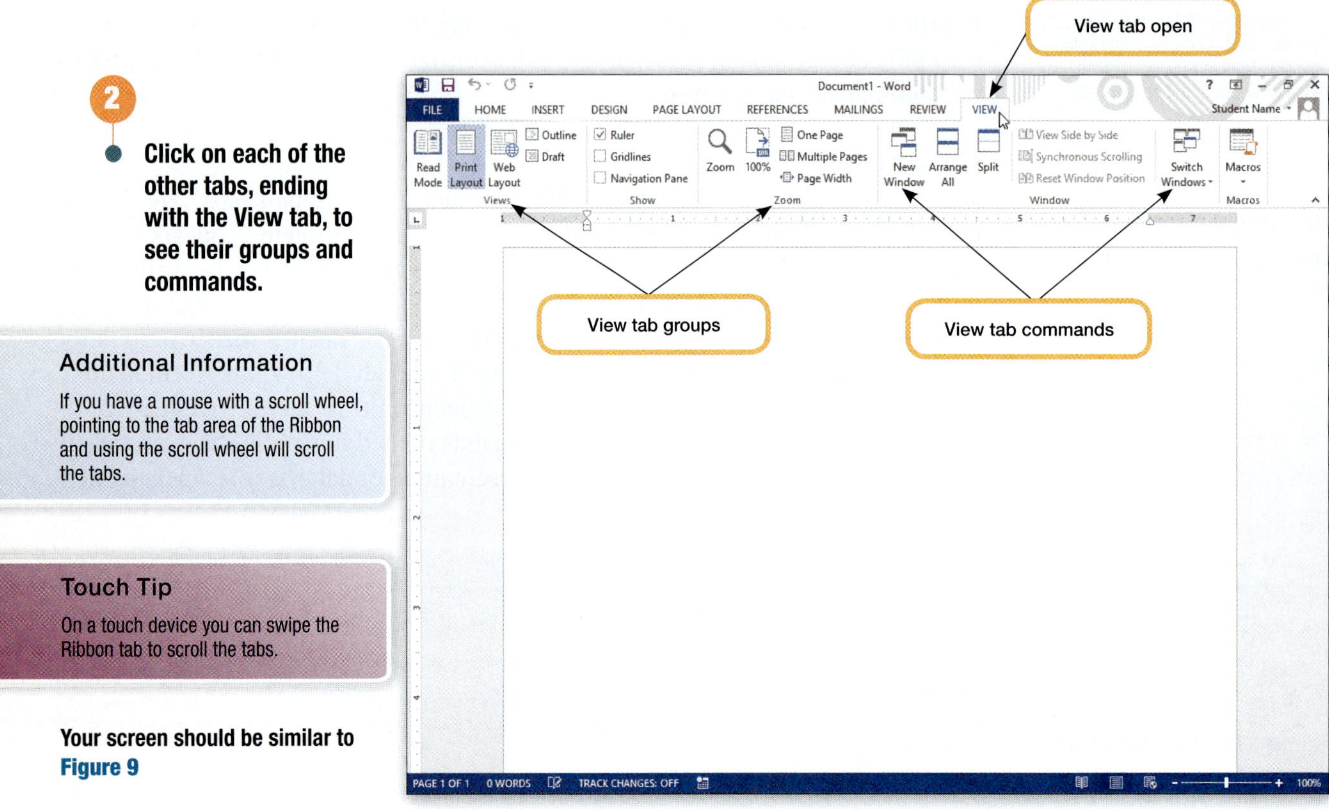

Figure 9

Each tab relates to a type of activity; for example, the View tab commands perform activities related to viewing the document. Within each tab, similar commands are grouped together to make it easy to find the commands you want to use.

Displaying Enhanced ScreenTips

Although command buttons display graphic representations of the action they perform, often the graphic is not descriptive enough. As you have learned, pointing to a button displays the name of the button and the keyboard shortcut in a ScreenTip. To further help explain what a button does, many buttons in the Ribbon display **Enhanced ScreenTips**. For example, the Paste button in the Clipboard group of the Home tab is a two-part button. Clicking on the upper part will immediately perform an action, whereas clicking on the lower part will display additional options. You will use this feature next to see the Enhanced ScreenTips.

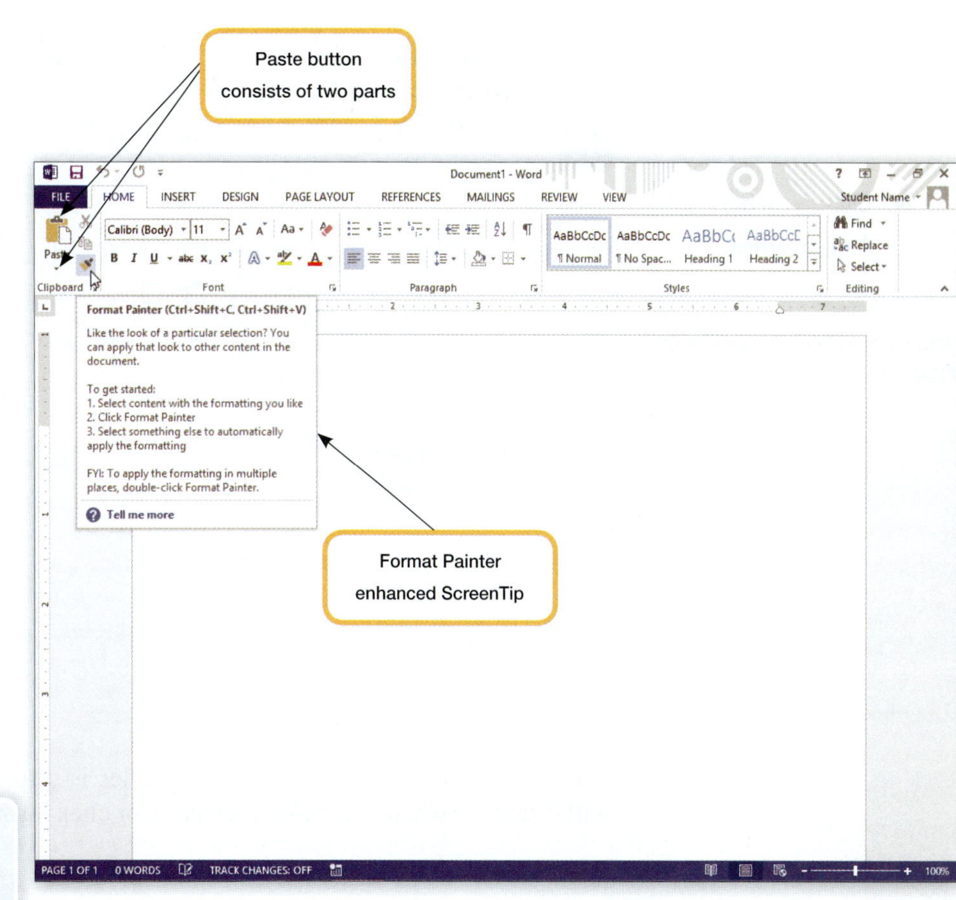

Figure 10

1

- **Click on the Home tab to open it.**
- **Point to the upper part of the Paste button in the Clipboard group.**
- **Point to the lower part of the Paste button in the Clipboard group.**
- **Point to Format Painter in the Clipboard group.**

Additional Information

Depending upon your screen resolution and size, the button may appear as Format Painter.

Your screen should be similar to Figure 10

Additional Information

Not all commands have keyboard shortcuts.

Additional Information

You will learn about using Help shortly.

Touch Tip

On a touch device, it may be difficult to touch the arrow only. To add space between buttons, turn on Touch Mode from the Quick Access toolbar.

Because the Paste button is divided into two parts, both parts display separate Enhanced ScreenTips containing the button name; the keyboard shortcut key combination, Ctrl + V; and a brief description of what action will be performed when you click on that part of the button. Pointing to Format Painter displays an Enhanced ScreenTip that provides more detailed information about the command including steps on how to use the feature. Enhanced ScreenTips help you find out what the feature does without having to look it up using Office Help, a built-in reference source. If a feature has a Help article, you can automatically access it by pressing F1 while the Enhanced ScreenTip is displayed or by choosing "Tell me more."

Using Command Buttons

Clicking on most command buttons immediately performs the associated action. Some command buttons, however, include an arrow as part of the button that affects how the button works. If a button includes an arrow that is separated from the graphic with a line when you point to the button (as in Bullets), clicking the button performs the associated default action and clicking the arrow displays a menu of options. If a button displays an arrow that is not separated from the graphic with a line when you point to it (as in Line and Paragraph Spacing), clicking the button immediately displays a menu of options. To see an example of a drop-down menu, you will open the Bullets menu.

1

- Click [▾] in the [Bullets] Bullets button.

Your screen should be similar to **Figure 11**

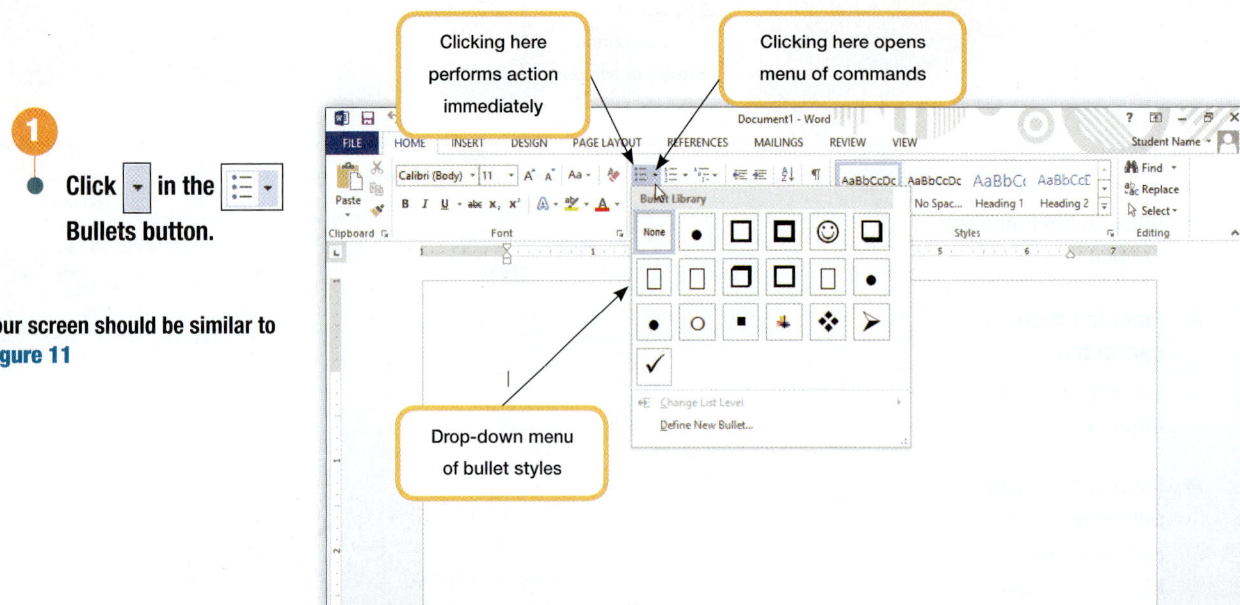

Figure 11

A drop-down menu of different bullet styles is displayed. The drop-down menu will disappear when you make a selection or click on any other area of the window.

2

- Click outside the Bullet menu to clear it.
- Click [Line and Paragraph Spacing] Line and Paragraph Spacing.

Your screen should be similar to **Figure 12**

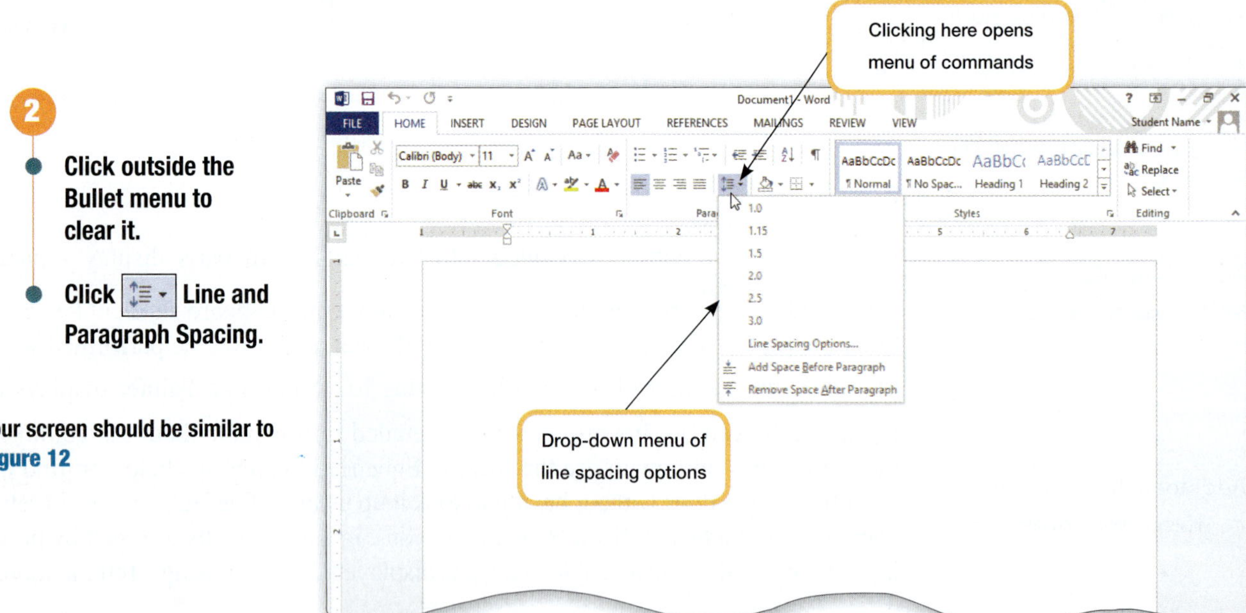

Figure 12

Another Method

You also can open tabs and choose Ribbon commands using the access key shortcuts. Press Alt or F10 to display the access key letters in KeyTips over each available feature. Then type the letter for the feature you want to use.

The menu of options opened automatically when you clicked [Line and Paragraph Spacing] Line and Paragraph Spacing.

Using the Dialog Box Launcher

Because there is not enough space, only the most used commands are displayed in the Ribbon. If more commands are available, a button, called the **dialog box launcher**, is displayed in the lower-right corner of the group. Clicking opens a dialog box or task pane of additional options.

1

- **Click outside the Line and Paragraph Spacing menu to clear it.**
- **Point to the of the Paragraph group to see the ScreenTip.**
- **Click of the Paragraph group.**

Your screen should be similar to Figure 13

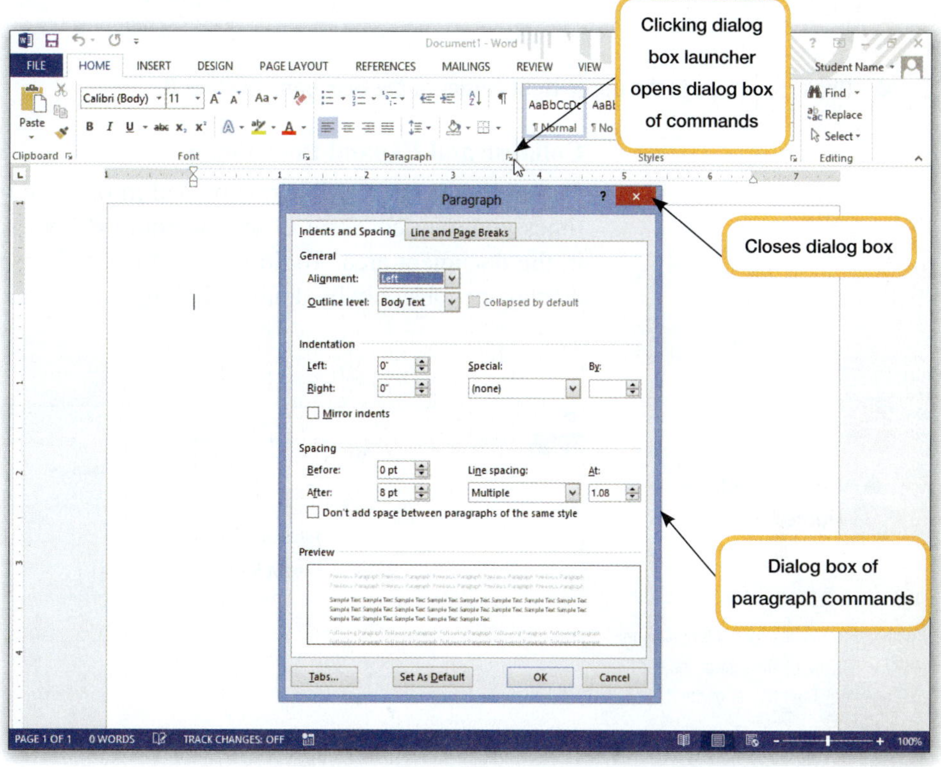

Figure 13

The Paragraph dialog box appears. It provides access to the more advanced paragraph settings options. Selecting options from the dialog box and clicking OK will close the dialog box and apply the options as specified. To cancel the dialog box, you can click Cancel or × Close in the dialog box title bar.

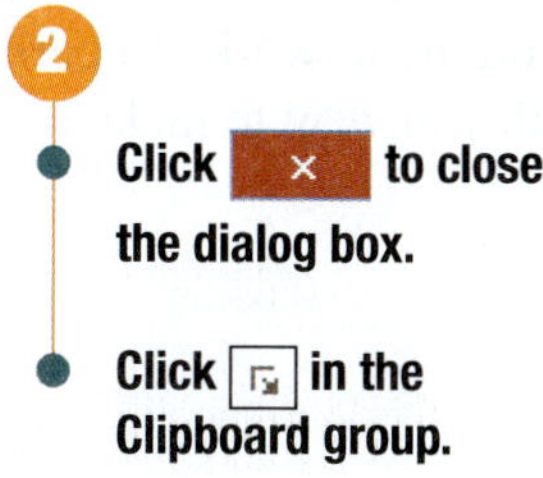

2

- **Click × to close the dialog box.**
- **Click in the Clipboard group.**

Your screen should be similar to Figure 14

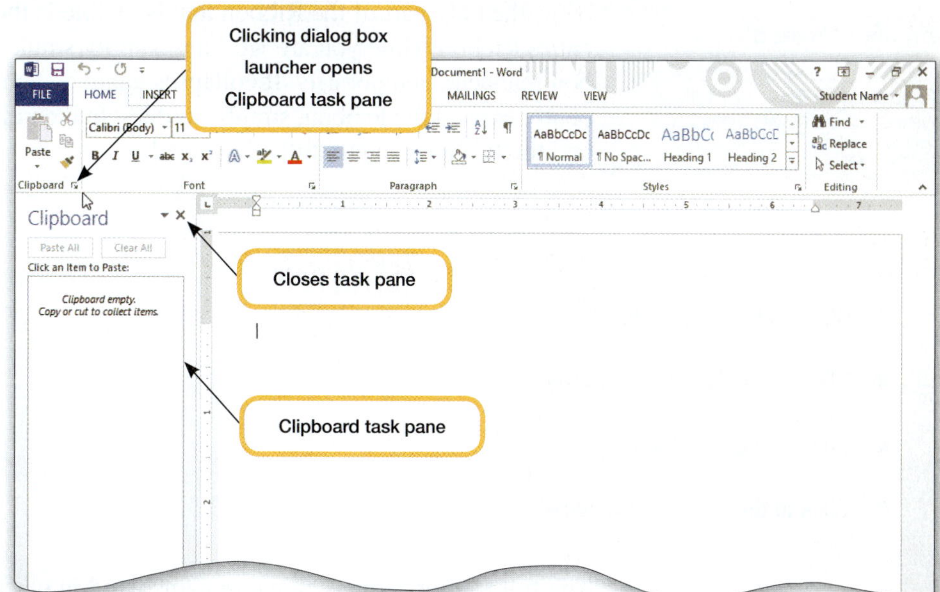

Figure 14

Additional Information

You will learn about using the features in the dialog boxes, the task panes, and the Clipboard as they are used in the labs.

A **task pane** is open (see Figure 14) that contains features associated with the Clipboard. Unlike a dialog box, a task pane is a separate window that can be sized and moved. Generally, task panes are attached or docked to one edge of the application window. Also, task panes remain open until you close them. This allows you to make multiple selections from the task pane while continuing to work on other areas of your document.

- **Click ☒ Close in the upper-right corner of the task pane to close it.**

Collapse and Expand the Ribbon

Currently, the entire Ribbon is pinned in place in the application window. Sometimes you may not want to see the entire Ribbon so that more space is available in the document area. To do this, you can collapse the Ribbon to minimize it to display the tabs only by double-clicking the active tab.

- **Double-click the Home tab.**

Another Method

Another way to collapse the Ribbon is to click ^ Collapse the Ribbon located at the bottom-right corner of the Ribbon.

Your screen should be similar to Figure 15

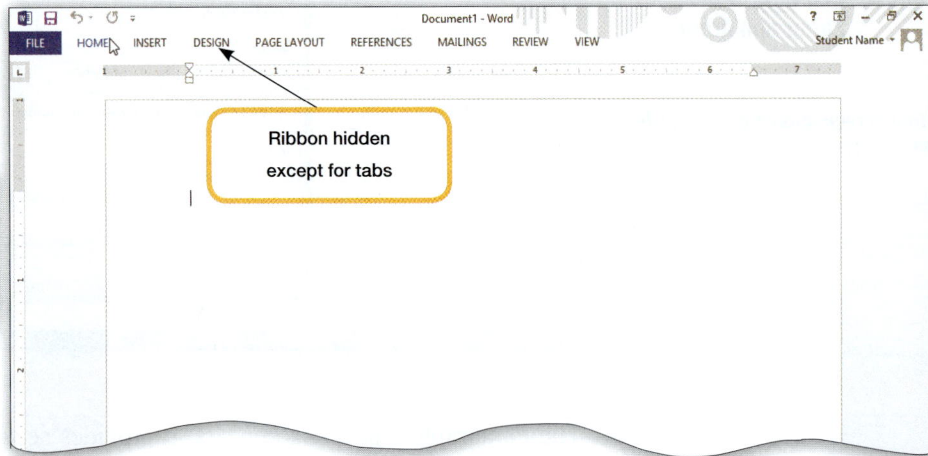

Figure 15

Another Method

You also can choose Collapse the Ribbon from the Ribbon's context menu or use the keyboard shortcut Ctrl + F1.

Now, the only part of the Ribbon that is visible is the tab area. Then, to access the entire Ribbon while you are working, simply single-click on any tab and the Ribbon reappears temporarily. It collapses again as you continue to work. To permanently expand the Ribbon, simply double-click on the tab you want to make active and the Ribbon is again fully displayed.

- **Click on the Insert tab.**
- **Click in the document window.**
- **Double-click the Home tab.**
- **Click in the document window.**

The full Ribbon reappears and remains fixed in place and the Home tab is active.

Using the Office Backstage

To the left of the Home tab in the Ribbon is the File tab. Unlike the other tabs that display a Ribbon of commands, the File tab opens the Office Backstage. The Office **Backstage** contains commands that allow you to work *with* your document, unlike the Ribbon that allows you to work *in* your document. The Backstage contains commands that apply to the entire document. For example, you will find commands to open, save, print, and manage your files and set your program options. The File tab is common to all the Office 2013 applications, although the options may vary slightly.

1

- **Click the File tab to open the Backstage.**
- **Click Info in the list of sidebar options.**

Your screen should be similar to Figure 16

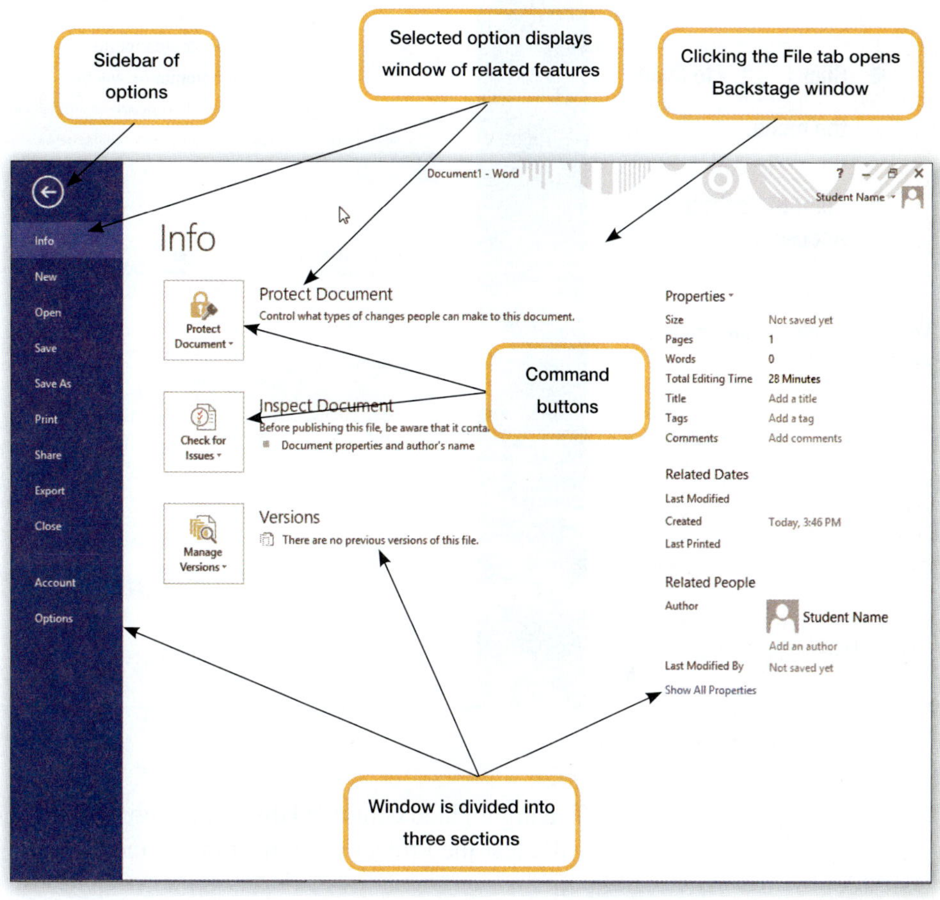

Figure 16

Another Method

You also can use the directional keys to move up, down, left, or right within Backstage and press Enter to choose a selected option or command.

The Backstage window is open and completely covers the application window. The left side of the window displays a list of options in a sidebar. Pointing to an option selects it and it appears highlighted. Clicking an option chooses it and displays related commands and features in the right side. Choosing some options opens a dialog box or immediately performs the associated action. The last two options in the sidebar are used to change account and program settings.

The Info window is open and displays information about the current document. The three command buttons are used to control changes that can be made to the document, check for issues related to distribution, and manage document versions for the current document. A description of these buttons and the current document settings is shown to the right of the button. Notice that the buttons display a ▾. This indicates that a menu of commands will be displayed when you click the button. The right side of the window displays a list of settings, called **properties**, associated with the document. The current properties displayed in the Info window show the initial or **default** properties associated with a new blank document.

Additional Information

You will learn more about document properties shortly.

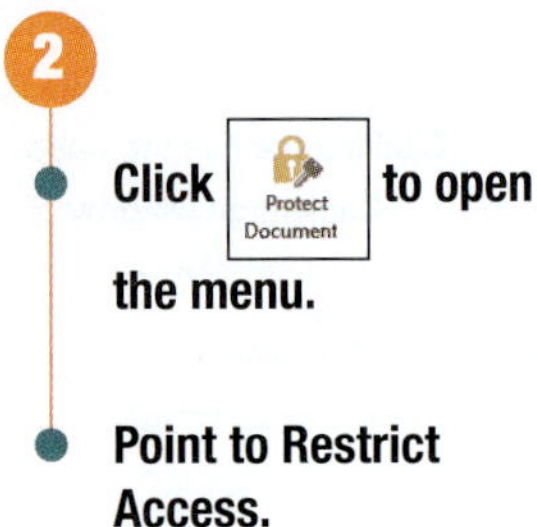

2

- **Click** Protect Document **to open the menu.**
- **Point to Restrict Access.**

Your screen should be similar to Figure 17

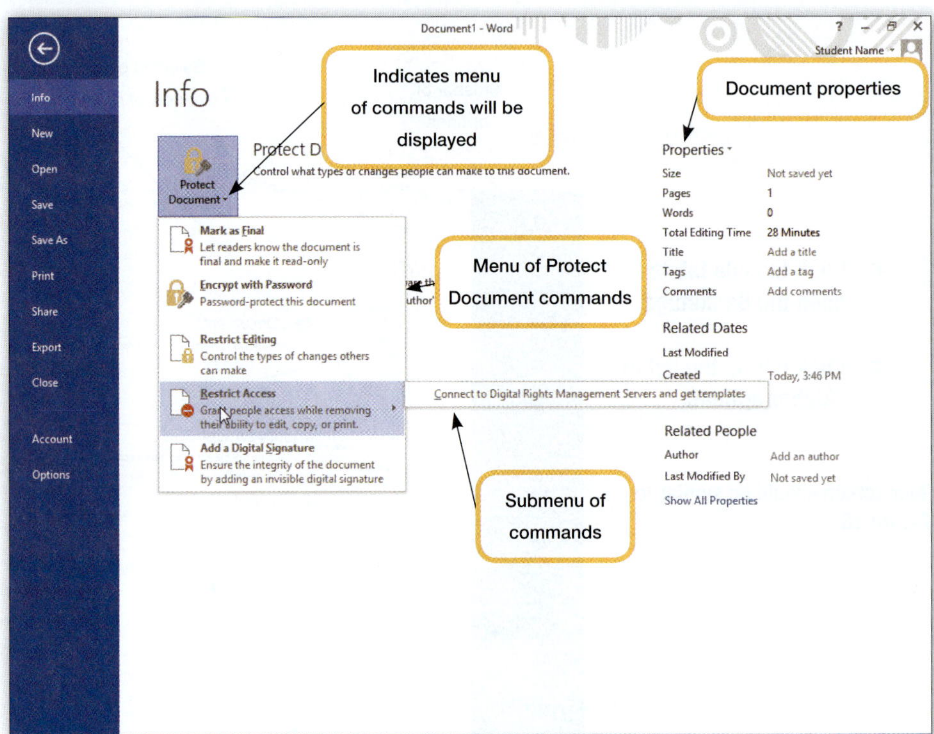

Figure 17

The highlighted command displays a submenu of additional commands. Next, you will clear the Protect Document menu and open the New window in Backstage.

3

- **Click** **Protect Document** **again to clear the submenu.**
- **Click the New option in the sidebar.**

Your screen should be similar to Figure 18

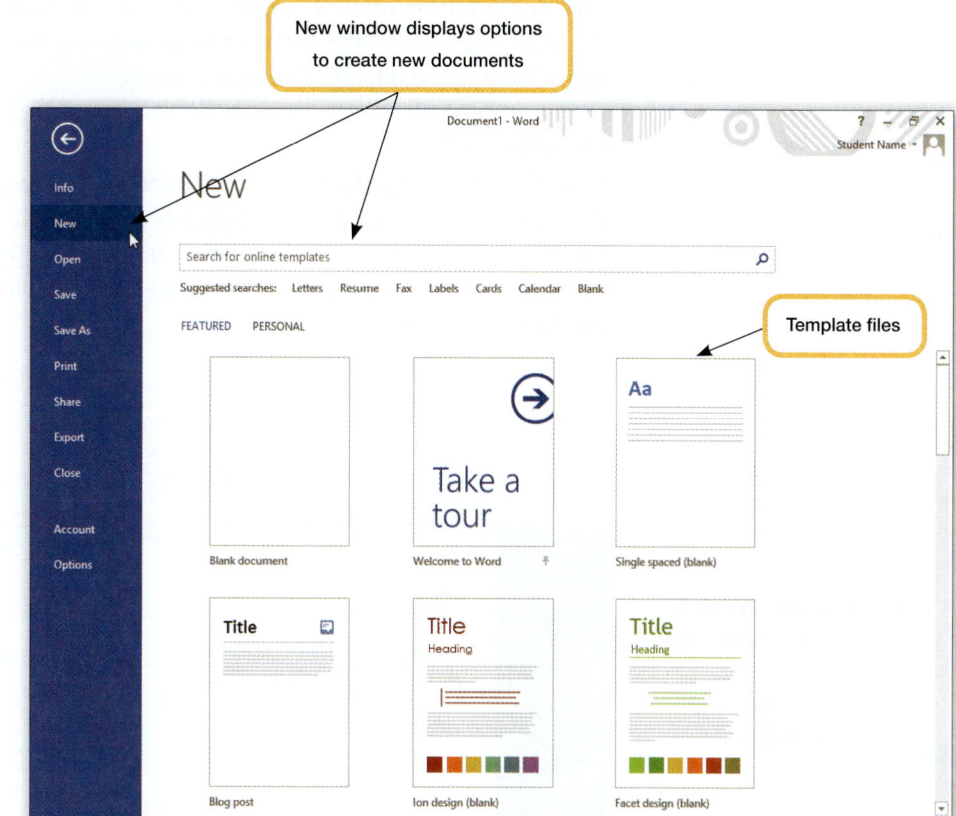

Figure 18

The Backstage window now displays options for creating a new document. It is very similar to the Start screen that appears when you first start Word 2013.

4

- **Click** ← **at the top of the sidebar.**

Another Method

You also can press Esc to close the Backstage window.

Backstage is closed and the document window is displayed again.

COMMON APPLICATION FEATURES

So far you have learned about using the Office 2013 user interface features. Next, you will learn about application features that are used to work in and modify documents and are the same or similar in all Office 2013 applications. These include how to open, close, and save files; navigate, scroll, and zoom a document; enter, select, edit, and format text; and document, preview, and print a file. To do this, you will open a Word document file and make a few changes to it. Then you will save and print the revised document. Once you have gained an understanding of the basic concepts of the common features using Word, you will be able to easily apply them in the other Office applications.

Opening a File

In all Office 2013 applications, you either need to create a new file using the blank document template or another template or open an existing file. Opening a file retrieves a file that is stored on your computer hard drive or an external storage location and places it in RAM (random-access memory) of your computer so it can be read and modified.

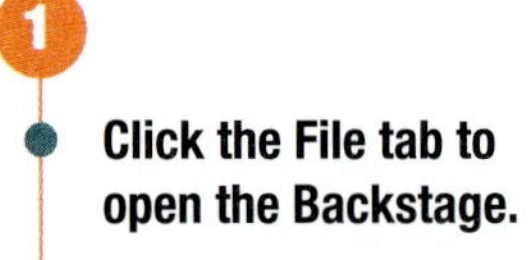

- **Click the File tab to open the Backstage.**
- **Click the Open option in the sidebar.**

Your screen should be similar to Figure 19

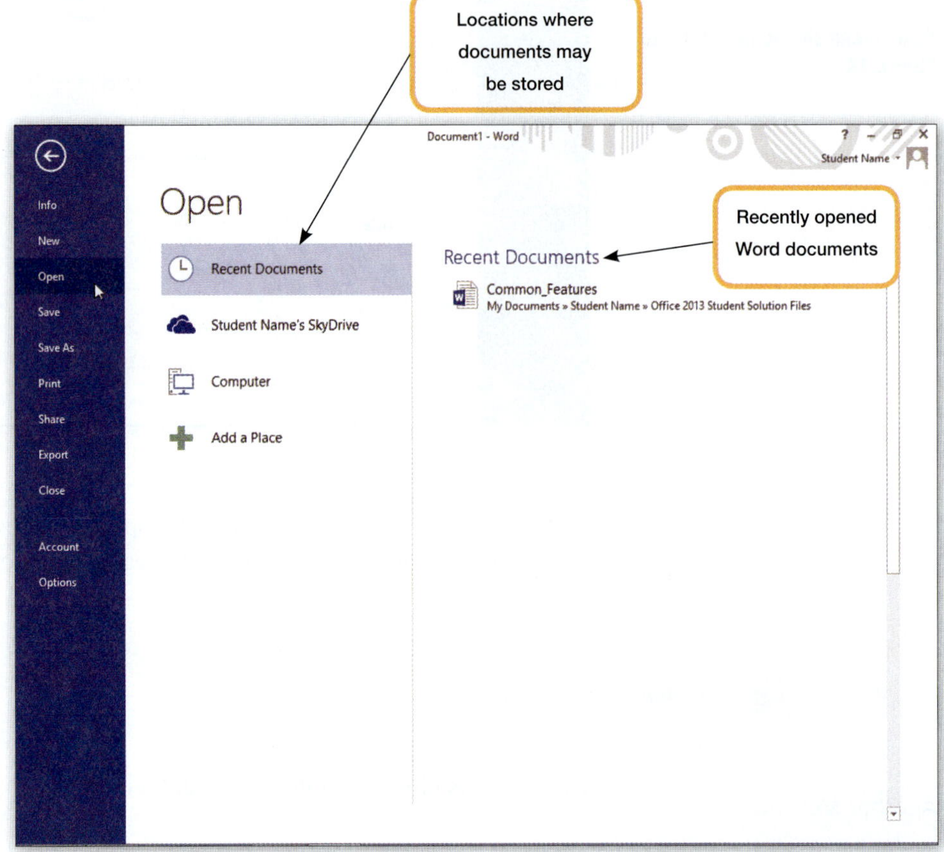

Figure 19

> **Additional Information**
> Microsoft SkyDrive and SharePoint are subscription file storage services that you can access anytime you are online.

The left side of the Open window displays locations where the file you want to open is stored. The location may be the hard drive of your computer, an external storage device, a local network, or in the cloud on SkyDrive or SharePoint. The **cloud** refers to any applications and services that are hosted and run on servers connected to the Internet. The Recent Documents option is selected by default and displays a list of file names of documents that have been recently opened in Word 2013 in the Recent Documents pane. Below the file name the path location of the file is displayed. If the file you want to open appears in the Recent Documents list, clicking on the file immediately opens it.

First you need to change to the location where your data files for completing these labs are stored.

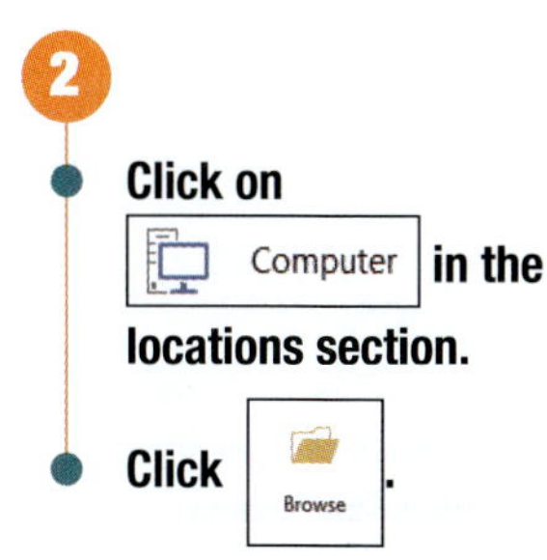

Your screen should be similar to **Figure 20**

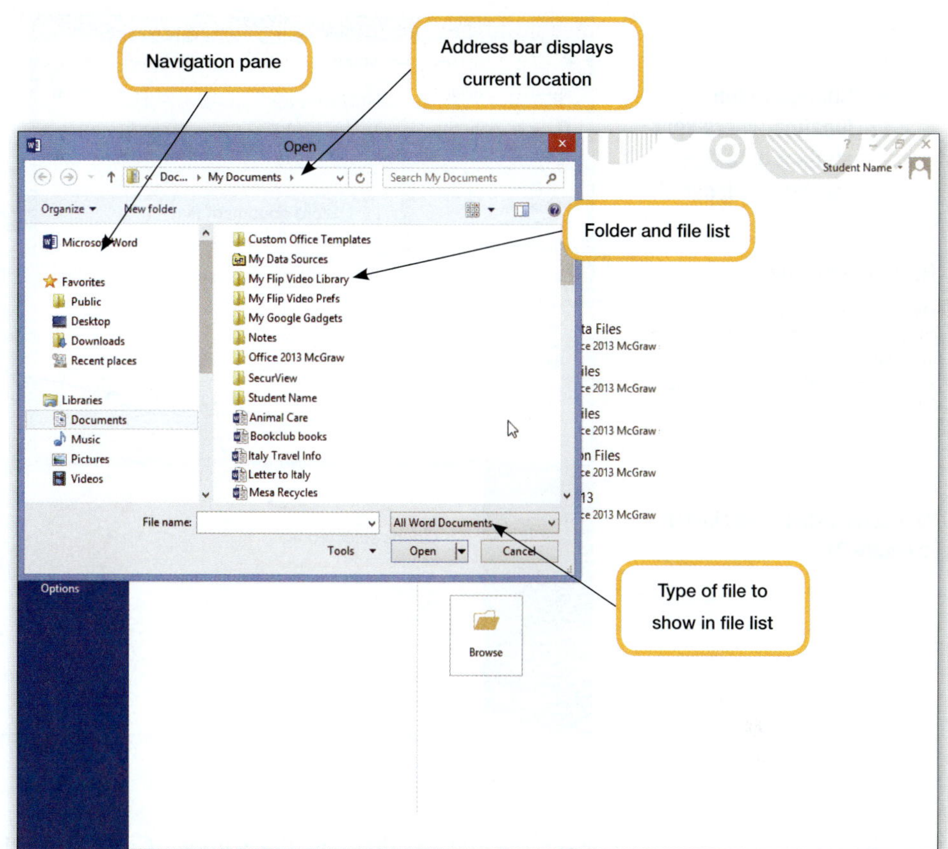

Figure 20

Additional Information

The Open dialog box is common to all programs using the Windows operating system. Your dialog box may look slightly different depending on the current View setting.

Additional Information

You will learn about the different file types shortly.

The Open dialog box is displayed in which you specify the location where the file you want to open is stored and the file name. The location consists of identifying the hard drive of your computer or an external storage device or a remote computer followed by folders and subfolders within that location. The Address bar displays the default folder as the location to open the file. The file list displays folder names as well as the names of any Word documents in the current location. Only Word documents are listed because All Word Documents is the specified file type in the File Type list box. In Excel and PowerPoint, only files of that application's file type would be displayed.

There are several methods that can be used to locate files. One is to use the Address bar to specify another location by either typing the complete folder name or path or by opening the drop-down list of previously accessed locations and clicking a new location. Another is to use the features in the Navigation pane, to choose a link to a Favorite item or location, to search the folders and files in the Libraries or to navigate through the hierarchical structure of drives and folders on your computer. Clicking a link or folder from the list displays files at that location in the file list. Then, from the file list, you can continue to select subfolders until the file you want to open is located.

You will open the file IO_Common Features that is supplied with your student data files for this lab.

Change to the location where your student data files for this lab are located.

Having Trouble?

The text assumes the location is on your computer in a folder named Introduction to Office. If your files are in a different location, your instructor will provide further directions.

Your screen should be similar to Figure 21

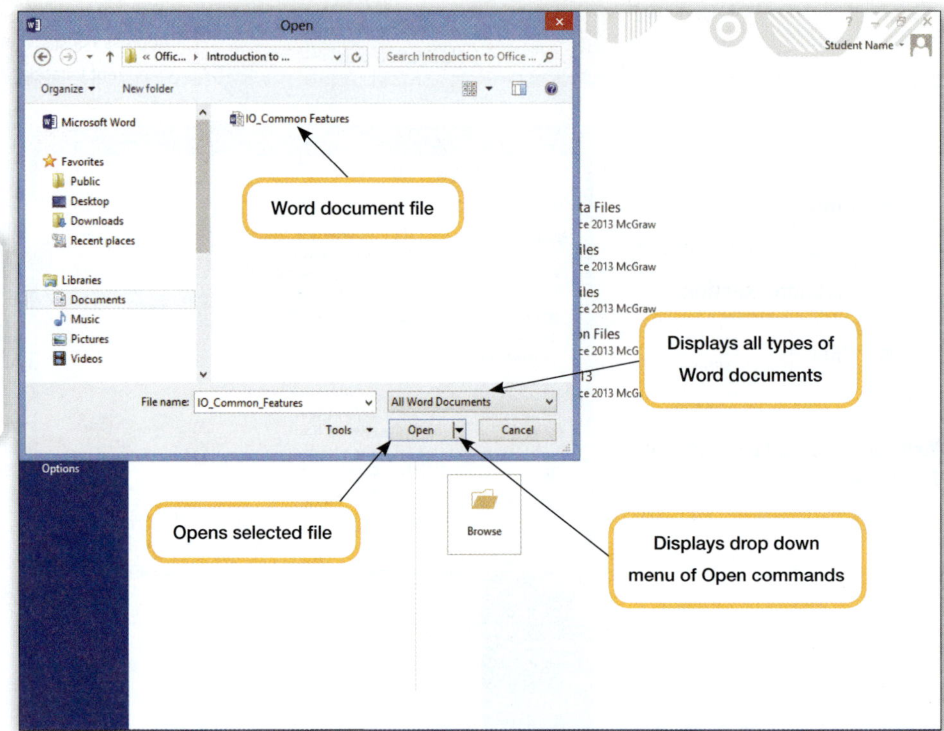

Figure 21

Now the file list displays the names of all Word files at that location. Next, you open the file by clicking on the file name to select it and clicking the Open button. In addition, in the Office applications you can specify how you want to open a file by choosing from the Open drop-down menu options described in the following table.

Open Options	Description
Open	Opens with all formatting and editing features enabled. This is the default setting.
Open Read-only	Opens file so it can be read or copied only, not modified in any way.
Open as Copy	Automatically creates a copy of the file and opens the copy with complete editing capabilities.
Open in Browser	Opens HTML type files in a web browser.
Open with Transform	Opens certain types of documents and lets you change it into another type of document.
Open in Protected View	Opens files from potentially unsafe locations with editing functions disabled.
Open and Repair	Opens file and attempts to repair any damage.

Another Method

You could also press Enter to open a selected file or double-click on the file name.

You will open the file IO_Common Features. Clicking the Open button opens the file using the default Open option so you can read and edit the file.

4

- **Select** IO_Common Features.
- **Click** Open.

Your screen should be similar to Figure 22

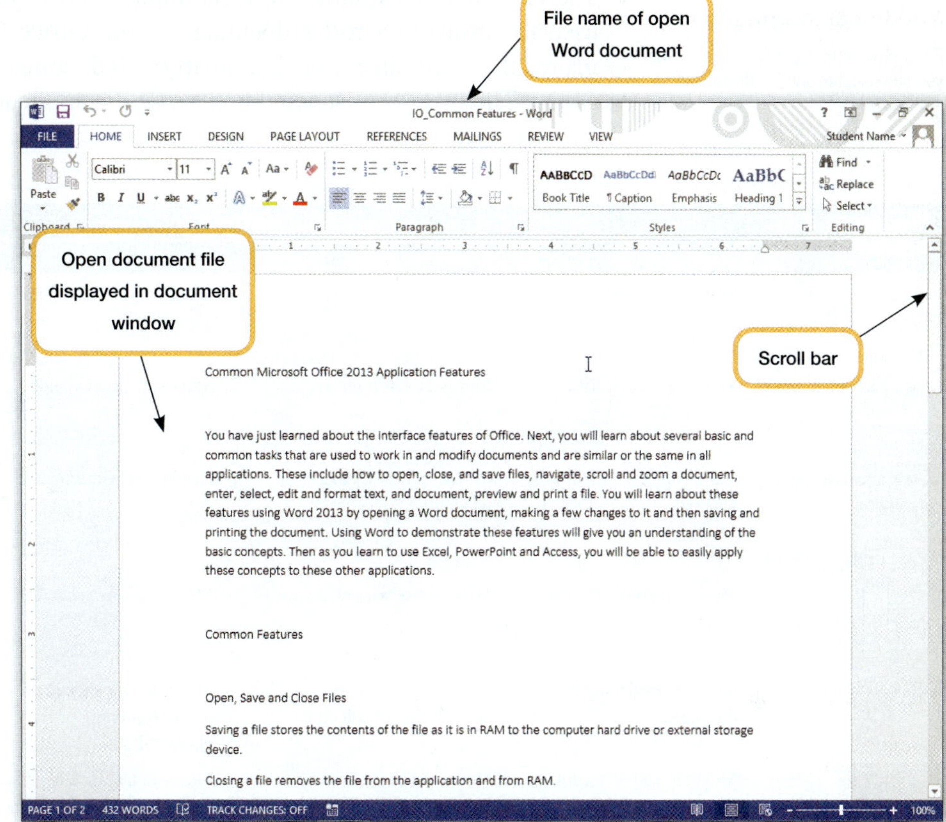

Figure 22

A Word document file describing the common Microsoft Office application features is displayed in the document window.

Scrolling the Document Window

As documents increase in size, they cannot be easily viewed in their entirety in the document window and much time can be spent moving to different locations in the document. All Office 2013 applications include features that make it easy to move around and view the information in a large document. The basic method is to scroll through a document using the scroll bar or keyboard. Both methods are useful, depending on what you are doing. For example, if you are entering text using the keyboard, using the keyboard method may be more efficient than using the mouse.

Additional Information

Scroll bars are also found in task panes and dialog boxes and operate similarly.

Touch Tip

With a touch device, you can touch the document and slide it up and down.

Additional Information

If you have a mouse with a scroll wheel, you can use it to scroll a document vertically.

The table below explains the basic mouse and keyboard techniques that can be used to vertically scroll a document in the Office 2013 applications. There are many other methods for navigating through documents that are unique to an application. They will be discussed in the specific application text.

Mouse or Key Action	Effect in:			
	Word	Excel	PowerPoint	Access
Click ▼ Or ↓	Moves down line by line.	Moves down row by row	Moves down slide by slide	Moves down record by record
Click ▲ Or ↑	Moves up line by line.	Moves up row by row	Moves up slide by slide	Moves up record by record
Click above/below scroll box Or Page Up/Page Down	Moves up/down window by window	Moves up/down window by window	Displays previous/next slide	Moves up/down window by window
Drag Scroll Box	Moves up/down line by line	Moves up/down row by row	Moves up/down slide by slide	Moves up/down record by record
Ctrl + Home	Moves to beginning of document	Moves to first cell in worksheet or beginning of cell entry	Moves to first slide in presentation or beginning of entry in placeholder	Moves to first record in table or beginning of field entry
Ctrl + End	Moves to end of document	Moves to last-used cell in worksheet or end of cell entry	Moves to last slide in presentation or to end of placeholder entry	Moves to last record in table or end of field entry

Additional Information

You also can scroll the document window horizontally using the horizontal scroll bar or the → and ← keys.

You will use the vertical scroll bar to view the text at the bottom of the Word document. When you use the scroll bar to scroll, the actual location in the document where you can work does not change, only the area you are viewing changes. For example, in Word, the cursor does not move and in Excel the cell you can work in does not change. To move the cursor or make another cell active, you must click in a location in the window. However, when you scroll using the keyboard, the actual location as identified by the position of the cursor in the document also changes. For example, in Word the cursor attempts to maintain its position in a line as you scroll up and down through the document. In Excel the cell you can work in changes as you move through a worksheet using the keyboard.

- **Click [▼] in the vertical scroll bar 10 times.**
- **Click at the beginning of the word Scroll in the Common Features section to move the cursor.**
- **Press [↓] 10 times to scroll the window and move the cursor down 10 lines.**

Your screen should be similar to Figure 23

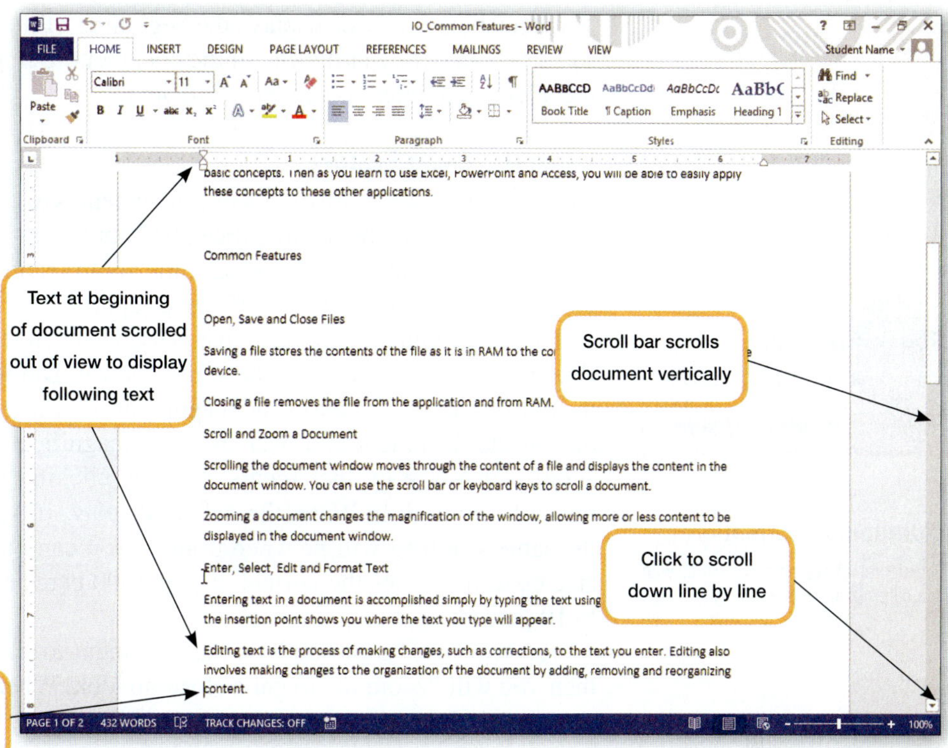

Figure 23

Having Trouble?

If your screen scrolls differently, this is a function of the type of monitor you are using.

The text at the beginning of the document has scrolled line by line off the top of the document window, and the following text is now displayed. In a large document, scrolling line by line can take a while. You will now try out several additional mouse and keyboard scrolling features that move by larger increments through the document.

- **Click below the scroll box in the scroll bar.**
- **Press [Ctrl] + [End] to move to the end of the last line of the document.**
- **Drag the scroll box to the top of the scroll bar.**

Your screen should be similar to Figure 24

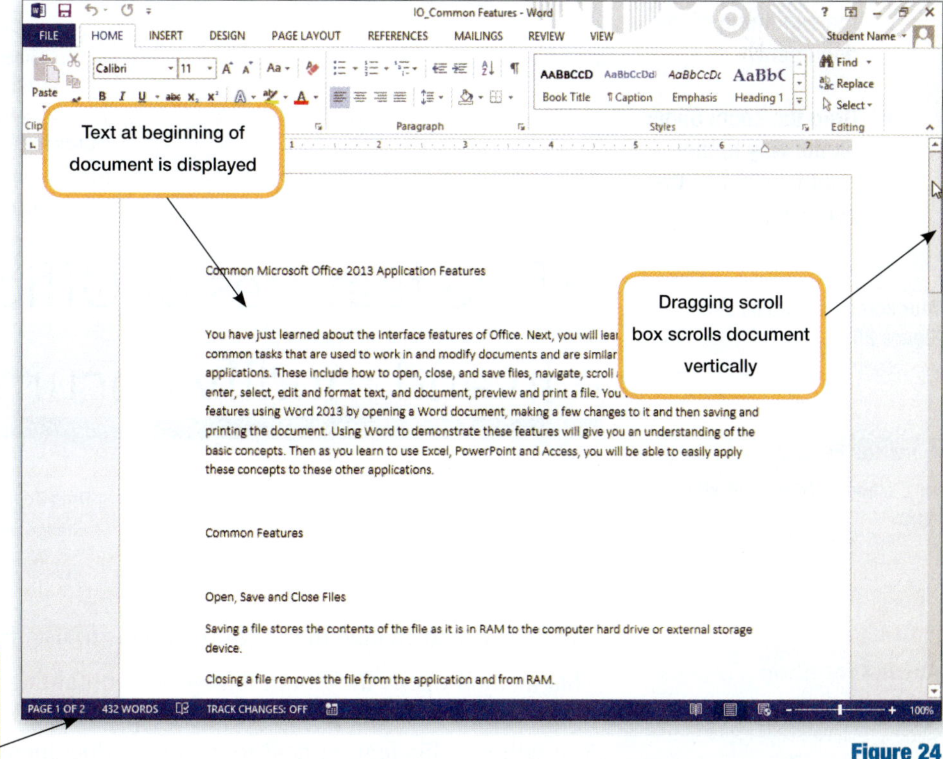

Figure 24

The document window displays the beginning of the document; however, the cursor is still on page 2 at the end of the document. Using these features makes scrolling a large document much more efficient.

Using the Zoom Feature

Another way to see more or less of a document is to use the zoom feature. Although this feature is available in all Office 2013 applications, Excel and PowerPoint have fewer options than Word. In Access, the zoom feature is available only when specific features are used, such as viewing reports.

Touch Tip

With a touch device, you can zoom in by stretching two fingers apart and zoom out by pinching two fingers together.

The Zoom Slider in the status bar is used to change the magnification. To use the Zoom Slider, click and drag the slider control. Dragging to the right zooms in on the document and increases the magnification whereas dragging to the left zooms out on the document and decreases the magnification. You also can change the zoom percentage by increments of 10 by clicking the + or - on each end of the slider control. In Word, the default display, 100 percent, shows the characters the same size they will be when printed. You can increase the onscreen character size up to five times the normal display (500 percent) or reduce the character size to 10 percent.

Additional Information

The degree of magnification varies with the different applications.

You will first "zoom out" on the document to get an overview of the file, and then you will "zoom in" to get a close-up look. When a document is zoomed, you can work in it as usual.

1

- **Click - in the Zoom Slider five times to decrease the zoom percentage to 50%.**
- **Press Ctrl + Home to move the cursor to the beginning of the document.**
- **Drag the Zoom Slider all the way to the right to increase the zoom to 500%.**

Your screen should be similar to Figure 25

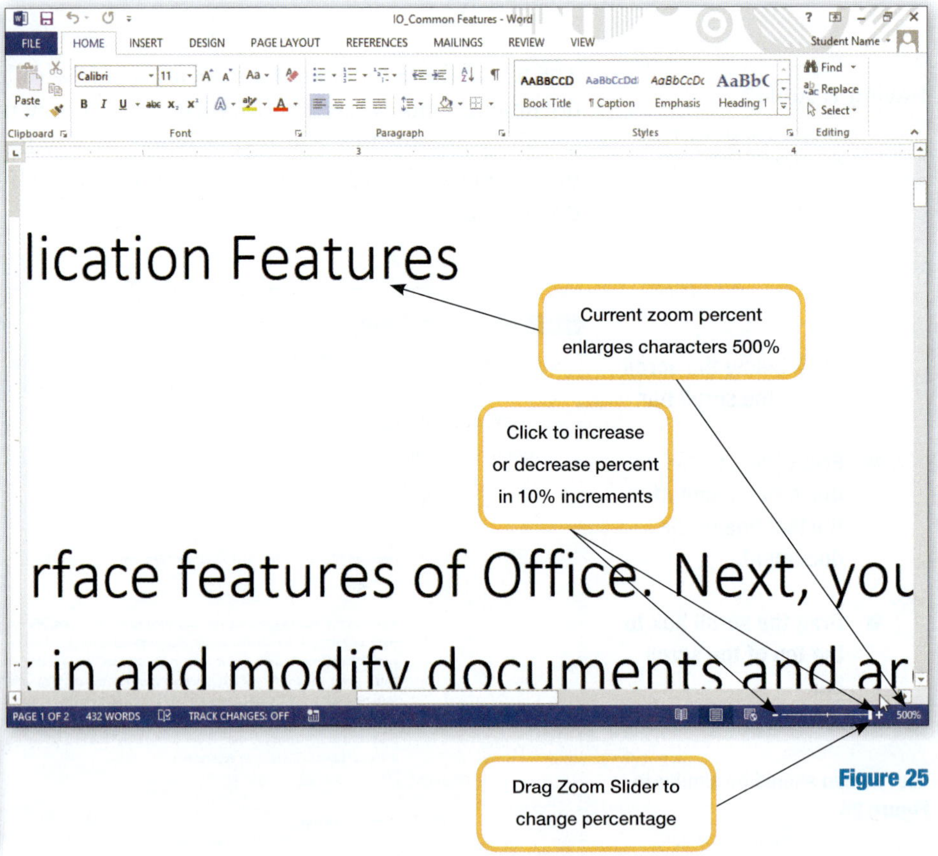

Figure 25

Another Method

You can also hold down Ctrl while using the scroll wheel on your mouse to zoom a document.

Another way to change the magnification is to use the Zoom button in the View tab. This method opens the Zoom dialog box containing several preset zoom options, or an option that lets you set a precise percentage using the Percent scroll box. You will use this feature next to zoom the document. This method is available in Word only.

Another Method

You can also click on the zoom percentage in the status bar to open the Zoom dialog box.

- Open the View tab.
- Click  in the Zoom group.
- Click Whole Page and note that the percent value in the Percent text box and the preview area reflect the new percentage setting.
- Click the ▲ scroll button in the Percent scroll box to increase the zoom percentage to 57.

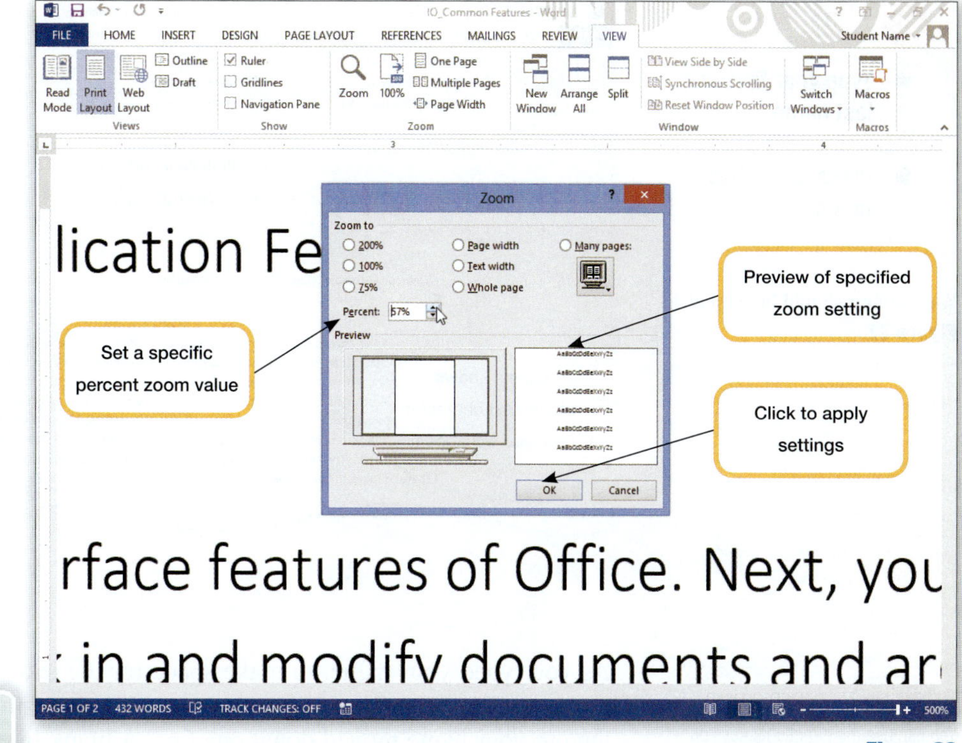

Figure 26

Another Method

You could also type a value in the Percent text box to specify an exact percentage.

Your screen should be similar to Figure 26

The Zoom dialog box preview areas show how the document will appear on your screen at the specified zoom percent. Not until you complete the command by clicking OK will the zoom percent in the document actually change. You will complete the command to apply the 57% zoom setting. Then, you will use the 100% button in the Zoom group to quickly return to the default zoom setting.

3

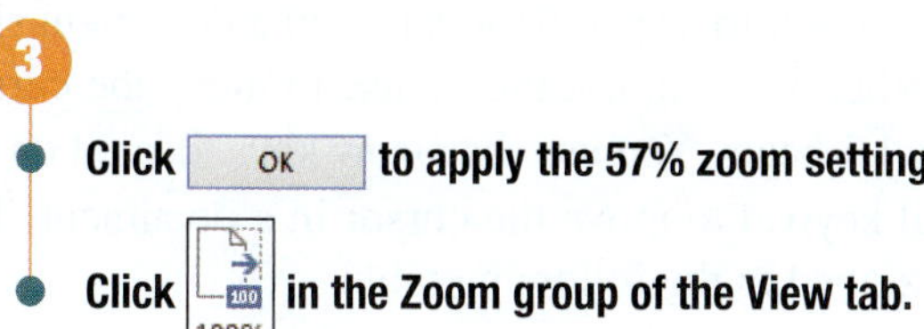

- Click OK to apply the 57% zoom setting.
- Click 100% in the Zoom group of the View tab.

The document is again at 100% magnification.

Entering and Editing Text

Touch Tip

With a touch device, a Touch keyboard appears when needed to enter text.

Now that you are familiar with the entire document, you will make a few changes to it. The keyboard is used to enter information into a document. In all applications, the location of the cursor shows you where the text will appear as you type. After text is entered into a document, you need to know how to move around within the text to edit or make changes to the text. Again, the process is similar for all Office applications.

Additional Information

The effect of pressing Enter varies in the different Office applications. For example, in Excel, it completes the entry and moves to another cell. You will learn about these differences in the individual application labs.

Currently, in this Word document, the cursor is positioned at the top of the document. You will type your name at this location. As you type, the cursor moves to the right and the characters will appear to the left of the cursor. Then you will press Enter to end the line following your name and press Enter again at the beginning of a line to insert a blank line.

- **Type your first and last name.**
- **Press Enter two times.**

Your screen should be similar to Figure 27

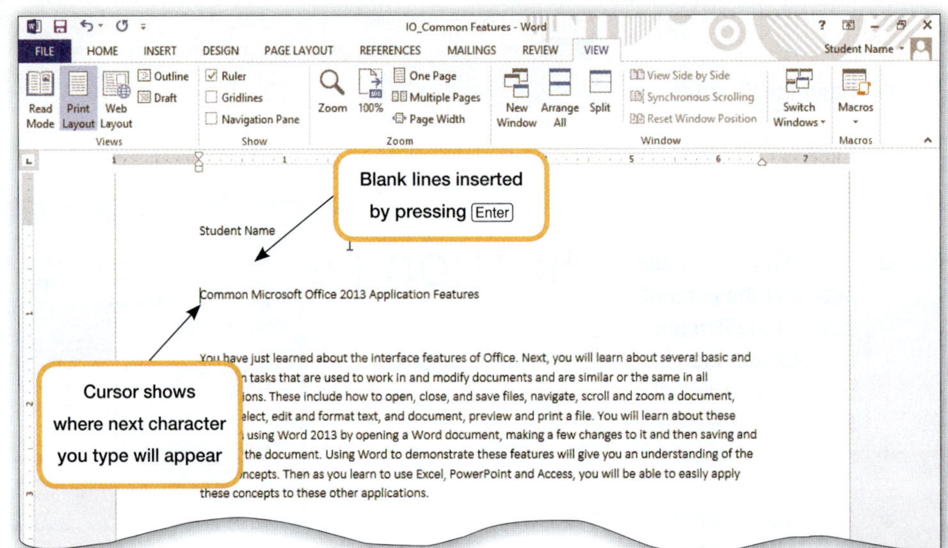

Figure 27

Additional Information

You can use the directional keys on the numeric keypad or the dedicated directional keypad area. If using the numeric keypad, make sure the Num Lock feature is off; otherwise, numbers will be entered in the document. The Num Lock indicator light above the keypad is lit when on. Press Num Lock to turn it off.

Touch Tip

With a touch device, tap in the text to place the cursor.

As you typed your name, to make space for the text on the line, the existing text moved to the right. Then, when you pressed Enter the first time, all the text following your name moved down one line. A blank line was inserted after pressing Enter the second time.

Next, you want to add a word to the first line of the first paragraph. To do this, you first need to move the cursor to the location where you want to make the change. The keyboard or mouse can be used to move through the text in the document window. Depending on what you are doing, one method may be more efficient than another. For example, if your hands are already on the keyboard as you are entering text, it may be quicker to use the keyboard rather than take your hands off to use the mouse.

You use the mouse to move the cursor to a specific location in a document simply by clicking on the location. When you can use the mouse to move the cursor, the mouse pointer is shaped as an I I-beam. You use the arrow keys located on the numeric keypad or the directional keypad to move the cursor in a document. The keyboard directional keys are described in the following table.

Key	Word/PowerPoint	Excel	Access
→	Right one character	Right one cell	Right one field
←	Left one character	Left one cell	Left one field
↑	Up one line	Up one cell	Up one record
↓	Down one line	Down one cell	Down one record
Ctrl + →	Right one word	Last cell in row	One word to right in a field entry
Ctrl + ←	Left one word	First cell in row	One word to left in a field entry
Home	Beginning of line	First cell in row	First field of record
End	End of line		Last field of record

Additional Information

Many of the keyboard keys and key combinations have other effects depending on the mode of operation at the time they are used. You will learn about these differences in the specific application labs as they are used.

In the first line of the first paragraph, you want to add the word "basic" before the word "interface" and the year "2013" after the word "Office." You will move to the correct locations using both the keyboard and the mouse and then enter the new text.

- **Click at the beginning of the word You in the first paragraph.**
- **Press → four times to move to the beginning of the second word.**
- **Press Ctrl + → five times to move to the beginning of the seventh word.**

Additional Information

Holding down a directional key or key combination moves quickly in the direction indicated, saving multiple presses of the key.

- **Type basic and press Spacebar.**

Having Trouble?

Do not be concerned if you make a typing error; you will learn how to correct them next.

- **Position the I-beam between the e in Office and the period at the end of the first sentence and click.**
- **Press Spacebar and type 2013**

Your screen should be similar to Figure 28

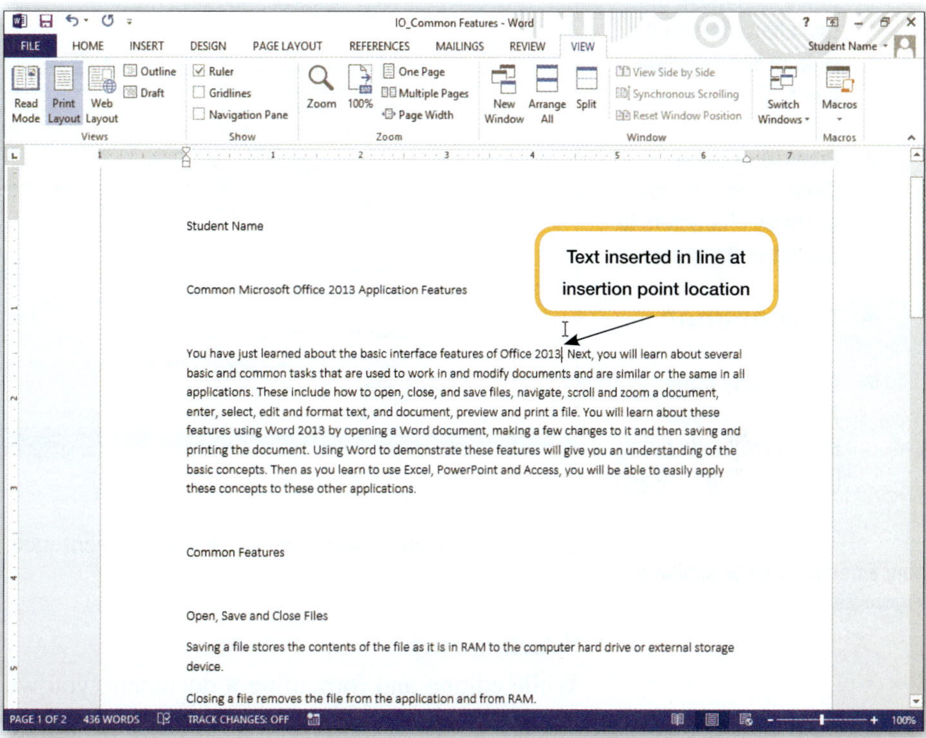

Figure 28

Next, you want to edit the text you just entered by changing the word "basic" to "common." Removing typing entries to change or correct them is one of the basic editing tasks. Corrections may be made in many ways. Two of the most basic editing keys that are common to the Office applications are the Backspace and Delete keys. The Backspace key removes a character or space to the left of the cursor. It is particularly useful when you are moving from right to left (backward) along a line of text. The Delete key removes the character or space to the right of the cursor and is most useful when moving from left to right along a line.

You will use these features as you make the correction.

3

- **Move the cursor between the s and i in "basic" (in the first sentence).**
- **Press Delete two times to remove the two characters to the right of the insertion point.**
- **Press Backspace three times to remove the three characters to the left of the cursor.**
- **Type common**
- **Correct any other typing errors you may have made using Backspace or Delete.**

Your screen should be similar to Figure 29

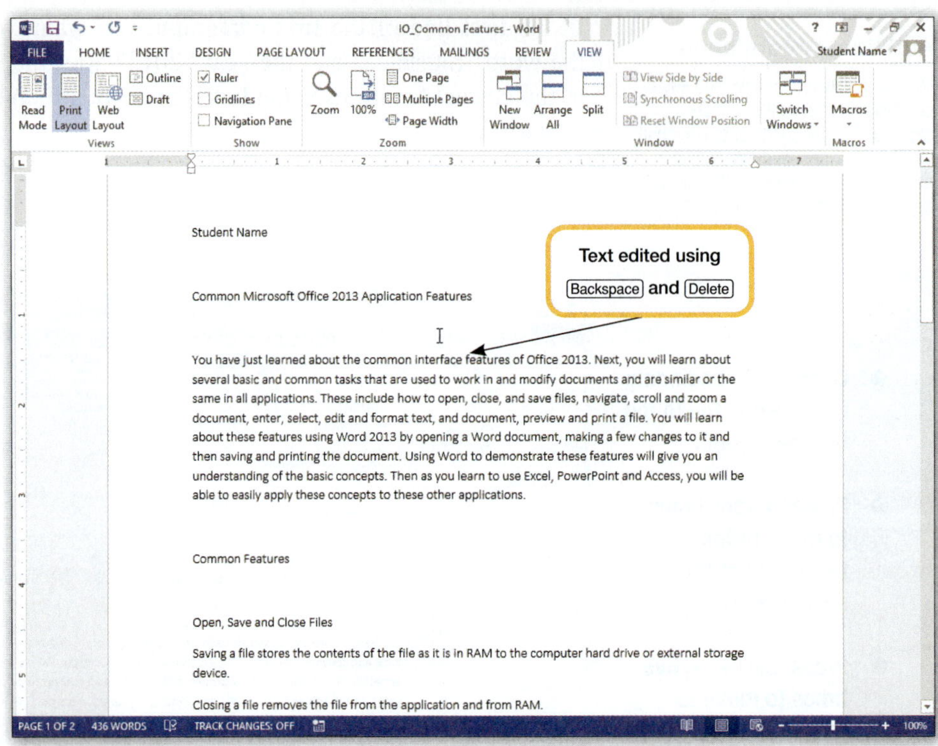

Figure 29

The word "basic" was deleted from the sentence and the word "common" was entered in its place.

Selecting Text

While editing and formatting a document, you will need to select text. Selecting highlights text and identifies the text that will be affected by your next action. To select text using the mouse, first move the cursor to the beginning or end of the text to be selected, and then drag to highlight the text you want selected. You can select as little as a single letter or as much as the entire document. You also can select text using keyboard features. The following table summarizes common mouse and keyboard techniques used to select text in Word.

Additional Information

The capability to select text is common to all Office 2013 applications. However, many of the features that are designed for use in Word are not available in the other applications. Some are available only when certain modes of operation are in effect or when certain features are being used.

Touch Tip

With a touch device, tap in the text to place the cursor and drag the selection handle to select.

To Select	Mouse	Keyboard
Next/previous space or character	Drag across space or character.	Shift + → / Shift + ←
Next/previous word	Double-click in the word.	Ctrl + Shift + → / Ctrl + Shift + ←
Sentence	Press Ctrl and click within the sentence.	
Line	Click to the left of a line when the mouse pointer is ↗.	
Multiple lines	Drag up or down to the left of a line when the mouse pointer is ↗.	
Text going backward to beginning of paragraph	Drag left and up to the beginning of the paragraph when the mouse pointer is ↗.	Ctrl + Shift + ↑
Text going forward to end of paragraph	Drag right and down to the end of the paragraph when the mouse pointer is ↗.	Ctrl + Shift + ↓
Paragraph	Triple-click on the paragraph or double-click to the left of the paragraph when the mouse pointer is ↗.	
Multiple paragraphs	Drag to the left of the paragraphs when the mouse pointer is ↗.	
Document	Triple-click or press Ctrl and click to the left of the text when the mouse pointer is ↗.	Ctrl + A

Having Trouble?

If you accidentally select the incorrect text, simply click anywhere in the document or press any directional key to clear the selection and try again.

You want to change the word "tasks" in the next sentence to "application features". Although you could use Delete and Backspace to remove the unneeded text character by character, it will be faster to select and delete the word. First you will try out several of the keyboard techniques to select text. Then you will use several mouse features to select text and finally you will edit the sentence.

1

- **Move the cursor to the beginning of the word "basic" in the second sentence.**
- **Press Shift + → five times to select the word basic.**
- **Press Shift + Ctrl + → to extend the selection word by word until the entire line is selected.**
- **Press Shift + Ctrl + ↓ to extend the selection to the end of the paragraph.**

Your screen should be similar to Figure 30

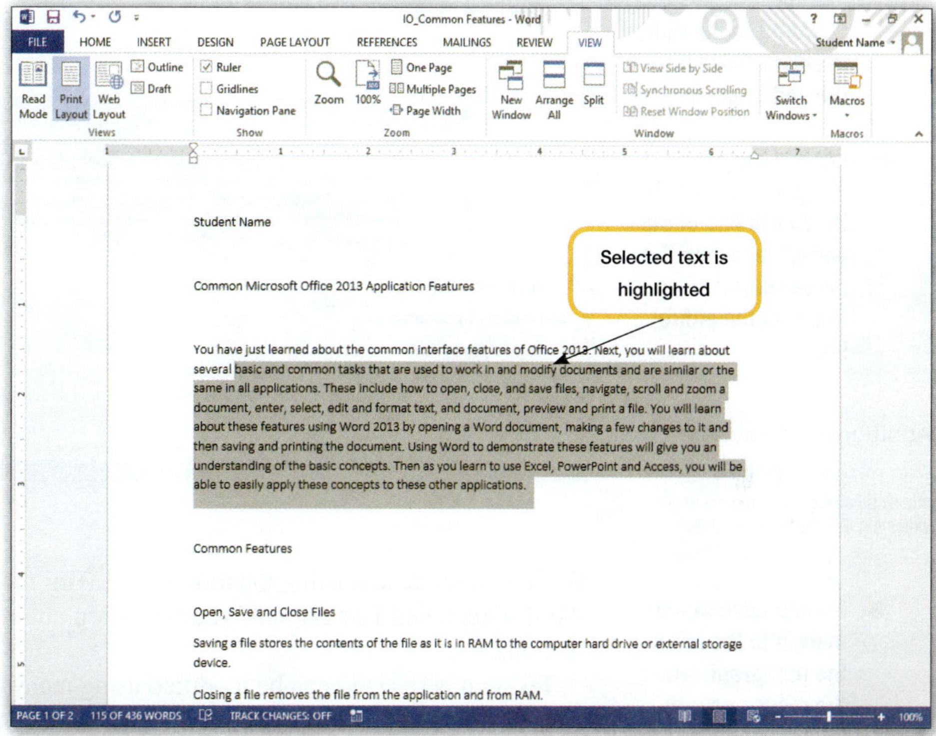

Figure 30

The text from the cursor to the end of the paragraph is selected. Next, you will clear this selection and then use the mouse to select text.

2

- **Click anywhere in the paragraph to clear the selection.**
- **Click at the beginning of the word "basic" and drag to the right to select the text to the end of the line.**
- **Click in the left margin to the left of the fourth line of the paragraph when the mouse pointer is ⇗ to select the entire line.**

Additional Information

When positioned in the left margin, the mouse pointer shape changes to ⇗, indicating it is ready to select text.

- **Double-click in the margin to the left of the paragraph when the mouse pointer is ⇗ to select the paragraph.**

Your screen should be similar to Figure 31

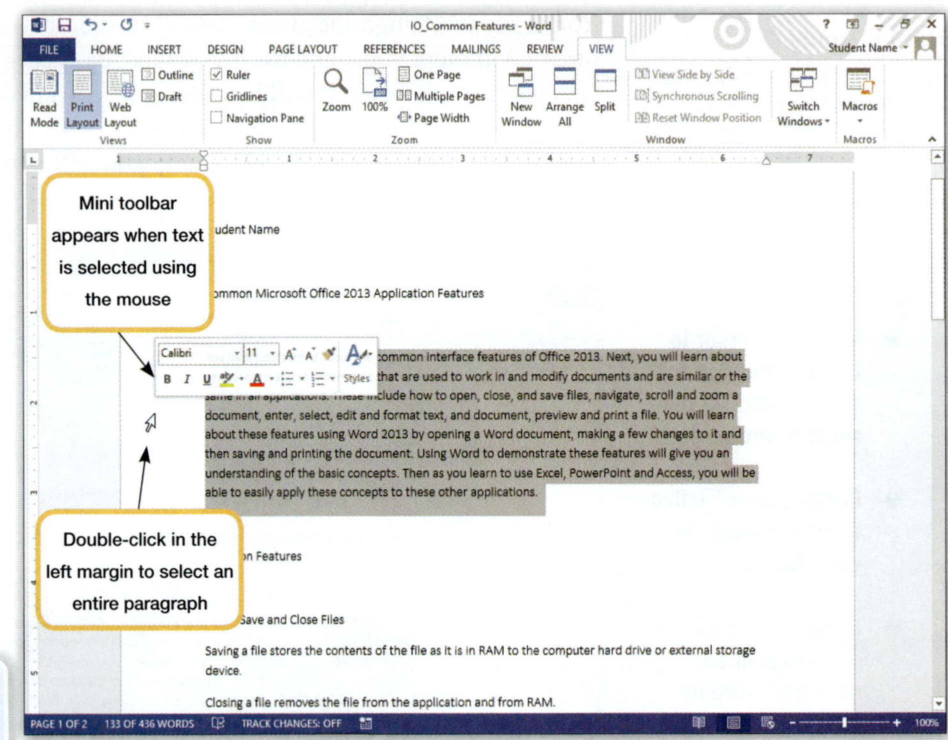

Figure 31

When you select text using the mouse, the **Mini toolbar** appears automatically in Word, Excel, and PowerPoint. You will learn about using this feature in the next section.

Text that is selected can be modified using many different features. In this case, you want to replace the word "tasks" in the second sentence with "application features".

- **Double-click on the word "tasks" in the second sentence.**
- **Type application features**

Your screen should be similar to Figure 32

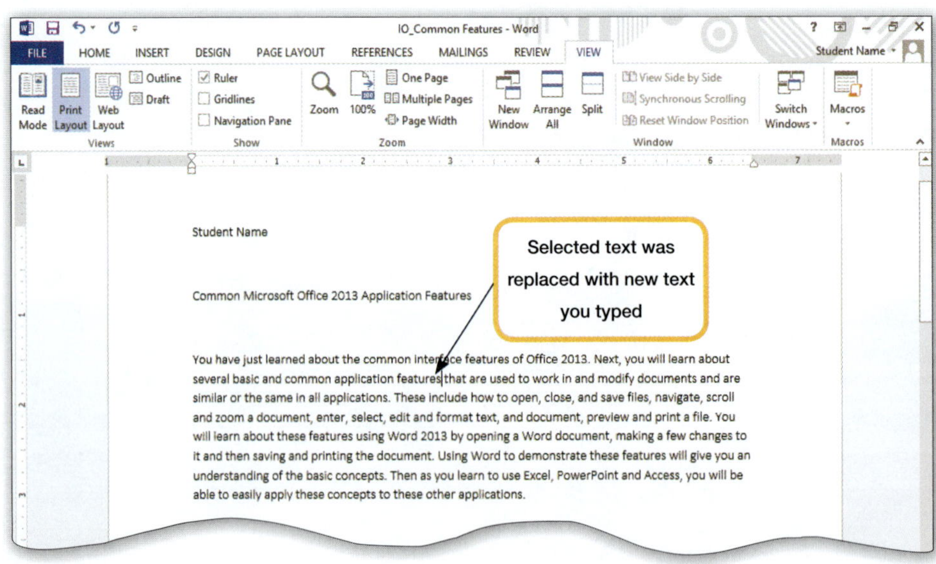

Figure 32

As soon as you began typing, the selected text was automatically deleted. The new text was inserted in the line by pushing the existing text to the right. Any text that could not fit on the line moved to the beginning of the next line. This is the **word wrap** feature. Although this feature is used mostly in Word, it is also used in the other applications.

Formatting Text

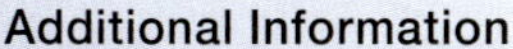

Additional Information

Font and text effects will be explained in more detail in each application lab.

An important aspect of all documents you create using Office 2013 is the appearance of the document. To improve the appearance you can apply many different formatting effects. The most common formatting features are font and character effects. A **font**, also commonly referred to as a **typeface**, is a set of characters with a specific design. The designs have names such as Times New Roman and Courier. Each font has one or more sizes. **Font size** is the height and width of the character and is commonly measured in points, abbreviated "pt." One point equals about 1/72 inch. **Character effects** are enhancements such as bold, italic, and color that are applied to selected text. Using font and character effects as design elements can add interest to your document and give readers visual cues to help them find information quickly.

First you want to change the font and increase the font size of the title of this document.

1

- **Click in the left margin next to the title line when the mouse pointer is ↗ to select it.**
- **Open the Home tab.**
- **Open the Calibri Font drop-down menu in the Font group.**
- **Point to the Arial Black font option in the menu.**

Your screen should be similar to Figure 33

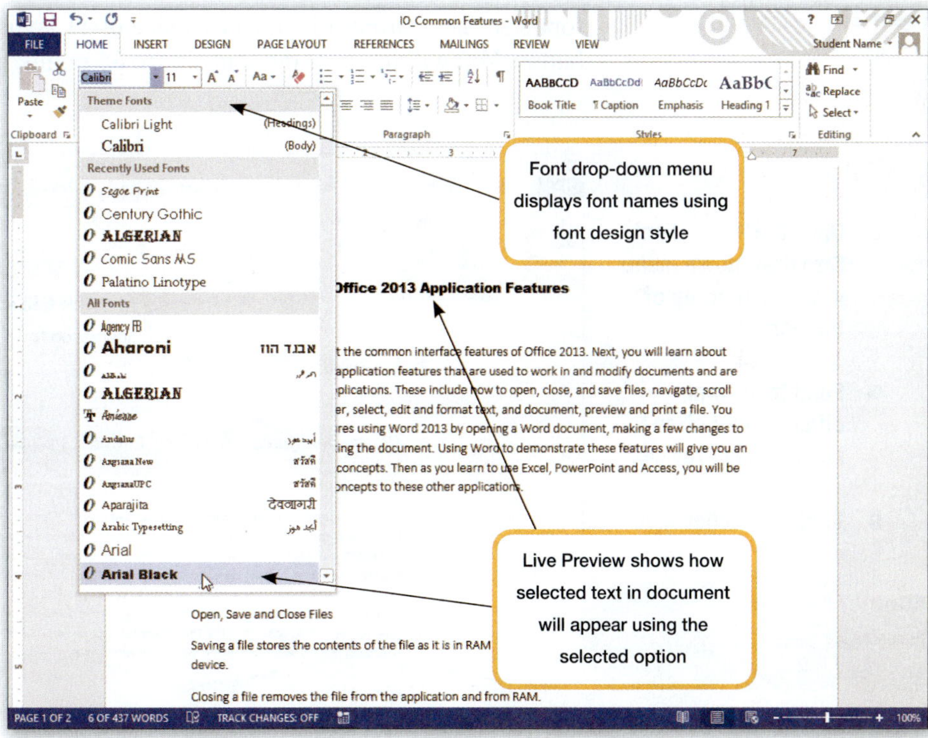

Figure 33

Additional Information

Live Preview is also available in Excel, Access, and PowerPoint.

As you point to the font options, the **Live Preview** feature shows you how the selected text in the document will appear if this option is chosen.

- Point to several different fonts in the menu to see the Live Preview.
- Scroll the menu and click Segoe Print to choose it.

Additional Information

Font names are listed in alphabetical order.

Having Trouble?

If this font is not available on your computer, choose a similar font.

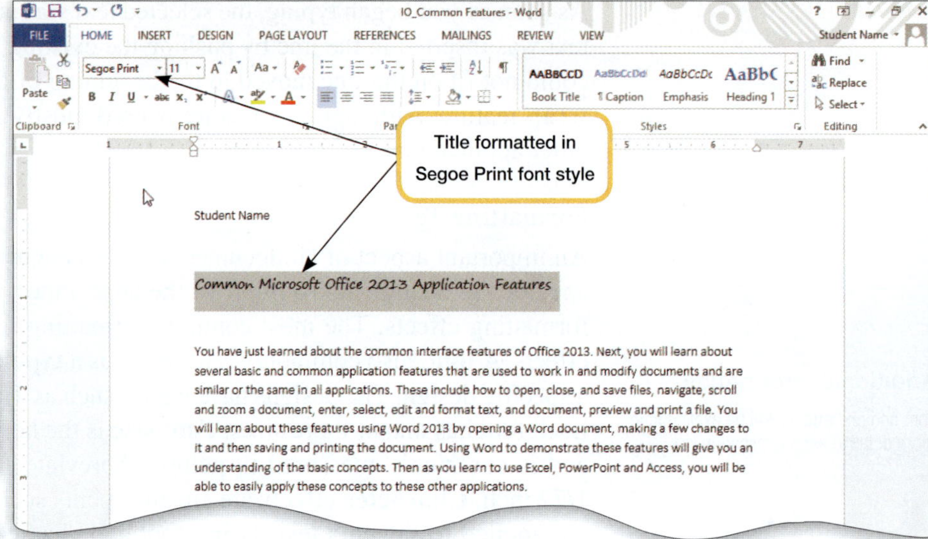

Figure 34

Your screen should be similar to Figure 34

The title appears in the selected font and the name of the font used in the selection is displayed in the Segoe Print Font button. Next you want to increase the font size. The current (default) font size of 11 is displayed in the 11 Font Size button. You will increase the font size to 16 points.

- Open the 11 Font Size drop-down menu in the Font group of the Home tab.
- Point to several different font sizes to see the Live Preview.
- Click 16 to choose it.

Another Method

The keyboard shortcut is Ctrl + Shift + P.

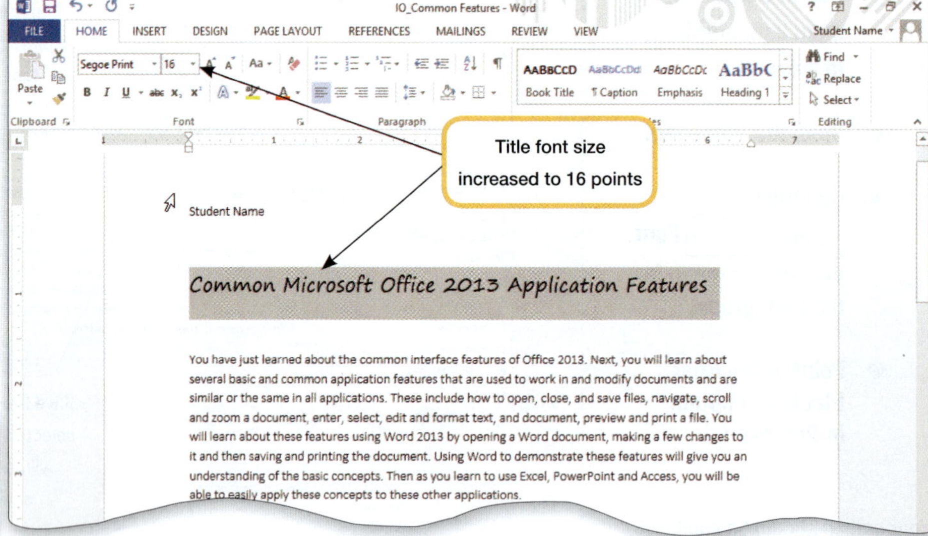

Figure 35

Your screen should be similar to Figure 35

Touch Tip

With a touch device, tap on the selected text, then tap on the formatting option.

Now the title stands out much more from the other text in the document. Next you will use the Mini toolbar to add formatting to other areas of the document. As you saw earlier, the Mini toolbar appears automatically when you select text. Initially the Mini toolbar appears dimmed (semi-transparent) so that it does not interfere with what you are doing, but it changes to solid when you point at it. It displays command buttons for often-used commands from the Font and Paragraph groups that are used to format a document.

4

- **Select the line "Common Features" and point to the Mini toolbar.**
- **Click [11] Font Size and choose 14.**
- **Click [B] Bold.**
- **Click [I] Italic.**
- **Click [U] Underline.**

Your screen should be similar to Figure 36

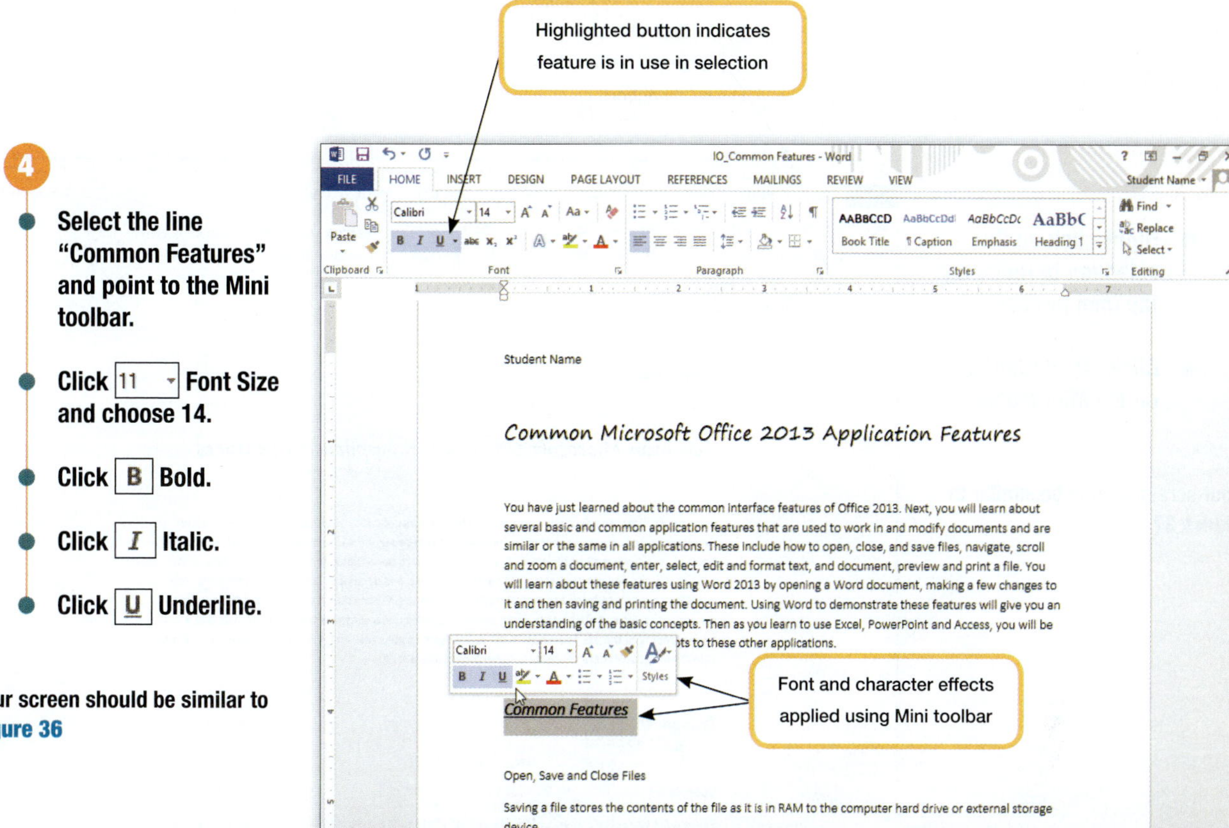

Figure 36

The increase in font size as well as the text effects makes this topic heading much more prominent. Notice the command button for each selected effect is highlighted, indicating the feature is in use in the selection.

Using the Mini toolbar is particularly useful when the Home tab is closed because you do not need to reopen the Home tab to access the commands. It remains available until you clear the selection or press Esc. If you do nothing with a selection for a while, the Mini toolbar will disappear. To redisplay it simply right-click on the selection again. This will also open the context menu.

You will remove the underline effect from the selection next.

5

- **Right-click on the selection to redisplay the Mini toolbar.**
- **Click U Underline on the Mini toolbar.**

Your screen should be similar to Figure 37

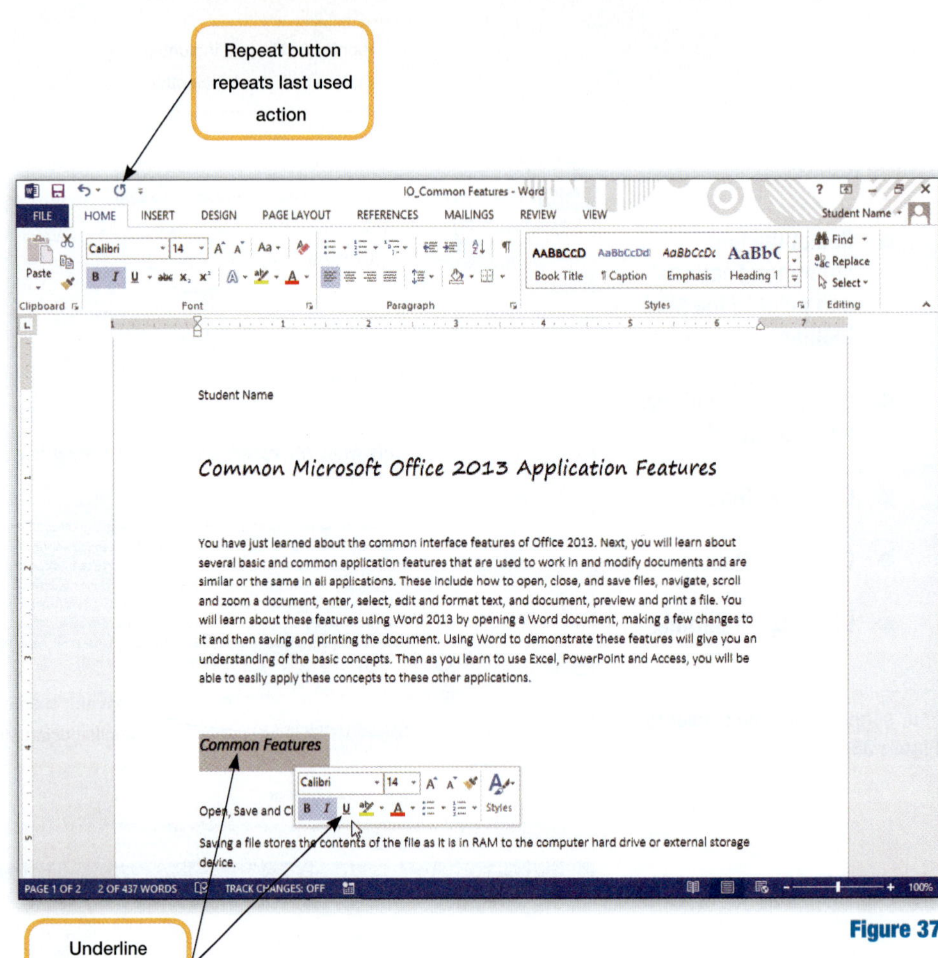

Figure 37

The context menu and Mini toolbar appeared when you right-clicked the selection. The context menu displayed a variety of commands that are quicker to access than locating the command on the Ribbon. The commands that appear on this menu change depending on what you are doing at the time. The context menu disappeared after you made a selection from the Mini toolbar. Both the Mini toolbar and context menus are designed to make it more efficient to execute commands.

Also notice that the Redo button in the Quick Access Toolbar has changed to a Repeat button. This feature allows you to quickly repeat the last-used command at another location in the document.

Undoing and Redoing Editing Changes

Instead of reselecting the U Underline command to remove the underline effect, you could have used Undo to reverse your last action or command. You will use this feature to restore the underline (your last action).

1

- **Click Undo in the Quick Access Toolbar.**

Another Method

The keyboard shortcut is Ctrl + Z.

Your screen should be similar to Figure 38

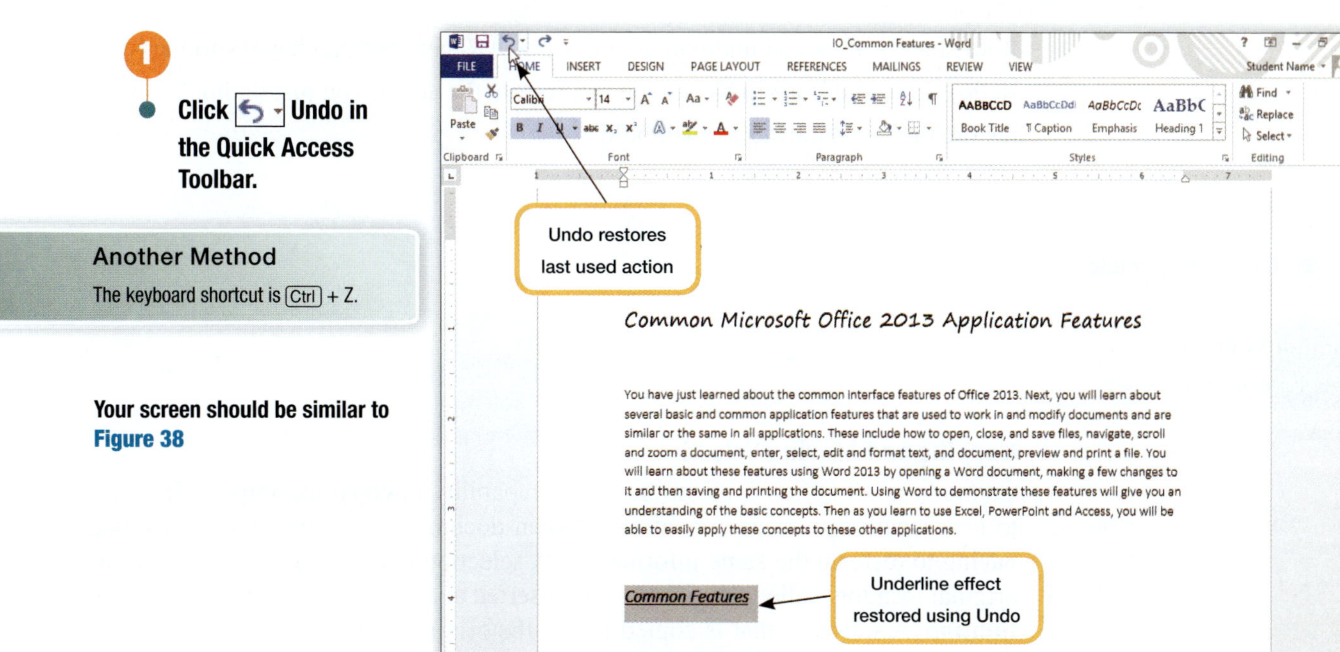

Figure 38

Undo reversed the last action and the underline formatting effect was restored. Notice that the Undo button includes a drop-down menu button. Clicking this button displays a menu of the most recent actions that can be reversed, with the most-recent action at the top of the menu. When you select an action from the drop-down menu, you also undo all actions above it in the menu.

2

- **Open the Undo drop-down menu.**
- **Choose Bold.**

Your screen should be similar to Figure 39

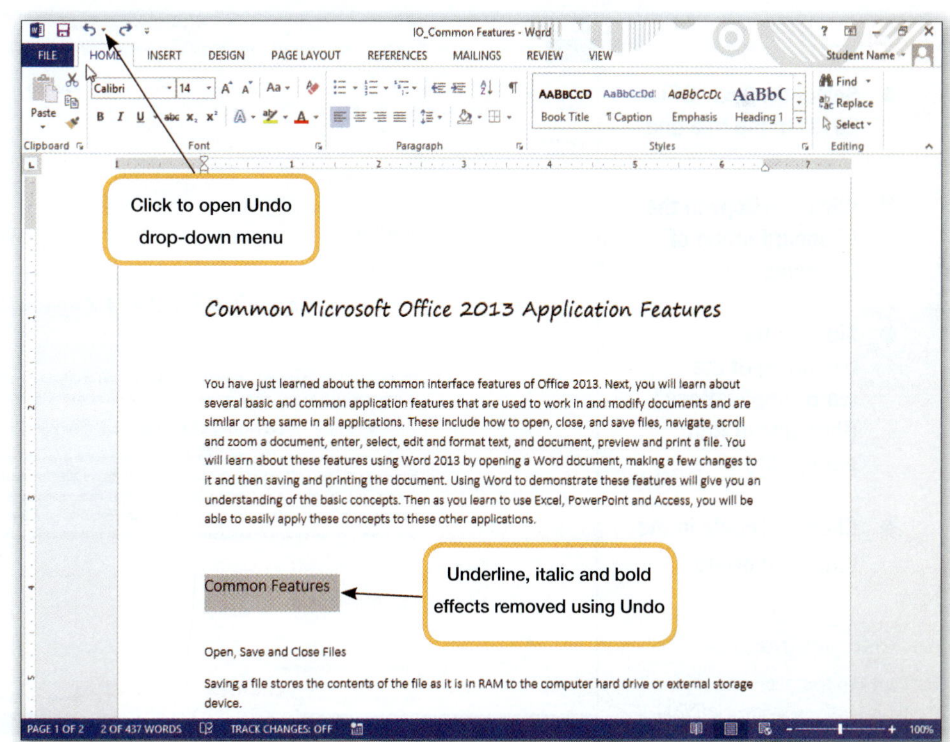

Figure 39

The underline, italic, and bold effects were all removed.

Immediately after you undo an action, the Repeat button changes to the Redo button and is available so you can restore the action you just undid. You will restore the last-removed format, bold.

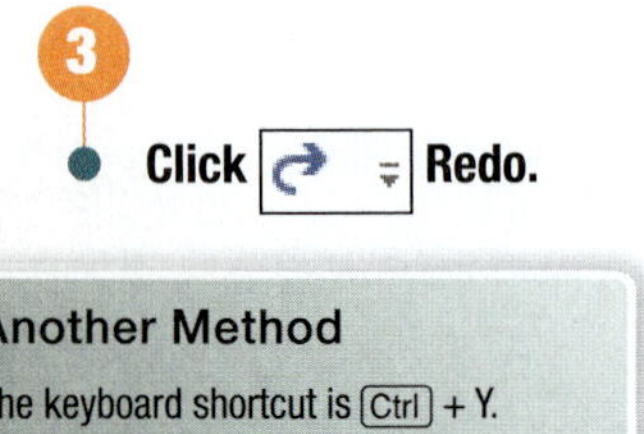

3

- Click Redo.

Another Method

The keyboard shortcut is Ctrl + Y.

Copying and Moving Selections

Common to all Office applications is the capability to **copy** and **move** selections to new locations in a document or between documents, saving you time by not having to recreate the same information. A selection that is moved is cut from its original location, called the **source**, and inserted at a new location, called the **destination**. A selection that is copied leaves the original in the source and inserts a duplicate at the destination.

Additional Information

You will learn about using the Office Clipboard in the individual application texts.

When a selection is cut or copied, the selection is stored in the system **Clipboard**, a temporary Windows storage area in memory. It is also stored in the **Office Clipboard**. The system Clipboard holds only the last cut or copied item, whereas the Office Clipboard can store up to 24 items that have been cut or copied. This feature allows you to insert multiple items from various Office documents and paste all or part of the collection of items into another document.

First, you will copy the text "Office 2013" to two other locations in the first paragraph.

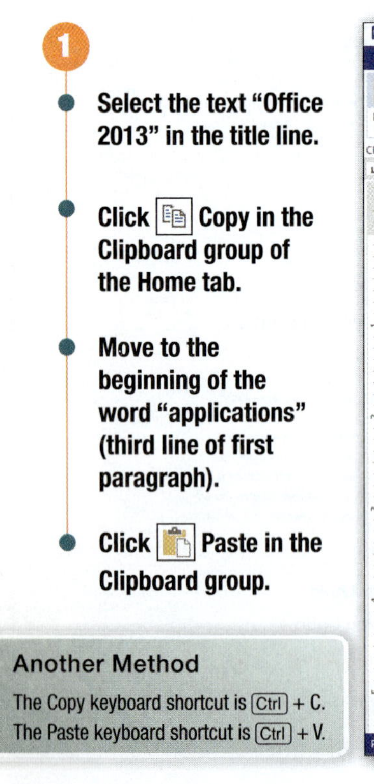

1

- Select the text "Office 2013" in the title line.
- Click Copy in the Clipboard group of the Home tab.
- Move to the beginning of the word "applications" (third line of first paragraph).
- Click Paste in the Clipboard group.

Another Method

The Copy keyboard shortcut is Ctrl + C.
The Paste keyboard shortcut is Ctrl + V.

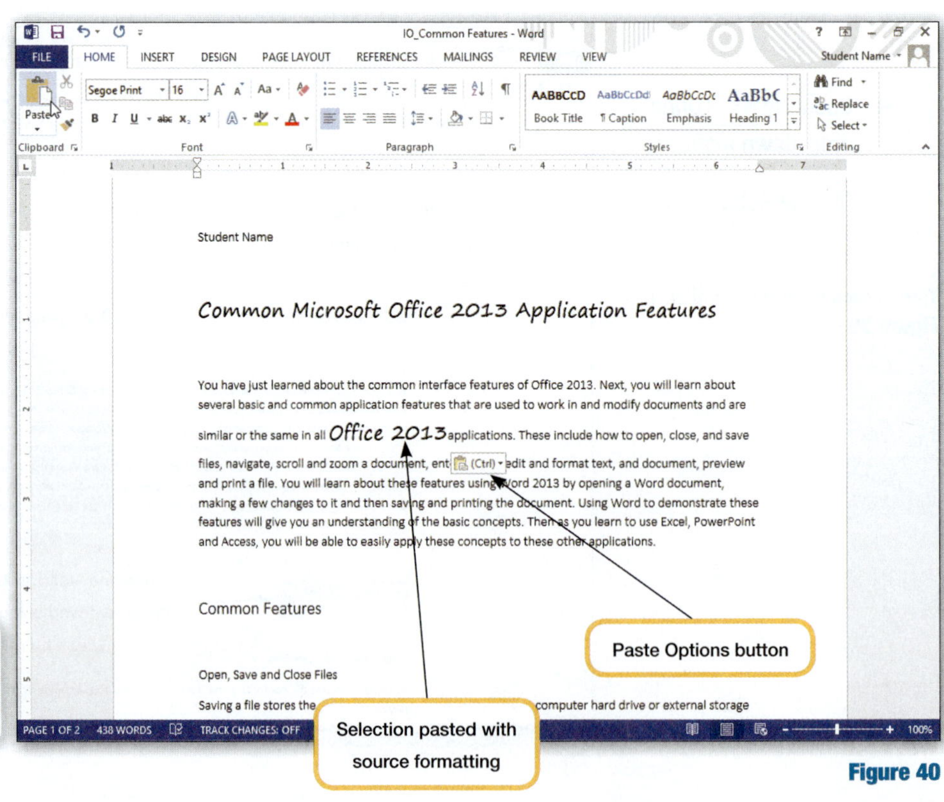

Figure 40

Your screen should be similar to Figure 40

The copied selection is inserted at the location you specified with the same formatting as it has in the title. The (Ctrl) Paste Options button appears automatically whenever a selection is pasted. It is used to control the format of the pasted item.

2

- **Click the (Ctrl) Paste Options button.**
- **If necessary, insert a blank space after the year.**

Your screen should be similar to Figure 41

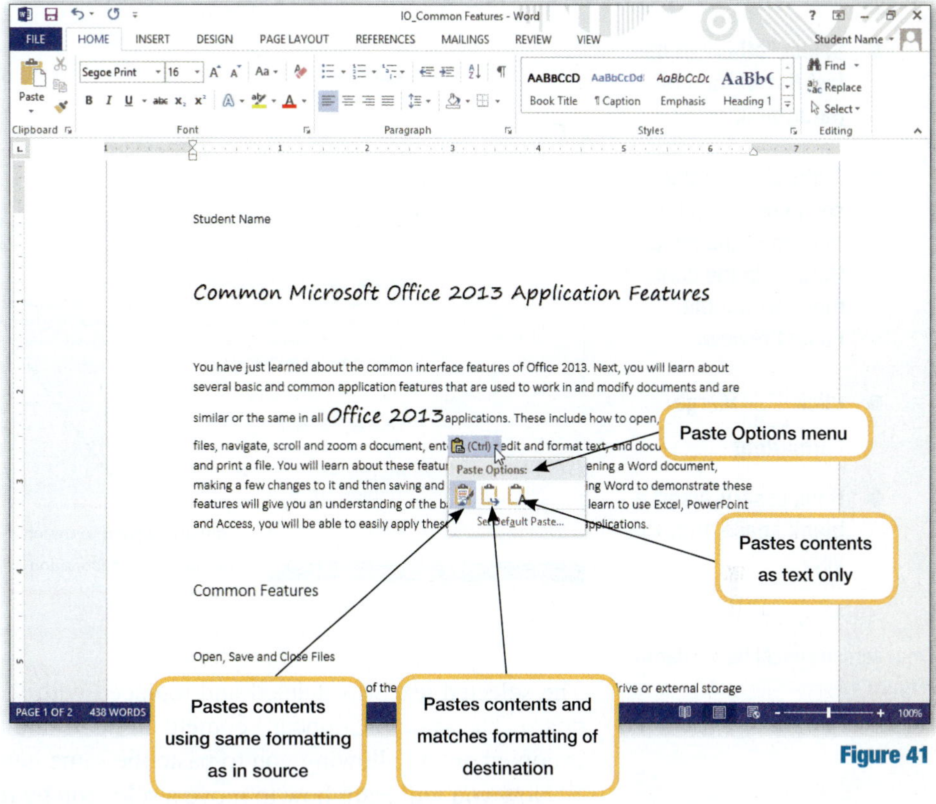

Figure 41

Additional Information

The Paste Options vary with the different applications. For example, Excel has 14 different Paste Options. The Paste Options feature is not available in Access and Paste Preview is not available in Excel.

The Paste Options are used to specify whether to insert the item with the same formatting that it had in the source, to change it to the formatting of the surrounding destination text, or to insert text only (from a selection that is a combination of text and graphics). The default as you have seen is to keep the formatting from the source. You want to change it to the formatting of the surrounding text. As you point to a Paste Options button, a **Paste Preview** will show how that option will affect the selection. Then you will copy it again to a second location.

3

- Click Merge Formatting.
- Select "other" in the last line of the first paragraph.
- Right-click on the selection and point to each of the Paste Options in the context menu to see the Paste Preview.
- Click Merge Formatting.
- If necessary, insert a blank space after the year.

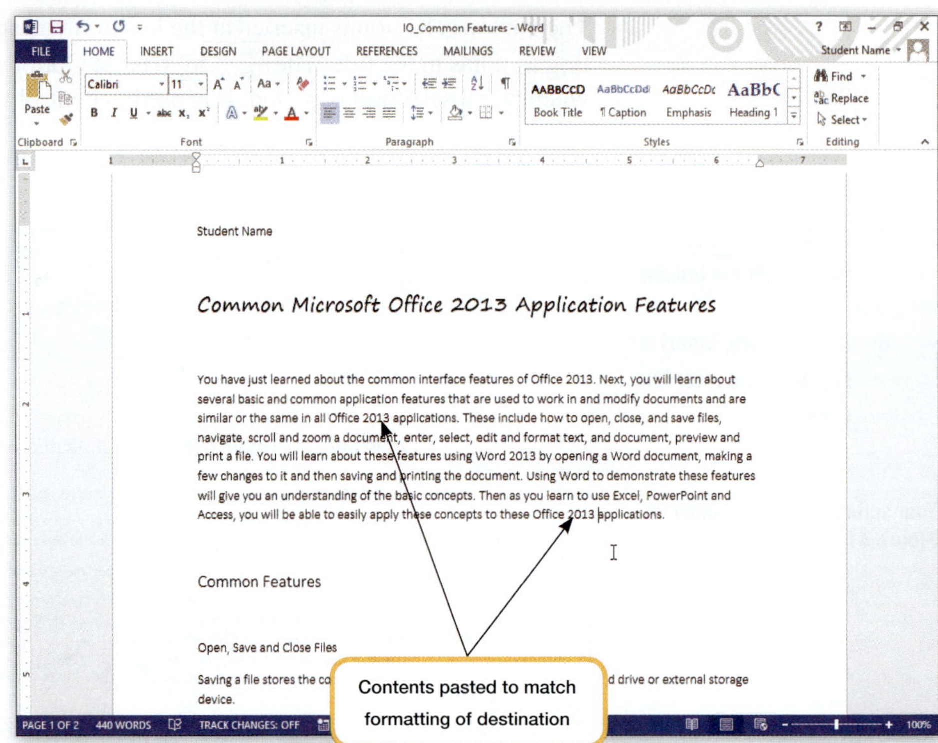

Figure 42

Your screen should be similar to Figure 42

The selected text was deleted and replaced with the contents of the system Clipboard. The system Clipboard contents remain in the Clipboard until another item is copied or cut, allowing you to paste the same item multiple times.

Now you will learn how to move a selection by rearranging several lines of text in the description of common features. You want to move the last sentence in the document, beginning with "Opening a file", to the top of the list. The Cut and Paste commands in the Clipboard group of the Home tab are used to move selections.

4

- **Scroll to see the end of the document.**
- **Double-click in the left margin next to the last sentence in the document to select it.**
- **Click [Cut icon] Cut in the Clipboard group.**

Another Method

The Cut keyboard shortcut is Ctrl + X. You also can choose Cut from the context menu.

Your screen should be similar to Figure 43

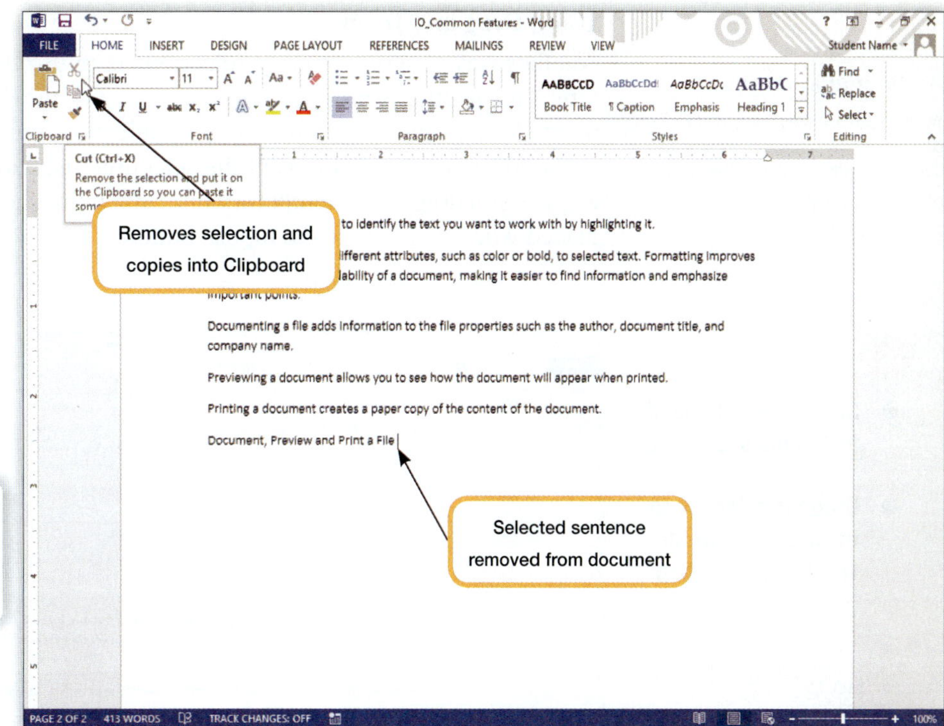

Figure 43

The selected paragraph is removed from the source and copied to the Clipboard. Next, you need to move the cursor to the location where the text will be inserted and paste the text into the document from the Clipboard.

5

- **Move to the beginning of the word "Saving" at the top of the Common Features list.**
- **Press Ctrl + V.**

Your screen should be similar to Figure 44

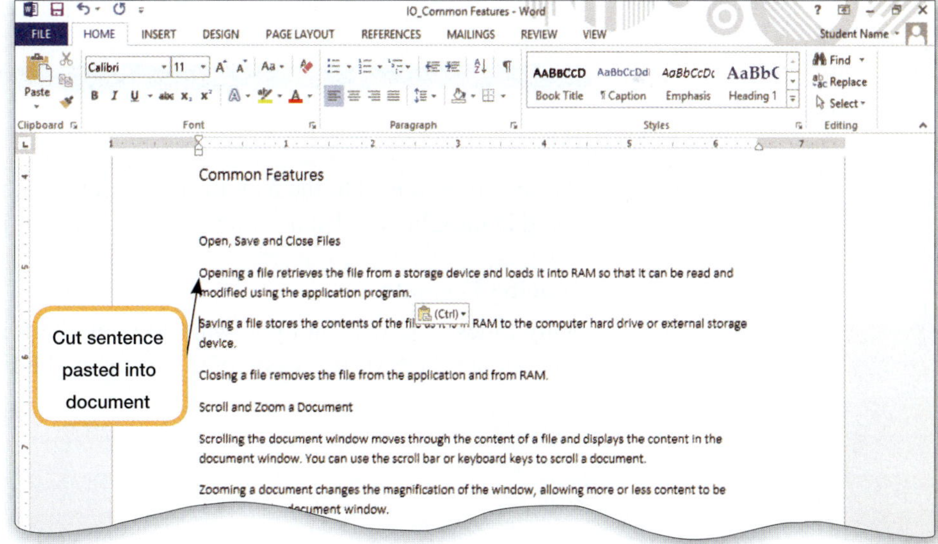

Figure 44

Additional Information

You also can move or copy by clicking the right mouse button in your highlighted selection. A context menu appears with the available move and copy options.

The cut sentence is reentered into the document at the cursor location. That was much quicker than retyping the whole sentence! Because the source has the same formatting as the text at the destination, the default setting to keep the source formatting is appropriate.

Using Drag and Drop

Another way to move or copy selections is to use the drag-and-drop editing feature. This feature is most useful for copying or moving short distances in a document. To use drag and drop to move a selection, point to the selection and drag it to the location where you want the selection inserted. The mouse pointer appears as  as you drag, and a temporary insertion point shows you where the text will be placed when you release the mouse button.

Additional Information

You also can use drag and drop to copy and paste a selection by holding down Ctrl while dragging. The mouse pointer shape is .

1

- **Select the last line of text in the document.**
- **Drag the selection to the beginning of the word "Documenting" (four lines up).**

Touch Tip

With a touch device, tap in the selection and then slide or drag the selection to move it.

Your screen should be similar to Figure 45

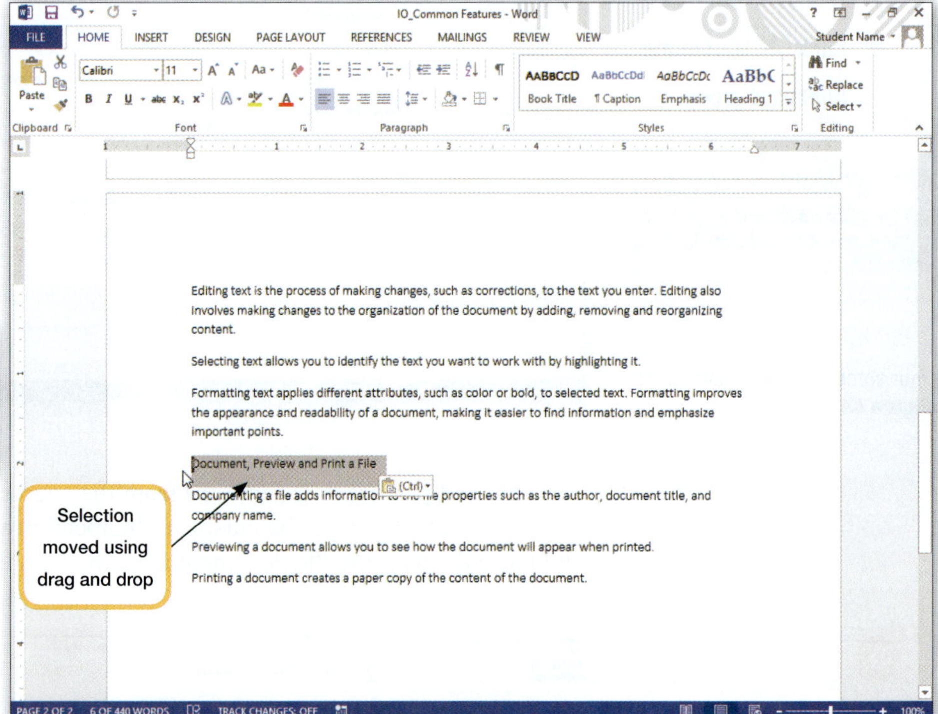

Figure 45

The selection moved to the new location. However, the selection is not copied and stored in the Clipboard and cannot be pasted to multiple locations in the document.

Copying Formats

Many times, you will find you want to copy the formats associated with a selection, but not the text. It is easy to do this using the **Format Painter** tool.

1

- **Apply bold and italic effects and increase the font size to 14 for the currently selected text.**
- **Click Format Painter in the Clipboard group.**
- **Scroll the document up and select the topic line of text "Enter, Select, Edit and Format text".**

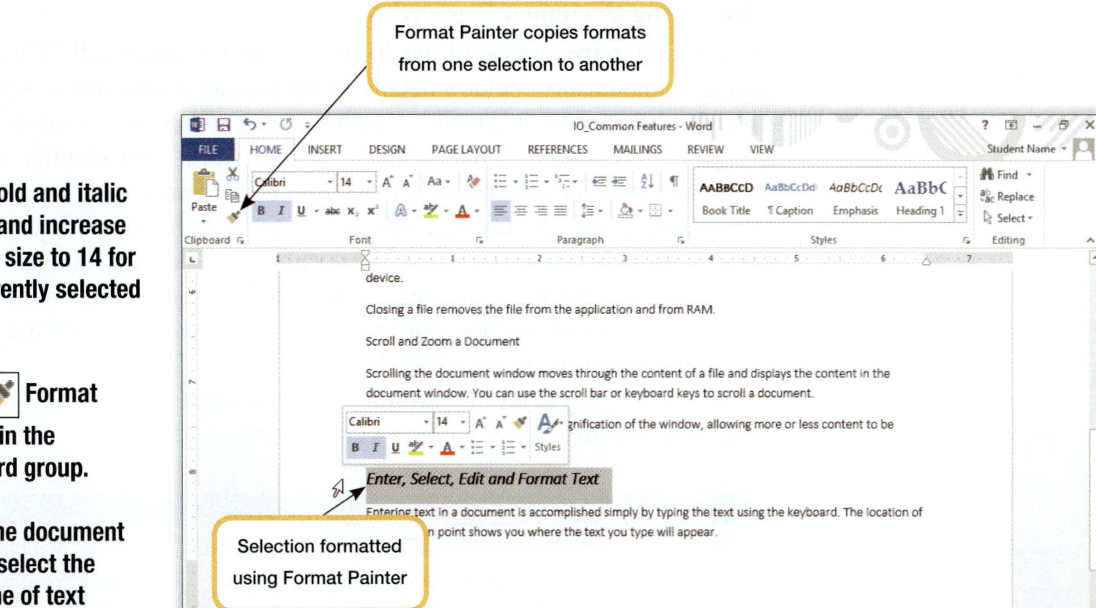

Figure 46

Additional Information

The mouse pointer appears as when this feature is on.

Your screen should be similar to **Figure 46**

The text you selected is formatted using the same formats. This feature is especially helpful when you want to copy multiple formats at one time. Next, you want to format the other topic heads in the Common Features list using the same formats. To do this, you can make the Format Painter "sticky" so that it can be used to copy the format multiple times in succession.

2

- **Double-click Format Painter in the Clipboard group.**
- **Select the remaining two topic heads in the Common Features list:**

  Scroll and Zoom a Document

  Open, Save and Close Files
- **Click Format Painter to turn off this feature.**
- **Clear the selection.**

Your screen should be similar to **Figure 47**

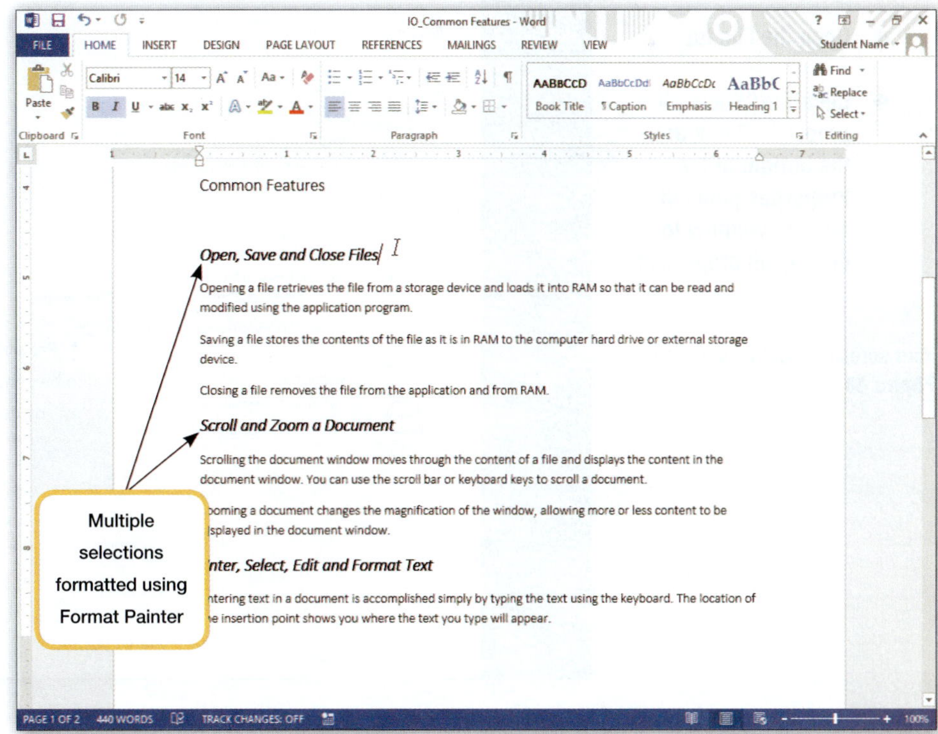

Figure 47

Specifying Document Properties

In addition to the content of the document that you create, all Office 2013 applications automatically include details about the document that describe or identify it called **metadata** or document **properties**. Document properties include details such as title, author name, subject, and keywords that identify the document's topic or contents (described below). Some of these properties are automatically generated. These include statistics such as the number of words in the file and general information such as the date the document was created and last modified. Others such as author name and tags or keywords are properties that you can specify. A **tag** or **keyword** is a descriptive word that is associated with the file and can be used to locate a file using a search.

By specifying relevant information as document properties, you can easily organize, identify, and search for your documents later.

Property	Action
Title	Enter the document title. This title can be longer and more descriptive than the file name.
Tags	Enter words that you associate with the presentation to make it easier to find using search tools.
Comments	Enter comments that you want others to see about the content of the document.
Categories	Enter the name of a higher-level category under which you can group similar types of presentations.
Author	Enter the name of the presentation's author. By default this is the name entered when the application was installed.

You will look at the document properties that are automatically included and add documentation to identify you as the author, and specify a document title and keywords to describe the document.

- **Open the File tab.**
- **Click the "Show all properties" link at the bottom of the Properties panel in the Info window to display all properties.**

Your screen should be similar to Figure 48

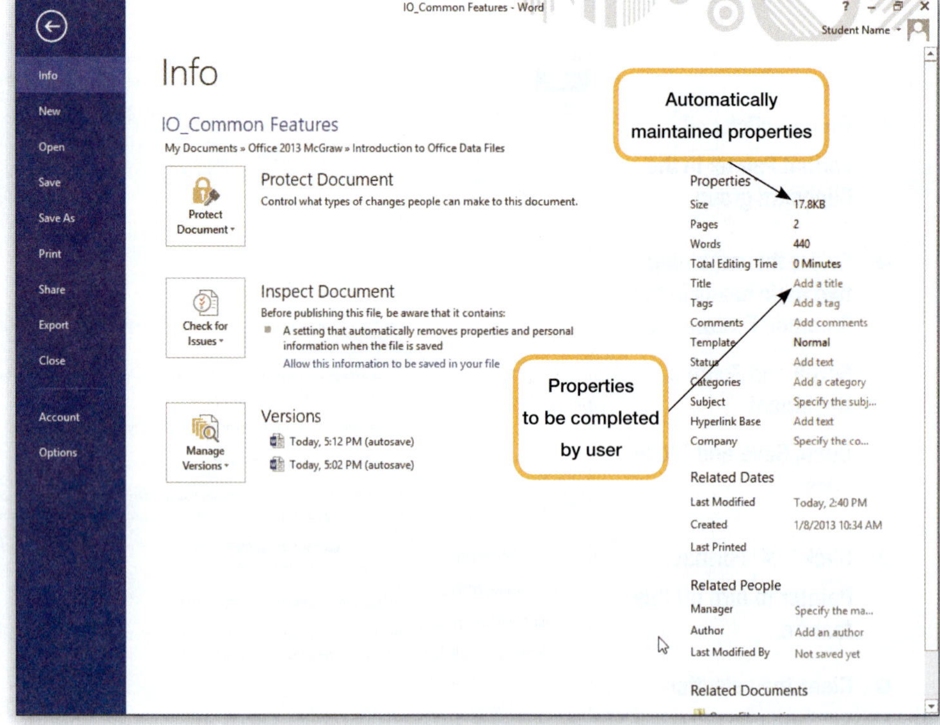

Figure 48

Additional Information

The document properties vary with the different Office applications. For example, the Word document includes a word count and a PowerPoint document includes a slide count.

The Properties panel in the right section of the Info tab is divided into four groups and displays the properties associated with the document. Properties such as the document size, number of words, and number of pages are automatically maintained. Others such as the title and tag properties are blank waiting for you to specify your own information.

You will add a title, a tag, and your name as the author name.

2

- **Click in the Title text box and type Common Office Features**
- **In the same manner, enter common, features, interface as the tags.**
- **Click in the Add an Author text box and enter your name.**
- **If necessary, click outside the search results box to clear it.**

Your screen should be similar to Figure 49

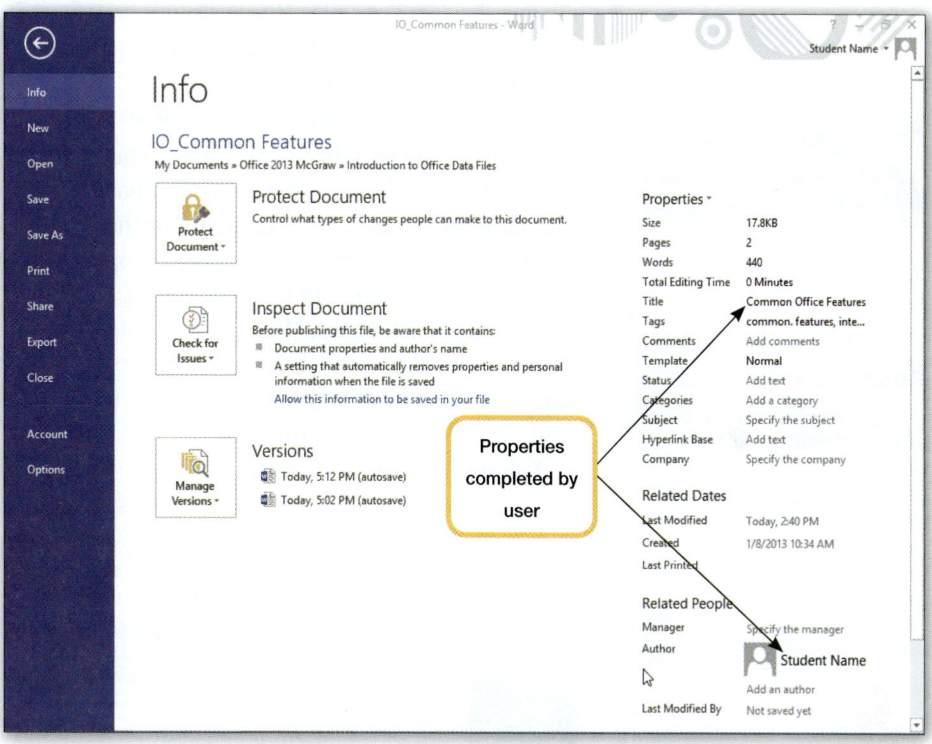

Figure 49

Additional Information

You can personalize your copy of the Office applications to include your name and initials as the author using the Options option on the File tab.

Once the document properties are specified, you can use them to identify and locate documents. You also can use the automatically updated properties for the same purpose. For example, you can search for all files created by a specified user or on a certain date.

Saving a File

As you enter and edit text to create a document in Word, Excel, and PowerPoint, the changes you make are immediately displayed onscreen and are stored in your computer's memory. However, they are not permanently stored until you save your work to a file on a disk. After a document has been saved as a file, it can be closed and opened again at a later time to be edited further. Unlike Word, Excel, and PowerPoint, where you start work on a new document and then save your changes, Access requires that you name the new database file first and create a table for your data. Then, it saves your changes to the data automatically as you work. This allows multiple users to have access to the most up-to-date data at all times.

Additional Information

You can specify different AutoRecover settings by choosing Options/Save in the Backstage and specifying the AutoRecover settings of your choice.

As a backup against the accidental loss of work from power failure or other mishap, Word, Excel, and PowerPoint include an AutoRecover feature. When this feature is on, as you work you may see a pulsing disk icon briefly appear in the status bar. This icon indicates that the program is saving your work to a temporary recovery file. The time interval between automatic saving can be set to any period you specify; the default is every 10 minutes. After a problem has occurred, when you restart the program, the recovery file is automatically opened containing all changes you made up to the last time it was saved by AutoRecover. You then need to save the recovery file. If you do not save it, it is deleted when closed. AutoRecover is a great feature for recovering lost work but should not be used in place of regularly saving your work.

Another Method

The keyboard shortcut for the Save command is Ctrl + S.

You will save the work you have done so far on the document. You use the Save or Save As commands to save files. The Save option on the File tab or the Save button on the Quick Access Toolbar will save the active file using the same file name by replacing the contents of the existing disk file with the document as it appears on your screen. The Save As option on the File tab is used to save a file using a new file name, to a new location, or as a different file type. This leaves the original file unchanged. When you create a new document, you can use either of the Save commands to save your work to a file on the disk. It is especially important to save a new document very soon after you create it because the AutoRecover feature does not work until a file name has been specified.

Additional Information

Saving a file is the same in all Office 2013 applications, except Access.

You will save this file using a new file name to your solution file location.

Click Save As in the sidebar of the Backstage.

Your screen should be similar to Figure 50

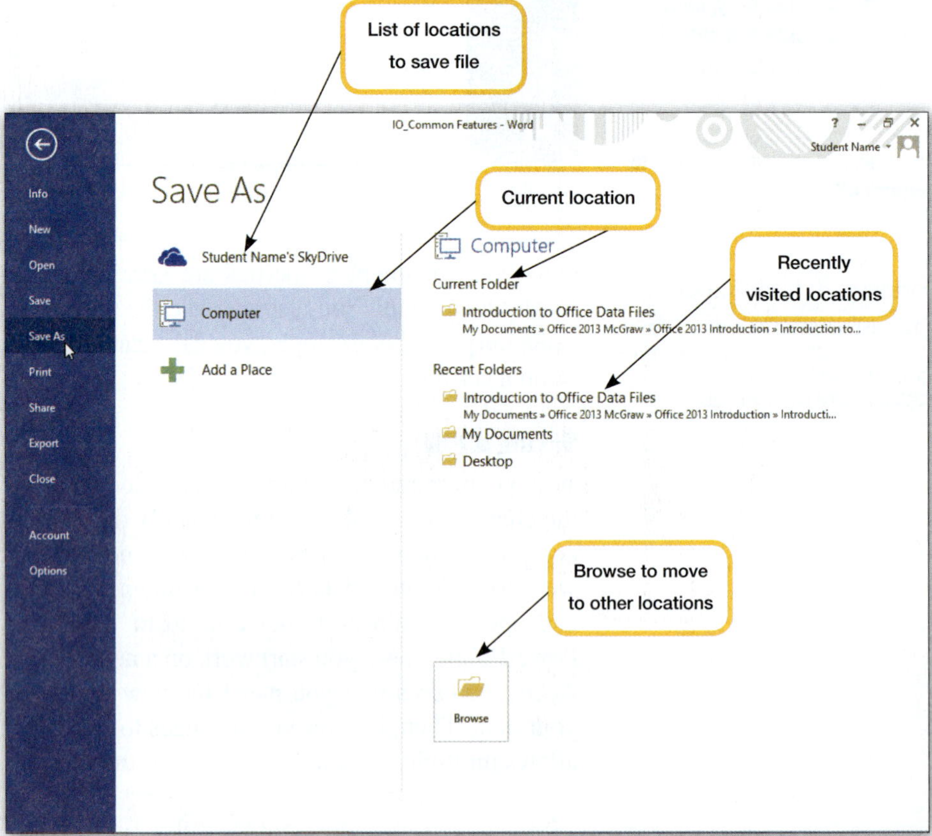

Figure 50

The Save As window is displayed in which you select the location where you want to save the file. Just as in the Open window, the location may be the hard drive of your computer, an external storage device, a local network, or in the cloud on SkyDrive or SharePoint. The location where the file was opened is the current location in the list. A list of current and recent folders is displayed in the right section. If the current folder location is where you want to save the file, clicking on the folder immediately opens it. If you need to open a different folder, click on it in the Recent Folders list or click Browse to locate the folder.

2

- **If necessary, select a different location from the list of locations.**
- **Select the folder from the Current Folder or Recent Folders list or click Browse.**

Your screen should be similar to Figure 51

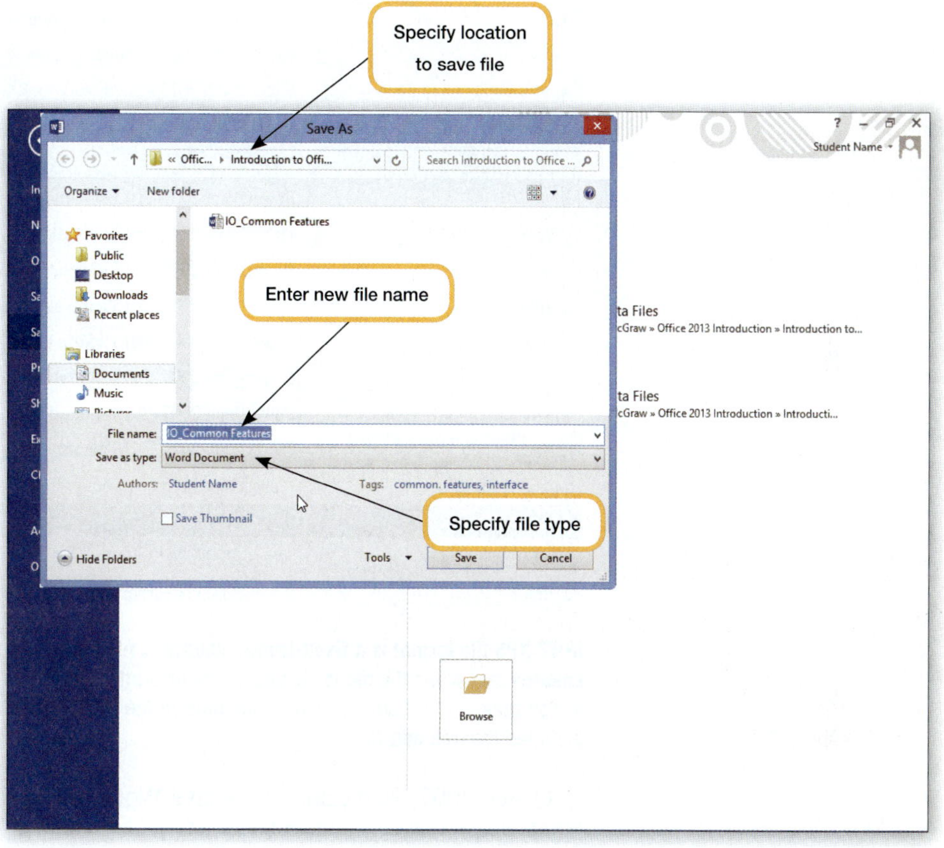

Figure 51

Having Trouble?

Do not be concerned if your Save As dialog box Save location and file details such as the size, type, and date modified are different. These features are determined by the Folder and dialog box settings on your computer.

Additional Information

You can set a default location to save a file by choosing Options/Save in the Backstage and specifying the default save location.

The Save As dialog box is used to specify the location where you will save the file and the file name. The Address bar displays the current folder location and the File name text box displays the name of the open file. The file name is highlighted, ready for you to enter a new file name. The Save as type box displays "Word Document" as the default format in which the file will be saved. Word 2013 documents are automatically saved using the file extension .docx. The file type you select determines the file extension that will be automatically added to the file name when the file is saved. The file types and extensions for the four Office 2013 applications are described in the following table.

Extensions	File Type
Word 2013	
.docx	Word 2007–2013 document without macros or code
.dotx	Word 2007–2013 template without macros or code
.docm	Word 2007–2013 document that could contain macros or code
.xps	Word 2007–2013 shared document (see Note)
.doc	Word 95–2003 document
Excel 2013	
.xlsx	Excel 2007–2013 default workbook without macros or code
.xlsm	Excel 2007–2013 default workbook that could contain macros
.xltx	Excel 2007–2013 template without macros
.xltm	Excel 2007–2013 template that could contain macros
.xps	Excel 2007–2013 shared workbook (see Note)
.xls	Excel 97–2003 workbook
PowerPoint 2013	
.pptx	PowerPoint 2007–2013 default presentation format
.pptm	PowerPoint 2007–2013 presentation with macros
.potx	PowerPoint 2007–2013 template without macros
.potm	PowerPoint 2007–2013 template that may contain macros
.ppam	PowerPoint 2007–2013 add-in that contains macros
.ppsx	PowerPoint 2007–2013 slide show without macros
.ppsm	PowerPoint 2007–2013 slide show that may contain macros
.thmx	PowerPoint 2007–2013 theme
.ppt	PowerPoint 2003 or earlier presentation
Access 2013	
.accdb	Access 2007–2013 database
.mdb	Access 2003 or earlier database

NOTE XPS file format is a fixed-layout electronic file format that preserves document formatting and ensures that when the file is viewed online or printed, it retains exactly the format that you intended. It also makes it difficult to change the data in the file. To save as an XPS file format, you must have installed the free add-in.

Office 2007, 2010, and 2013 save Word, Excel, and PowerPoint files using the XML format (Extensible Markup Language) and a four-letter file extension. This format makes your documents safer by separating files that contain macros (small programs in a document that automate tasks) to make it easier for a virus checker to identify and block unwanted code or macros that could be dangerous to your computer. It also makes file sizes smaller by compressing the content upon saving and makes files less susceptible to damage. In addition, XML format makes it easier to open documents created with an Office application using another application.

Previous versions of Word, Excel, and PowerPoint did not use XML and had a three-letter file extension. If you plan to share a file with someone using an Office 2003 or earlier version, you can save the document using the three-letter file type; however, some features may be lost. Otherwise, if you save it as a four-letter file type, the recipient may not be able to view all features. There also may be loss of features for users of Office 2007 (even though it has an XML file type) because the older version does not support several of the new features in Office 2013. Office 2013 includes a feature that checks for compatibility with previous versions and advises you what features in the document may be lost if opened by an Office 2007 user or if the document is saved in the 2003 format.

If you have an Office Access 2007 (.accdb) database that you want to save in an earlier Access file format (.mdb), you can do so as long as your .accdb database

Additional Information

Depending upon your Office 2013 setup, a prompt to check for compatibility may appear automatically when you save a file.

Additional Information

Using Save As in Access creates a copy of the open database file and then opens the copy. Access automatically closes the original database.

does not contain any multivalued lookup fields, offline data, or attachments. This is because older versions of Access do not support these new features. If you try to convert an .accdb database containing any of these elements to an .mdb file format, Access displays an error message.

First you may need to change the location to the location where the file will be saved. The same procedures you used to specify a location to open a file are used to specify the location to save a file. Then, you will change the file name to Common Features using the default Word document type (.docx).

3

- **If necessary, select the location where you save your solution files.**
- **If necessary, drag in the File Name text box to highlight the existing file name.**
- **Type Common Features**
- **Click Save.**

Your screen should be similar to Figure 52

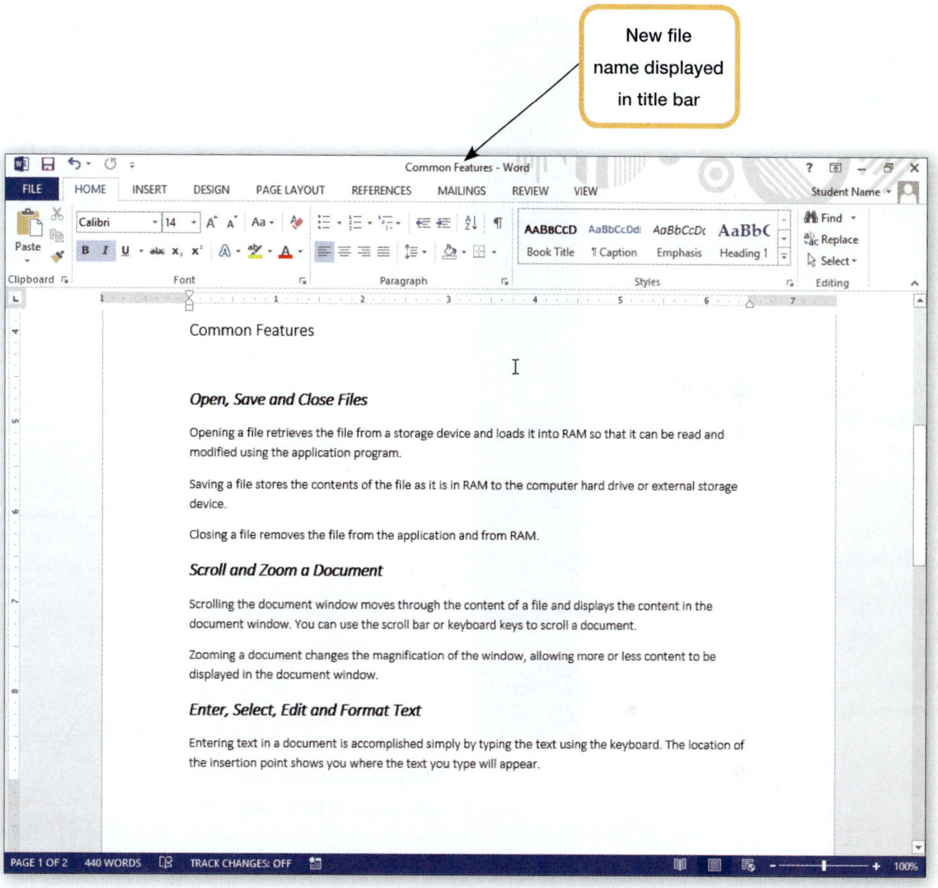

New file name displayed in title bar

Figure 52

Additional Information

Windows file names can contain letters, numbers, and spaces; however, the symbols \, /, ?, :, *, ", <, and > cannot be used. The file name can be entered in either uppercase or lowercase letters and will appear exactly as you type it.

The document is saved as Common Features.docx at the location you selected, and the new file name is displayed in the Word application window title bar. Depending upon your Windows setup, the file extension also may be displayed in the title bar.

Printing a Document

Once a document appears how you want, you may want to print a hard copy for your own reference or to give to others. All Office 2013 applications include the capability to print and have similar options. You will print this document next.

1 Open the File tab and choose Print.

Another Method

The keyboard shortcut for the Print command is Ctrl + P.

Your screen should be similar to Figure 53

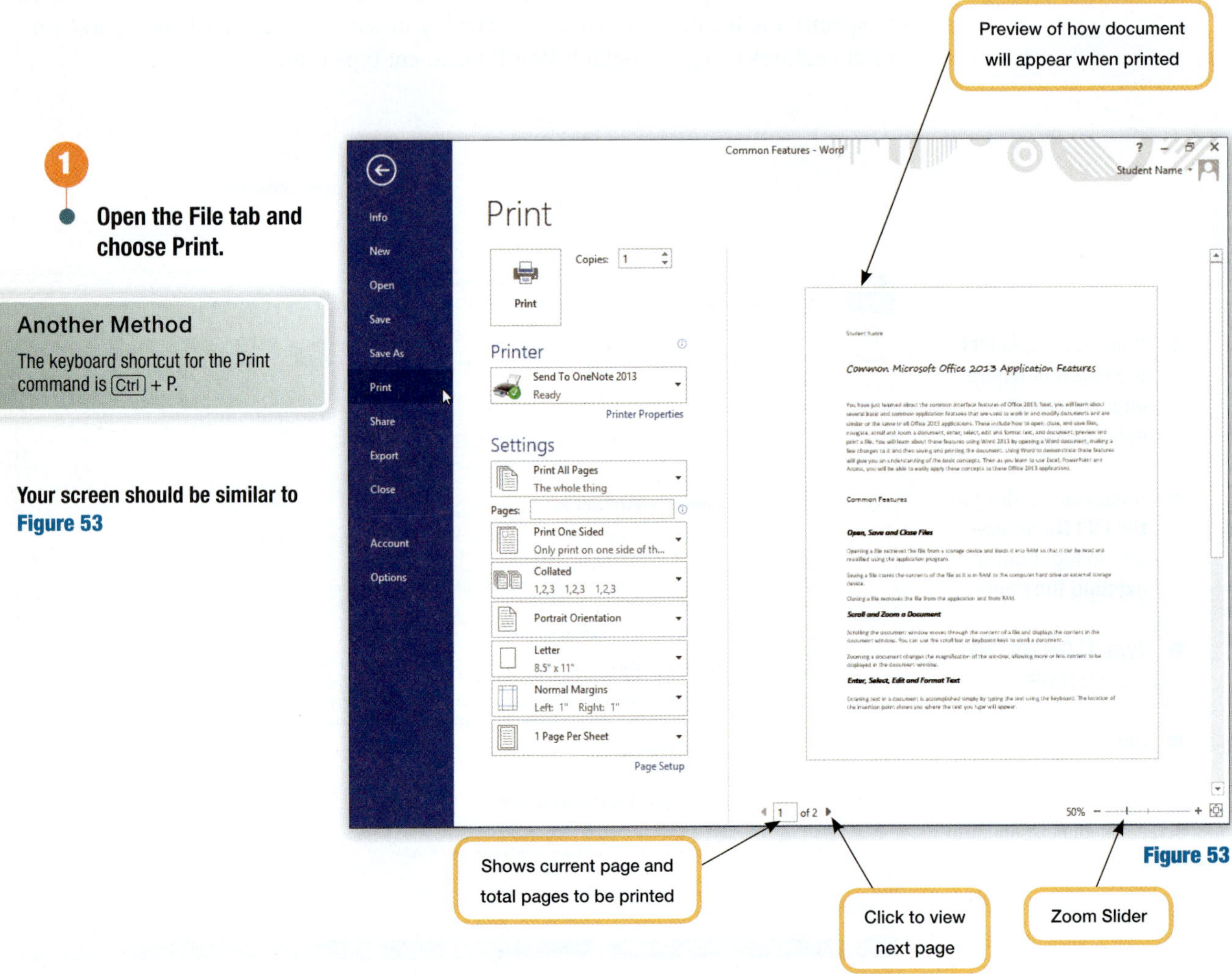

Figure 53

The right section of the Print page displays a preview of the current page of your document. To save time and unnecessary printing and paper waste, it is always a good idea to preview each page of your document before printing. Notice below the preview, the page scroll box shows the page number of the page you are currently viewing and the total number of pages. The scroll buttons on either side are used to scroll to the next and previous pages. Additionally, a Zoom Slider is available to adjust the size of the preview.

2

- **Click ▶ to view the second page of the document.**
- **Increase the zoom to 70%.**

Your screen should be similar to Figure 54

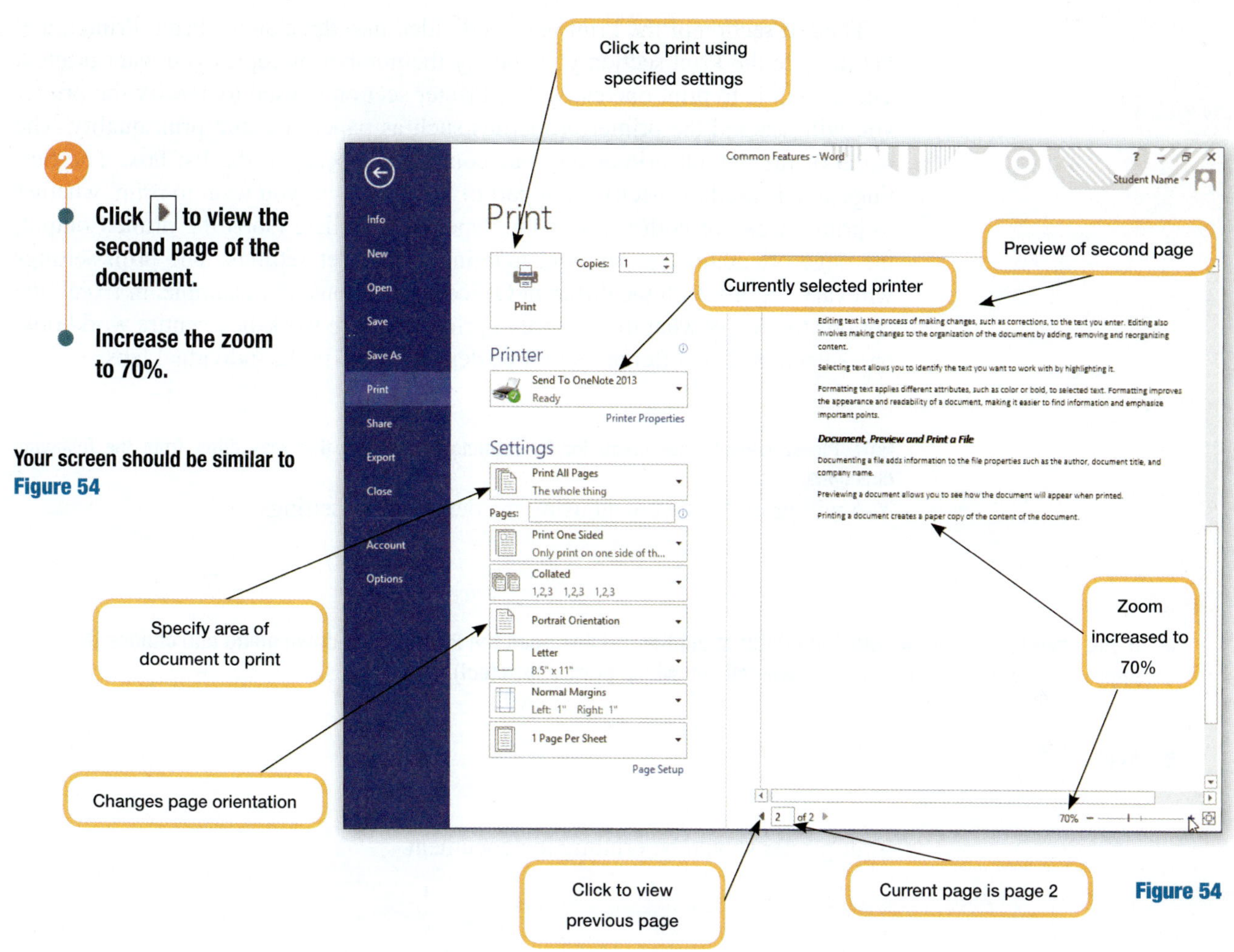

Figure 54

If you see any changes you want to make to the document, you would need to close the File tab and make the changes. If the document looks good, you are ready to print.

The left section of the Print page is divided into three areas: Print, Printer, and Settings. In the Print section you specify the number of copies you want printed. The default is to print one copy. The Printer section is used to specify the printer you will use and the printer properties such as paper size and print quality. The name of the default printer on your computer appears in the list box. The Settings area is used to specify what part of the document you want to print, whether to print on one or both sides of the paper or to collate (sort) the printed output, the page orientation, paper size, margins, and sheet settings. The print settings will vary slightly with the different Office applications. For example, in Excel, the options to specify what to print are to print the entire worksheet, entire workbook, or a selection. The differences will be demonstrated in the individual labs.

NOTE Please consult your instructor for printing procedures that may differ from the following directions.

You will print the document using the default print settings.

3

- **If you need to change the selected printer to another printer, open the Printer drop-down menu and choose the appropriate printer (your instructor will tell you which printer to select).**
- **Click Print.**

Your printer should be printing the document.

Closing a File

Finally, you want to close the document.

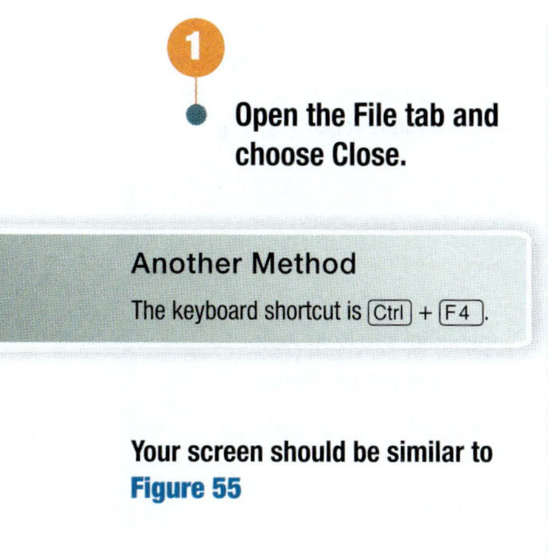

1 Open the File tab and choose Close.

Another Method

The keyboard shortcut is Ctrl + F4.

Your screen should be similar to Figure 55

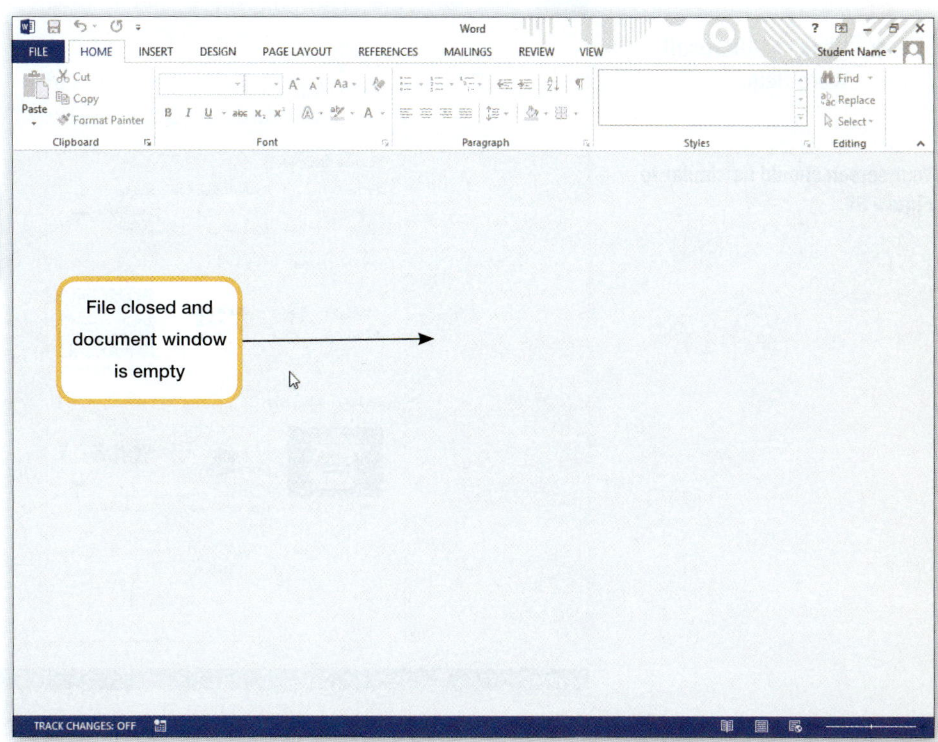

Figure 55

Additional Information

Do not click ✕ Close in the window title bar as this closes the application.

Now the Word window displays an empty document window. Because you did not make any changes to the document since saving it, the document window closed immediately. If you had made additional changes, the program would display a dialog box asking whether you wanted to save the file before closing it, to close the file without saving the changes or to cancel the action. This prevents the accidental closing of a file that has not been saved first.

USING OFFICE HELP

Another Method

You also can press F1 to access Help.

The ? in the upper-right corner of the Ribbon is used to access the Microsoft Help system. This button is always visible even when the Ribbon is hidden. Because you are using the Microsoft Word 2013 application, Microsoft Word Help will be accessed.

Click [?] Microsoft Word Help.

Your screen should be similar to Figure 56

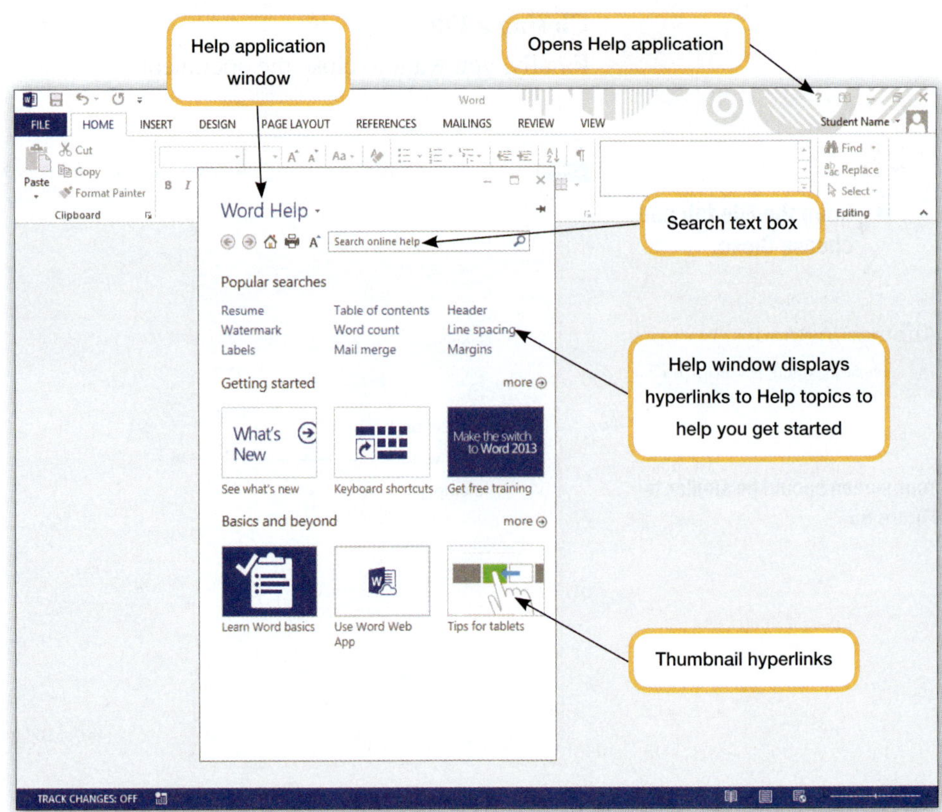

Figure 56

Additional Information

Because Help is an online feature, the information is frequently updated. Your screens may display slightly different information than those shown in the figures in this lab.

The Word Help feature is a separate application and is opened and displayed in a separate window. If you are connected to the Internet, the Microsoft Office Online website, Office.com, is accessed and help information from this site is displayed in the window. If you are not connected, the offline help information that is provided with the application and stored on your computer is located and displayed. Generally, the listing of topics is similar but fewer in number.

Additional Information

Depending on the size of your Help window, you may need to scroll the window to see all the Help information provided.

Selecting Help Topics

The Home window is displayed and provides several ways you can get help. The first is to type in the Search text box a word or phrase about a topic you want help on. A second is to select a topic from the Popular searches list. Each topic is a **hyperlink** or connection to the information located on the Office.com website or in Help on your computer. When you point to a hyperlink, it appears underlined and the mouse pointer appears as 👆. Clicking the hyperlink accesses and displays the information associated with the hyperlink. A third method is to click one of the thumbnail hyperlinks in the Getting Started or Basics and beyond sections to access information about these topics.

1

- Click the "Learn Word basics" thumbnail.
- Scroll the Help window to see the "Choose a template" topic.

Your screen should be similar to Figure 57

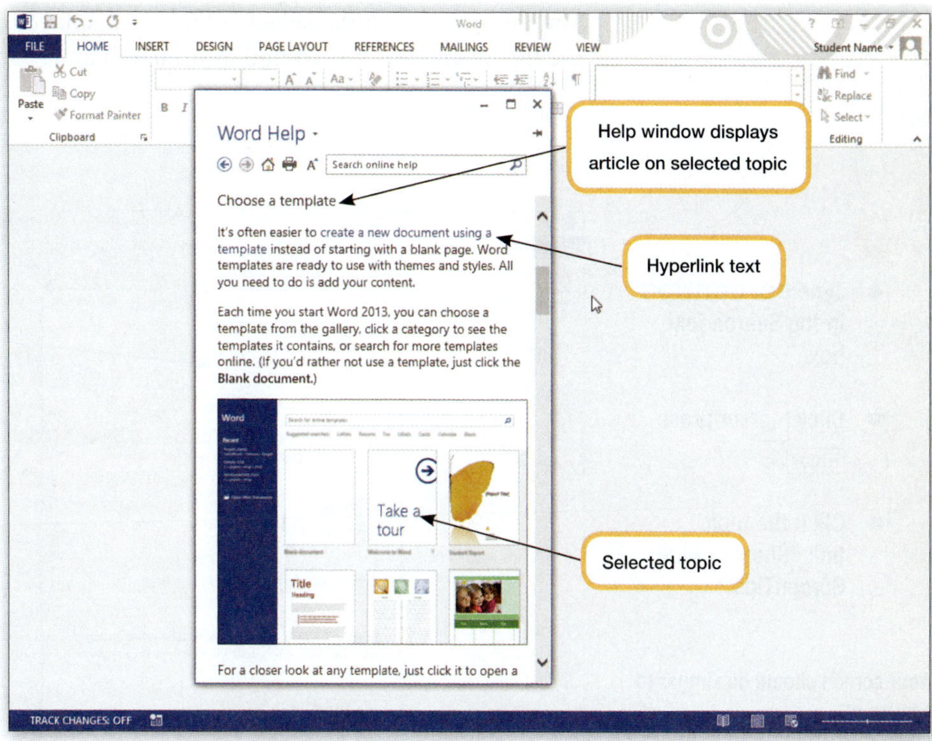

Figure 57

An article containing information about basic features of Word 2013 is displayed. Notice the colored text "create a new document using a template." This indicates the text is a hyperlink to more information about this topic.

2

- Click "create a new document using a template."
- Scroll the window and read the information about this topic.
- Scroll back to the top of the window.

Your screen should be similar to Figure 58

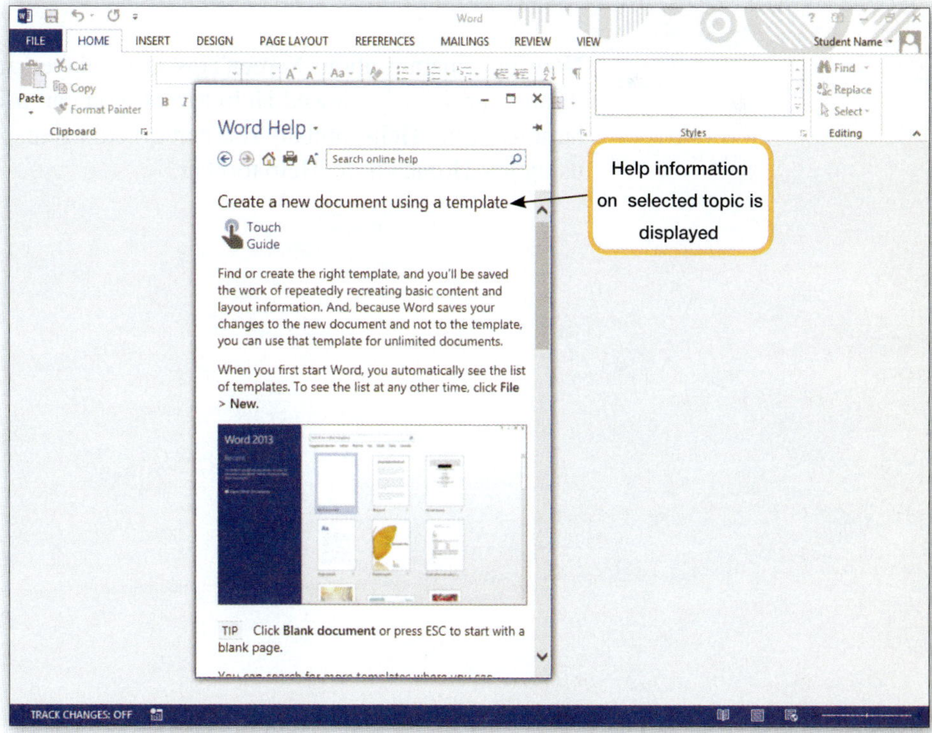

Figure 58

The information on the selected topic is displayed in the window. Next, you will use the Search text box to find information about ScreenTips.

3

- **Type screentips in the Search text box.**
- **Click [search icon] or press Enter.**
- **Click the topic link "Show or hide ScreenTips."**

Your screen should be similar to Figure 59

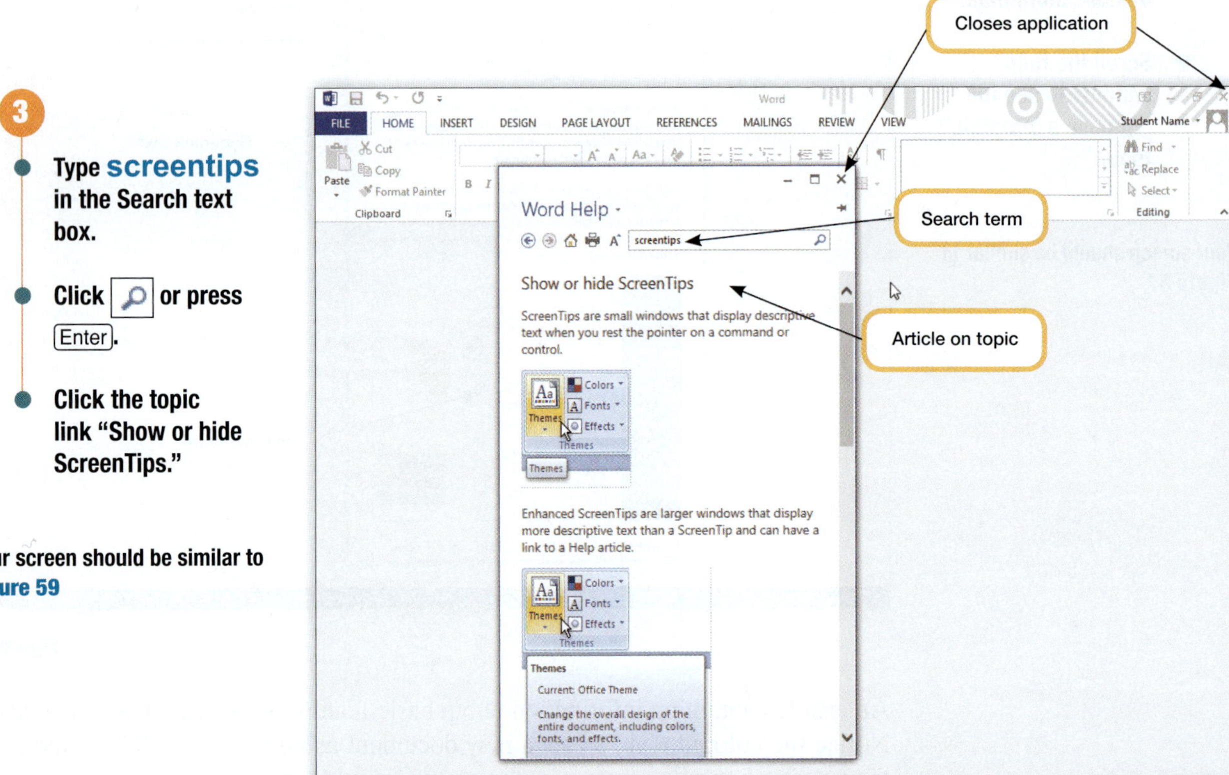

Figure 59

Now information about ScreenTips is displayed in the Help window. To move through previously viewed Help topics, you can use the [Back icon] Back and [Forward icon] Forward buttons in the Help toolbar. You can quickly redisplay the opening Help window using [Home icon] Home on the Help toolbar.

4

- Click Back two times to display the last two previously viewed topics.
- Click Home in the Help window toolbar.

Your screen should be similar to Figure 60

Figure 60

The Help Home window is displayed again.

EXITING AN OFFICE 2013 APPLICATION

Now you are ready to close the Help window and exit the Word program. The Close button located on the right end of the window title bar can be used to exit most application windows. If you attempt to close an application without first saving your document, a dialog box appears asking if you want to save your work before exiting the application, not to save your latest changes to the document or to cancel the action. If you do not save your work and you exit the application, any changes you made since last saving it are lost.

1

- **Click Close in the Help window title bar to close the Help window.**
- **Click Close in the Word window title bar to exit Word.**

Another Method

The keyboard shortcut for the Exit command is Alt + F4.

The program window is closed and the Windows desktop is visible again.

KEY TERMS

Backstage IO.27
buttons IO.16
character effects IO.43
Clipboard IO.48
cloud IO.3, 30
commands IO.20
context menu IO.19
contextual tabs IO.22
copy IO.48
cursor IO.17
database IO.8
default IO.28
destination IO.48
dialog box launcher IO.25
document window IO.17
edit IO.3
Enhanced ScreenTips IO.22
fields IO.8
font IO.43
font size IO.43
format IO.4
Format Painter IO.52
groups IO.20
hyperlink IO.64
insertion point IO.17
keyboard shortcut IO.18
keyword IO.54
Live Preview IO.43
metadata IO.54
Mini toolbar IO.42, IO.44
move IO.48
Office Clipboard IO.48
on-demand tabs IO.22
Paste Preview IO.49
properties IO.28, 54
Quick Access Toolbar IO.16
records IO.8
Ribbon IO.17
ScreenTip IO.18
scroll bar IO.17
shortcut menu IO.19
slide IO.11
slide shows IO.11
source IO.48
status bar IO.17
tables IO.8
tabs IO.20
tag IO.54
task pane IO.26
template IO.15
tooltip IO.18
typeface IO.43
user interface IO.14
View buttons IO.17
word wrap IO.43
worksheet IO.6
Zoom Slider IO.17

COMMAND SUMMARY

Command/Button	Shortcut	Action
Quick Access Toolbar		
Undo	Ctrl + Z	Restores last change
Redo	Ctrl + Y	Restores last Undo action
Repeat	Ctrl + Y	Repeats last action

COMMAND SUMMARY (CONTINUED)

Command/Button	Shortcut	Action
[Word icon]		Displays a menu of commands to open, close, and size the application window.
? Microsoft Word Help	F1	Opens Microsoft Help
File tab		
Info		Displays document properties
New		Starts a new document file
Open	Ctrl + O	Opens existing file
Save	Ctrl + S or [Save icon]	Saves document using same file name
Save As	F12	Saves document using a new file name, type, and/or location
Print	Ctrl + P	Prints document using specified settings
Close	Ctrl + F4 or [X]	Closes document
View tab		
Zoom group Zoom		Changes magnification of document
Home tab		
Clipboard group Paste	Ctrl + V	Inserts copy of Clipboard at location of cursor
Cut	Ctrl + X	Removes selection and copies to Clipboard
Copy	Ctrl + C	Copies selection to Clipboard
Format Painter		Duplicates formats of selection to other locations
Font group Calibri Font	Ctrl + Shift + F	Changes typeface
11 Font Size	Ctrl + Shift + P	Changes font size
B Bold	Ctrl + B	Adds/removes bold effect
I Italic	Ctrl + I	Adds/removes italic effect
U Underline	Ctrl + U	Adds/removes underline effect

LAB EXERCISES

Hands-On Exercises

STEP-BY-STEP

EXPLORING EXCEL 2013

1. In this exercise you will explore the Excel 2013 application and use many of the same features you learned about while using Word 2013 in this lab.
   a. Start Office Excel 2013 and choose Blank workbook.
   b. What shape is the mouse pointer when positioned in the document window area? ____________
   c. Excel has ____________ tabs. Which tabs are not the same as in Word?
   ____
   d. Open the Formulas tab. How many groups are in the Formulas tab? ____________
   e. Which tab contains the group to work with charts? ____________
   f. From the Home tab, click the Number group dialog box launcher. What is the name of the dialog box that opens? ____________ How many number categories are there? ____________ Close the dialog box.
   g. Display ScreenTips for the following buttons located in the Alignment group of the Home tab and identify what action they perform.
   ____
   ____
   ____
   h. Open the Excel Help window. From the Help window choose "Learn Excel Basics" and then choose "Enter data manually in worksheet cells" and answer the following:
      - What is the definition of worksheet? Hint: Click on the hyperlinked term "worksheet" to view a definition.
      ____
      - What four types of data can be entered in a worksheet? ____________, ____________, ____________, ____________
   i. Read the topic "Quick Start: Edit and enter data in a worksheet." If you have an Internet connection, click the Watch the video link and view the video. Close your browser window.
   j. Enter the term "formula" in the Search text box. Look at several articles and answer the following question: All formula entries begin with what symbol? ____________
   k. Redisplay the "Enter data manually in worksheet cells" topic. Return to the Home page.
   l. Close the Help window. Exit Excel.

EXPLORING POWERPOINT 2013

2. In this exercise you will explore the PowerPoint 2013 application and use many of the same features you learned about while using Word 2013 in this lab.

   a. Start PowerPoint 2013 and choose Blank presentation.
   b. PowerPoint has ____________ tabs. Which tabs are not the same as in Word?
   ____
   c. Open the Animations tab. How many groups are in this tab? ____________
   d. Which tab contains the group to work with themes? ____________
   e. Click on the text "Click to add title." Type your name. Select this text and change the font size to 72; add italic and bold. Cut this text. Click in the box containing "Click to add subtitle" and paste the cut selection. Use the Paste Options to keep the source formatting.
   f. Click on the text "Click to add title" and type the name of your school. Select the text and apply a font of your choice.
   g. Open the PowerPoint Help window. From the Help window, choose "Learn PowerPoint Basics." Read the information in this article:
      - In the "Insert a new slide" topic, click the link to "Add, rearrange, and delete slides."
      - What is a layout?

      ____
   h. Enter the term "menus" in the Search text box. What do the commands in the Animations tab do?
   ____
   i. Display the Help Home window again. Close the Help window. Exit PowerPoint and do not save the changes you made to the presentation.

LAB EXERCISES

EXPLORING ACCESS 2013

3. As noted in this Introduction to Microsoft Office 2013, when you start Access 2013 you need to either open an existing database file or create and name a new database. Therefore, in this exercise, you will simply explore the Access 2013 Help information without opening or creating a database file.
   a. Use the Start menu to start Office Access 2013.
   b. Click [?] Help in the Access Start window.
   c. Choose the topic "Basic tasks for an Access 2013 desktop database."
      - In the first paragraph, what are three examples of kinds of information that can be stored in a database?
        ____________, ____________, and ____________.
   d. In the Search box enter "table." Choose the topic "Introduction to tables" and from the Overview answer the following questions:
      - What is a database?
        ____
      - What are the three parts of a table?
        ____________, ____________, and ____________.
      - A field is also commonly called a ____________.
      - Each row in a table is also called a ____________.
   e. Close the Help window. Exit Access.

ON YOUR OWN

USING TOUCH IN OFFICE

1. In addition to the Help information you used in this lab, Office 2013 Help also includes online tutorials. Selecting a Help topic that starts a tutorial will open the browser program on your computer. You will use one of these tutorials to learn more about using touch features.
   Start Word 2013. Open Help and choose "Learn Word basics" from the Help Home window. Click on the Touch Guide. The Office Touch Guide web page is opened in your browser. Read the information in this article. When you are done, close the browser window, close Help, and exit Word 2013.

Creating a Presentation Lab 1

Objectives

After completing this lab, you will know how to:

1. Use a template to create a presentation.
2. View and edit a presentation.
3. Copy and move selections.
4. Move, copy, and delete slides.
5. Increase and decrease list levels.
6. Create a numbered list.
7. Check spelling.
8. Size and move placeholders.
9. Change fonts and formatting.
10. Insert, size, move, and modify graphics.
11. Run a slide show.
12. Document a file.
13. Preview and print a presentation.

CASE STUDY

Animal Rescue Foundation

You are the volunteer coordinator at the local Animal Rescue Foundation. This nonprofit organization rescues unwanted pets from local animal shelters and finds foster homes for them until a suitable adoptive family can be found. The agency has a large volunteer group called the Animal Angels that provides much-needed support for the foundation.

The agency director has decided to launch a campaign to increase community awareness about the foundation. As part of the promotion, you have been asked to create a powerful and persuasive presentation to entice more members of the community to join Animal Angels.

The agency director has asked you to preview the presentation at the weekly staff meeting tomorrow and has asked you to present a draft of the presentation by noon today.

To help you create the presentation, you will use Microsoft PowerPoint 2013, a graphics presentation application that is designed to create presentation materials such as slides, overheads, and handouts. In addition, your presentation can be designed to incorporate the latest high-definition (HD) and widescreen technology. Using PowerPoint 2013, you can create a high-quality and interesting onscreen presentation with pizzazz that will dazzle your audience.

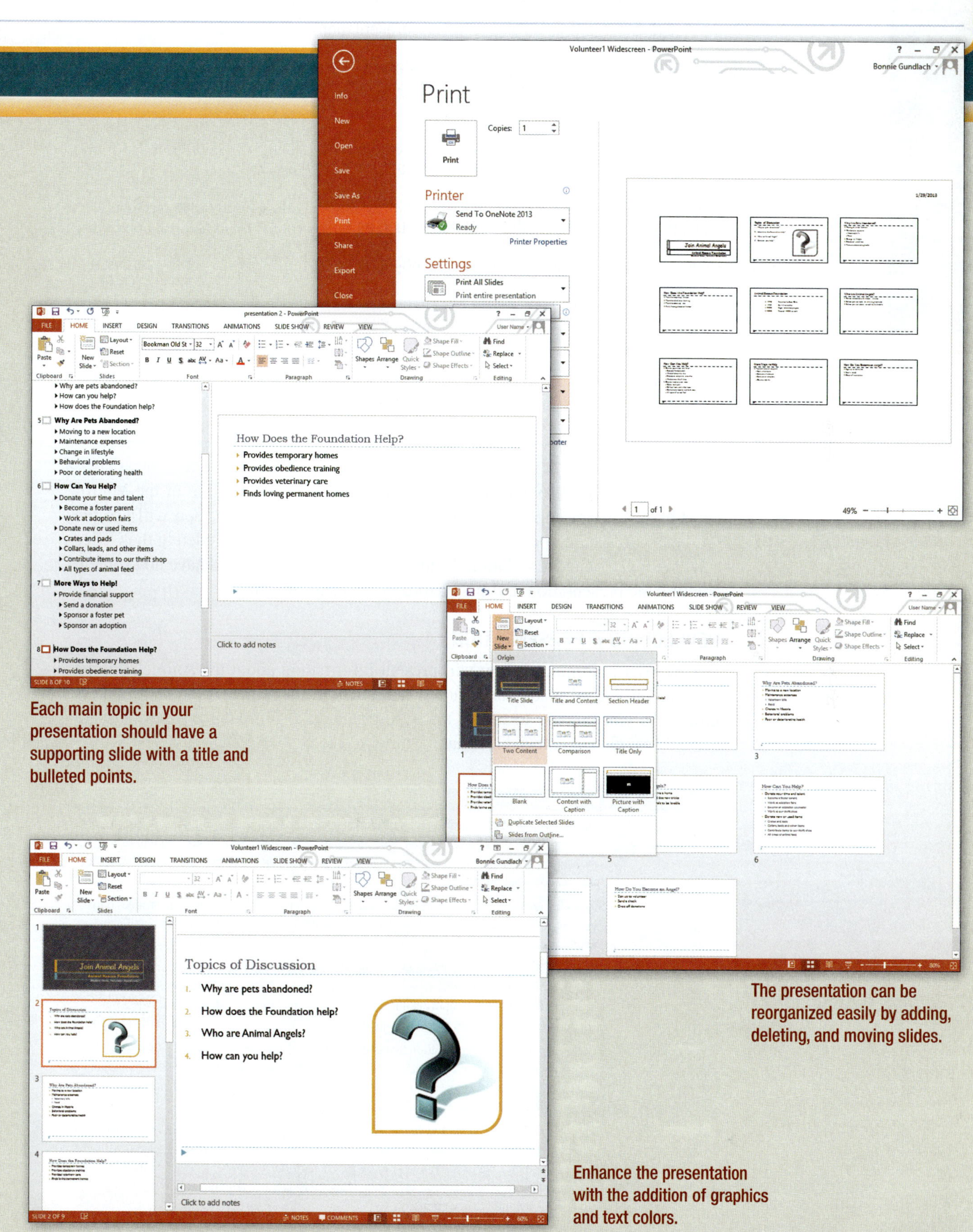

Each main topic in your presentation should have a supporting slide with a title and bulleted points.

The presentation can be reorganized easily by adding, deleting, and moving slides.

Enhance the presentation with the addition of graphics and text colors.

Concept Preview

The following concepts will be introduced in this lab:

1 **Slide** A slide is an individual "page" of your presentation.

2 **Spelling Checker** The spelling checker locates all misspelled words, duplicate words, and capitalization irregularities as you create and edit a presentation, and proposes possible corrections.

3 **AutoCorrect** The AutoCorrect feature makes some basic assumptions about the text you are typing and, based on those assumptions, automatically corrects the entry.

4 **Layout** A layout defines the position and format for objects and text on a slide. A layout contains placeholders for the different items such as bulleted text, titles, charts, and so on.

5 **Graphic** A graphic is a nontext element or object such as a drawing or picture that can be added to a slide.

Starting a New Presentation

The Animal Rescue Foundation has just installed the latest version of the Microsoft Office suite of applications, Office 2013, on its computers. You will use the graphics presentation program, Microsoft PowerPoint 2013, included in the Office suite, to create your presentation. Using this program, you should have no problem creating the presentation in time for tomorrow's staff meeting.

DEVELOPING A PRESENTATION

During your presentation, you will present information about the Animal Rescue Foundation and why someone should want to join the Animal Angels volunteer group. As you prepare to create a new presentation, you should follow several basic steps: plan, create, edit, enhance, and rehearse.

Step	Description
Plan	The first step in planning a presentation is to understand its purpose. You also need to find out the length of time you have to speak, who the audience is, what type of room you will be in, and what kind of audiovisual equipment is available. These factors help to determine the type of presentation you will create.
Create	To begin creating your presentation, develop the content by typing your thoughts or notes into an outline. Each main idea in your presentation should have a supporting slide with a title and bulleted points.
Edit	While typing, you will probably make typing and spelling errors that need to be corrected. This is one type of editing. Another type is to revise the content of what you have entered to make it clearer, or to add or delete information. To do this, you might insert a slide, add or delete bulleted items, or move text to another location.
Enhance	You want to develop a presentation that grabs and holds the audience's attention. Choose a design that gives your presentation some dazzle. Wherever possible, add graphics to replace or enhance text. Add effects that control how a slide appears and disappears and that reveal text in a bulleted list one bullet at a time.
Rehearse	Finally, you should rehearse the delivery of your presentation. For a professional presentation, your delivery should be as polished as your materials. Use the same equipment that you will use when you give the presentation. Practice advancing from slide to slide and then back in case someone asks a question. If you have a mouse available, practice pointing or drawing on the slide to call attention to key points.

After rehearsing your presentation, you may find that you want to go back to the editing or enhancing phase. You may change text, move bullets, or insert a new slide. As you make changes, rehearse the presentation again to see how the changes affect your presentation. By the day of the presentation, you will be confident about your message and at ease with the materials.

EXPLORING THE POWERPOINT DOCUMENT WINDOW

During the planning phase, you have spoken with the foundation director regarding the purpose of the presentation and the content in general. The purpose of your presentation is to educate members of the community about the organization and to persuade many to volunteer. In addition, you want to impress the director by creating a professional presentation that will use the new widescreen and high-definition (HD) technology the organization recently purchased.

Just as in some of the other Microsoft Office 2013 applications, you can start with a blank template or use one of the predesigned templates.

1

- **Start the PowerPoint 2013 application.**
- **If necessary, maximize the window.**

Having Trouble?

See "Common Office 2013 Interface Features," page IO.14, for information on how to start the application and use features that are common to all 2013 Office applications.

Your screen should be similar to Figure 1.1

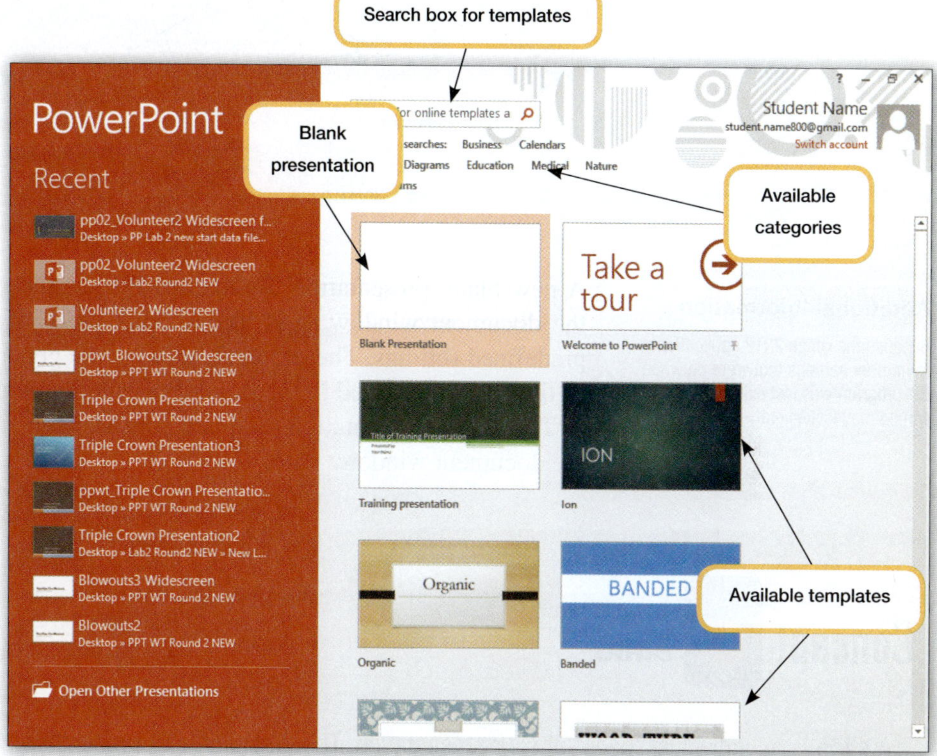

Figure 1.1

You decide to try to create your first presentation using the Blank Presentation template. It is the simplest and most generic of the templates. Because it has minimal design elements, it is good to use when you first start working with PowerPoint, as it allows you to easily add your own content and design changes.

2

- **Choose Blank Presentation.**
- **If necessary, click ≜ NOTES in the status bar to display the notes pane.**

Your screen should be similar to Figure 1.2

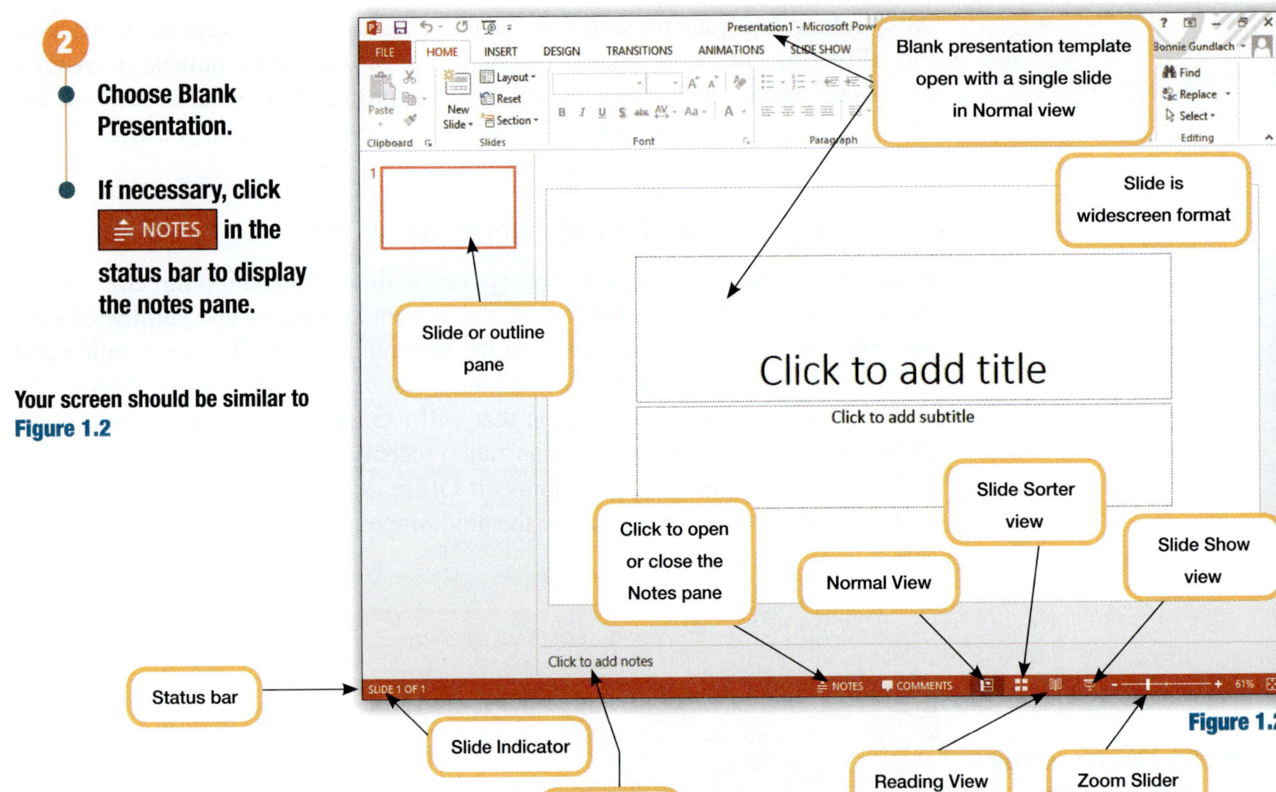

Figure 1.2

Additional Information

Because the Office 2013 applications remember settings that were on when the program was last exited, your screen may look slightly different.

A new blank presentation file, named Presentation1, is opened and displayed in the document window. It is like a blank piece of paper that already has many predefined settings. These default settings are generally the most commonly used settings and are stored in the Blank Presentation template file.

The Blank Presentation template consists of a single slide that is displayed in the document window.

Concept 1 Slide

A **slide** is an individual "page" of your presentation. The first slide of a presentation is the title slide, which is used to introduce your presentation. Additional slides are used to support each main point in your presentation. The slides give the audience a visual summary of the words you speak, which helps them understand the content and keeps them engaged. The slides also help you, the speaker, organize your thoughts and prompt you during the presentation.

When you first start PowerPoint, it opens in a view called Normal view. A **view** is a way of looking at a presentation and provides the means to interact with the presentation. PowerPoint provides several views you can use to look at and modify your presentation. Depending on what you are doing, one view may be preferable to another.

View	Button	Description
Normal		Provides three working areas of the window that allow you to work on all aspects of your presentation in one place.
Outline		Displays content of presentation in outline form in the Outline tab making it easier to focus on content rather than design.
Slide Sorter		Displays a miniature of each slide to make it easy to reorder slides, add special effects such as transitions, and set timing between slides.
Reading View		Displays each slide in final form within the PowerPoint window so you can see how it will look during a presentation but still have access to the Windows desktop.
Slide Show		Displays each slide in final form using the full screen space so you can practice or present the presentation.

Normal view is displayed by default because it is the main view you use while creating a presentation. Normal view has three working areas: Slides or outline pane, Slide window, and Notes pane. These areas allow you to work on all components of your presentation in one convenient location. The **Slides pane** displays a miniature version or **thumbnail** of each slide. When selected, the **Outline pane** displays the slide's content in outline form rather than as a slide thumbnail. The **Slide window** displays the selected slide. Notice the blank slide shape is rectangular. This is the default **widescreen** slide size (16:9) and is used to create a presentation that can take advantage of new widescreen technology, including HD features and equipment. Standard slide size (4:3) is also available. In this size, slides are squarer and are designed to be displayed on traditional-size screens. The **Notes pane,** when displayed, appears below the Slide window. It is used to enter notes that apply to the current slide and can be opened and closed by clicking NOTES on the status bar.

Below the document window is the status bar, which displays the slide indicator, messages and information about various PowerPoint settings, buttons to change the document view, and a window zoom feature. The **slide indicator** on the left side of the status bar identifies the number of the slide that is displayed in the Slide pane, along with the total number of slides in the presentation. You will learn about the other features of the status bar shortly.

ENTERING AND EDITING TEXT

Notice the blank slide contains two boxes with dotted borders. These boxes, called **placeholders**, are containers for all the content that appears on a slide. Slide content consists of text and **objects** such as, graphics, tables and charts. In this case, the placeholders are text placeholders that are designed to contain text and display standard **placeholder text** messages that prompt the user to enter a title and subtitle.

As suggested, you will enter the title for the presentation. As soon as you click on the placeholder, the placeholder text will disappear and will be replaced by the text you type.

1

- **Click the "Click to add title" placeholder.**

Your screen should be similar to Figure 1.3

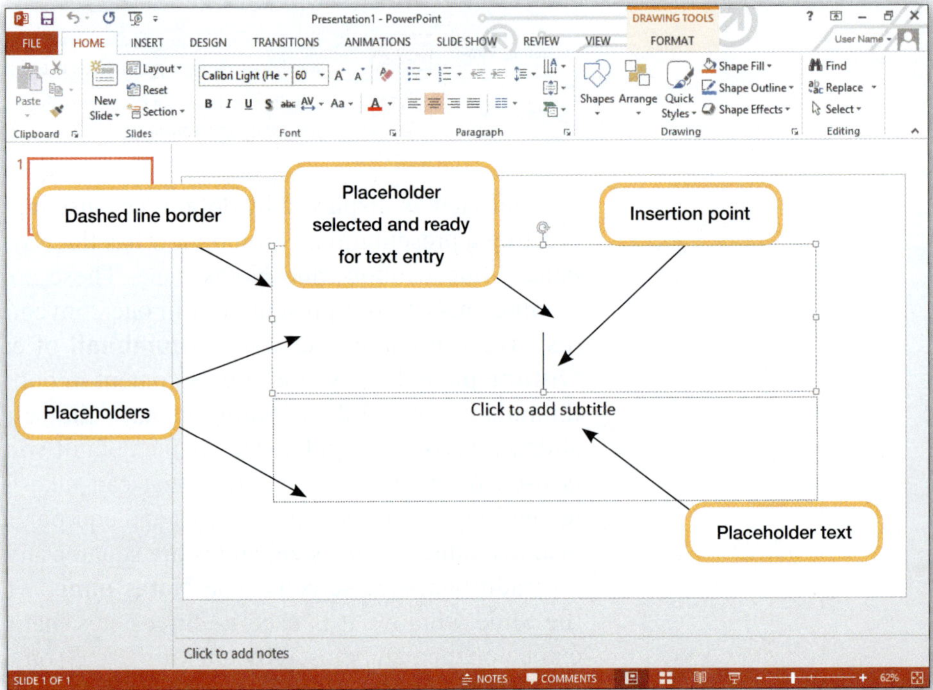

Figure 1.3

Notice that the placeholder is surrounded with a dashed-line border. This indicates that you can enter, delete, select, and format the object inside the placeholder. Because this placeholder contains text, the insertion point is displayed to show your location in the text and to allow you to select and edit the text. Additionally, the mouse pointer appears as a I to be used to position the insertion point.

Next you will type the title text you want to appear on the slide. Then you will enter the subtitle.

Additional Information

A solid border indicates that you can format the placeholder box itself. Clicking the dashed-line border changes it to a solid border.

Having Trouble?

See the section "Entering and Editing Text" on page IO.37 in the Introduction to Microsoft Office 2013 to review this feature.

2

- **Type Join Animal Angels**

Having Trouble?

If you make a typing error, press Backspace to delete the characters back to the error and retype the entry.

- **Click in the "Click to add subtitle" placeholder and type Animal Rescue Foundation**

Your screen should be similar to Figure 1.4

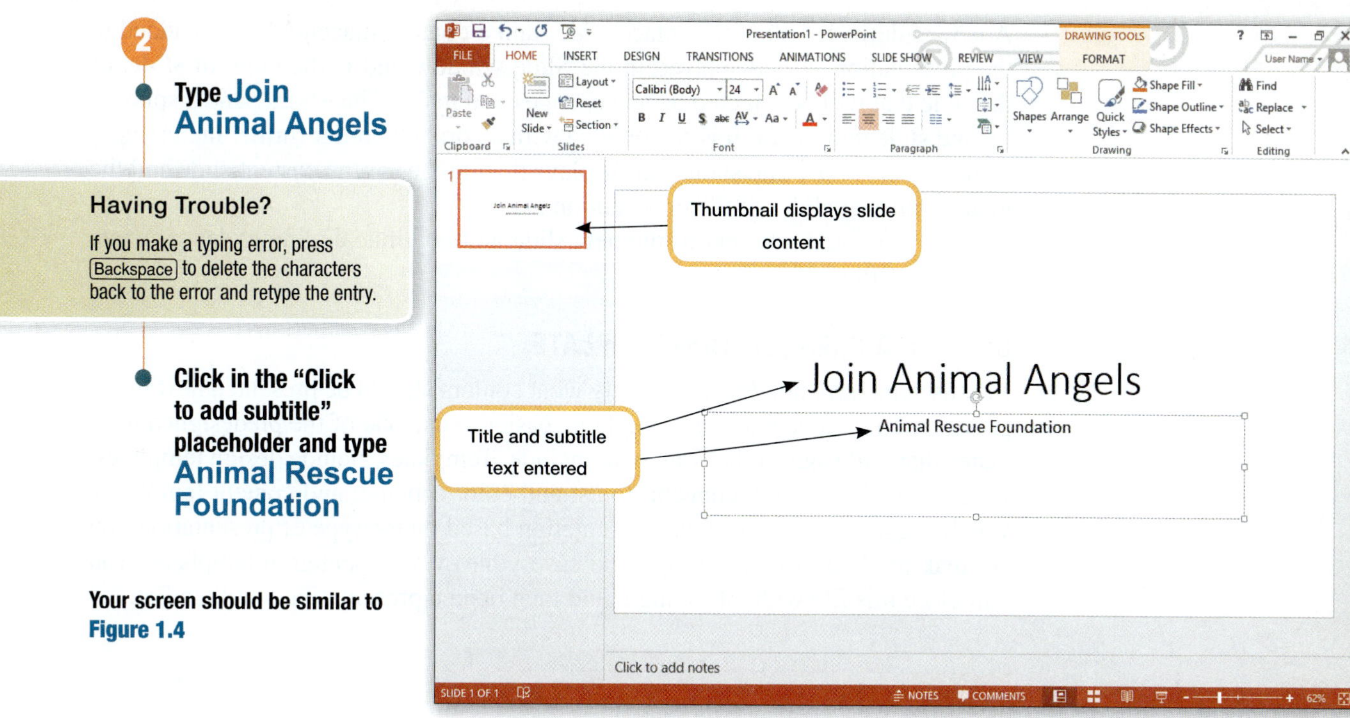

Figure 1.4

The content for the first slide is complete. Notice that the thumbnail of the slide in the Slides pane now displays the text you just entered.

INSERTING A SLIDE

Next you want to add the content for a second slide. To continue creating the presentation, you need to add another slide.

1

- **If necessary, open the Home tab.**
- **Click the upper section of New Slide button in the Slides group.**

Additional Information

The New Slide button has two sections. Clicking the upper section inserts the default slide layout. The lower section opens a menu of options.

Another Method

You also can use the keyboard shortcut Ctrl + M to insert a new slide.

Your screen should be similar to Figure 1.5

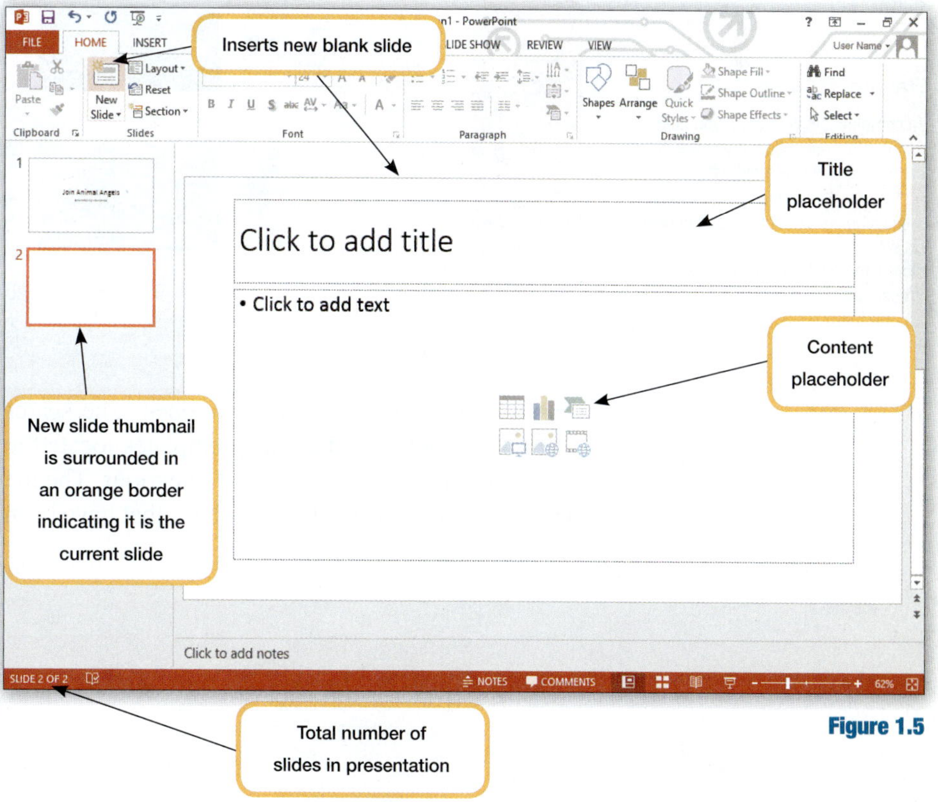

Inserts new blank slide

Title placeholder

Click to add title

• Click to add text

Content placeholder

New slide thumbnail is surrounded in an orange border indicating it is the current slide

Click to add notes

SLIDE 2 OF 2

Total number of slides in presentation

Figure 1.5

A new slide with a slide title placeholder and a content placeholder was added to the presentation. It is displayed in the Slide window and is the **current slide**, or the slide that will be affected by any changes you make. The Slides pane displays a second slide thumbnail. It is surrounded with an orange border further indicating it is the current slide. The status bar displays the number of the current slide and the total number of slides in the presentation.

Now you could add text to the new slide and continue adding slides to create the presentation.

OPENING A PRESENTATION TEMPLATE

Because you have not decided exactly what content should be presented next in the presentation, you decide that it might be easier to use one of the predesigned templates that will suggest the content to include. Templates include design templates, which provide a design concept, fonts, and color scheme; and content templates, which suggest content for your presentation based on the type of presentation you are making. You also can design and save your own presentation templates. You will close this file without saving it and then open a presentation template file.

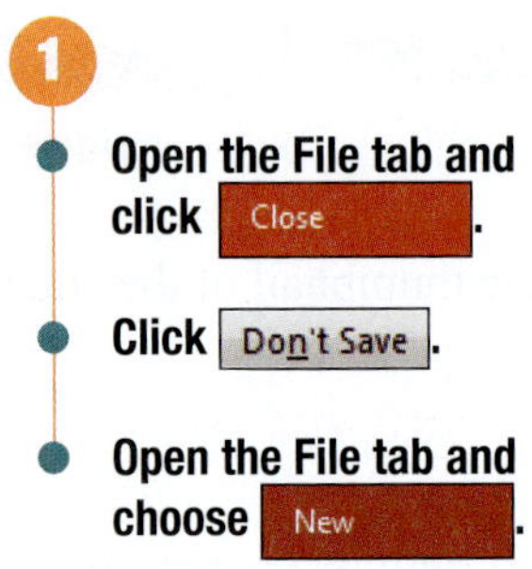

Your screen should be similar to Figure 1.6

Having Trouble?

To complete steps 2 and 3 you need an Internet connection. If you are not connected to the Internet, choose Open, change to the location containing your data files, and double-click on the file pp01_Training. Then skip to the next section, Viewing the Presentation.

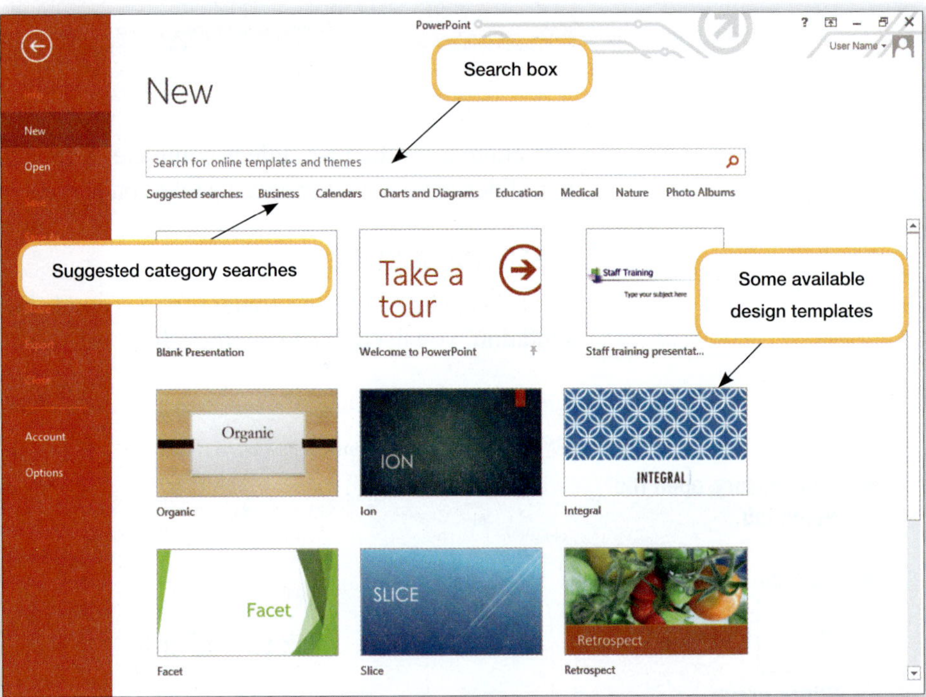

Figure 1.6

The New presentation window is open. The search box at the top of the window is used to quickly find content templates located in a specific category. Below the search box are links to suggested categories. The main window area displays several design templates as well as templates that have been recently opened.

Additional Information

The template categories and files may vary as the content from the Office.com website is updated frequently.

You will look for templates in the business category that will help you create a basic business presentation. When you open a category, examples of the content and/or design templates will be displayed. Before deciding on the template you will use, you will look at some of the available templates.

2

- **Choose Business from the suggested searches list of links.**

Your screen should be similar to Figure 1.7

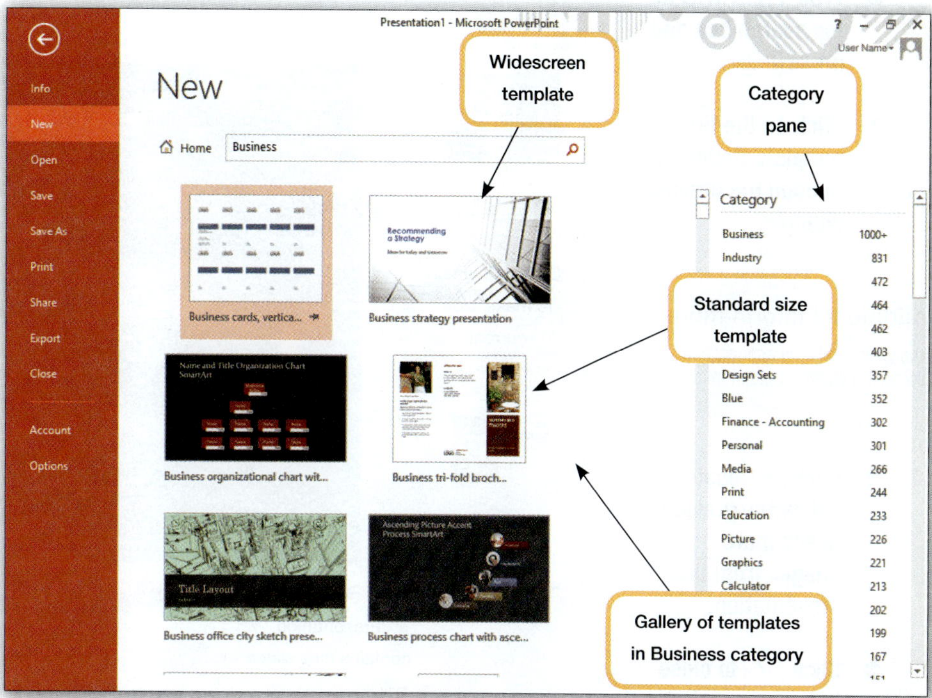

Figure 1.7

Thumbnail images representing the first slide in each template file are displayed. Notice that the thumbnails are different shapes and sizes. Templates can have either portrait or landscape orientation and can be either standard or widescreen in size.

You find the Business category contains a large number of templates. To narrow the number of selections, you can choose another more specific category from the Category pane or type a more specific search term in the search box.

- Type Training in the search box and press Enter.
- Click on the first template thumbnail to open the preview window.

Additional Information

The template name appears in a ScreenTip when you point to it.

- Click ▶ located below the preview to see more images from the presentation.
- Click ✕ to close the preview window.
- Locate and preview the Training seminar presentation (shown in Figure 1.8).
- Click .

Another Method

You also can double-click on the thumbnail to download the template file.

Your screen should be similar to Figure 1.8

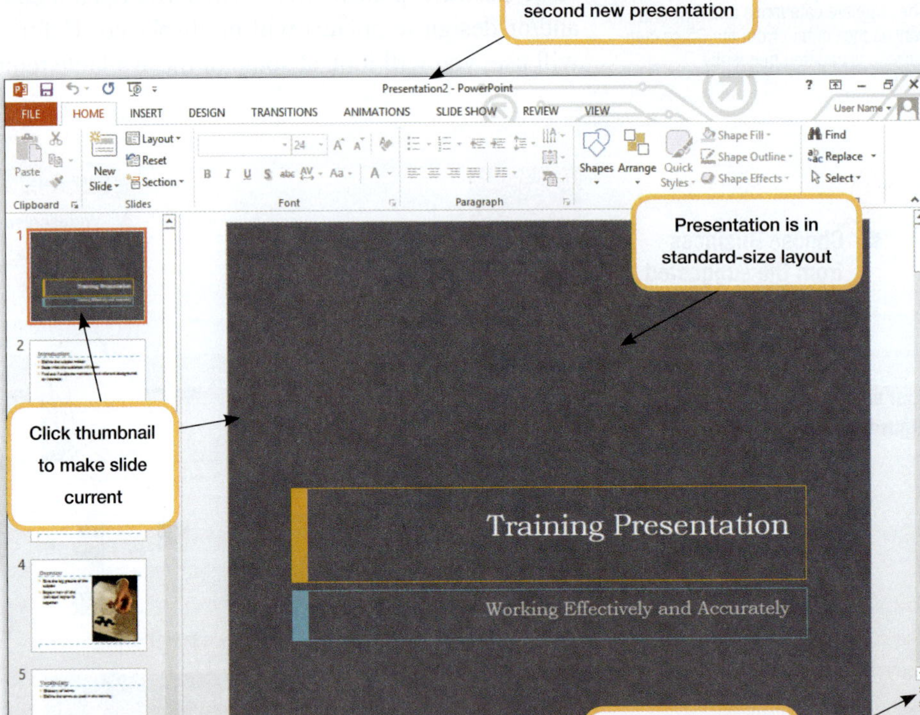

Figure 1.8

The template file is downloaded and opened in PowerPoint. It contains a total of nine slides. Because this is the second new presentation you have worked on since starting PowerPoint 2013, the default file name is Presentation2. You think the design of the template looks good and you will begin your presentation for the volunteers using the content in this template as a guide.

CHANGING SLIDE SIZE

This template uses standard-size slides in its layout. Because you know that during the meeting you will be using equipment that supports widescreen features, you will change the slide size to widescreen before adding the presentation content. This will make your editing process easier since you will already be using the correct format. If necessary, you can always convert back to standard later; however, adjustments to your slides may be required. It's always best to start in the layout that will be used in order to avoid having to make many modifications later.

1

- **Open the Design tab.**
- **Click** Slide Size **in the Customize group.**
- **Choose** Widescreen (16:9)**.**
- **If necessary, click** [icon] **at the right end of the status bar to fit the slide to the current window.**
- **Point to the splitter bar between the Slide tab and the Slide pane, and when the mouse pointer is shaped as ⟺, drag to the right to increase the width of the pane to show four slides.**

Your screen should be similar to Figure 1.9

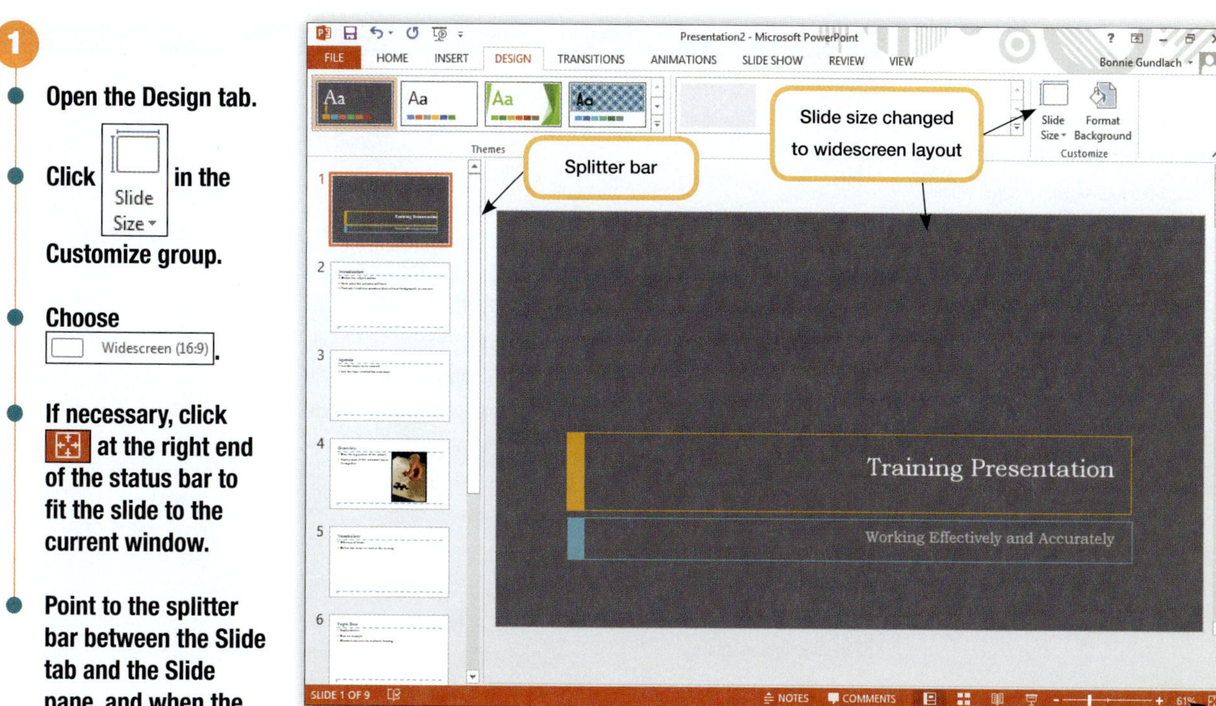

Figure 1.9

The slide size is now the rectangular shape used with widescreen equipment. Additionally, by increasing the width of the Slide tab, you can more easily see the slide content.

MOVING AMONG SLIDES

You want to look at the slides in the presentation to get a quick idea of their content. There are many ways to move from slide to slide in PowerPoint. Most often, the quickest method is to click on the slide thumbnail in the Slides pane. Clicking on a slide in the Slides pane displays it in the Slide window and makes it the current slide. However, if your hands are already on the keyboard, you may want to use the keyboard directional keys. The table on the next page shows both keyboard and mouse methods to move among slides in Normal view.

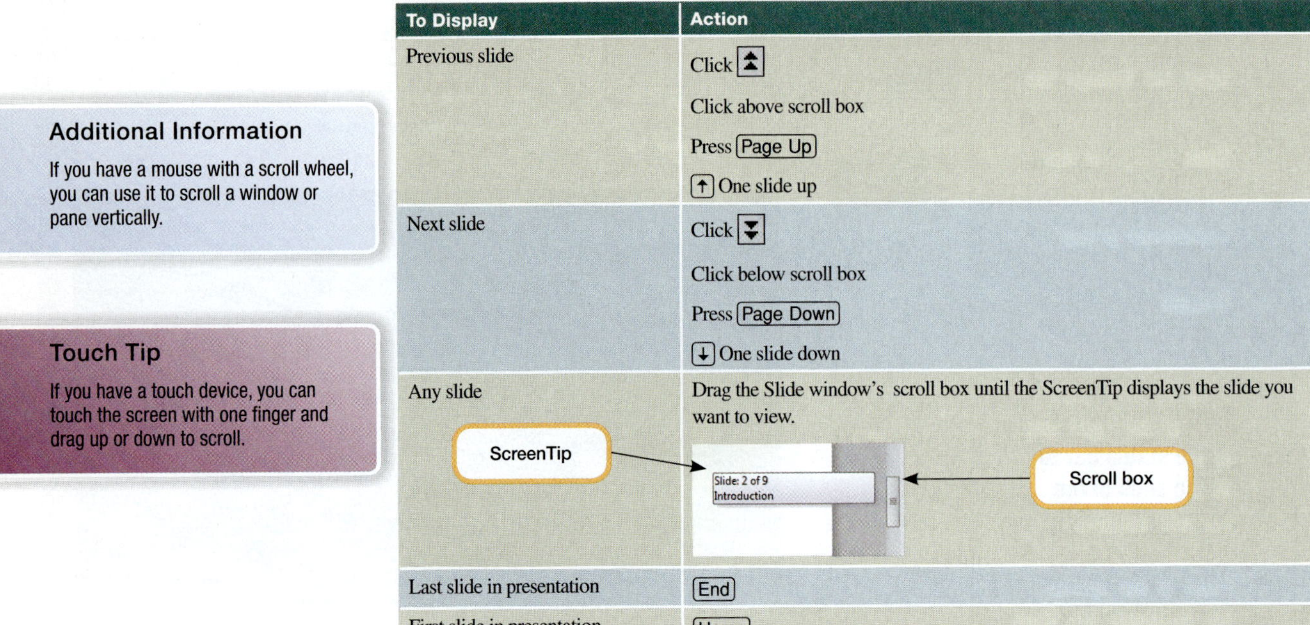

Additional Information

If you have a mouse with a scroll wheel, you can use it to scroll a window or pane vertically.

Touch Tip

If you have a touch device, you can touch the screen with one finger and drag up or down to scroll.

To Display	Action
Previous slide	Click [⏫] Click above scroll box Press Page Up ↑ One slide up
Next slide	Click [⏬] Click below scroll box Press Page Down ↓ One slide down
Any slide	Drag the Slide window's scroll box until the ScreenTip displays the slide you want to view.
Last slide in presentation	End
First slide in presentation	Home

You will try out several of these methods as you look at the slides in the presentation. First you will use the Slides pane. This pane makes it easy to move from one slide to another.

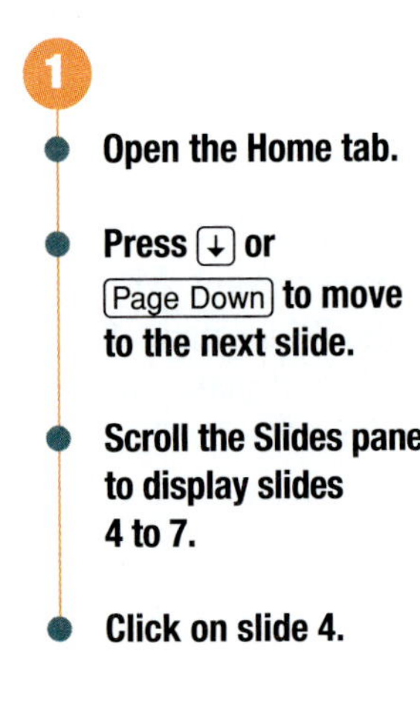

1

- **Open the Home tab.**
- **Press ↓ or Page Down to move to the next slide.**
- **Scroll the Slides pane to display slides 4 to 7.**
- **Click on slide 4.**

Your screen should be similar to Figure 1.10

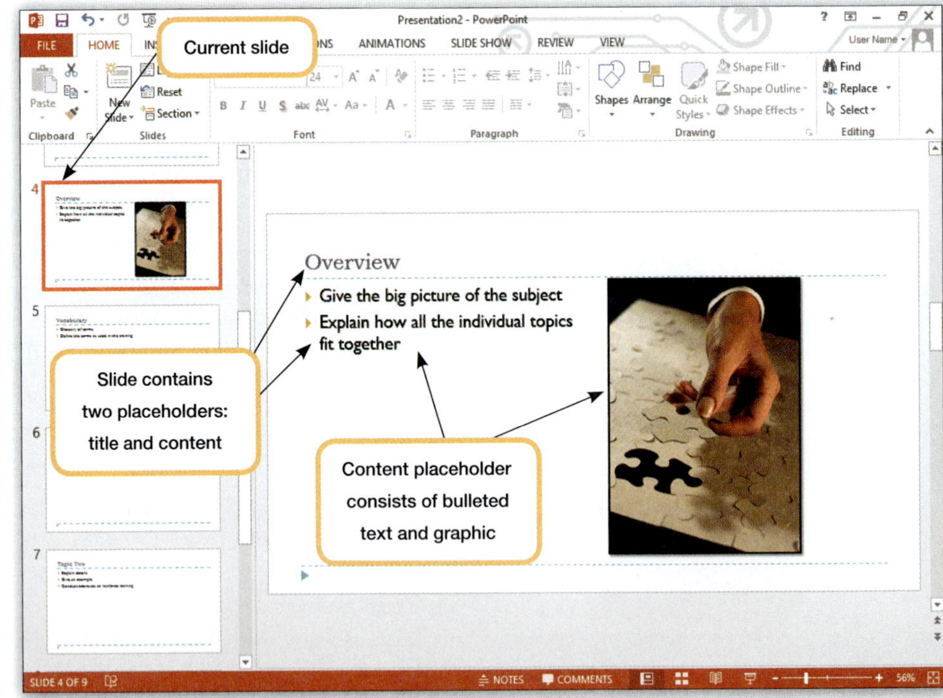

Figure 1.10

Slide 4 is the current slide and is displayed in the Slide window. This slide contains two placeholders: title and content. The content placeholder consists of two bulleted items as well as a graphic. Next you will use the Slide window scroll bar to display the next few slides.

2

- **Click** ▼ **Next Slide to display slide 5.**

Having Trouble?

The ▲ Previous Slide and ▼ Next Slide buttons are located at the bottom of the Slide window's vertical scroll bar.

- **Drag the scroll box and stop when the ScreenTip displays Slide 6 of 9.**
- **Click below the scroll box to display slide 7.**
- **Press** End **to display the last slide.**

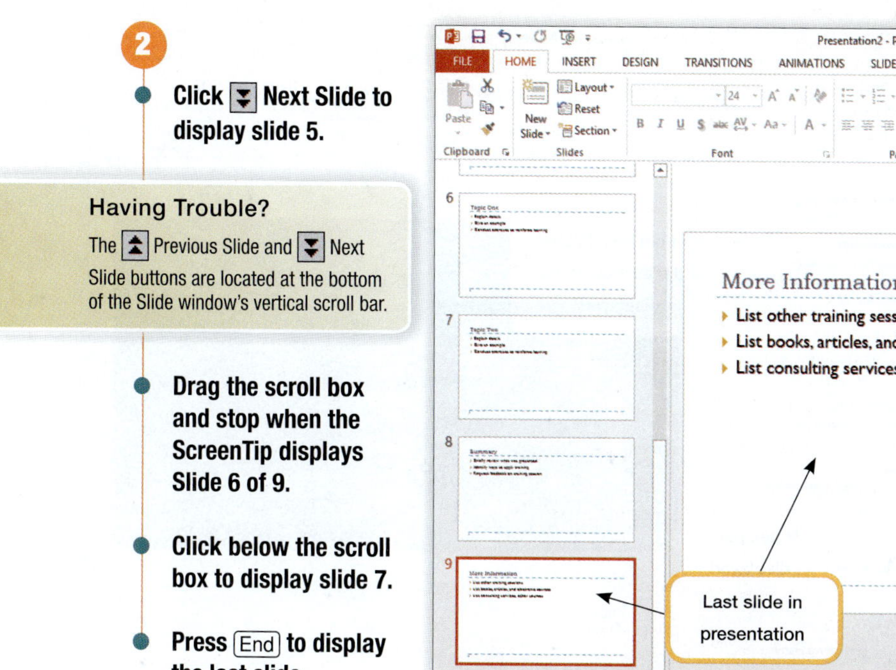

Your screen should be similar to Figure 1.11

Figure 1.11

You can see this template will help you to create your presentation because the content provides some basic guidance as to how to organize a presentation.

Editing a Presentation

Now you need to edit the presentation to replace the sample content with the appropriate information for your presentation. Editing involves making text changes and additions to the content of your presentation. It also includes making changes to the organization of content. This can be accomplished quickly by rearranging the order of bulleted items on slides as well as the order of slides.

USING OUTLINE VIEW

You have already entered text in a slide in the Slide window in Normal view. Another way to make text-editing changes is to use Outline view. Outline view displays the content of the presentation in outline form in the Outline pane, making it easy to see the organization of your presentation as you enter and edit content. The first change you want to make is to enter a title for the presentation on slide 1. First, you will open Outline view and select the sample title text on the slide in the Outline pane and delete it.

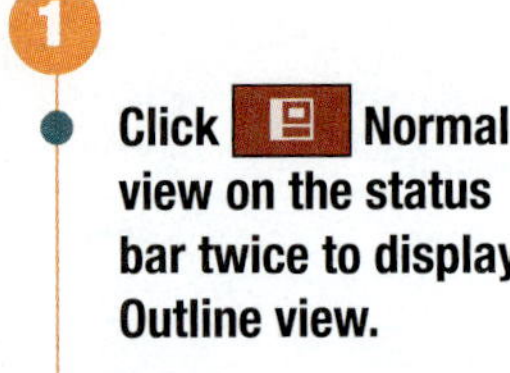

- **Click Normal view on the status bar twice to display Outline view.**

Another Method

You also can choose Outline View from the View tab to display the Outline tab.

- **Scroll the Outline pane to the top to display the text for slide 1.**
- **Click anywhere on the text for slide 1 in the Outline pane to make it the current slide.**
- **Select the text "Training Presentation" on slide 1 in the outline pane.**

Having Trouble?

Refer to the topic "Selecting Text" on page IO.40 in the Introduction to Microsoft Office 2013 to review these features.

Additional Information

The Mini toolbar appears automatically when you select text.

- **Press Delete.**

Your screen should be similar to Figure 1.12

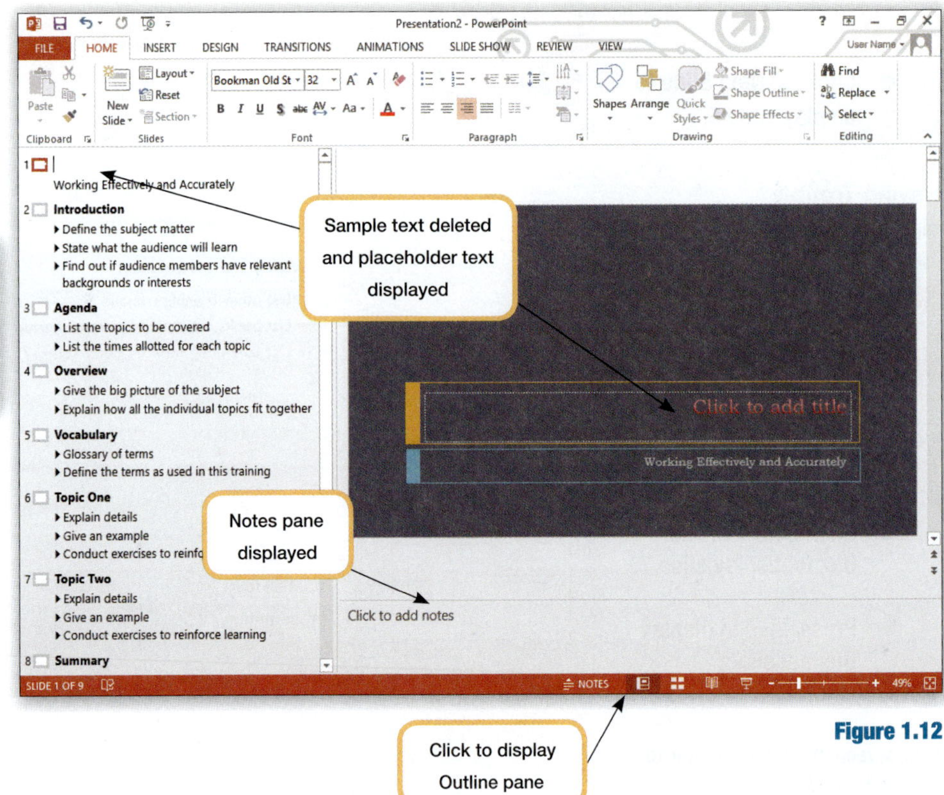

Figure 1.12

When in Normal view, clicking Normal view switches between displaying the Slides pane and the Outline pane. In Outline view, the Slides pane is replaced with the Outline pane. Unlike the Slides pane that displays a miniature version of each slide, the Outline pane displays the text on the slides only. Also notice that the Notes pane is now displayed. Changing views automatically displays the Notes pane.

The sample text is deleted. As you change the text content in the Outline pane, it also appears in the slide displayed in the Slide window. Notice that although you deleted the sample text, the slide still displays the title placeholder text.

You will enter the title and subtitle for the presentation next.

2

- **Type** Join Animal Angels

Having Trouble?

If you make a typing error, use Backspace or Delete to correct the errors.

- **Select the text "Working Efficiently and Accurately" on the second line of slide 1 in the Outline pane and type** Animal Rescue Foundation

Touch Tip

If you have a touch device, you can tap in text and then drag the selection handle to select text.

Your screen should be similar to Figure 1.13

Additional Information

If you click the slide icon to the right of the slide number in the Outline pane, all text on the slide is selected.

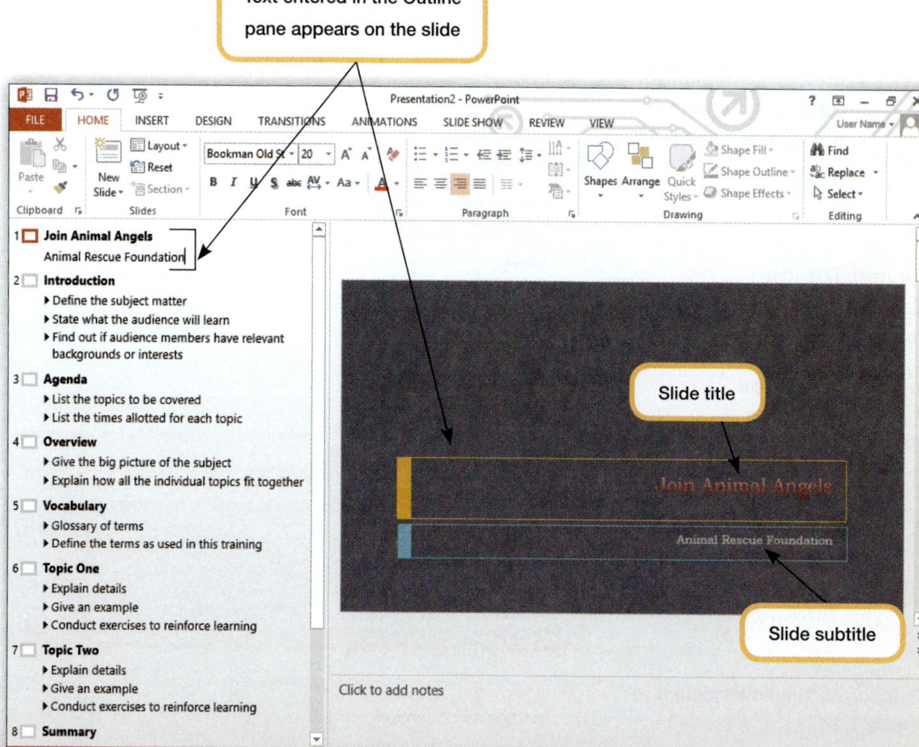

Figure 1.13

As soon as you pressed a key, the selected text was deleted and replaced with the text you typed. When entering the title for a slide, it is a common practice to use title case, in which the first letter of most words is capitalized.

The next change you want to make is on the Introduction slide. The sample text recommends that you define the subject of the presentation and what the audience will learn. You will replace the sample text next to the first bullet with the text for your slide. In the Outline pane, you can select an entire paragraph and all sub-paragraphs by pointing to the left of the line and clicking when the mouse pointer is a ✥.

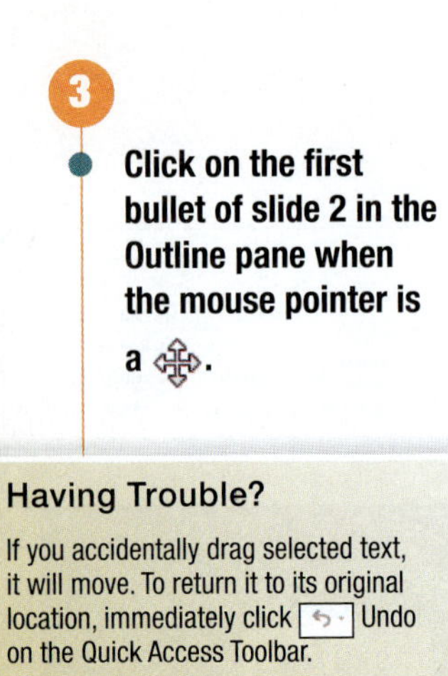

3

- Click on the first bullet of slide 2 in the Outline pane when the mouse pointer is a ✥.

> **Having Trouble?**
>
> If you accidentally drag selected text, it will move. To return it to its original location, immediately click ↶ Undo on the Quick Access Toolbar.

- Type **Your Name, Volunter** (this word is intentionally misspelled) **Coordinator**

Your screen should be similar to **Figure 1.14**

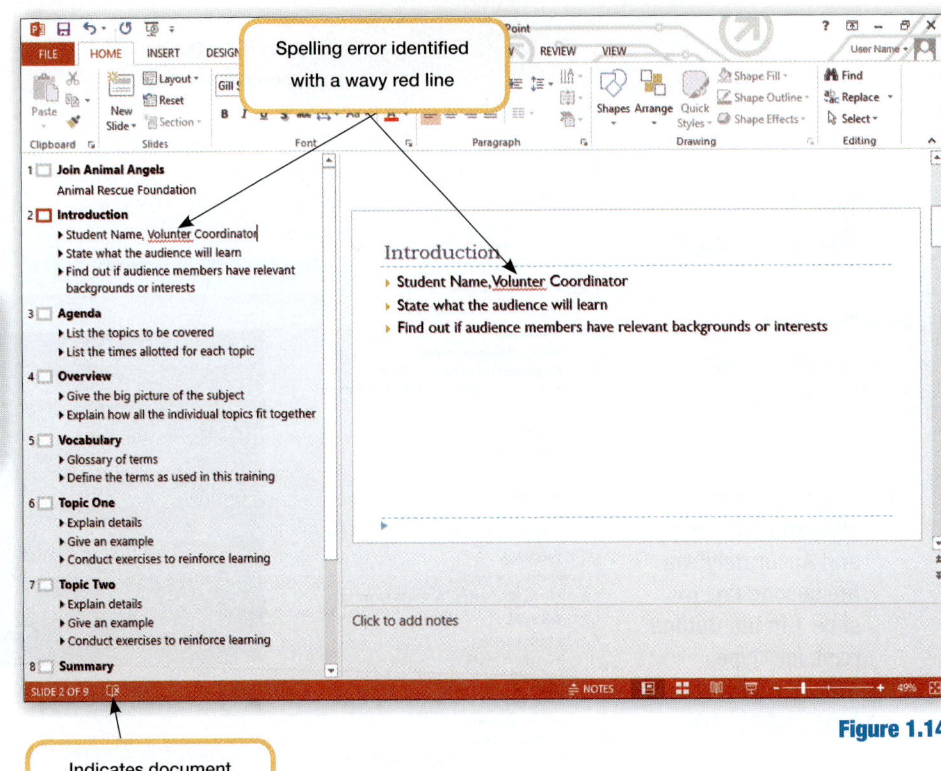

Figure 1.14

CORRECTING ERRORS

As you enter text, the program checks each word for accuracy. In this case, a spelling error was located. PowerPoint identified the word as misspelled by underlining it with a wavy red line. The Spelling indicator in the status bar also shows a spelling error has been detected in the document.

> **Having Trouble?**
>
> Do not be concerned if the spelling checker identifies your name as misspelled.

> **Having Trouble**
>
> If the Spelling indicator is not displayed, right click on the status bar and choose Spell Check from the context menu.

Concept  Spelling Checker

The **spelling checker** locates all misspelled words, duplicate words, and capitalization irregularities as you create and edit a presentation, and proposes possible corrections. This feature works by comparing each word to a dictionary of words. If the word does not appear in the main dictionary or in a custom dictionary, it is identified as misspelled. The **main dictionary** is supplied with the program; a **custom dictionary** is one you can create to hold words you commonly use, such as proper names and technical terms, that are not included in the main dictionary.

If the word does not appear in either dictionary, the program identifies it as misspelled by displaying a red wavy line below the word. You can then correct the misspelled word by editing it. Alternatively, you can display a list of suggested spelling corrections for that word and select the correct spelling from the list to replace the misspelled word in the presentation.

To quickly correct the misspelled word, you can select the correct spelling from a list of suggested spelling corrections displayed on the shortcut menu.

1

Right-click on the misspelled word in the Outline pane to display the shortcut menu.

Your screen should be similar to Figure 1.15

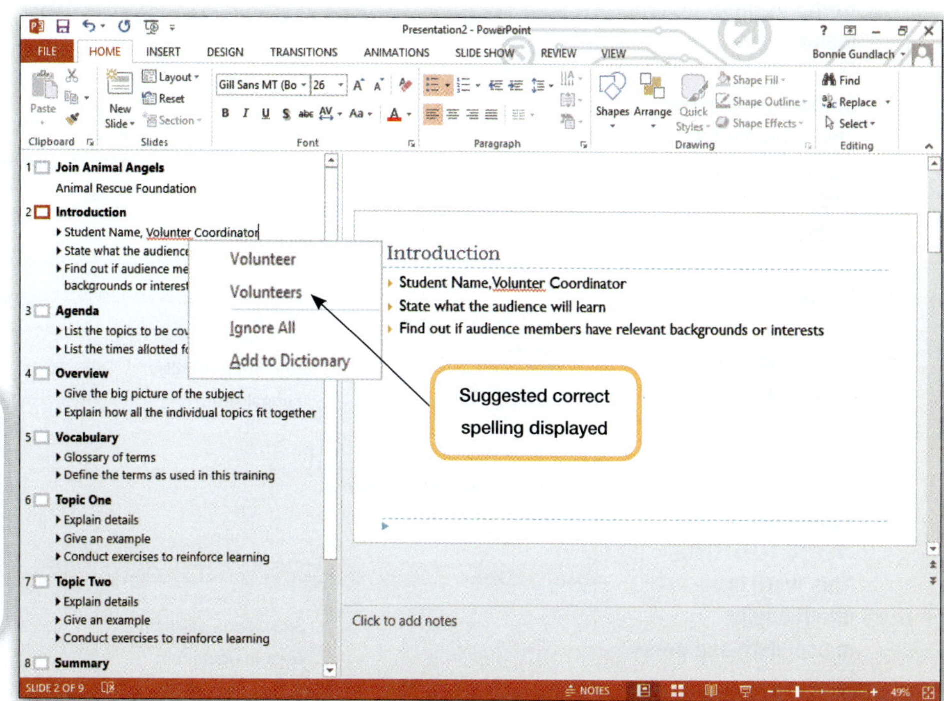

Figure 1.15

Additional Information

Sometimes the spelling checker cannot suggest replacements because it cannot locate any words in its dictionary that are similar in spelling. Other times the suggestions offered are not correct. If either situation happens, you must edit the word manually.

The shortcut menu displays two suggested correct spellings. The menu also includes two related menu options described below.

Option	Effect
Ignore All	Instructs PowerPoint to ignore the misspelling of this word throughout the rest of this session.
Add to Dictionary	Adds the word to the custom dictionary list. When a word is added to the custom dictionary, PowerPoint will always accept that spelling as correct.

Additional Information

The spelling checker works just as it does in the other Microsoft Office 2013 applications.

You will replace the word with the correct spelling and then enter the information for the second bullet.

- Choose "Volunteer" from the shortcut menu.
- In the Outline pane, select the text in the second bullet on slide 2 by clicking the bullet.
- Press Delete.
- In the Outline pane, select the text in the second bullet on slide 2.
- Type **volunteer oppotunities** (this word is intentionally misspelled) and press Spacebar.

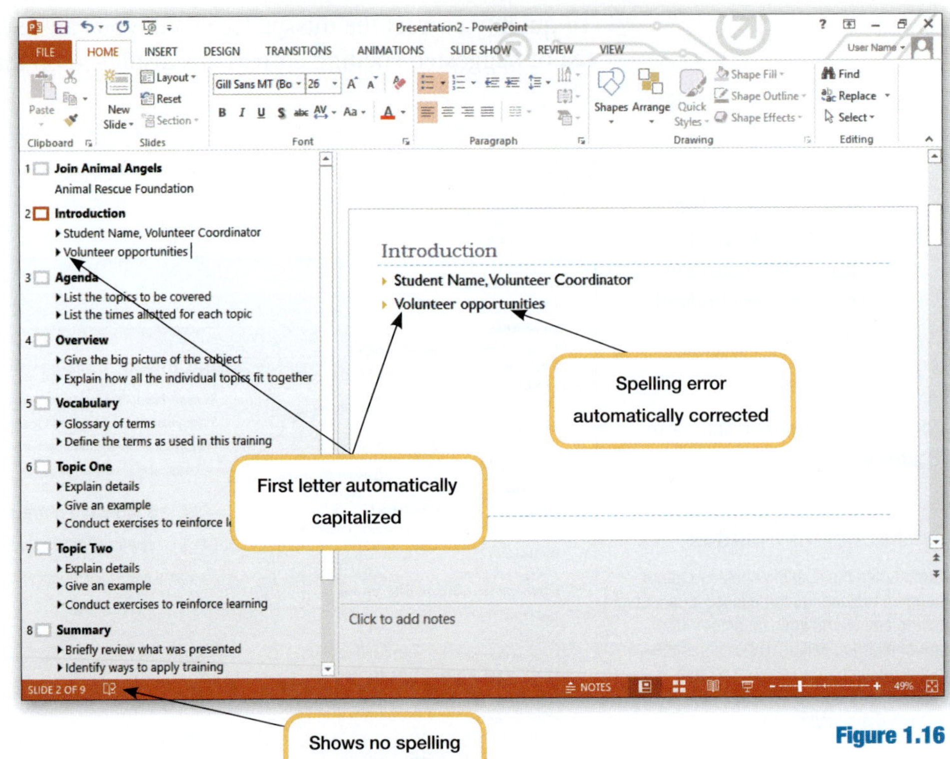

Figure 1.16

Your screen should be similar to Figure 1.16

Additional Information

Bulleted items in a presentation are capitalized in sentence case format. Ending periods, however, are not included.

Notice that the first letter of "volunteer" was automatically capitalized. Also notice that the incorrect spelling of the word "oppotunities" was corrected. These corrections are part of the AutoCorrect feature of PowerPoint.

Concept 3 AutoCorrect

The **AutoCorrect** feature makes some basic assumptions about the text you are typing and, based on those assumptions, automatically corrects the entry. The AutoCorrect feature automatically inserts proper capitalization at the beginning of sentences and in the names of days of the week. It also will change to lowercase letters any words that were incorrectly capitalized due to the accidental use of the Caps Lock key. In addition, it also corrects many common typing and spelling errors automatically.

One way the program makes corrections automatically is by looking for certain types of errors. For example, if two capital letters appear at the beginning of a word, the second capital letter is changed to a lowercase letter. If a lowercase letter appears at the beginning of a sentence, the first letter of the first word is capitalized. If the name of a day begins with a lowercase letter, the first letter is capitalized.

Another way the program makes corrections is by automatically replacing a misspelled word with the correct spelling in situations where the spelling checker offers only one suggested spelling correction. AutoCorrect also checks all words against the AutoCorrect list, a built-in list of words that are commonly spelled or typed incorrectly. If it finds the entry on the list, the program automatically replaces the error with the correction. For example, the typing error "aboutthe" is automatically changed to "about the" because the error is on the AutoCorrect list. You also can add words to the AutoCorrect list that you want to be corrected automatically. Any such words are added to the list on the computer you are using and will be available to anyone who uses the machine after you.

COPYING AND MOVING SELECTIONS

You are now ready to enter the text for the next slide in your presentation by entering the three main topics of discussion. You want to enter a new slide title, Topics of Discussion, with three bulleted items describing the topics to be discussed. Two placeholder bullets with sample text are displayed. You will edit these and then add a third bulleted item.

1

- **Move to slide 3.**
- **In the Outline pane, replace the sample title, Agenda, with Topics of Discussion**
- **Select and replace the text in the first bullet with Why are pets abandoned?**
- **Select and replace the text in the second bullet with How can you help?**
- **Press Enter.**

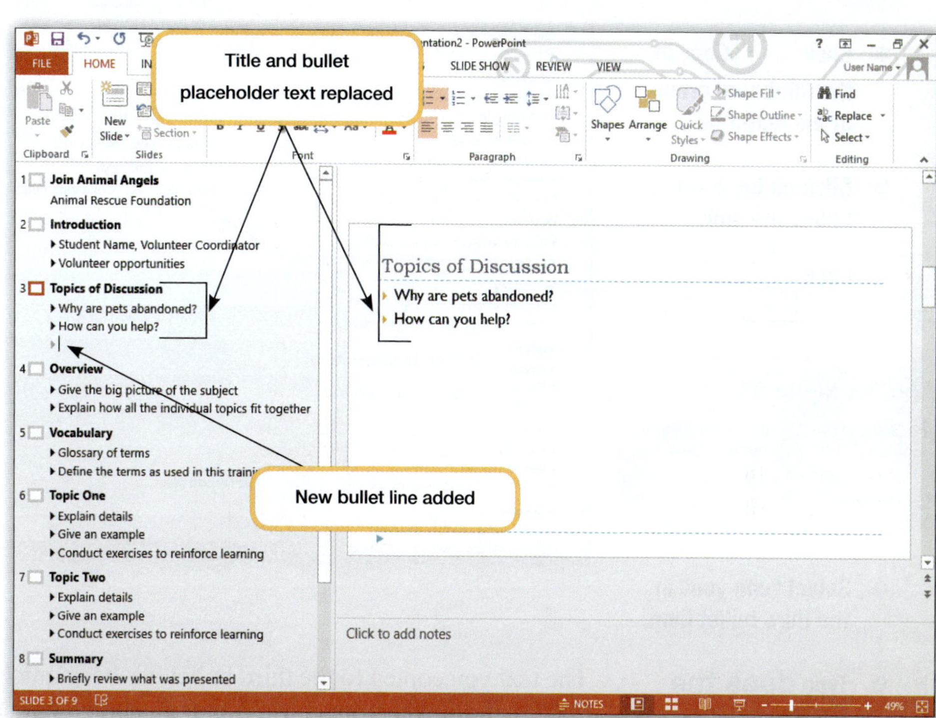

Figure 1.17

Having Trouble?

If you accidentally insert an extra bullet and blank line, press Backspace twice to remove them.

A new bulleted line is automatically created whenever you press Enter at the end of a bulleted item. Because the text you want to enter for this bullet is similar to the text in the second bullet, you decide to save time by copying and pasting the bullet text. Then you will modify the text in the third bullet.

Your screen should be similar to Figure 1.17

Having Trouble?

Refer to "Copying and Moving Selections" on page IO.47 in the Introduction to Microsoft Office 2013 to review this feature.

2

- **Select the second bulleted item.**
- **Click [Copy icon] Copy in the Clipboard group of the Home tab.**
- **Click on the third bullet line and click [Paste].**

Another Method

You also can press Ctrl + C to copy a selection and Ctrl + V to paste a selection.

- **Select "can you" in the third bullet item.**
- **Type does the Foundation**
- **If necessary, select and delete the fourth blank bullet line.**

Your screen should be similar to Figure 1.18

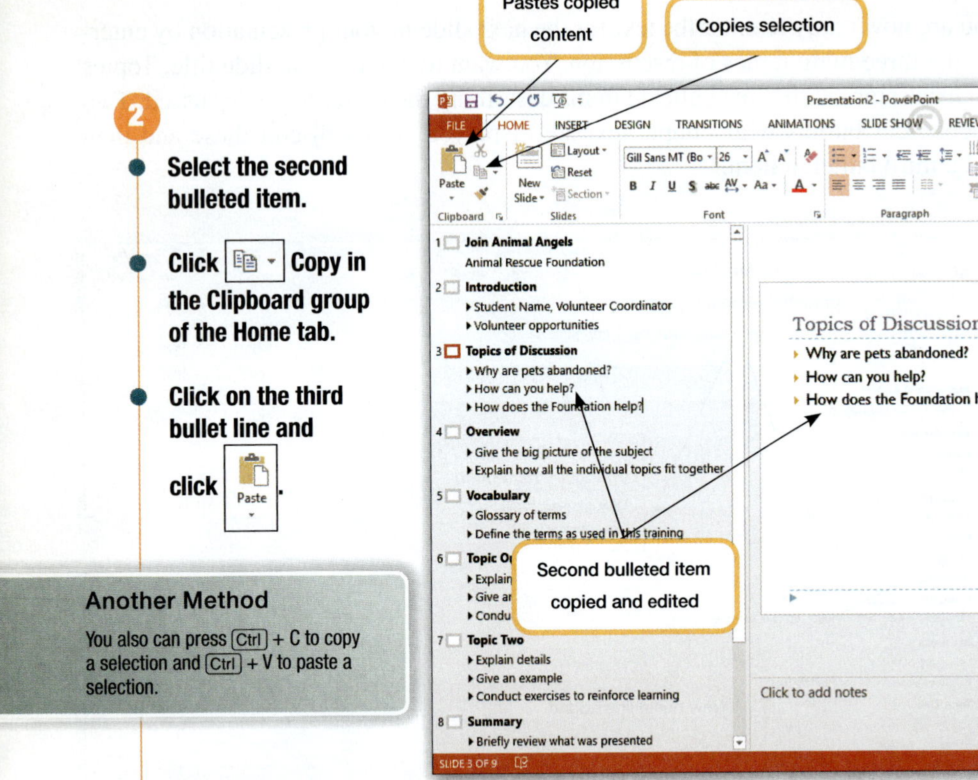

Figure 1.18

The text you copied to the third bullet has been quickly modified. Copying is especially helpful when the entries are long and complicated.

As you review what you have entered so far in your presentation, you decide that it would be better to introduce yourself on the first slide. Rather than retyping this information, you will move your introduction from slide 2 to slide 1. You will do this using drag and drop.

3

- **In the Outline pane, press Enter at the end of the subtitle in slide 1 to create a blank line.**
- **Select the first bulleted item on slide 2.**
- **Drag the selection to the blank line on slide 1.**

Another Method

You can also use  Cut or Ctrl + X to cut a selection and then paste it to the new location.

- **Move to the blank line at the end of slide 1 and press Backspace to delete it.**

Your screen should be similar to Figure 1.19

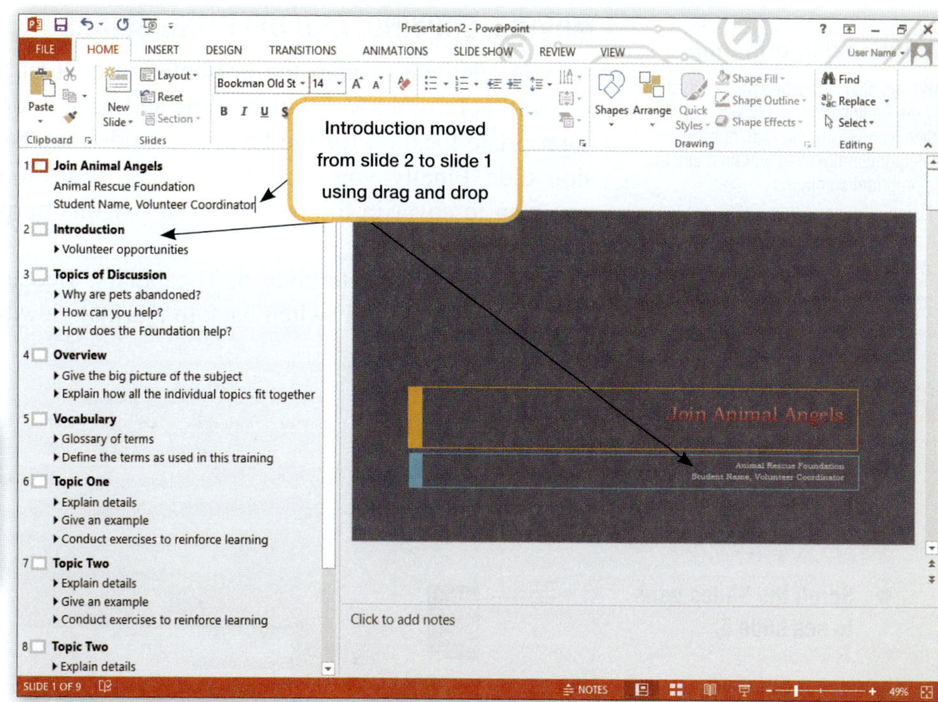

Figure 1.19

Because the Outline pane lets you see the content in multiple slides at once, it makes it easy to see the organization of the presentation and to quickly make text changes within and between slides.

Before continuing, you will save your work to a file named Volunteer.

Having Trouble?

Review saving files in the "Saving a File" section on page IO.54 in the Introduction to Microsoft Office 2013.

4

- **Open the File tab and click Save As.**
- **Select the location where you will save your solution files.**
- **Replace the proposed file name in the File Name text box with Volunteer.**
- **Click Save.**

Additional Information

The file extensions may or may not be displayed, depending upon your Windows folder settings.

The presentation is now saved to the location you specified in a new file named Volunteer. The view in use at the time the file is saved also is saved with the file. The file is saved with the default file extension of .pptx. You can also save PowerPoint presentations as an image file using the .gif, .tif, or .jpg file extension. When you save a presentation as an image file, you are given the choice to save the Current Slide Only or Every Slide as an image, in which case each slide will be saved as a separate image file.

MOVING, COPYING, AND DELETING SLIDES

Additional Information

You can also delete and move slides in the Outline pane by clicking on the slide icon next to the slide number to select the entire slide and then use the appropriate command.

As you continue to plan the presentation content and organization, you decide you will not use the Vocabulary slide and want to delete it. You also think a more appropriate location for the Overview slide may be above the Topics of Discussion slide. Finally, you plan to have three slides to present the three main topics you plan to cover in the presentation. For this purpose, you want to add a third topic slide.

First you will delete slide 5, Vocabulary. Because you are not working with slide content, you will switch back to Normal view to make these changes.

1

- **Click**  **Normal to display the Slides pane in Normal view.**
- **Scroll the Slides pane to see slide 5.**
- **Click on slide 5 to select the slide.**
- **Press Delete.**

Another Method

You can also choose Delete Slide from the selected slide's context menu.

Your screen should be similar to Figure 1.20

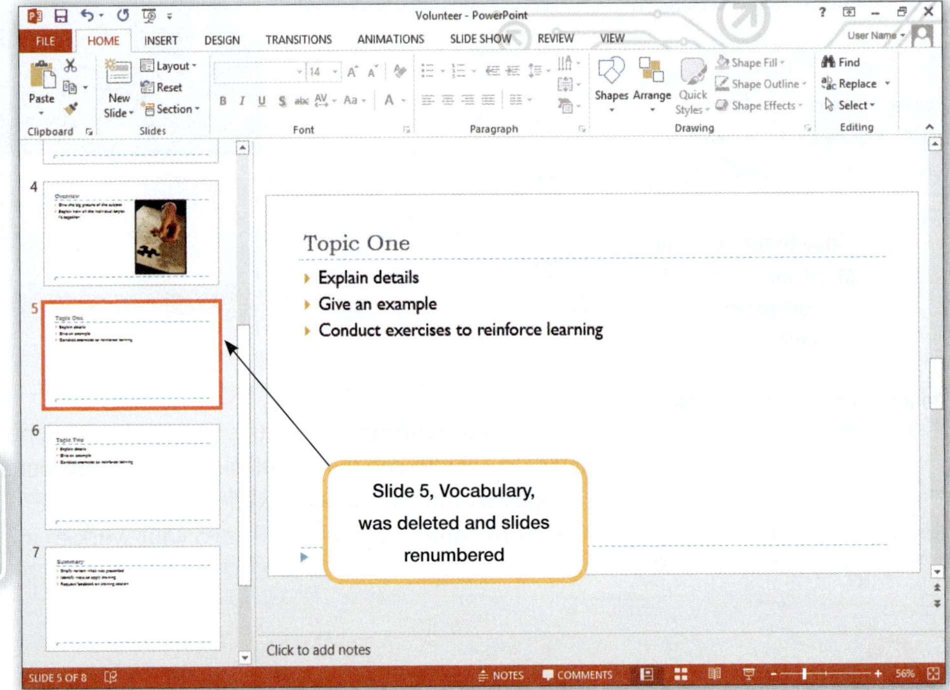

Figure 1.20

The slide has been deleted and all subsequent slides renumbered.

Next, you will move the Overview slide (4) above slide 3 using drag and drop.

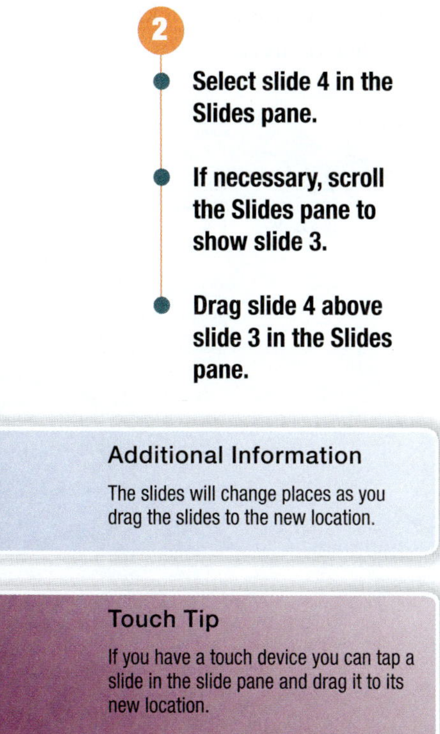

2

- **Select slide 4 in the Slides pane.**
- **If necessary, scroll the Slides pane to show slide 3.**
- **Drag slide 4 above slide 3 in the Slides pane.**

Additional Information

The slides will change places as you drag the slides to the new location.

Touch Tip

If you have a touch device you can tap a slide in the slide pane and drag it to its new location.

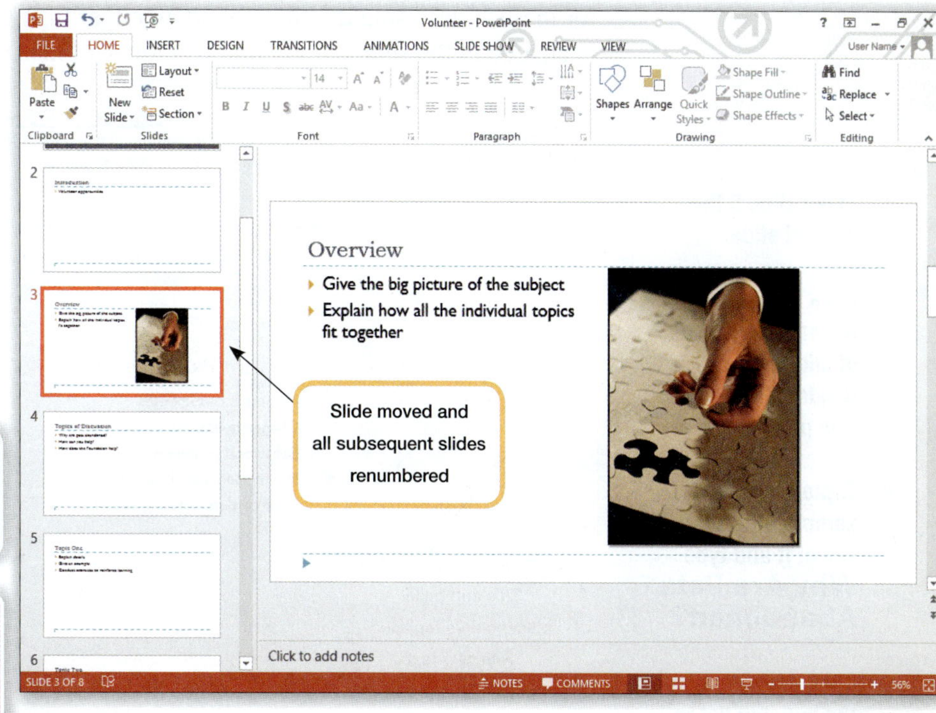

Figure 1.21

Your screen should be similar to Figure 1.21

The Overview slide is now slide 3, and, again, all following slides are appropriately renumbered. Finally, you will make a copy of slide 6.

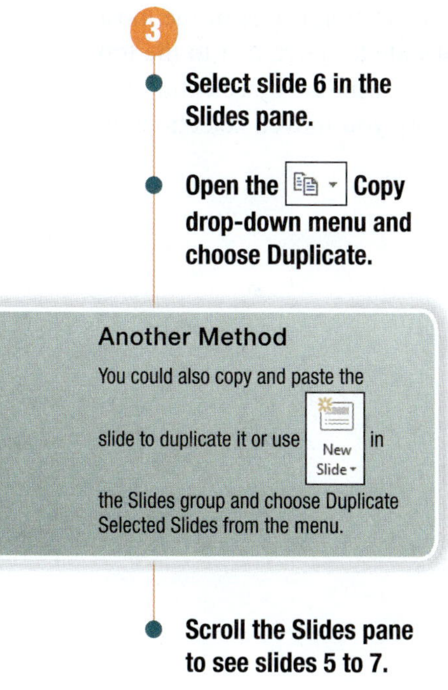

3

- **Select slide 6 in the Slides pane.**
- **Open the Copy drop-down menu and choose Duplicate.**

Another Method

You could also copy and paste the slide to duplicate it or use New Slide in the Slides group and choose Duplicate Selected Slides from the menu.

- **Scroll the Slides pane to see slides 5 to 7.**

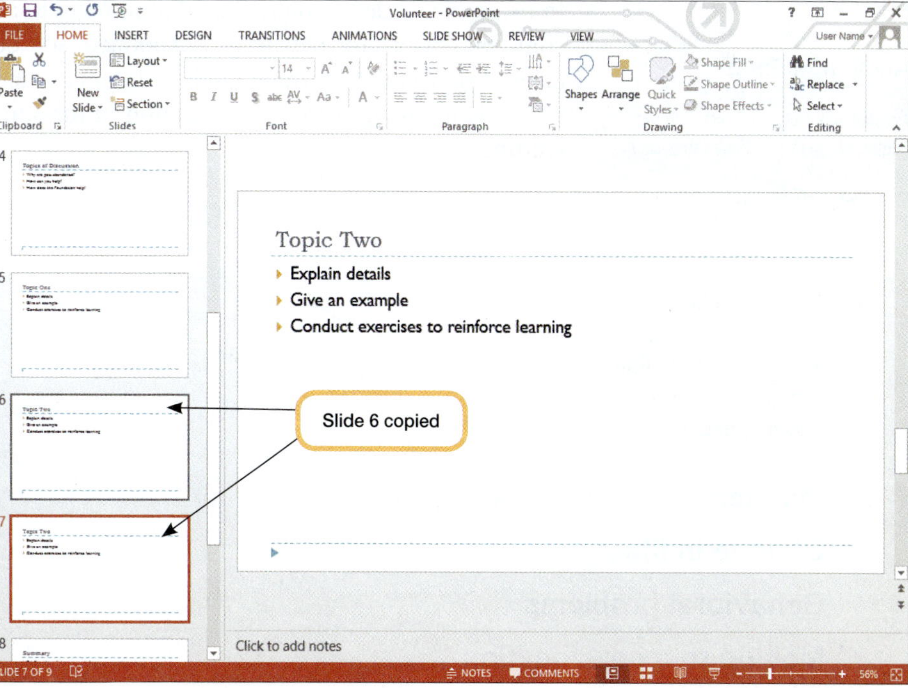

Figure 1.22

Your screen should be similar to Figure 1.22

There are now three topic slides. The duplicate slide was inserted directly below the slide that was copied and is the selected slide.

MOVING, DEMOTING, AND PROMOTING BULLETED ITEMS

Now you are ready to enter the text for the three topic slides. You will enter the text for these slides using the Slide window rather than Outline view. Simply clicking in an area of the slide in the Slide window will make it the active area.

1

- **Make slide 5 the current slide.**
- **Click anywhere in the sample title text of slide 5 in the Slide window to select the title placeholder.**
- **Triple-click on the sample title to select it and type Why Are Pets Abandoned?**
- **Click anywhere on the bulleted list to select the content placeholder.**
- **Drag to select all the text in the content placeholder.**

Another Method

You also can click Select in the Editing group of the Home tab or use the shortcut key Ctrl + A to select everything in a placeholder box.

- **Enter the following bulleted items (press Enter after each line, except the last, to create a new bullet):**

Maintenance expenses

Change in lifestyle

Behavioral problems

Moving to a new location

Poor or deteriorating health

Your screen should be similar to Figure 1.23

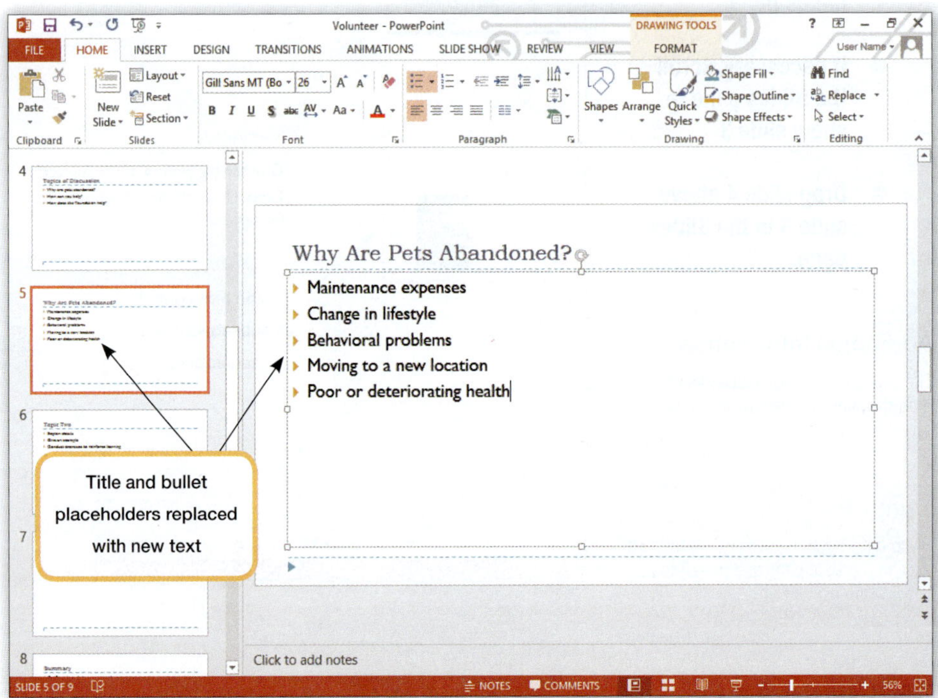

Figure 1.23

In reviewing slide 5, you realize that moving to a new location is one of the most common reasons for pets to be abandoned, so you decide to move that to the top of the list. You can rearrange bulleted items in the Slide window by selecting the item and dragging it to a new location in the same way you moved selections in Outline view.

2

- **Select all the text in the fourth bulleted item in the Slide window.**
- **Drag the selection to the beginning of the first bulleted item.**

Your screen should be similar to Figure 1.24

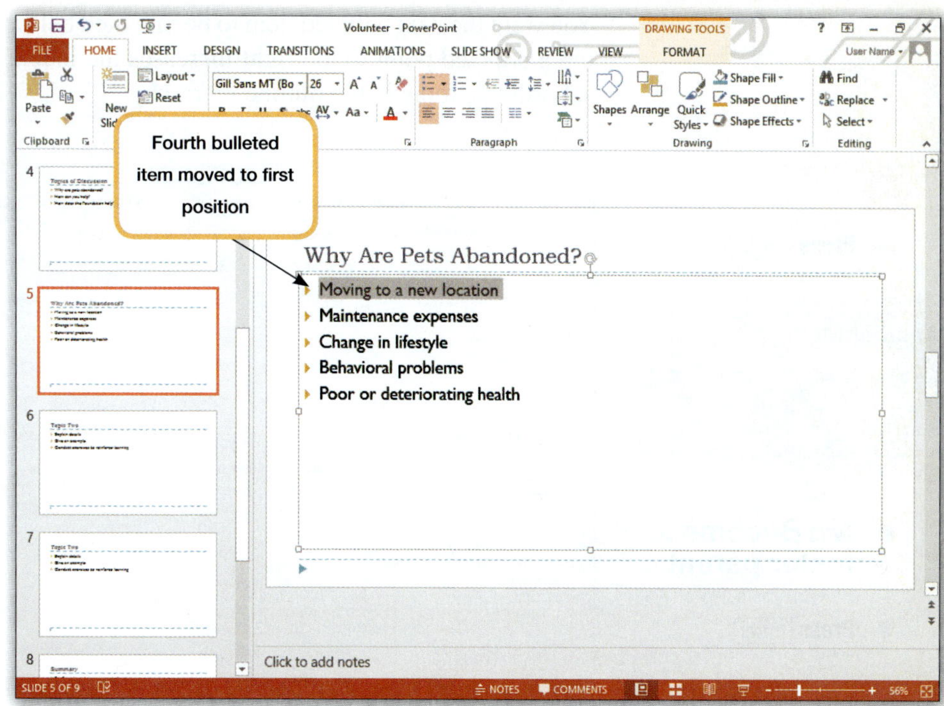

Figure 1.24

The fourth bullet is now the first bulleted item in the list.

ADJUSTING LIST LEVELS

In the next slide, you will enter information about how people can help the Animal Rescue Foundation.

1

- **Make slide 6 the current slide.**
- **Replace the sample title text with How Can You Help?**
- **Select all the text in the bulleted text placeholder.**
- **Type Donate your time and talent**
- **Press Enter.**

Your screen should be similar to Figure 1.25

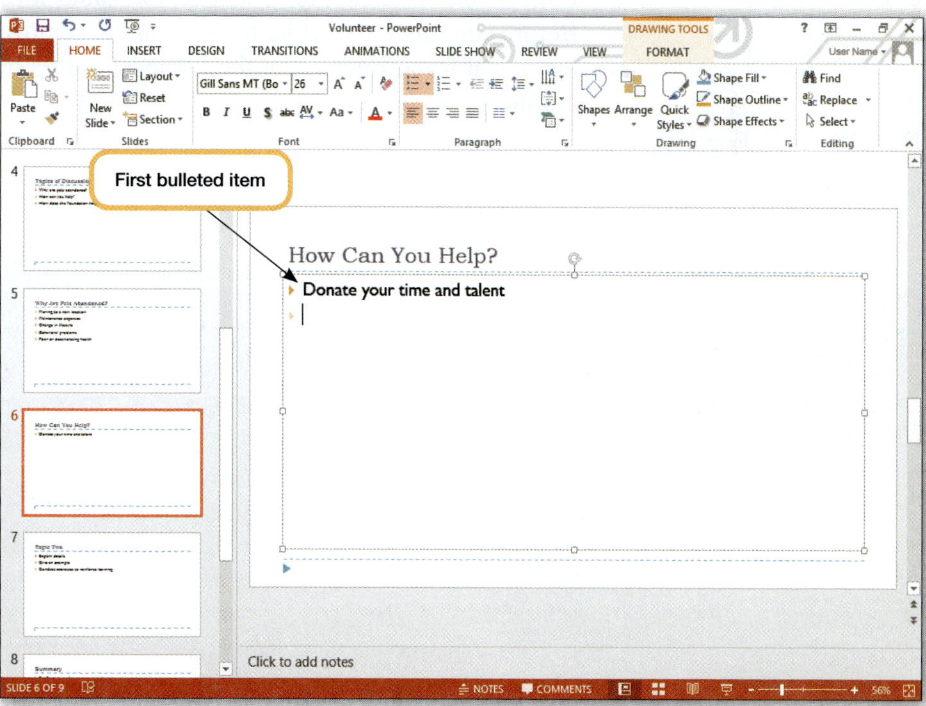

Figure 1.25

You want the next bulleted item to be indented below the first bulleted item. Indenting a bulleted point to the right increases the indent level and makes it a lower or subordinate topic in the outline hierarchy.

2

- Press Tab.

Another Method

You also can click Increase List Level in the Paragraph group of the Home tab.

- Type **Become a foster parent**
- Press Enter.
- Type **Work at adoption fairs**
- Press Enter.

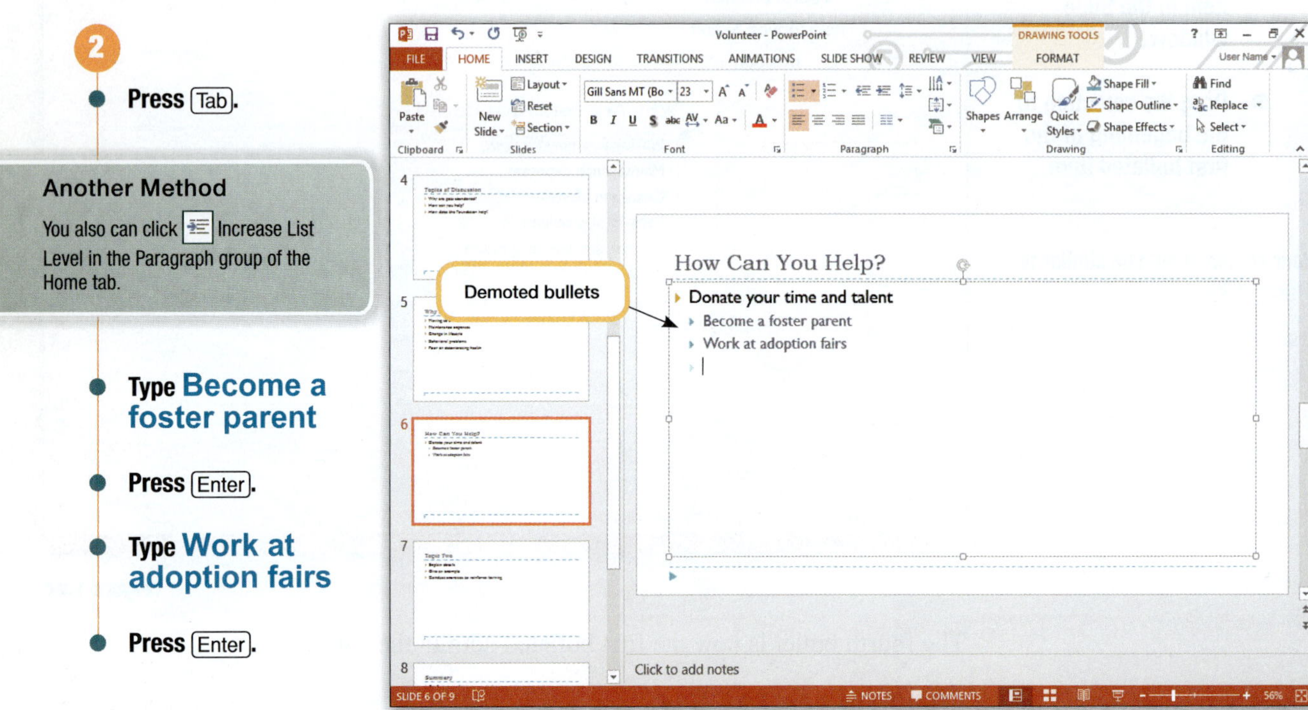

Your screen should be similar to **Figure 1.26**

Figure 1.26

PowerPoint continues to indent to the same level until you cancel the indent. Before entering the next item, you want to remove the indentation by decreasing the indent level. Decreasing the list level moves it to the left, or up a level in the outline hierarchy.

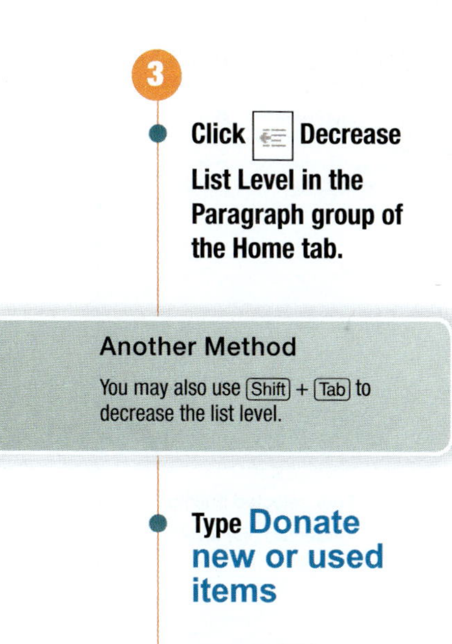

3

- Click [icon] **Decrease List Level** in the Paragraph group of the Home tab.

Another Method

You may also use Shift + Tab to decrease the list level.

- Type **Donate new or used items**
- Press Enter.
- Enter the next four bulleted items:

  Crates and pads

  Collars, leads, and other items

  Contribute items to our thrift shop

  All types of animal feed

Your screen should be similar to **Figure 1.27**

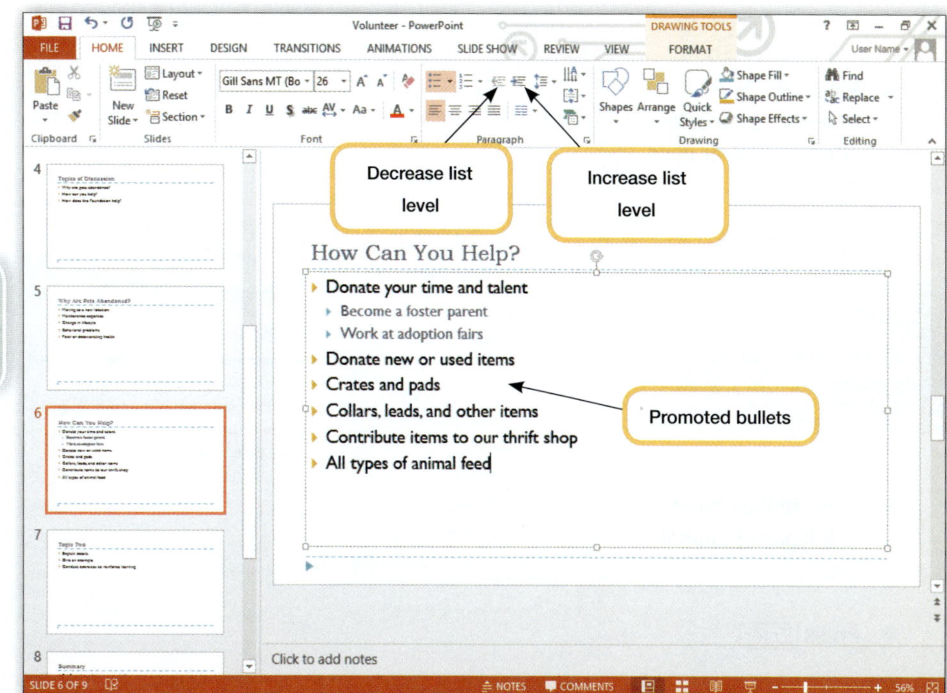

Figure 1.27

You also can increase or decrease list levels after the text has been entered. The insertion point must be at the beginning of the line to be adjusted, or all the text must be selected. You will increase the level of the last four bulleted items.

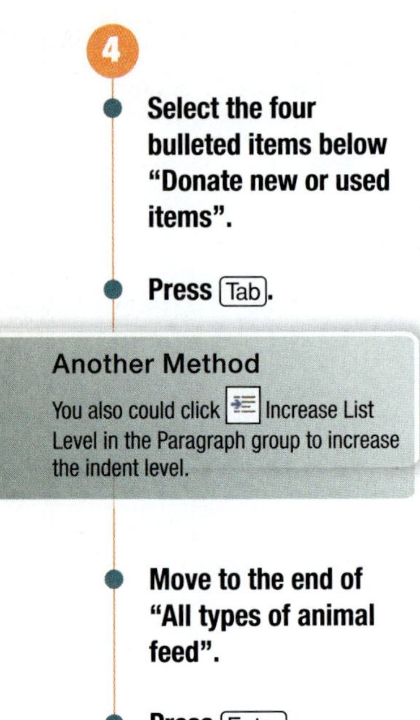

4

- **Select the four bulleted items below "Donate new or used items".**
- **Press Tab.**

Another Method

You also could click Increase List Level in the Paragraph group to increase the indent level.

- **Move to the end of "All types of animal feed".**
- **Press Enter.**

Your screen should be similar to Figure 1.28

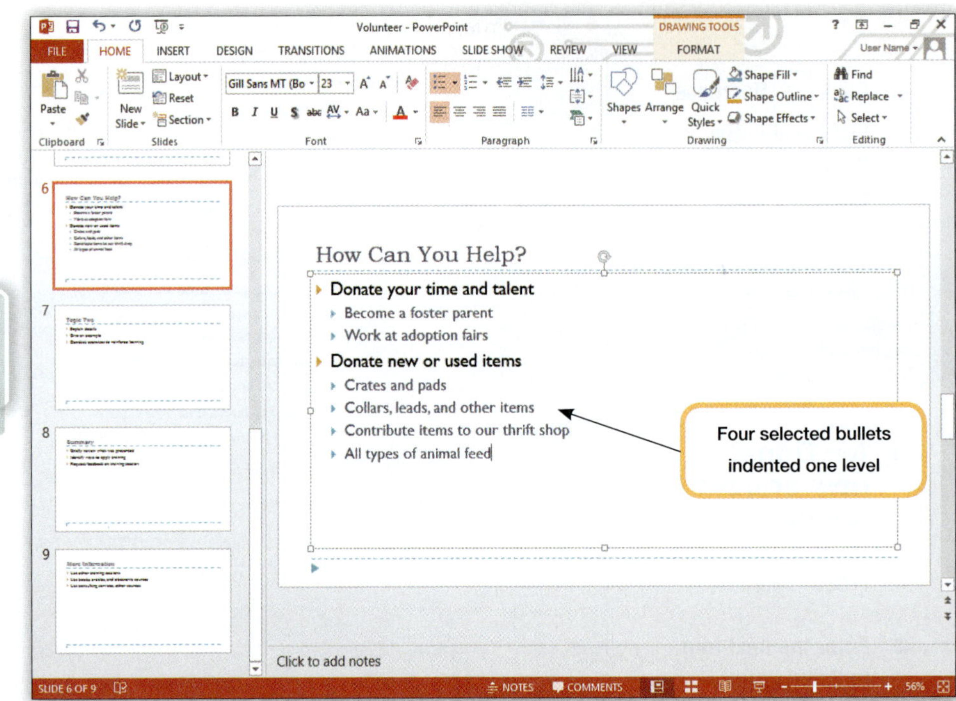

Figure 1.28

The list level of the four selected items has been indented one level. Next you will add more items to the bulleted list.

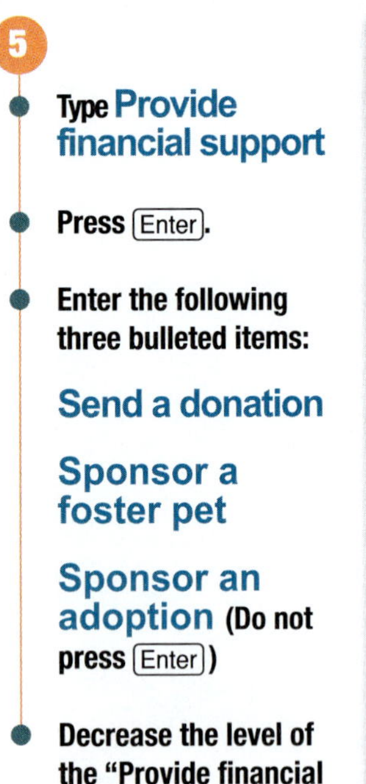

5

- **Type Provide financial support**
- **Press Enter.**
- **Enter the following three bulleted items:**

  Send a donation

  Sponsor a foster pet

  Sponsor an adoption (Do not press Enter)

- **Decrease the level of the "Provide financial support" bullet.**

Your screen should be similar to Figure 1.29

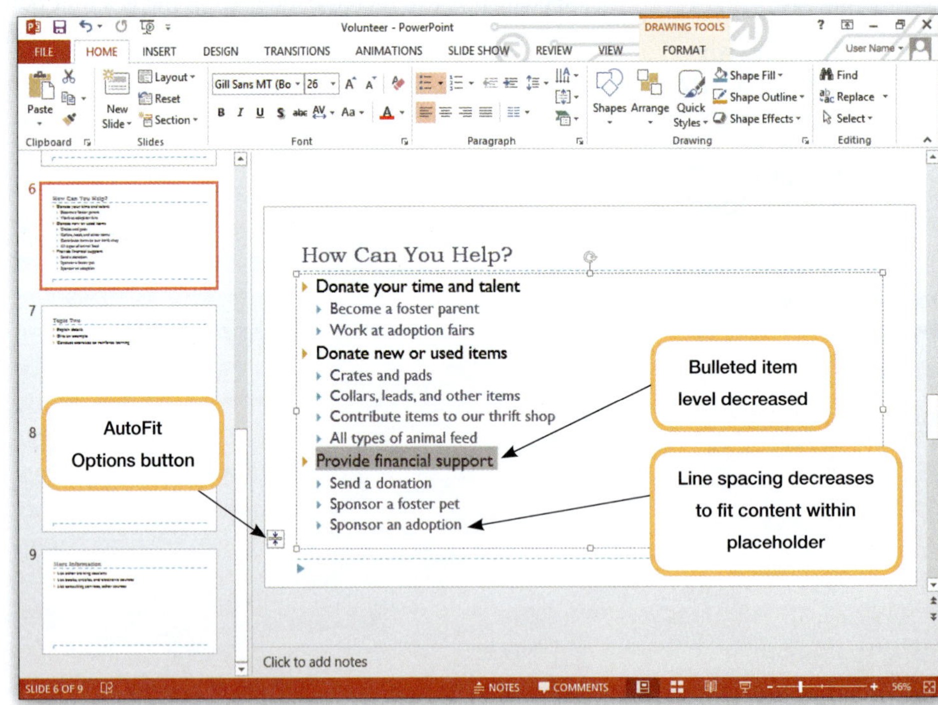

Figure 1.29

As you entered bulleted items, the line spacing of the text decreased to fit all the content in the placeholder. This feature is known as AutoFit and is "on" by default. When this adjustment occurs, an AutoFit Options button appears at the bottom left corner of the placeholder. It provides options that allow you to turn this feature on and off or to control the AutoFit options.

SPLITTING TEXT BETWEEN SLIDES

Although using AutoFit made all the content fit inside the placeholder, you decide that 10 bulleted items are too many for a single slide. Generally, when creating slides, it is a good idea to limit the number of bulleted items on a slide to six. It also is recommended that the number of words on a line should not exceed five.

You decide to split the slide content between two slides. To make this change, you need to change to Outline view and indicate where to start a new slide by moving the insertion point to the end of the item you want to be the last item on the current slide.

1

- **Change to Outline view.**
- **If necessary, scroll the Outline pane so that slides 6 and 7 are visible.**
- **Move the insertion point to the end of the item "All types of animal feed" on slide 6.**
- **Press Enter.**
- **Click Decrease List Level twice to decrease the indent level of the blank line.**

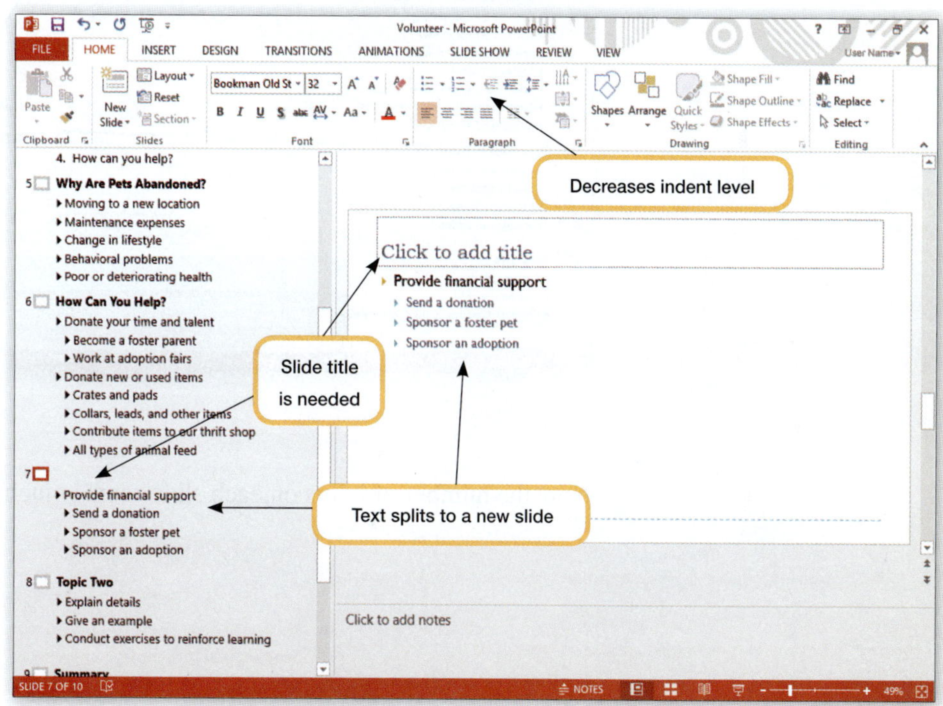

Figure 1.30

Your screen should be similar to Figure 1.30

A new slide, with a title placeholder, is inserted into the presentation. The items from the previous slide, beginning with where you positioned the insertion point, were moved to the new slide. Sometimes, when splitting text between slides, the content may not split appropriately and you may still need to make adjustments to the slides. You will add a title to the new slide.

2

- **On slide 7, replace the title placeholder with More Ways to Help!**

Your screen should be similar to Figure 1.31

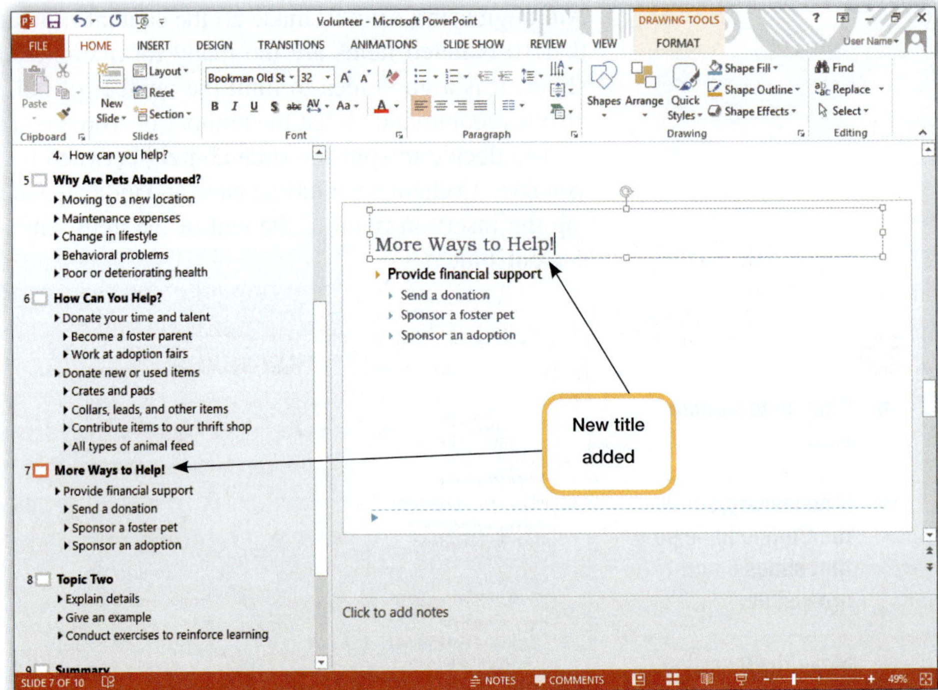

Figure 1.31

Now the number of items on each slide seems much more reasonable.

Finally, you will add the text for the third topic slide.

- **Make slide 8 current.**
- **Enter the slide title** How Does the Foundation Help?
- **Enter the following bulleted items:**

  Provides temporary homes

  Provides obedience training

  Provides veterinary care

  Finds loving permanent homes
- **Scroll the Outline pane to see slides 4 through 8.**

Your screen should be similar to Figure 1.32

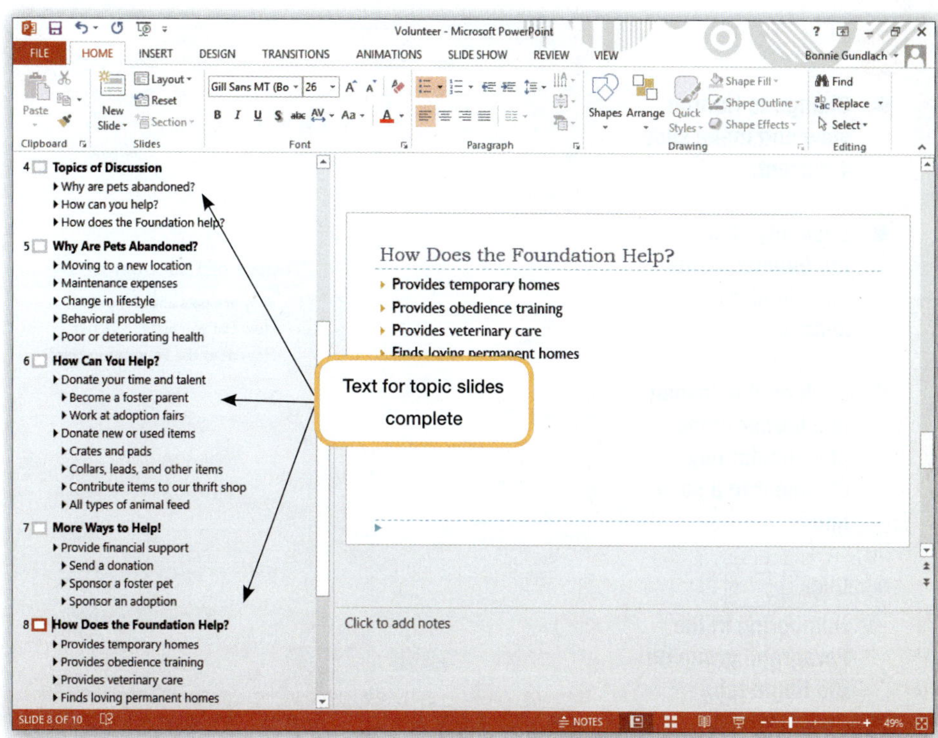

Figure 1.32

The text for the three topic slides reflects the order of the topics in the Topics of Discussion slide.

CREATING A NUMBERED LIST

After looking at slide 4, you decide that it would be better if the topics of discussion were a numbered list. You can easily change the format of the bulleted items to a numbered list using the Numbering command in the Paragraph group on the Home tab.

1

- **Change to Normal view and make slide 4 current.**
- **Click anywhere in the bulleted items placeholder on slide 4.**
- **Click on the dashed-line border of the placeholder box to change it to a solid line.**
- **Click [Numbering button] Numbering in the Paragraph group on the Home tab.**

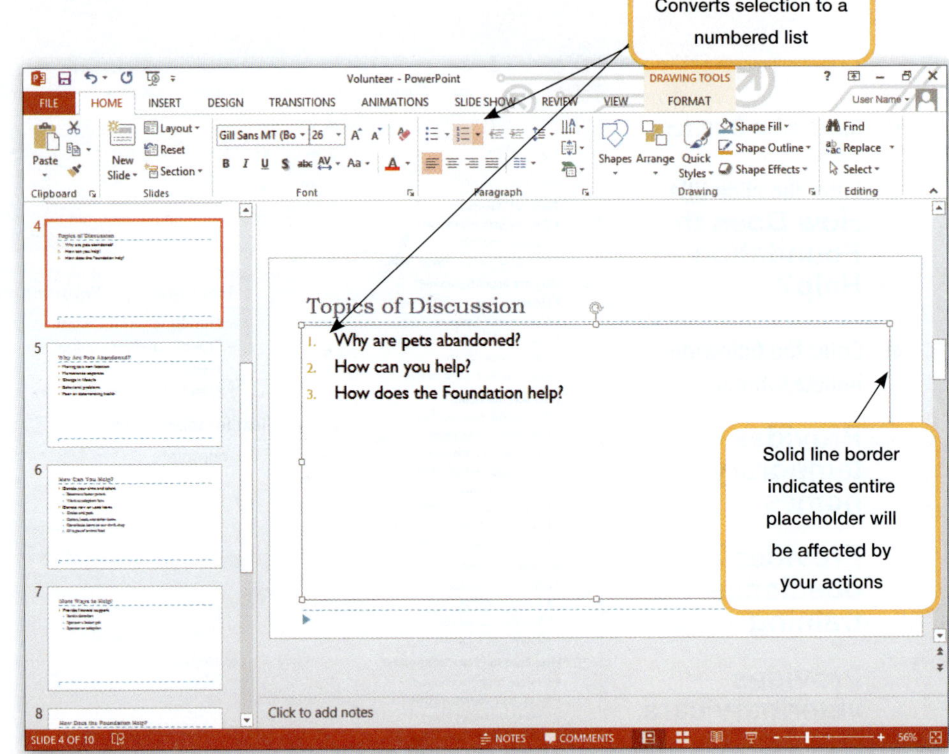

Figure 1.33

Your screen should be similar to Figure 1.33

Notice the insertion point does not appear in the placeholder box. This is because a solid line around the placeholder indicates your action will affect the entire placeholder rather than individual parts, such as the text, of the placeholder. The bullets have been replaced with an itemized numbered list.

CHANGING LINE SPACING

Since there are only three items in the numbered list, you decide to increase the line spacing on this slide. Even if more items are added later, the new spacing will still be appropriate. Because you want the line spacing to affect all text within the placeholder, you still want to have the entire placeholder box selected. Otherwise, only the line spacing of the line you are on would change.

1

- If necessary, click the dashed line border of the placeholder box to change it to a solid line.
- Click [Line Spacing icon] Line Spacing in the Paragraph group.
- Choose 1.5 from the drop-down menu.

Your screen should be similar to Figure 1.34

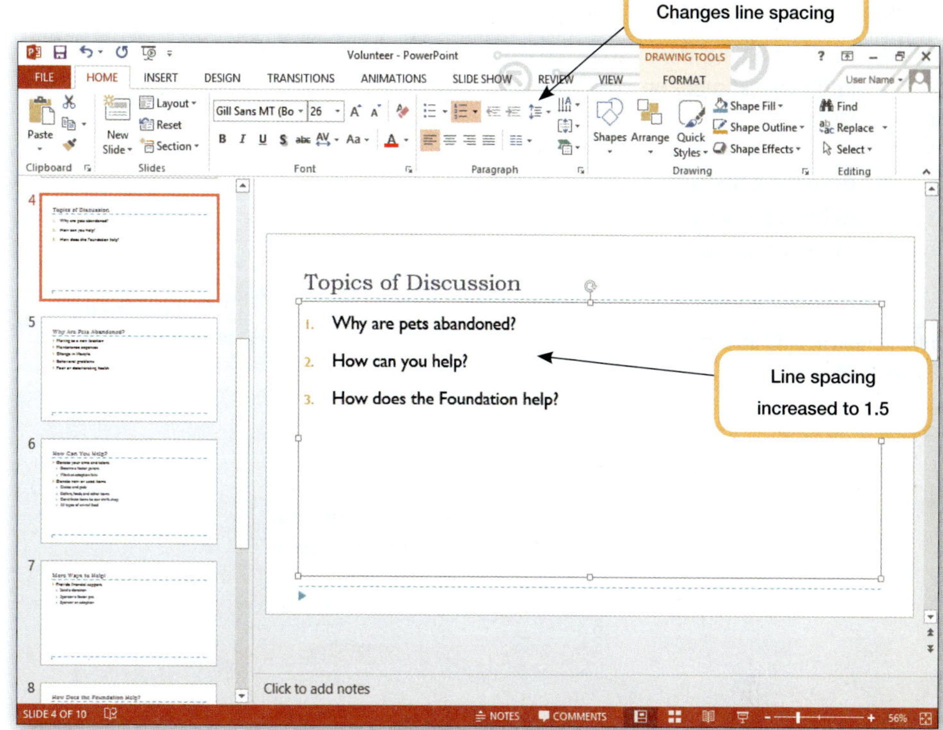

Figure 1.34

MOVING, DEMOTING, AND PROMOTING NUMBERED ITEMS

Now it is obvious to you that you entered the topics in the wrong order. You want to present the information about the Foundation before information about how individuals can help. Just like a bulleted item, an item in a numbered list can be moved easily by selecting it and dragging it to a new location.

1

- **Select the third item in the placeholder on slide 4.**
- **Drag the selection up to the beginning of the second line.**

Your screen should be similar to Figure 1.35

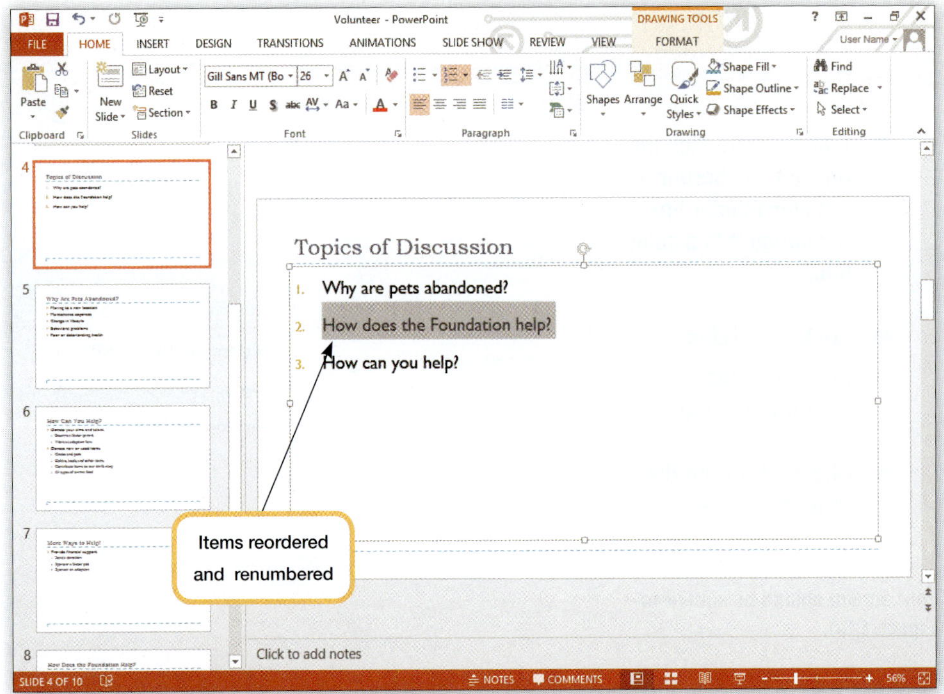

Figure 1.35

As soon as you clicked inside the placeholder, the insertion point appeared and the solid-line border changed to a dashed-line border, indicating you can edit the contents of the placeholder. The third item in the numbered list is now the second item, and PowerPoint automatically renumbered the list for you.

You now realize that you forgot to include the Animal Angels volunteer group as a topic to be discussed. You will add it to the Topics of Discussion slide as a subtopic below the "How can you help?" topic.

2

- **Open Outline view to review the slide content.**
- **In the Outline pane, click at the end of the third numbered list item on slide 4 and press Enter.**
- **Press Tab and type Who are Animal Angels?**

Your screen should be similar to Figure 1.36

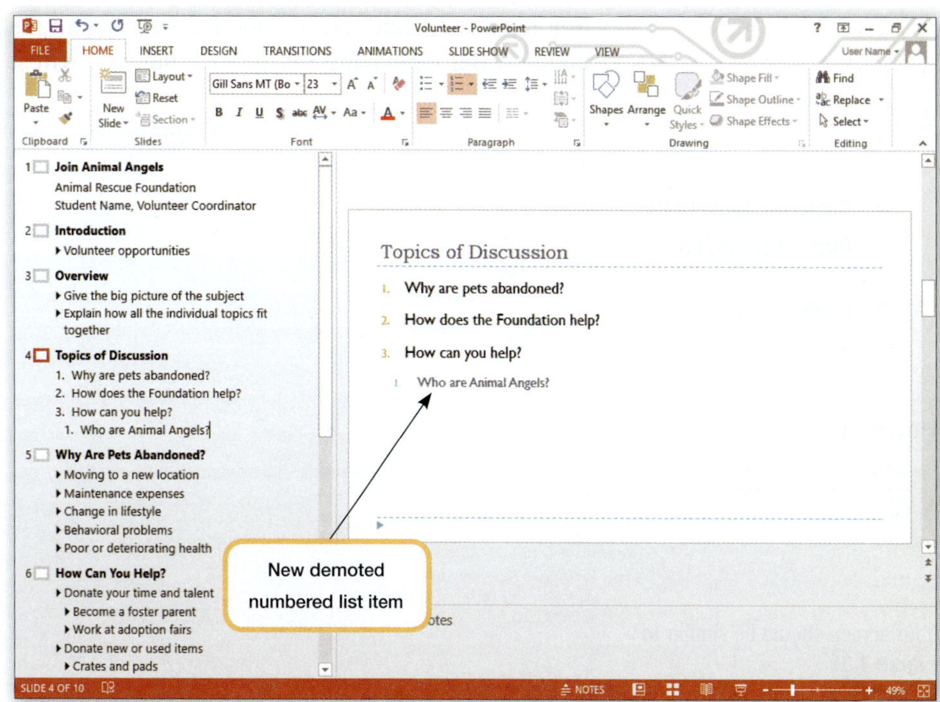

Figure 1.36

The numbering for the subtopic begins with 1 again. The new item is too important to be indented on the list, so you will decrease the list level to the same level as the other items.

3

- **In the Slide window, select the entire fourth line.**
- **Press Shift + Tab to decrease the list level of the fourth line.**
- **Drag the selected item to the beginning of the third line.**

Your screen should be similar to Figure 1.37

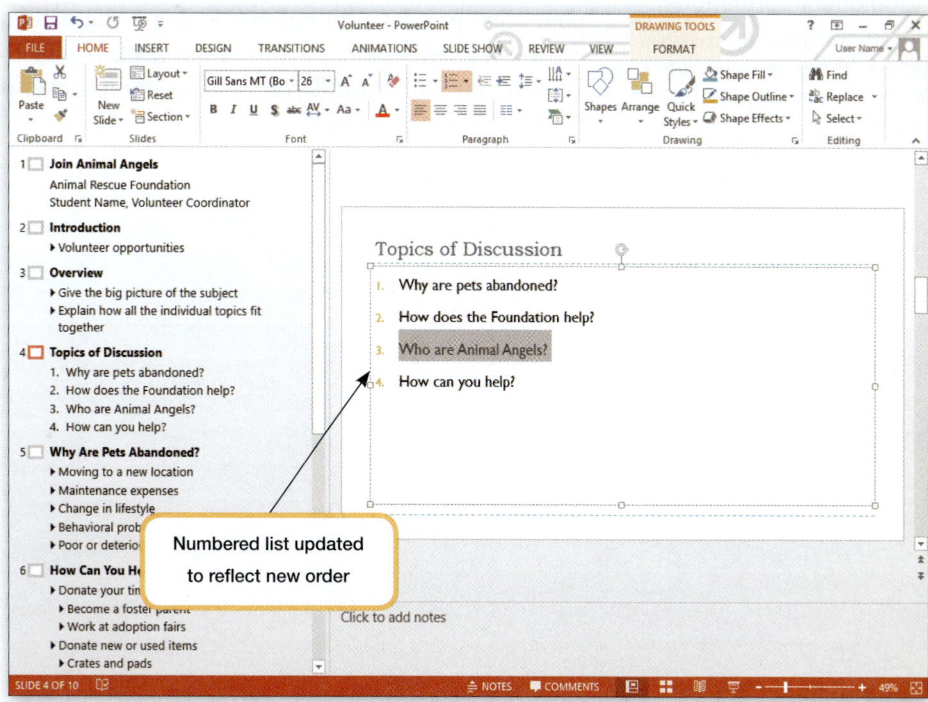

Figure 1.37

The numbered list has again been appropriately adjusted.

You have just been notified about an important meeting that is to begin in a few minutes. Before leaving for the meeting, you will save and close the presentation.

4

- **Click [Save] Save in the Quick Access bar.**
- **Open the File tab and click Close.**

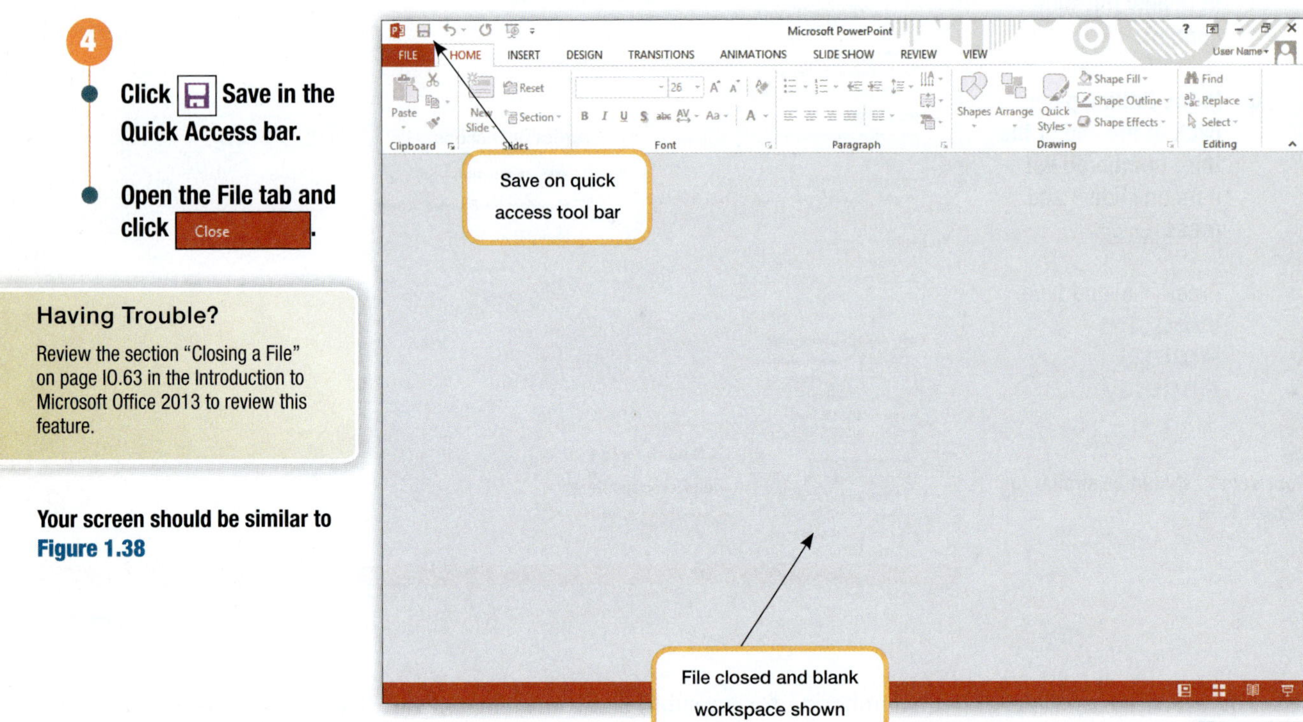

Figure 1.38

Having Trouble?

Review the section "Closing a File" on page IO.63 in the Introduction to Microsoft Office 2013 to review this feature.

Your screen should be similar to Figure 1.38

Additional Information

If you are ending your lab session now, click × at the upper-right corner of the window or press Alt + F4 to exit the program.

The presentation is closed, and an empty workspace is displayed. Always save your slide presentation before closing a file or leaving the PowerPoint program. As a safeguard against losing your work if you forget to save the presentation, PowerPoint will remind you to save any unsaved presentation before closing the file or exiting the program.

Opening an Existing Presentation

After returning from your meeting, you continued to work on the presentation. You revised the content of several of the slides and added information for several new slides. Then you saved the presentation using a new file name. You will open this file to see the changes and will continue working on the presentation.

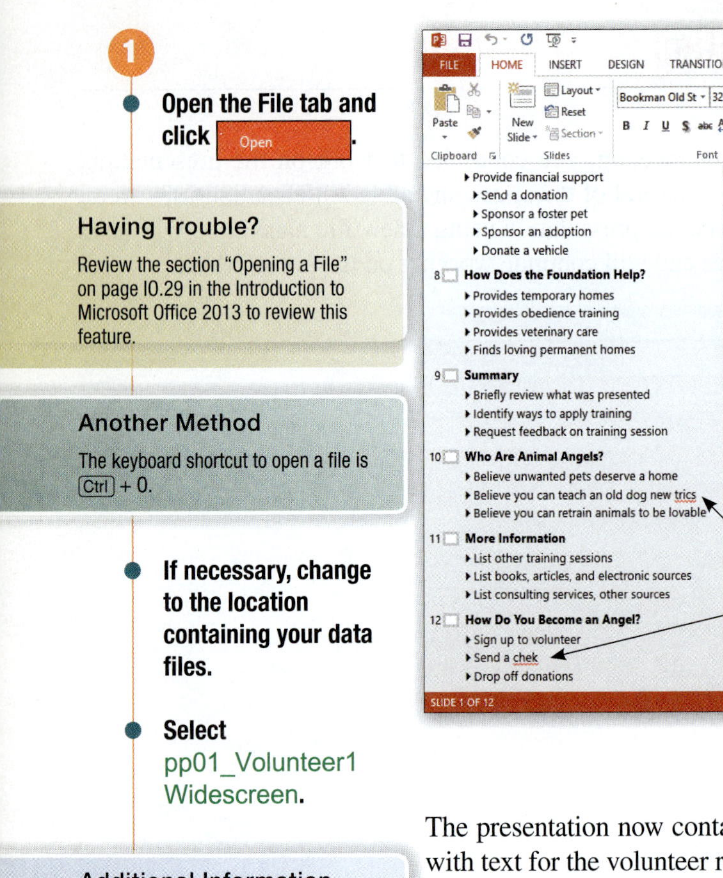

1

- **Open the File tab and click Open.**

Having Trouble?

Review the section "Opening a File" on page IO.29 in the Introduction to Microsoft Office 2013 to review this feature.

Another Method

The keyboard shortcut to open a file is Ctrl + O.

- **If necessary, change to the location containing your data files.**
- **Select pp01_Volunteer1 Widescreen.**

Additional Information

You also can quickly open a recently used file by selecting it from the Recent Presentations list.

- **Click Save.**
- **Open Outline view.**
- **Replace "Student Name" in slide 1 with your name.**
- **Scroll the Outline pane to see the additional content that has been added to the presentation.**

Your screen should be similar to Figure 1.39

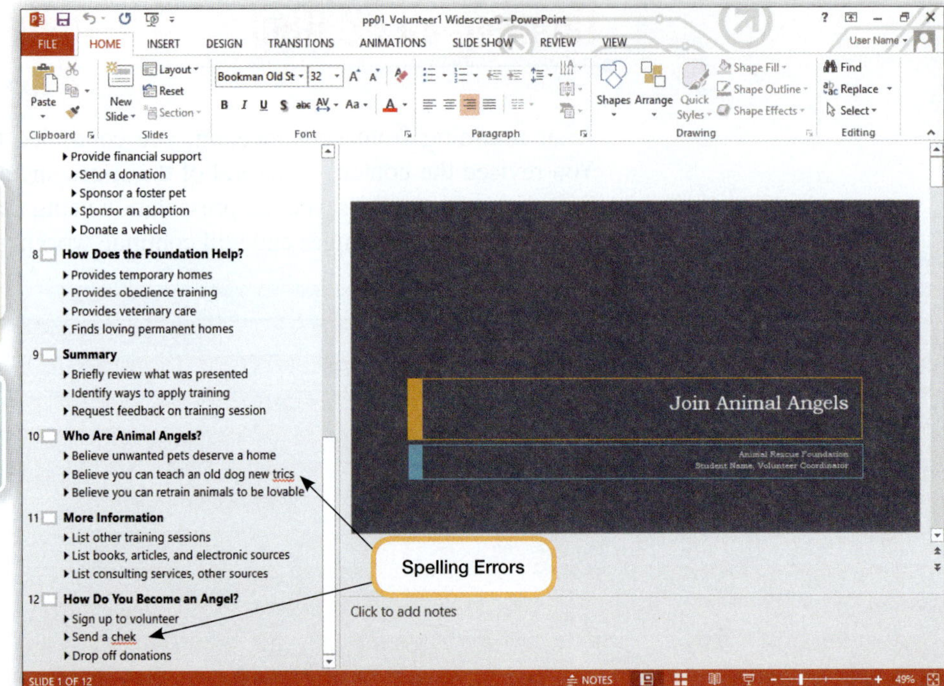

Figure 1.39

The presentation now contains 12 slides, and all the sample text has been replaced with text for the volunteer recruitment presentation, except for slides 3, 9, and 11.

Using Spelling Checker

Additional Information

Unlike Word 2013, Powerpoint does not check for grammar errors.

As you entered the information on the additional slides, you left some typing errors uncorrected. To correct the misspelled words, you can use the shortcut menu to correct each individual word or error, as you learned earlier. However, in many cases, you may find it more efficient to wait until you are finished writing before you correct any spelling or grammatical errors. To do this, you can manually turn on the spelling checker to locate and correct the spelling on all slides of the presentation at once.

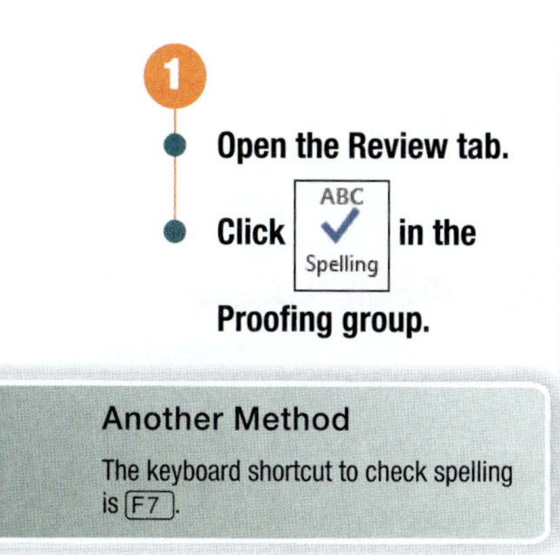

1
- **Open the Review tab.**
- **Click** ABC Spelling **in the Proofing group.**

Another Method

The keyboard shortcut to check spelling is F7.

Your screen should be similar to Figure 1.40

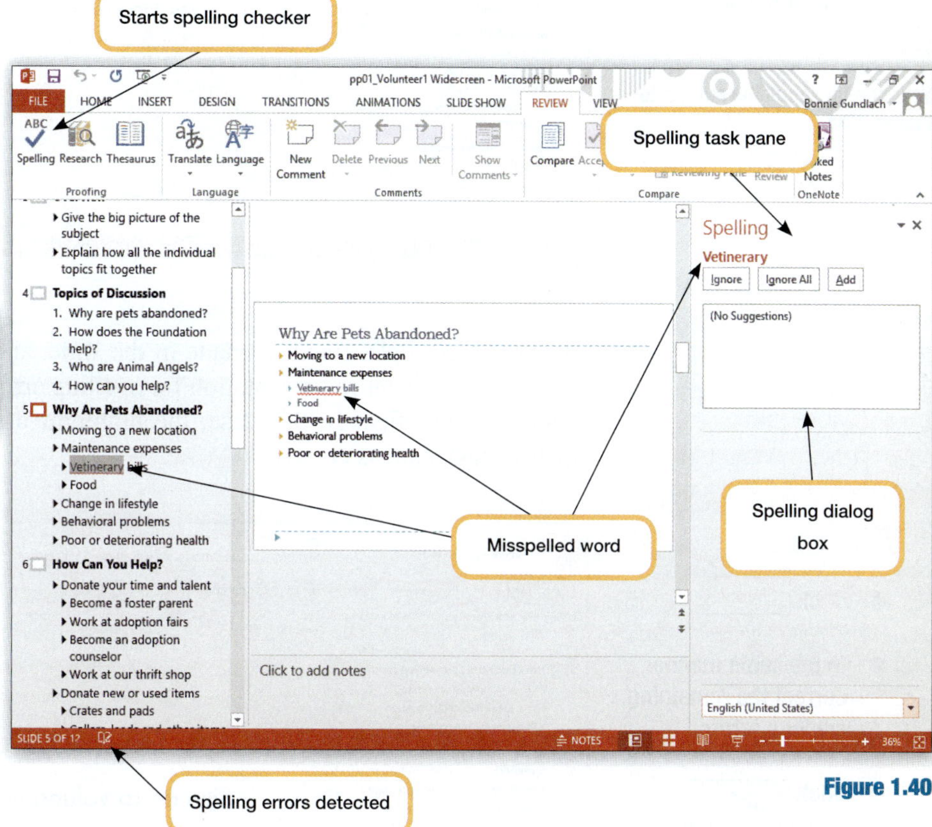

Figure 1.40

Additional Information

The spelling checker identifies many proper names and technical terms as misspelled. To stop this from occurring, use the Add option to add those names to the custom dictionary.

The program jumps to slide 5; highlights the first located misspelled word, "Vetinerary," in the Outline pane; and opens the Spelling task pane. The misspelled word is displayed at the top of the task pane. The Suggestions list box typically displays the words the spelling checker has located in the dictionary that most closely match the misspelled word.

In this case, the spelling checker does not display any suggested replacements because it cannot locate any words in the dictionaries that are similar in spelling. When there are no suggestions or none of the suggestions is correct, you must edit the word yourself by typing the correction in the slide.

2

- Type **Veterinary** to make the correction.

Additional Information

The replacement text should be entered exactly as you want it to appear, including capitalization.

- Click **Resume** in the Spelling pane.

Your screen should be similar to Figure 1.41

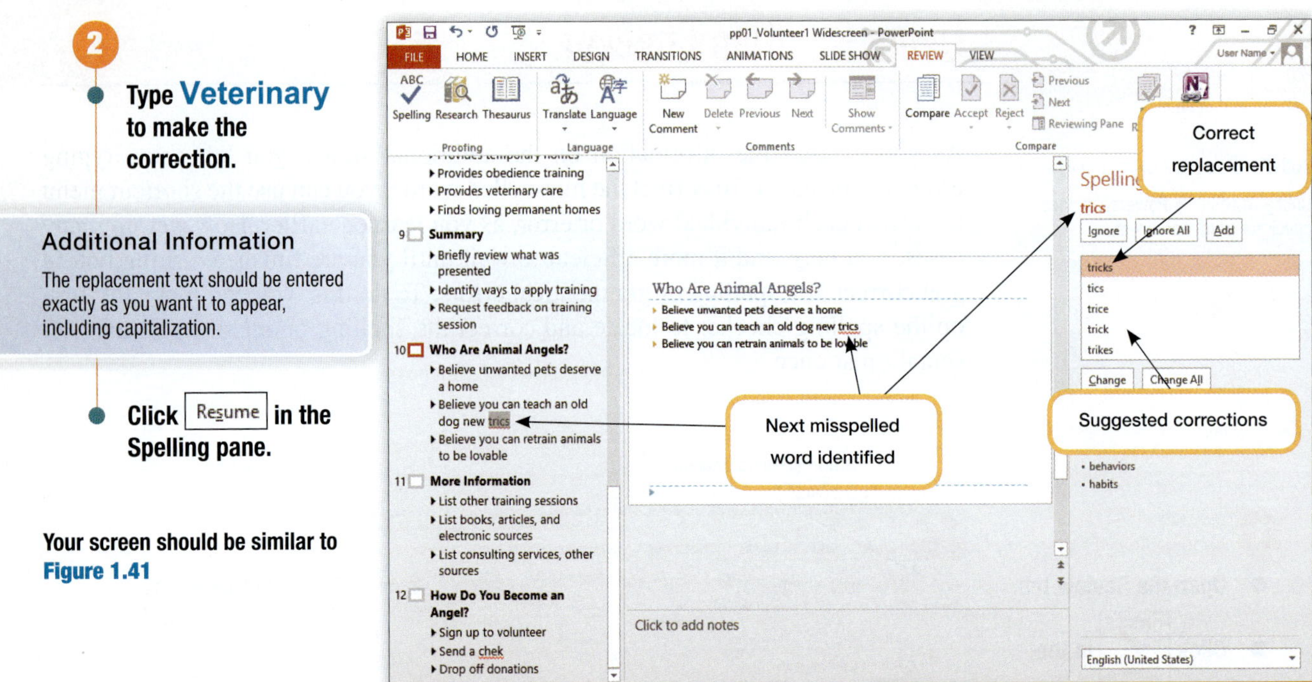

Figure 1.41

The corrected replacement is made in the slide, and the spelling checker continues to check the entire presentation for spelling errors. The next misspelled word, "trics," is identified. In this case, the highlighted suggested replacement in the Spelling task pane is correct.

3

- Click **Change**.
- In the same manner, correct the remaining spelling errors.
- Click **OK** in response to the message telling you that the spell check is complete.
- Open the File tab, click **Save As**, and save the revised presentation as **Volunteer1 Widescreen** to your solution file location.

Your screen should be similar to Figure 1.42

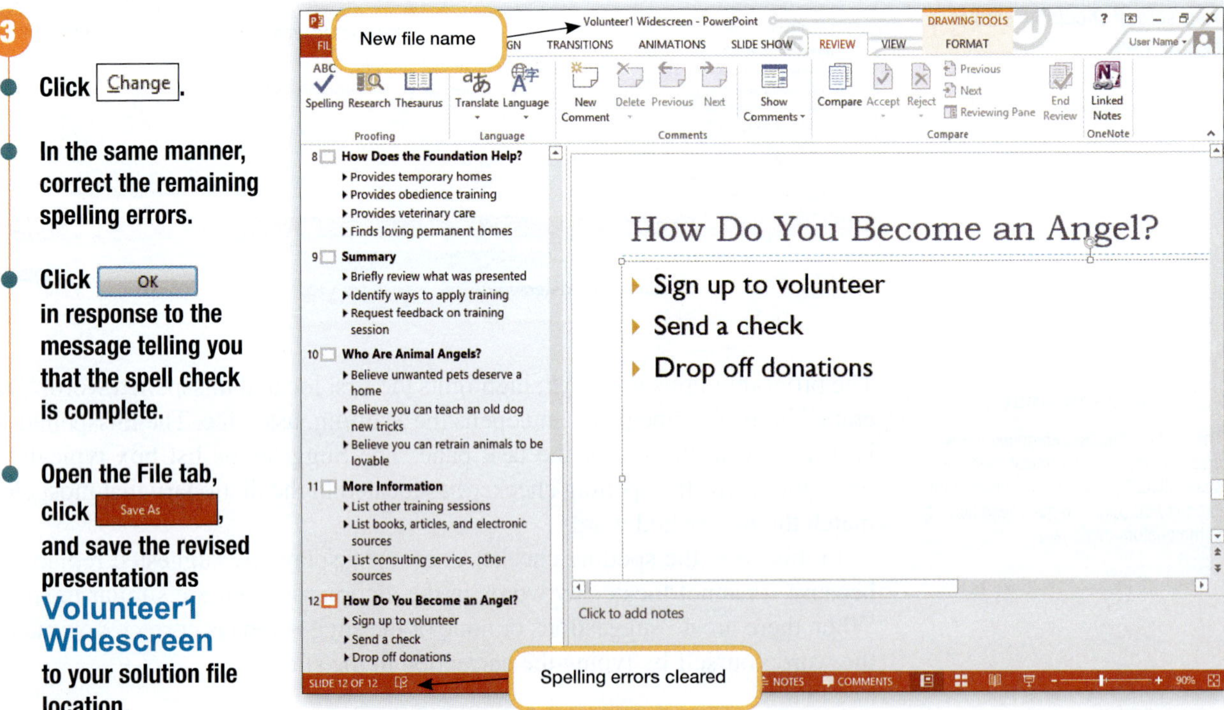

Figure 1.42

The Spelling indicator in the status bar shows that all spelling errors have been resolved.

Using Slide Sorter View

To get a better overall picture of the presentation, you will switch to Slide Sorter view. This view displays thumbnail images of each slide in the Slide window and is particularly useful for rearranging slides to improve the flow and organization of the presentation. Clicking on a thumbnail selects the slide and makes it the current slide.

1

- **Click [Slide Sorter icon] Slide Sorter in the status bar.**

Another Method

You also could switch to Slide Sorter view by clicking [Slide Sorter] in the Presentation Views group of the View tab.

- **Click on 100% in the status bar, choose 66% from the Zoom dialog box, and click OK.**
- **Click on slide 1.**

Your screen should be similar to Figure 1.43

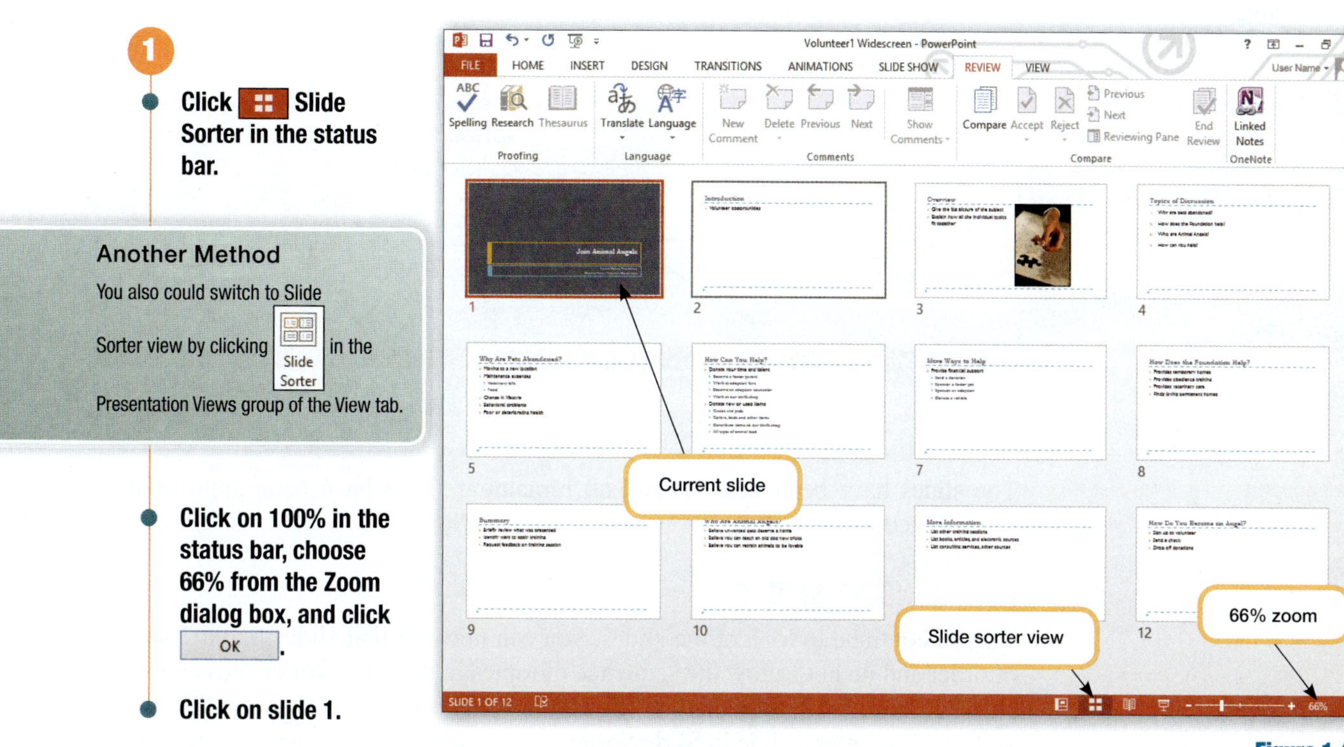

Figure 1.43

The currently selected slide, slide 1, appears with an orange border around it. Viewing all the slides side by side helps you see how your presentation flows. You realize that the second slide is no longer necessary because you added your name to the opening slide. You also decide to delete the original slides 3, 9, and 11 because you plan to add any necessary information to other slides.

Having Trouble?

Do not be concerned if your screen displays a different number of slides per row. This is a function of the size of your monitor and your monitor settings.

SELECTING AND DELETING SLIDES

In Slide Sorter view, it is easy to select and work with multiple slides at the same time. To select multiple slides, hold down Ctrl while clicking on each slide to select it.

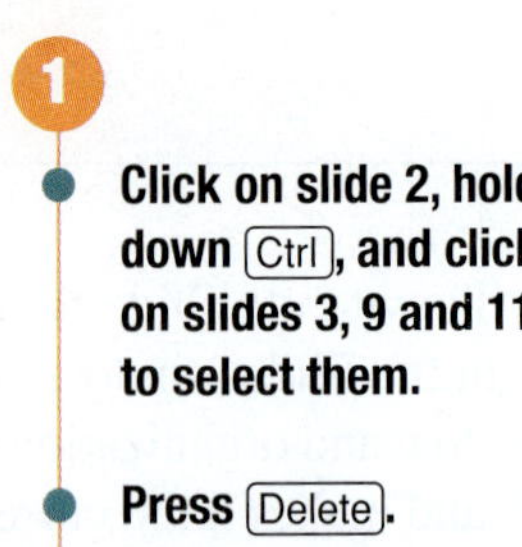

- **Click on slide 2, hold down Ctrl, and click on slides 3, 9 and 11 to select them.**
- **Press Delete.**
- **Increase the zoom to 80%.**

Additional Information

The zoom setting for each view is set independently and remains in effect until changed to another zoom setting.

Your screen should be similar to Figure 1.44

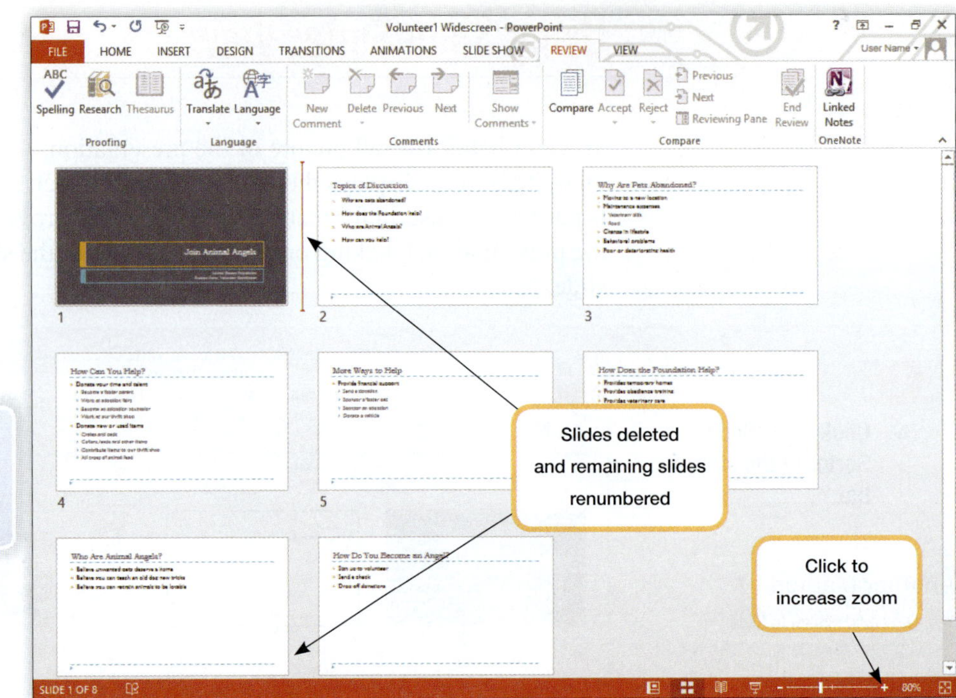

Figure 1.44

The slides have been deleted, and all remaining slides have been appropriately renumbered.

REARRANGING SLIDES

As you continue to look at the slides, you can now see that slides 6 and 7 are out of order and do not follow the sequence of topics in the Topics of Discussion slide. You will correct the organization of the slides by moving slides 6 and 7 before slide 4. To reorder a slide in Slide Sorter view, you drag it to its new location using drag and drop. As you drag the mouse, Live Preview shows you where the slide will be placed when you release the mouse button.

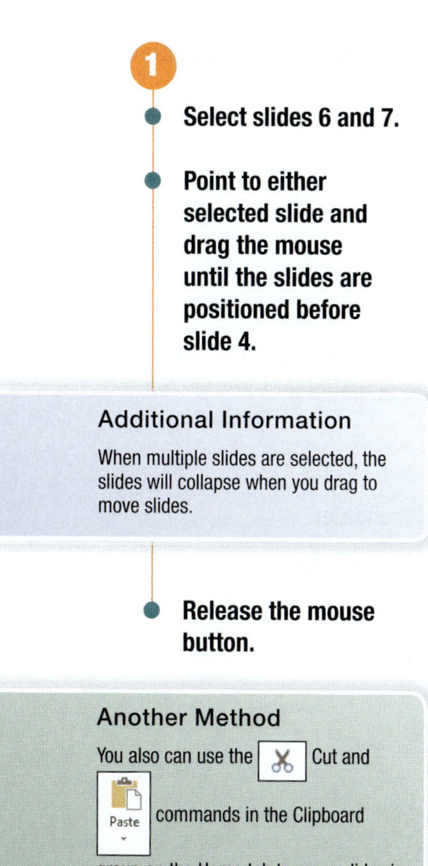

1

- Select slides 6 and 7.
- Point to either selected slide and drag the mouse until the slides are positioned before slide 4.

Additional Information

When multiple slides are selected, the slides will collapse when you drag to move slides.

- Release the mouse button.

Another Method

You also can use the Cut and Paste commands in the Clipboard group on the Home tab to move slides in Slide Sorter view.

Your screen should be similar to Figure 1.45

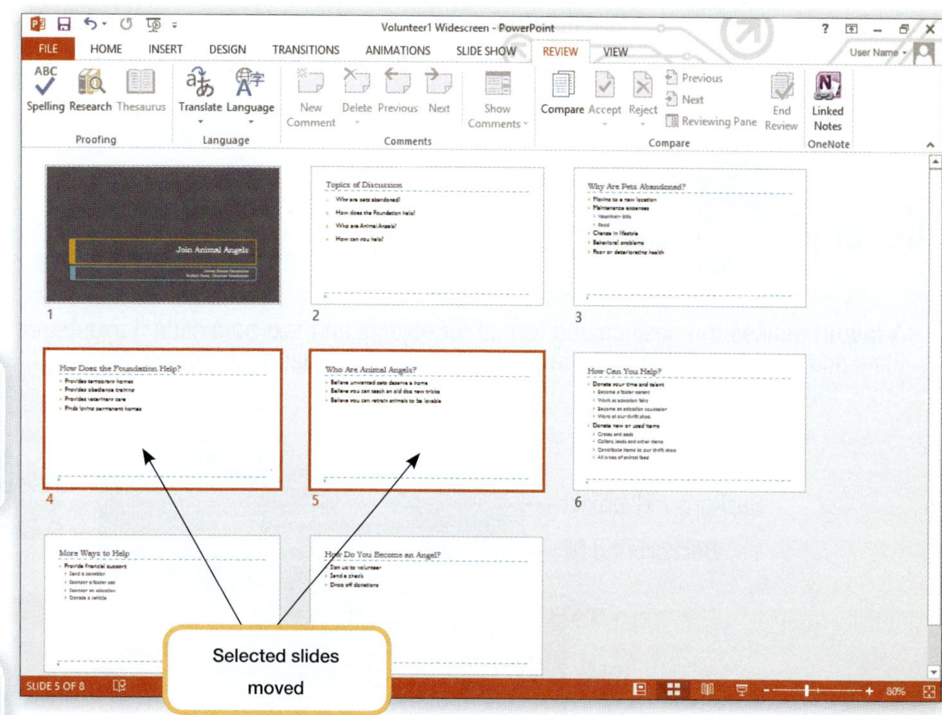

Figure 1.45

The slides now appear in the order in which you want them.

SELECTING A SLIDE LAYOUT

During your discussion with the foundation director, it was suggested that you add a slide showing the history of the organization. To include this information in the presentation, you will insert a new slide after slide 4. A new slide is inserted after the current or selected slide.

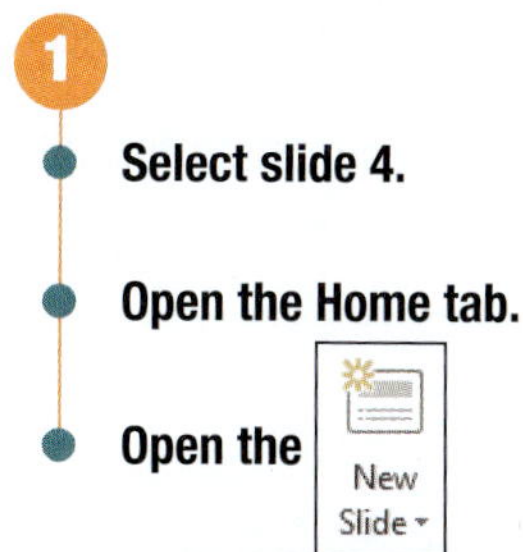

1

- Select slide 4.
- Open the Home tab.
- Open the New Slide drop-down menu in the Slides group.

Your screen should be similar to Figure 1.46

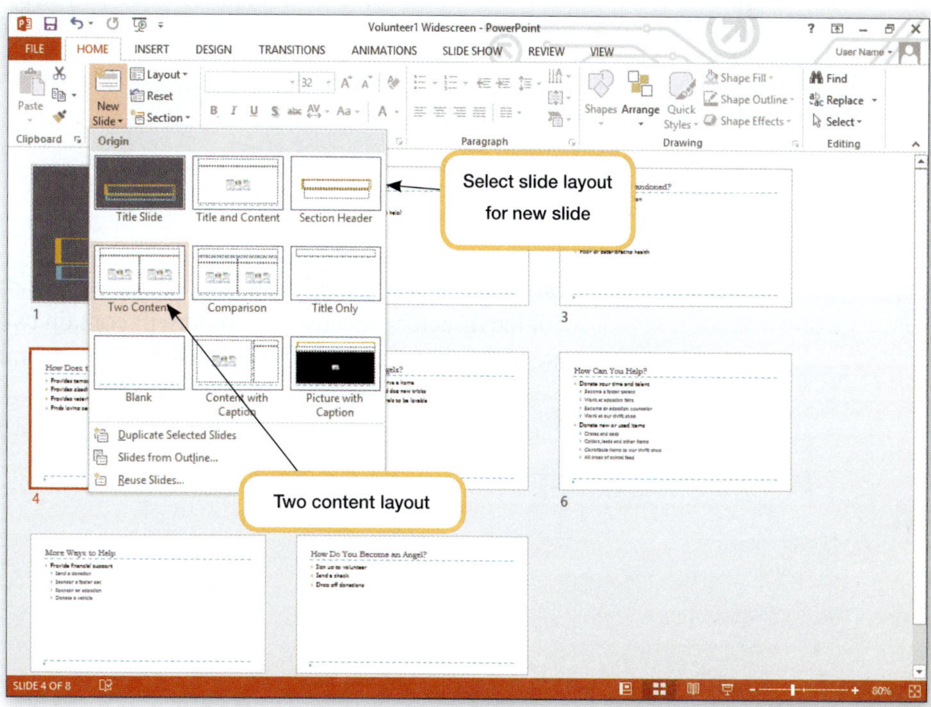

Figure 1.46

The drop-down menu displays nine built-in slide layouts. The number of available layouts varies with the template you are using.

Concept 4 Layout

A layout defines the position and format for objects and text on a slide. Layouts provide placeholders for slide titles and slide content such as text, tables, diagrams, charts, or clip art. Many of these placeholders are shown in the following diagram.

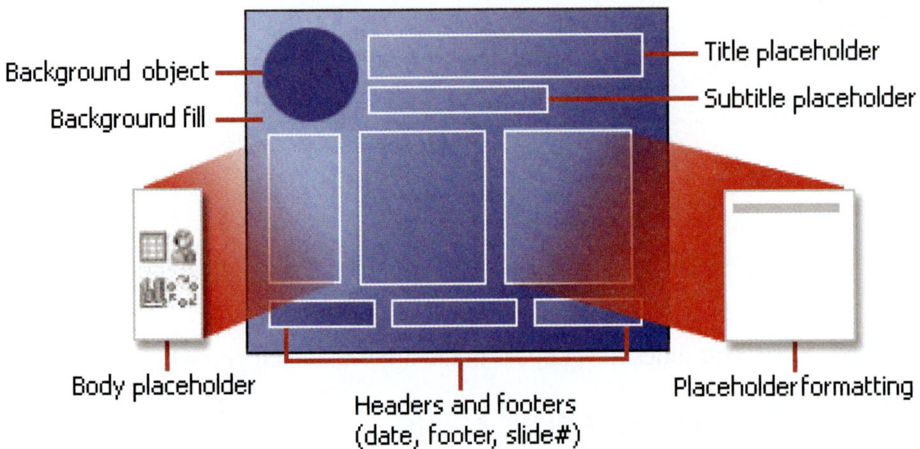

You can change the layout of an existing slide by selecting a new layout. If the new layout does not include placeholders for objects that are already on your slide (for example, if you created a chart and the new layout does not include a chart placeholder), you do not lose the information. All objects remain on the slide, and the selected layout is automatically adjusted by adding the appropriate type of placeholder for the object. Alternatively, as you add new objects to a slide, the layout automatically adjusts by adding the appropriate type of placeholder. You also can rearrange, size, and format placeholders on a slide any way you like to customize the slide's appearance.

To make creating slides easy, use the predefined layouts. The layouts help you keep your presentation format consistent and, therefore, more professional.

You need to choose the layout that best accommodates the changes you discussed with the director. Because this slide will contain two columns of text about the history of the organization, you will use the Two Content layout.

2

- **Choose Two Content.**
- **Change to Normal view.**

Additional Information

The current slide does not change when you switch views.

Your screen should be similar to Figure 1.47

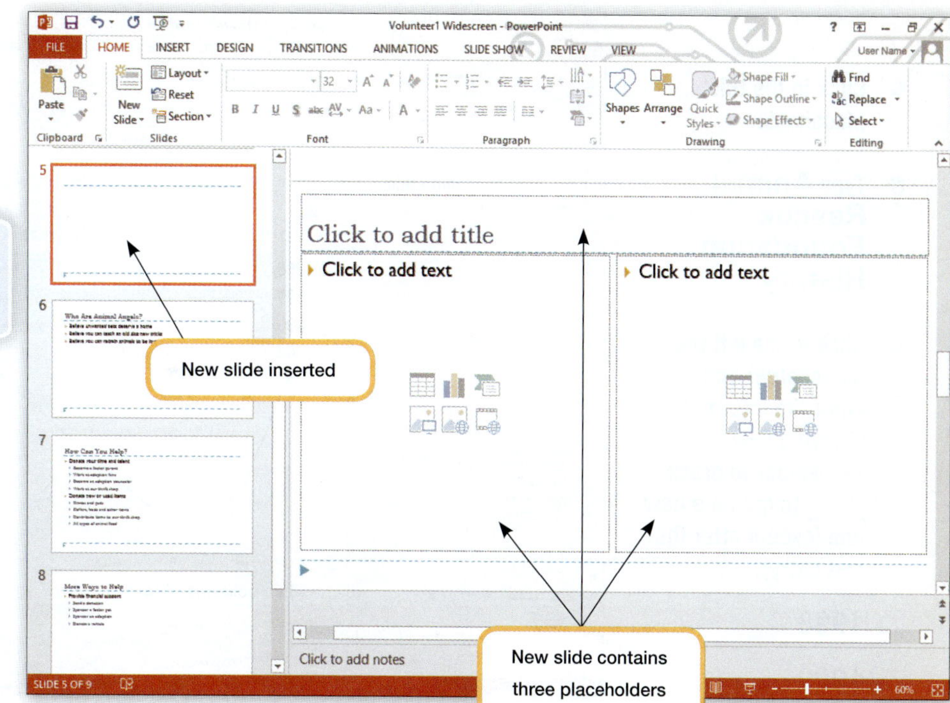

Figure 1.47

A new Two Content slide is inserted with the same design elements as the other slides in the presentation. The Two Content layout contains three placeholders, but unlike the template slides, the placeholders on the inserted slide do not contain sample text. When you select the placeholder, you can simply type in the text without having to select or delete any sample text.

CHANGING A PLACEHOLDER

You will add text to the slide presenting a brief history of the Animal Rescue Foundation. First, you will enter the slide title and then the list of dates and events.

1

- Click in the title placeholder.
- Type **Animal Rescue Foundation History**
- Click in the left text placeholder and enter the information shown below. Remember to press Enter to create a new line (except after the last entry).

1998

1999

2000

2008

- In the same manner, enter the following text in the right text placeholder:

Founded by Steve Dow

Built first shelter

Began volunteer program

Rescued 3000 animals!

Your screen should be similar to **Figure 1.48**

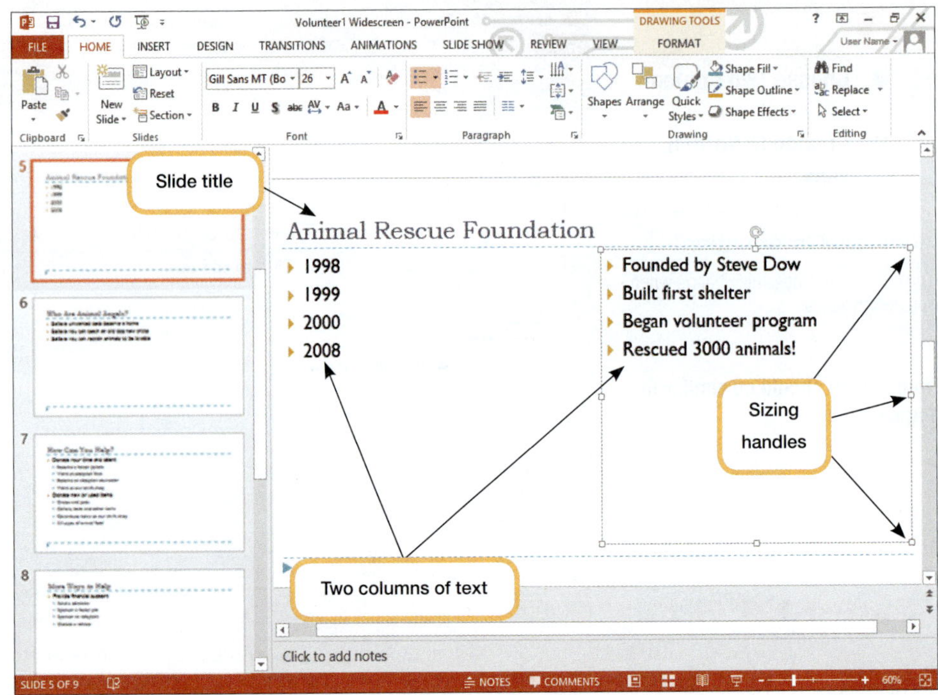

Figure 1.48

Notice that the left placeholder is much too big for the content and leaves too much space between the columns of information. To fix this, you can adjust the size of the placeholders.

SIZING A PLACEHOLDER

The four squares that appear at the corners and sides of a selected placeholder's border are **sizing handles** that can be used to adjust the size of the placeholder. Dragging the corner sizing handles will adjust both the height and width at the same time, whereas the center handles adjust the associated side borders. When you point to the sizing handle, the mouse pointer appears as ⤡, indicating the direction in which you can drag the border to adjust the size.

You will decrease the width of the left placeholder and the height of both placeholders.

1

- Select the left text placeholder and drag the right-center sizing handle to the left as in Figure 1.49.
- With the left placeholder still selected, hold down Shift while clicking on the right placeholder to select both.
- Use the bottom-middle sizing handle of either selected placeholder to decrease the height of the placeholders as in Figure 1.49.

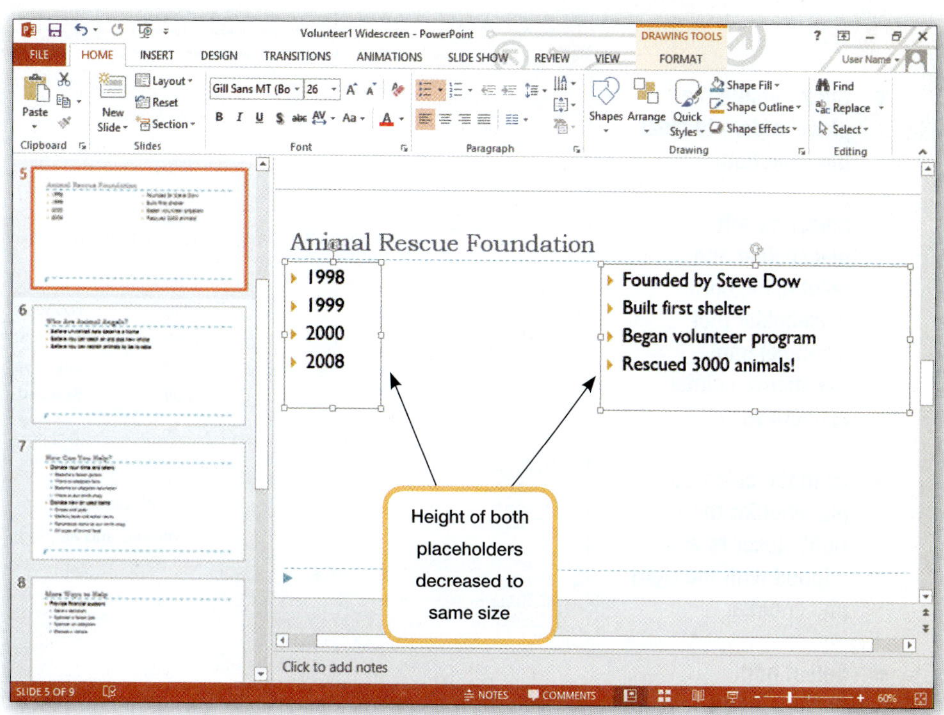

Figure 1.49

Your screen should be similar to Figure 1.49

MOVING AND ALIGNING A PLACEHOLDER

Next, you will decrease the blank space between the two columns. Then you will move both placeholders so they appear more centered in the space. An object can be moved anywhere on a slide by dragging the placeholder's border. The mouse pointer appears as ✥ when you can move a placeholder. As you drag the placeholder, red Smart Guide alignment lines appear when two objects are close to even, to help you evenly align the selected object with another. They also appear when you move an object close to the left or right margin of the slide to help you align the object with the margins.

1

- Click outside the placeholders to clear the selection.
- Select the left placeholder and point to the border placeholder (not a handle) until the mouse pointer appears as ✥.
- Drag the selected placeholder to the right closer to and aligned with the right placeholder.
- Select both placeholders and drag to align them with the left margin.
- Position the placeholders as in Figure 1.50.

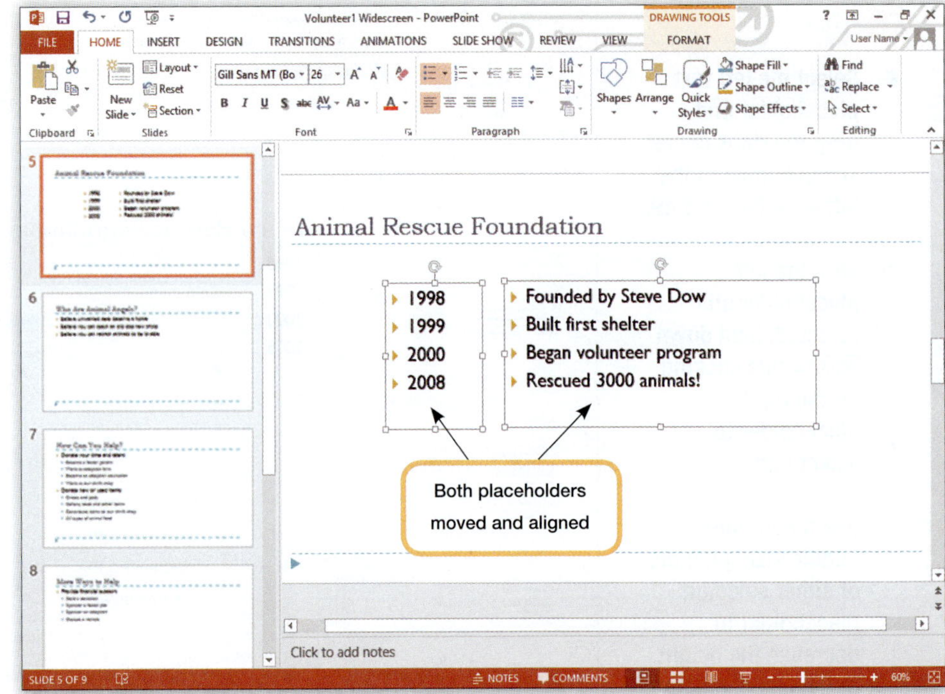

Figure 1.50

Another Method

You also can use Align Align in the Arrange group of the Format tab to evenly align two selected objects.

Your screen should be similar to Figure 1.50

ADDING AND REMOVING BULLETS

Next, you will remove the bullets from the items on the history slide. You can quickly apply and remove bullets using Bullets in the Paragraph group on the Home tab. This button applies the bullet style associated with the design template you are using. Because the placeholder items already include bullets, using this button will remove them.

- With both text placeholders still selected, click Bullets from the Paragraph group in the Home tab to remove all bullets.

Your screen should be similar to **Figure 1.51**

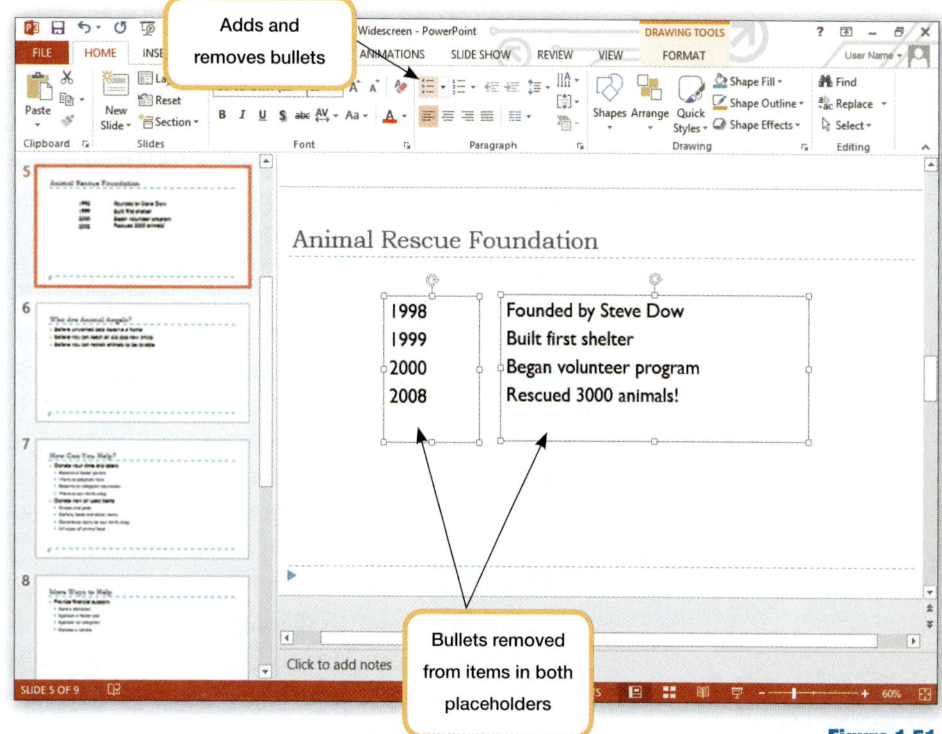

Figure 1.51

The bullets are removed from all the items in both placeholders. Now, however, you think it would look better to add bullets back to the years in the first column.

2

- Select the four years in the left column.
- Click Bullets from the Paragraph group in the Home tab.
- Click outside the selected placeholder to deselect it.
- Save the presentation again.

Your screen should be similar to **Figure 1.52**

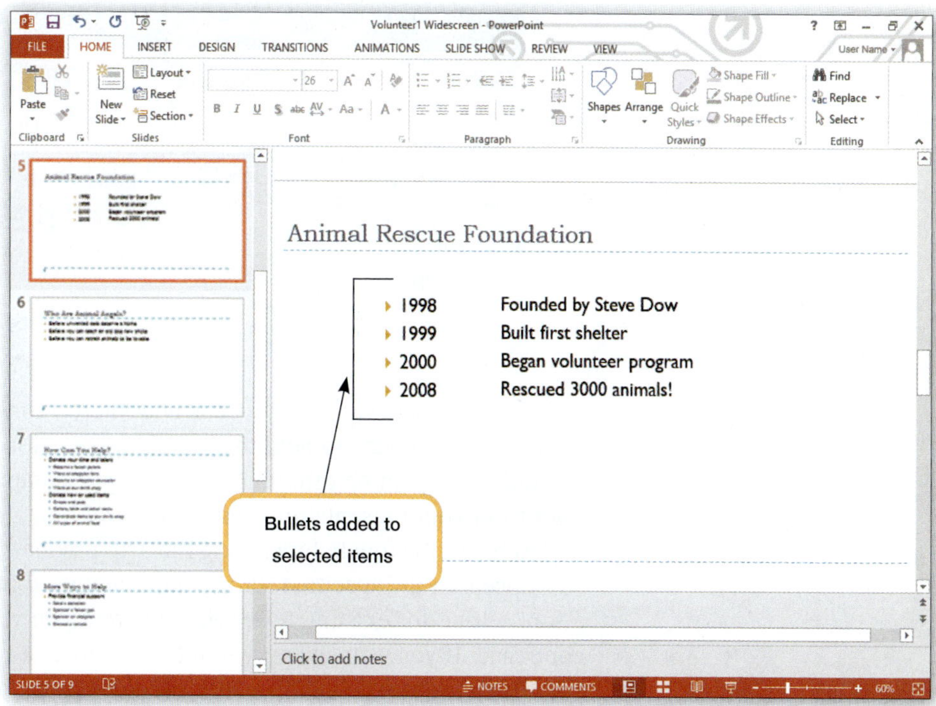

Figure 1.52

Bullets appear before the selected text items only.

Formatting Slide Text

The next change you want to make to the presentation is to improve the appearance of the title slide. Although the design template you are using already includes many formatting features, you want this slide to have more impact.

Applying different formatting to characters and paragraphs can greatly enhance the appearance of the slide. **Character formatting** features affect the selected characters only. They include changing the character style and size, applying effects such as bold and italics, changing the character spacing, and adding animated text effects. **Paragraph formatting** features affect an entire paragraph. A paragraph is text that has an Enter at the end of it. Each item in a bulleted list, title, and subtitle is a paragraph. Paragraph formatting features include the position of the paragraph or its alignment between the margins, paragraph indentation, spacing above and below a paragraph, and line spacing within a paragraph.

CHANGING FONTS

First, you will improve the appearance of the presentation title by changing the font of the title text. There are two basic types of fonts: serif and sans serif. **Serif fonts** have a flair at the base of each letter that visually leads the reader to the next letter. Two common serif fonts are Courier New and Garamond. Serif fonts generally are used for text in paragraphs. **Sans serif fonts** do not have a flair at the base of each letter. Calibri and Helvetica are two common sans serif fonts. Because sans serif fonts have a clean look, they are often used for headings in documents.

Having Trouble?

Refer to the section "Formatting Text" on page IO.43 in the Introduction to Microsoft Office 2013 to review this feature.

Each font can appear using a different font size. Several common fonts in different sizes are shown in the following table.

Font Name	Font Type	Font Size
Calibri	Sans serif	This is 10 pt. This is 16 pt.
Courier New	Serif	This is 10 pt. This is 16 pt.
Garamond	Serif	This is 10 pt. This is 16 pt.

Using fonts as a design element can add interest to your presentation and give your audience visual cues to help them find information quickly. It is good practice to use only two or three different fonts in a presentation, because too many can distract from your presentation content and can look unprofessional.

To change the font before typing the text, use the command and then type. All text will appear in the specified setting until another font setting is selected. To change a font setting for existing text, select the text you want to change and then use the command. If you want to apply font formatting to a word, simply move the insertion point to the word and the formatting is automatically applied to the entire word. To apply formatting to all the text in a placeholder, select the entire placeholder first.

Additional Information

The font used in the title is Bookman Old Style as displayed in the Bookman Old St Font button. It is automatically used in all headings in this template.

The Bookman Old St Font button in the Font tab or on the Mini toolbar that appears when you select text is used to change the font style. As you select a font from the drop-down menu, a live preview of how the selected font will appear is displayed in the document.

1

- **Select the Title placeholder on slide 1.**
- **Click the border of the placeholder to change it to a solid line.**
- **Open the**  **Font drop-down list in the Font group of the Home tab.**
- **Point to several fonts to see the live preview.**

Your screen should be similar to Figure 1.53

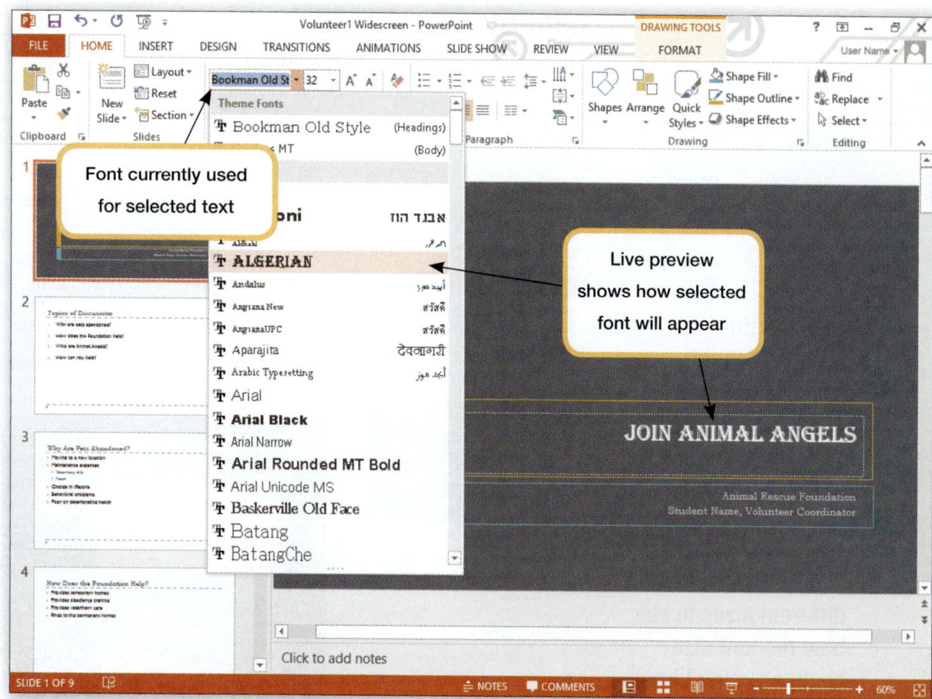

Figure 1.53

All the text in the placeholder appears in the font style selected. With Live Preview, you can see how the text will look with the selected font before you choose the one that you want. You want to change the font to a design that has a less serious appearance.

2

- **Scroll the menu and choose Comic Sans MS.**

> **Another Method**
>
> You can also select text and make format changes using the Mini toolbar.

Your screen should be similar to Figure 1.54

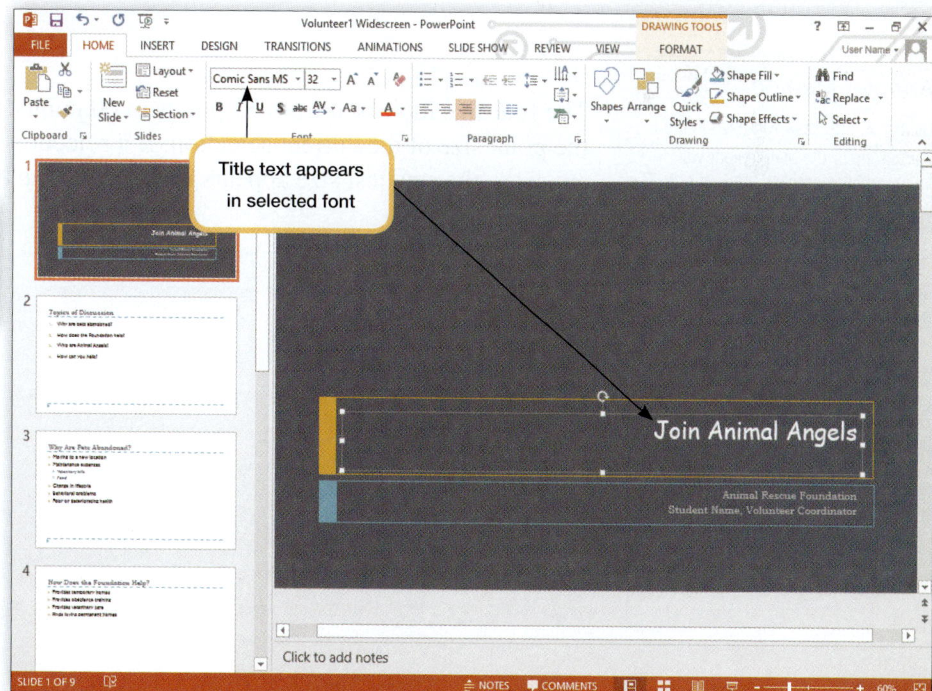

Figure 1.54

The title has changed to the new font style, and the Font button displays the font name used in the current selection.

CHANGING FONT SIZE

You also want to increase the size of the title text.

- With the title placeholder still selected, open the [32 ▾] Font Size drop-down list in the Font group of the Home tab.
- Point to several different sizes to see how the font size changes using Live Preview.
- Choose 60.

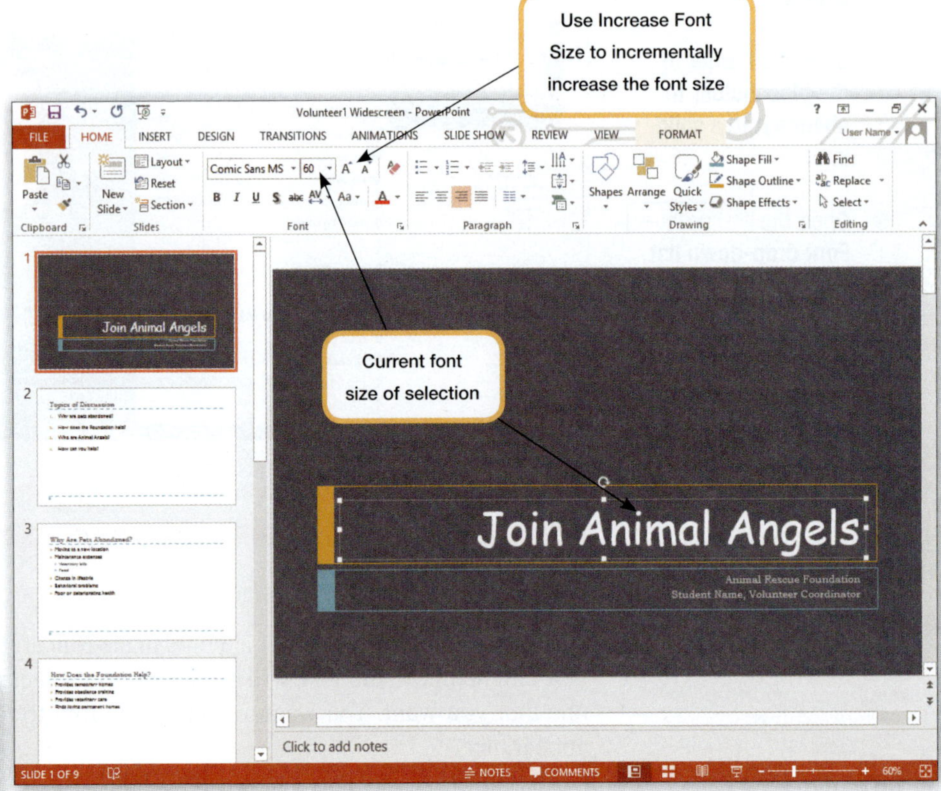

Figure 1.55

Another Method

You also could use [32 ▾] Font Size in the Mini toolbar.

Another Method

Using [A˄] Increase Font Size in the Font group or the Mini toolbar will incrementally increase the font size. The keyboard shortcut is Ctrl + Shift + >.

Your screen should be similar to Figure 1.55

The font size increased from 32 points to 60 points. The Font Size button displays the point size of the current selection. If a selection includes text in several different sizes, the smallest size appears in the Font Size button followed by a plus sign.

Additional Information

Use [A˅] Decrease Font Size or Ctrl + Shift + < to incrementally decrease the point size of selected text.

APPLYING TEXT EFFECTS

Next, you want to further enhance the title slide by adding **text effects** such as color and shadow to the title and subtitle. The following table describes some of the effects and their uses. The Home tab and the Mini toolbar contain buttons for many of the formatting effects.

Format	Example	Use
Bold, italic	***Bold Italic***	Adds emphasis
Underline	Underline	Adds emphasis
Superscript	"To be or not to be."[1]	Used in footnotes and formulas
Subscript	H_2O	Used in formulas
Shadow	Shadow	Adds distinction to titles and headings
Color	Color Color Color	Adds interest

You decide to add color and a shadow effect to the main title first.

1

- **With the title placeholder still selected, click [S] Text Shadow in the Font group.**

Additional Information

Many formatting commands are toggle commands. This means the feature can be turned on and off simply by clicking on the command button.

- **Open the [A] Font Color menu to display a gallery of colors.**

- **Choose Gold, Accent 1, Lighter 40% in the Theme Colors section.**

Additional Information

A ScreenTip displays the name of the color when you point to it.

Your screen should be similar to Figure 1.56

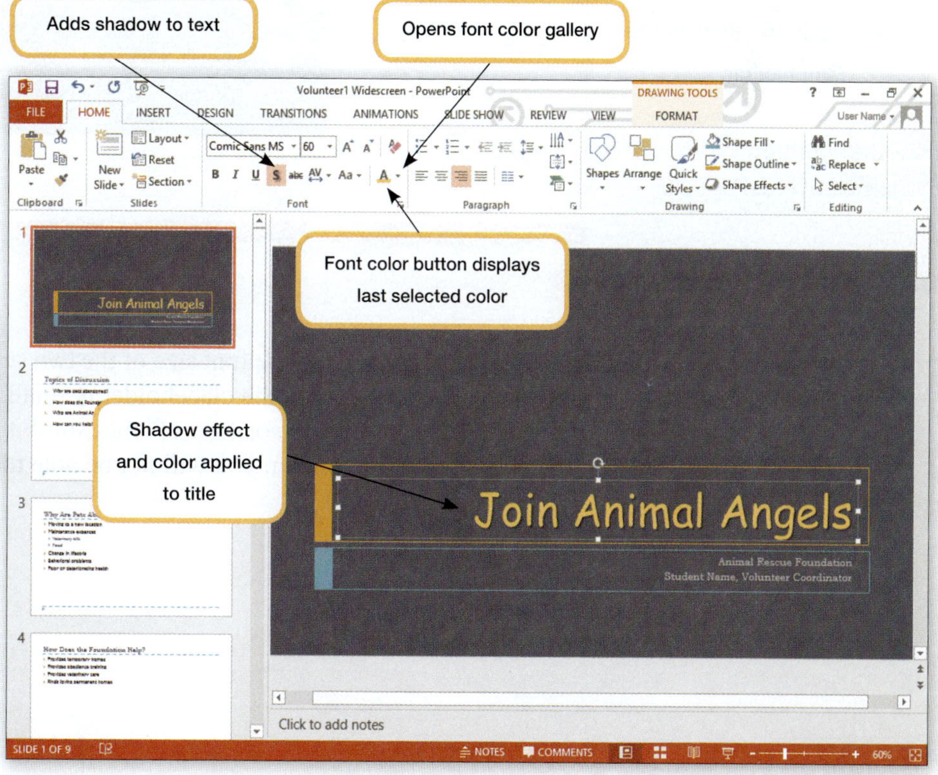

Figure 1.56

The selected color and slight shadow effect make the title much more interesting. Also notice the color in the Font Color button is the gold color you just selected. This color can be quickly reapplied to other selections now simply by clicking the button.

Next you will enhance the two lines in the Subtitle placeholder by applying a different effect to each line.

2

- **Select the text "Animal Rescue Foundation".**
- **Open the A Font Color gallery in the Mini toolbar.**
- **Choose Gold, Accent 1 in the Theme Colors section.**
- **Click B Bold on the Mini toolbar.**

Another Method

The keyboard shortcut is Ctrl + B.

Your screen should be similar to Figure 1.57

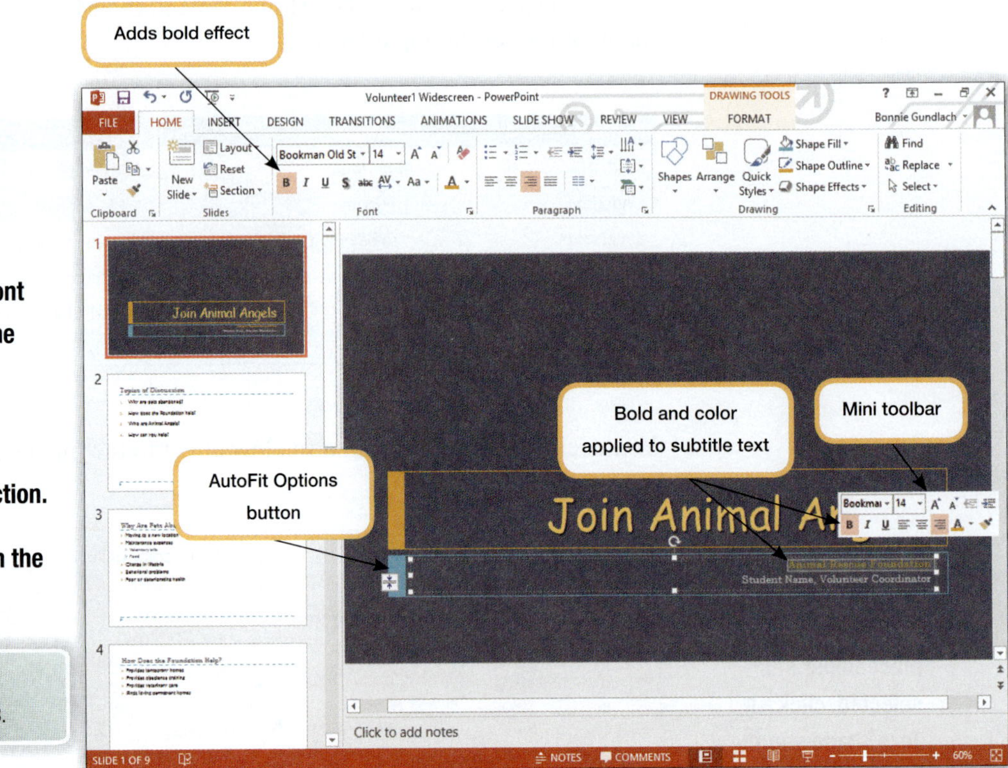

Figure 1.57

Next you want to increase the font size of the two subtitle lines and add a few additional text effects. Because the placeholder is small, you will first need to increase the size of the placeholder or turn off the AutoFit to placeholder feature. If you leave the AutoFit feature on, you will not be able to increase the font size.

- **Click Autofit and choose Stop Fitting Text to This Placeholder.**

Having Trouble?

If the Mini toolbar is no longer displayed, right-click on the selection to display it again.

- **Change the font size to 32.**
- **Select the entire second line of the subtitle.**
- **Click Italic.**
- **Click Increase Font Size.**
- **Click somewhere outside the placeholder.**
- **Save the presentation.**

Your screen should be similar to Figure 1.58

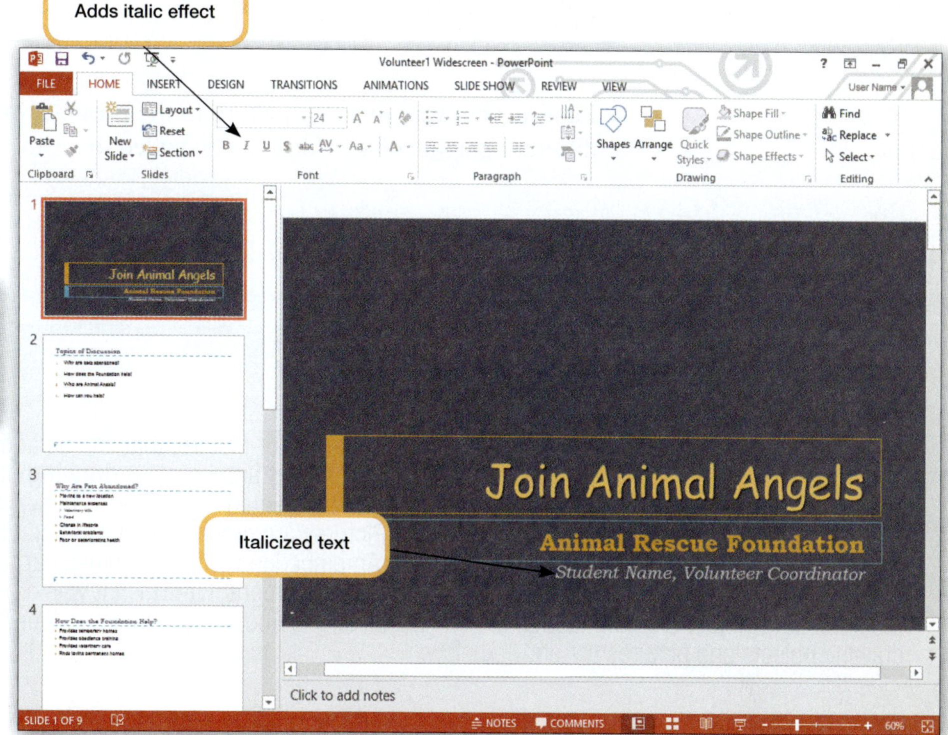

Figure 1.58

Now the title slide has much more impact.

Working with Graphics

Finally, you want to add a picture to the presentation. A picture is one of several different graphic objects that can be added to a slide.

Concept  Graphics

A **graphic** is a nontext element or object, such as a drawing or picture, that can be added to a slide. A graphic can be a simple drawing object consisting of shapes such as lines and boxes. A **drawing object** is part of your presentation document. Many simple drawing objects can be created using PowerPoint. A **picture** is an image such as a graphic illustration or a scanned photograph. Pictures are graphics that were created from another program and are inserted in a slide as **embedded objects**. An embedded object becomes part of the presentation file and can be opened and edited using the **source program**, the program in which it was created. Any changes made to the embedded object are not made to the original picture file because they are independent. Several examples of drawing objects and pictures are shown below.

Photograph

Graphic illustration

Drawing object

Add graphics to your presentation to help the audience understand concepts and to add interest.

Digital images created using a digital camera are one of the most common types of graphic files. You also can create graphic files using a scanner to convert printed documents, including photographs, to an electronic format.

Graphic files can be obtained from your computer or a computer network and a variety of online sources. All types of graphics, including clip art, photographs, and other types of images, can be found on the Internet. **Clip art** are simple drawings created using a graphics program. Remember that any images you locate on the Internet are protected by copyright and should only be used with permission. You can also purchase CDs or access to stock image sites containing graphics.

Additional Information

When your computer is connected to a scanner, you also can scan a picture and insert it directly into a slide without saving it as a file first.

INSERTING A PICTURE FROM YOUR COMPUTER

You want to add a graphic of a question mark you have stored on your computer to slide 2.

1

- **Make slide 2 current.**
- **Open the Insert tab.**
- **Click** Pictures **in the Images group.**
- **Navigate to the location of your student files and double-click** pp01_Question Mark1.

Your screen should be similar to Figure 1.59

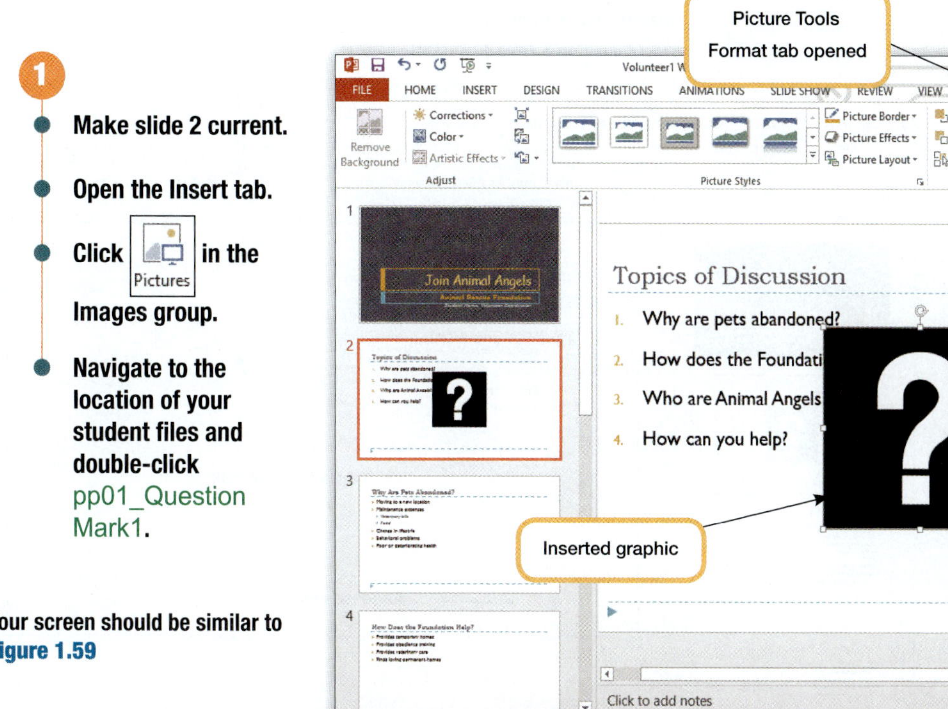

Figure 1.59

The question mark graphic is inserted on the slide and is a selected object that can be sized and moved like any other object. Because graphic objects are inserted as **floating objects** in the **drawing layer**, a separate layer from the placeholder, it may cover some of the content in the placeholder. This allows graphics to be positioned precisely on the slide, including above and below other graphics and text. The Picture Tools Format tab automatically appears and can be used to modify the selected picture object.

> **Having Trouble?**
> If you do not have an Internet connection, insert the picture pp01_Question Mark2 and skip to the next section, Deleting, Sizing, and Moving a Graphic.

INSERTING A GRAPHIC FROM ONLINE SOURCES

You decide you want to search online sources for a graphic of a question mark that might be more interesting.

1
- **Open the Insert tab.**
- **Click Online Pictures in the Images group.**

> **Having Trouble?**
> Your Clip Art task pane may already display graphics if this feature was previously used while the application was still running.

Your screen should be similar to Figure 1.60

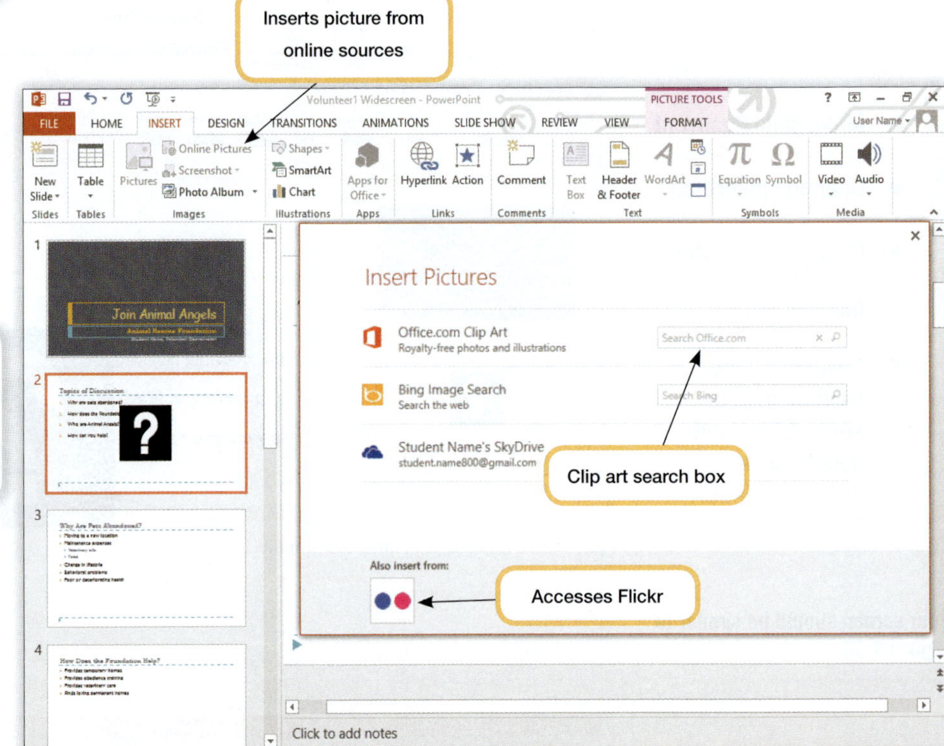

Figure 1.60

The Insert Pictures window provides several methods to locate online graphics. The first is to use Microsoft's Office.com clip art website. The second is to use Microsoft's search engine Bing to search the web. A third is to access your SkyDrive account to locate pictures you have stored at that location. Finally, you can access Flickr, an online photo management and sharing website, for pictures you have uploaded to an account with the website.

You will use the Office.com website to search for question mark pictures by entering a word or phrase that is representative of the type of picture you want to locate in the Search Office.com text box. Enter a specific search term to get fewer results that are more likely to meet your requirements.

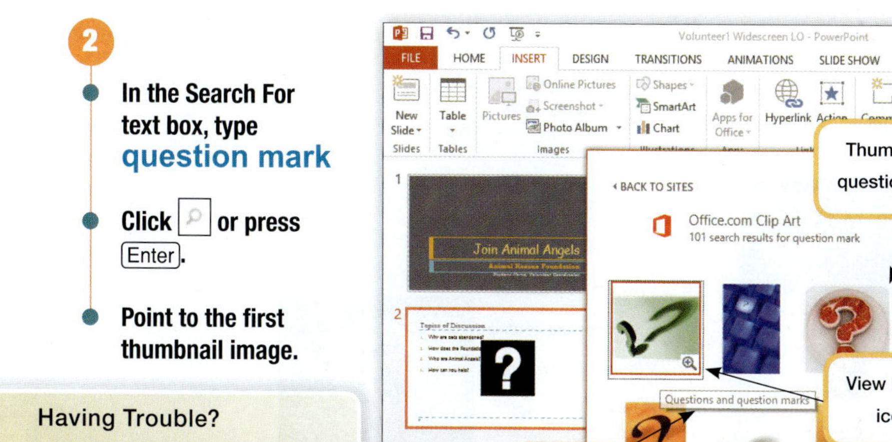

2

- In the Search For text box, type **question mark**
- Click [search icon] or press Enter.
- Point to the first thumbnail image.

Having Trouble?

Because the online selection of clip art is continuously changing, the thumbnails displayed on your screen may not match those shown in Figure 1.61.

Your screen should be similar to Figure 1.61

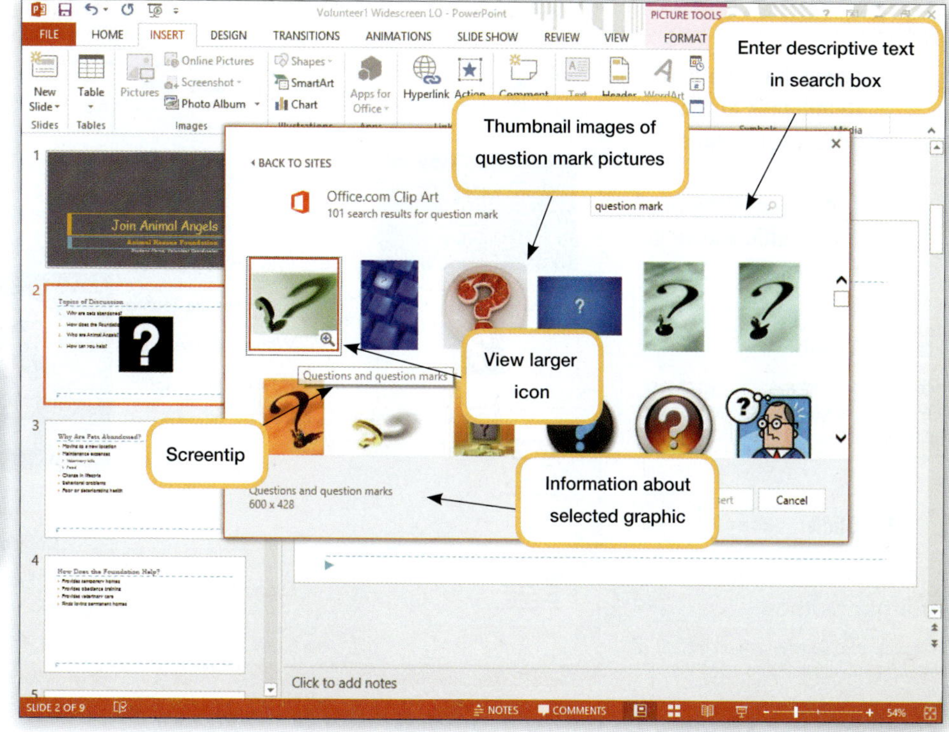

Figure 1.61

The program searches the Office.com Clip Art gallery for clip art and graphics that match your search term and displays thumbnails of all located graphics. Pointing to a thumbnail displays a ScreenTip containing a descriptive title associated with the graphic. At the bottom of the window, it displays the title and information about the picture properties. Additionally, because it is sometimes difficult to see the detail in the graphic, you can preview it in a larger size by clicking the [View Larger icon] View Larger icon.

3

- **Scroll the gallery of thumbnails to view additional images.**
- **Locate and click on the graphic shown in Figure 1.62.**

Having Trouble?

If this graphic is not available just choose a question mark graphic that you like from the gallery.

- **Click** Insert.

Another Method

You could also double-click on the graphic to both select and insert it in the slide.

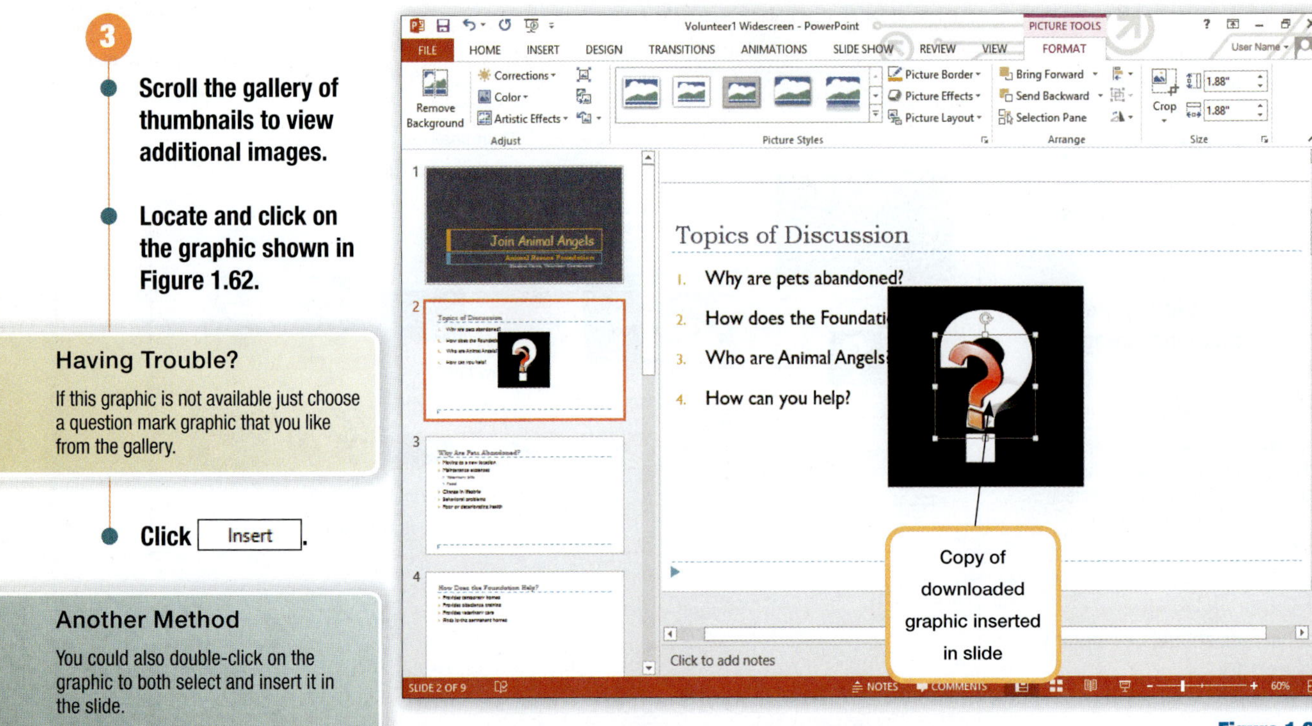

Figure 1.62

Your screen should be similar to Figure 1.62

The clip art image is downloaded and inserted in the center of the slide and may be on top of the other graphic.

DELETING, SIZING, AND MOVING A GRAPHIC

There are now two graphics in the slide. You decide to use the graphic from the online site and need to remove the original graphic. To do this, you select the graphic and delete it.

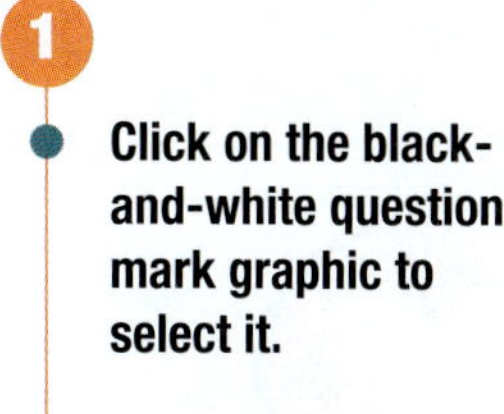

1

- **Click on the black-and-white question mark graphic to select it.**
- **Press Delete.**

Your screen should be similar to Figure 1.63

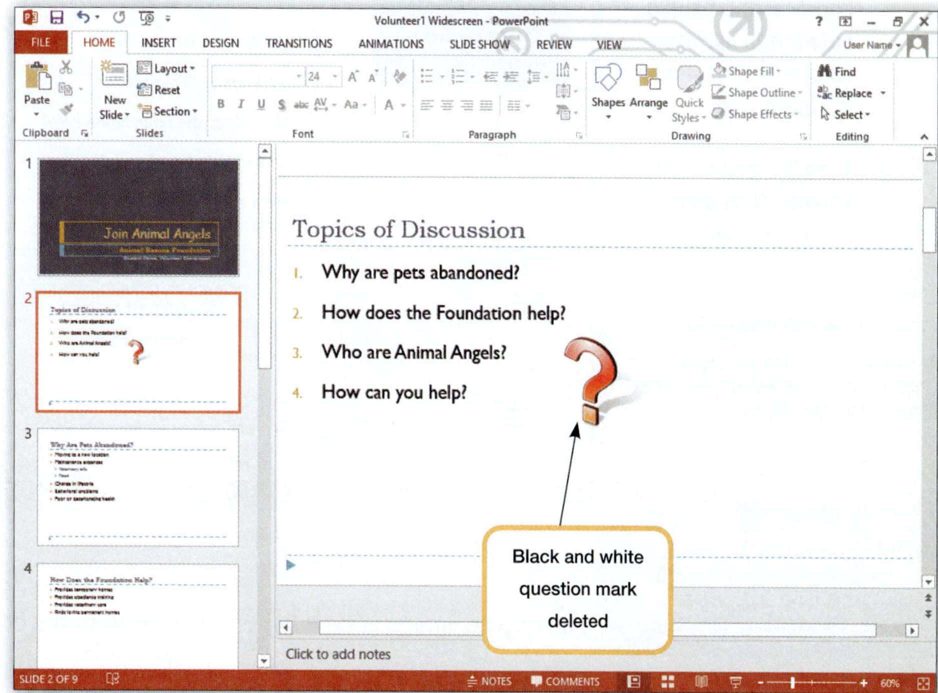

Figure 1.63

Additional Information

Be careful when increasing the size of a picture (bitmap) image, as it can lose sharpness and appear blurry if enlarged too much.

Next, you need to size and position the remaining graphic on the slide. A graphic object is sized and moved just like a placeholder. You want to increase the graphic size and move it to the right on the slide.

2

- **Click on the graphic to select it.**
- **Drag the top left corner sizing handle outward to increase its size to that shown in Figure 1.64.**
- **Drag the graphic to position it as shown in Figure 1.64.**

Additional Information

To maintain an object's proportions while resizing it, hold down (Shift) while dragging the sizing handle.

Another Method

You also can size a graphic by entering exact values in the Shape Height and Shape Width text boxes in the Size group of the Picture Tools Format tab.

Your screen should be similar to Figure 1.64

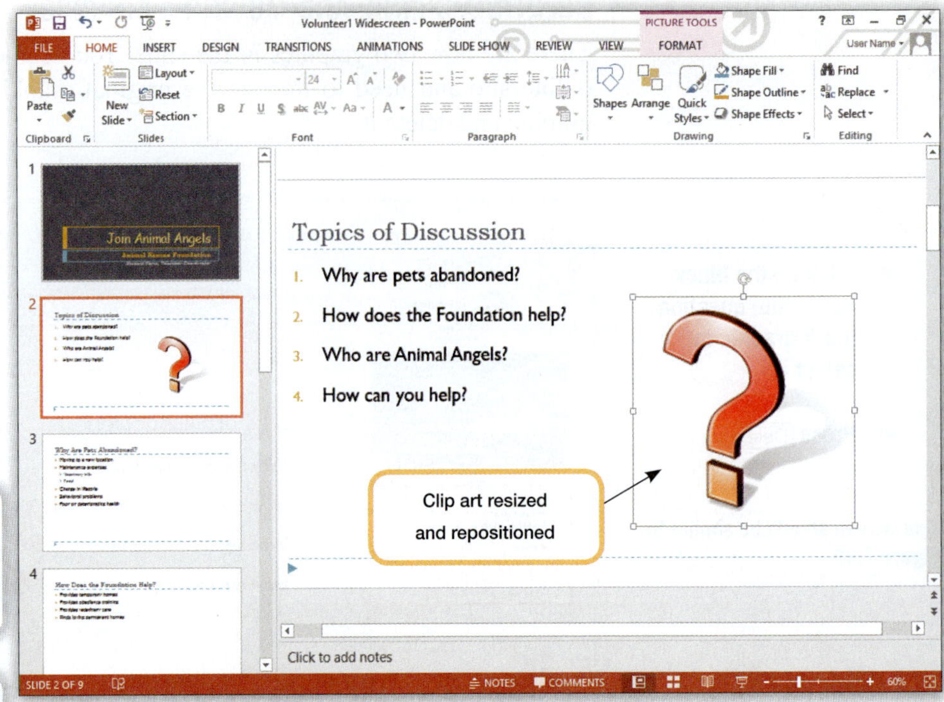

Figure 1.64

The clip art image is now larger and placed in the correct position on the slide.

ADDING GRAPHIC EFFECTS

The Picture Tools Format tab is used to customize the look of the graphic to suit your presentation. The first enhancement you would like to make is to change the color of the question mark so it coordinates with the slide design.

1

- With the clip art selected, click  in the Adjust group of the Picture Tools Format tab.
- Point to the choices in the Recolor gallery to see live previews.
- Choose Aqua, Accent color 2 Dark (second row, third from left).

Your screen should be similar to **Figure 1.65**

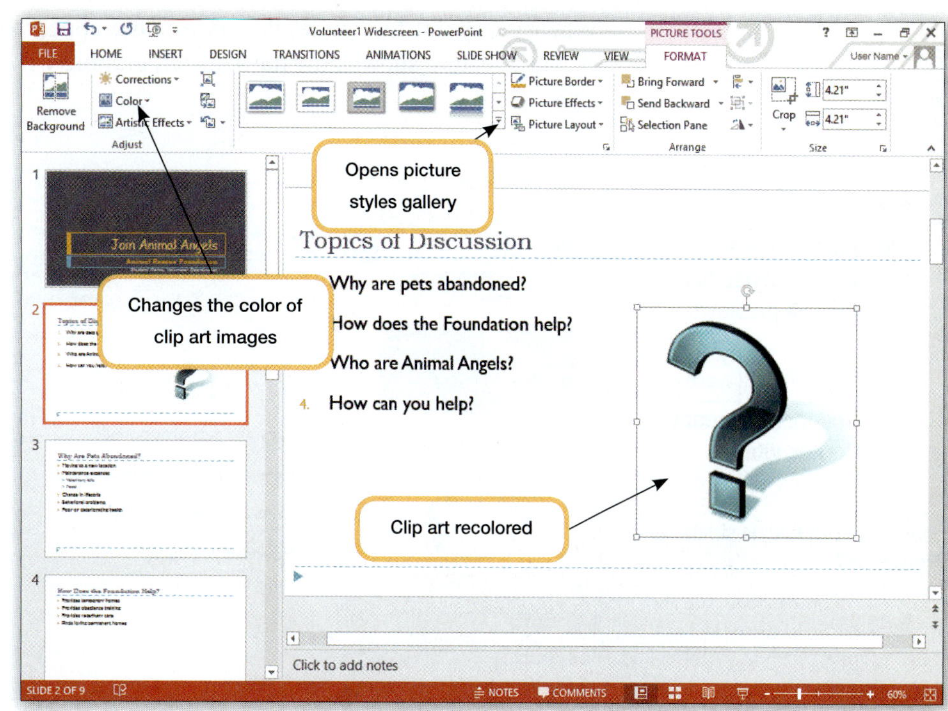

Figure 1.65

Next, you want to enhance the graphic by applying a picture style to it. A **style** is a combination of formatting options that can be applied in one easy step. In the case of **picture styles**, the combinations consist of border, shadow, and shape effects. You also can create your own picture style effects by selecting specific style elements, such as borders and shadows, individually using the Picture Effects, Picture Border, and Picture Layout commands.

2

- Click More in the Picture Styles group to open the Picture Styles gallery.

Your screen should be similar to **Figure 1.66**

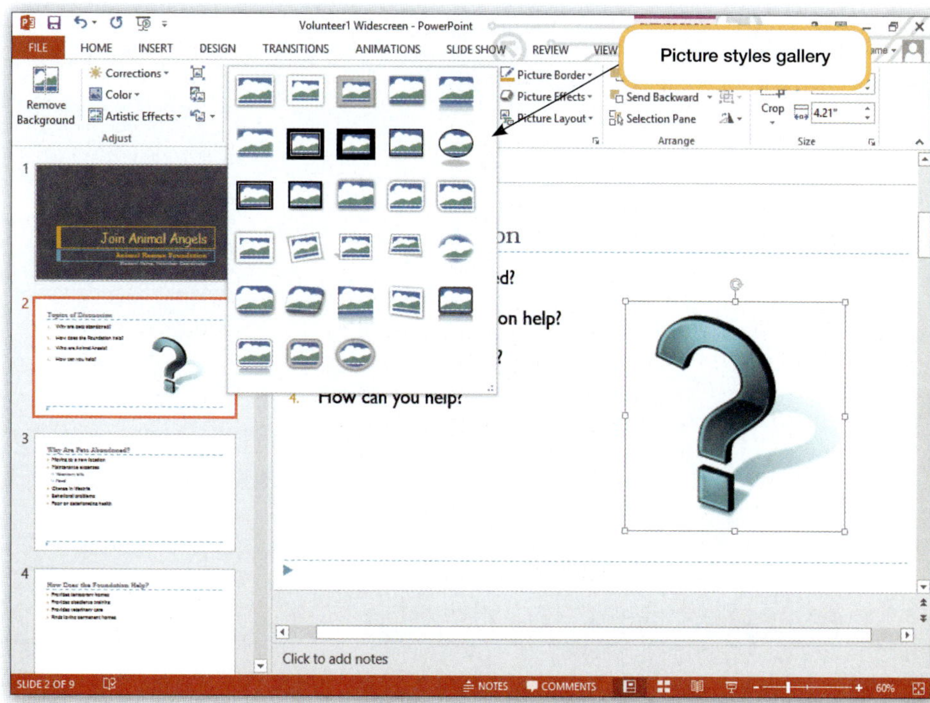

Figure 1.66

When you point to a style, the style name appears in a ScreenTip, and the Live Preview feature shows how the selected graphic will look with the selected picture style.

3

- **Point to several picture styles to see the live previews.**
- **Choose the [icon] Rounded Diagonal Corner, white.**

Your screen should be similar to Figure 1.67

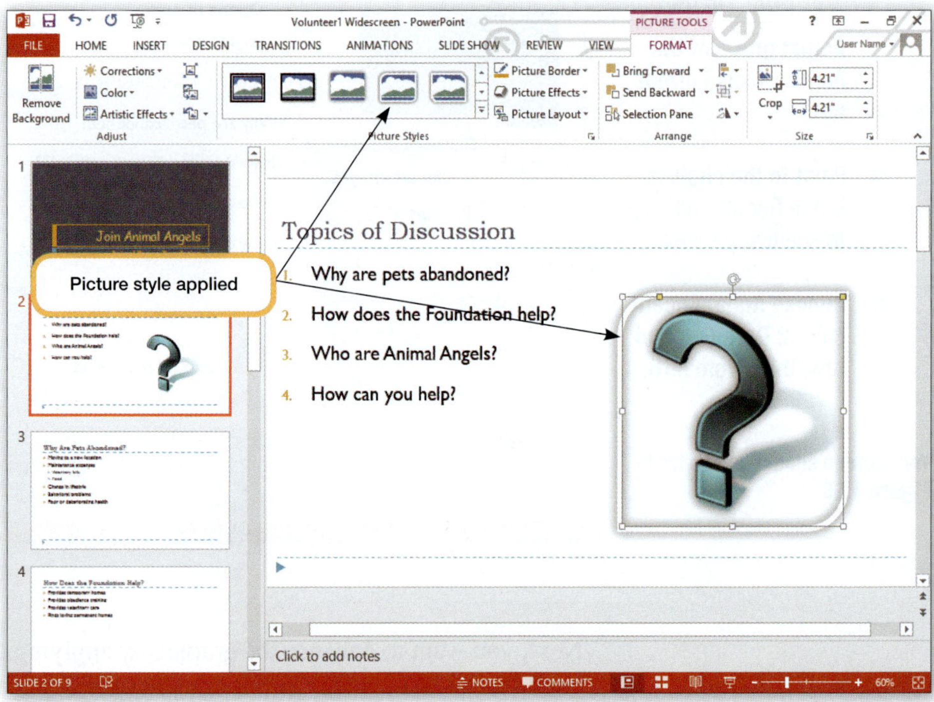

Figure 1.67

As you look at the picture, you decide to change the color of the border and remove the shadow.

4

- If necessary, select the graphic and open the Picture Tools Format tab.
- Click Picture Border in the Picture Styles group.
- Choose Gold, Accent 1 from the Theme Colors group.
- Click Picture Effects in the Picture Styles group.
- From the Shadow group, choose No Shadow.
- Click outside the graphic to deselect the object.
- Save the presentation.

Your screen should be similar to Figure 1.68

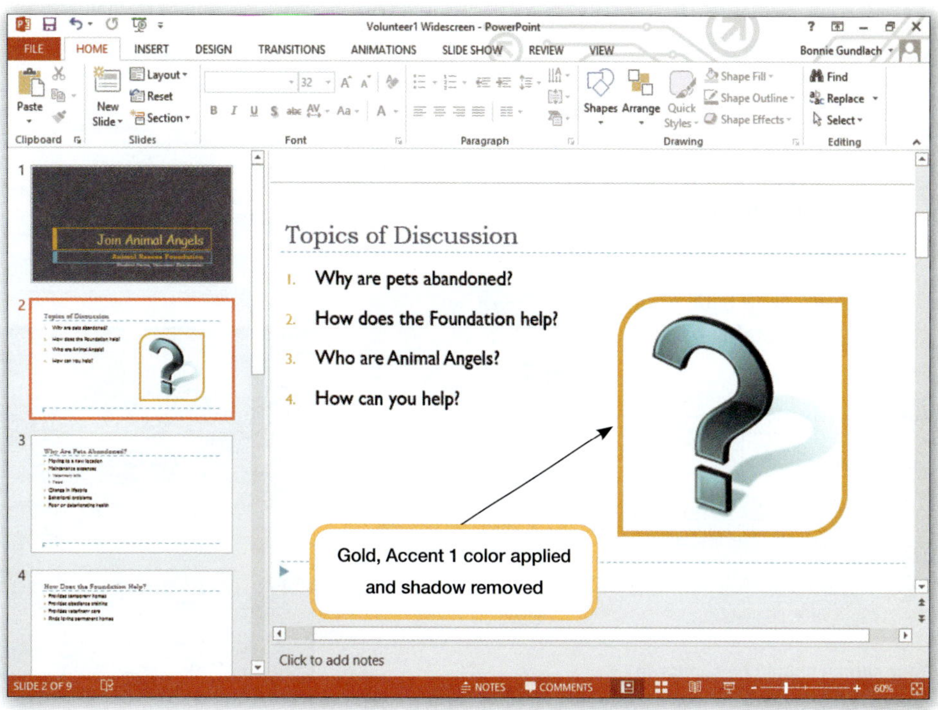

Figure 1.68

The addition of a customized graphic image gives your presentation a more polished look. Now that the slides are in the order you want and formatted, you would like to see how the presentation will look when viewed by an audience.

Rehearsing a Presentation

Rather than projecting the presentation on a large screen as you would to present it for an audience, a simple way to rehearse a presentation is to view it on your computer screen as a **slide show**. A slide show displays each slide full screen and in order. While the slide show is running during this rehearsal, you can plan what you will say while each slide is displayed.

USING SLIDE SHOW VIEW

When you view a slide show, each slide fills the screen, hiding the PowerPoint application window, so you can view the slides as your audience would. You will begin the slide show starting with the first slide.

1

Select slide 1 in the Slides pane.

Click Slide Show (in the status bar).

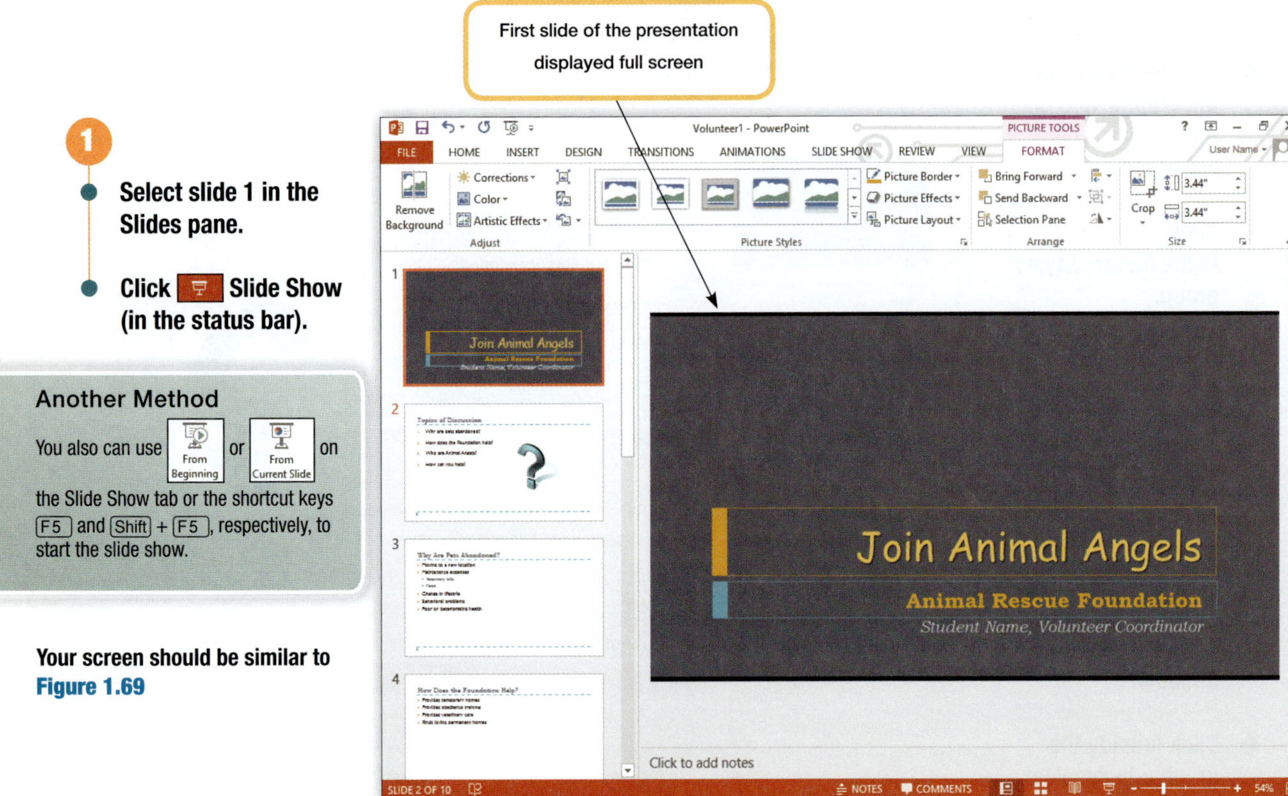

Another Method

You also can use From Beginning or From Current Slide on the Slide Show tab or the shortcut keys F5 and Shift + F5, respectively, to start the slide show.

Your screen should be similar to Figure 1.69

Figure 1.69

Additional Information

Using From Current Slide on the Slide Show tab runs the slide show beginning with the currently selected slide.

The presentation title slide is displayed full screen, as it will appear when projected on a screen using computer projection equipment. The easiest way to see the next slide is to click the mouse button. You also can use the keys shown below to move to the next or previous slide.

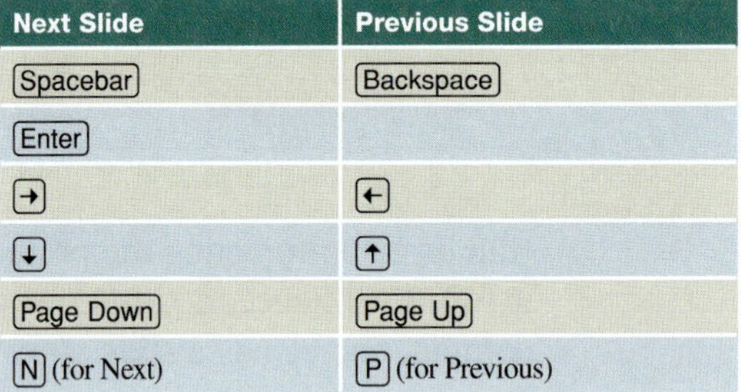

Next Slide	Previous Slide
Spacebar	Backspace
Enter	
→	←
↓	↑
Page Down	Page Up
N (for Next)	P (for Previous)

You also can select Next, Previous, or Last Viewed from the shortcut menu. Additionally, moving the mouse pointer to the lower-left corner of the window in Slide Show displays the Slide Show toolbar. Clicking or moves to the previous or next slide, and opens the shortcut menu.

2

- **Click to display the next slide.**
- **Using each of the methods described, slowly display the entire presentation.**
- **When the last slide displays a black window, click again to end the slide show.**

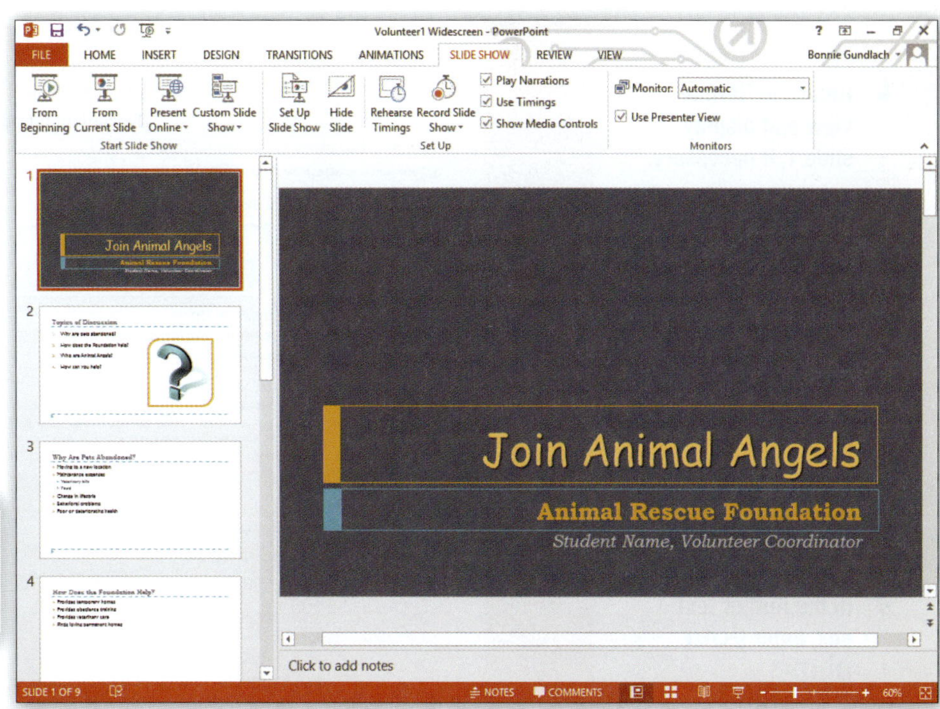

Figure 1.70

Additional Information

You can press Esc or use End Show on the shortcut menu at any time to end the slide show.

Your screen should be similar to Figure 1.70

After the last slide is displayed, the program returns to the view you were last using, in this case, Normal view.

Documenting a File

Having Trouble?

Refer to the section "Specifying Document Properties" on page IO.53 in the Introduction to Microsoft Office 2013 to review this feature.

Finally, you want to update the presentation file properties by adding your name as the author, the title, and a tag.

1

- Return to Normal view and display slide 1, if necessary.
- Open the File tab and, if necessary, click Info.
- In the Title text box, enter **Join Animal Angels**
- In the Tags text box, enter **Volunteer, Recruit**
- In the Author text box, enter **your name**
- Click anywhere outside the text box.

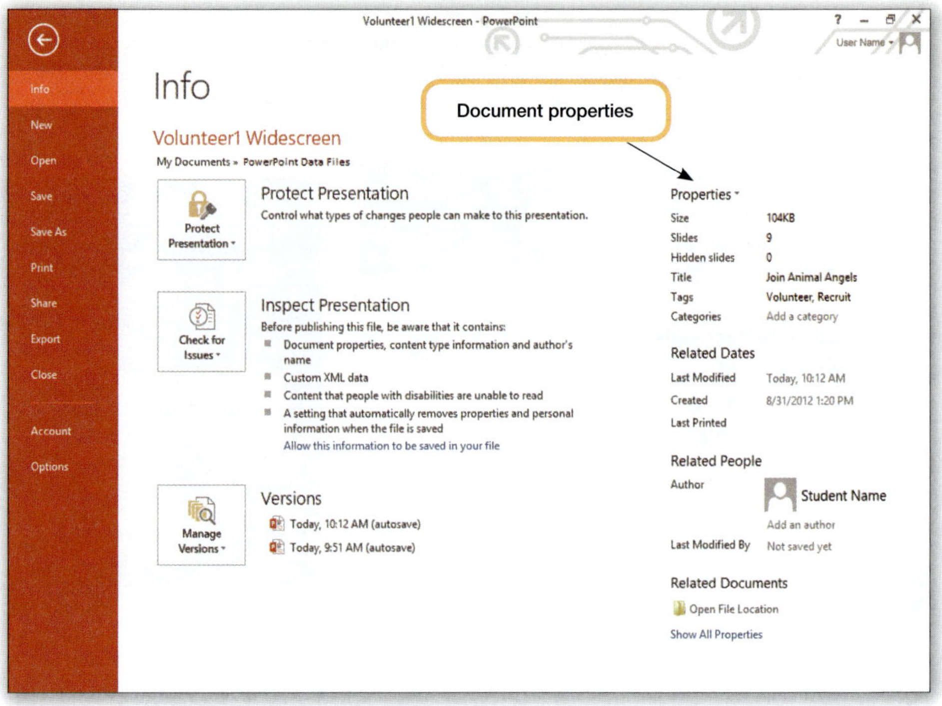

Your screen should be similar to Figure 1.71

Figure 1.71

Previewing and Printing the Presentation

Although you still plan to make many changes to the presentation, you want to provide a printed copy of the presentation to the foundation director to get feedback regarding the content and layout.

PRINTING A SLIDE

Although your presentation looks good on your screen, it may not look good when printed. Shading, patterns, and backgrounds that look good on the screen can make your printed output unreadable. Fortunately, PowerPoint displays a preview of how your printed output will appear as you specify the print settings. This allows you to make changes to the print settings before printing and reduces unnecessary paper waste.

Having Trouble?

Refer to the section "Printing a Document" on page IO.59 in the Introduction to Microsoft Office 2013 to review basic printing features.

1

Click 

from the File tab.

Your screen should be similar to Figure 1.72

Figure 1.72

The Print window displays the print options in the left pane that are used to modify the print settings. The preview area displays the first slide in the presentation as it will appear when printed using the current settings. It appears in color if your selected printer is a color printer; otherwise, it appears in grayscale (shades of gray). Even if you have a color printer, you can print the slides in grayscale or pure black and white. You want to print using the black-and-white option. The page scroll box shows the page number of the page you are currently viewing and the number of total pages. The scroll buttons on either side are used to scroll to the next and previous pages.

The other change you want to make to the print settings is to print only the first slide in the presentation. To do this, you will change the settings to print the current slide only.

Additional Information

Use grayscale when your slides include patterns whose colors you want to appear in shades of gray.

2

- If you need to select a different printer, open the Printer drop-down list and select the appropriate printer.
- Click 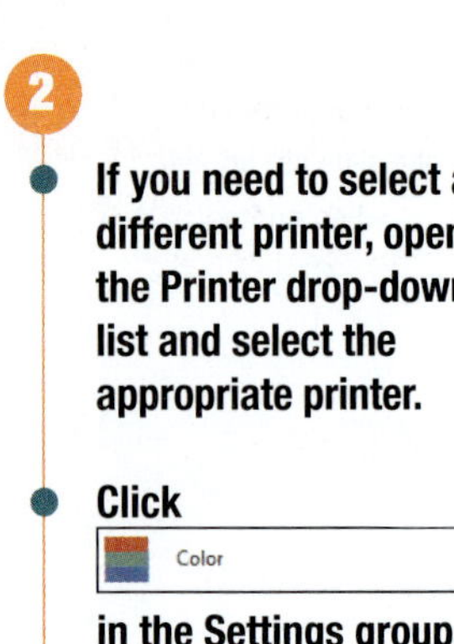 in the Settings group.
- Choose Pure Black and White.
- Click Print All Slides (Print entire presentation) in the Settings area.
- Choose Print Current Slide from the submenu.

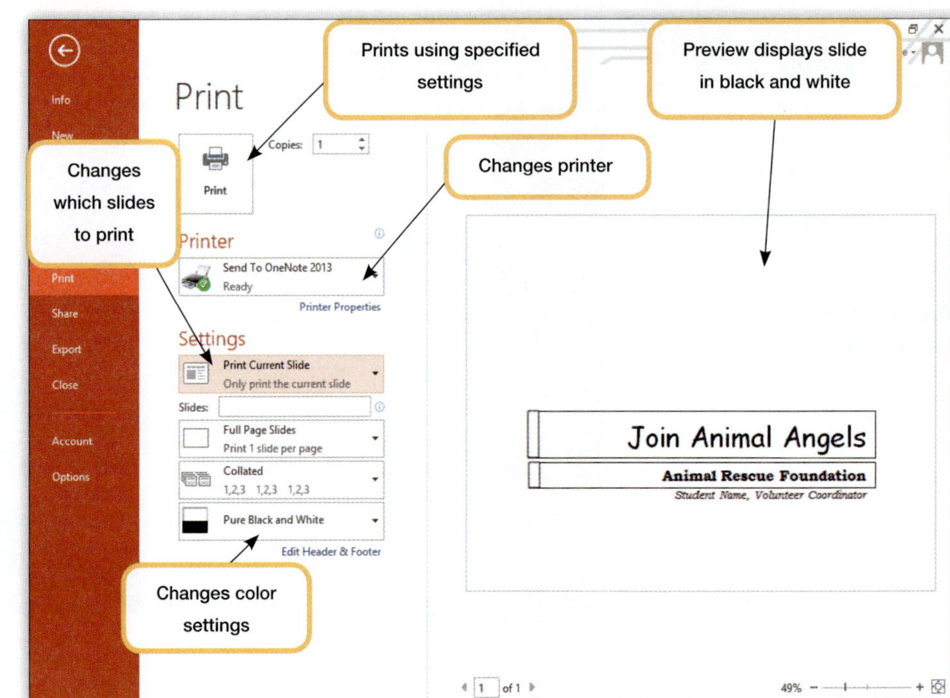

Figure 1.73

Another Method

You could also type **1** in the Slides text box to select only the title slide.

Your screen should be similar to Figure 1.73

The preview area displays how the slide will look when printed in black and white. Notice the page scroll box in the preview area now shows 1 of 1, indicating that only the first slide will be printed.

Additional Information

Please consult your instructor for printing procedures that may differ from the following directions.

3

- If necessary, make sure your printer is on and ready to print.
- Click .

A printing progress bar appears in the status bar, indicating that the program is sending data to the printer and the title slide should be printing.

PRINTING HANDOUTS

You also can change the type of printed output from full page slides to any one of the output settings described in the table below. Only one type of output can be printed at a time.

Additional Information
You will learn about notes in Lab 2.

Output Type	Description
Full Page Slides	Prints one slide on a page.
Notes Pages	Prints the slide and the associated notes on a page.
Outline	Prints the slide content as it appears in Outline view.
Handouts	Prints multiple slides on a page.

To help the foundation's director get a better feel for the flow of the presentation, you decide to also print out the presentation as a handout. The handout format will allow him to see each slide as it appears onscreen.

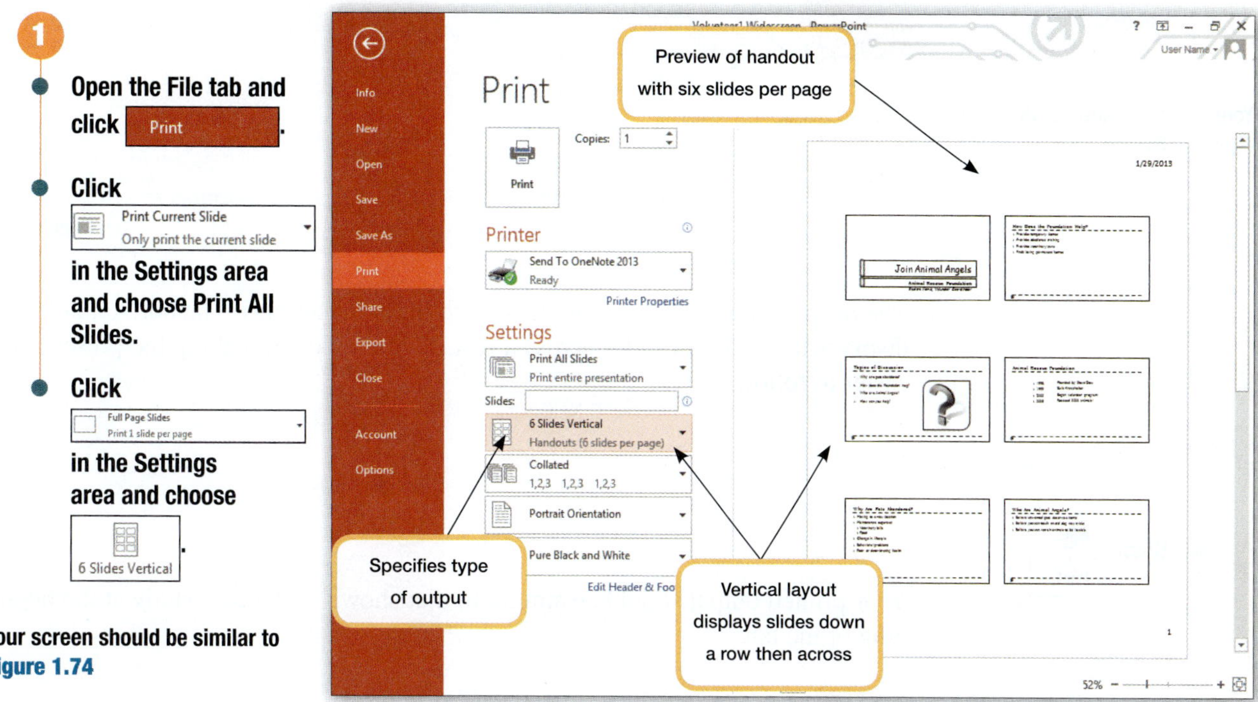

Figure 1.74

Additional Information

The Orientation setting will override the Slide Layout setting. So, even if you leave the Slide Layout setting as 6 Slides Vertical, the presentation will print horizontal to match the Orientation setting.

The preview area shows the handouts as they will print. The vertical arrangement of the slides displays the slides down a row and then across. You decide to change the orientation from the default of portrait to landscape so that the slides print across the length of the paper, to change the arrangement to horizontal, and also to increase the number of slides per page so that the entire presentation fits on one page.

2

- Click 6 Slides Vertical Handouts (6 slides per page) and choose 9 Slides Horizontal.
- Click Portrait Orientation and choose Landscape Orientation.
- Change the Color setting to Pure Black and White, if necessary.

Your screen should be similar to Figure 1.75

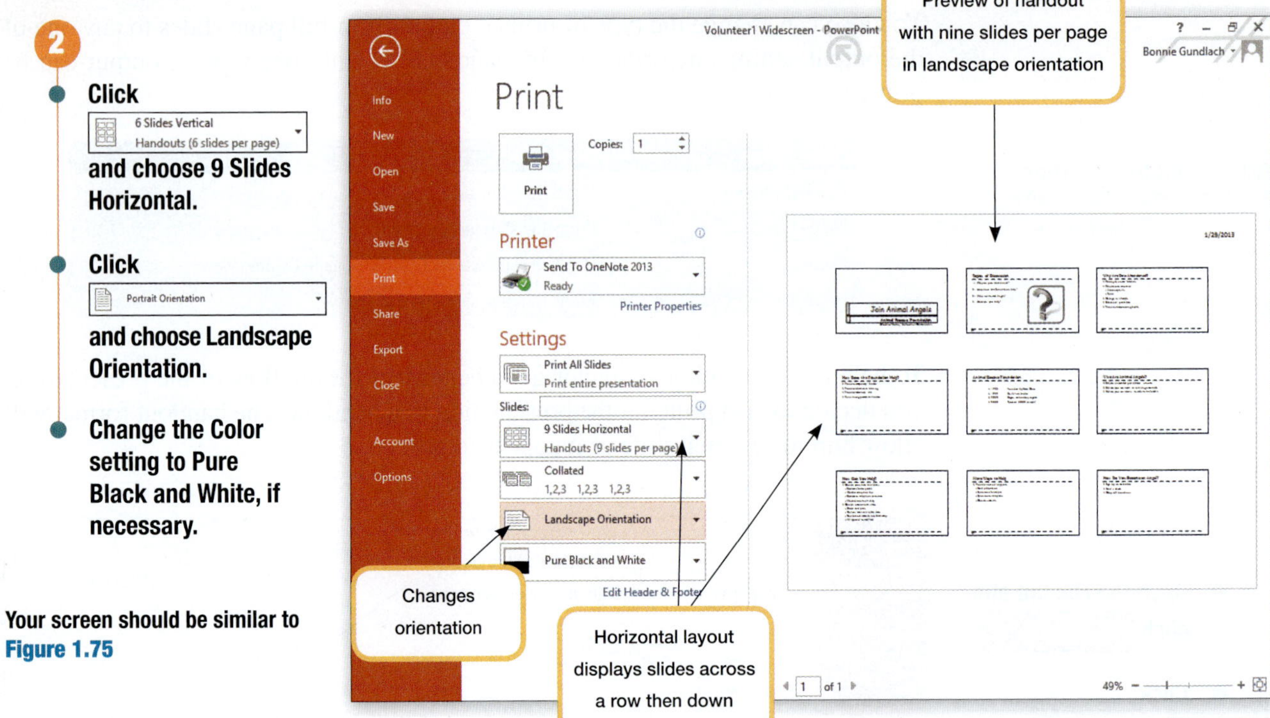

Figure 1.75

The preview area reflects your changes to the print settings. The horizontal layout displays the slides in order across a row and then down, making the presentation easier to follow.

3

- Click 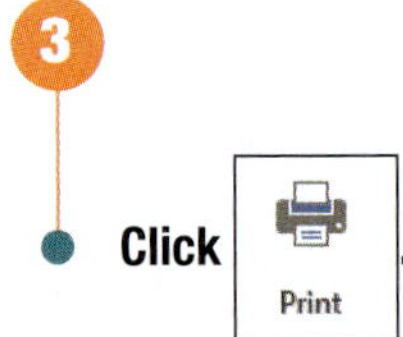.

Your printed output should be similar to that shown in the case study at the beginning of the lab.

PRINTING AN OUTLINE

The final item you want to print is an outline of the presentation. An outline will make it easier for the director to provide feedback on the overall organization of the presentation.

1

- Open the File tab and choose Print.
- Change the Color setting to Pure Black and White again, if necessary.
- Change the orientation to Portrait Orientation.
- Click

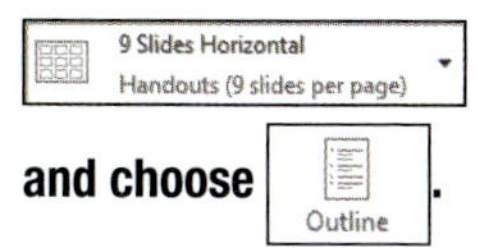

and choose Outline.
- Ensure that the correct printer is selected and ready.

Your screen should be similar to Figure 1.76

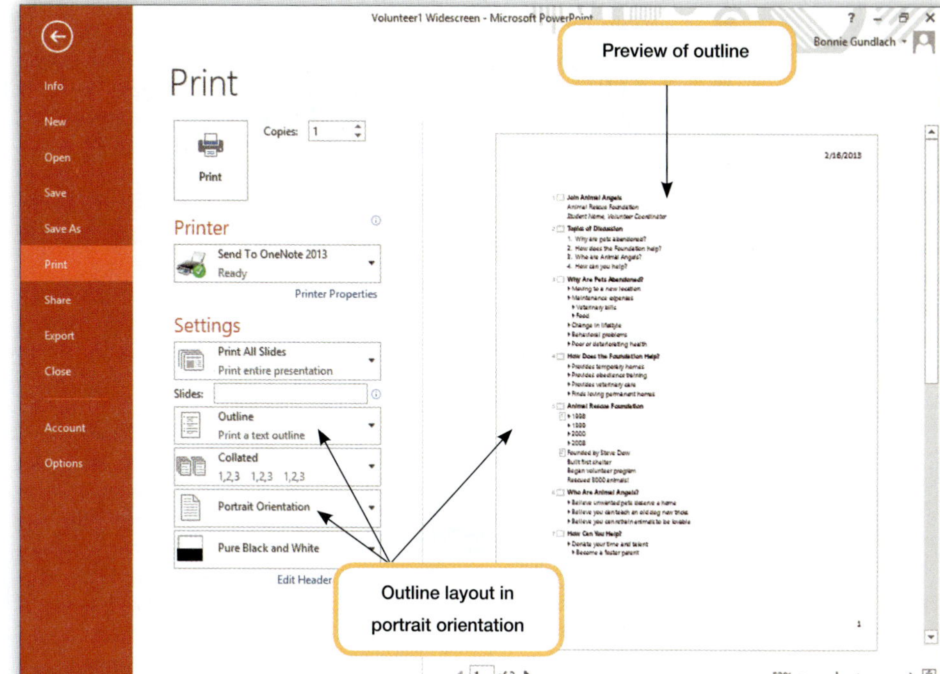

Figure 1.76

2

- Click

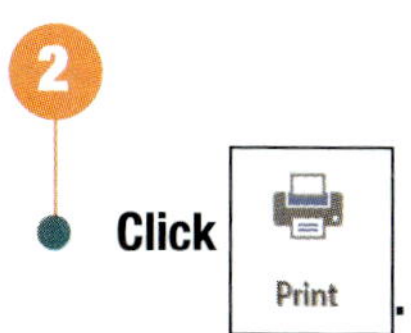

The printed outline will be a two-page document that looks similar to the preview.

Exiting PowerPoint

1

- Click ✕ Close in the title bar.
- If asked to save the file again, click Save.

You have finished working on the presentation for now and will exit the PowerPoint program.

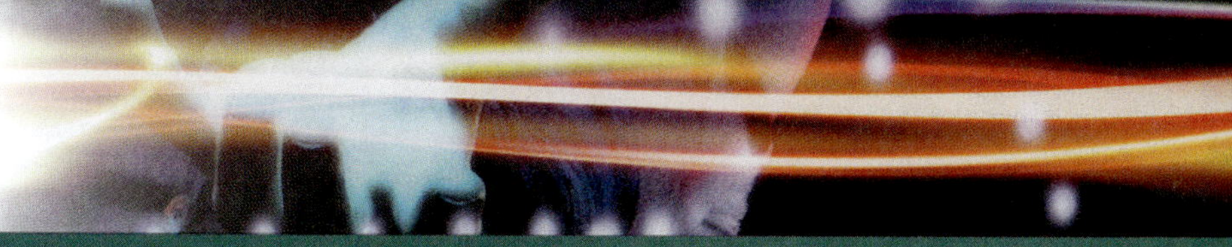

EXPLORE YOUR CAREER OPTIONS

Account Executive

Sales is an excellent entry point for a solid career in any company. Account executive is just one of many titles that a sales professional may have; field sales and sales representative are two other titles. Account executives take care of customers by educating them on the company's latest products, designing solutions using the company's product line, and closing the deal to make the sale and earn their commission. These tasks require the use of effective PowerPoint presentations that educate and motivate potential customers. The salary range of an account executive is limited only by his or her ambition; salaries range from $30,000 to more than $120,540. To learn more about this career, visit the website for the Bureau of Labor Statistics of the U.S. Department of Labor.

Lab 1 CONCEPT SUMMARY

Creating a Presentation

Slide (PP1.7)

A slide is an individual "page" of your presentation.

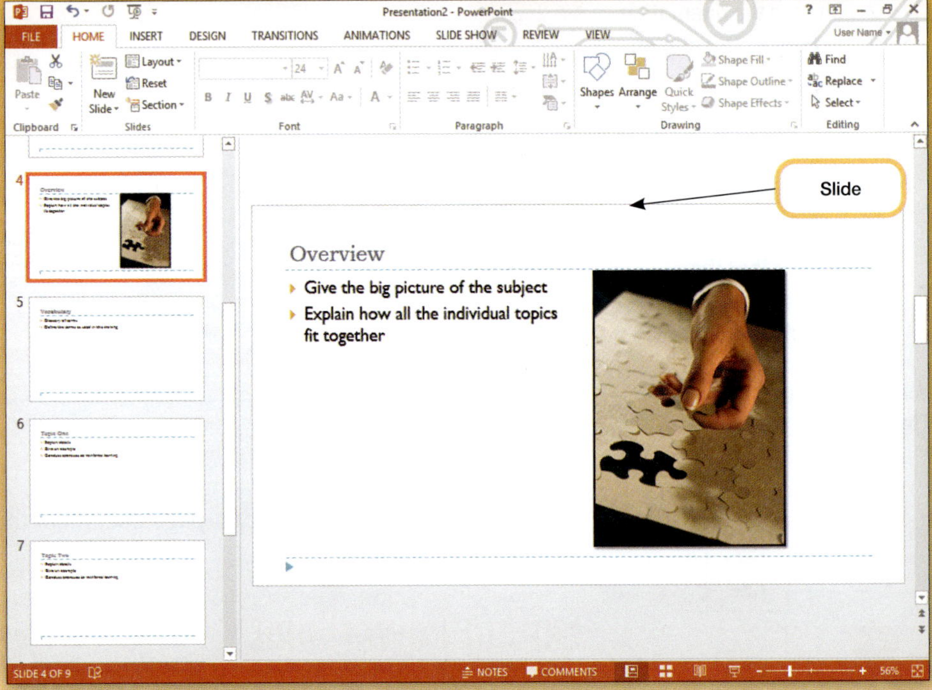

Spelling Checker (PP1.18)

The spelling checker locates most misspelled words, duplicate words, and capitalization irregularities as you create and edit a presentation, and proposes possible corrections.

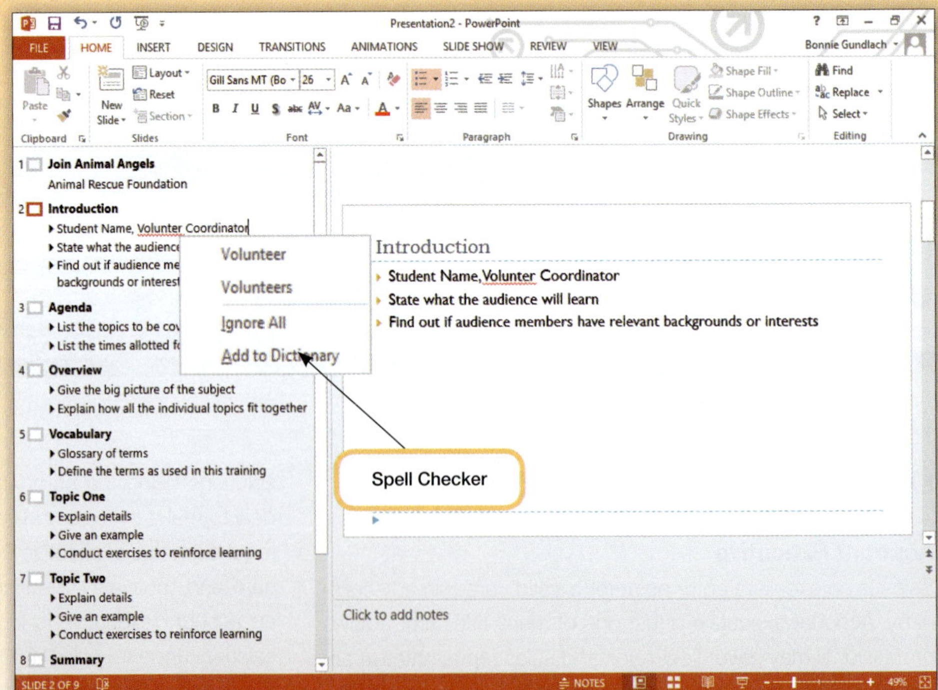

AutoCorrect (PP1.20)

The AutoCorrect feature makes some basic assumptions about the text you are typing and, based on those assumptions, automatically corrects the entry.

Layout (PP1.46)

A layout defines the position and format for objects and text on a slide. A layout contains placeholders for the different items such as bulleted text, titles, charts, and so on.

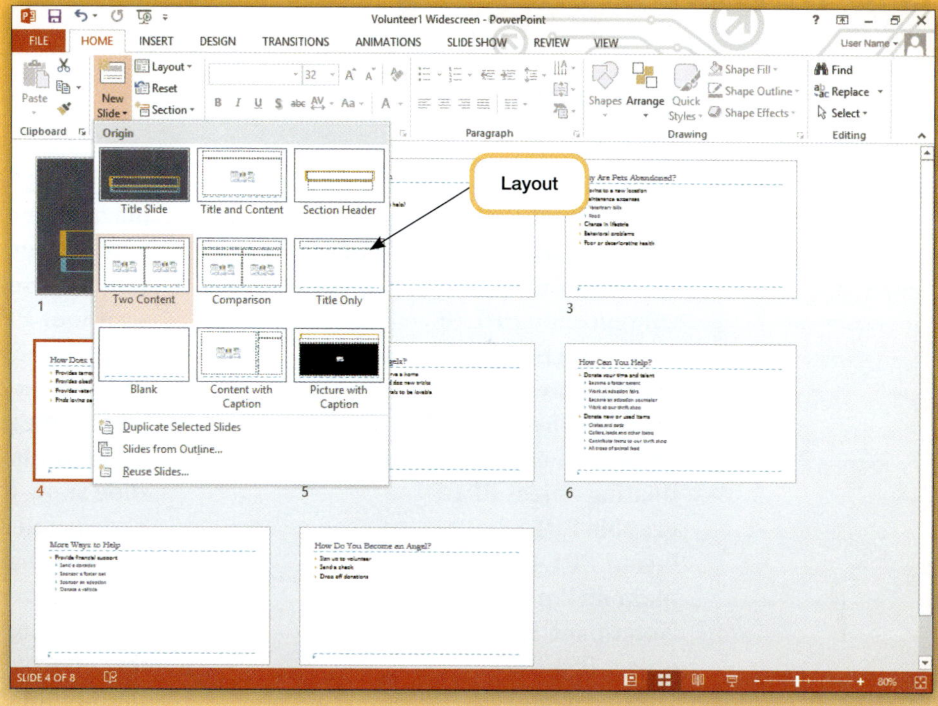

Graphic (PP1.58)

A graphic is a nontext element or object, such as a drawing or picture, that can be added to a slide.

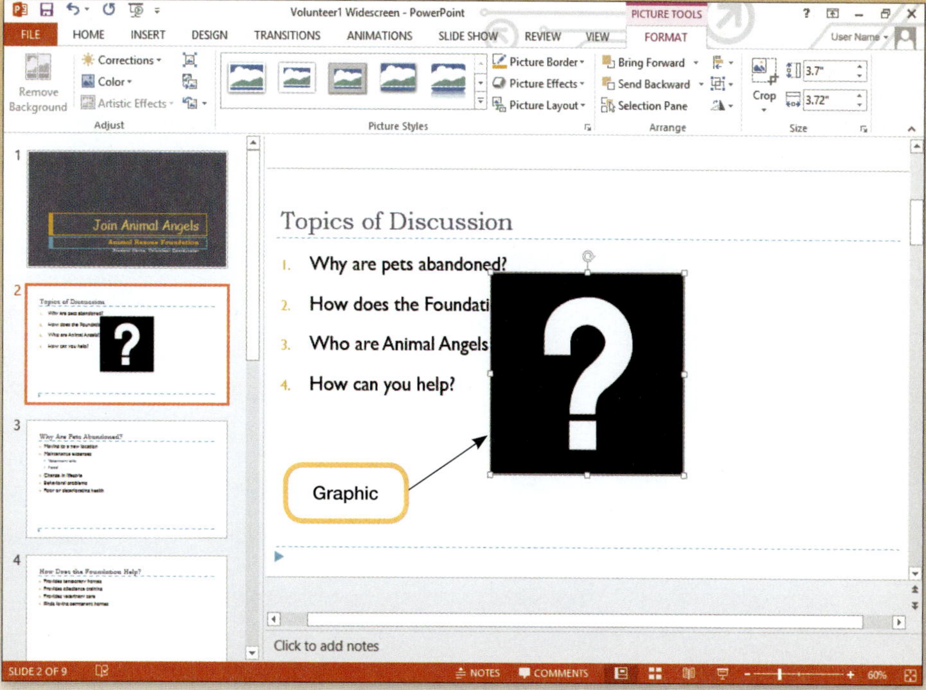

KEY TERMS

AutoCorrect PP1.20
character formatting PP1.52
clip art PP1.58
current slide PP1.10
custom dictionary PP1.18
drawing layer PP1.59
drawing object PP1.58
embedded object PP1.58
floating object PP1.59
graphic PP1.58
layout PP1.46
main dictionary PP1.18
Notes pane PP1.7
object PP1.8
Outline pane PP1.7
paragraph formatting PP1.52
picture PP1.58
picture style PP1.65
placeholder PP1.8
placeholder text PP1.8
sans serif font PP1.52
serif font PP1.52
sizing handles PP1.48
slide PP1.6
Slide indicator PP1.7
Slide window PP1.7
slide show PP1.67
Slides pane PP1.7
source program PP1.58
spelling checker PP1.18
style PP1.65
text effects PP1.54
thumbnail PP1.7
view PP1.7
widescreen PP1.7

COMMAND SUMMARY

Command	Shortcut	Action
File tab		
Save	Ctrl + S	Saves presentation
Save As	F12	Saves presentation using new file name and/or location
Open	Ctrl + O	Opens existing presentation
Close		Closes presentation
Info		Document properties
New	Ctrl + N	Opens New Presentation dialog box
Print	Ctrl + P	Opens print settings and a preview pane
Exit		Closes PowerPoint
Quick Access Toolbar		
Save	Ctrl + S	Saves presentation
Undo	Ctrl + Z	Reverses last action
Home tab		
Clipboard group		
Paste	Ctrl + V	Pastes item from Clipboard
Cut	Ctrl + X	Cuts selection to Clipboard
Copy	Ctrl + C	Copies selection to Clipboard
Slides group		
New Slide	Ctrl + M	Inserts new slide with selected layout
Layout		Changes layout of a slide
Font group		
Bookman Old St Font		Changes font type
32 Size		Changes font size

LAB REVIEW

COMMAND SUMMARY (CONTINUED)

Command	Shortcut	Action
A		Increases font size
A		Decreases font size
I		Italicizes text
U		Underlines text
S		Applies a shadow effect
A		Changes font color
Paragraph group Bullets/Bullets		Formats bulleted list
Numbering/Bulleted		Formats numbered lists
Decrease List Level		Decreases the indent level
Increase List Level		Increases the indent level
Editing group Select / Select All	Ctrl + A	Selects everything in the placeholder box
Insert tab		
Images group Pictures		Inserts picture from your computer
Online Pictures		Finds and inserts pictures from a variety of online sources
Design tab		
Customize group Slide Size		Selects standard, widescreen, or custom slide size

COMMAND SUMMARY (CONTINUED)

Command	Shortcut	Action
Slide Show tab		
Start Slide Show group		
From Beginning	F5	Displays presentation starting with the first slide
From Current Slide	Shift + F5	Displays presentation starting with the current slide
Review tab		
Proofing group		
ABC Spelling	F7	Spell-checks presentation
View tab		
Presentation Views group		
Normal		Switches to Normal view
Slide Sorter		Switches to Slide Sorter view
Outline View		Switches pane view to Outline
Picture Tools Format tab		
Adjust group		
Color		Modifies the color of the picture
Picture Styles group		
More		Opens Picture styles gallery to choose an overall visual style for a picture
Picture Layout		Changes layout of a drawing
Picture Border		Applies a border style to picture
Picture Effects		Applies a visual effect to picture

LAB EXERCISES

SCREEN IDENTIFICATION

1. In the following PowerPoint screen, letters identify important elements. Enter the correct term for each screen element in the space provided.

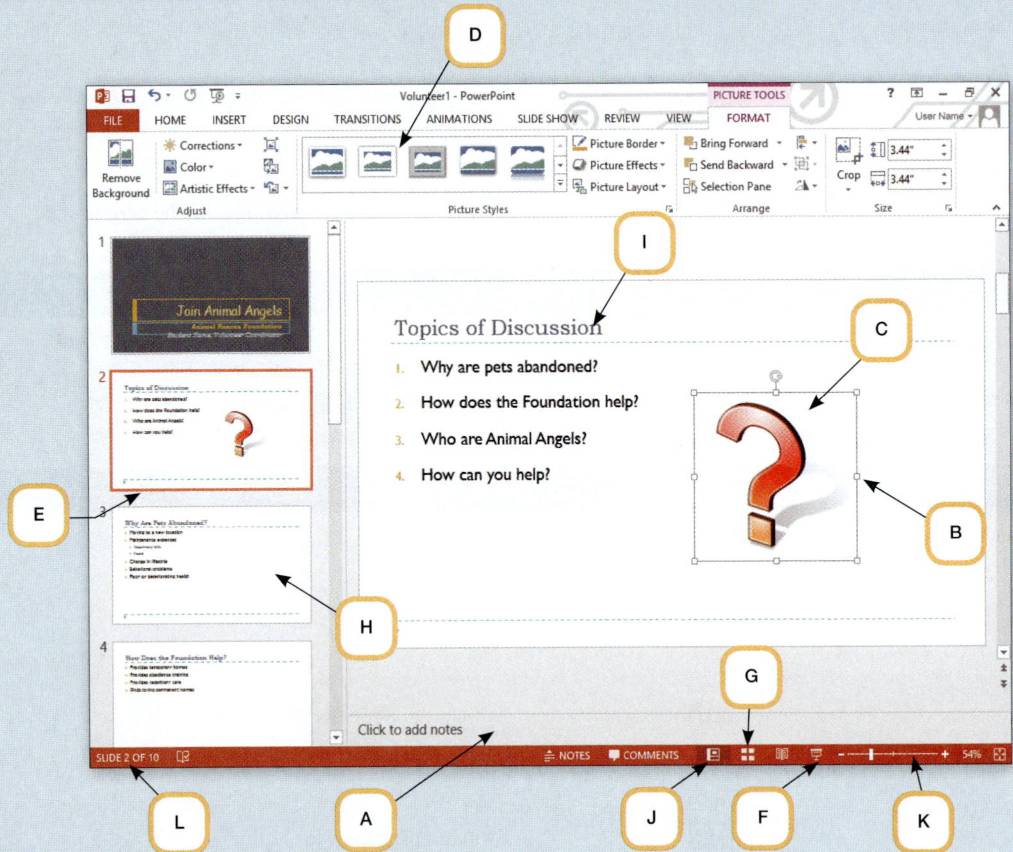

Possible answers for the screen identification are:

Graphic	Presentation template
Slide indicator	Zoom slider
Picture Styles	Sizing handle
Slide Show view	Slides tab
Slide Sorter view	Note pane
Slide title	Thumbnail
Current slide	Normal view

A. ____________ **G.** ____________
B. ____________ **H.** ____________
C. ____________ **I.** ____________
D. ____________ **J.** ____________
E. ____________ **K.** ____________
F. ____________ **L.** ____________

MATCHING

Match the item on the left with the correct description on the right.

1. thumbnail	____ a. small image
2. Notes pane	____ b. sample text that suggests the content for the slide
3. slide	____ c. moves the slide back to the previous slide in a presentation
4. placeholder text	____ d. individual page of a presentation
5. AutoFit	____ e. displays each slide as a thumbnail
6. Previous Slide button	____ f. indents a bulleted point to the right
7. Slides pane	____ g. defines the position and format for objects and text that will be added to a slide
8. template	____ h. includes space to enter notes that apply to the current slide
9. tab	____ i. a preset, formatted presentation on which you can base your presentation
10. layout	____ j. tool that automatically resizes text to fit within the placeholder

TRUE/FALSE

Circle the correct answer to the following questions.

1. The Previous Slide and Next Slide buttons are located at the bottom of the horizontal scroll bar. **True False**
2. PowerPoint will continue to indent to the same level when you demote a bulleted point until you cancel the indent. **True False**
3. Content templates focus on the design of a presentation. **True False**
4. Widescreen is the default for a new, blank presentation. **True False**
5. A layout contains placeholders for different items such as bulleted text, titles, and charts. **True False**
6. PowerPoint identifies a word as misspelled by underlining it with a wavy blue line. **True False**
7. PowerPoint limits the type of output you can print from your presentation to slides only. **True False**
8. You can rely on AutoCorrect to ensure your document is error free. **True False**
9. After the final slide is displayed in Slide Sorter view, the program will return to the view you were last using. **True False**
10. Graphics are objects, such as charts, drawings, pictures, and scanned photographs, that provide visual interest or clarify data. **True False**

LAB EXERCISES

FILL-IN

Complete the following statements by filling in the blanks with the correct terms.

1. A(n) ________________ is an individual "page" of your presentation.
2. A(n) ________________ is a miniature of a slide.
3. ________________ is a feature of PowerPoint that enables all text to fit within a placeholder.
4. ________________ is a PowerPoint feature that advises you of misspelled words as you add text to a slide and proposes possible corrections.
5. A(n) ________________ is a file containing predefined settings that can be used as a pattern to create many common types of presentations.
6. ________________ define the position and format for objects and text that will be added to a slide.
7. When selected, a placeholder is surrounded with eight ________________.
8. Use ________________ to modify the level of indented items.
9. The ________________ can be adjusted to increase or decrease the size of the slides on your computer screen.
10. The size of a(n) ________________ can be changed by dragging its sizing handles.

MULTIPLE CHOICE

Circle the correct response to the questions below.

1. The keyboard shortcut to view a slide show is ________________.
   a. F5
   b. Alt + V
   c. F3
   d. Ctrl + V
2. The step in the development of a presentation that focuses on determining the length of your speech, the audience, the layout of the room, and the type of audiovisual equipment available is ________________.
   a. editing
   b. creating
   c. planning
   d. enhancing
3. If you want to provide copies of your presentation to the audience showing multiple slides on a page, you would print ________________.
   a. note pages
   b. handouts
   c. slides
   d. outline area

4. The ________________ feature makes some basic assumptions about the text you are typing and, based on those assumptions, automatically corrects the entry.
   a. grammar checker
   b. AutoCorrect
   c. spelling checker
   d. template
5. When the spelling checker is used, you can create a(n) ________________ dictionary to hold words that you commonly use but are not included in the main dictionary.
   a. official
   b. common
   c. personal
   d. custom
6. A ________________ is a nontext element or object, such as a drawing or picture, that can be added to a slide.
   a. slide
   b. template
   c. text box
   d. graphic
7. ________________ view is used to work on most aspects of your presentation.
   a. Normal
   b. Outline
   c. Slide
   d. Slide Sorter
8. A ________________ is a file containing predefined settings that can be used as a pattern to create many common types of presentations.
   a. presentation
   b. slide
   c. template
   d. graphic
9. A(n) ________________ is an onscreen display of your presentation.
   a. slide
   b. handout
   c. outline
   d. slide show
10. ________________ displays a miniature of each slide to make it easy to reorder slides, add special effects such as transitions, and set timing between slides.
    a. Slide Show view
    b. Slide Sorter view
    c. Reading view
    d. Normal view

LAB EXERCISES

Hands-On Exercises

RATING SYSTEM

★ Easy

★★ Moderate

★★★ Difficult

STEP-BY-STEP

TRIPLE CROWN PRESENTATION ★

1. Kevin Mills works at Adventure Travel Tours. He is working on a presentation about lightweight hiking to be presented to a group of interested clients. Kevin recently found some new information to add to the presentation. He also wants to rearrange some slides and make a few other changes to improve the appearance of the presentation. The handouts of your completed presentation will be similar to those shown here.

   a. Open the file pp01_Triple Crown. Save the presentation as Triple Crown Presentation. Run the slide show.

   b. Enter your name in the subtitle on slide 1.

   c. Spell-check the presentation, making the appropriate corrections.

   d. Change the layout of slide 5 to Title Only.

   e. Move slide 6 before slide 5.

   f. Insert an appropriate photograph from online sources on slide 4. Size and position it appropriately.

   g. Insert a new slide using the Two Content layout after slide 4.

h. Enter the title **Less is More**. Insert an appropriate photograph on hiking from online sources in the right content placeholder. Move to slide 4 and select the second promoted bullet, "Where to cut weight:" and its subpoints. Cut this text and paste it in the left content placeholder of slide 5.

i. Change the layout of slide 7 to Title and Content layout. Add the following text in the text placeholder: **Contact Steve Johnson at Adventure Travel Tours or visit us on the web at www.AdventureTravelTours.com/hiking**.

j. Run the slide show.

k. Save the presentation. Print the slides in landscape orientation as handouts (four per page).

EMERGENCY DRIVING TECHNIQUES ★★

2. The Department of Public Safety holds monthly community outreach programs. Next month's topic is about how to handle special driving circumstances, such as driving in rain or snow. You are responsible for presenting the section on how to handle tire blowouts. You have organized the topics to be presented and located several clip art graphics that will complement the talk. Now you are ready to begin creating the presentation. Handouts of the completed presentation are shown here.

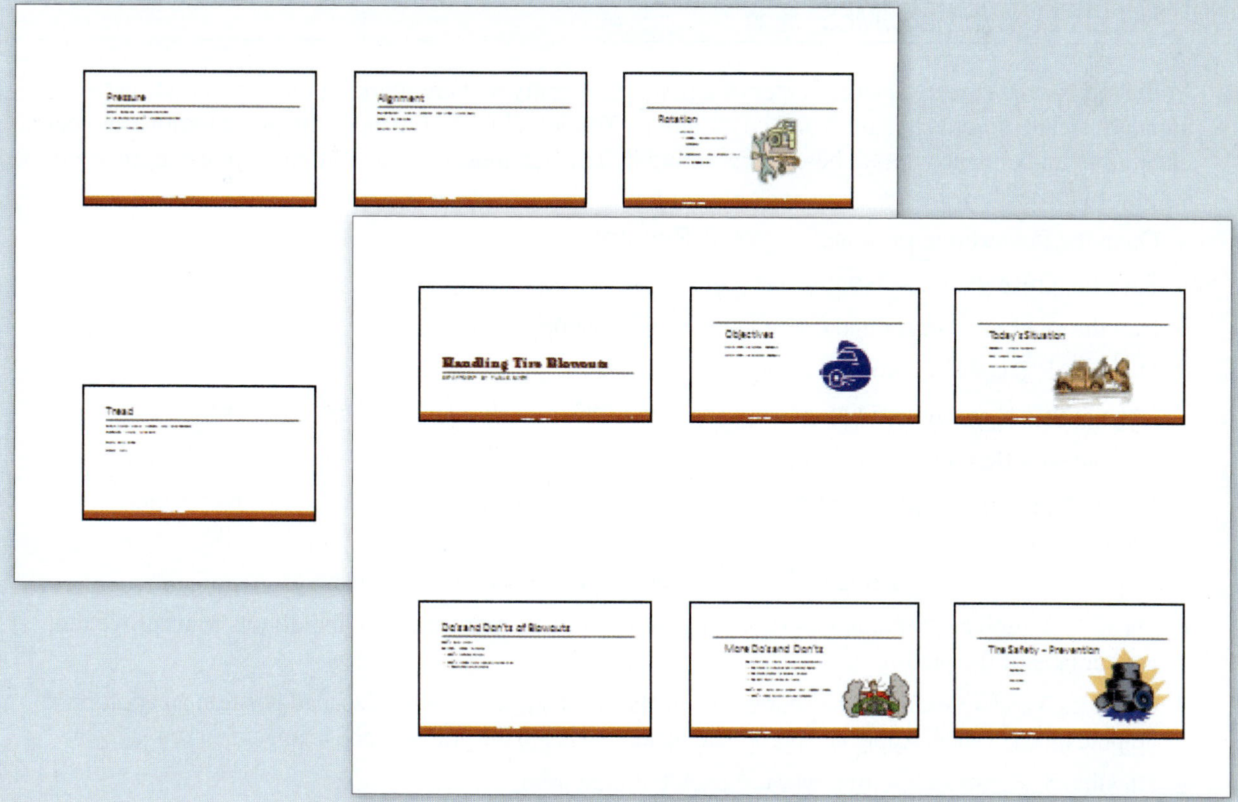

a. Open the PowerPoint presentation pp01_Handling Blowouts.
b. Save the presentation as Handling Blowouts.
c. Change format to widescreen.
d. Run the spelling checker and correct any errors.
e. On slide 1, replace "Student Name" with your name and increase font size to 16.
   Increase the title text to 54 pt.
   Change title text color to Orange, Accent 2, Darker 50%.
f. On slide 5:
   Promote bullet 4.
   Demote the last bullet.
   Resize and reposition the graphic if necessary.
g. On slide 6, insert a graphic on the theme of tires and position it in the lower-right corner of the slide.
h. On slide 3, change the color of the clip art to Orange Accent color 1 Dark. Apply the Reflected Perspective Right picture style to the clip art image.
i. Save the presentation.
j. Run the slide show.
k. Print the slides as handouts (six per page, horizontal) and close the presentation.

WRITING EFFECTIVE RÉSUMÉS ★★

3. You work for the career services center of a major university and are working on a presentation to help students create effective résumés and cover letters. You are close to finishing the presentation but need to clean it up and enhance it a bit before presenting it. The handouts of your completed presentation will be similar to those shown here.
   a. Open the PowerPoint presentation pp01_Resume.
   b. Save the presentation as Resume1.
   c. Run the spelling checker and correct any spelling errors.
   d. On slide 1: Display in Normal view.
      Change title font size to 54 pt. Modify the size of the placeholder to ensure the text fits.
      Change subtitle font size to 24 pt.
      Insert graphic image pp01_Success from your student data files location. Size and position appropriately.
      Apply an appropriate picture style to the selected graphic and change its color.
   e. On slide 2, replace "Student Name" with your name. Use picture styles and effects to improve the appearance of the picture.
   f. On slides 3 and 4, search online sources on the theme of success. Insert, size, and position an appropriate graphic on each slide. Apply an appropriate picture styles to the graphics and change their colors.
   g. On slide 5, capitalize the first word of each bulleted item.

h. On slide 6, split the slide content into two so slide 7 begins with the "Other" bulleted item. Add title to Slide 7: More Resume Headings.

i. On slide 10, reorganize the bulleted items so "Types of cover letters" is the first item.

j. To match the slide order with the way the topics are now introduced, move slide 13 before slide 11.

k. On slide 13: Break each bulleted item into two or three bullets each as appropriate.

   Capitalize the first word of each bulleted item.

   Remove any commas and periods at the end of the bullets.

l. Save the presentation.

m. Run the slide show.

n. Print the slides as handouts (nine per page, horizontal, in landscape orientation) and close the presentation.

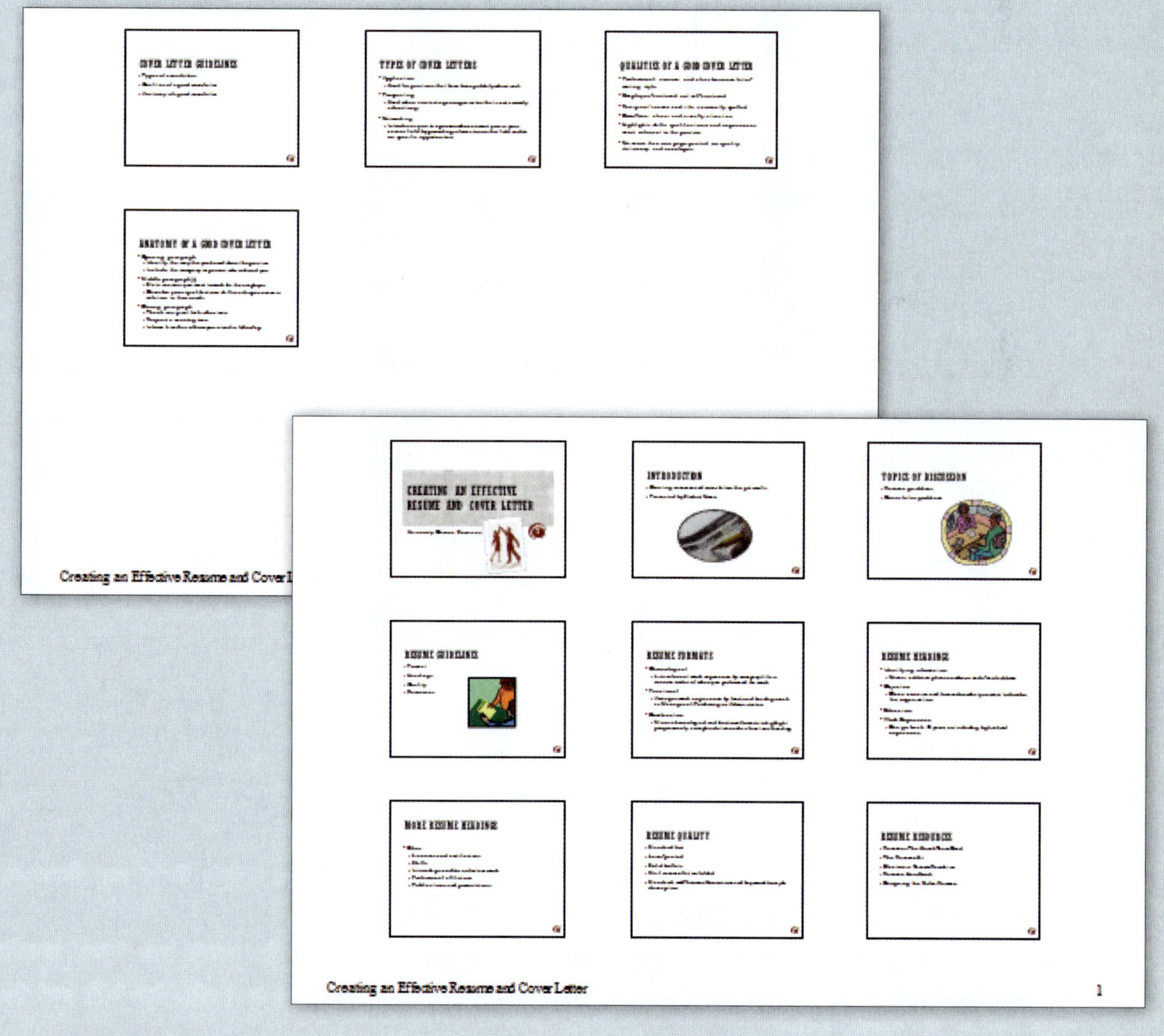

LAB EXERCISES

EMPLOYEE ORIENTATION ★★★

4. As the front desk manager of the Beachside Inn, you want to make a presentation to your new employees about the amenities your hotel offers its guests as well as information on activities and dining in the area. The purpose of this presentation is to enable employees to answer the many questions that are asked by the guests about both the hotel and the town. The handouts of your completed presentation will be similar to those shown here.

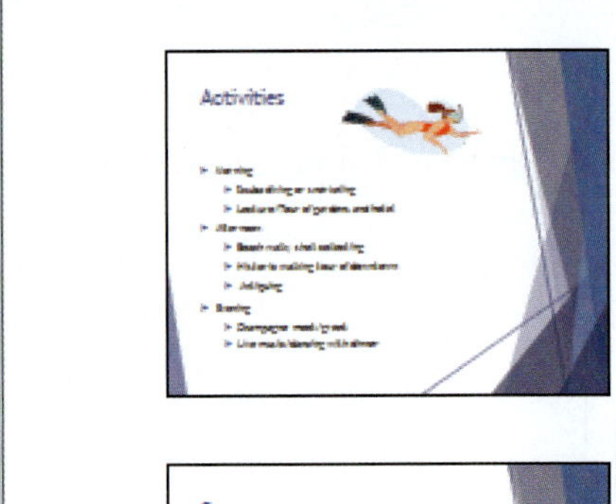

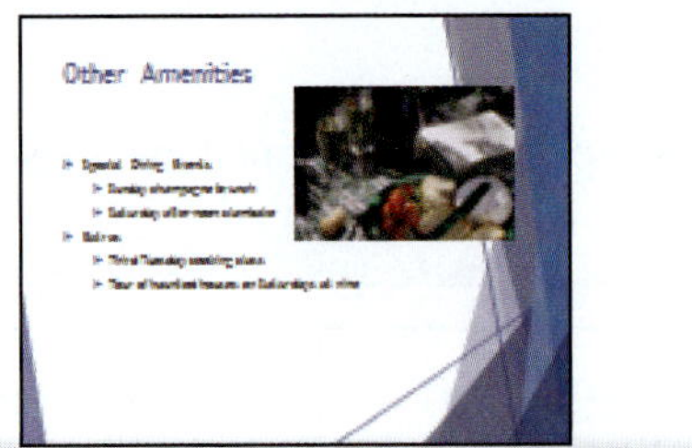

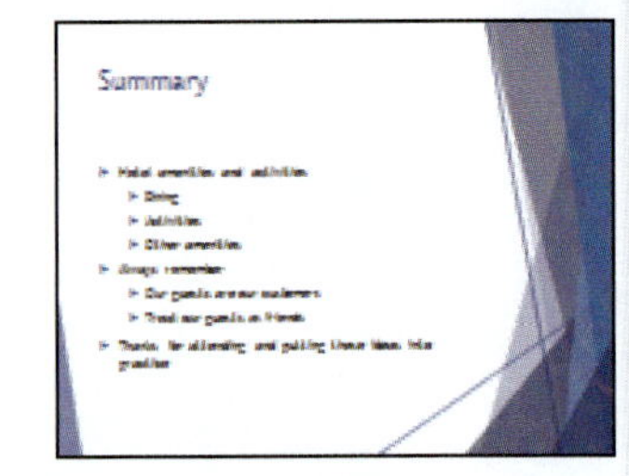

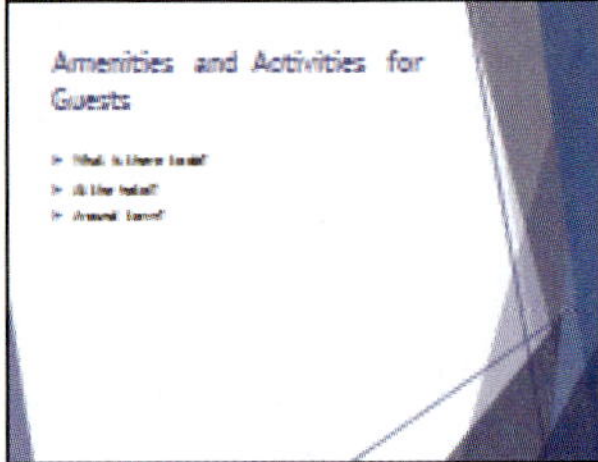

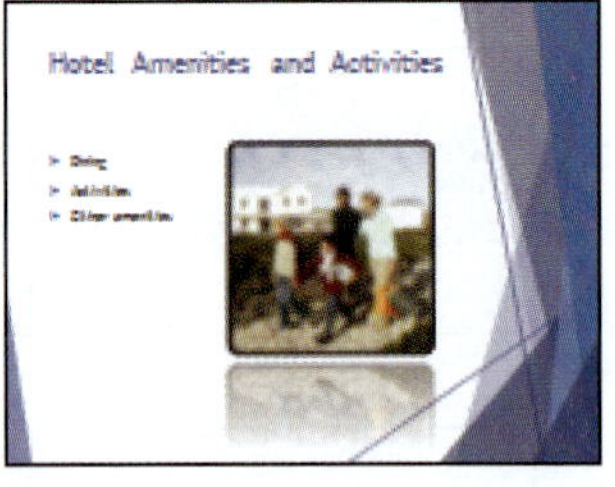

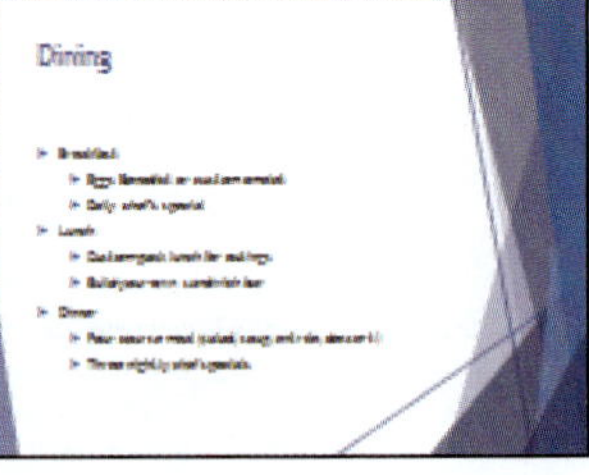

a. Open pp01_Beachside Inn.

b. Save the presentation as Beachside Inn Orientation.

c. On slide 1:

   Enter **Beachside Inn** as the company name. Set the font to Lucinda Sans; apply Bold and Shadow. Change the font color to Dark Purple, Text 2, Darker 25%, and size 54.

   Insert, size, and position a clip art image suitable as a hotel logo in place of the "your logo here" graphic.

   Insert a line after the title. Type your name on the line, and change the font to Trebuchet MS and the font size to 20. Apply italics.

d. On slide 2:

Enter **Amenities and Activities for Guests** as the title.

Enter the sample bulleted text **What is there to do?** as the first bullet.

Enter **At the hotel?** as the second bullet.

Enter **Around town?** as the third bullet.

Remove the remaining bulleted items.

e. Insert a new slide after slide 2. In this slide:

Set the layout to Title and Content.

Enter **Hotel Amenities and Activities** as the title.

Enter **Dining** as the first bullet.

Enter **Activities** as the second bullet.

Enter **Other amenities** as the third bullet.

Insert, size, and position a clip art image suitable for a hotel at the bottom center of the slide. Apply picture styles and effects.

f. Insert a new slide after slide 3. In this slide:

Set the layout to Title and Content.

Enter **Dining** as the title.

Enter **Breakfast** as the first bullet under Dining.

Enter **Eggs Benedict or custom omelet** and demote to appear as the first bullet under Breakfast.

Enter **Daily chef's special** as the second bullet under Breakfast.

Enter **Lunch** and promote to appear as the second bullet under Dining.

Enter **Custom-pack lunch for outings** and demote to appear as the first bullet under Lunch.

Enter **Build-your-own sandwich bar** as the second bullet under Lunch.

Enter **Dinner** and promote to appear as the third bullet under Dining.

Enter **Four-course meal (salad, soup, entrée, dessert)** as the first bullet under Dinner.

Enter **Three nightly chef specials** as the second bullet under Dinner.

g. Insert a new slide after slide 4. In this slide:

Set the layout to Title and Content.

Enter **Activities** as the title.

Enter **Morning** as the first bullet under Activities.

Enter **Scuba diving or snorkeling** and demote to appear as the first bullet under Morning.

Enter **Lecture/Tour of gardens and hotel** as the second bullet under Morning.

Enter **Afternoon** and promote to appear as the second bullet under Activities.

Enter **Beach walk; shell collecting** as the first bullet under Afternoon.

Enter **Historic walking tour of downtown** as the second bullet under Afternoon.

Enter **Antiquing** as the third bullet under Afternoon.

Enter **Evening** and promote to appear as the third bullet under Activities.

Enter **Champagne meet/greet** and demote to appear as the first bullet under Evening.

Enter **Live music/dancing with dinner** as the second bullet under Evening.

Add a graphic reflecting one of the mentioned activities to this slide.

h. Insert a new slide after slide 5. In this slide:

Set the layout to Title and Content.

Enter **Other Amenities** as the title.

Enter **Special dining events** as the first bullet under Other Amenities.

Enter **Sunday champagne brunch** and demote to appear as the first bullet under Special Dining Events.

Enter **Saturday afternoon clambake** as the second bullet under Special Dining Events.

Enter **Extras** and promote to appear as the second bullet for Other Amenities.

Enter **Third Tuesday cooking class** and demote to appear as the first bullet under Extras.

Enter **Tour of haunted houses on Saturdays at nine** as the second bullet under Extras.

Insert, size, and position a clip art image suitable for a hotel at the bottom center of the slide. Apply picture styles and effects.

i. Delete slides 7 through 13.

j. On the Summary slide 7.

Enter **Hotel amenities and activities** as the first bullet under Summary.

Enter **Dining** and demote to appear as the first bullet under Hotel amenities and activities.

Enter **Activities** as the second bullet under Hotel amenities and activities.

Enter **Other amenities** as the third bullet under Hotel amenities and activities.

Enter **Always remember** and promote to appear as the second bullet under Summary.

Enter **Our guests are our customers** and demote to appear as the first bullet under Always remember.

Enter **Treat our guests as friends** as the second bullet under Always remember.

Enter **Thanks for attending and putting these ideas into practice** and promote to appear as the third bullet under Summary.

Delete any remaining bullet placeholders.

k. Save the presentation.

l. Run the slide show.

m. Print the slides as handouts (four per page, horizontal, in landscape orientation).

WORKPLACE ISSUES ★★★

5. Tim is preparing for his lecture on "Workplace Issues" for his Introduction to Computers class. He uses PowerPoint to create presentations for each of his lectures. He has organized the topics to be presented, and located several clip art graphics that will complement the lecture. He is now ready to begin creating the presentation. Several slides of the completed presentation are shown here.

   a. Open a new presentation using the Training Presentation template. If you don't have access to the Internet, you can use the file pp01_Training.

   b. Save the presentation as Workplace Issues.

   c. On slide 1:

      Change the title to **Workplace Issues - Lecture 4**. Change the font size to 54 and apply a bold effect.

      Change **Your Name** to your name. Change the font size of this line to 28.

      Insert, size, and position a graphic image suitable for the theme of an office meeting. Apply a picture style to the image.

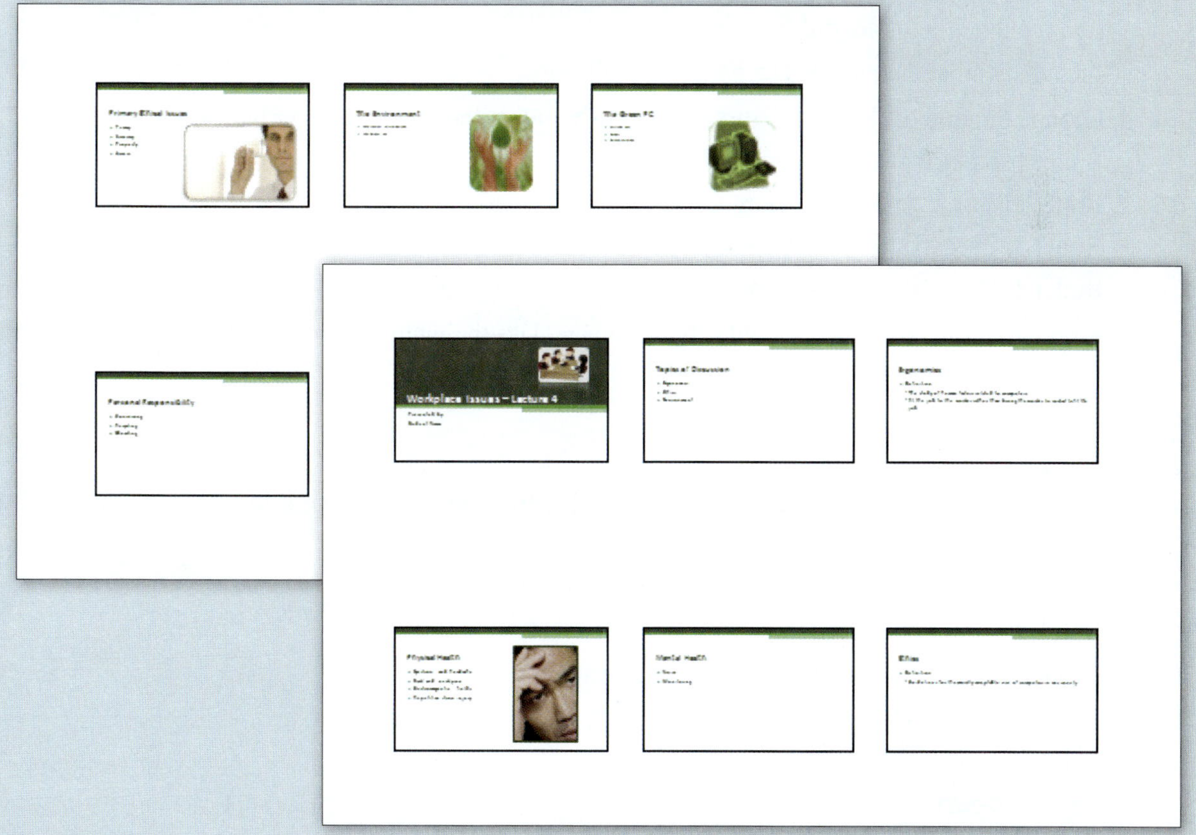

LAB EXERCISES

d. On slide 2:

Enter **Topics of Discussion** as the title text.

Enter **Ergonomics** as bullet 1.

Enter **Ethics** as bullet 2.

Enter **Environment** as bullet 3.

e. On slide 3:

Enter **Ergonomics** as the title.

Enter **Definition** as the first bullet.

Enter **Fit the job to the worker rather than forcing the worker to contort to fit the job** as the second bullet.

Enter **The study of human factors related to computers** as the third bullet.

Delete the last bullet.

f. Change the order of bullets 2 and 3 on slide 3.

Demote bullets 2 and 3.

g. On slide 4:

Change the title to **Mental Health**.

Include two bulleted items: **Noise** and **Monitoring**.

h. Change the title of slide 5 to **Physical Health** and include the following bulleted items:

Bullet 1: **Eyestrain and headache**

Bullet 2: **Back and neck pain**

Bullet 3: **Electromagnetic fields**

Bullet 4: **Repetitive strain injury**

Insert, size, and position a suitable clip art image. Use the picture formatting tools to customize the image to suit the presentation.

i. On slide 6:

Change the title to **Ethics**.

Include two bullets: **Definition** and **Guidelines for the morally acceptable use of computers in our society**.

Demote bullet 2.

Delete the third bullet.

j. Change the title of slide 7 to **Primary Ethical Issues**.

Enter **Privacy** as bullet 1.

Enter **Accuracy** as bullet 2.

Enter **Property** as bullet 3.

Enter **Access** as bullet 4.

Insert, size, and position a suitable clip art image. Use the picture formatting tools to customize the image to suit the presentation.

k. Insert a new Two Content layout slide between slides 7 and 8. On the new slide 8:

Enter **The Environment** as the title.

Enter **The Energy Star Program** as the first bullet.

Enter **The Green PC** as the second bullet.

In the right placeholder, insert, size, and position a suitable graphic. Use the picture formatting tools to customize the image to suit the presentation.

l. Create a duplicate of slide 8. On the new slide 9:

Enter **The Green PC** as the title.

Enter **System Unit** as the first bullet.

Enter **Display** as the second bullet.

Enter **Manufacturing** as the third bullet.

In the right placeholder, insert, size, and position an appropriate graphic.

m. Add a new slide after slide 9. Use the Title and Content layout.

Enter **Personal Responsibility** as the title.

Enter **Conserving** as the first bullet.

Enter **Recycling** as the second bullet.

Enter **Educating** as the third bullet.

n. In Slide Sorter view, move slide 5 before slide 4.

o. Delete slides 11-17.

p. Save the presentation.

q. Run the slide show.

r. Print the slides as handouts (six per page in landscape orientation).

ON YOUR OWN

INTERNET POLICY PRESENTATION ★

1. You are working in the information technology department at International Sales Incorporated. Your manager has asked you to give a presentation on the corporation's Internet policy to the new-hire orientation class. Create your presentation with PowerPoint, using the information in the Word file pp01_Internet Policy as a resource. Use a template of your choice. When you are done, run the spelling checker, then save your presentation as Internet Policy and print it.

LAB EXERCISES

TELEPHONE TRAINING COURSE ★★

2. You are a trainer with Super Software, Inc. You received a memo from your manager alerting you that many of the support personnel are not using proper telephone protocol or obtaining the proper information from customers who call in. Your manager has asked you to conduct a training class that covers these topics. Using the Word document pp01_Memo data file as a resource, prepare the slides for your class. When you are done, save the presentation as Phone Etiquette and print the handouts. Be sure to use a design theme, graphics, and widescreen format.

VISUAL AIDS ★★

3. You are a trainer with Super Software, Inc. Your manager has asked you to prepare a presentation on various visual aids that may be used in presentations. Using the pp01_VisualAids data file as a resource, create an onscreen presentation using an appropriate template. Select a widescreen template, or modify the template you like to widescreen so your presentation can be showcased with new technology. Add graphics that illustrate each type of visual aid. Include your name on the title slide. When you are done, save the presentation as Presentation Aids and print the handouts.

WEB DESIGN PROPOSAL ★★★

4. Your company wants to create a website, but it is not sure whether to design its own or hire a web design firm to do it. You have been asked to create a presentation to management relaying the pros and cons of each approach. To gather information, search the web for the topic "web design," and select some key points about designing a web page from one of the "how-to" or "tips" categories. Use these points to create the first part of your presentation, and call it something like "Creating Our Own web Page." Then search the web for the topic "web designers," and select two web design firms. Pick some key points about each firm (for example, websites they have designed, design elements they typically use, and/or their design philosophy). Finally, include at least one slide that lists the pros and cons of each approach. Include your name on the title slide. When your presentation is complete, save it as Web Design and print the slides as handouts.

   You will expand on this presentation in On Your Own Exercise 4 of Lab 2.

CAREERS WITH ANIMALS ★★★

5. You have been volunteering at the Animal Rescue Foundation. The director has asked you to prepare a presentation on careers with animals to present to local schools in hopes that some students will be inspired to volunteer at the foundation. Using the Word document pp01_Animal Careers data file as a resource, create the presentation. Add photos or other graphics where appropriate. When you are done, save the presentation as Careers with Animals and print the handouts.

Modifying and Refining a Presentation Lab 2

Objectives

After completing this lab, you will know how to:

1. Find and replace text.
2. Create and enhance a table.
3. Crop and enhance graphic objects.
4. Create and enhance shapes.
5. Create a text box.
6. Change the theme.
7. Modify slide masters.
8. Add animation, sound, and transitions.
9. Control a slide show.
10. Add speaker notes.
11. Add and hide slide footers.
12. Use Presenter view.
13. Customize print settings.

CASE STUDY

Animal Rescue Foundation

The Animal Rescue Foundation director was very impressed with your first draft of the presentation to recruit volunteers and asked to see the presentation onscreen. While viewing it together, you explained that you plan to make many more changes to improve the appearance of the presentation. For example, you plan to use a different color theme and to include more art and other graphic features to enhance the appearance of the slides. You also explained that you will add more action to the slides using the special effects included with PowerPoint to keep the audience's attention.

The director suggested that you include more information on ways that volunteers can help. Additionally, because the organization has such an excellent adoption rate, the director wants you to include a table to illustrate the success of the adoption program.

PowerPoint 2013 gives you the design and production capabilities to create a first-class onscreen presentation. These features include artist-designed layouts and color themes that give your presentation a professional appearance. In addition, you can add your own personal touches by modifying text attributes, incorporating art or graphics, and including animation to add impact, interest, and excitement to your presentation.

Displaying information in tables makes data easy to understand.

Pictures add interest and enhance the appearance of the slide.

Animations and transitions add action to a slide show.

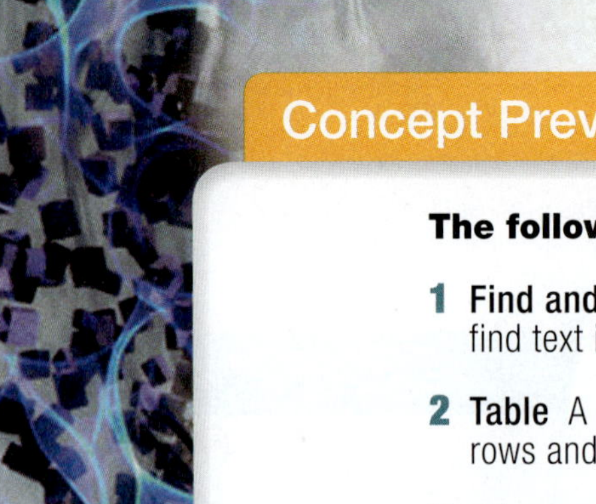

Concept Preview

The following concepts will be introduced in this lab:

1. **Find and Replace** To make editing easier, you can use the Find and Replace feature to find text in a presentation and replace it with other text.
2. **Table** A table is used to organize information into an easy-to-read format of horizontal rows and vertical columns.
3. **Alignment** Alignment controls the position of text entries within a space.
4. **Theme** A theme is a predefined set of formatting choices that can be applied to an entire document in one simple step.
5. **Master** A master is a special slide or page that stores information about the formatting for all slides or pages in a presentation.
6. **Animations** Animations are special effects that add action to text and graphics so they move around on the screen during a slide show.

Finding and Replacing Text

After meeting with the foundation director, you want to update the content to include the additional information on ways that volunteers can help the Animal Rescue Foundation.

1

- **Start PowerPoint 2013.**
- **Open the file** pp02_Volunteer2 Widescreen **from your data file location.**
- **If necessary, switch to Normal view.**
- **Replace Student Name in slide 1 with your name.**
- **Scroll the Slide window to view the content of the revised presentation.**

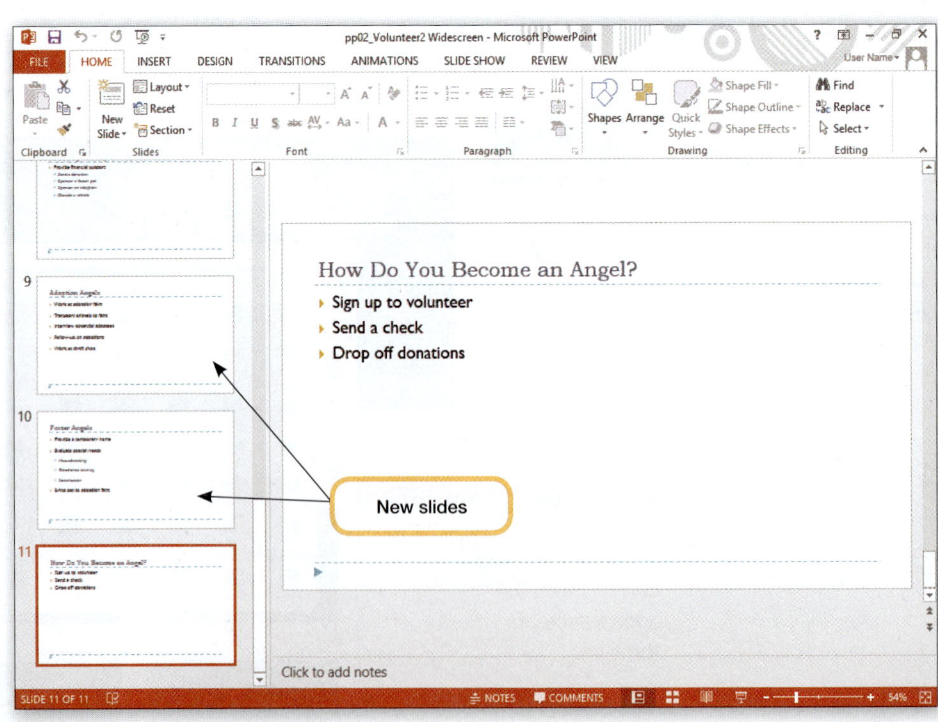

Figure 2.1

Your screen should be similar to **Figure 2.1**

You added two new slides, 9 and 10, with more information about the Animal Angels volunteer organization, bringing the total number of slides in the presentation to 11. As you reread the content of the presentation, you decide to edit the text by finding the word "pet" and replacing it with the word "animal." To do this, you will use the Find and Replace feature.

Concept  Find and Replace

To make editing easier, you can use the **Find and Replace** feature to find text in a presentation and replace it with other text. The Find feature will locate and identify any text string you specify in the presentation by highlighting it. When used along with the Replace feature, not only will the string be identified, but it will be replaced with the replacement text you specify if you choose. For example, suppose you created a lengthy document describing the type of clothing and equipment needed to set up a world-class home gym, and then you decided to change "sneakers" to "athletic shoes." Instead of deleting every occurrence of "sneakers" and typing "athletic shoes," you can use the Find and Replace feature to perform the task automatically.

The Replace feature also can be used to replace a specified font in a presentation with another. When using this feature, however, all text throughout the presentation that is in the specified font is automatically changed to the selected replacement font.

The Find and Replace feature is fast and accurate; however, use care when replacing so that you do not replace unintended matches.

FINDING TEXT

First, you will use the Find command to locate all occurrences of the word "pet" in the presentation.

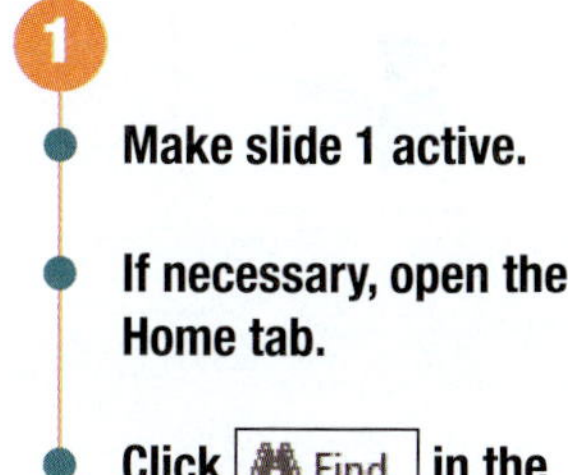

1
- **Make slide 1 active.**
- **If necessary, open the Home tab.**
- **Click Find in the Editing group.**

Another Method

The keyboard shortcut is Ctrl + F.

Your screen should be similar to Figure 2.2

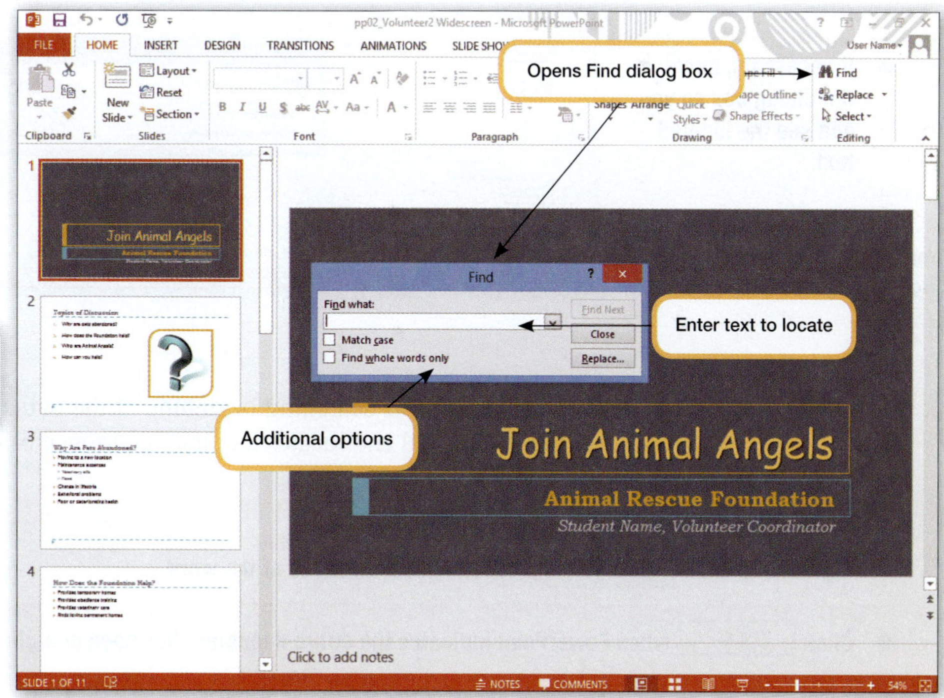

Figure 2.2

In the Find dialog box, you enter the text you want to locate in the Find what text box. The two options described in the following table allow you to refine the procedure that is used to conduct the search.

Option	Effect on Text
Match Case	Distinguishes between uppercase and lowercase characters. When selected, finds only those instances in which the capitalization matches the text you typed in the Find what box.
Find Whole Words Only	Distinguishes between whole and partial words. When selected, locates matches that are whole words and not part of a larger word. For example, finds "cat" only and not "catastrophe," too.

You want to find all occurrences of the complete word "pet." You will not use either option described above, because you want to locate all words regardless of case and because you want to find "pet" as well as "pets" in the presentation.

2

- **Type pet in the Find what text box.**
- **Click Find Next.**

Additional Information

You can also press Enter after specifying the search term to begin the search.

- **If necessary, move the dialog box so you can see the located text.**

Your screen should be similar to Figure 2.3

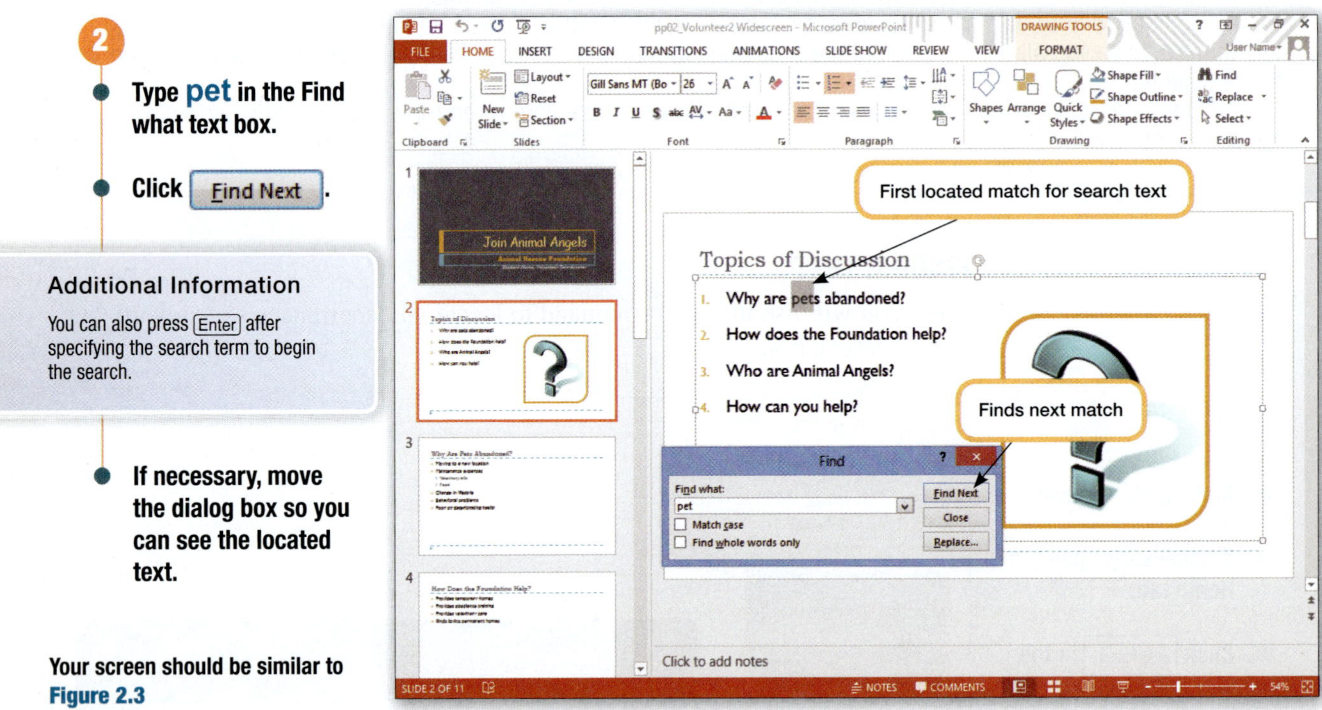

Figure 2.3

PowerPoint begins searching beginning at the cursor location for all occurrences of the text to find and locates the first occurrence of the word "pet."

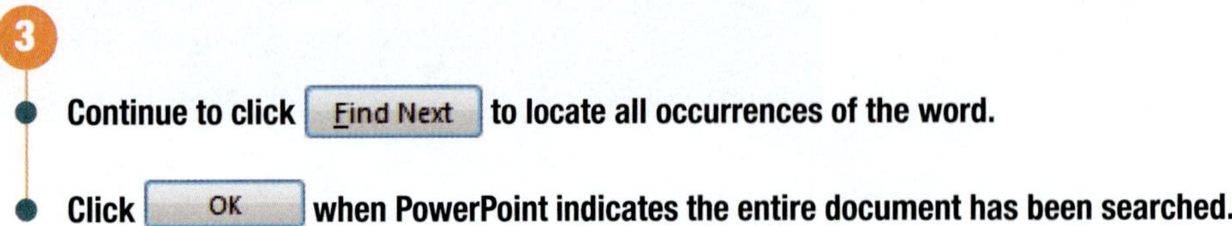

3

- **Continue to click Find Next to locate all occurrences of the word.**
- **Click OK when PowerPoint indicates the entire document has been searched.**

The word "pet" is used five times in the document. Using the Find command is a convenient way to quickly navigate through a document to locate and move to specified information.

REPLACING TEXT

You want to replace selected occurrences of the word "pet" with "animal" throughout the presentation. You will use the Replace feature to specify the text to enter as the replacement text.

1 **Click** [Replace] **in the Editing group.**

Another Method

The keyboard shortcut to replace text is Ctrl + H.

Your screen should be similar to Figure 2.4

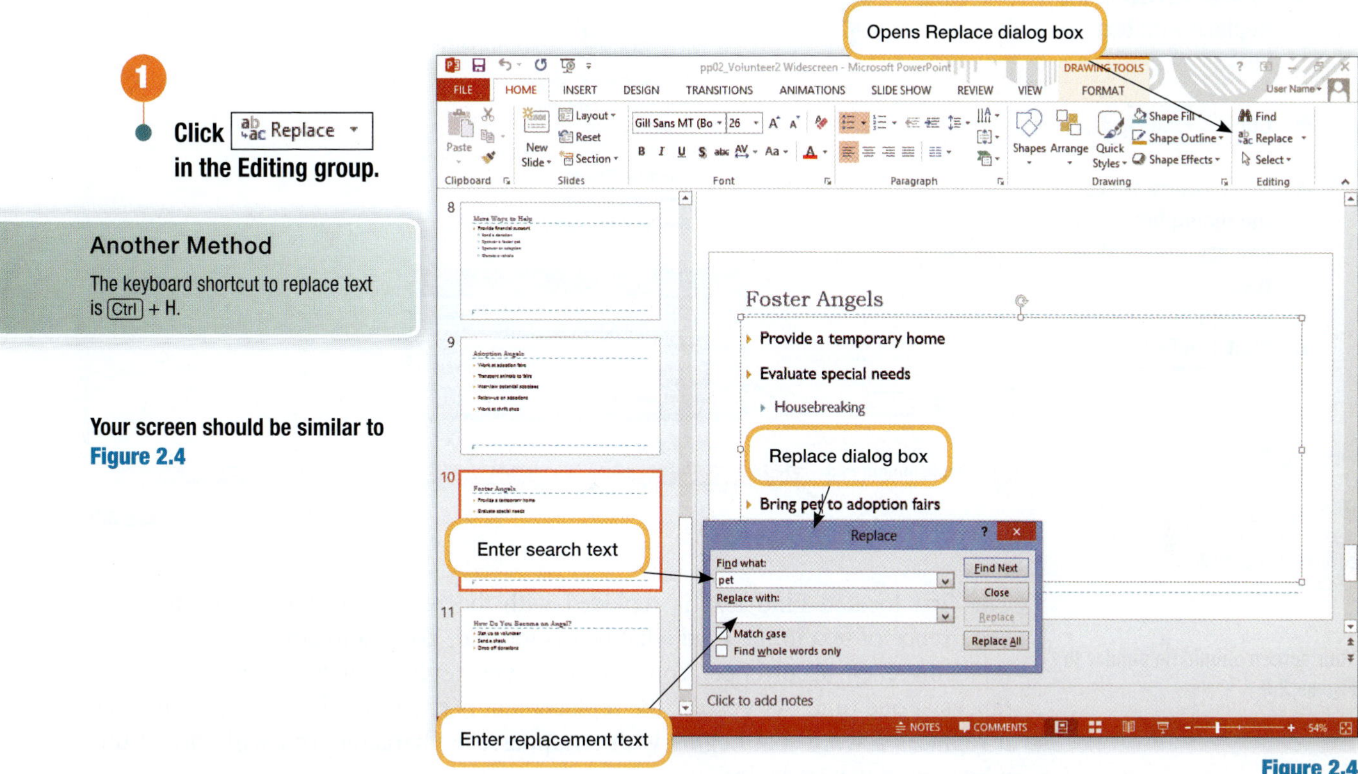

Figure 2.4

The Find dialog box changes to the Replace dialog box, and the search text you entered is still specified in the Find what text box. You can now enter the replacement text in the Replace with text box. The replacement text must be entered exactly as you want it to appear in your presentation.

- Press Tab or click in the Replace with text box.
- Type **animal** in the Replace with text box.
- Click Find Next.
- If necessary, move the dialog box so you can see the located text.
- Click Replace.

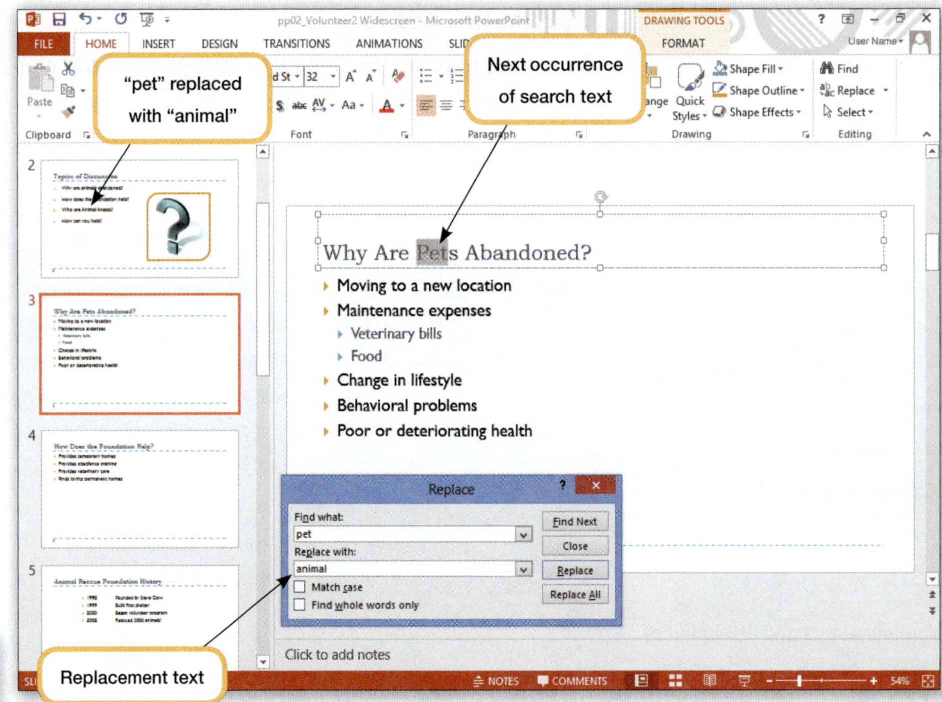

Figure 2.5

Having Trouble?

Click Find Next to move to the next occurrence if the search does not advance automatically.

Your screen should be similar to Figure 2.5

The first located Find text is replaced with the replacement text, and the next occurrence of text in the Find what box is located. You could continue finding and replacing each occurrence. You will, however, replace all the remaining occurrences at one time. As you do, the replacement is entered in lowercase even when it replaces a word that begins with an uppercase character. You will correct this when you finish replacing.

3

- Click Replace All to continue.
- Click OK in response to the finished searching dialog box.
- Click Close to close the Replace dialog box.
- Edit the word "animals" to "Animals" in slide 3.
- Click somewhere outside the placeholder.
- Save the presentation as Volunteer2 Widescreen to your solution file location.

Your screen should be similar to Figure 2.6

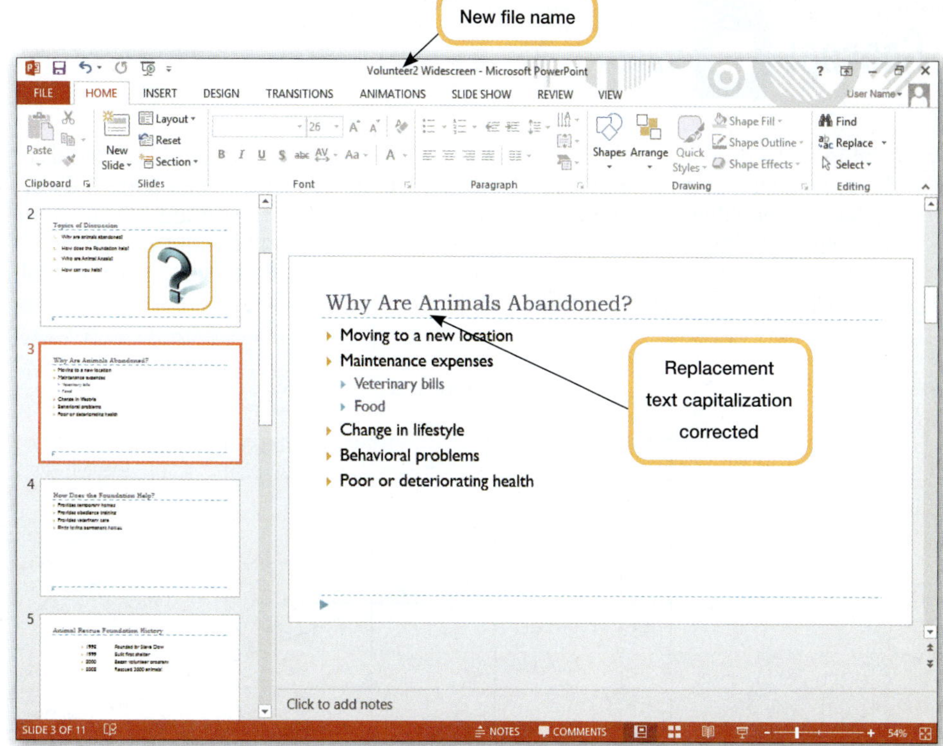

Figure 2.6

If you plan to change all occurrences, it is much faster to use Replace All. Exercise care when replacing all occurrences, however, because the search text you specify might be part of another word and you may accidentally replace text you want to keep.

Creating a Simple Table

During your discussion with the director, he suggested that you add a slide containing data showing the success of the adoption program. The information in this slide will be presented using a table layout.

Concept 2 Table

A **table** is used to organize information into an easy-to-read format of horizontal rows and vertical columns. The intersection of a row and column creates a **cell** in which you can enter data or other information. Cells in a table are identified by a letter and number, called a **table reference**. Columns are identified from left to right beginning with the letter A, and rows are numbered from top to bottom beginning with the number 1. The table reference of the top-leftmost cell is A1 because it is in the first column (A) and first row (1) of the table. The third cell in column B is cell B3. The fourth cell in column C is C4.

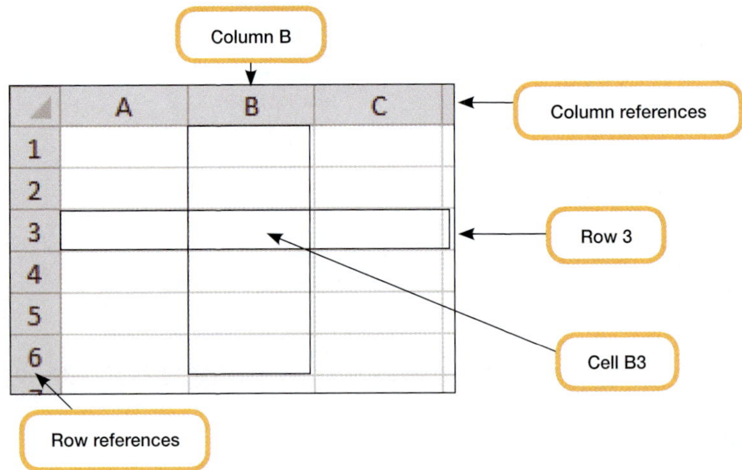

Tables are a very effective method for presenting information. The table layout organizes the information for readers and greatly reduces the number of words they have to read to interpret the data. Use tables whenever you can to make the information in your presentation easier to read.

The table you will create will display columns for the year and for the number of rescues and adoptions. The rows will display the data for the past four years. Your completed table will be similar to the one shown here.

Year	Rescues	Adoptions
2012	3759	3495
2013	3847	3784
2014	3982	3833
2015	4025	3943

CREATING A TABLE SLIDE

To include this information in the presentation, you will insert a new slide after slide 5. Because this slide will contain a table showing the adoption data, you will use the Title and Content layout.

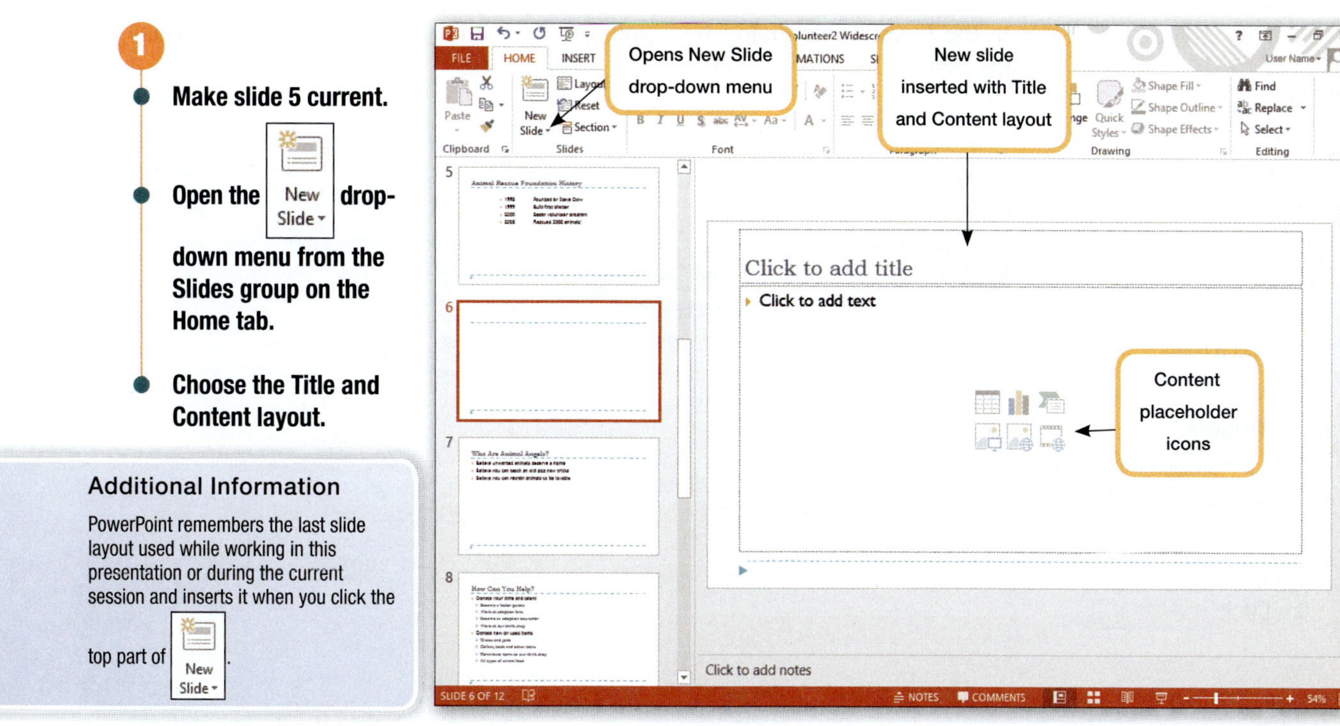

1

- **Make slide 5 current.**
- **Open the New Slide drop-down menu from the Slides group on the Home tab.**
- **Choose the Title and Content layout.**

Additional Information

PowerPoint remembers the last slide layout used while working in this presentation or during the current session and inserts it when you click the top part of New Slide.

Your screen should be similar to Figure 2.7

Figure 2.7

Six icons appear inside the content placeholder, each representing a different type of content that can be inserted. Clicking an icon opens the appropriate feature to add the specified type of content.

INSERTING THE TABLE

First, you will add a slide title, and then you will create the table to display the number of adoptions and rescues.

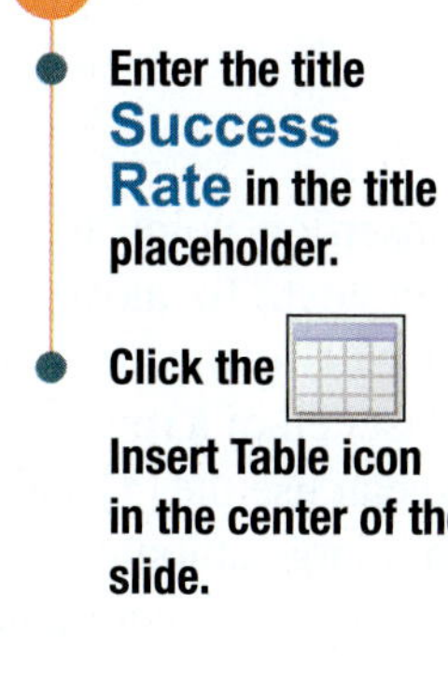

1

- **Enter the title Success Rate in the title placeholder.**
- **Click the Insert Table icon in the center of the slide.**

Your screen should be similar to Figure 2.8

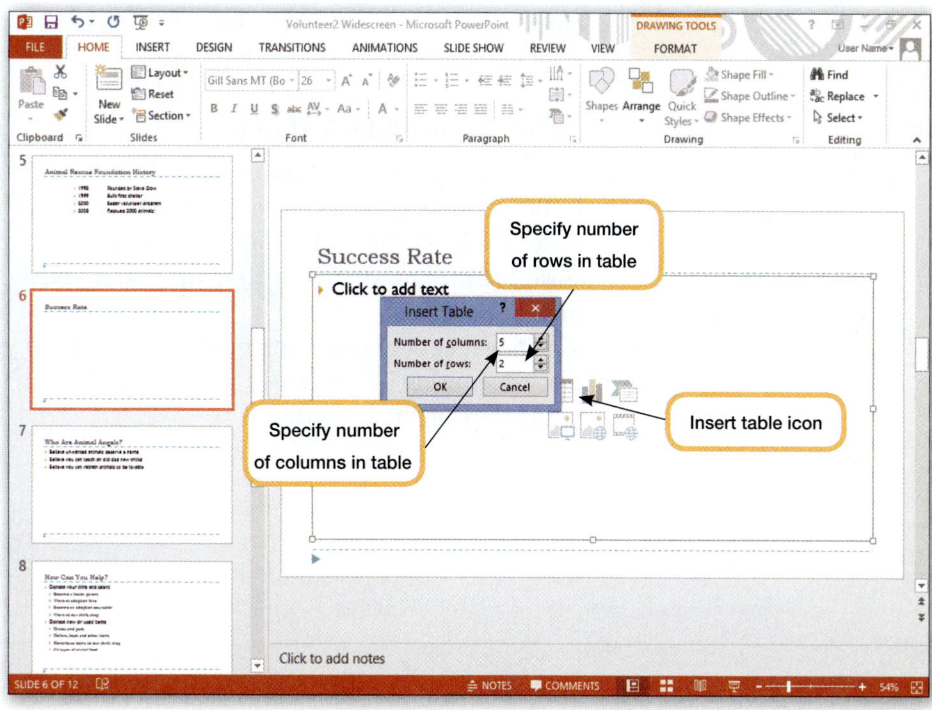

Figure 2.8

In the Insert Table dialog box, you specify the number of rows and columns for the table.

2

- **Specify 3 columns and 5 rows.**

Having Trouble?

You can type in the number or use the scroll buttons to increase or decrease the number.

- **Click OK.**

Your screen should be similar to Figure 2.9

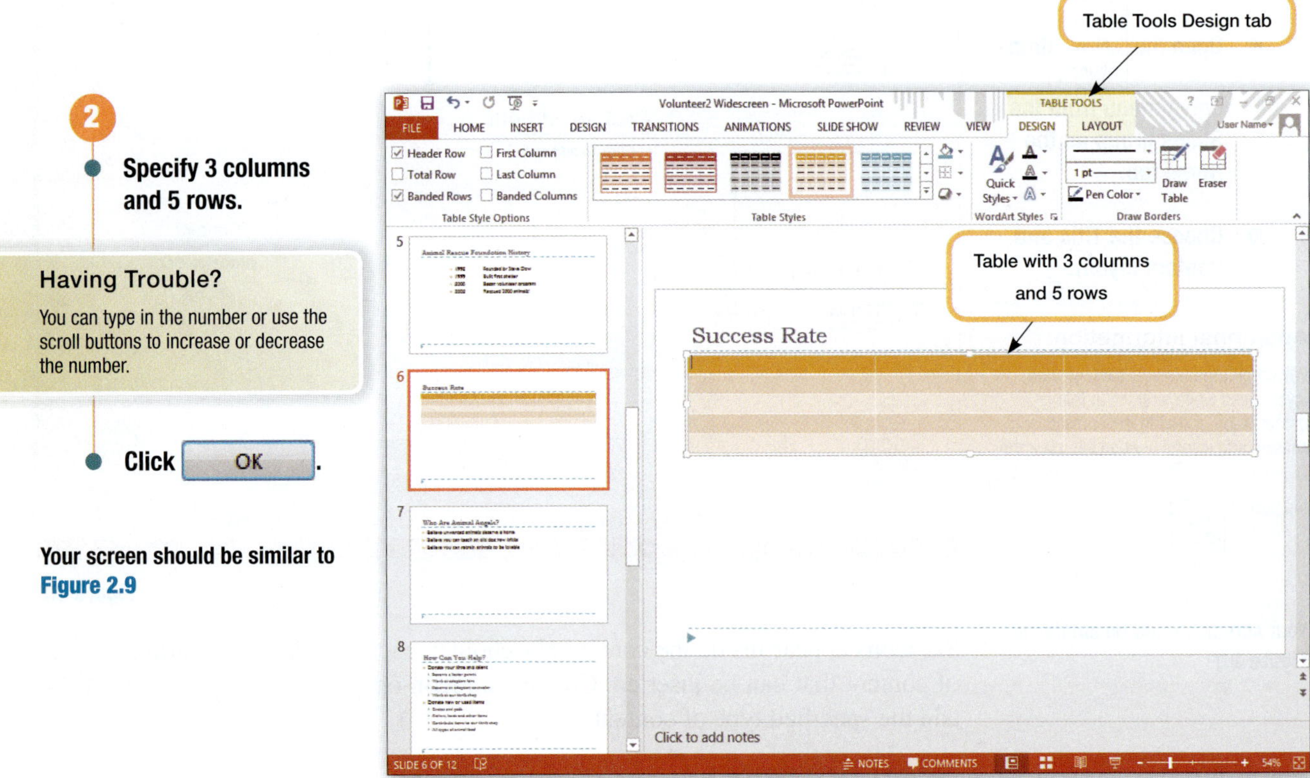

Figure 2.9

A basic table consisting of three columns and five rows is displayed as a selected object. In addition, the Table Tools Design tab opens in anticipation that you will want to modify the design of the table.

ENTERING DATA IN A TABLE

Now you can enter the information into the table. The insertion point appears in the top-left corner cell, cell A1, ready for you to enter text. To move in a table, click on the cell or use Tab to move to the next cell to the right and Shift + Tab to move to the cell to the left. If you are in the last cell of a row, pressing Tab takes you to the first cell of the next row. You also can use the ↑ and ↓ directional keys to move up or down a row. When you enter a large amount of text in a table, using Tab to move is easier than using the mouse because your hands are already on the keyboard.

1

- Type Year

- Press Tab or click on the next cell to the right.

Having Trouble?

Do not press Enter to move to the next cell, as this adds a new line to the current cell. If this happens, press Backspace to remove it.

Your screen should be similar to Figure 2.10

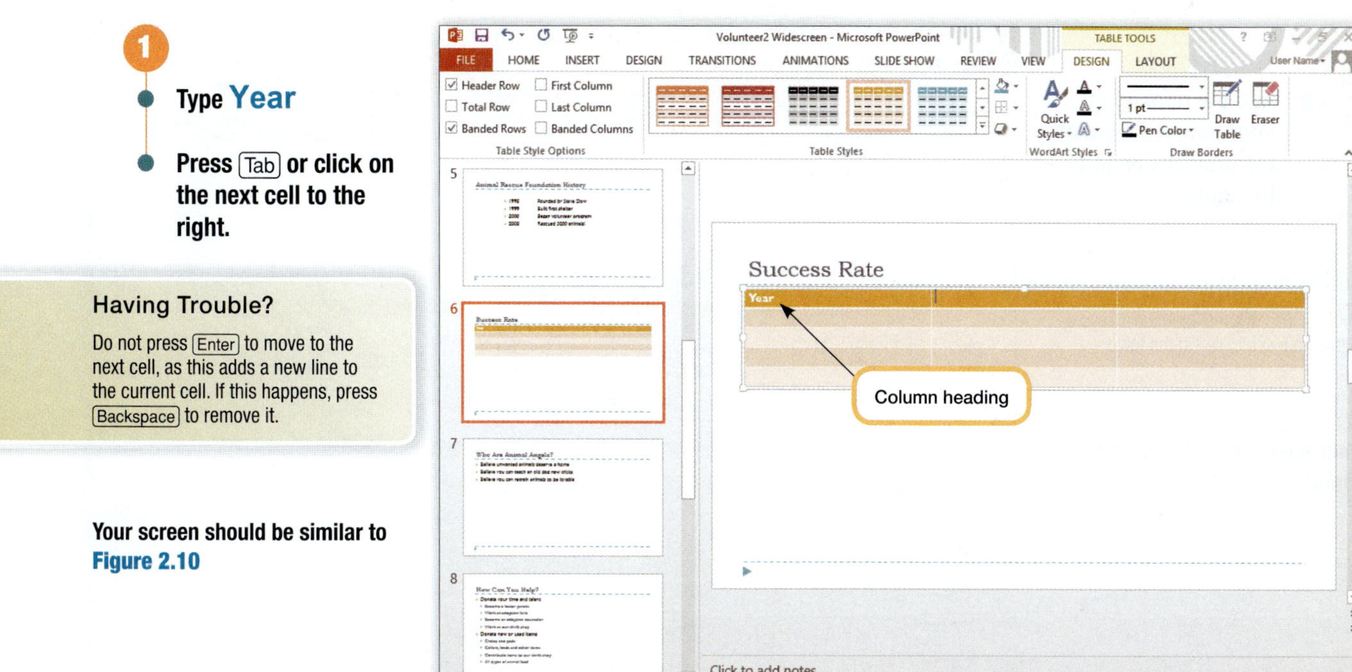

Figure 2.10

Next, you will complete the information for the table by entering the data shown below.

	Column A	Column B	Column C
Row 1	Year	Rescues	Adoptions
Row 2	2012	3759	3495
Row 3	2013	3847	3784
Row 4	2014	3982	3833
Row 5	2015	4025	3943

Add the remaining information shown on the previous page to the table.

Additional Information

You can also use the directional keys to move from cell to cell in the table.

Your screen should be similar to Figure 2.11

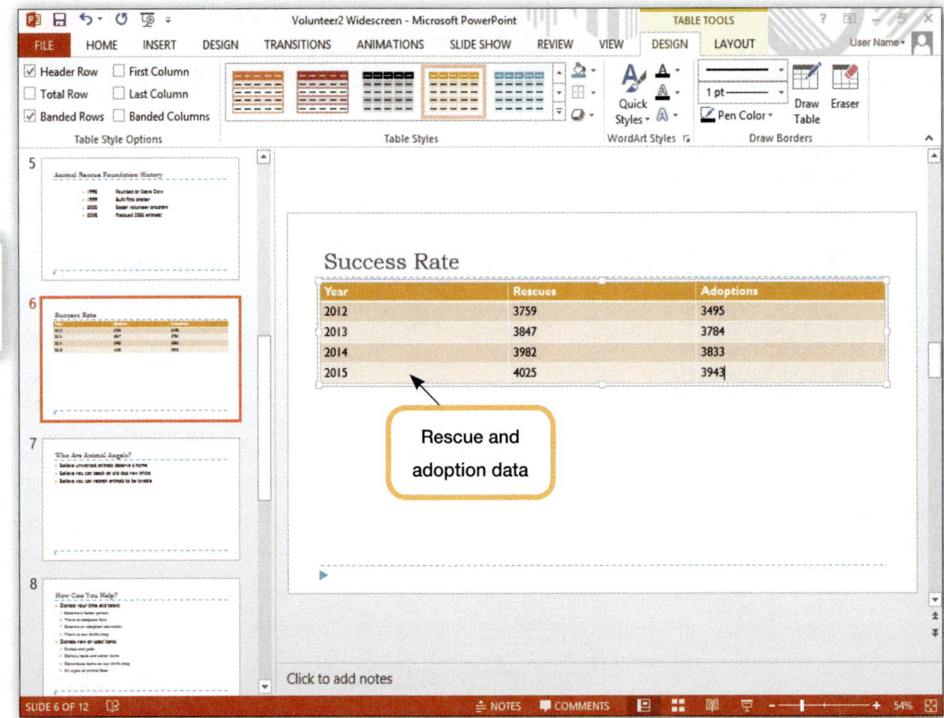

Figure 2.11

You are happy with the table but would like to increase the font size of the text to make it more readable onscreen. The size of the font in a table can be changed like any other text on a slide. However, selecting text in a table is slightly different. The following table describes how to select different areas of a table.

Area to Select	Procedure
Cell	Drag across the contents of the cell.
Row	Drag across the row or click in front of the row when the mouse pointer is a ➡.
Column	Drag down the column or click in front of the row when the mouse pointer is a ⬇.
Multiple cells, rows, or columns	Drag through the cells, rows, or columns when the mouse pointer is a ⬈ or I.
	Or select the first cell, row, or column, and hold down ⇧Shift while clicking on another cell, row, or column.
Contents of next cell	Press Tab.
Contents of previous cell	Press ⇧Shift + Tab.
Entire table	Drag through all the cells or click anywhere inside the table and press Ctrl + A. Alternatively, select the entire table as an object first by clicking on the table border.

Because you want to increase the font size of all the text in the table, you will select the table as an object. The insertion point will not display in the table when the entire table is selected.

3

- **Click on the table border to select it as an object.**
- **Open the Home tab.**
- **Click A^ Increase Font Size in the Font group four times.**

Your screen should be similar to Figure 2.12

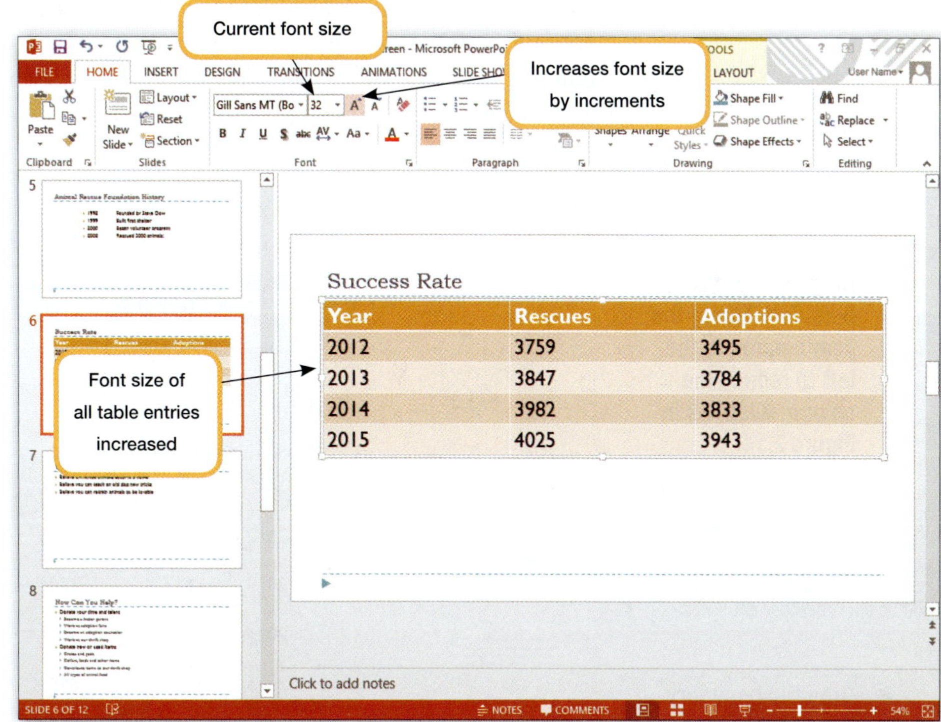

Figure 2.12

The font size has quickly been increased by four units, and at 32 points the text is much easier to read.

SIZING THE TABLE AND COLUMNS

You now want to increase the overall size of the table to better fill the space on the slide and then adjust the size of the columns to fit their contents.

1

- **Drag the lower-right corner sizing handle down to increase the table size as in Figure 2.13.**

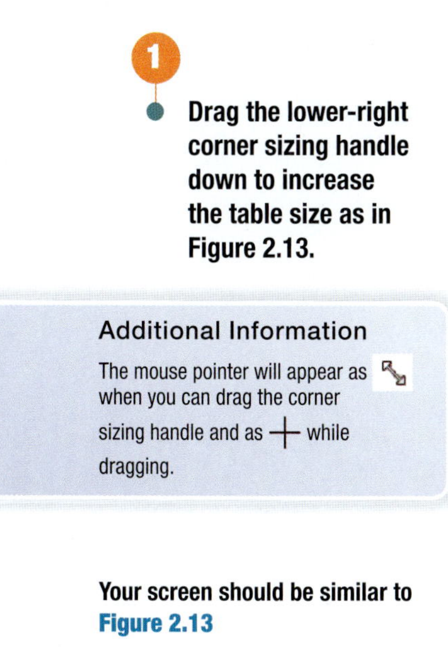

Additional Information

The mouse pointer will appear as ⤡ when you can drag the corner sizing handle and as + while dragging.

Your screen should be similar to Figure 2.13

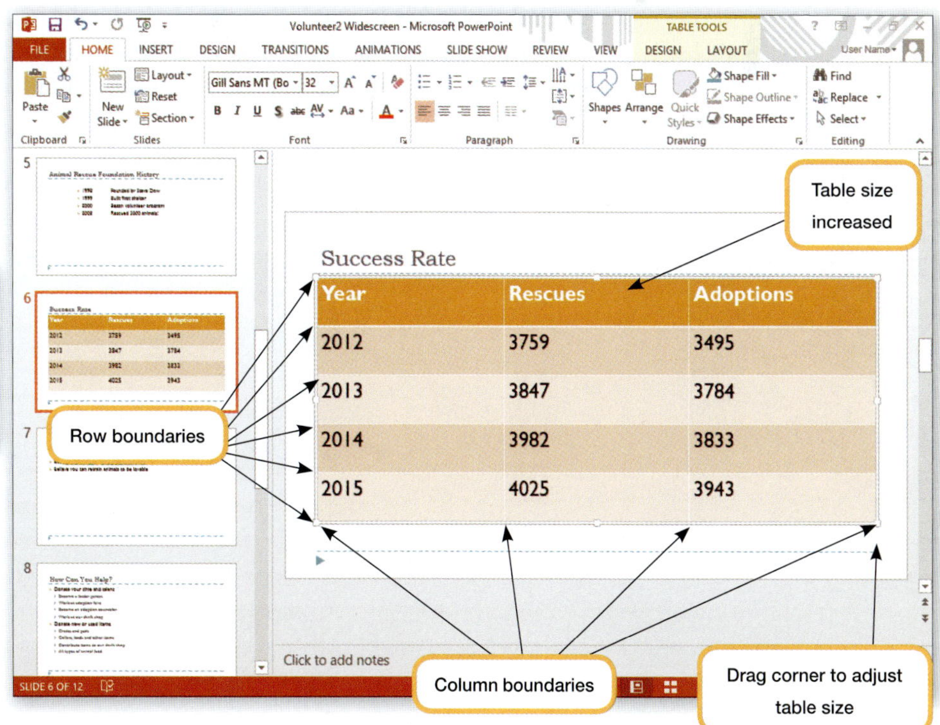

Figure 2.13

To adjust the individual column width or row height, you drag the row and column boundaries. The mouse pointer appears as a ⫲ when you can size the column and ÷ when you can size the row. The mouse pointer appears as a ✥ when you can move the entire table.

2

- **Drag the right column boundary line of the year column to the left to reduce the column width as in Figure 2.14.**

Additional Information

You also can double-click on the boundary line to automatically size the width to the largest cell entry.

- **Drag the boundary lines of the other two columns to the left to reduce the column widths as in Figure 2.14.**

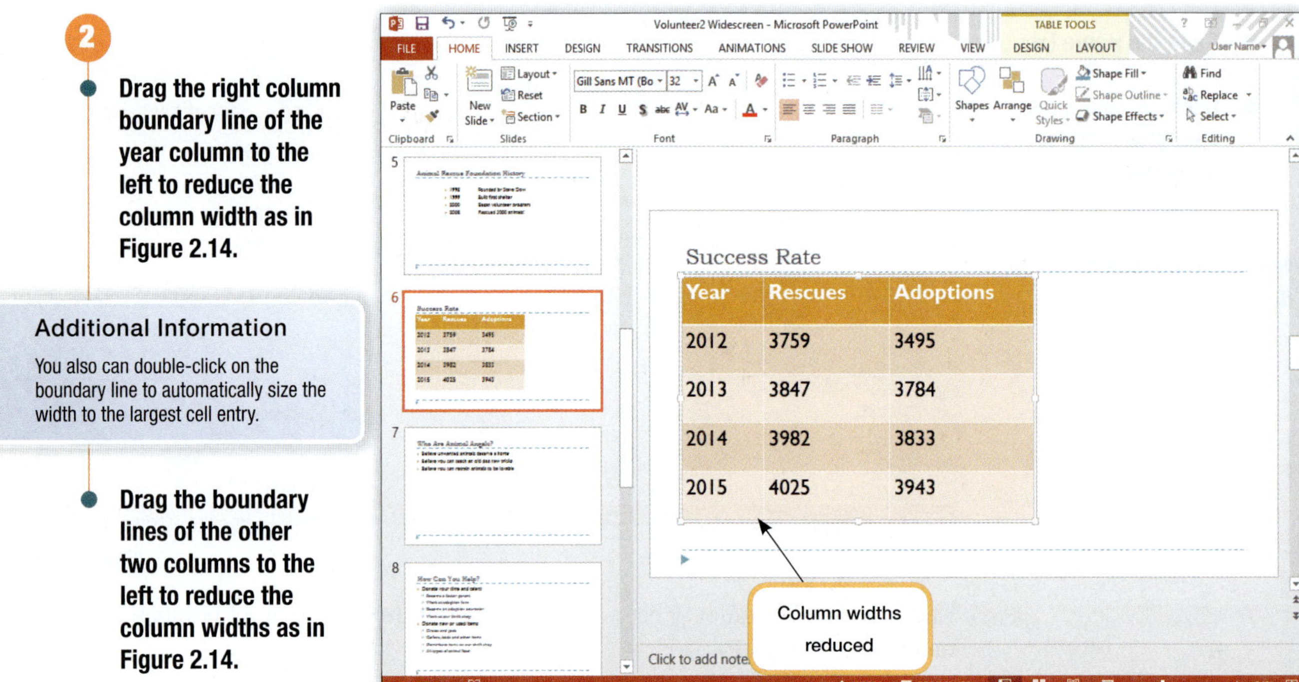

Your screen should be similar to Figure 2.14

Figure 2.14

Now the columns are more appropriately sized to the data they display and the overall table size is good. You decide it would look best to align the table in the center of the slide as well. You could do this manually by moving the object to center it. A more precise method is to use the built-in alignment feature.

3

- **Open the Table Tools Layout tab.**
- **Click [Align] in the Arrange group to display the drop-down menu.**

Having Trouble?

You may need to click [Arrange] to open the group.

- **Choose Align Center.**

Your screen should be similar to Figure 2.15

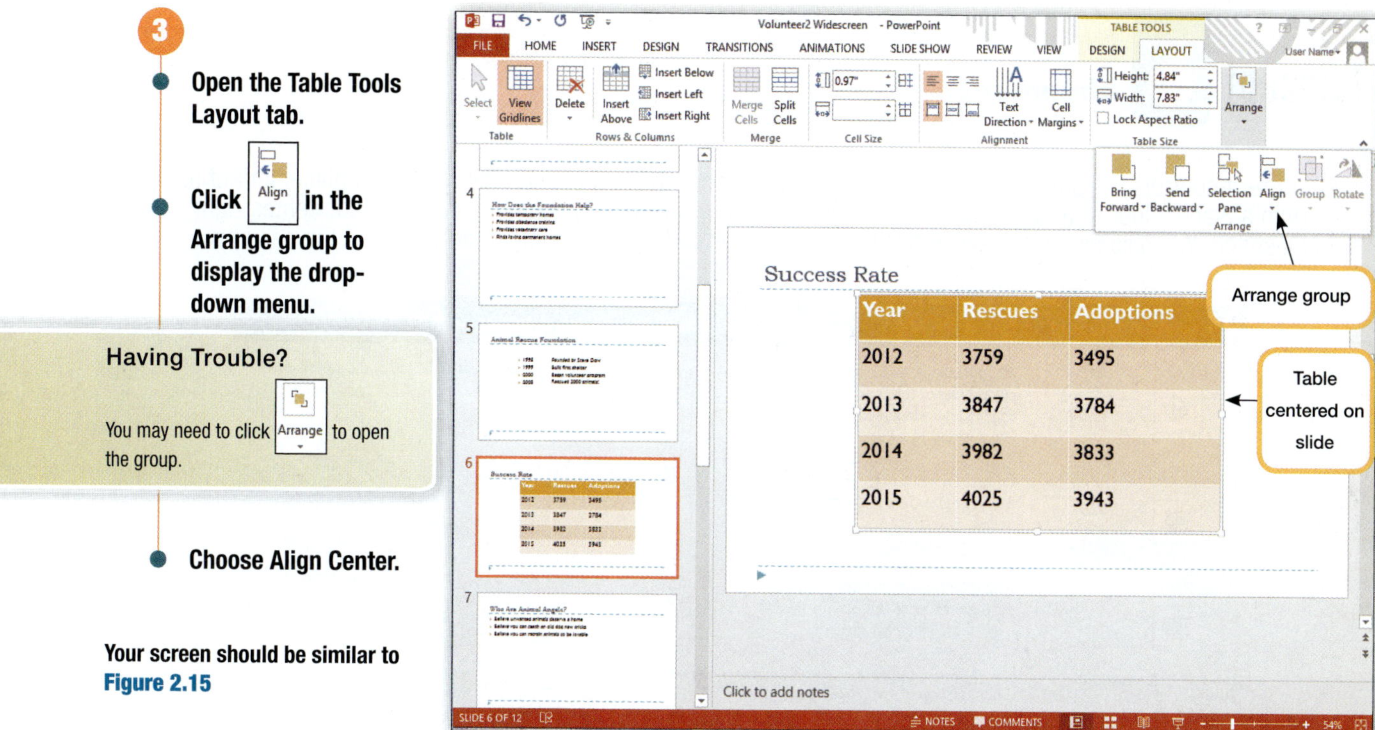

Figure 2.15

ALIGNING TEXT IN CELLS

The next change you want to make is to center the text and data in the cells. To do this, you can change the alignment of the text entries.

Concept 3 Alignment

Alignment controls the position of text entries within a space. You can change the horizontal placement of an entry in a placeholder or a table cell by using one of the four horizontal alignment settings: left, center, right, and justified. You also can align text vertically in a table cell with the top, middle, or bottom of the cell space.

Horizontal Alignment	Effect on Text	Vertical Alignment	Effect on Text
Align Left	Aligns text against the left edge of the placeholder or cell, leaving the right edge of text, which wraps to another line, ragged.	Align Top	Aligns text at the top of the cell space.
Center	Centers each line of text between the left and right edges of the placeholder or cell.	Center Vertically	Aligns text in the middle of the cell space.
Align Right	Aligns text against the right edge of the placeholder or cell, leaving the left edge of multiple lines ragged.	Align Bottom	Aligns text at the bottom of the cell space.
Justify	Aligns text evenly with both the right and left edges of the placeholder.		

The commands to change alignment are in the Paragraph group of the Home tab and in the Alignment group of the TableTools Layout tab. Additionally, you can use the shortcuts shown below or the Mini toolbar.

Alignment	Keyboard Shortcut
Left	Ctrl + L
Center	Ctrl + E
Right	Ctrl + R
Justify	Ctrl + J

The data in the table is not centered within the cells. You want to center the cell entries both horizontally and vertically in their cell spaces.

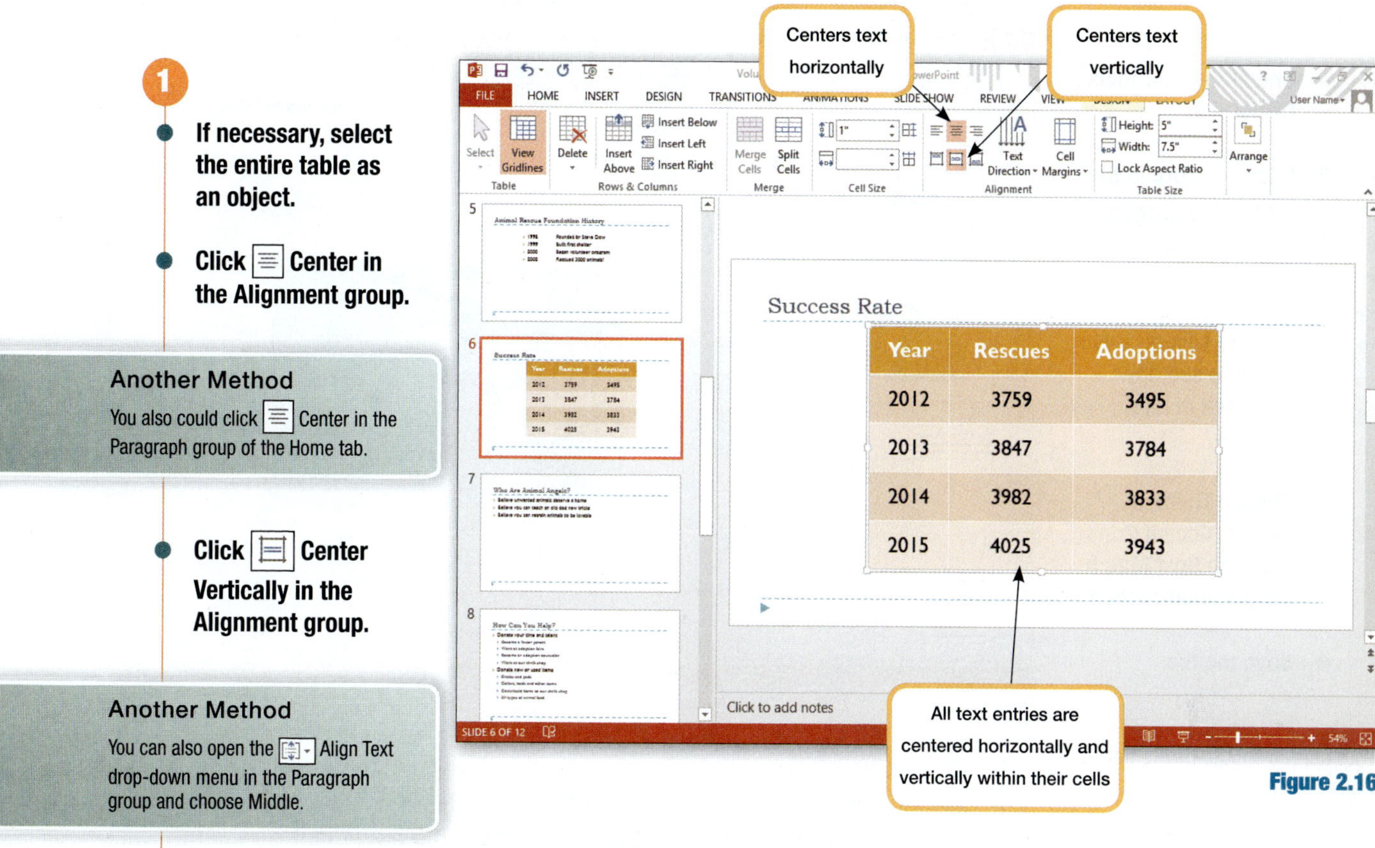

Figure 2.16

1

- **If necessary, select the entire table as an object.**
- **Click Center in the Alignment group.**

Another Method

You also could click Center in the Paragraph group of the Home tab.

- **Click Center Vertically in the Alignment group.**

Another Method

You can also open the Align Text drop-down menu in the Paragraph group and choose Middle.

- **Drag the table to position it as in Figure 2.16.**

Your screen should be similar to Figure 2.16

ENHANCING THE TABLE

Next, you will add color and other formatting changes to the table. To quickly make these enhancements, you will apply a table style. Like picture styles, **table styles** are combinations of shading colors, borders, and visual effects such as shadows and reflections that can be applied in one simple step. You also can create your own table style effects by selecting specific style elements such as borders and shadows individually using the Shading, Borders, and Effects commands from the Table Styles group on the Table Tools Design tab.

1

- Open the Table Tools Design tab.
- Click [▾] More in the Table Styles group to display the Table Styles gallery.
- Point to several table styles to see how they look in Live Preview.
- Choose Themed Style 1, Accent 2 from the Best Match for Document group.
- Save the file.

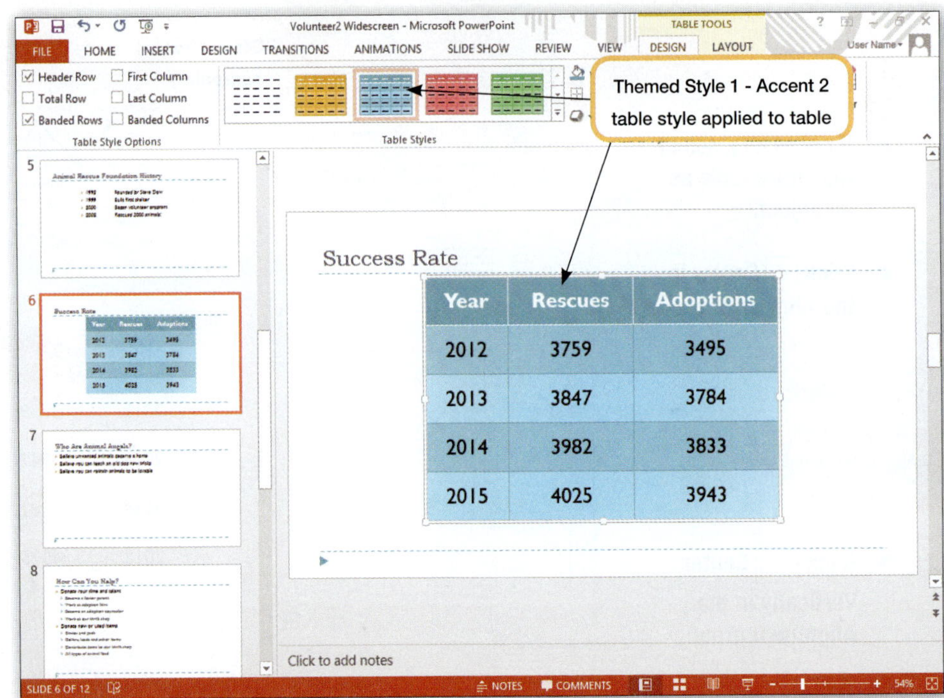

Figure 2.17

Your screen should be similar to Figure 2.17

The selected table style has been applied to the table. The enhancements added to the table greatly improve its appearance, and the table now displays the information in an attractive and easy-to-read manner.

Cropping and Enhancing Pictures

Now you are ready to further enhance the presentation by adding to the title slide a picture of a dog that is up for adoption. You will improve the appearance of the picture by cropping it and enhancing it with a picture style.

INSERTING A GRAPHIC

You will first insert the picture of the dog from a file on your computer.

1

- **Select slide 1.**
- **Open the Insert tab.**
- **Click Pictures in the Images group.**
- **Change the location to your data file location.**
- **If necessary, change the view to Large Icons.**

Having Trouble?

If necessary, click [change view button] and choose Large Icon.

Your screen should be similar to Figure 2.18

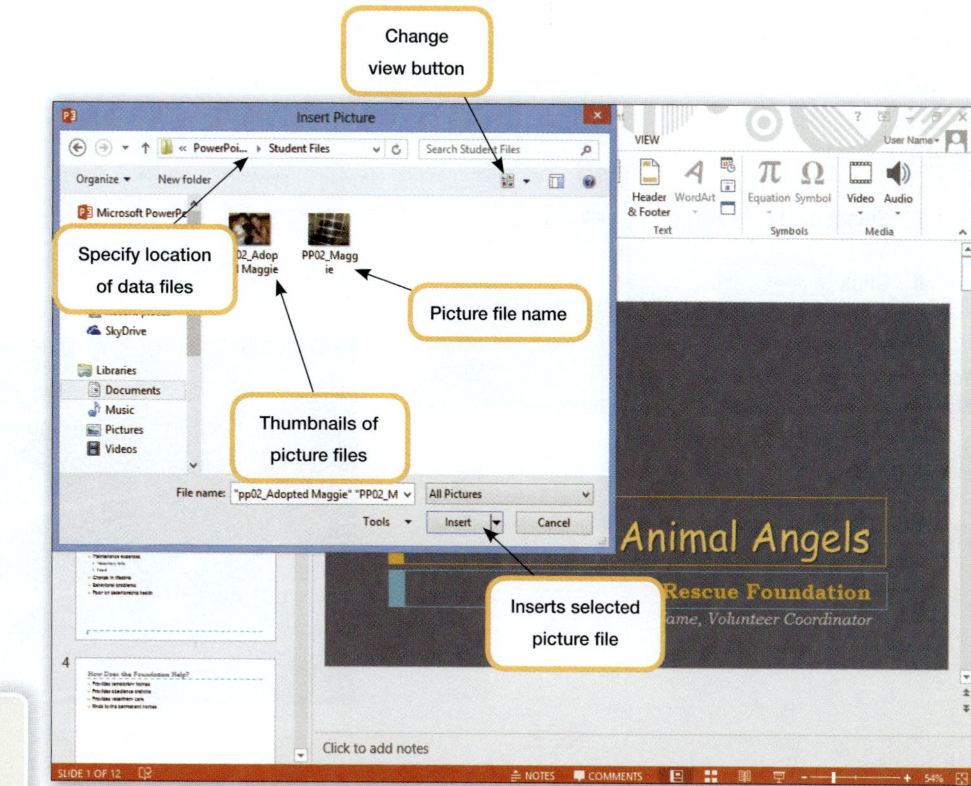

Figure 2.18

Having Trouble?

Your screen may display additional picture files.

A thumbnail preview of each picture is displayed above the file name.

- **Select** pp02_Maggie
- **Click** Insert.

Your screen should be similar to Figure 2.19

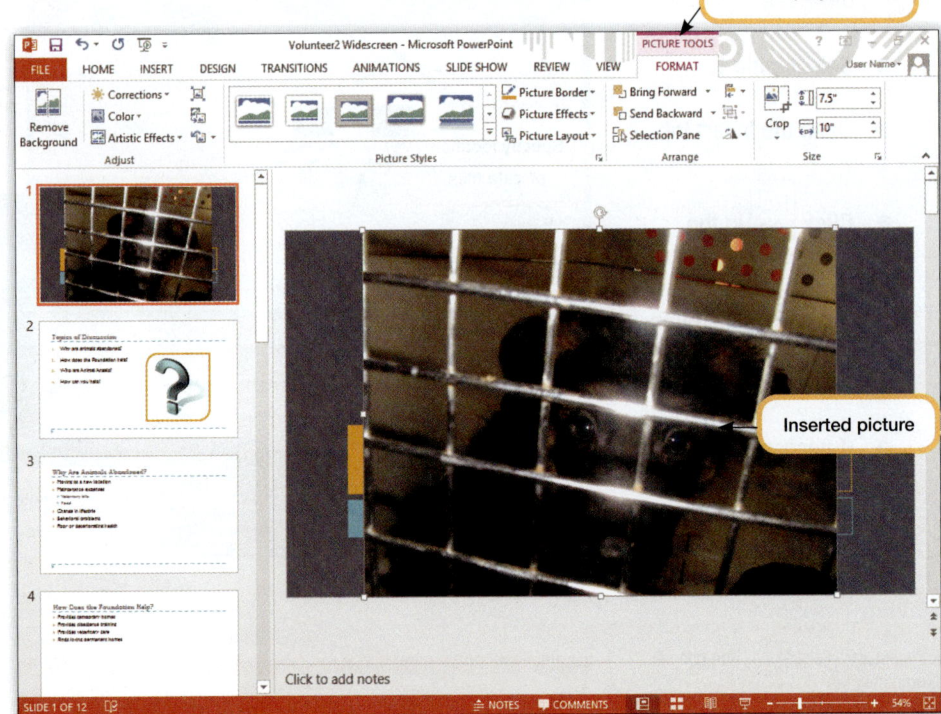

Figure 2.19

The Picture Tools Format tab is automatically displayed in the Ribbon, in anticipation that you may want to modify the graphic. You will decrease the size of the picture first.

Drag the bottom-right corner sizing handle inward to decrease its size to that shown in Figure 2.20.

Additional Information

To maintain an object's proportions while resizing it, hold down Shift while dragging the sizing handle.

Your screen should be similar to Figure 2.20

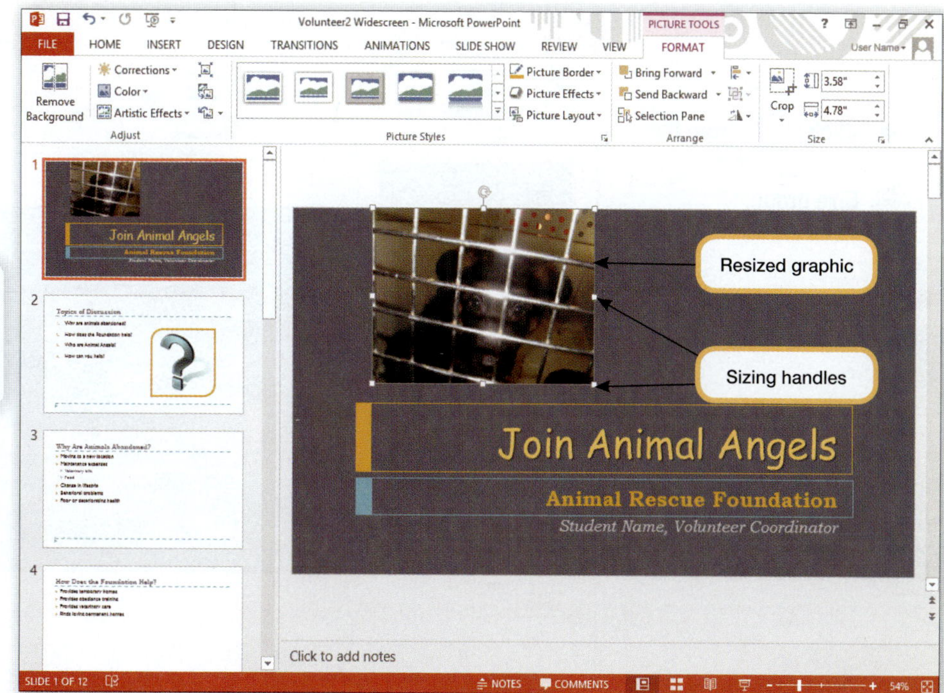

Figure 2.20

CROPPING A GRAPHIC

Next, you decide that you can draw more attention to Maggie by cropping the picture. Trimming or removing part of a picture is called **cropping**. Cropping removes the vertical or horizontal edges of a picture to help focus attention on a particular area. You will remove the upper part of the picture by cropping it to show Maggie only.

1

- Click [Crop] from the Size group.

Another Method

The Crop tool is also on the picture's context menu.

Additional Information

The mouse pointer appears as [icon] or [icon] when it is used to crop a picture.

- Point to the upper-left corner of the photo, and when the mouse pointer changes to a [icon], drag down and inward slightly to just above Maggie's head.

- Click [Crop] from the Size group to turn off this feature.

Your screen should be similar to Figure 2.21

Additional Information

Be careful when increasing the size of a picture (bitmap) image, as it can lose sharpness and appear blurry if enlarged too much.

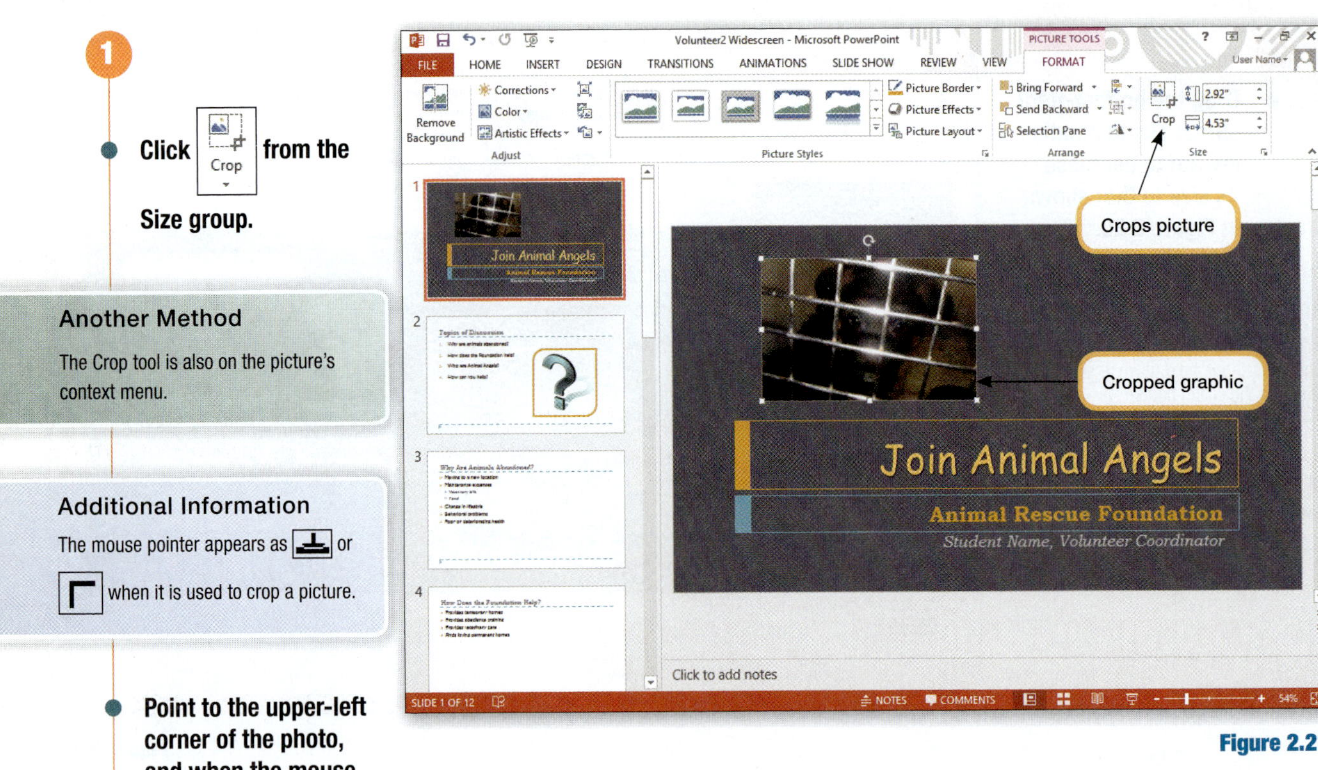

Figure 2.21

The upper part of the picture has been removed, leaving the Maggie's head as the focus of attention. Even after a picture has been cropped, the cropped parts remain as part of the picture file. This allows you to readjust how the picture was cropped. To permanently delete the cropped parts use the Compress Pictures command in the Adjust group and save the file. This also reduces the file size and prevents others from viewing the cropped parts of the picture.

Next you want to increase the graphic's size and position it centered in the space above the title.

2

- **Size the picture as in Figure 2.22 (approximately 3 by 4.75 inches).**

Additional Information

The Shape Height and Shape Width buttons in the Size group display the current shape's size as you drag.

- **Open the [Align Objects] Align Objects drop-down menu in the Arrange group of the Picture Tools Format tab and choose Align Center.**
- **If necessary, position the graphic vertically on the slide as shown in Figure 2.22.**

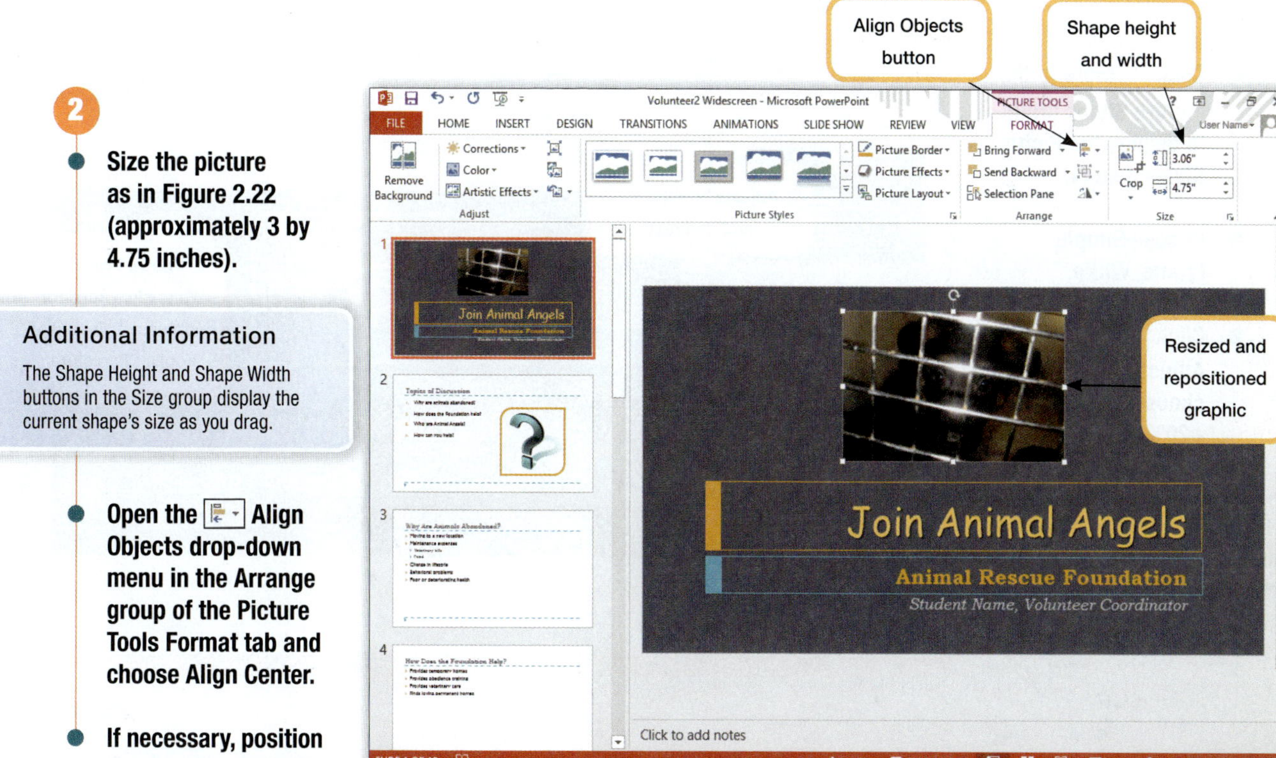

Figure 2.22

Your screen should be similar to Figure 2.22

ENHANCING A PICTURE

Finally, you want to enhance the picture by selecting a picture style and then improve the brightness of the picture so that the dog stands out better.

1

- Click More in the Picture Styles group to display the Picture Styles gallery.
- Choose Simple Frame, White.
- Click Corrections in the Adjust group and choose Brightness: +20% Contrast: 0% (Normal).

Your screen should be similar to Figure 2.23

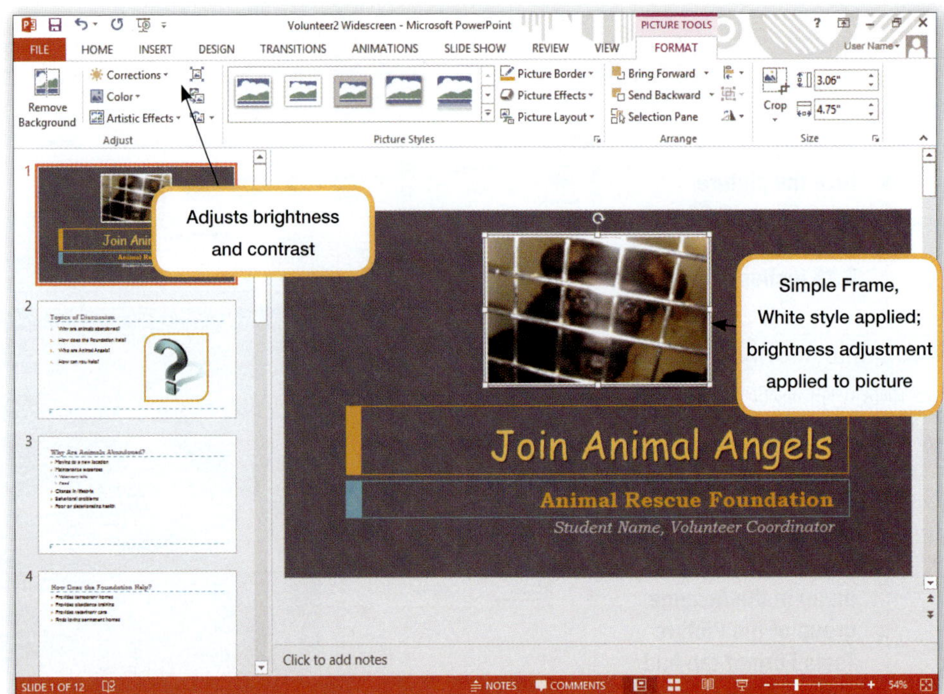

Figure 2.23

The addition of the picture style and adjustment of the brightness greatly improves the appearance of the picture and makes the title slide much more interesting and effective.

Inserting and Enhancing Shapes

At the end of the presentation, you want to add a concluding slide. This slide needs to be powerful, because it is your last chance to convince your audience to join Animal Angels.

ADDING A SHAPE

To create the concluding slide, you will duplicate slide 1 and replace the picture with another showing Maggie's adoption. You will also add a graphic of a heart that you will create using one of the ready-made shapes supplied with PowerPoint. These shapes include rectangles and circles, lines, a variety of basic shapes, block arrows, flowchart symbols, stars and banners, action buttons, and callouts.

1

- Duplicate slide 1.
- Move slide 2 to the end of the presentation.
- Select the picture and press Delete.
- Insert the picture pp02_Adopted Maggie from your student file location.
- Crop the picture as in Figure 2.24.
- Increase the brightness 20%.
- Choose the Simple Frame, White (the first choice) from the Picture Styles gallery.
- Size and position the picture as in Figure 2.24.

Your screen should be similar to Figure 2.24

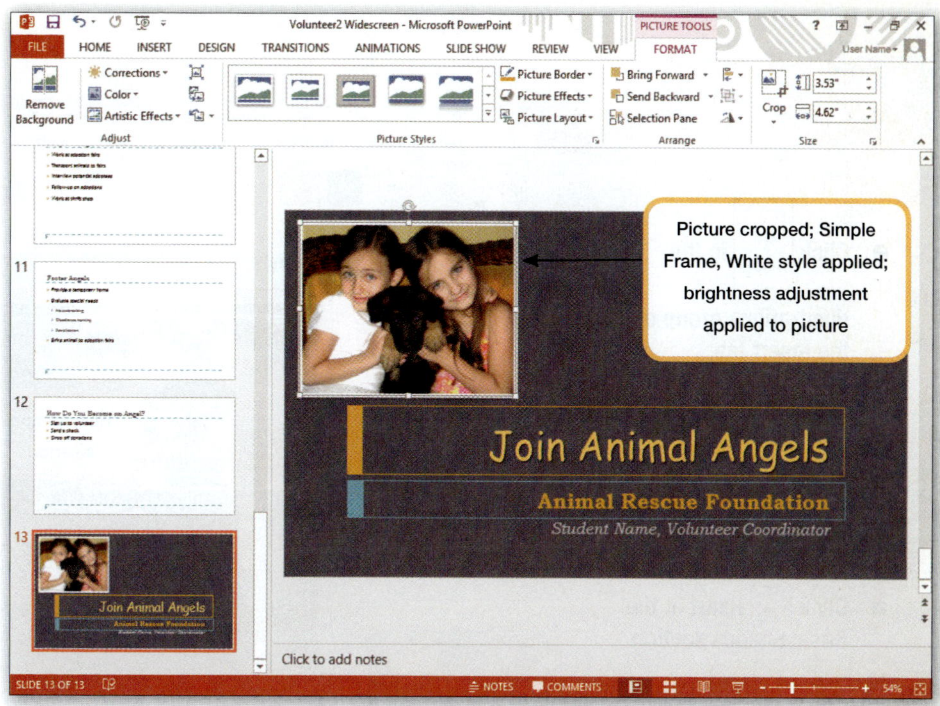

Figure 2.24

The picture is cropped, framed, sized, and positioned in the upper-left corner of the slide. In the space to the right you will insert a heart shape by selecting the shape from the Shapes gallery on the Insert tab. When inserting a shape, the mouse pointer appears as + when pointing to the slide. Then, to insert the shape, click on the slide and drag to increase the size.

2

- **Click** Shapes **in the Illustrations group of the Insert tab.**

Another Method

You also can access the Shapes gallery from the Drawing group of the Home tab.

- **Click** ♡ **Heart in the Basic Shapes section.**

Additional Information

The selected shape will be added to the Recently Used Shapes section of the Shapes gallery.

- **Click above the title on the slide and drag to insert and enlarge the heart shape.**

Another Method

To maintain the height and width proportions of the shape, hold down (Shift) while you drag.

- **Size and position the heart shape as in Figure 2.25.**

Additional Information

A shape can be sized and moved just like any other object.

Your screen should be similar to Figure 2.25

Additional Information

Many more shapes are available from the Office.com Clip Art gallery.

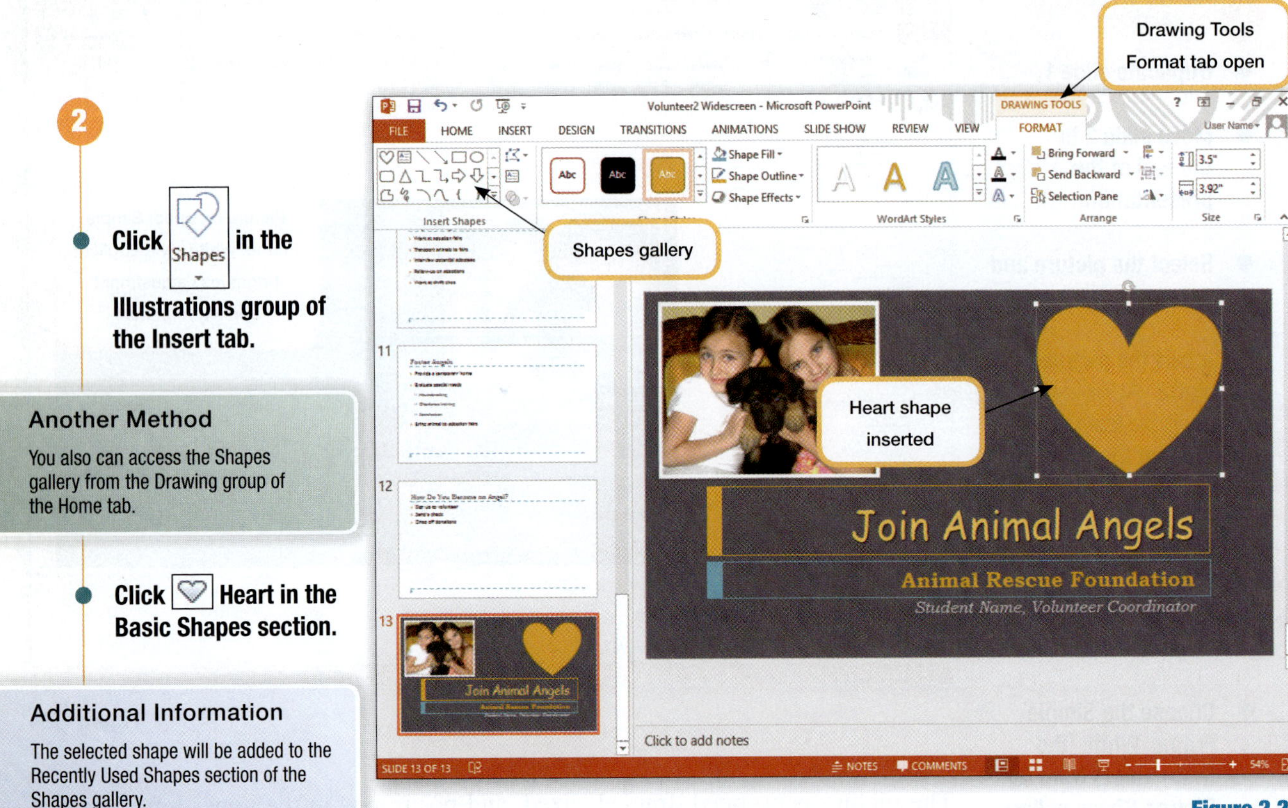

Figure 2.25

The heart shape is inserted and the Drawing Tools Format tab is available.

ENHANCING A SHAPE

Next, you will enhance the heart graphic's appearance by selecting a shape style and adding a reflection. Just like the other styles in PowerPoint 2013, **shape styles** consist of combinations of fill colors, outline colors, and effects.

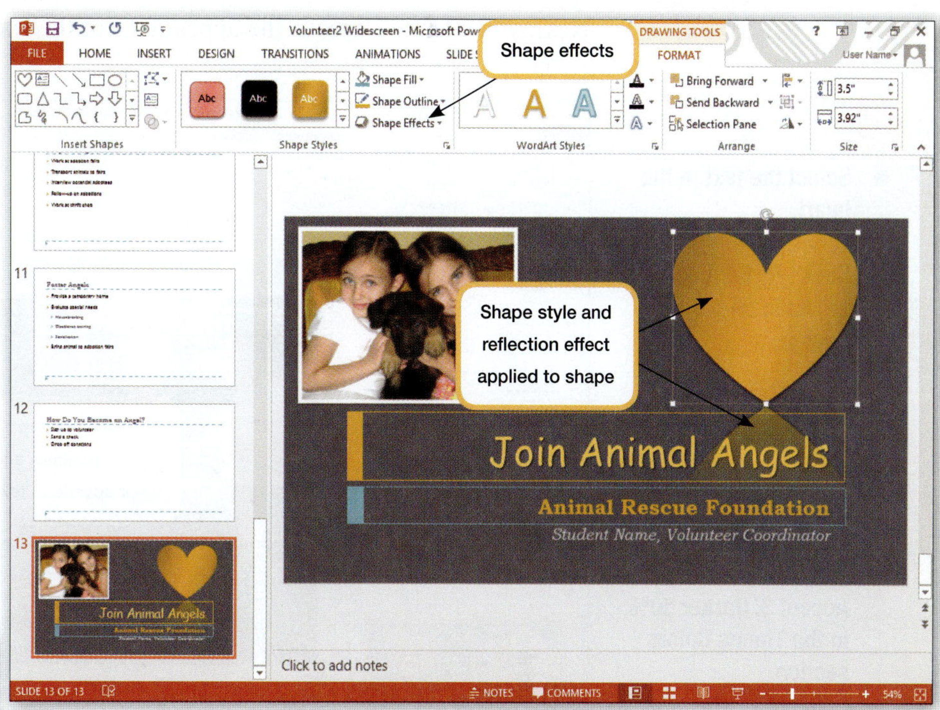

Figure 2.26

1. Open the Drawing Tools Format tab.
   - Click More in the Shape Styles group to open the Shape Styles gallery.
   - Choose Moderate Effect, Gold Accent 1.
   - Click Shape Effects and choose Half Reflection, 4 pt offset from the Reflection gallery.

Additional Information

The offset controls the amount of space between the object and the reflection.

Your screen should be similar to Figure 2.26

The addition of style and reflection effects greatly improves the appearance of the heart.

ADDING TEXT TO A SHAPE

Next, you will add text to the heart object. Text can be added to all shapes and becomes part of the shape; when the shape is moved, the text moves with it.

1. Right-click on the heart shape to open the context menu, and choose Edit Text.
   - Type **Open Your Heart**

Having Trouble?

If the inserted text does not fit into the heart shape, increase the size of the heart.

Your screen should be similar to Figure 2.27

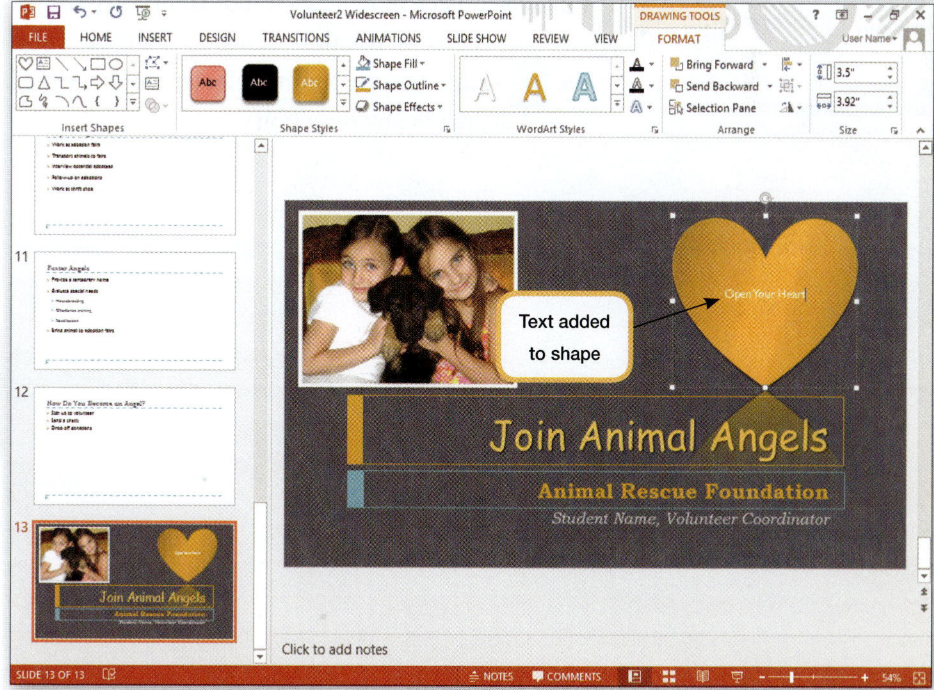

Figure 2.27

Next, you want to improve the appearance of the text using character effects.

2

- Select the text in the heart.
- Click **B** Bold and *I* Italic on the Mini toolbar.
- Increase the font size to 24 points.
- Open the A Font Color gallery and choose Rose, Accent 3, Darker 50% in the Theme Colors section.
- Click outside the heart to deselect the shape.

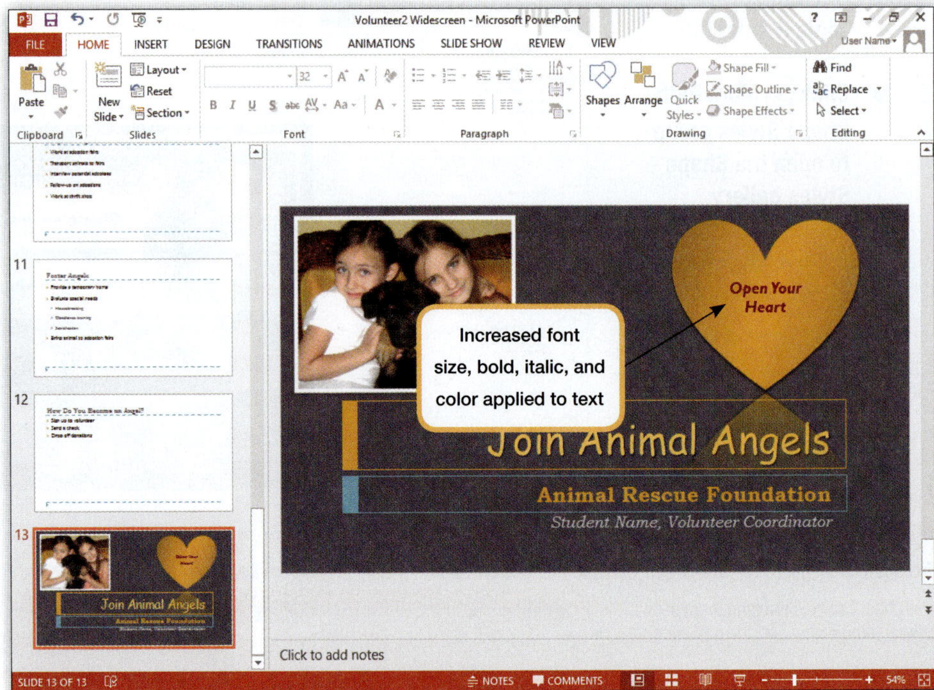

Figure 2.28

Your screen should be similar to Figure 2.28

Additional Information

Holding down (Shift) while slowly dragging the rotate handle rotates the object in 15-degree increments.

Another Method

You also can use Rotate Objects in the Arrange group of the Drawing Tools Format tab to rotate an object.

ROTATING THE OBJECT

Finally, you want to change the angle of the heart shape and the picture. You can rotate an object 90 degrees left or right, flip it vertically or horizontally, or specify an exact degree of rotation. You will change the angle of the heart to the right using the **rotate handle** for the selected object, which allows you to rotate the object to any degree in any direction.

1

- Select the heart shape.
- Drag the rotate handle to the right slightly.

Additional Information

The mouse pointer appears as [icon] when positioned on the rotate handle, and Live Preview shows how the object will look as you rotate it.

- Select the picture.
- Drag the rotate handle to the left slightly.

Having Trouble?

You may need to reposition and/or slightly resize the graphics.

Your screen should be similar to Figure 2.29

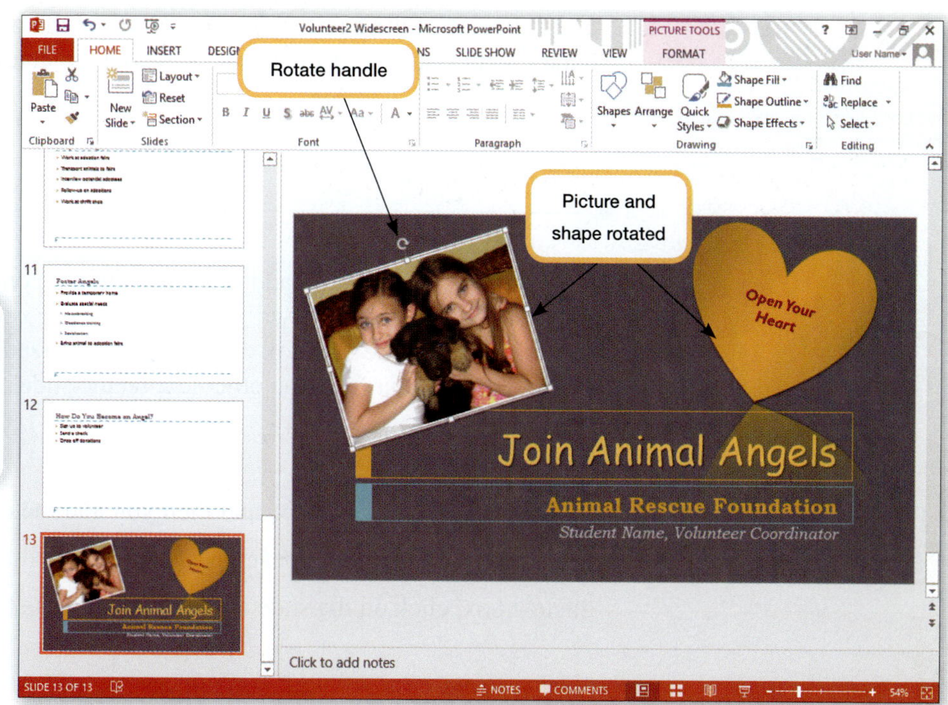

Figure 2.29

The angle of the graphics is an interesting addition to the slide.

USING COLOR MATCHING

You decide the color of the heart you added is too dark, and you'd like to match the lighter yellow in the girl's shirt. PowerPoint 2013 includes an **eyedropper tool** that makes it easy to copy a color from an object in the slide and apply it to any shape.

1

- Select the heart shape.
- Click [Shape Fill] in the Drawing group of the Home tab.
- Choose Eyedropper.

Additional Information

The insertion point changes to [icon] with a small box that shows the color you are pointing to.

- Point to the light yellow color in the girl's blouse, and when the ScreenTip displays Light Yellow, click to choose it.

Your screen should be similar to Figure 2.30

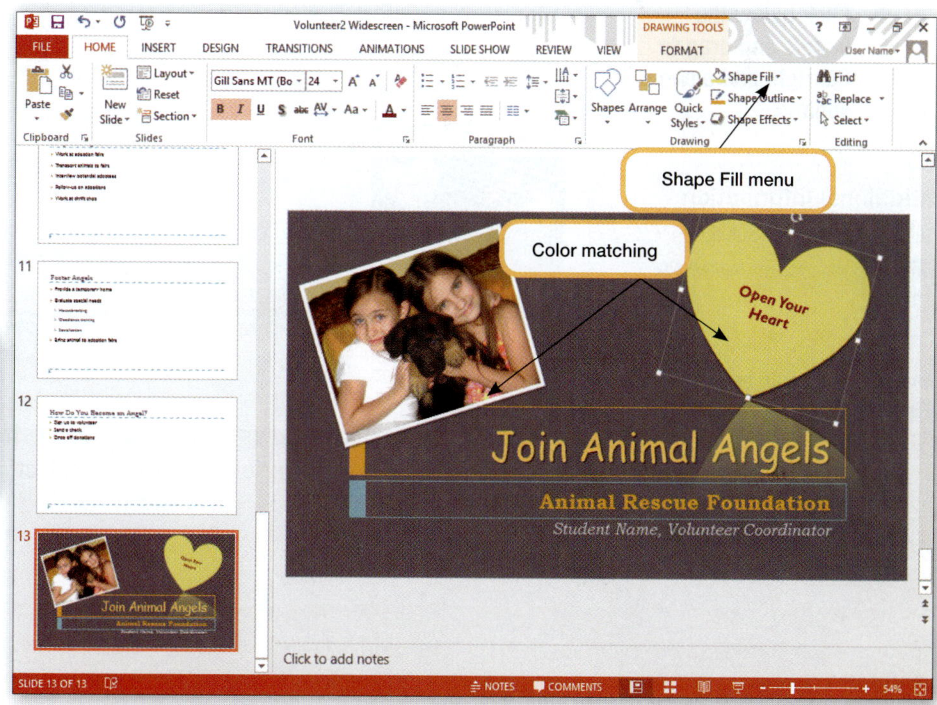

Figure 2.30

Another Method

You also can use Shape Fill on the Drawing Tools Format tab to access the eyedropper tool.

The fill color of the heart shape now matches the light yellow in the blouse. The darker text inside the heart "pops," and your concluding slide stands out.

Working with Text Boxes

On slide 12, you want to add the foundation's contact information. To make it stand out on the slide, you will put it into a text box. A **text box** is a container for text or graphics. The text box can be moved, resized, and enhanced in other ways to make it stand out from the other text on the slide.

CREATING A TEXT BOX

First you create the text box, and then you add the content. When inserting a text box, the mouse pointer appears as ↓ when pointing to the slide. Then, to create the text box, click on the slide and drag to increase the size.

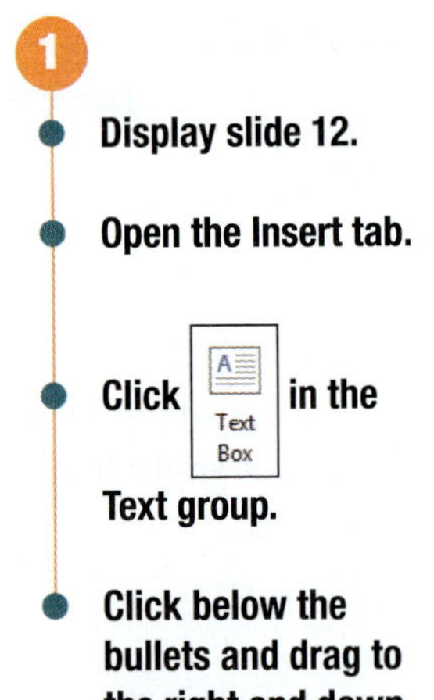

1

- **Display slide 12.**
- **Open the Insert tab.**
- **Click Text Box in the Text group.**
- **Click below the bullets and drag to the right and down slightly.**

Additional Information

The mouse pointer appears as + when dragging to create the text box.

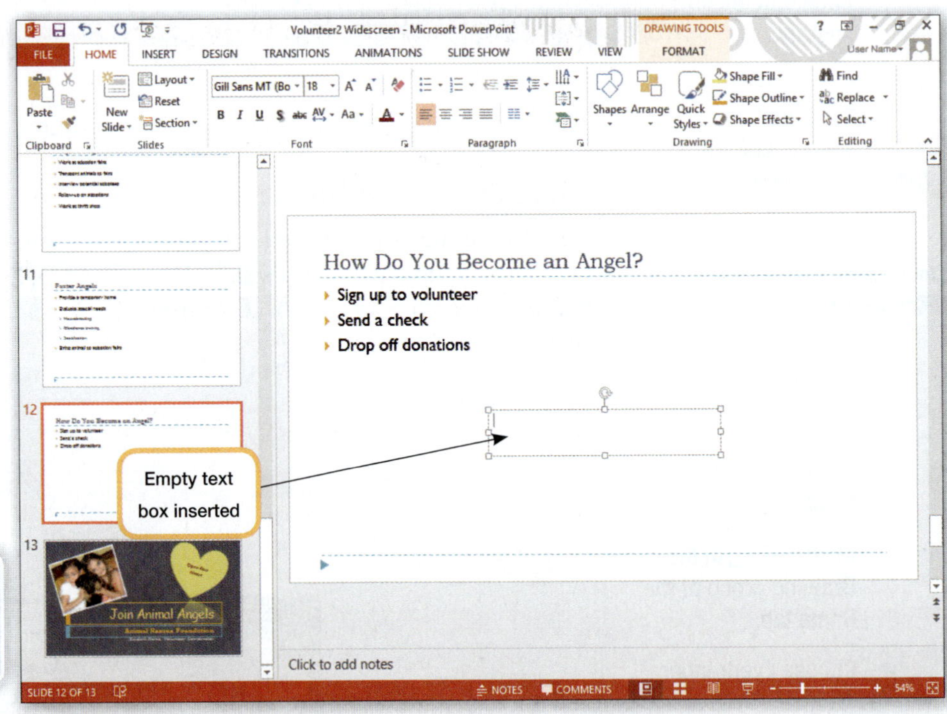

Figure 2.31

Your screen should be similar to Figure 2.31

The text box is created and is a selected object. It is surrounded with a dashed border indicating you can enter, delete, select, and format the text inside the box.

ADDING TEXT TO A TEXT BOX

The text box displays an insertion point, indicating that it is waiting for you to enter the text. As you type the text, the text box will automatically resize as needed to display the entire entry.

- **Type the organization's name and address shown below in the text box. Press Enter to start a new line.**

Having Trouble?

If your text box displays a solid border and no cursor, when you start to type, the cursor will appear and it will change to a dashed border.

Animal Rescue Foundation

1166 Oak Street

Lakeside, NH 03112

(603) 555-1313

- **Click on the text box border to select the entire object and increase the font size to 24 points and bold.**
- **If necessary, increase the width of the text box to display the name of the foundation on a single line.**

Additional Information

You also could copy text from another location and paste it into the text box.

Your screen should be similar to Figure 2.32

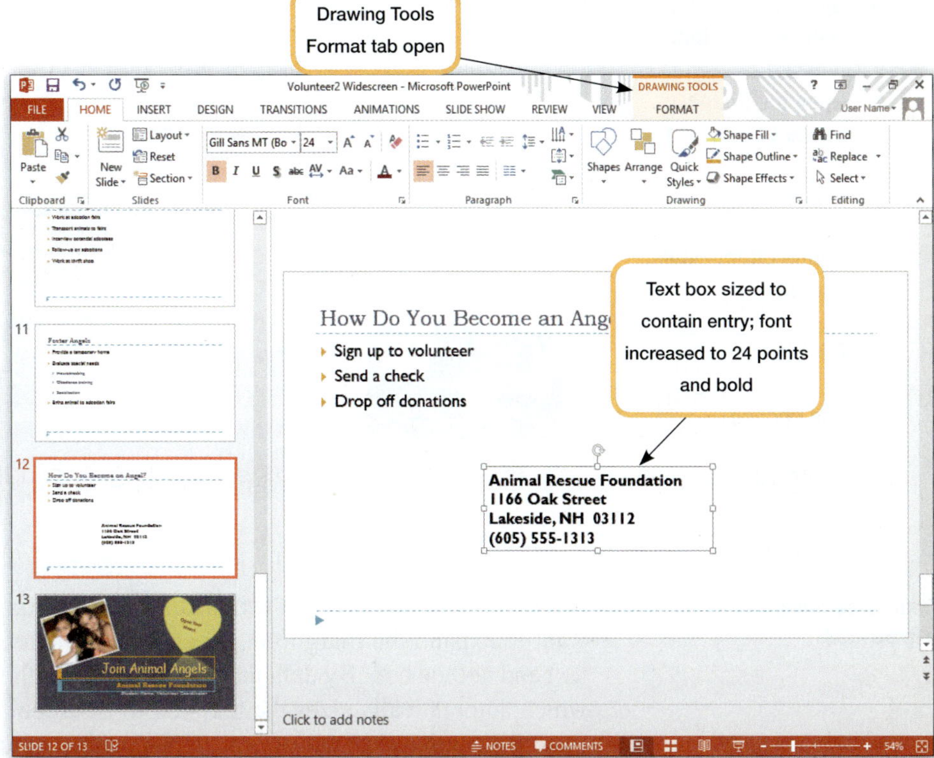

Figure 2.32

The text box is now more prominent and the content is easier to read.

ENHANCING THE TEXT BOX

Like any other object, the text box can be sized and moved anywhere on the slide. It also can be enhanced by adding styles and effects. You want to change the color and add a bevel effect around the box to define the space.

1

- If necessary, select the text box as an object (solid border).
- Open the Drawing Tools Format tab.
- Open the Shape Styles gallery and choose Abc Subtle Effect - Gold, Accent 1.
- Click Shape Effects and choose Angle from the Bevel group.

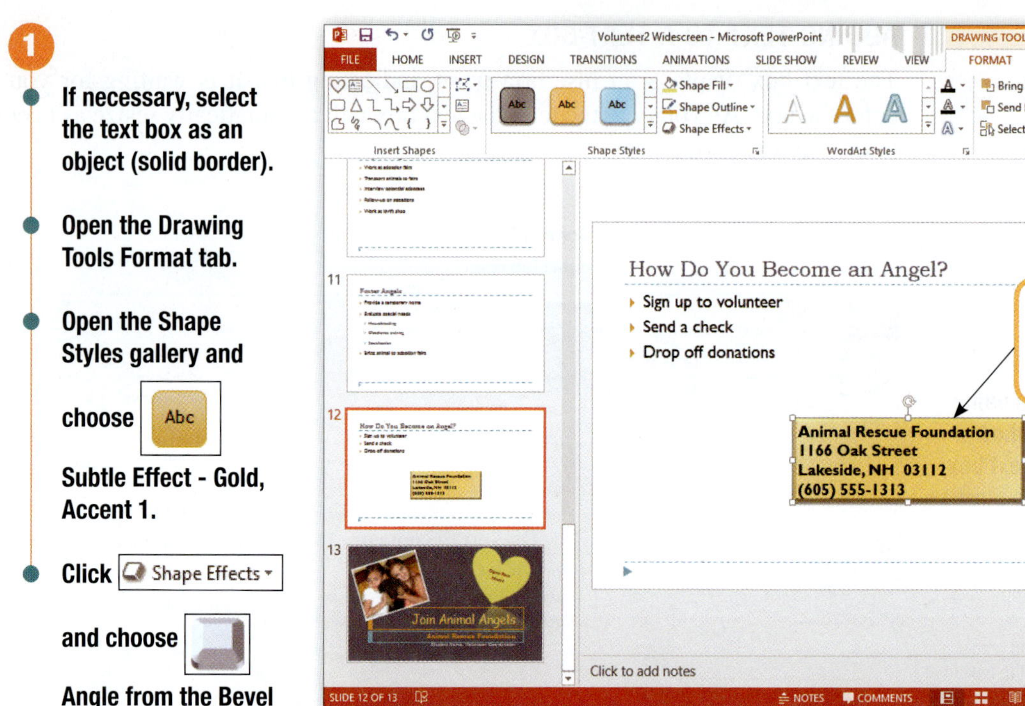

Figure 2.33

Your screen should be similar to Figure 2.33

Next, you will position the text within the text box and the box on the slide. You want to expand the margin on either side of the text to focus the attention on the text and not the box. By default, PowerPoint uses the AutoFit feature on text boxes, which automatically sizes the text box to fit around the text. You will turn off the AutoFit feature so that you control the position of the text.

2

- Right-click within the text of the text box and choose Format Text Effects.
- Click Textbox from the Format Shape pane and choose Do Not AutoFit.
- Change the left and right margins to .3.
- Choose Middle Centered from the Vertical Alignment drop-down box.
- Close the Format Shape pane.
- Adjust the size of the text box to display the information as in Figure 2.34.
- Move the text box to the position shown in Figure 2.34.
- Deselect the text box.
- Save the presentation.

Your screen should be similar to **Figure 2.34**

NOTE If you are ending your session now, exit PowerPoint 2013. When you begin again, open this file.

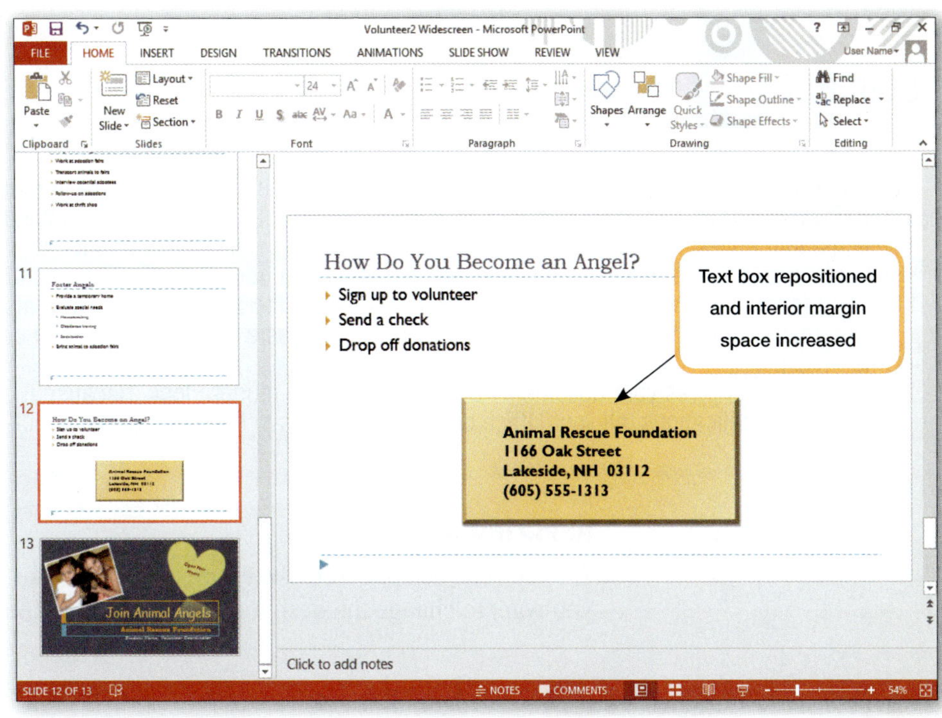

Figure 2.34

The information in the text box now stands out from the other information on the slide.

Changing the Presentation Design

When you first started this presentation, you used a PowerPoint template that included sample text as well as color and design elements. Now you are satisfied with the presentation's basic content and organization, but you would like to change its design style and appearance by applying a different theme.

Concept 4 Theme

A **theme** is a predefined set of formatting choices that can be applied to an entire document in one simple step. PowerPoint includes 29 named, built-in themes consisting of different combinations of colors, background designs, font styles, and layouts. Each theme uses a unique set of colors, fonts, and effects. Each theme consists of 12 colors that are applied to specific elements in a document. Each font component includes body and heading fonts. Each effects component includes different line and fill effects. You also can create your own custom themes by modifying an existing theme and saving it as a custom theme. The default presentation uses the Office Theme.

Using themes gives your documents a professional and modern look. Because themes are shared across Office 2013 applications, all your Office documents can have the same uniform look.

APPLYING A THEME

A theme can be applied to the entire presentation or to selected slides. In this case, you want to change the design for the entire presentation.

1

- **Display slide 1.**
- **Open the Design tab.**
- **Click ▾ More in the Themes group to open the Themes gallery.**
- **Point to**  **Wisp in the Office section of the gallery.**

Your screen should be similar to Figure 2.35

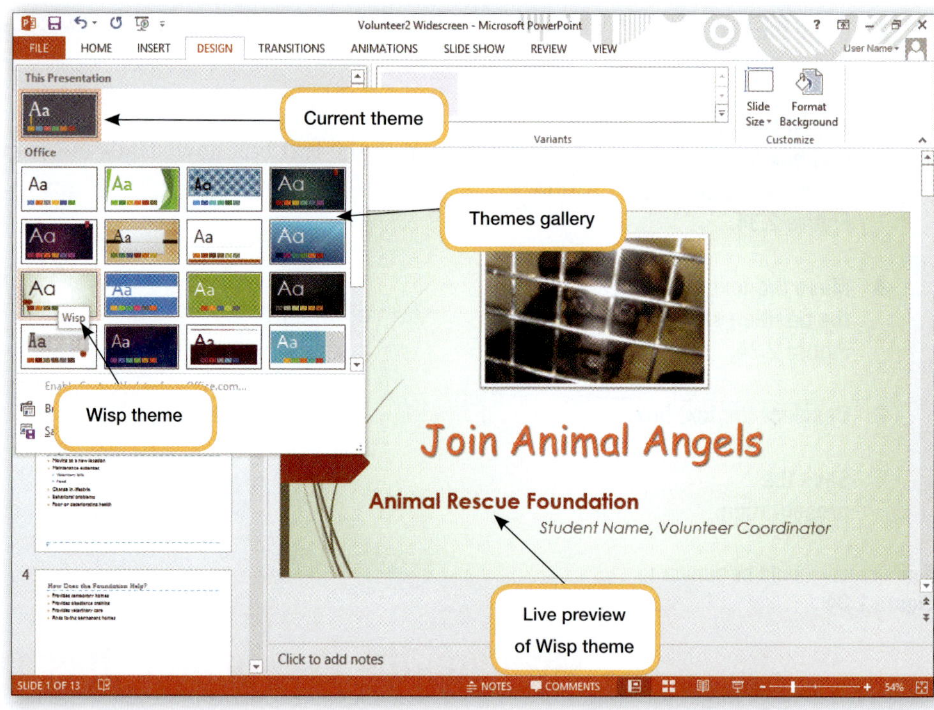

Figure 2.35

The Themes gallery displays thumbnails of each theme in the Office section. The This Presentation area displays the Origin theme that is currently used in the presentation. This is the theme associated with the presentation template you used to start the presentation. Pointing to a thumbnail displays a Live Preview of the presentation in the selected theme. As you can see, the slide colors, background designs, font styles, and overall layout of the slide are affected by the theme.

You will preview several other themes, and then use the Facet theme for the presentation.

- **Preview several other themes.**
- **Choose the Facet theme.**

Your screen should be similar to Figure 2.36

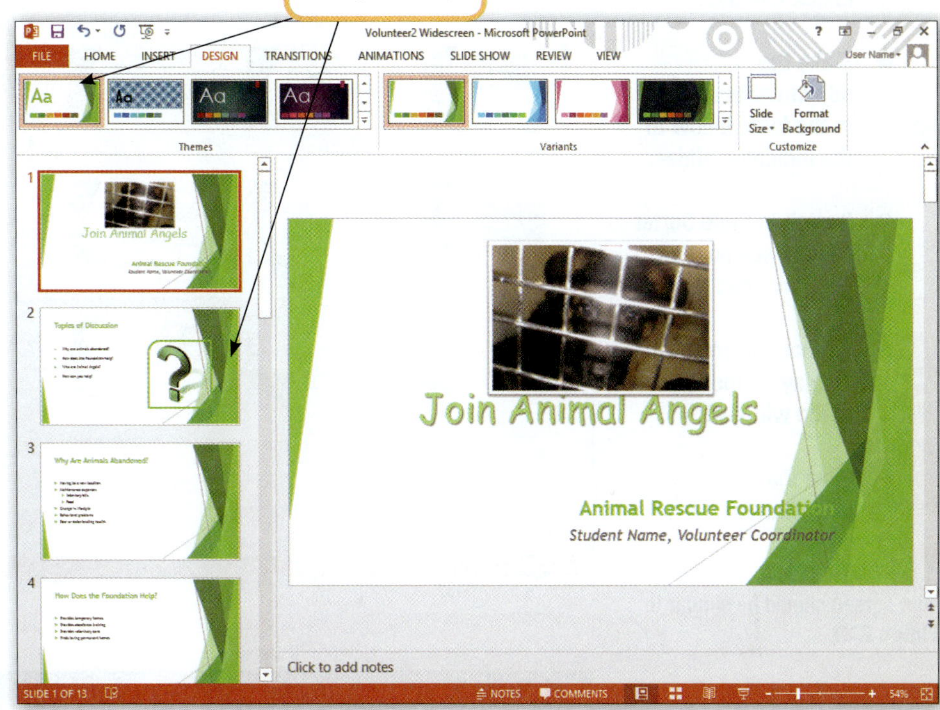

Figure 2.36

Additional Information

To apply a theme to selected slides, preselect the slides to apply the themes to in the Slide pane, and use the Apply to Selected Slides option from the theme's shortcut menu.

The Facet theme has been applied to all slides in the presentation. When a new theme is applied, the text styles, graphics, and colors that are included in the design replace the previous design settings. Consequently, the layout may need to be adjusted. For example, the slide title on slide 1 will need to be repositioned and and the picture size adjusted.

However, if you had made individual changes to a slide, such as changing the font of the title, these changes are not updated to the new theme design. In this case, the title font is still the Comic Sans MS that you selected in Lab 1; however, it has a different point size.

3

- **Select each slide and check the layout.**
- **Make the adjustments shown in the table below to the indicated slides.**
- **Switch to Slide Sorter view to see how all your changes look.**
- **Reduce the zoom to display all the slides in the window.**
- **Save the presentation.**

Your screen should be similar to Figure 2.37

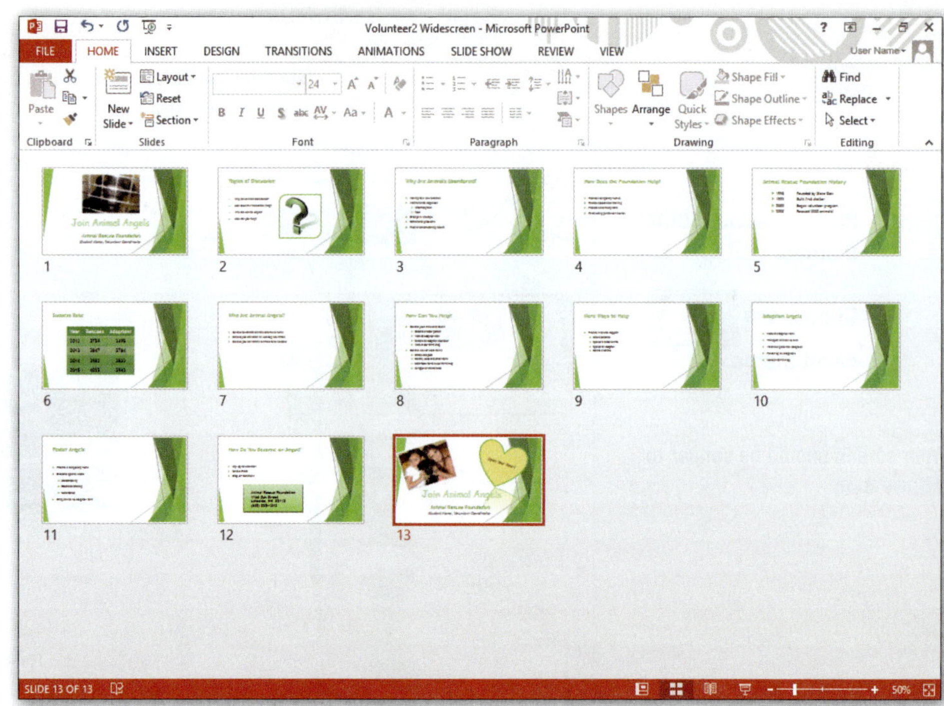

Figure 2.37

Slide	Adjustment
1	Move the title box down and the subtitle box to the left. If necessary, make the subtitle box smaller. Increase the size of the graphic slightly. Realign the graphic to the center of the slide.
2	If needed, adjust the position of the text content placeholder so the bullets align with the title text. If needed, adjust the size of the graphic and reposition it slightly.
5	If necessary, move the title placeholder down slightly to the same position on the slide as the title on the other slides. Select both content placeholders and move them slightly to the left, and increase the font size to 24 points.
6	Appropriately adjust the size and position of the table.
8	Move the content placeholder up slightly.
12	Adjust the position of the text box as needed.
13	If necessary, rotate, move, and resize both graphics to fit the slide. Reposition the title and subtitle placeholder boxes appropriately on the slide.

SELECTING THEME VARIANTS

By default, the Facet theme uses a green color palette with a white background. In addition, each theme includes a set of variations from which you can choose different color palettes and font families. You will change the variant to one that includes a more interesting background.

1

- **Display slide 1 in Normal view.**
- **Open the Design tab.**
- **Point to each of the four variants and look at the live previews.**
- **Select the last variant.**

Your screen should be similar to Figure 2.38

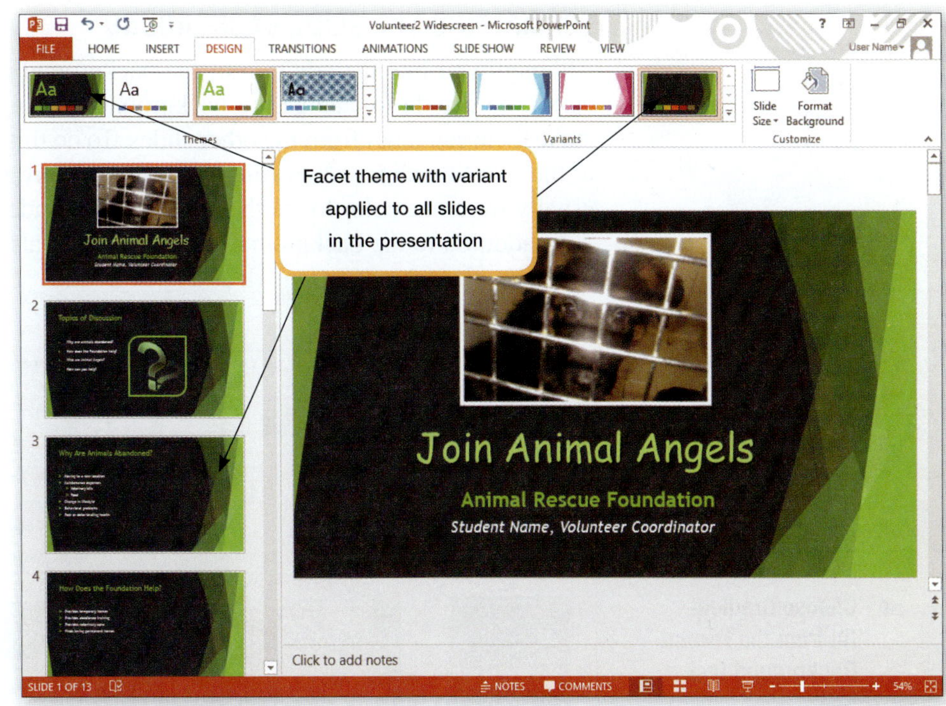

Figure 2.38

The selected variant includes light green and white text with a dark blue-gray background on all slides.

FORMATTING THE SLIDE BACKGROUND

Although you like the addition of the background color, you think it is a bit too dark. You decide to change the background shading in the first and last slide to make them stand out from the other slides. To do this, you will add a gradient color to the two title slides. A **gradient** is a gradual progression of colors and shades, usually from one color to another or from one shade to another of the same color.

In addition to the background colors, you can also use texture and pattern fills, a picture, clip art, or watermark as a background.

1

- **Click** 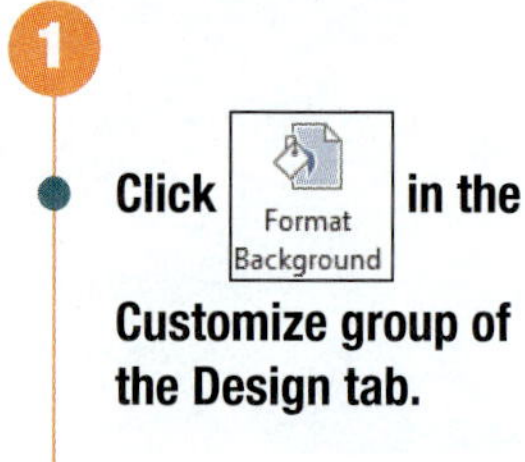

in the Customize group of the Design tab.

- **Choose Gradient fill from the Format Background task pane.**

Your screen should be similar to Figure 2.39

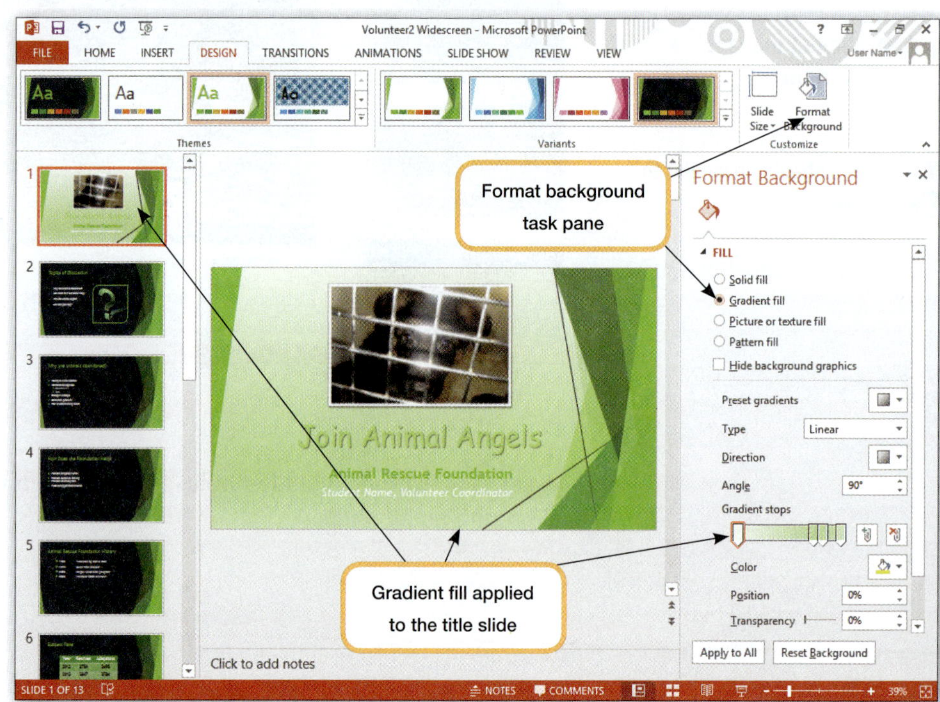

Figure 2.39

Since the original theme (Facet) uses shades of green, the gradient background shows a white to light green progression. The type of fill used by default is linear, from top to bottom. You will make a simple modification of the color so that the progression goes from blue-gray to green and from bottom to top.

2

- Click [icon] Color and choose Blue-Gray, Background 2, Lighter 60%.
- Click [icon] Direction and choose Linear Up (second row, second item).
- Display slide 13 and choose Gradient Fill.
- Close the Format Background pane.
- Change the color of the title and first subtitle line on slides 1 and 13 to Red, Accent 5, Darker 25%.
- Save the presentation.

Your screen should be similar to Figure 2.40

Figure 2.40

When you selected Gradient Fill on the last slide, the changes you made to slide 1 automatically applied to slide 13. Now, both title slides have the same effects for consistency, and both slides stand out.

Working with Master Slides

While viewing the slides, you think the slide appearance could be further improved by changing the font color and bullet design on all slides. Although you can change each slide individually, you can make the change much faster to all the slides by changing the slide master.

Concept 5 Master

A **master** is part of a template that stores information about the formatting for the three key components of a presentation—slides, speaker notes, and handouts. Each component has a master associated with it. The masters are described below.

Slide master	Defines the format and layout of text and objects on a slide, text and object placeholder sizes, text styles, backgrounds, color themes, effects, and animation.
Handout master	Defines the format and placement of the slide image, text, headers, footers, and other elements that will appear on every handout.
Notes master	Defines the format and placement of the slide image, note text, headers, footers, and other elements that will appear on all speaker notes.

Any changes you make to a master affect all slides, handouts, or notes associated with that master. Each theme comes with its own slide master. When you apply a new theme to a presentation, all slides and masters are updated to those of the new theme. Using the master to modify or add elements to a presentation ensures consistency and saves time.

You can create slides that differ from the slide master by changing the format and placement of elements in the individual slide rather than on the slide master. For example, when you changed the font settings of the title on the title slide, the slide master was not affected. Only the individual slide changed, making it unique. If you have created a unique slide, the elements you changed on that slide retain their uniqueness, even if you later make changes to the slide master. That is the reason that the title font did not change when you changed the theme.

MODIFYING THE SLIDE MASTER

You will change the title text font color and the bullet style in the slide master so that all slides in the presentation will be changed.

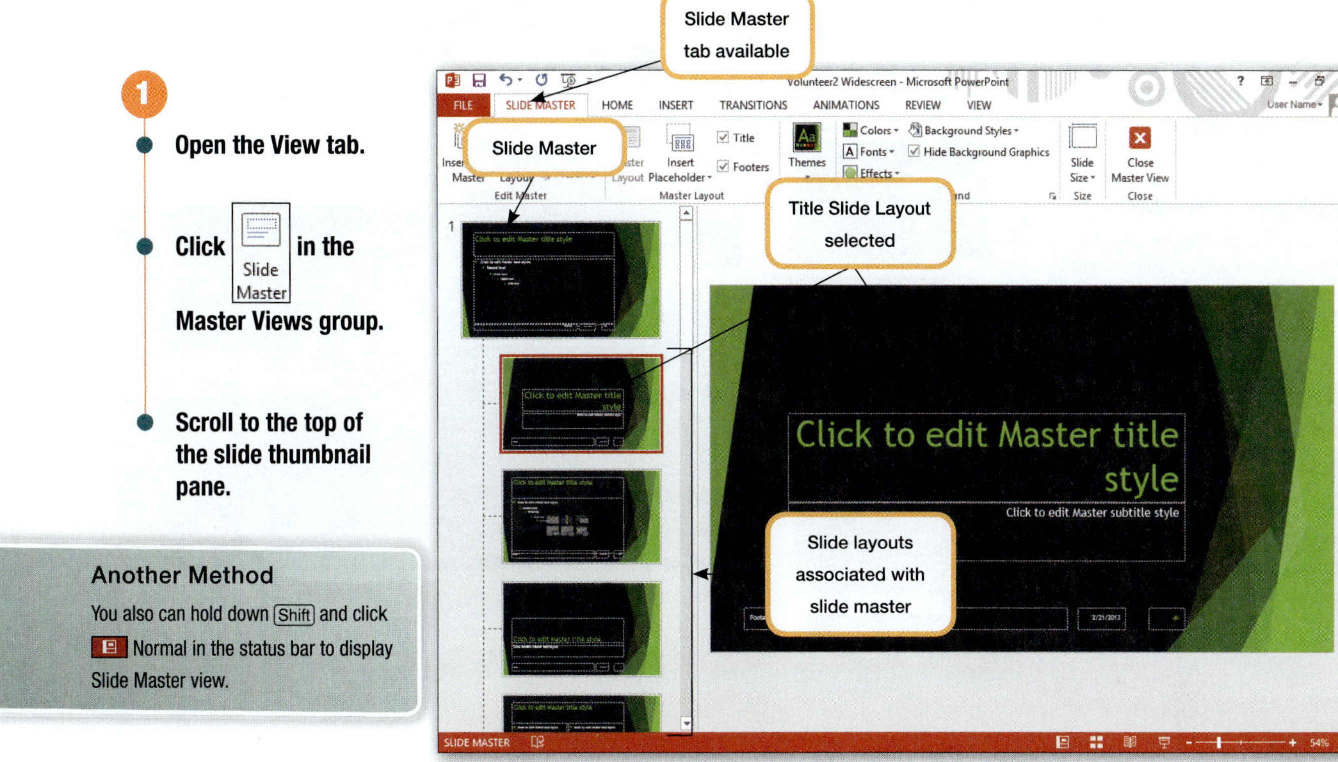

1

- **Open the View tab.**
- **Click Slide Master in the Master Views group.**
- **Scroll to the top of the slide thumbnail pane.**

Another Method

You also can hold down Shift and click Normal in the status bar to display Slide Master view.

Your screen should be similar to Figure 2.41

Figure 2.41

Additional Information

Every presentation contains at least one slide master. Each slide master contains one or more built-in or custom layouts.

Slide Master view consists of two panes: the slide thumbnail pane on the left containing slide thumbnails for the slide master and for each of the layouts associated with the slide master and the Slide pane on the right displaying the selected slide. In the slide thumbnail pane, the slide master is the large thumbnail at the top of the pane. It stores information about the theme and slide layouts of a presentation. Below the slide master are the layouts associated with the slide master. The slide master and all supporting layouts appear in the current theme, Facet, with the color variant you selected. Each slide layout displays a different layout arrangement. The thumbnail for the Title Slide Layout is selected, and the Slide pane displays the slide.

If you modify the slide master, all layouts beneath the slide master are also changed. If you modify a slide layout, although you are essentially also modifying the slide master, the changes affect only that layout under the slide master. You want to change the slide master so that your changes affect all the associated layouts.

2

- **Point to the thumbnails to see the ScreenTip.**

Additional Information

The ScreenTip identifies the selected master or layout and the slides where it is used in the presentation.

- **Click on the Facet Slide Master thumbnail to select it.**

Your screen should be similar to Figure 2.42

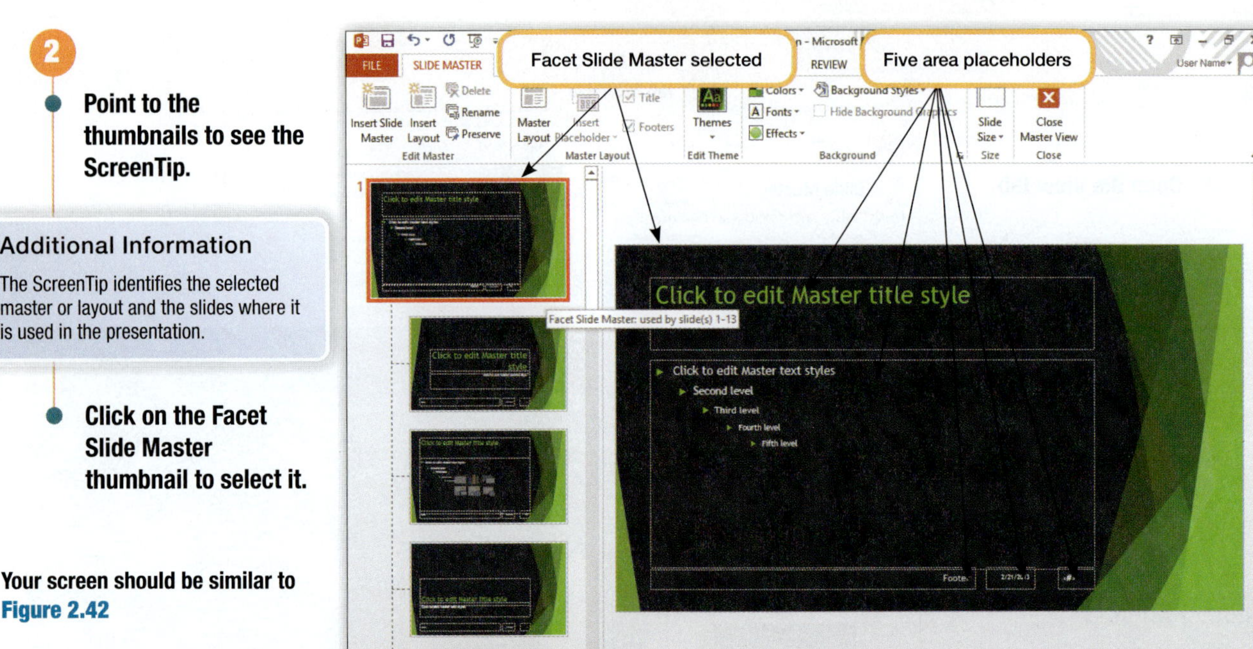

Figure 2.42

The Facet Slide Master consists of five area placeholders that control the appearance of all slides: title, content, date, slide number, and footer. The title and content areas display sample text to show you how changes you make in these areas will appear. You make changes to the slide master in the same way that you change any other slide. First you will change the font color and size for the title text throughout the presentation.

3

- **Click on the title area placeholder border to select it.**

Having Trouble?

Do not select an individual item within the content area or the changes will be applied to that item only.

- **Open the Home tab.**
- **Change the font color to Gold, Accent 3 and bold.**

Your screen should be similar to Figure 2.43

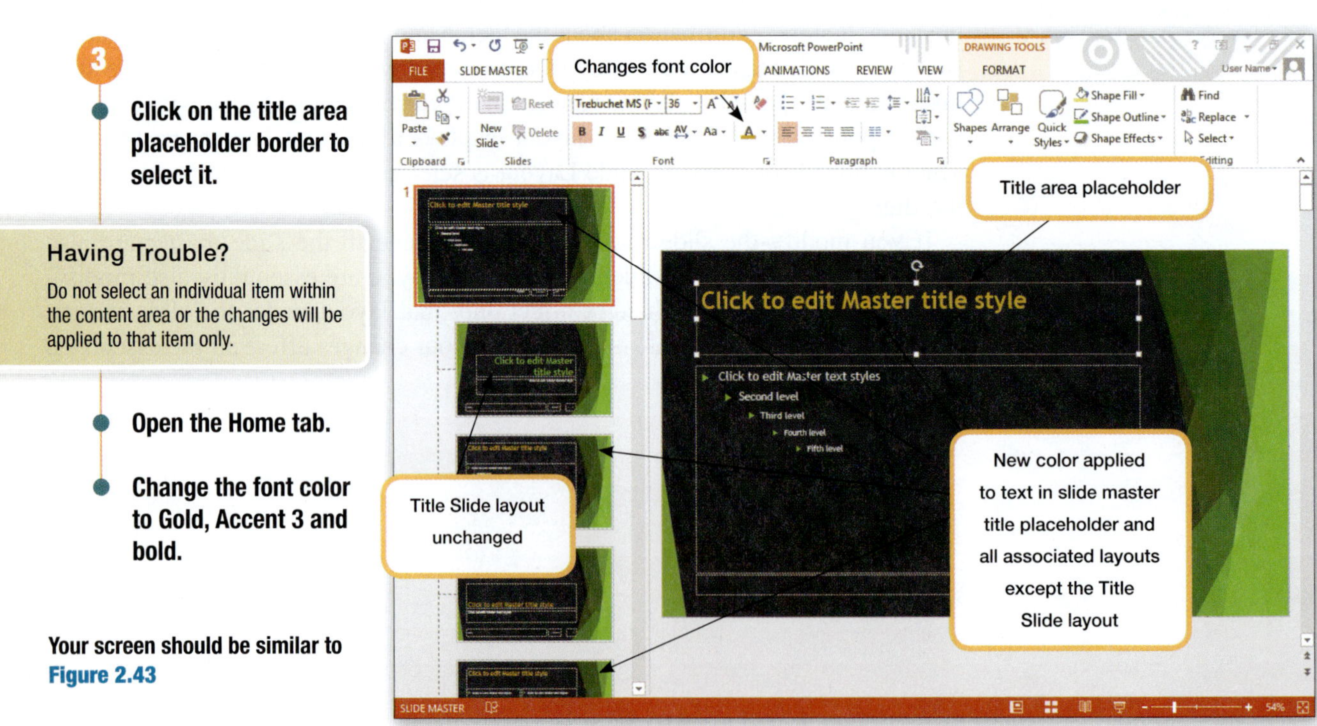

Figure 2.43

4

- Click on the content area placeholder border to select it.
- Open the Bullets drop-down menu.
- Choose Bullets and Numbering.
- Click Picture... .
- In the Office.com clip art search box, type bullets and press Enter.

Having Trouble?

If you do not have Internet access, select another bullet design from the basic designs provided.

Your screen should be similar to **Figure 2.44**

Notice that the font changes appear in all layouts below the slide master except the Title Slide layout. This is because you changed the format of the title on the individual slides which overrides the changes made to the master slide.

Next, you will modify the content area placeholder to change the bullet style, increase the font size, and modify the position of the placeholder.

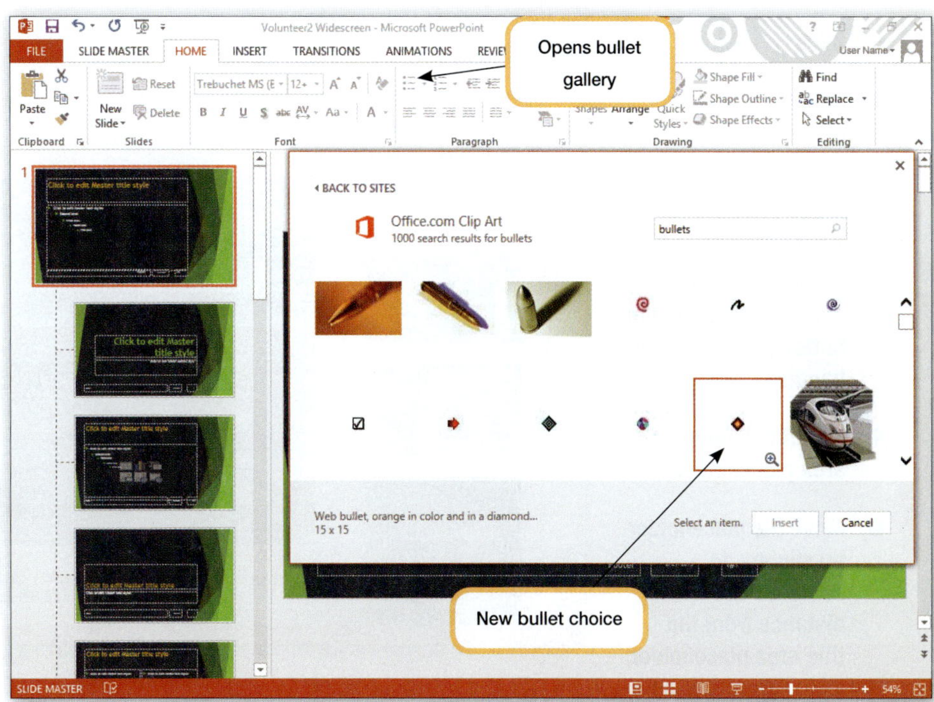

Figure 2.44

From the search results, you select the bullet design you want to use from the bullet styles listed. You will use a diamond-shaped bullet design.

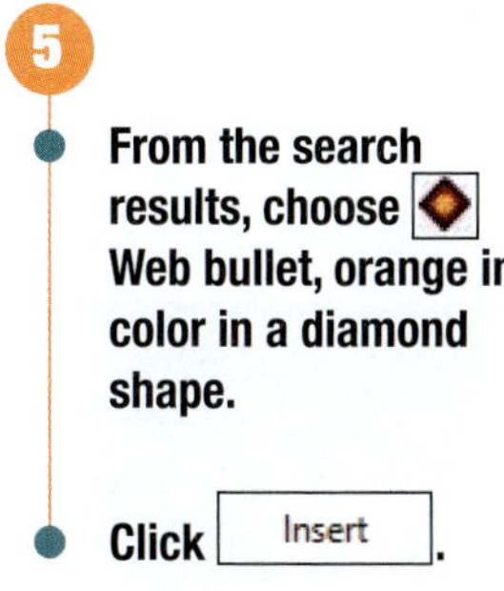

5

- From the search results, choose Web bullet, orange in color in a diamond shape.
- Click Insert .

Your screen should be similar to **Figure 2.45**

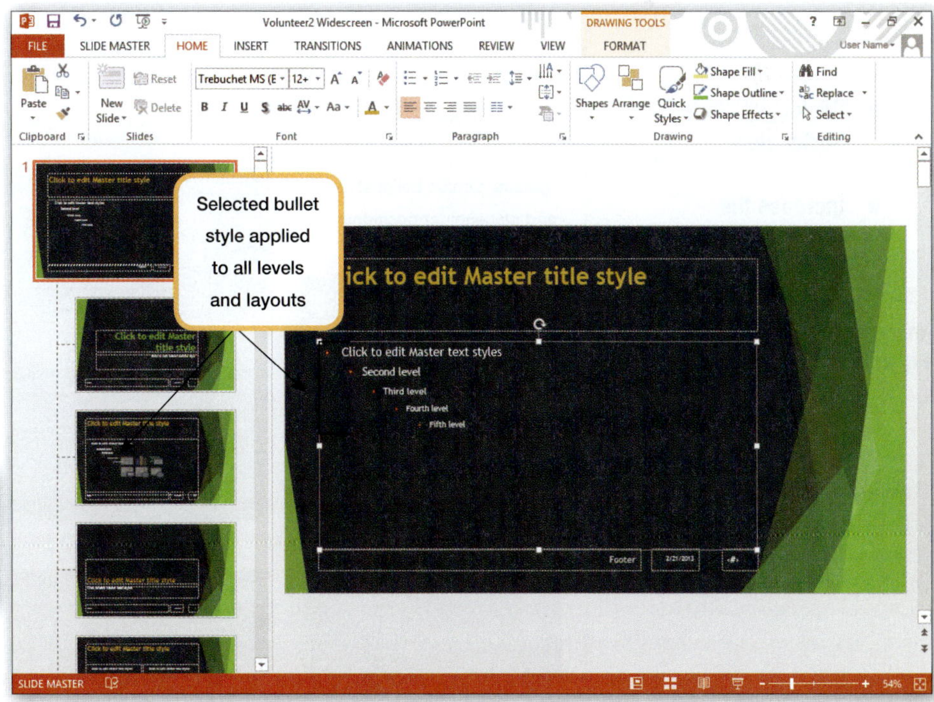

Figure 2.45

Additional Information

You can apply different bullet styles to each level by selecting each level individually.

6

- If necessary, select the content area placeholder.
- Click [A˄] twice.
- Select the title area placeholder.
- Click [A˅] once.
- Decrease the height of the title area placeholder using the bottom, middle sizing handle.
- Select the content area placeholder.
- Move the placeholder up slightly, to decrease the distance from the title area placeholder, as in Figure 2.46.

The selected bullet style has been applied to all levels of items in the content area and to all layouts under the slide master that have bulleted items. Next, you will increase the font size and adjust the size and position of the title and content area placeholders.

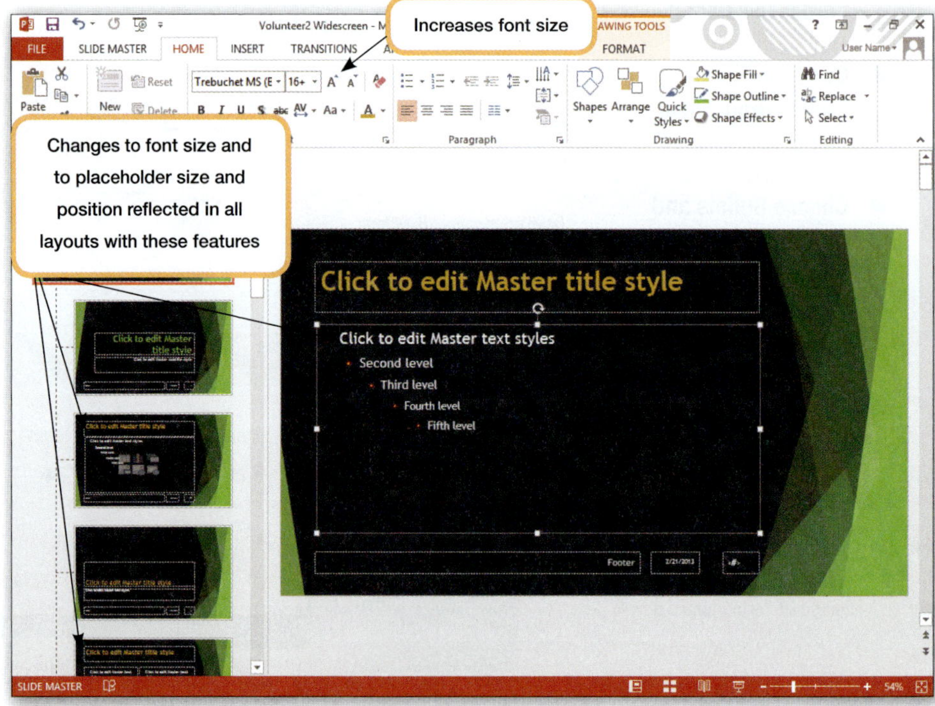

Figure 2.46

Your screen should be similar to Figure 2.46

Now you want to see how all the changes you have made to the slide master have affected the actual slides in the presentation.

7

- Click [Slide Sorter] Slide Sorter view.
- Increase the magnification to 90%.

Your screen should be similar to Figure 2.47

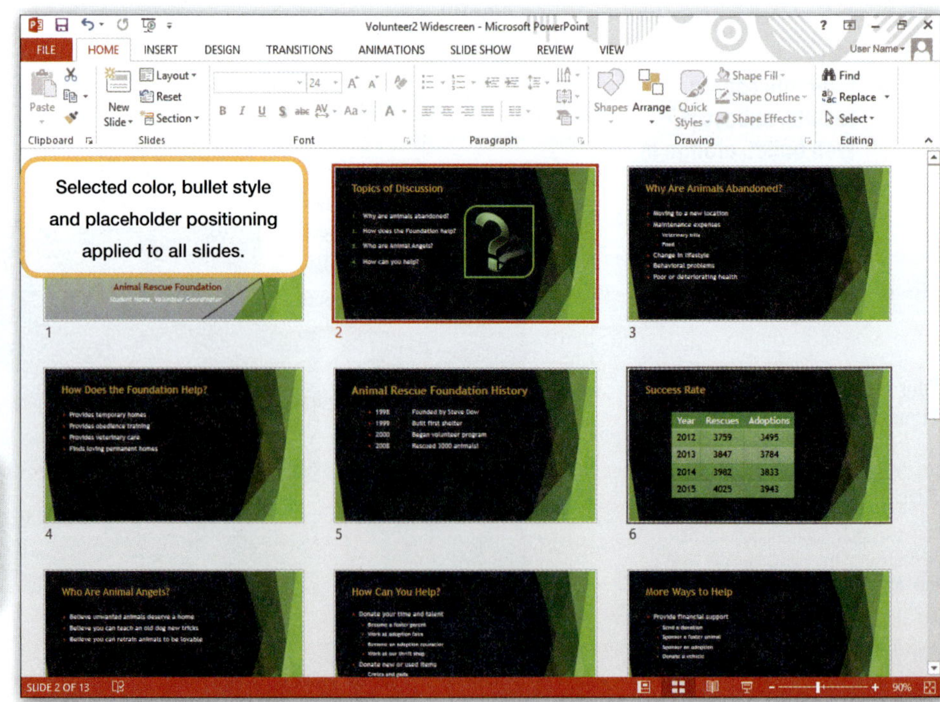

Figure 2.47

Having Trouble?

With the changes made to the master slide, you may need to resize or reposition a graphic.

You can now see that the changes you made to the bullet style, font color and size, and positioning of the placeholders in the slide master are reflected in all slides in the presentation with the exception of the Title Layout slides. Using the slide master allows you to quickly make global changes to your presentation.

You will run the slide show next to see how the changes you have made look full screen.

8

- **Run the slide show beginning with slide 1.**
- **Click on each slide to advance through the presentation.**
- **If necessary, fix any slides that did not display correctly.**
- **Save the presentation.**

Now that you are happy with the look of the presentation, you want to incorporate animation effects to change the way the text appears on the slides.

Animating the Presentation

You are pleased with the changes you have made to the presentation so far. However, you have several places in mind where using animation will make the presentation more interesting.

Concept  Animations

Animations are special effects that add action to text and graphics so they move around on the screen during a slide show. Animations provide additional emphasis for items or show the information on a slide in phases. There are two basic types of animations: object animations and transitions.

Object animations are used to display each bullet point, text, paragraph, or graphic independently of the other text or objects on the slide. You set up the way you want each element to appear (to fly in from the left, for instance) and whether you want the other elements already on the slide to dim or shimmer when a new element is added. For example, because your audience is used to reading from left to right, you could select animations that fly text in from the left. Then, when you want to emphasize a point, bring a bullet point in from the right. That change grabs the audience's attention.

Transitions control the way that the display changes as you move from one slide to the next during a presentation. You can select from many different transition choices. You may choose Dissolve for your title slide to give it an added flair. After that, you could use Wipe Right for all the slides until the next to the last, and then use Dissolve again to end the show. As with any special effect, use slide transitions carefully.

When you present a slide show, the content of your presentation should take center stage. You want the animation effects to help emphasize the main points in your presentation—not draw the audience's attention to the special effects.

ADDING TRANSITION EFFECTS

First, you want to add a transition effect to the slides. Although you can add transitions in Normal view, you will use Slide Sorter view so you can more easily preview the action on the slides.

1

- **Switch to Slide Sorter view, if necessary.**
- **Select slide 1.**
- **Open the Transitions tab.**
- **Click [▾] More in the Transition to This Slide group to open the Transitions gallery.**

Your screen should be similar to Figure 2.48

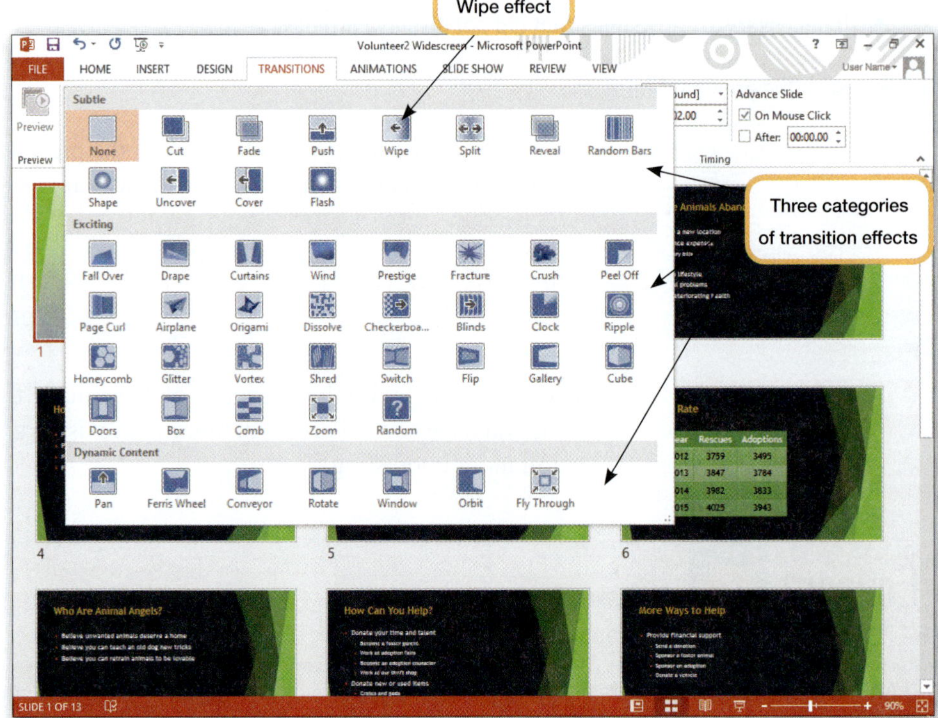

Figure 2.48

There are three transition categories, Subtle, Exciting, and Dynamic Content, with each containing variations on the category effect. You want to use a simple transition effect that will display as each slide appears. As you choose a transition effect a Live Preview of the effect is displayed on the selected slide.

Additional Information

Use the None transition option to remove transition effects.

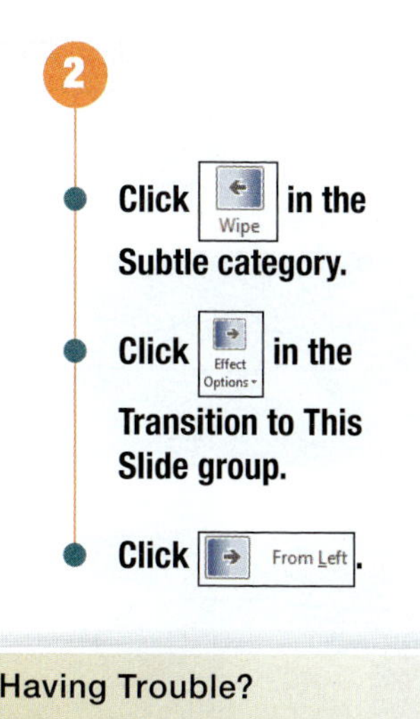

2

- Click Wipe in the Subtle category.
- Click Effect Options in the Transition to This Slide group.
- Click From Left.

Having Trouble?

If you want to see the transition effect again, click [icon] below the slide in Slide Sorter view.

Your screen should be similar to Figure 2.49

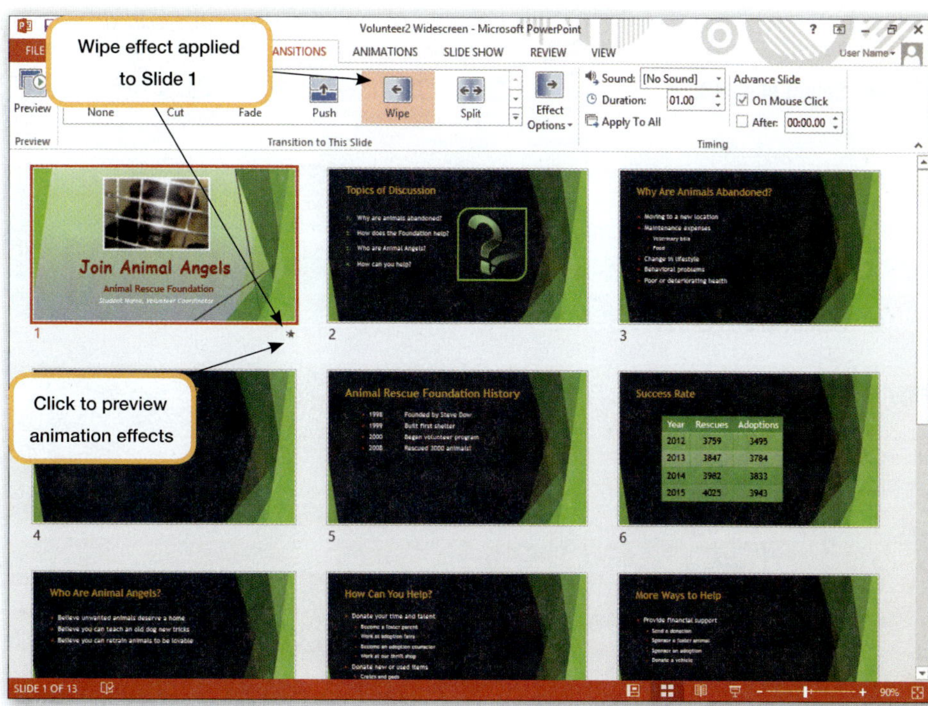

Figure 2.49

Another Method

You can also see the transition effect that is applied to a slide by selecting the slide and clicking Preview in the Preview group of the Transitions tab.

Additional Information

You also can select transition effects from the Transitions gallery by scrolling the list in the Transition to This Slide group.

The selected slide displays the Wipe Left transition effect. This effect displays the next slide's content by wiping over the previous slide from the right with the new slide content. You will use the Wipe Right transition effect on slide 13. You also want to try different transition effects on the other slides using the Random transition effect, which randomly displays a different transition effect for each slide.

3

- Select slide 13.
- Click Wipe in the Transition to This Slide group.
- Select slides 2–12.

Having Trouble?

Select slide 2 and hold down ⇧Shift while selecting slide 12.

- Choose Random in the Exciting group.

Your screen should be similar to Figure 2.50

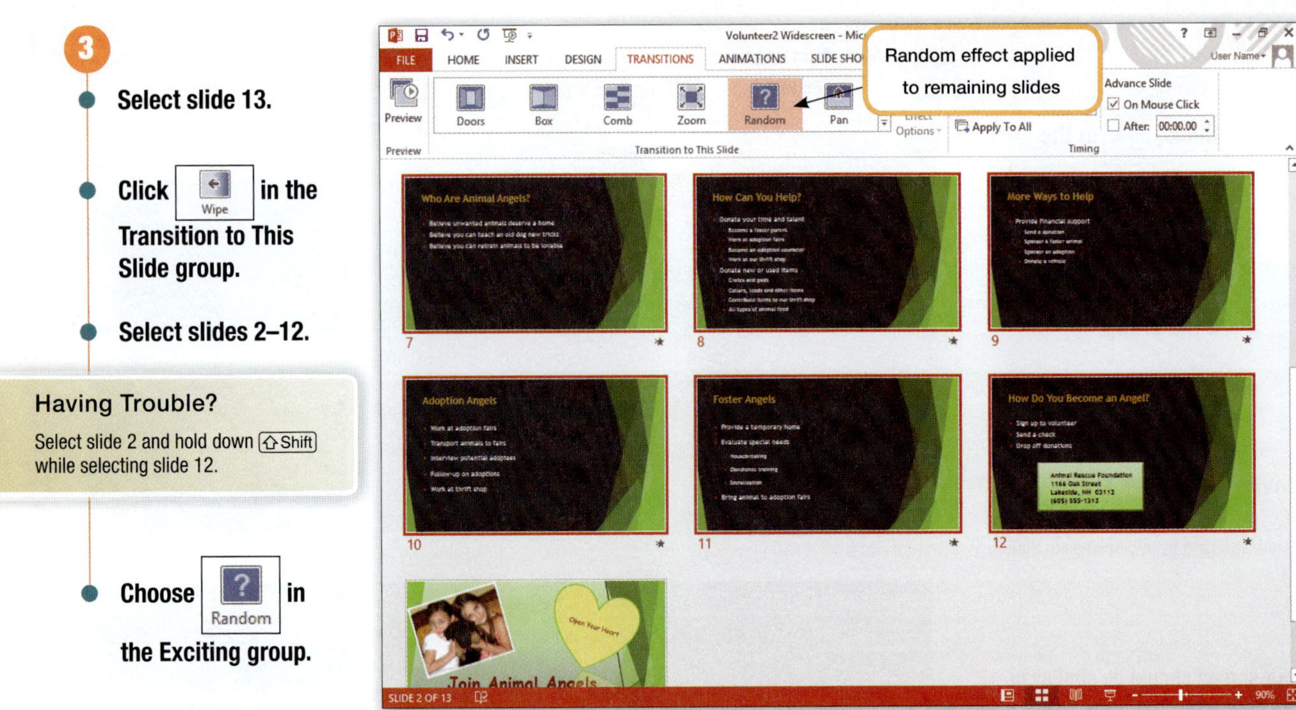

Figure 2.50

The transition animation effects associated with the selected slides were individually previewed beginning with slide 2, and each slide now displays a transition icon.

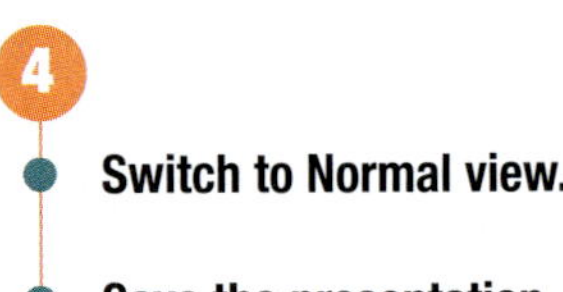

4

- Switch to Normal view.
- Save the presentation.

Notice an animation icon appears below each slide number in the Slides pane.

ANIMATING AN OBJECT

Next, you want to add an animation effect to the heart shape on the final slide. There are four different types of animation effects, described below. Animation effects can be used by themselves or in combination with other effects.

Type	Effect
Entrance	Makes an object appear on the slide using the selected effect.
Exit	Makes an object leave the slide using the selected effect.
Emphasis	Makes an object more noticeable by applying special effects to the object such as changing the text size and colors or adding bold or underlines.
Motion Path	Makes an object move in a selected pattern such as up, down, or in a circle.

- **Display slide 13 in Normal view.**
- **Select the heart shape.**
- **Open the Animations tab.**
- **Open the Animations gallery and click on several effects to see the Live Preview.**
- **Choose Fly In.**

Your screen should be similar to Figure 2.51

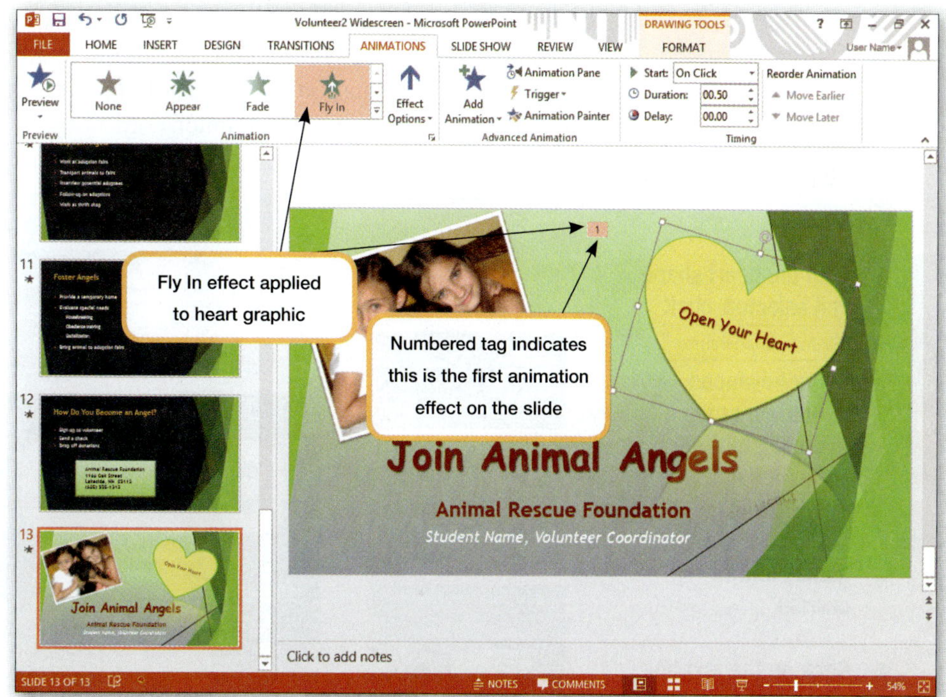

Figure 2.51

As you add animated items to a slide, each item is numbered. The number determines the order in which they display. A nonprinting numbered tag appears on the slide near each animated item that correlates to the effects in the list. This number does not appear during a slide show.

Next, you want to change the Fly In effect to come in from the left and to run slower.

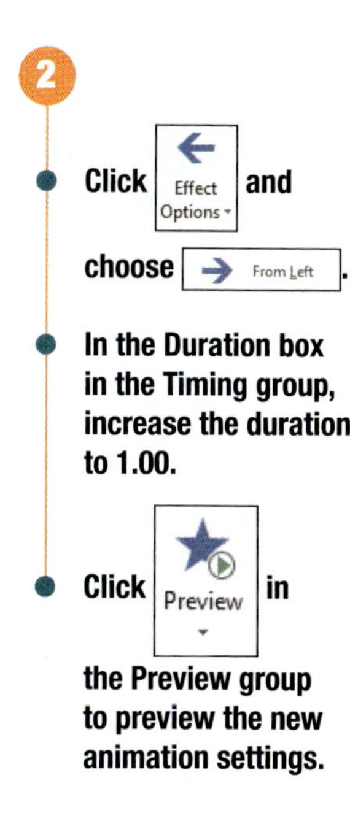

2

- **Click Effect Options and choose From Left.**
- **In the Duration box in the Timing group, increase the duration to 1.00.**
- **Click Preview in the Preview group to preview the new animation settings.**

Your screen should be similar to Figure 2.52

Figure 2.52

You like the way the animation effect livens up the final slide of the presentation, so you decide to apply the same effect to the text box on slide 12. Since you plan to use the same animation settings for both slides, the easiest way to duplicate an effect is to use the Animation Painter.

3

- **With the heart shape still selected, click [Animation Painter] in the Advanced Animation group to duplicate the animation effect of the heart shape.**
- **Make slide 12 current.**
- **Click on the text box to apply the copied effects.**

Your screen should be similar to Figure 2.53

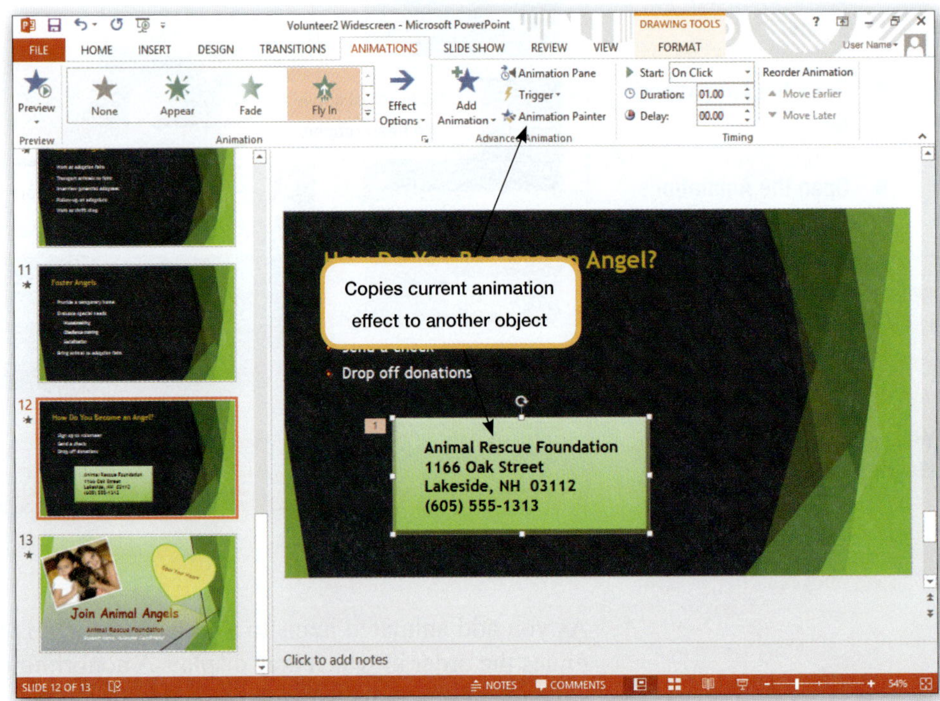

Figure 2.53

The Fly In animation effect is applied to the text box and previewed for you.

ADDING SOUND EFFECTS

Now that you have added animations to your presentation, you decide to give the animation on slide 13 extra emphasis by adding sound to the animation effect. To add the more advanced animation effects, you need to display the Animation pane.

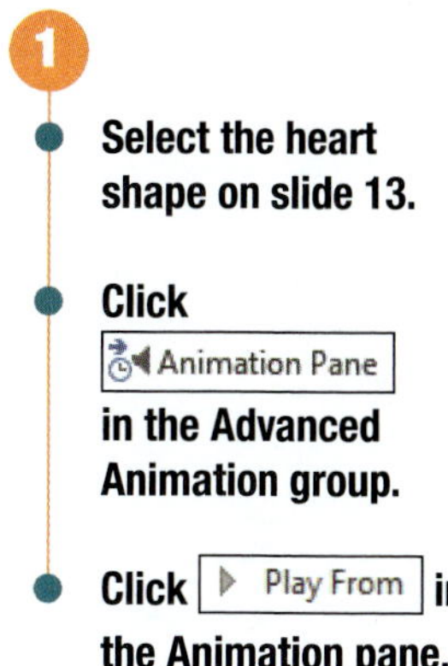

1

- Select the heart shape on slide 13.
- Click Animation Pane in the Advanced Animation group.
- Click Play From in the Animation pane.

Your screen should be similar to **Figure 2.54**

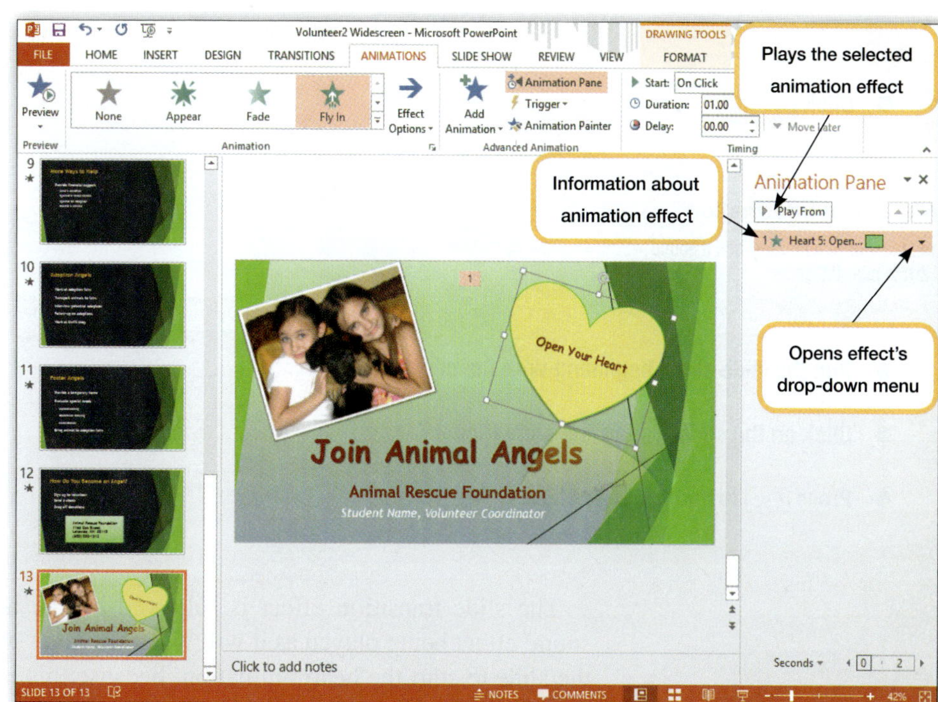

Figure 2.54

The Animation pane shows information about each animation effect on a slide. This includes the type of effect, the order of multiple effects in relation to one another, the name of the object affected, and the duration of the effect. It also is used to manage the animations and to add advanced effects to existing animations. You will use it to add a sound to the Fly In effect.

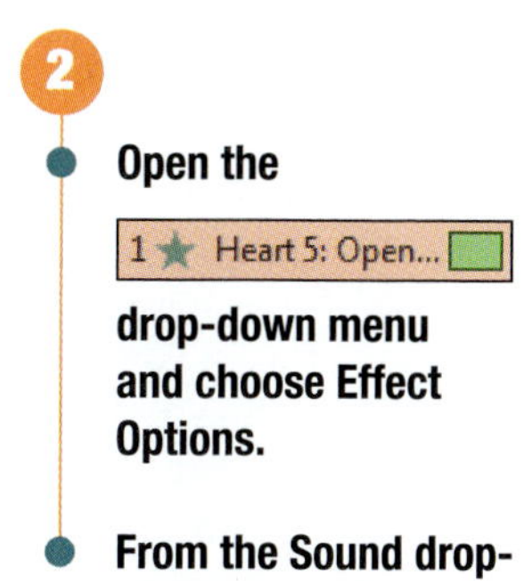

2

- Open the 1 Heart 5: Open... drop-down menu and choose Effect Options.
- From the Sound drop-down list choose Chime.

Your screen should be similar to **Figure 2.55**

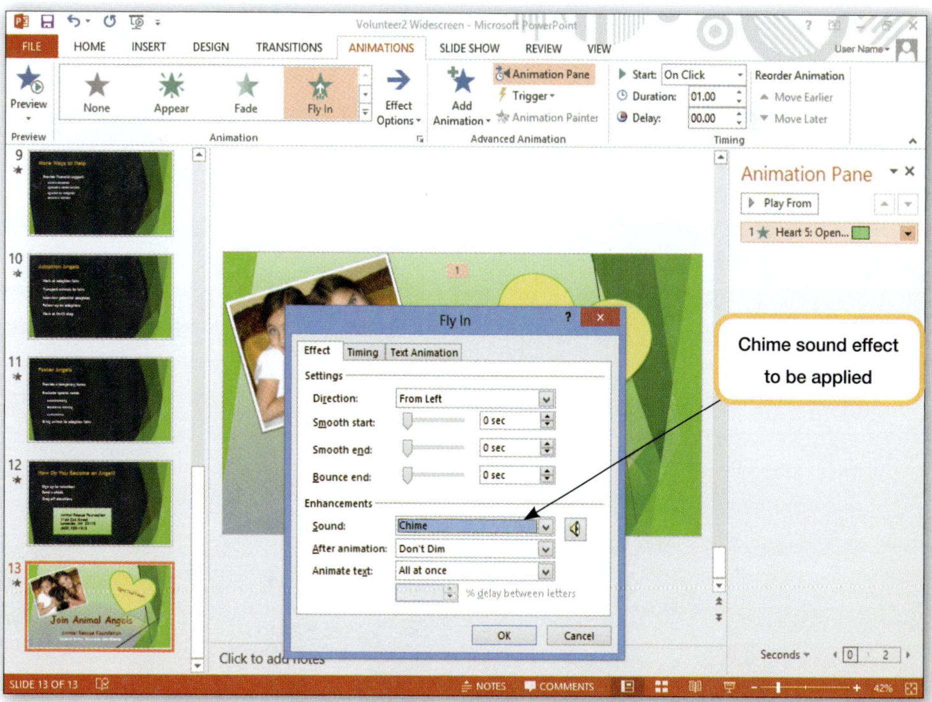

Figure 2.55

The Fly In dialog box is used to change the default settings associated with the selected effect. In this case, you are adding the Chime sound to the animation.

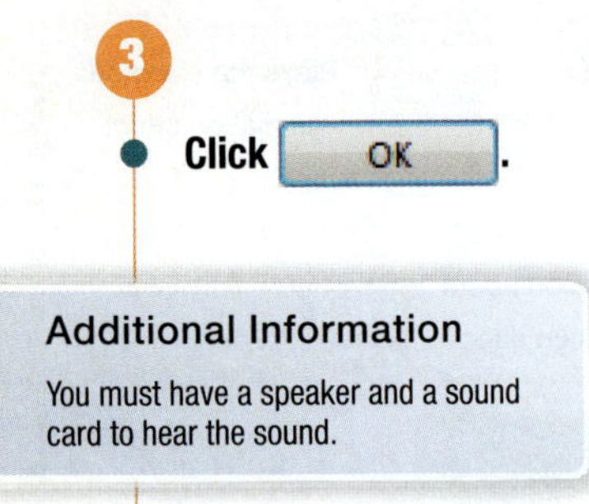

Additional Information

You must have a speaker and a sound card to hear the sound.

- **Run the slide show beginning with the current slide.**
- **Click on the slide to start the animation.**
- **Press Esc to end the slide show.**

The slide transition effect is followed by the heart fly-in animation and the sound effect being played as it will when the slide show is run. You had to click on the slide to start the heart animation, because this is the default setting to start an animation.

ANIMATING A SLIDE MASTER

The next effect you want to add to the slides is an animation effect that will display each bullet or numbered item progressively on a slide. When the animation is applied to a slide, the slide initially shows only the title. The bulleted text appears as the presentation proceeds. You want to add this effect to all the slides that have bulleted items (slides 2–4 and 7–12). However, you do not want slide 5, which contains the foundation's history, to display with an animation because you want the history to appear all at the same time.

To apply the animation to the bulleted items, you could add the effect to each slide individually. However, when there are many slides, it is faster to add the effect to the slide master so all slides based on the selected slide layout display the effect. You will move to slide 2, the first slide in the presentation to use bullets, and apply the animation effects to the associated slide layout under the slide master.

1

- **Make slide 2 current.**
- **Change to Slide Master view.**
- **Point to the selected slide layout thumbnail to see the ScreenTip and confirm that the correct slides will be affected (Title and Content Layout: used by slide(s) 2 – 4, 6 – 12).**
- **Select the content placeholder.**
- **Open the Animations tab.**
- **Scroll the Animation gallery and click Wipe.**

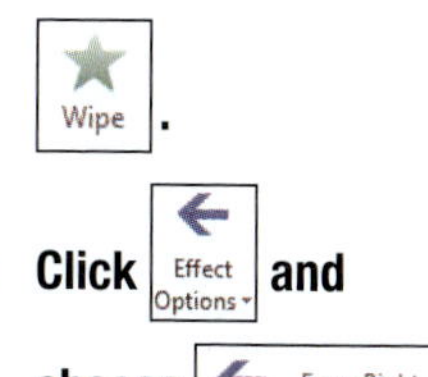

- **Click Effect Options and choose From Right.**

Your screen should be similar to Figure 2.56

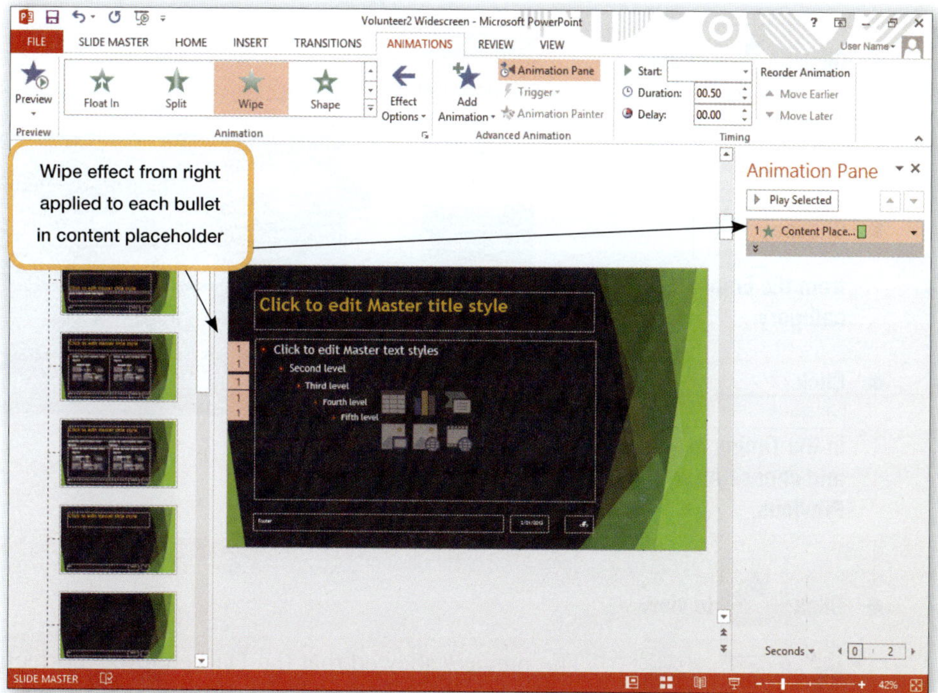

Figure 2.56

Animation icons appear next to each bulleted item in the content placeholder, and the Animation pane displays the information about the animation. The preview demonstrated how this effect will appear on the slide. Although the slide master preview does not show it, each bullet will appear individually on the slide. You can confirm this because a number tab appears next to each bullet in the content area indicating that the effect will be applied to each line.

You also want to add a second animation effect to give more emphasis to the bulleted items. You will add the Darken animation effect and change the Start timing setting associated with the effect. The Start settings control the method used to advance the animation for each bullet item while you run the slide show. The default Start setting, On Click, means you need to click the mouse to start each animation effect. You want the Darken effect to begin automatically after the first animation effect is finished.

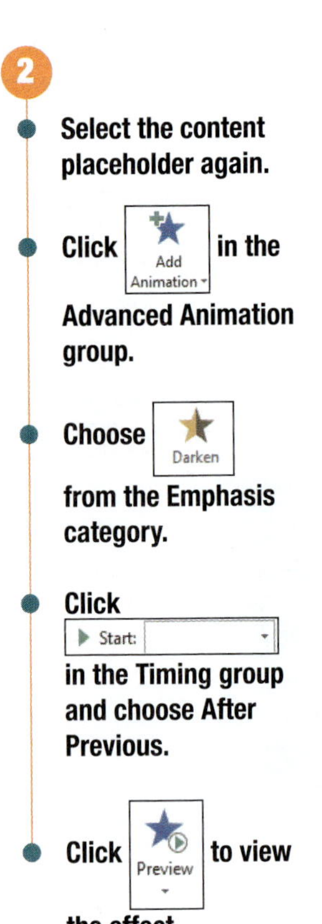

2

- **Select the content placeholder again.**
- **Click Add Animation in the Advanced Animation group.**
- **Choose Darken from the Emphasis category.**
- **Click Start: in the Timing group and choose After Previous.**
- **Click Preview to view the effect.**

Your screen should be similar to Figure 2.57

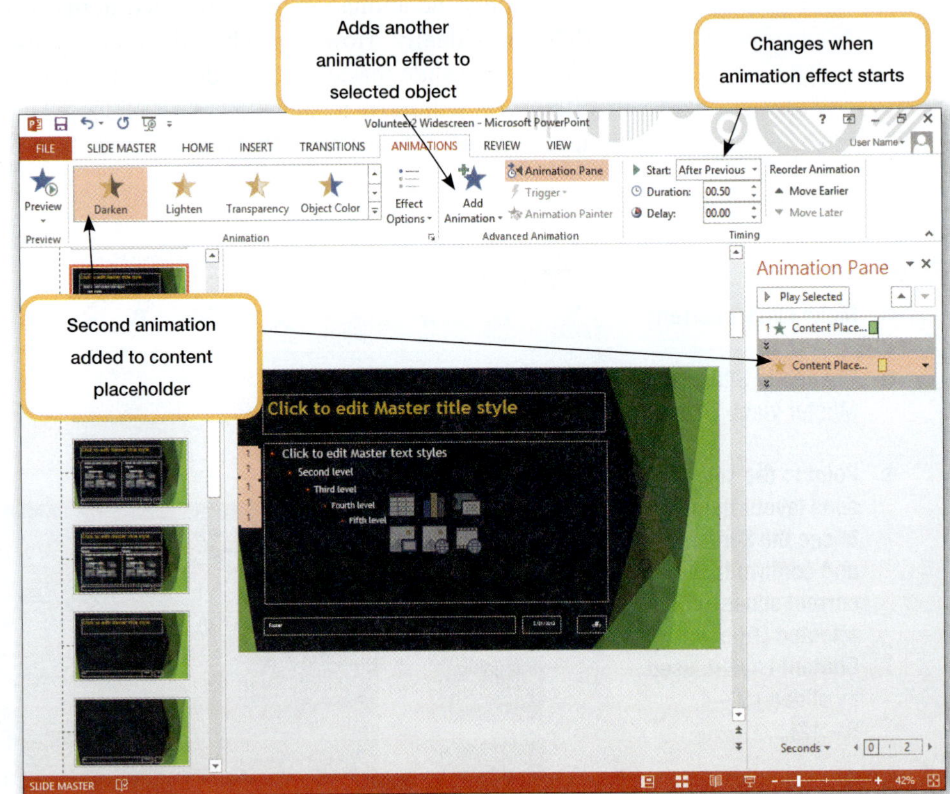

Figure 2.57

The preview showed that the Darken effect correctly started after the Wipe effect ended. You are concerned, however, that the timing for the Wipe effect is too fast and the Darken emphasis is too subtle. You will lengthen the duration for the Wipe effect and change the Darken emphasis to another.

3

- **Click on** 1 ★ Content Place... **in the Animation pane to select it.**
- **Increase the Duration setting in the Timing group to 3.00.**
- **Click on** ★ Content Place... **in the Animation pane to select it.**
- **Choose** Bold Reveal **from the Emphasis group of the Animation gallery.**
- **Click** Play Selected.

Your screen should be similar to Figure 2.58

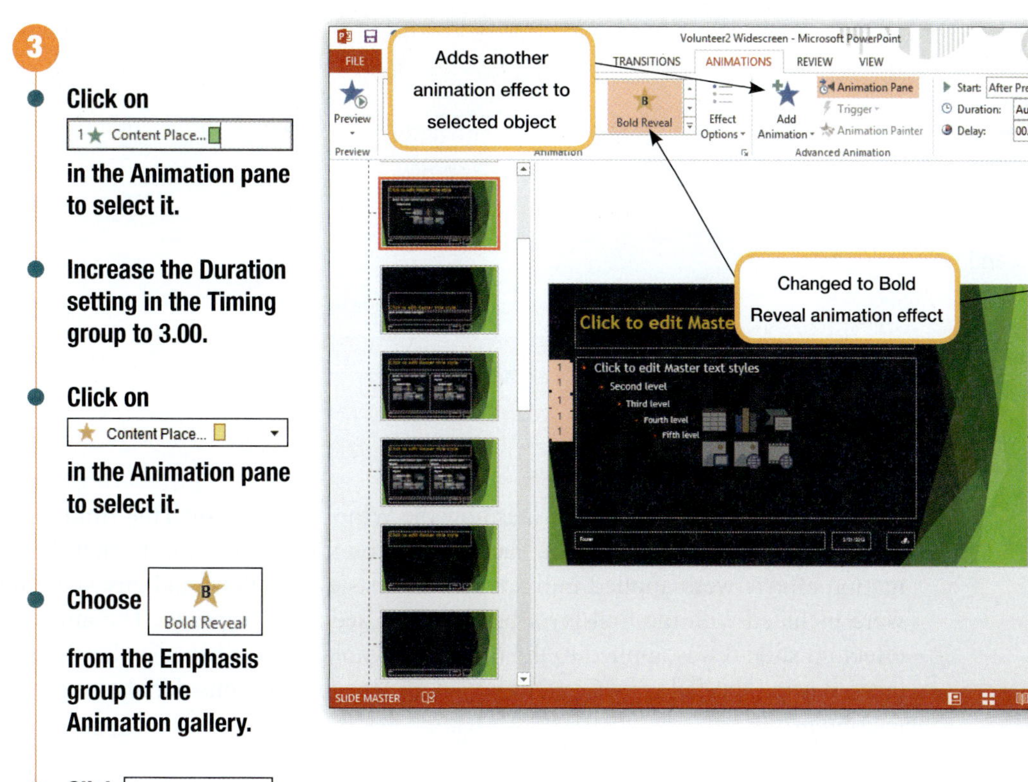

Figure 2.58

The changes in the animation effects are shown in the Animation pane and have been applied to slides 2–4 and 6–12. To check how the animation effects actually appear in a slide, you will return to Normal view and preview the animations.

Additional Information

The bar in each effect in the Animation pane indicates the length of the duration.

4

- **Change to Normal view and preview the animation on slides 2 and 11.**
- **Move to slide 5 and verify that there are no animations associated with it.**
- **Play the animation on slide 6.**

On slide 2, the preview demonstrates how the Wipe effect and then the Bold Reveal emphasis appears one-by-one on each bullet. You noticed on slide 11 that the animation effects were applied individually to first-level bullets, and any subbullets were included with the first-level bullets. This seems appropriate. The animation effect on slide 6 was applied to the table as a whole. This is because the slide was created using the Title and Content layout and the table is considered a single bulleted item.

CHANGING AND REMOVING ANIMATION EFFECTS

You want to remove the animation from slide 6. However, because the animation is associated with the slide master, removing it would remove it from all slides using that layout. Instead, you will change the slide layout to another layout that does not have an animation associated with it. Then you will add some other animation effects to this slide and apply these same effects to slide 5.

1

- Change the slide layout of slide 6 to the Title Only layout.

Having Trouble?
Open the Home tab and click Layout.

- Center the table in the slide space.
- Select the title placeholder and apply the Fly In from Left animation.
- Change the Start setting to With Previous and change the duration to 1.00.
- Apply the Random Bars animation with a duration of 2.00 to the table object.
- Preview the animations.
- Use the Animation Painter to copy the animation from the title placeholder of slide 6 to the title placeholder of slide 5.
- Use the Animation Painter to copy the table animation from slide 6 to both content placeholders on slide 5.

Additional Information
To apply the animation to multiple objects, double-click Animation Painter. When you are done, click Animation Painter again to turn it off.

- Preview the animations on slide 5.

Your screen should be similar to Figure 2.59

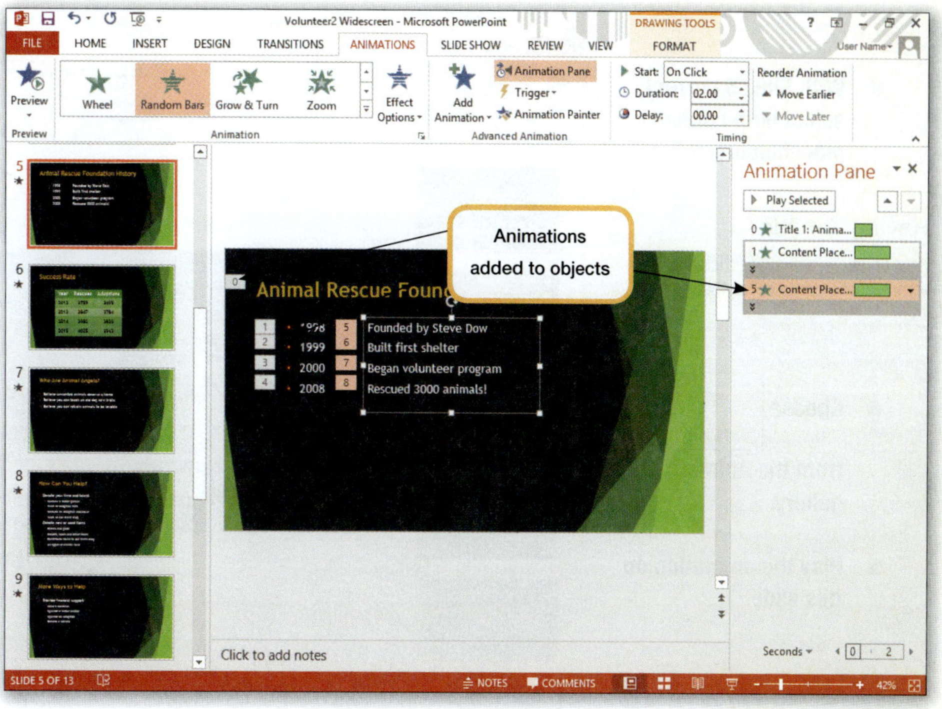

Animations added to objects

Figure 2.59

You like the title animation; however, you decide to remove the animations associated with the two content placeholders.

2

- **With Slide 5 current, select both content placeholders.**

Having Trouble?

Hold down Shift while clicking on each placeholder to select them both.

- **Choose [None] from the Animation gallery.**
- **Play the animation on this slide.**

Your screen should be similar to Figure 2.60

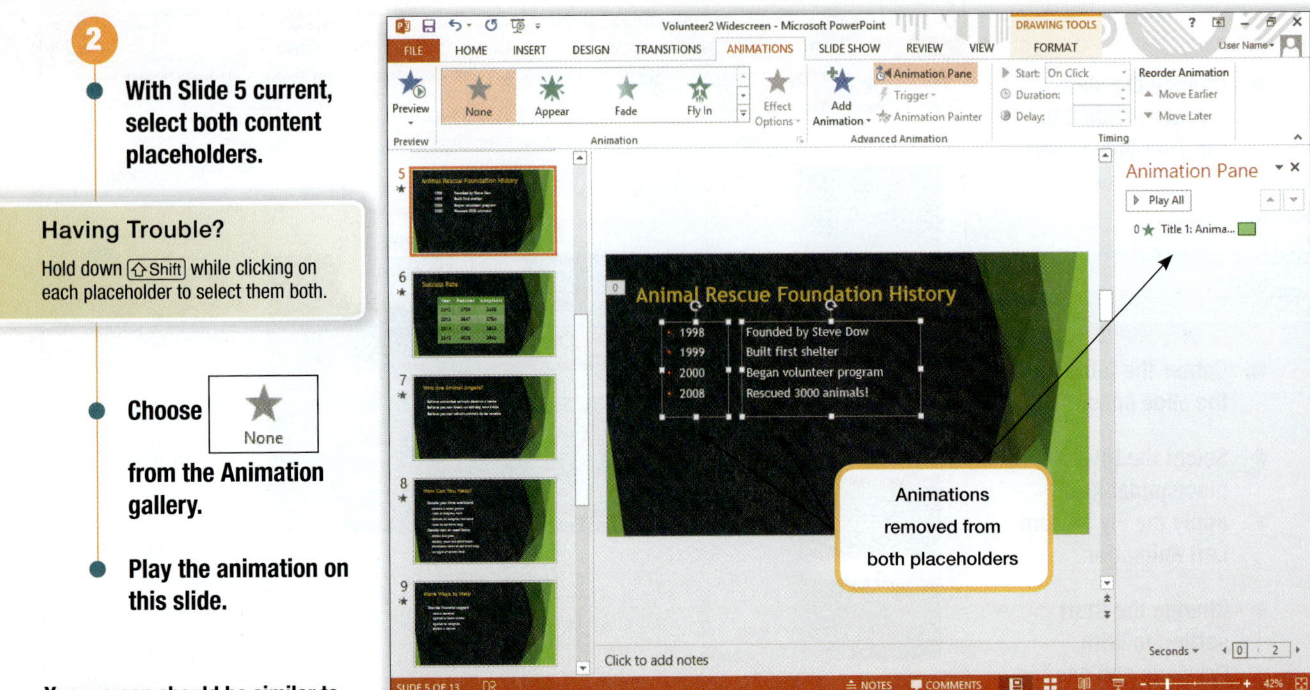

Figure 2.60

Now the only animation on this slide is the Fly In affect of the title placeholder. Be careful when using animations, as sometimes too many animation effects distract from the slide content. You think your animation changes will add interest without making the presentation appear too lively.

3

- **Close the Animation pane.**
- **Save the presentation.**

To see how the transitions and animations work together, you will run the slide show next.

Preparing for the Slide Show

As you run the slide show to see the animation effects, you will also practice preparing for the presentation. As much as you would like to control a presentation completely, the presence of an audience usually causes the presentation to change course. PowerPoint has several ways to control a slide show during the presentation.

NAVIGATING IN A SLIDE SHOW

Running the slide show and practicing how to control the slide show help you to have a smooth presentation. For example, if someone has a question about a previous slide, you can go backward and redisplay it. You will try out some of the features you can use while running the slide show.

1

- **Start the slide show from the beginning.**
- **Click to advance to slide 2.**
- **Click 4 times to display the four bullets.**

Your screen should be similar to Figure 2.61

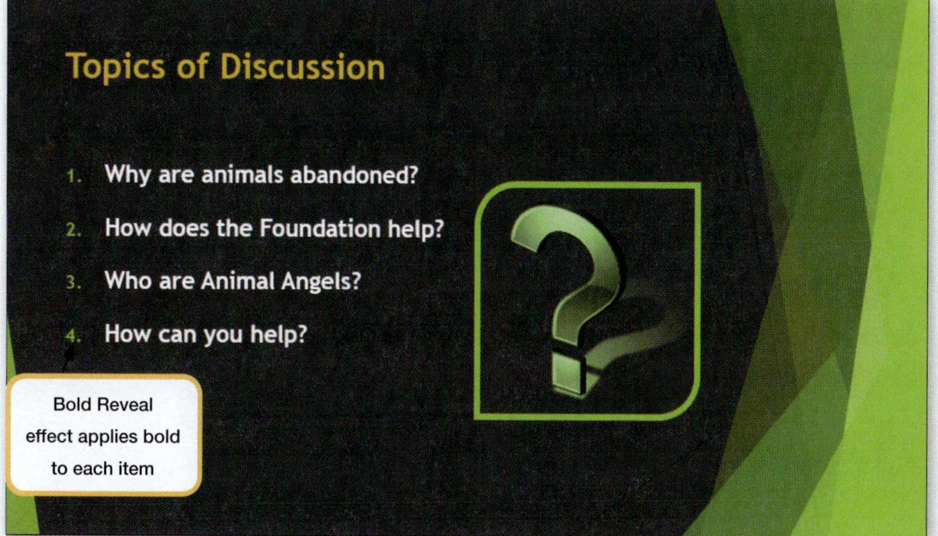

Figure 2.61

Another Method

You can also use the mouse wheel to move forward or backward through a presentation.

The first slide appeared using the Wipe From Left transition effect associated with the slide. The second slide appeared using a random transition effect. Each bulleted item on slide 2 appeared when you clicked using the Wipe animation effect, and the Bold Reveal animation effect started automatically as soon as the last bullet appeared.

When an animation is applied to the content area of a slide, the content items are displayed only when you click or use any of the procedures to advance to the next slide. This is because the default setting to start an animation is On Click. This allows the presenter to focus the audience's attention and to control the pace of the presentation. The Bold Reveal associated with slide 2 started automatically because you changed the Start setting to After Previous.

2

- **Continue to click or press** `Spacebar` **until the title of slide 8, "How Can You Help?" appears.**
- **Press** `Backspace` **(5 times).**

Additional Information

You can return to the first slide in the presentation by holding down both mouse buttons for two seconds.

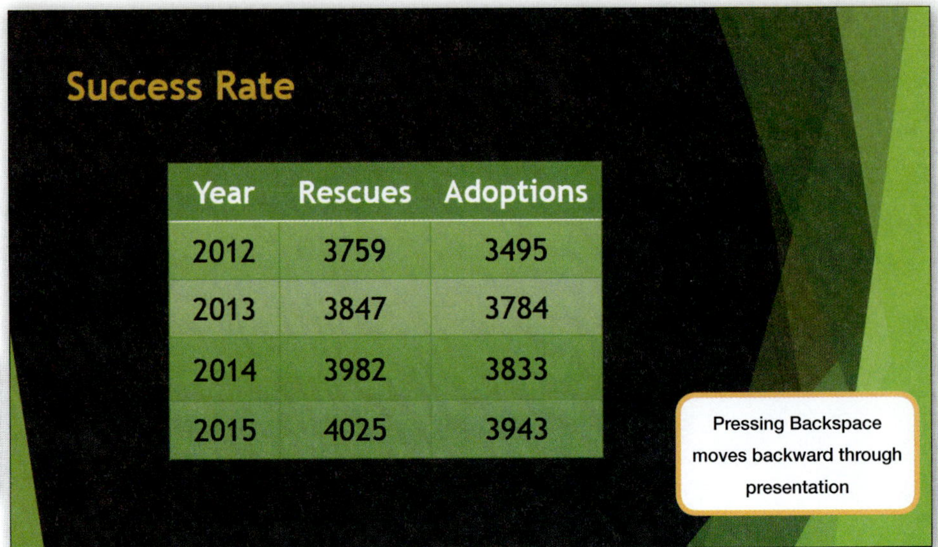

Your screen should be similar to Figure 2.62

Figure 2.62

You returned the onscreen presentation to slide 6, but now, because the audience has already viewed slide 7, you want to advance to slide 8. To go to a specific slide number, you type the slide number and press `Enter`.

3

- **Type 8 and press** `Enter`**.**

Another Method

You also can choose Go to Slide from the shortcut menu and select a slide to display.

- **Click two times to display the bulleted items.**
- **Click again to display slide 9.**

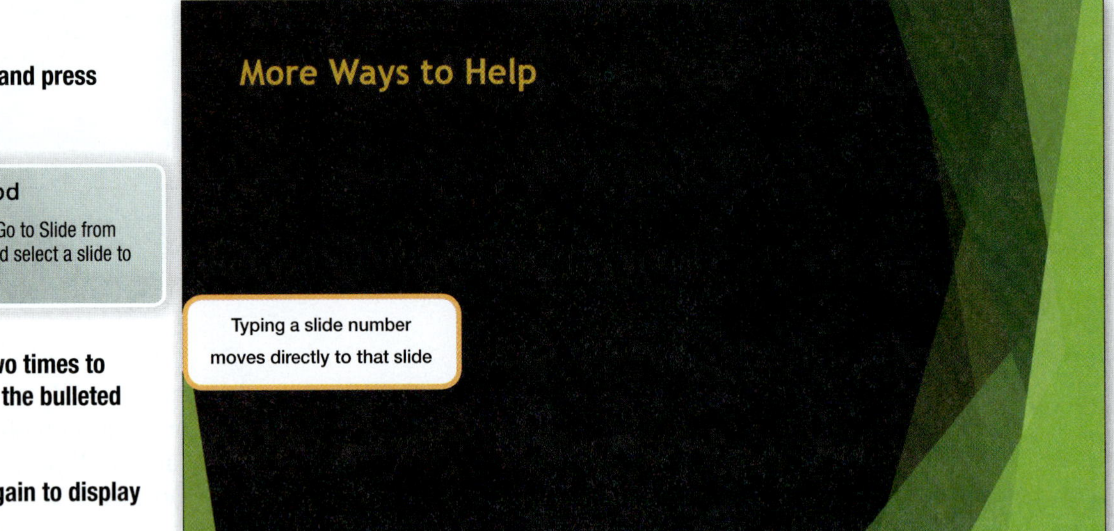

Your screen should be similar to Figure 2.63

Figure 2.63

Slide 9, More Ways to Help, is displayed.

Sometimes a question from an audience member can interrupt the flow of the presentation. If this happens to you, you can black out the screen to focus attention on your response.

- **Press b or B.**

Additional Information

You also can white out the screen by pressing W.

The screen goes to black while you address the topic. When you are ready to resume the presentation, you can bring the slide back.

- **Click, or press b.**
- **Click to display the bulleted items on slide 9.**

ADDING FREEHAND ANNOTATIONS

During your presentation, you may want to point to an important word, underline an important point, or draw check marks next to items that you have covered. To do this, you can use the mouse pointer during the presentation. When you move the mouse, the mouse pointer appears and the **Slide Show control bar** (shown on Figure 2.64) is displayed in the lower-left corner of the screen.

Icon	Description
	Displays the previous slide.
	Displays the next slide.
	Provides pen and laser pointer tools to add annotations to slides.
	Shows thumbnails of all slides, making it easy to quickly jump to any slide.
	Zooms in to a portion of the slide to show greater detail.
	Provides options to hide/show Presenter view, black or white out the screen, change display and arrow settings, and end the slide show.

The mouse pointer in its current shape can be used to point to items on the slide. You also can change it to a laser pointer, a pen, or a highlighter.

1

- **Move the mouse on your desktop to display the mouse pointer and the Slide Show control bar.**
- **Click in the Slide Show control bar to display the Pointer Options menu.**

Another Method

You also can select Pointer Options from the shortcut menu.

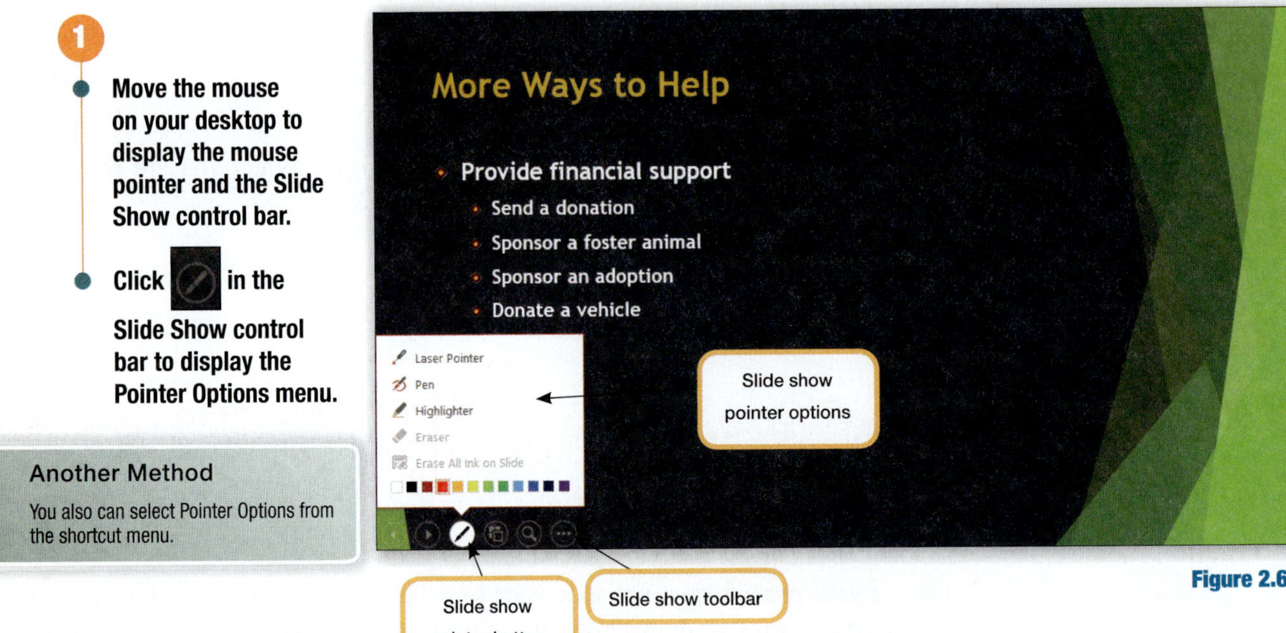

Figure 2.64

Your screen should be similar to Figure 2.64

The pointer options are described in the following table.

Pointer Options	Effect
Laser Pointer	Changes the mouse pointer to a red laser tip for emphasis.
Pen	Changes the mouse pointer to a ballpoint pen for annotation.
Highlighter	Changes the mouse pointer to a highlighter.
Eraser	Changes the mouse pointer to an eraser to remove selected annotations.
Erase All Ink on Slide	Removes all annotations from the slide.

You will try out several of the freehand annotation features to see how they work. To use the slide annotation features, first select the pointer style and then drag the pointer in the direction you want to draw.

- **Choose Pen.**

> **Another Method**
>
> You also can use Ctrl + P to display the Pen.

- **Point near the word "Send" and then drag until a circle is drawn around the word "Send".**
- **Choose Light Blue from the Colors bar of the Pointer Options menu.**
- **Draw three lines under the word "Help"**
- **Choose Highlighter from the Pointer Options menu and highlight the word "donation".**

Your screen should be similar to Figure 2.65

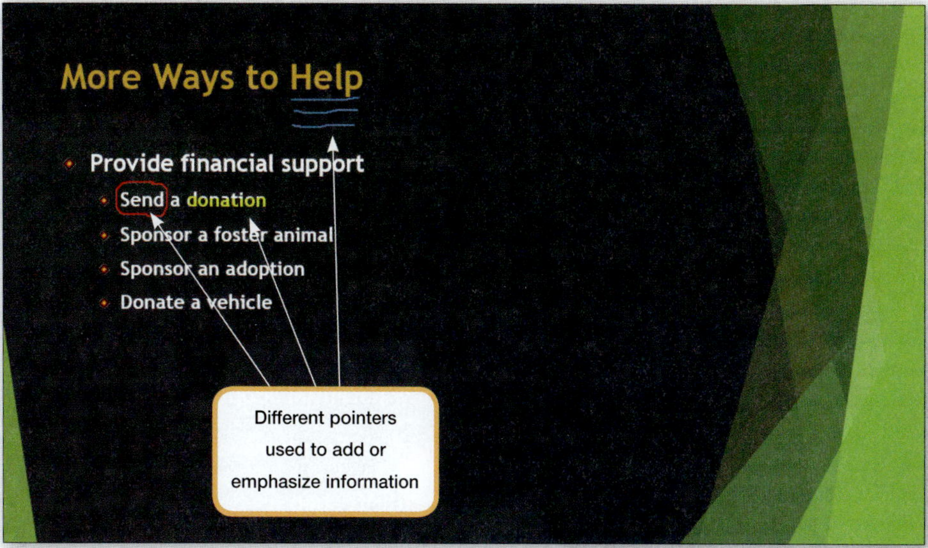

Figure 2.65

The freehand annotation feature allows you to point out and emphasize important information on a slide during the presentation.

- **Practice using the freehand annotator to draw any shapes you want on the slide.**
- **To erase the annotations, choose Erase All Ink on Slide from the Pointer Options menu.**

> **Another Method**
>
> The keyboard shortcut to erase annotations is E.

- **To turn off freehand annotation, click on the tool you are using in the Pointer Options menu to toggle it off or press Esc.**

> **Another Method**
>
> You also can use Ctrl + A to display the arrow or right-click on the slide to display the shortcut menu; select Pointer Options, Arrow Options; and choose Automatic to turn off freehand annotation.

Another feature that you can use to emphasize information on a slide is to change the mouse pointer to a laser pointer.

4

- Click to display the five bulleted items on slide 10.
- Choose Laser Pointer from the Pointer Options menu.

Additional Information

You can control the color of the laser light by clicking Set Up Slideshow on the Slide Show tab. You can then click the Laser pointer color drop-down list to choose a different color.

- Use the laser pointer to point to the first bulleted item on the slide.

Your screen should be similar to Figure 2.66

Another Method

If you press Ctrl and hold down the left mouse button, you can temporarily turn on the laser pointer.

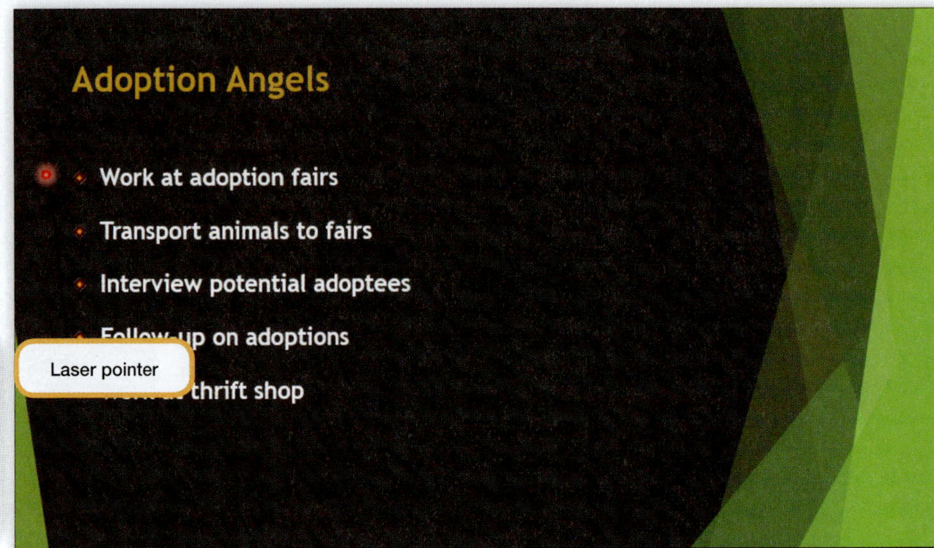

Figure 2.66

The laser pointer is much brighter than the regular mouse pointer.

If you do not erase annotations before ending the presentation, you are prompted to keep or discard the annotations when you end the slide show. If you keep the annotations, they are saved to the slides and will appear as part of the slide during a presentation.

Adding Speaker Notes

When making your presentation, there are some critical points you want to be sure to discuss. To help you remember the important points, you can add notes to a slide and then print the **notes pages**. These pages display the notes below a small version of the slide they accompany. You can create notes pages for some or all of the slides in a presentation. You decide to add speaker notes on slide 9 to remind you to suggest foster care donations.

1

- **Press Esc to end the slide show.**
- **Display slide 9 in Normal view.**
- **Increase the size of the Notes pane to that shown in Figure 2.67.**

Having Trouble?

Adjust the size of the notes pane by dragging the pane splitter bar.

- **Click in the Notes pane and type the following:**

Suggested foster animal donations per month

Cat: $10

Dog: $15/small $20/medium $25/large

Having Trouble?

Press Enter to begin a new line and Tab to separate the dollar amounts.

Your screen should be similar to Figure 2.67

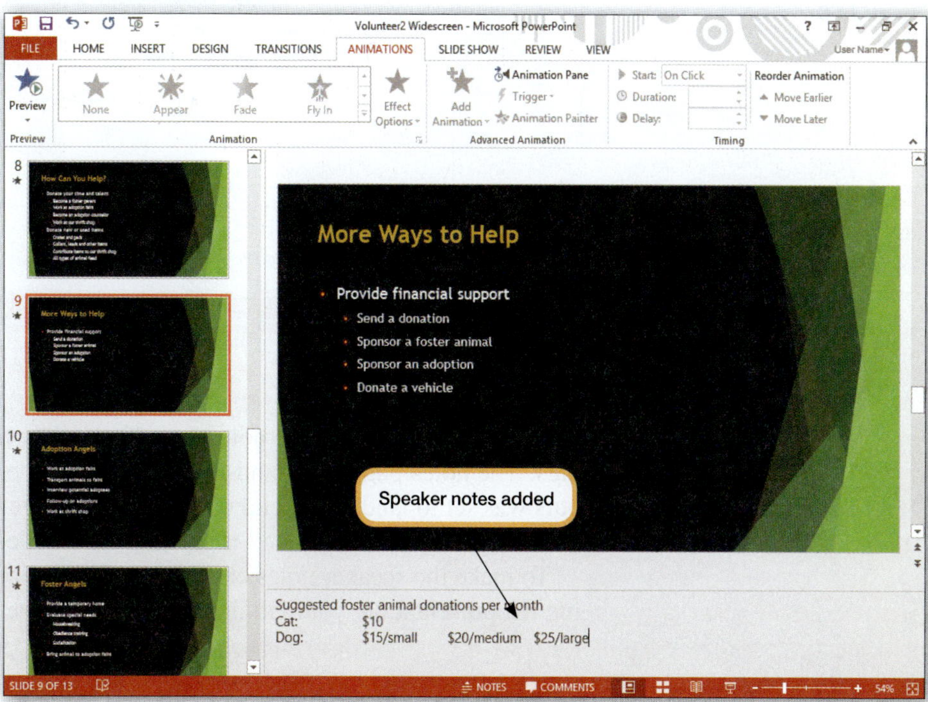

Figure 2.67

You will preview the notes page to check its appearance before it is printed.

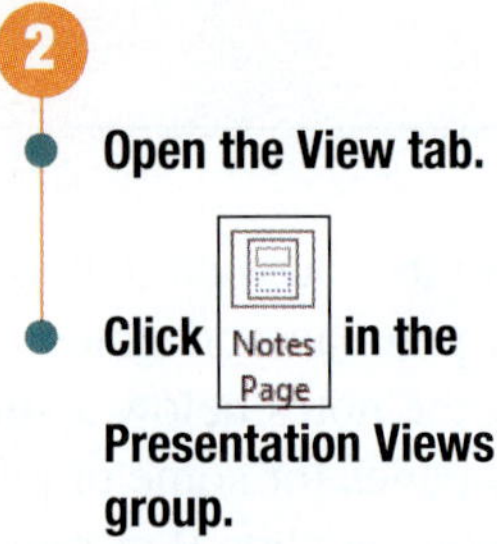

- Open the View tab.
- Click [Notes Page] in the the Presentation Views group.

Your screen should be similar to Figure 2.68

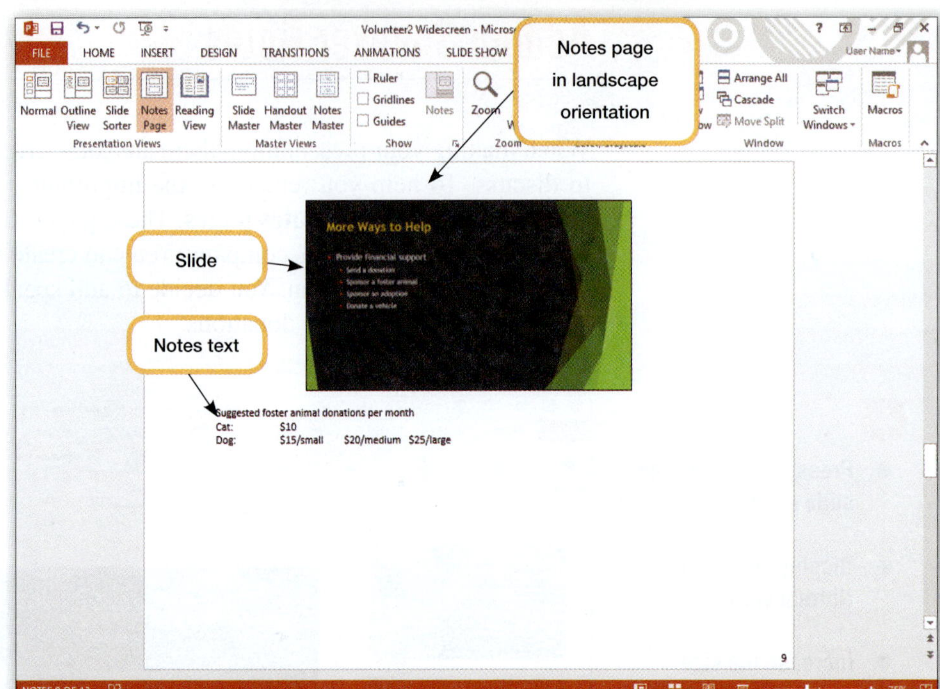

Figure 2.68

The notes pages display the note you added below the slide that the note accompanies. The notes page is in landscape orientation because the orientation for handouts was set to landscape (end of Lab 1). The page orientation setting affects both handouts and notes pages and is saved with the file.

To make the speaker notes easier to read in a dimly lit room while you are making the presentation, you will increase the font size of the note text.

3

- Click on the note text to select the placeholder.
- Click on the placeholder border to select the entire object.
- Increase the font size to 20.
- Click outside the note text border.

Your screen should be similar to Figure 2.69

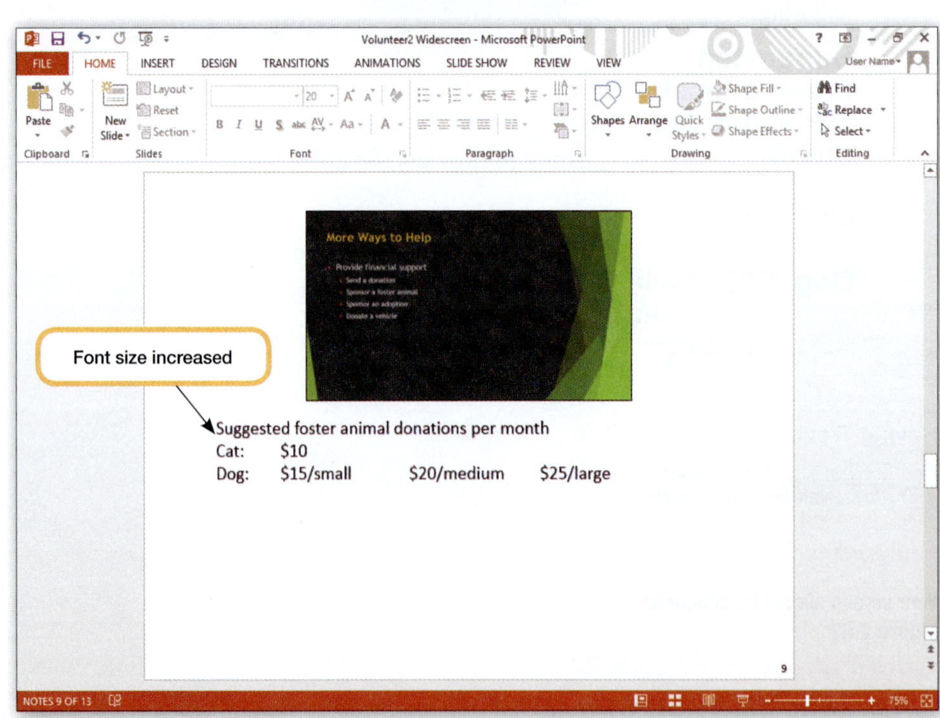

Figure 2.69

Adding Headers and Footers

Currently, the only information that appears in the footer of the notes page is the page number. You want to include additional information in the header and footer of the notes and handouts. The header and footer typically display information inside the margin space at the top and bottom of each printed page. Additionally, slides also may include header and footer information.

ADDING A HEADER TO A NOTES PAGE

You want to include the date and your name in the header of the notes pages.

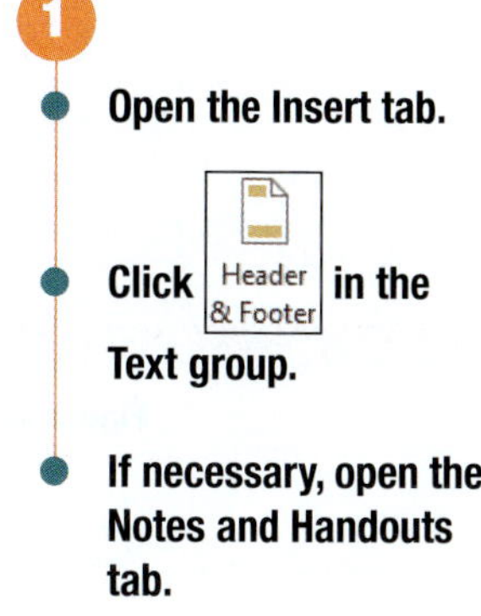

1

- **Open the Insert tab.**
- **Click Header & Footer in the Text group.**
- **If necessary, open the Notes and Handouts tab.**

Your screen should be similar to Figure 2.70

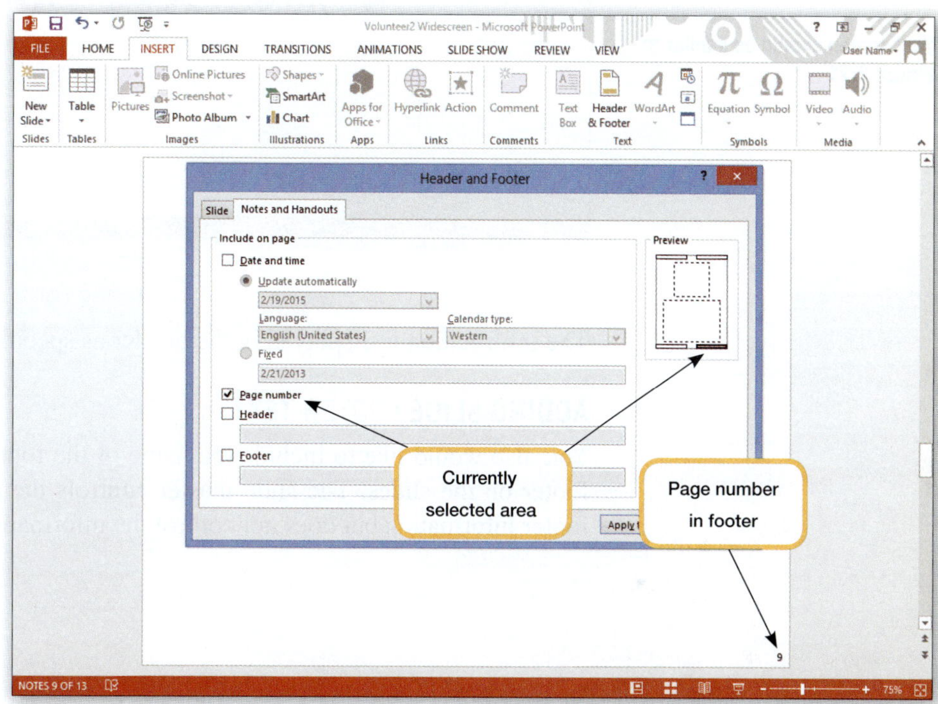

Figure 2.70

On notes and handouts, you can include header text and a page number. The Preview box identifies the four areas where this information will appear and identifies the currently selected areas, in this case page number, in bold.

2

- **Choose Date and Time to turn on this option and, if necessary, choose Update Automatically.**
- **Choose Header and enter your name in the Header text box.**
- **Click Apply to All.**

Your screen should be similar to Figure 2.71

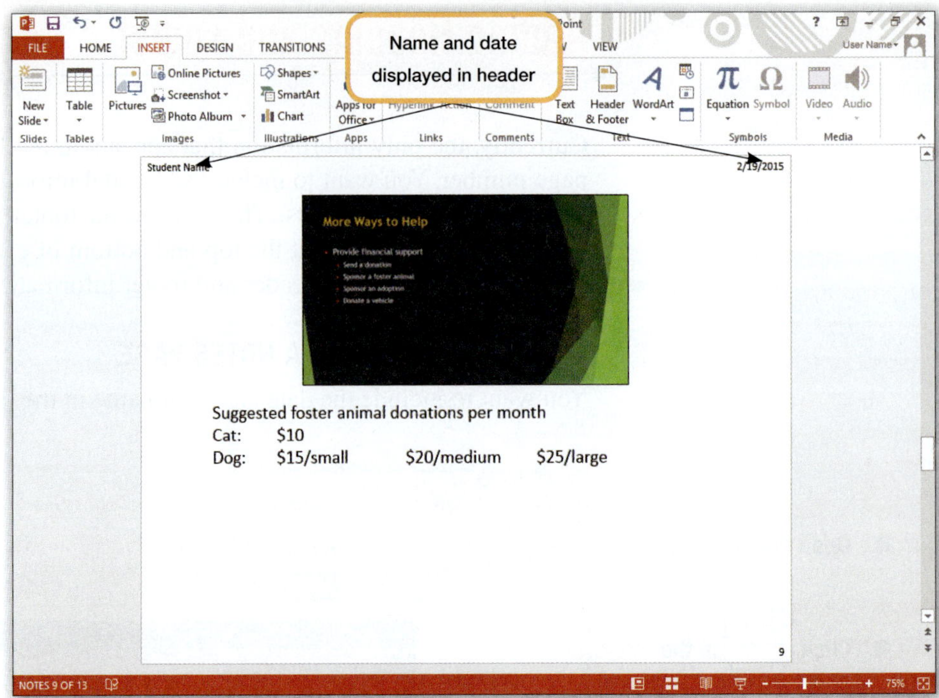

Figure 2.71

The information is displayed in the header as specified.

ADDING SLIDE FOOTER TEXT

You also would like to include the name of the foundation and slide number in a footer on the slides. The slide master controls the placement and display of the footer information but does not control the information that appears in those areas.

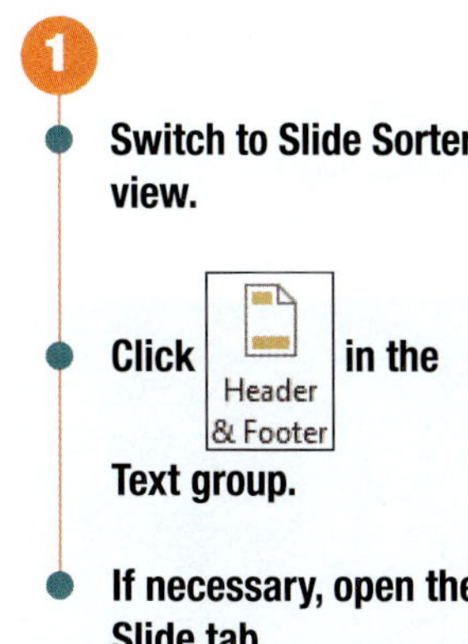

1

- **Switch to Slide Sorter view.**
- **Click** Header & Footer **in the Text group.**
- **If necessary, open the Slide tab.**

Your screen should be similar to Figure 2.72

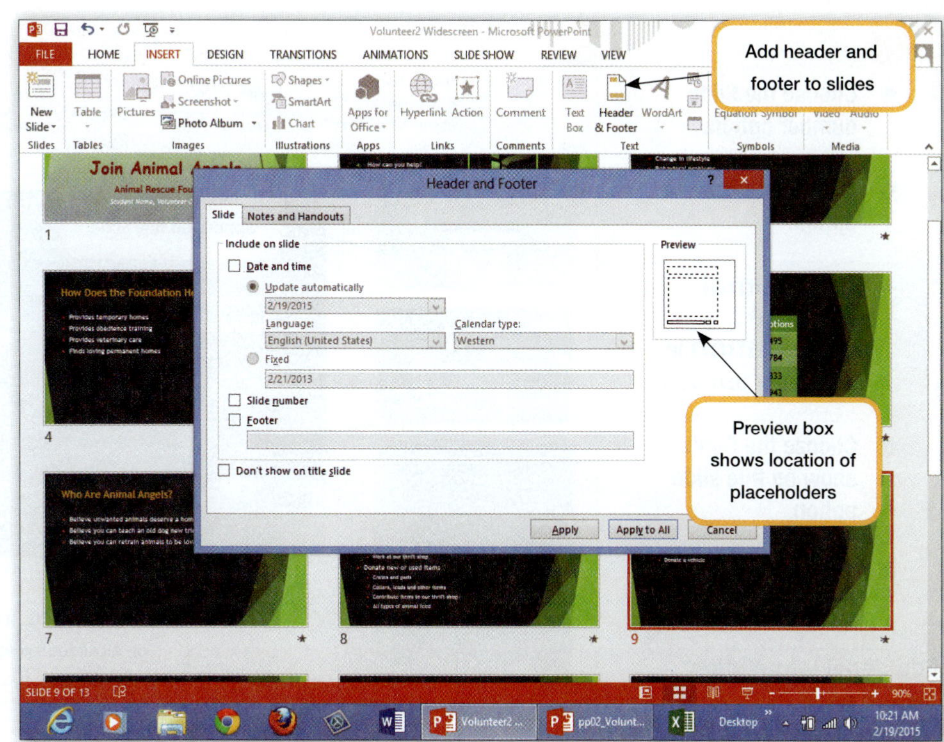

Figure 2.72

Slides can display the date and time, slide number, or footer text. The Preview box shows the location of the placeholders for each of these elements on the selected slide. When specified, this information can be displayed on all slides or selected slides only. You also can turn off the display of this information in title slides only. You would like to add the foundation name in the footer and the slide number to all slides, except the title slides.

2

- **Choose the Slide number option.**
- **Choose the Footer option.**
- **Type Animal Rescue Foundation in the Footer text box.**
- **Choose the Don't show on title slide option.**
- **Click Apply to All.**

Additional Information

The Apply command button applies the settings to the current slide or selected slides only.

- **Double-click slide 3.**
- **Scroll the Slides pane to the top.**
- **Save the presentation.**

Your screen should be similar to Figure 2.73

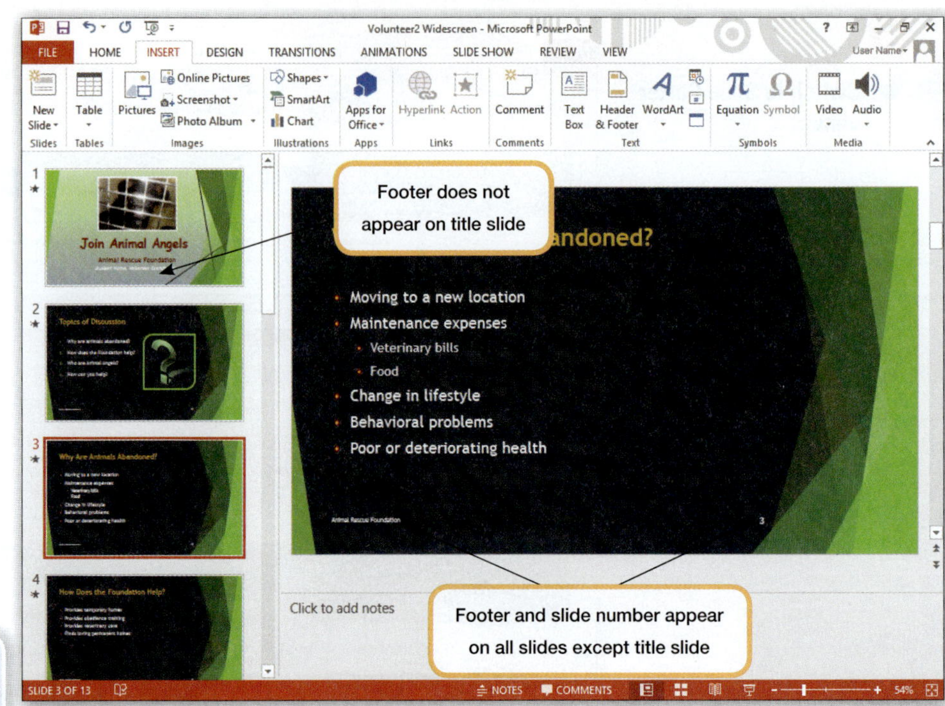

Figure 2.73

Additional Information

You can also delete the footer and slide number placeholders from individual slides to remove this information.

The foundation name and slide number appear in placeholders at the bottom of the slide. No footer information is displayed on the first or last slides in the presentation because they use the Title Slide layout.

USING PRESENTER VIEW

Finally, you will check the presentation again in Slide Show view using **Presenter view.** This view shows the full-screen slide show on one monitor for the audience and a "speaker view" on another monitor. Presenter view shows the current slide, a preview of the next slide, the speaker notes, a timer, and additional features to help you present the materials. It allows you to see your notes on your screen while your audience sees only the slide. This is quite helpful as you want to remember to emphasize key points in your presentation and add pertinent information, as you did on slide 9 with the suggested donation amounts.

You will start the slideshow with slide 9, switch to Presenter view, and try out the features available. If you have two monitors, Presenter view automatically displays on the other monitor. If you have only one monitor, you can use Alt + F5 to switch between views to try it out.

1

- **Make slide 9 current and start the slide show.**
- **Click once to display bulleted items.**
- **Click More slide show options in the Slide Show control bar.**
- **Choose Show Presenter View.**

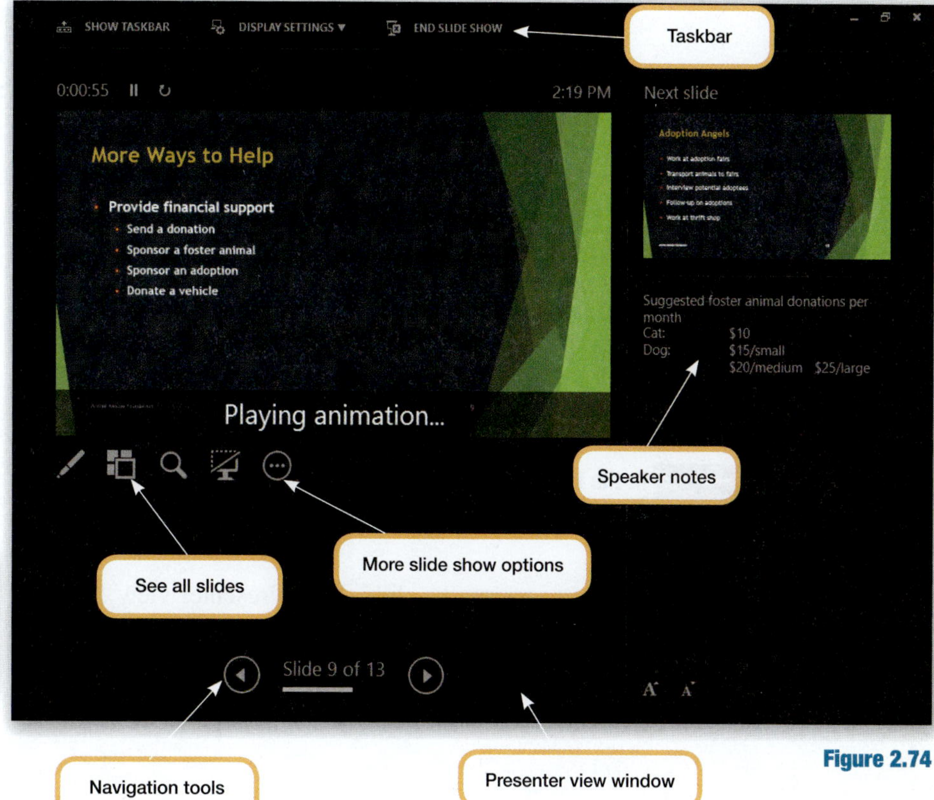

Figure 2.74

Having Trouble?

Press Alt + F5 to switch between Slide Show and Presenter view windows.

Your screen should be similar to Figure 2.74

Presenter view opens in a separate window and consists of three sections. The current slide is displayed in the large main section, the next slide in the upper-right section, and the notes page for the current slide in the lower-right section. The top of the Presenter view window contains a taskbar providing options to display the Windows taskbar, to select display settings, and to end the slide show. Below the taskbar is the timer that shows the time elapsed since the slide show started and pause and restart timer buttons. The current time is displayed on the far right of the same line.

Below the current slide is the control bar containing the same buttons as in the Slide Show window. This allows you to control the slide show using Presenter view rather than from the Slide Show window, making it much less obtrusive. They are always visible and easy to use.

At the bottom of the Presenter view window, a slide count shows which slide you are currently viewing of the total slides in the presentation and two navigation buttons to move to the previous or next slide. Additionally, the Increase Font Size and Decrease Font Size buttons below the Notes section can be used to increase or decrease the size of the text in that section.

You will now try out several of the features in Presenter view.

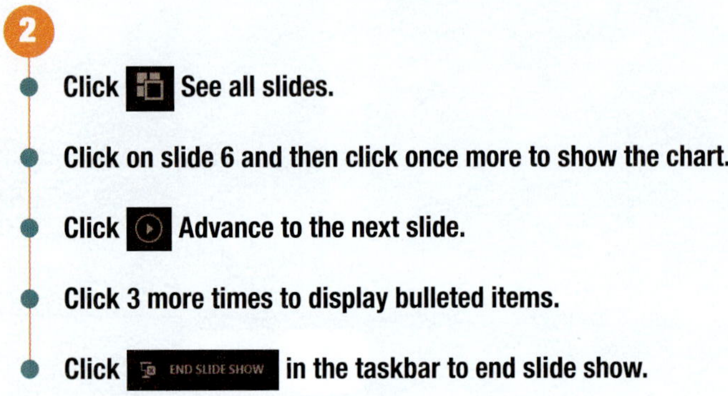

As you ran the slide show, Presenter view displayed information about the animations and transitions that were running.

Customizing Print Settings

You have created both slides and a notes page for the presentation and have seen how Presenter view works. Now you want to print the notes page and some of the slides. Customizing the print settings by selecting specific slides to print and scaling the size of the slides to fill the page are a few of the ways to make your printed output look more professional.

PRINTING NOTES PAGES

First you will print the notes page for the slide on which you entered note text.

1

- **Make slide 9 current.**
- **Open the File tab and choose Print.**
- **If necessary, select the printer.**
- **Choose Print Current Slide as the slide to print.**
- **Choose Notes Pages as the layout.**
- **Change the orientation to Portrait Orientation.**
- **If necessary, change the color setting to Grayscale.**

Your screen should be similar to Figure 2.75

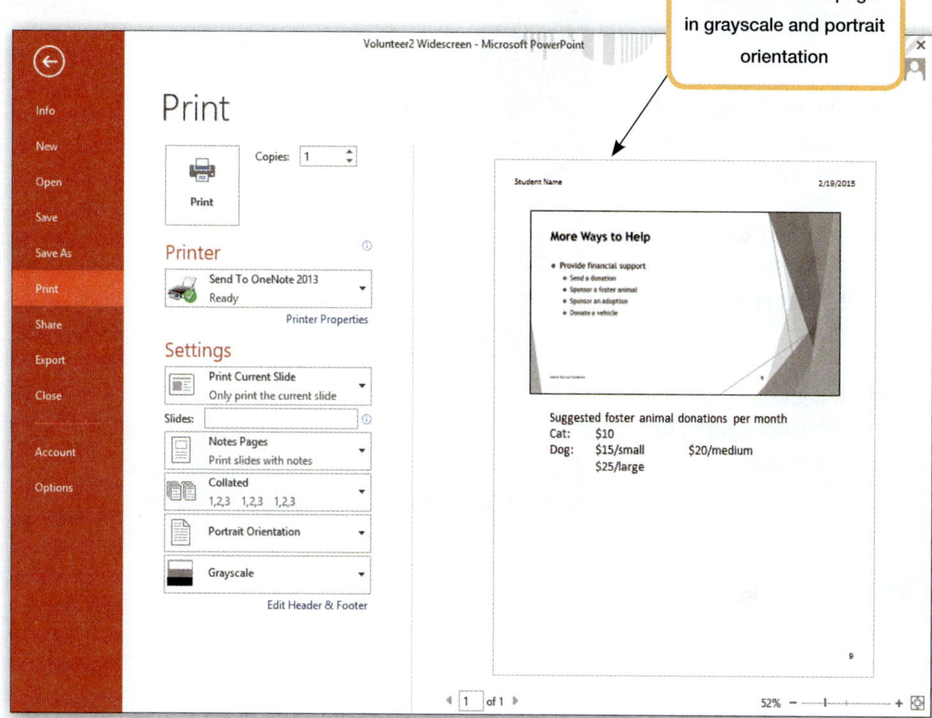

Figure 2.75

The notes page is displayed in grayscale and in portrait orientation, as it will appear when printed.

2

- **Click** 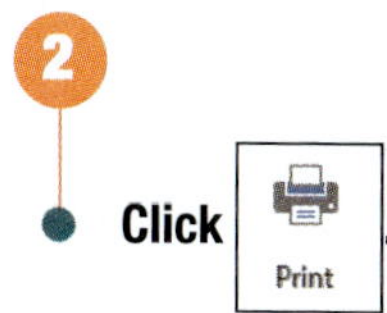.

Additional Information

To print multiple Notes pages, enter the slide number of each slide (separated by commas) you want to print in the Slides text box.

PRINTING SELECTED SLIDES

Next you will print a few selected slides to be used as handouts. You will change the orientation to portrait and scale the slides to fit the paper size.

1

- **Open the File tab and choose Print.**
- **In the Slides text box, type 1,6,12,13**

Additional Information

The print setting automatically changes to Custom Range.

- **Specify Handouts 4 Slides Horizontal as the layout.**
- **Choose Scale to Fit Paper from the Layout drop-down menu.**
- **If necessary, change the color setting to Grayscale.**

Your screen should be similar to Figure 2.76

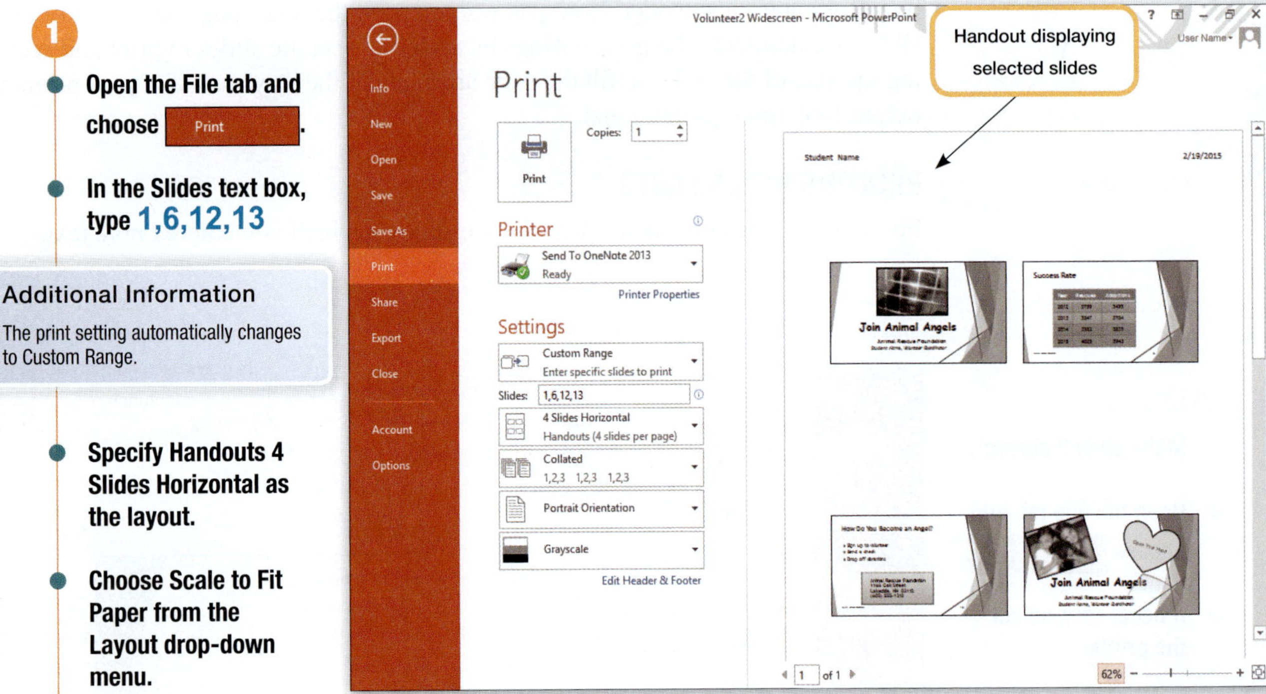

Figure 2.76

The four selected slides are displayed in portrait orientation, and the slide images were sized as large as possible to fill the page.

2

- **Print the handout.**
- **Open the File tab and if necessary, choose** Info**.**
- **In the Properties pane, enter your name in the Author text box.**
- **If necessary, in the Tags text box, enter Volunteer, Recruit**
- **Save the completed presentation.**
- **Exit PowerPoint.**

The view you are in when you save the file is the view that will be displayed when the file is opened.

FOCUS ON CAREERS

EXPLORE YOUR CAREER OPTIONS

Communications Specialist

Are you interested in technology? Could you explain technology in words and pictures? Communications specialists, also known as public relations specialists, assist sales and marketing management with communications media and advertising materials that represent the company's products and services to customers. In high-tech industries, you will take information from scientists and engineers and use PowerPoint to transform the data into eye-catching presentations that communicate effectively. You also may create brochures, develop websites, create videos, and write speeches. If you thrive in a fast-paced and high-energy environment and work well under the pressure of deadlines, then this job may be for you. Typically a bachelor's degree in journalism, advertising, or communications is desirable. Typical salaries range from $38,400 to $98,000, depending on the industry. To learn more about this career, visit the website for the Bureau of Labor Statistics of the U.S. Department of Labor.

Lab 2 CONCEPT SUMMARY

Modifying and Refining a Presentation

Find and Replace (PP2.5)

To make editing easier, you can use the Find and Replace feature to find text in a presentation and replace it with other text as directed.

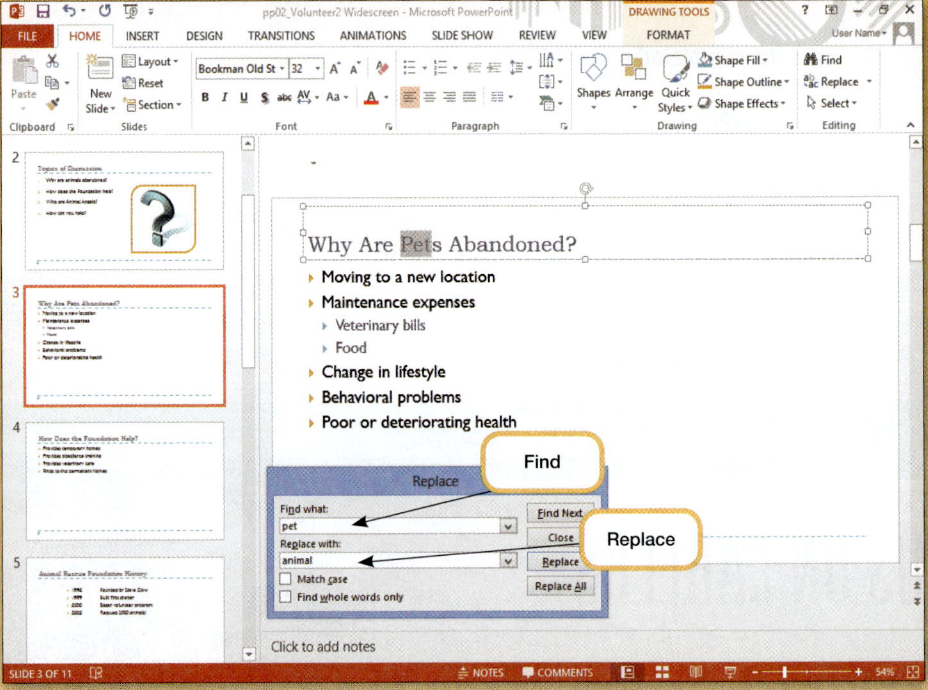

Table (PP2.10)

A table is used to organize information into an easy-to-read format of horizontal rows and vertical columns.

Alignment (PP2.18)

Alignment controls how text entries are positioned within a space.

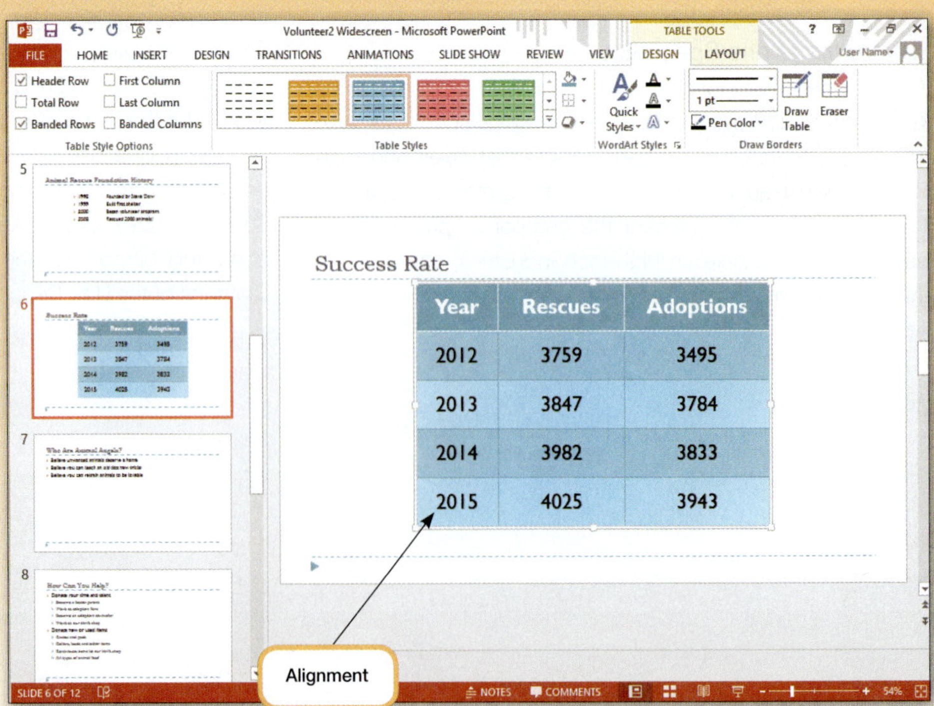

Theme (PP2.36)

A theme is a predefined set of formatting choices that can be applied to an entire document in one simple step.

Master (PP2.42)

A master is a special slide or page that stores information about the formatting for all slides in a presentation.

Animations (PP2.47)

Animations are special effects that add action to text and graphics so they move around on the screen during a slide show.

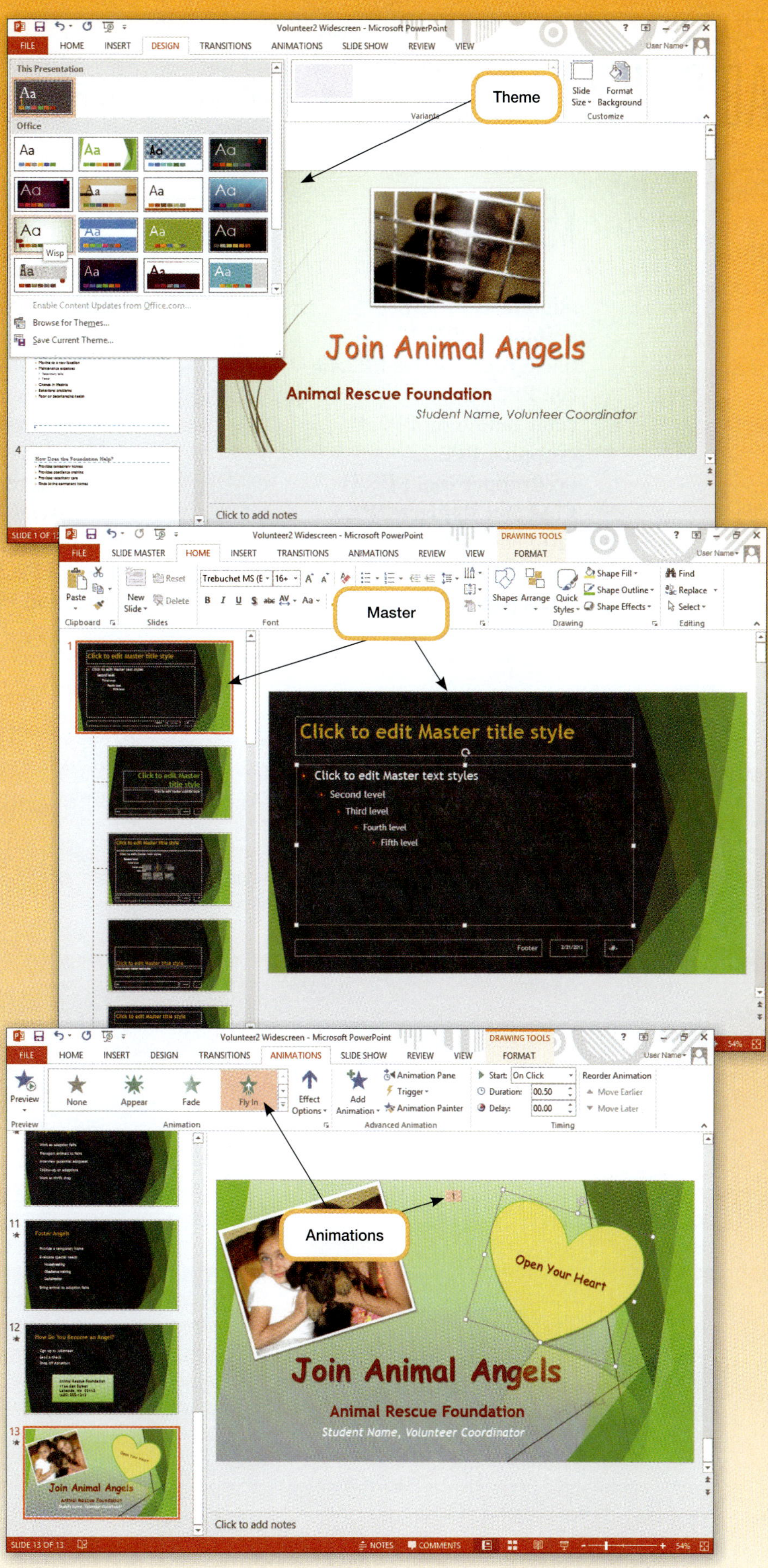

KEY TERMS

alignment PP2.18
animation PP2.47
background styles PP2.40
cell PP2.10
color matching PP2.31
cropping PP2.23
eyedropper tool PP2.31
Find and Replace PP2.5
gradient PP2.40
master PP2.42
notes pages PP2.67
object animations PP2.47
presenter view PP2.73
rotate handle PP2.30
shape styles PP2.28
slide Show control bar PP2.63
table PP2.10
table reference PP2.10
table styles PP2.19
text box PP2.32
theme PP2.36
transition PP2.47

COMMAND SUMMARY

Command	Shortcut	Action
Home tab		
Paragraph group		
Align Left	Ctrl + L	Aligns text to the left
Align Center	Ctrl + E	Centers text
Align Right	Ctrl + R	Aligns text to the right
Justify	Ctrl + J	Aligns text to both the left and right margins
Align Text		Sets vertical alignment of text
Drawing group		
Shapes		Inserts a shape
Shape Fill		Fills the selected shape with a solid color, gradient, picture, or texture
Shape Effects		Applies a visual effect to the selected shape, such as shadow, glow, or reflection
Editing group		
Find	Ctrl + F	Finds specified text
Replace	Ctrl + H	Replaces located text with replacement text
Insert tab		
Images group		
Pictures		Inserts picture from a file
Online Pictures		Finds and inserts a picture from a variety of online sources
Illustrations group		
Shapes		Inserts a shape
Text group		
Text Box		Inserts text box or adds text to selected shape
Header & Footer		Inserts a header and footer

COMMAND SUMMARY (CONTINUED)

Command	Shortcut	Action
Design tab		
Themes group		
More		Opens gallery of themes
Variants group		
More button		Customizes the look of the current theme
Transitions tab		
Preview group		
Preview		Displays the transition effect
Transition to This Slide group		
Effect Options		Opens a gallery of effect options
		Opens gallery of transition effects
Animations tab		
Preview group		
Preview		Displays the transition effect
Animation group		
Effect Options		Opens a gallery of effect options
		Opens a gallery of animation effects
Advanced Animation group		
Add Animation		Adds an animation effect to an object
Animation Pane		Opens the Animation pane
Animation Painter		Copies animation effect to another object
Timing group		
Start:		Sets the trigger for the animation
Duration: 01.00		Controls the amount of time for the animation to complete
View tab		
Presentation Views group		
Notes Page		Displays current slide in Notes view to edit the speaker notes

COMMAND SUMMARY (CONTINUED)

Command	Shortcut	Action
Slide Master		Opens Slide Master view to change the design and layout of the master slides
Drawing Tools Format tab		
Shapes Styles group More		Opens the Shape Styles gallery to select a visual style to apply to a shape
Shape Effects		Applies a visual effect to a shape
Arrange group or		Rotates or flips the selected object
Picture Tools Format tab		
Adjust group Color		Recolors picture
Compress Pictures		Compresses pictures in the document to reduce its size; permanently deletes cropped parts of a picture
Picture Styles More		Opens Picture Styles gallery to select an overall visual style for picture
Picture Effects		Applies a visual effect to picture
Arrange group Align		Changes placement of selected objects on slide
Size group Crop		Crops off unwanted section of a picture
Table Tools Design tab		
Table Styles group More		Opens the Table Styles gallery to choose a visual style for a table
Shading		Colors background behind selected text or paragraph
Border		Applies a border style
Effects		Applies a visual effect to the table such as shadows and reflections
Table Tools Layout tab		
Alignment group Center		Centers the text within a cell
Center Vertically		Centers the text vertically within a cell
Arrange group Align		Aligns edges of multiple selected objects

LAB EXERCISES

MATCHING

Match the item on the left with the correct description on the right.

1. object animation ____ a. adds text to a slide as an object
2. master ____ b. organizes information into an easy-to-read format of horizontal rows and vertical columns
3. Animation Painter ____ c. allows you to spin an object to any degree in any direction
4. theme ____ d. controls the way the display changes as you move from one slide to the next
5. rotate handle ____ e. predefined set of formatting choices that can be applied to an entire document
6. gradient ____ f. the progressive change of color
7. transition ____ g. motion, such as clip art that flies in from the left
8. table ____ h. special effects that add action to text and graphics
9. text box ____ i. quickly copies an animation effect and applies it to a different object
10. animation ____ j. slide that stores information about the formatting for all slides or pages in a presentation

TRUE/FALSE

Circle the correct answer to the following questions.

1.	Using masters, you are able to easily apply formatting changes to a selected group of slides.	**True**	**False**
2.	You cannot insert a table into PowerPoint, only graphics or other objects.	**True**	**False**
3.	Alignment controls the position of text entries in a placeholder.	**True**	**False**
4.	Find and Replace makes it difficult to locate specific words or phrases.	**True**	**False**
5.	A master is a special slide on which the formatting for selected slides or pages in your presentation is defined.	**True**	**False**
6.	When adding text to a text box in PowerPoint, the text box will lengthen automatically to display the entire entity.	**True**	**False**
7.	When you create a footer, it is automatically applied to every slide in the presentation.	**True**	**False**
8.	You can print 12 slides per page using notes pages.	**True**	**False**
9.	Tables contain rows and columns.	**True**	**False**
10.	A theme can be applied to selected slides in a presentation.	**True**	**False**

FILL-IN

Complete the following statements by filling in the blanks with the correct terms.

1. A(n) ______________________ is a container for text or graphics.
2. ______________________ provides access to a combination of different formatting options such as edges, gradients, line styles, shadows, and three-dimensional effects.
3. ______________________ lets you see your notes while your audience is viewing your slide.
4. ______________________ add action to text and graphics so they move on the screen.
5. The ______________________ allows you to add or highlight information on a slide during the slide show.
6. ______________________ controls the position of text entries within a space.
7. A(n) ______________________ is part of a template that stores information about the formatting for the three key components of a presentation—slides, speaker notes, and handouts.
8. Object ______________________ are used to display each bullet point, text, paragraph, or graphic independently of the other text or objects on the slide.
9. Use a(n) ______________________ or ______________________ on a slide to display information such as the date or slide number.
10. The ______________________ slide is a special slide that stores information about the formatting for all slides or pages in a presentation.

LAB EXERCISES

MULTIPLE CHOICE

Circle the letter of the correct response to the questions below.

1. To help you remember the important points during a presentation, you can add comments to slides and use ____________________.
   a. animation
   b. Normal view
   c. slide handouts
   d. Presenter view

2. If you want to display information in columns and rows, you would create a ____________________.
   a. slide layout
   b. shape
   c. table
   d. text box

3. A(n) ____________________ is a predefined set of formatting choices that can be applied to an entire document in one simple step.
   a. theme
   b. animation
   c. slide layout
   d. master

4. ____________________ add action to text and graphics so they move around on the screen.
   a. Animations
   b. Slides
   c. Transitions
   d. Masters

5. The ____________________ defines the format and placement of the slide image, note text, headers, footers, and other elements that will appear on all speaker notes.
   a. handouts master
   b. title master
   c. slide master
   d. notes master

6. ____________________ control the way that the display changes as you move from one slide to the next during a presentation.
   a. Graphics
   b. Transitions
   c. Animations
   d. Slide masters

7. You can change the horizontal placement of an entry in a placeholder or a table cell by using one of the four horizontal alignment settings: left, center, right, and ____________________.
   a. located
   b. marginalized
   c. highlighted
   d. justified

8. The best way to apply changes to every slide in your presentation is to ____________________.
   a. use slide sorter view
   b. change the title slide layout
   c. change each slide individually
   d. modify the theme slide master
9. If you wanted to add a company logo on each slide in your presentation, you would place it on the ____________________.
   a. notes page
   b. master
   c. handout
   d. outline slide
10. To substitute one word for another in a presentation, you would use the ____________________ feature.
   a. Find and Replace
   b. Duplicate
   c. Copy
   d. Locate and Move

LAB EXERCISES

Hands-On Exercises

RATING SYSTEM	
★	Easy
★★	Moderate
★★★	Difficult

STEP-BY-STEP

ENHANCING A STAFF TRAINING PRESENTATION ★

1. You are working on the staff training presentation for the Mountain View Inn. You have already created the introductory portion of the presentation and need to reorganize the topics and make the presentation more visually appealing. Three slides from your modified presentation will be similar to those shown here.

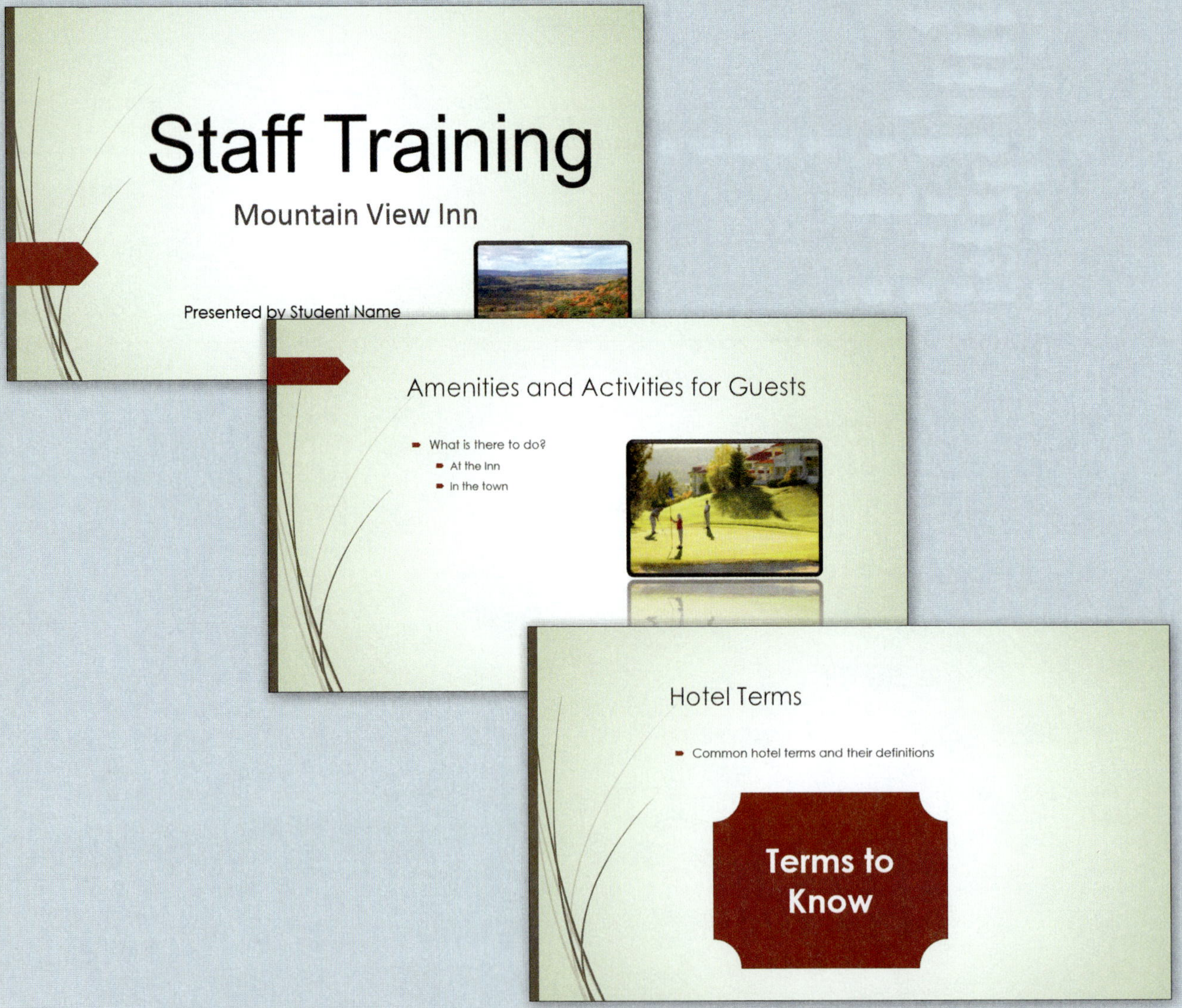

a. Open the file pp02_Mountain View Staff Training.
b. Save the file as Mountain View Training.
c. Run the slide show to see the progress so far.
d. Spell-check the presentation, making the appropriate corrections.
e. Find and replace any occurrence of "city" with the word **town**.
f. In slide 1:

   Insert a text box below the subtitle.

   Type **Presented by Your Name**.

   Set the font size to 24 and position the text box appropriately on the slide.

   Add the following speaker note: **Be sure to introduce yourself and play the name game**.
g. In slide 4:

   Add a shape of your choice to emphasize the text on the inserted shape.

   Enter and format the text **Terms to Know** within the inserted shape.

   Position and size the shape appropriately. Add an animation effect of your choice to the shape.
h. In slide 5:

   Set the Picture Style to Reflected Bevel, Black.

   Set the Picture Effect to Half Reflection, 4 pt offset.
i. Move slide 4 after slide 12.
j. Change the design of the slides to one of your choice from the Themes gallery. Check all slides and make any needed adjustments.
k. Duplicate slide 1 and move it to the end of the presentation. Delete the speaker note from slide 15.
l. Add a transition effect of your choice to all slides. Add an animation effect and sound to the first slide.
m. Using the theme master slide, increase title font one increment and content font by three increments.
n. Add your name to the File properties. Save the file.
o. Print slides 1, 4, 12, and 15 as handouts (four slides horizontal in portrait orientation).

LAB EXERCISES

EMERGENCY DRIVING TECHNIQUES ★

2. To complete this problem, you must have completed Step-by-Step Exercise 2 in Lab 1. You have completed the first draft of the presentation on tire blowouts, but you still have some information to add. Additionally, you want to make the presentation look better using many of the presentation features. Several slides of the modified presentation are shown here.

   a. Open the presentation Handling Blowouts, which was saved at the end of Step-by-Step Exercise 2 in Lab 1. If necessary, switch to Normal view.

   b. Save the file as Blowouts2.

   c. In Slide Master view, make the following adjustments to the Title Slide Layout:

      Delete the page number placeholder.

      Change the font of the title and subtitle to Tahoma or a similar font. Add a shadow.

      Decrease the title text to 54 pt.

      Change title text color to Orange, Accent 2, Darker 50%.

   d. On the Title and Content Layout master slide, delete the date placeholder, and move the student name placeholder to line up with the left edge of the of the title placeholder. Left justify the student name text. Ensure the slide number placeholder is right justified and in line with the right edge of the content placeholder.

e. Make the same changes as in Step d to the Title, Text, and Content Layout master (the last one). Move the page number placeholder to line up with the right edge of the right content placeholder. If necessary, resize the page number placeholder to fit within the brown bar.

f. On slide 6, replace the = in the title with a right-facing block arrow AutoShape. Add a Fly In from the Left animation to the AutoShape. Modify slide title text as necessary to fit on one line.

g. Change the shape fill color of the arrow to Ice Blue, Background 2, Darker 75%.

h. Duplicate the title slide and move it to the end of the presentation. Add a drawing object to this slide that includes the text **Drive Safely!** Modify the shape style.

i. Select an animation scheme of your choice to add transition effects to all the slides. Run the slide show.

j. Add the following note to slide 7 in a point size of 18:

Underinflation is the leading cause of tire failure.

Maximum inflation pressure on tire is not recommended pressure.

k. Add the following note to slide 10 in a point size of 18:

Penny test–tread should come to top of Lincoln's head.

l. Add file documentation and save the completed presentation.

m. Print the notes page for slide 7. Print slides 1, 6, and 11 as handouts with three slides per page.

ENHANCING THE ASU PRESENTATION ★★

3. Bonnie is the Assistant Director of New Admissions at Arizona State University. Part of her job is to make presentations at community colleges and local high schools about the university. She has already created the introductory portion of the presentation and needs to reorganize the topics and make the presentation more visually appealing. Several slides of the modified presentation are shown here.

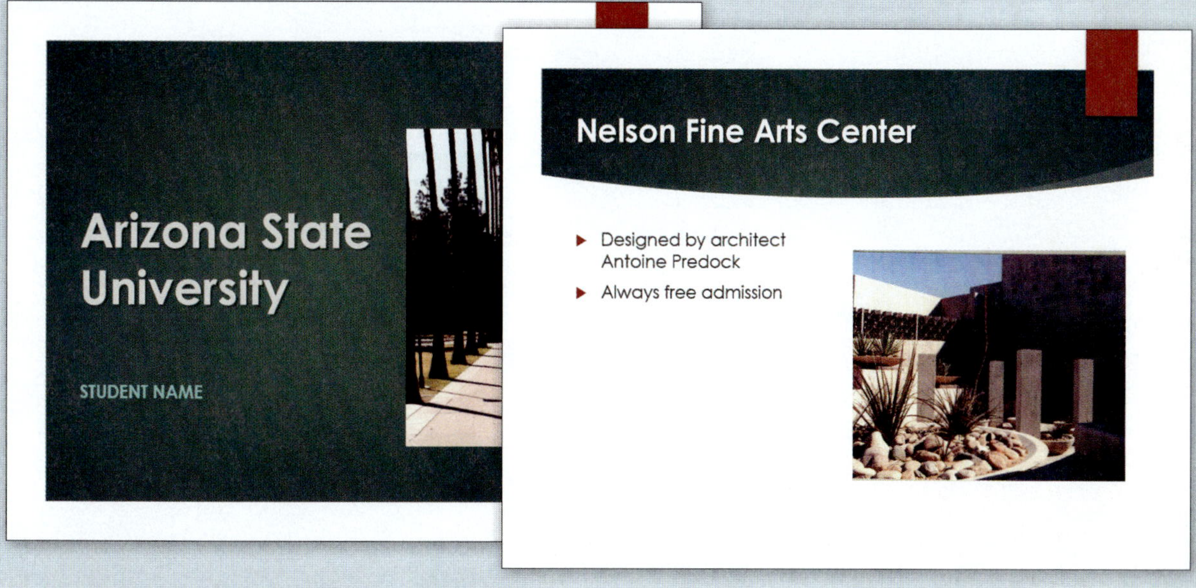

LAB EXERCISES

a. Open the file pp02_ASU Presentation.

b. Save the file as ASU Presentation1.

c. Run the slide show to see what Bonnie has done so far.

d. Spell-check the presentation, making the appropriate corrections.

e. Move slide 5 before slide 4.

f. Use the Find and Replace feature to locate all occurrences of "Arizona State University" and replace them with "ASU" on all slides except the first and second slides.

g. Enter your name as the subtitle in slide 1. Insert the picture pp02_PalmWalk on the title slide. Size the picture and position the placeholders on the slide appropriately.

h. Demote all the bulleted items on slides 8 and 9 except the first item.

i. Change the document theme to one of your choice. Choose a theme variant of your choice. If necessary, reposition graphics and change font sizes.

j. Modify the text color of all the titles in the presentation using the slide master.

k. Duplicate slide 1 and move the duplicate to the end of the presentation. Replace your name with **Apply Now!**

l. Bonnie would like to add some picture of the building at the end of presentation. Switch to Slide Sorter view and select slides 12, 13, and 14. Apply the Two Content layout. Insert the picture pp02_Student Services in slide 12, the picture pp02_Library in slide 13, and the picture pp02_Fine Arts in slide 14 from your student file location.

m. Add a custom animation and sound to the picture on the title slide.

n. Apply random transitions to all slides in the presentation.

o. Apply the Fly In From Right build effect to all slides with bullet items.

p. Run the slide show.

q. Add file documentation and save the presentation. Print slides 1, 2, and 12–15 as handouts (six per page).

ENHANCING THE TRIPLE CROWN PRESENTATION ★★★

4. To complete this exercise, you must have completed Step-by-Step Exercise 1 in Lab 1. Kevin's work on the Triple Crown Presentation was well received by his supervisor. She would like to see some additional information included in the presentation, including a table of upcoming qualifying hikes. Four slides from your updated presentation will be similar to those shown here.

Triple Crown Challenge

Adventure Travel Tours

Student Name

Qualifying Hikes

Hike	Location	Distance	Date	Guide
Death Valley	California	35 miles	August 25, 2015	Kevin Mills
Paria Canyon	Page, AZ	40 miles	September 29, 2015	Kevin Mills
Bryce to Zion	Utah	95 miles	October 20, 2015	Tracey Lynn

Student Name

Lightweight Backpacking

- Why go lightweight?
  - More miles
  - Less strain
  - Less impact on the environment

Student Name

Adventure is Waiting!

Adventure Travel Tours

Student Name

Call us Today!

Student Name

8

a. Open the file Triple Crown Presentation.

b. Save the file as Triple Crown Presentation2.

c. Change the document theme to one of your choice. Choose a theme variant of your choice. If necessary, reposition graphics and change font sizes.

d. Using the slide master, change the text color of the titles and subtitles. Change the bullet styles.

e. Use the Find and Replace command to replace any occurrence of "Paria Canyon" with **Emerald Pools**.

f. Replace slide 3 with a new Title and Content slide. In this slide:

Enter the title **Qualifying Hikes**.

Create a table with five columns and four rows.

Enter the following information in the table:

Hike	**Location**	**Distance**	**Date**	**Guide**
Death Valley	**California**	**35 miles**	**August 25, 2015**	**Kevin Mills**
Paria Canyon	**Page, AZ**	**40 miles**	**September 29, 2015**	**Kevin Mills**
Bryce to Zion	**Utah**	**95 miles**	**October 20, 2015**	**Tracey Lynn**

Adjust the column and row size as needed.

Center the cell entries both horizontally and vertically in their cell spaces.

Change the table style to one of your choice.

Position the table appropriately.

g. Add a footer that does not display the date and time but does display your name and the slide number on all slides except the title slide.

h. Add the Float In animation to the graphics on slides 4 and 5. Add an animation effect of your choice to all slides that include bullets. Add a transition effect of your choice to all slides.

i. Duplicate slide 1 and place the copy at the end of the presentation. In this slide:

Change the title to **Adventure is Waiting!**

Add the slide footer. (*Hint:* Use Copy and Paste to copy your name and the slide number to the final slide.)

Add a shape of your choice to the final slide with the text: **Call us Today!**

j. Add the following information to the file properties:

Author: **Your Name**

Title: **Triple Crown Presentation**

k. Save the file.

l. Print slides 1, 3, 5, and 8 as a handout with four slides, horizontal, on one page.

COMPLETING THE WORKPLACE ISSUES PRESENTATION ★★★

5. To complete this problem, you must have completed Step-by-Step Exercise 5 in Lab 1. Tim has completed the first draft of the presentation for his class lecture on workplace issues, but he still has some information he wants to add to the presentation. Additionally, he wants to make the presentation look better using many of the PowerPoint design and slide show presentation features. Several slides of the modified presentation are shown here.

Workplace Issues
Lecture 4

Topics of Discussion
Ergonomics
Ethics
Environment

Workplace Issues
Lecture 4
Presented by Student Name
End of Class

LAB EXERCISES

a. Open the presentation Workplace Issues, which was saved at the end of Step-by-Step Exercise 5 in Lab 1. If necessary, switch to Normal view.

b. Save the file as Workplace Issues2.

c. Change the design template to Organic. Change the theme variant to one of your choice. Modify fonts and graphics as appropriate.

d. Change to Slide Sorter view and check the slide layouts. Make the following adjustments:

   Title Slide Layout (in Slide Master view):

      Delete the date area and number area placeholders.

      Change the text color of the subtitle to a color of your choice and bold it.

   Slide master:

      Change the bullet style to a picture style of your choice.

      Reduce the size of the object area placeholder and center it on the slide.

      Increase font size of content text.

   Slide 1:

   Change the font of the title to Verdana or a similar font. Apply the shadow effect.

e. Check the slide layouts again in Slide Sorter view and fix the placement and size of the placeholders as needed.

f. Apply the Two Content layout to slide 2. Insert the clip art pp02_Arrows into the slide. Modify the graphic color to coordinate with the colors in your color scheme. Add a custom animation and sound to the graphic.

g. Change the angle of the graphic in slide 4.

h. Duplicate the title slide and move it to the end of the presentation. Delete the graphic and add a drawing object to this slide that includes the text **End of Class**. Format the object and text appropriately.

i. Add transition effects to all the slides. Run the slide show.

j. Add the following notes to slide 3 in a point size of 18:

   Computers used to be more expensive—focus was to make people adjust to fit computers

   Now, people are more expensive—focus is on ergonomics

   Objective—design computers and use them to increase productivity and avoid health risks

   Physical as well as mental risks

k. Add a bullet format to the notes on slide 3.

l. Add file documentation and save the completed presentation.

m. Print the notes page for slide 3. Print slides 1, 2, 6, and 11 as handouts with four slides per page.

ON YOUR OWN

CLUTTER CONTROL ★

1. You work for a business that designs and builds custom closet solutions. You have been asked to prepare a presentation for new clients that will help them prepare for the construction phase. Clients need to organize and categorize their items before the crews arrive on-site; your presentation will serve as an organization guide. Research ideas on reducing clutter on the web. Add transitions, animations, and a theme that will catch the viewer's attention. Include your name and the current date in a slide footer. Save the presentation, early and often, as Custom Closets, and print the presentation as handouts, nine per page.

DREAM VACATION ★★

2. For a class project, you have been asked to plan your "dream vacation." Choose your destination, and do some research on the web to create a presentation illustrating key tourist attractions, fun things to do, dining experiences, hotel choices, and travel costs and arrangements. Start a new presentation and add appropriate text content. Include a table. Add transitions, graphics, animations, and a theme that will catch the viewer's attention. Include your name and the current date in the slide footer. Save the presentation, early and often, as Dream Vacation and print the handouts.

ENHANCING THE CAREERS WITH ANIMALS PRESENTATION ★★★

3. To add interest to the Careers with Animals presentation that you created in Lab 1, On Your Own Exercise 5, select a theme and color theme of your choice. Add graphics, animation, sound, and transitions that will hold your audience's interest. Add speaker notes with a header that displays your name. Include your name and the current date in a slide footer. Modify the format to widescreen; be sure to check all slides and make any necessary modifications. Add appropriate documentation to the file, save the presentation, early and often, as Careers with Animals2, print the presentation as handouts, and print the notes pages for only the slides containing notes.

ENHANCING THE INTERNET POLICY PRESENTATION ★★★

4. After completing the Internet Policy presentation you created in Lab 1, On Your Own Exercise 1, you decide it could use a bit more sprucing up. You want to add some information about personal computing security. Do some research on the web to find some helpful tips on protecting personal privacy and safeguarding your computer. Enter this information in one or two slides. Add some animated graphics and transitions to help liven up the presentation. Make these and any other changes that you think would enhance the presentation. Add a table and format it appropriately. Include speaker notes for at least one slide. Add appropriate documentation to the file. Save the file, early and often, as Internet Policy2; print the presentation as handouts, nine per page; and print the notes pages (with a header displaying your name and the current date) for only the slides containing notes.

LAB EXERCISES

ENHANCING THE WEB DESIGN PRESENTATION ★★★

5. After completing the Web Design presentation in Lab 1, On Your Own Exercise 4, you decide it needs a bit more sprucing up. First of all, it would be more impressive as an onscreen presentation with a custom design. Also, the pros and cons information would look better as a table, and a few animated clip art pictures, nonstandard bullets, builds, and transitions wouldn't hurt. Make these and any other changes that you think would enhance the presentation. Include speaker notes for at least one slide. Include your name and the current date in a slide footer. Add appropriate documentation to the file and save it, early and often, as Web Design2. Print the presentation as handouts and print the notes pages for only the slides containing notes.

Working Together: Copying, Embedding, and Linking between Applications

CASE STUDY

Animal Rescue Foundation

The director of the Animal Rescue Foundation has reviewed the PowerPoint presentation you created and has asked you to include an adoption success rate chart that was created using Excel. Additionally, the director has provided a list of dates for the upcoming volunteer orientation meetings that he feels would be good content for another slide.

Frequently you will find that you want to include information that was created using a word processing, spreadsheet, or database application in your slide show. As you will see, you can easily share information between applications, saving you both time and effort by eliminating the need to re-create information that is available in another application while you create the new slides. The new slides containing information from Word and Excel are shown here.

NOTE The Working Together section assumes that you already know how to use Microsoft Word and Excel 2013 and that you have completed PowerPoint Lab 2.

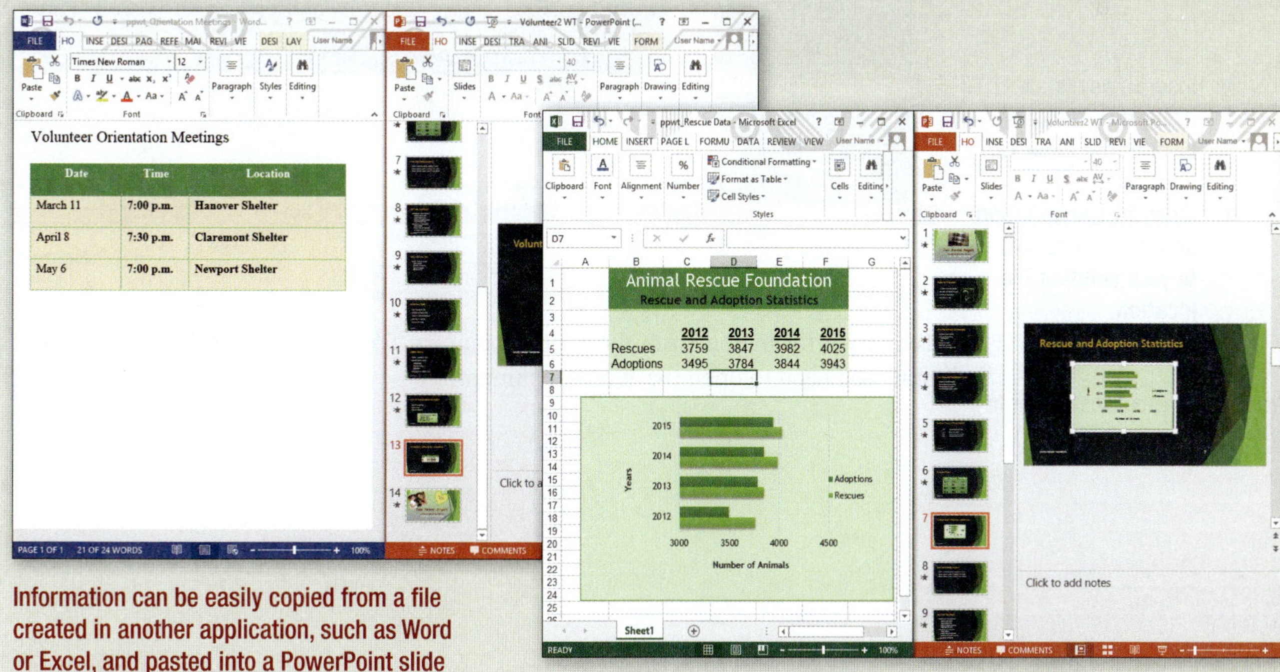

Information can be easily copied from a file created in another application, such as Word or Excel, and pasted into a PowerPoint slide as a linked or embedded object.

Copying between Applications

The director prepared the list of orientation meeting dates and locations in a document using Word 2013. As you have learned, all the Microsoft Office system applications have a common user interface, such as similar Ribbons and commands. In addition to these obvious features, the applications have been designed to work together, making it easy to share and exchange information between applications.

Rather than retype information, you will copy the list from the Word document into the presentation. You also can use the same commands and procedures to copy information from PowerPoint or other Office applications into a Word document.

COPYING FROM WORD TO A POWERPOINT SLIDE

First, you need to modify the PowerPoint presentation to include a new slide for the orientation meeting dates.

1

- **Start PowerPoint 2013.**
- **Open the presentation Volunteer2 Widescreen (saved at the end of Lab 2).**

Having Trouble?

If this file is not available, open ppwt_Volunteer2 Widescreen. Be sure to change Student Name on the first slide to your name.

- **Insert a new slide using the Title Only layout after slide 12.**
- **Save the presentation as Volunteer2 WT to your solution file location.**

Your screen should be similar to Figure 1

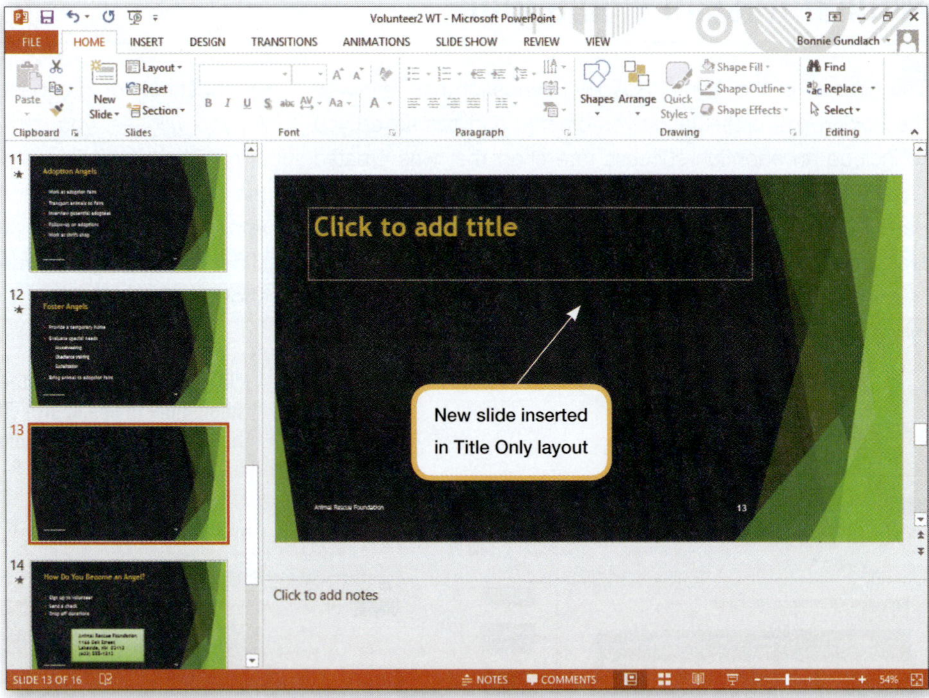

Figure 1

To copy information from the Word document file into the PowerPoint presentation, you need to open the Word document.

2

- **Start Word 2013.**
- **Open the document** ppwt_Orientation Meetings
- **If necessary, maximize the window, hide the rulers, and set the magnification to 100%.**

Having Trouble?

Open the View tab, and uncheck Ruler in the Show group.

Your screen should be similar to Figure 2

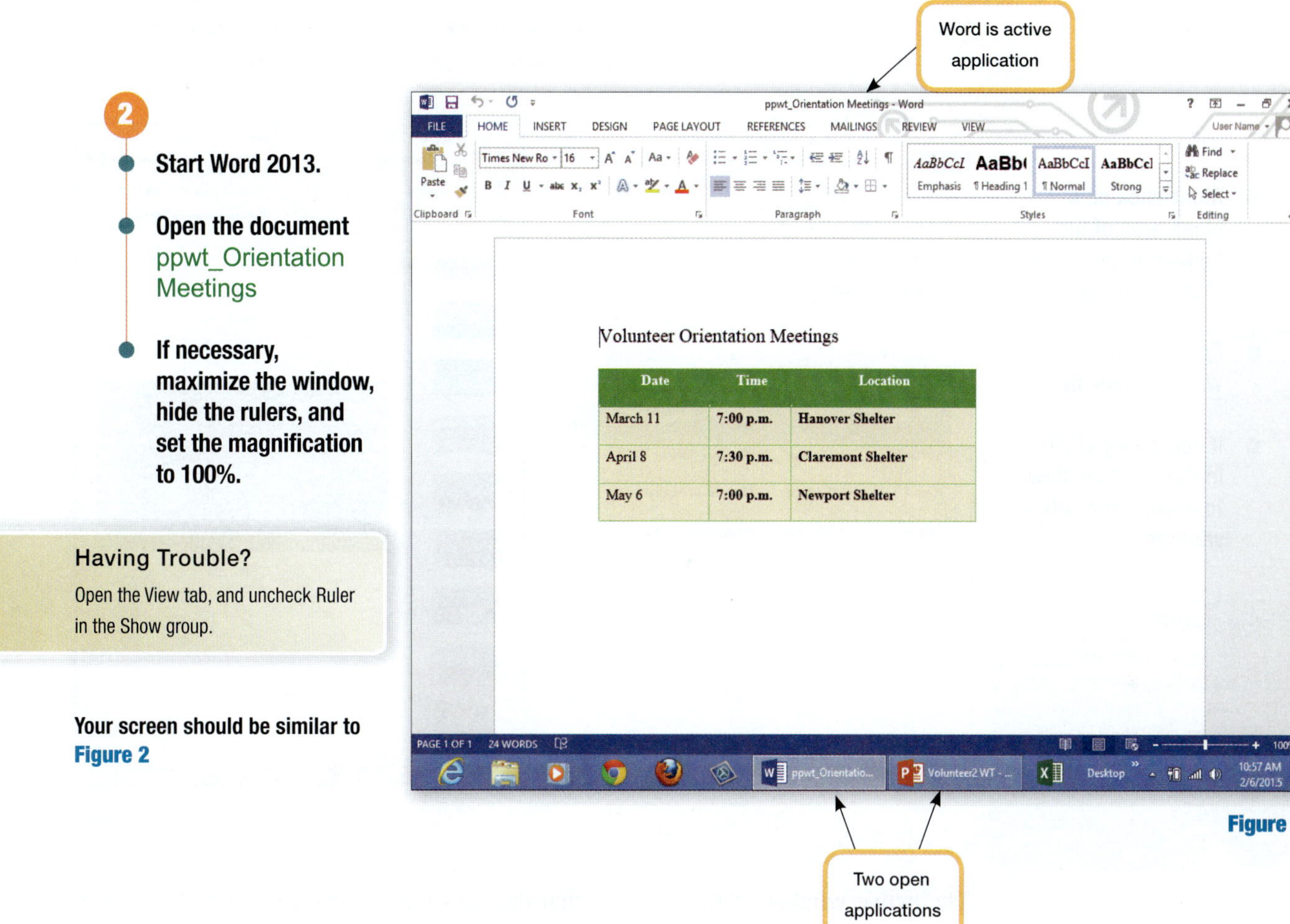

Figure 2

There are now two open applications, Word and PowerPoint. PowerPoint is open in a window behind the Word application window. Both application buttons are displayed in the taskbar. There are also two open files, ppwt_Orientation Meetings in Word and Volunteer2 WT in PowerPoint. Word is the active application, and ppwt_Orientation Meetings is the active file. To make it easier to work with two applications, you will display the windows next to each other to view both on the screen at the same time.

3

- **Right-click on a blank area of the taskbar to open the shortcut menu.**
- **Choose Show Windows Side by Side.**
- **If necessary, click in the Word window to make it the active window.**

Another Method

With Microsoft Windows 7 or 8, you also can use the Snap feature to quickly tile your windows. Simply drag the Word application window all the way to the left side of the screen and the PowerPoint window all the way to the right. The windows will automatically resize so that they each take up half the screen.

Your screen should be similar to Figure 3

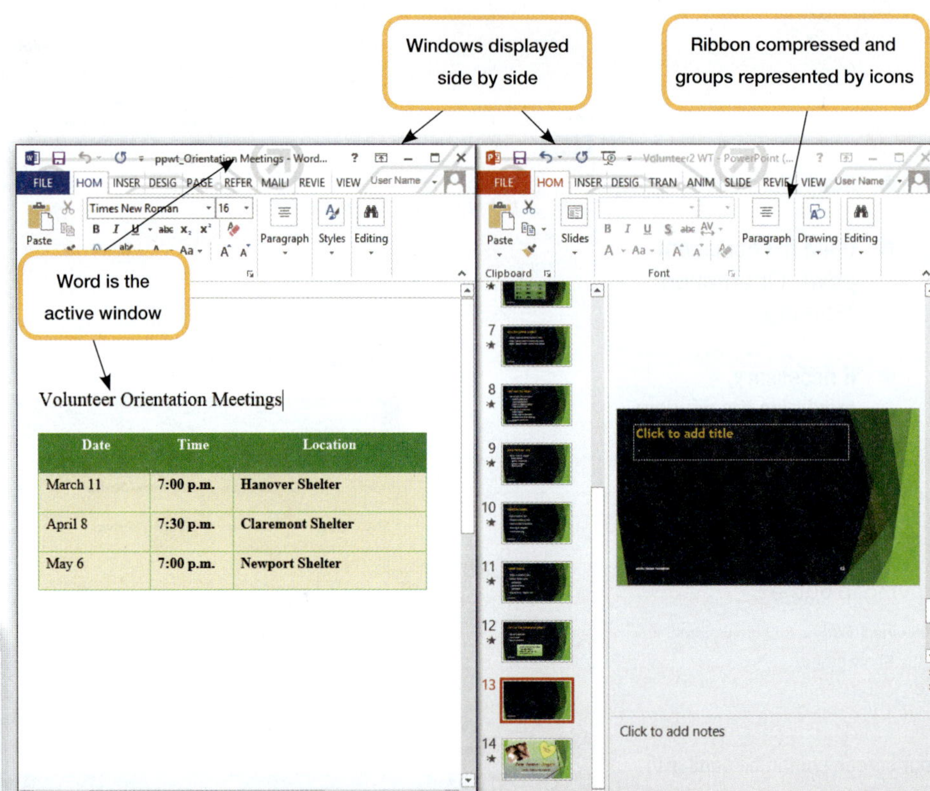

Figure 3

The active window is the window that displays the insertion point and does not have a dimmed title bar. It is the window in which you can work. Because the windows are side by side and there is less horizontal space in each window, the Ribbon groups are compressed. To access commands in these groups, simply click on the group button and the commands appear in a drop-down list.

First, you will copy the title from the Word document into the title placeholder of the slide. While using the Word and PowerPoint applications, you have learned how to use cut, copy, and paste to move or copy information within the same document. You can also perform these same operations between documents in the same application and between documents in different applications. The information is pasted in a format that the application can edit, if possible.

4

- Select the title "Volunteer Orientation Meetings."
- Click Copy on the Home tab in Word.
- Click on the PowerPoint window to make it the active window.
- Right-click in the title placeholder in the Slide window in PowerPoint.
- Click Use Destination Theme in the Paste Options area of the shortcut menu to apply the slide formatting to the title.

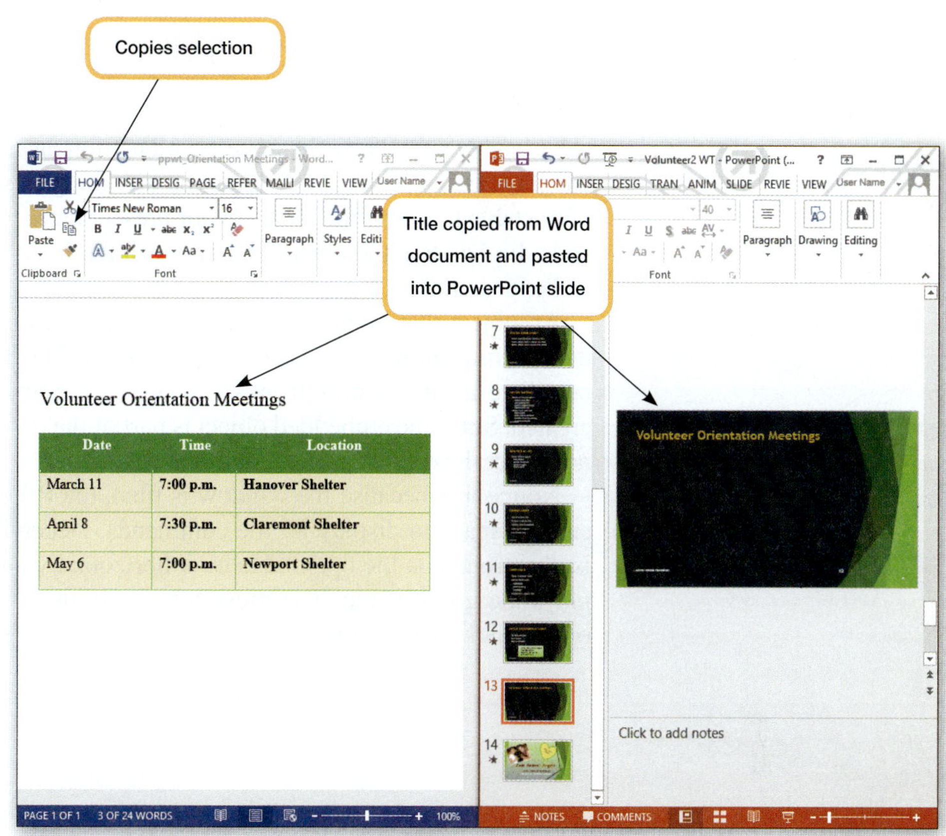

Figure 4

Another Method

You also could use drag and drop to copy the text to the slide.

- Click on the slide to deselect the placeholder.

Your screen should be similar to Figure 4

The title has been copied into the slide and can be edited and manipulated within PowerPoint. Because you used the Use Destination Theme paste option, the formats associated with the slide master were applied to the copied text.

Additional Information

You could also click Reset in the Slides group of the Home tab to quickly convert all the text on the slide to match the presentation's theme.

Embedding a Word Table in a PowerPoint Slide

Next, you want to copy the table of orientation dates and place it below the title in the slide. Because you know that you are going to want to change the formatting of the table to match the look of your presentation, you will **embed** the table in the slide. Embedding the object will give you the freedom to modify the table's shape and appearance.

An object that is embedded is stored in the file in which it is inserted, called the **destination file**, and becomes part of that file. The embedded object can then be edited using features from the source program, the program in which it was created. Since the embedded object is part of the destination file, modifying it does not affect the original file, called the **source file**.

Notice that because the window is tiled, the Ribbon is smaller and there is not enough space to display all the commands. Depending on how small the Ribbon is, the groups on the open tab shrink horizontally and show a single icon that displays the group name. The most commonly used commands or features are left open. Clicking the icon opens the group and displays the commands.

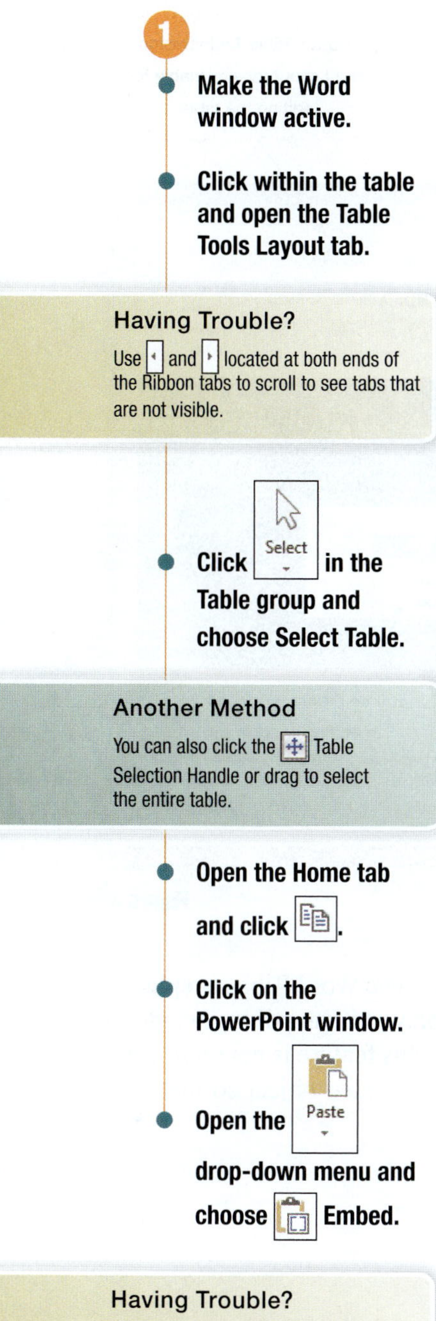

1

- **Make the Word window active.**
- **Click within the table and open the Table Tools Layout tab.**

Having Trouble?

Use ◂ and ▸ located at both ends of the Ribbon tabs to scroll to see tabs that are not visible.

- **Click Select in the Table group and choose Select Table.**

Another Method

You can also click the Table Selection Handle or drag to select the entire table.

- **Open the Home tab and click .**
- **Click on the PowerPoint window.**
- **Open the Paste drop-down menu and choose Embed.**

Having Trouble?

See "Copying and Moving Selections," on page IO.47 in the Introduction to Microsoft Office for more information on the Paste Options feature.

Your screen should be similar to Figure 5

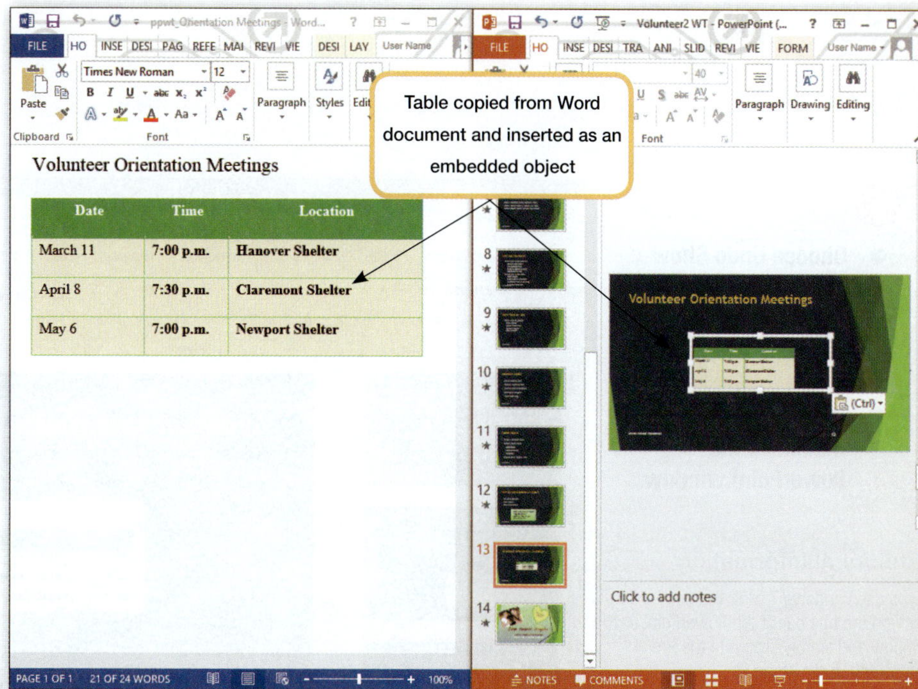

Figure 5

The table, including the table formatting, is copied into the slide as an embedded object that can be manipulated. The object container is larger than the table it holds.

EDITING AN EMBEDDED OBJECT

As you look at the table, you decide to change the size and appearance of the table. To do this, you will edit the embedded object using the source program.

- Choose Undo Show Side by Side from the taskbar shortcut menu.

- If necessary, maximize the PowerPoint window.

Additional Information

If you use Windows 7 or 8, you can click on the title bar of the PowerPoint window and simply drag it to the top of the screen to maximize it.

- Double-click the table.

Your screen should be similar to **Figure 6**

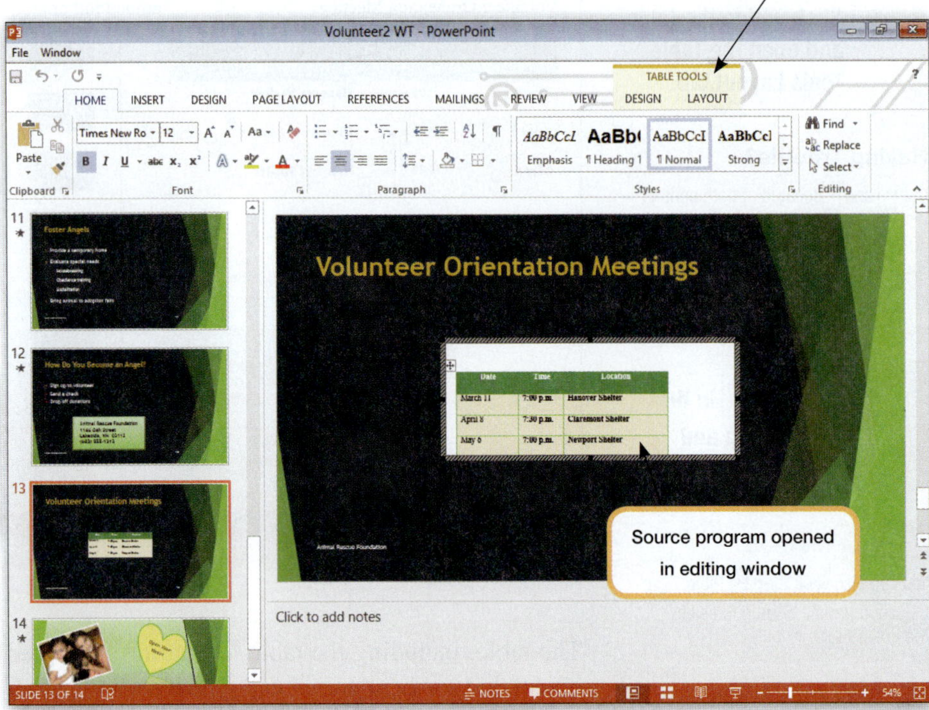

Figure 6

The source program, in this case Word 2013, is opened. The Word Ribbon replaces the PowerPoint Ribbon. The embedded object is displayed in an editing window. If your table does not display gridlines, this is because this feature is not on in your application. First, you will increase the size of the embedded object so that you can increase the size of the table within it.

Additional Information

You must have the source program on your system to be able to open and edit an embedded object.

Additional Information

If you want to see gridlines in your table, open the Layout tab and click 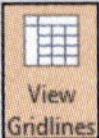.

- **Drag the sizing handle to increase the object's size as in Figure 7.**

Your screen should be similar to Figure 7

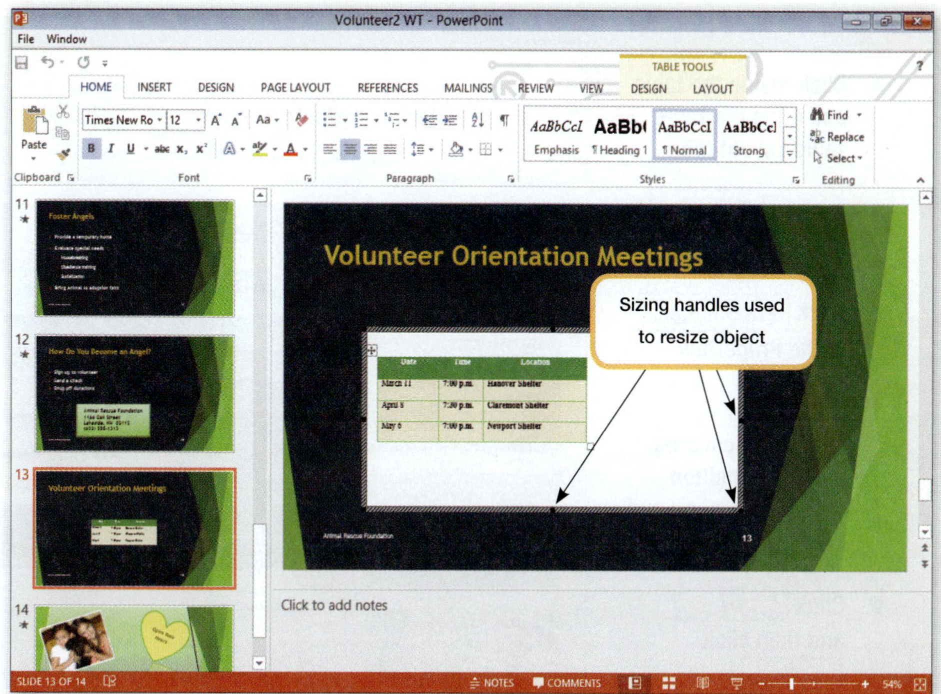

Figure 7

Now that the embedded object's container is larger, you can resize and reposition the table within the container.

- **Click inside the table and open the Table Tools Layout tab.**
- **Click**  **in the Table group.**
- **Click Positioning... in the Properties dialog box.**
- **In the Vertical area, open the Position drop-down menu and choose Top.**
- **Click OK and then click OK.** 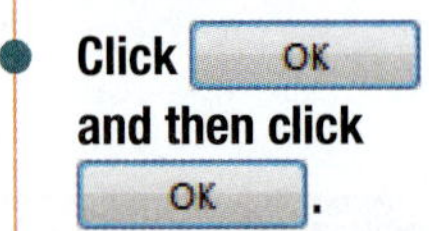
- **Scroll the window to see the entire table.**

Having Trouble?

Use the directional keys or the scroll wheel to adjust it vertically.

- **Slowly drag the bottom-right corner sizing handle of the table to increase the size of the table in the object's container.**

Having Trouble?

If you can't see the table's bottom-right corner sizing handle, try clicking in the table and scrolling up and down until it appears.

Having Trouble?

If the table gets too large to fit in the container, click Undo to reset it and try again.

Your screen should be similar to Figure 8

Embedded object is repositioned and sized

Table sizing handle

Figure 8

Next, you will use the Word commands to edit the object. You want to apply a different table design style and change the appearance of the text in the table.

4

- Open the Table Tools Design tab.
- Click More in the Table Styles group.
- Choose Grid Table 5, Dark-Accent 2 from the Table Styles gallery (fifth row, third column).
- Drag to select the entire table and open the Table Tools Layout tab.
- In the Alignment group, choose Align Center Left.
- With the table still selected, open the Home tab and click A four times to increase the font size to 20.
- Drag to select the first row of table headings and click A three times to increase the font size to 26.
- Click anywhere outside the object to close the source program.
- Position the object as in Figure 9 and deselect it.

Your screen should be similar to Figure 9

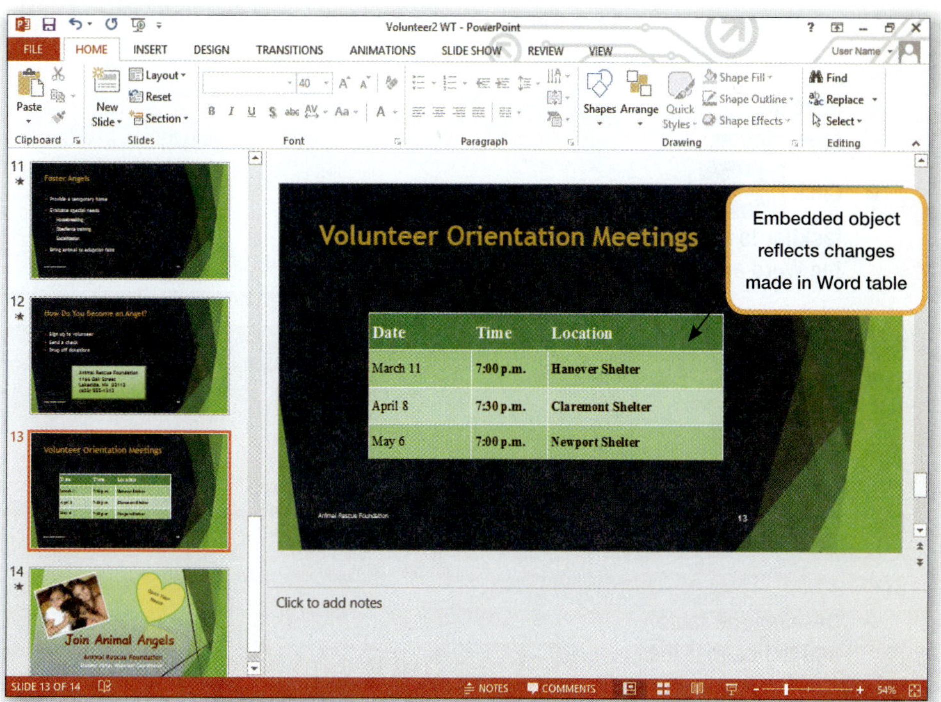

Figure 9

The embedded object in the PowerPoint slide is updated to reflect the changes you made in the Word table.

5

- Save the presentation.
- Click [Word taskbar button] in the taskbar to switch to the Word application.

Having Trouble?

Don't worry if your Word application taskbar image looks different than this one. Applications will look different depending on which version of Windows is installed on the computer you are using.

- Deselect the table and notice that the source file has not been affected by the changes you made to the embedded object.
- Exit Word.

Linking between Applications

Next, you want to copy the chart of the rescue and adoption data into the presentation. You will insert the chart object into the slide as a **linked object**, which is another way to insert information created in one application into a document created by another application. With a linked object, the actual data is stored in the source file (the document in which it was created). A graphic representation or picture of the data is displayed in the destination file (the document in which the object is inserted). A connection between the information in the destination file and the source file is established by creating a link. The link contains references to the location of the source file and the selection within the document that is linked to the destination file.

When changes are made in the source file that affect the linked object, the changes are automatically reflected in the destination file when it is opened. This connection is called a **live link**. When you create linked objects, the date and time on your machine should be accurate. This is because the program refers to the date of the source file to determine whether updates are needed when you open the destination file.

LINKING AN EXCEL CHART TO A POWERPOINT PRESENTATION

The chart of the rescue and adoption data will be inserted into another new slide following slide 6.

1

- **Insert a new slide following slide 6 using the Title Only layout.**
- **Start Excel 2013 and open the workbook** ppwt_Rescue Data **from your data files.**
- **Display the application windows side by side.**

Your screen should be similar to Figure 10

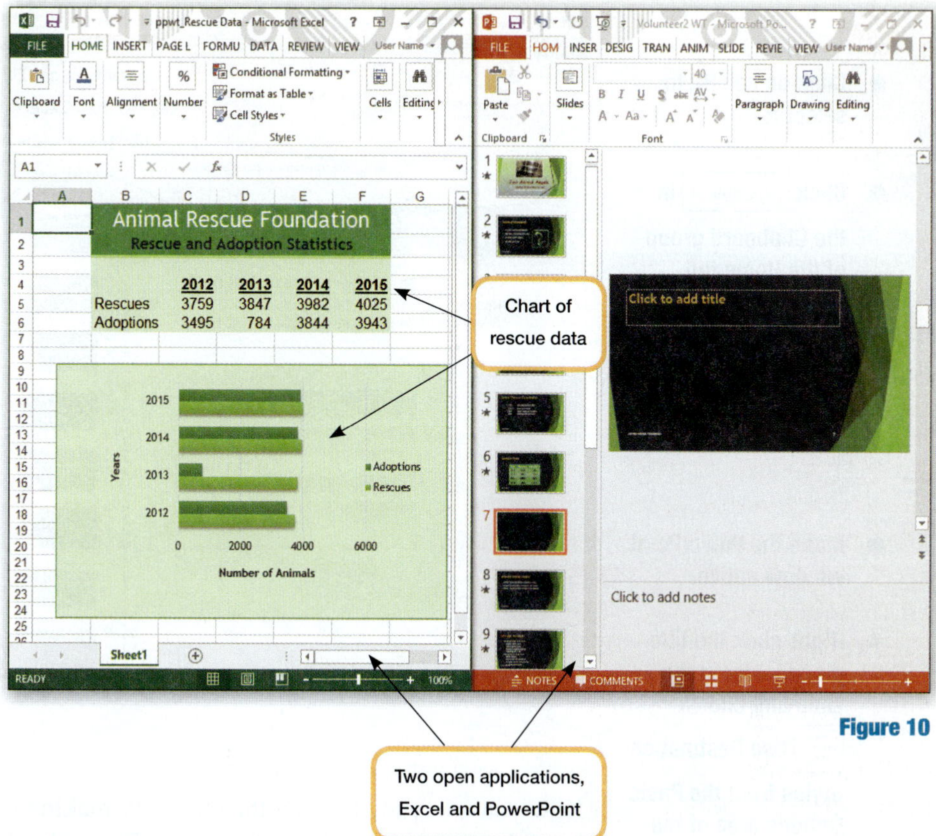

Figure 10

The worksheet contains the rescue and adoption data for the past four years as well as a bar chart of the data. Again, you have two open applications, PowerPoint and Excel. Next you will copy the second title line from the worksheet into the slide title placeholder.

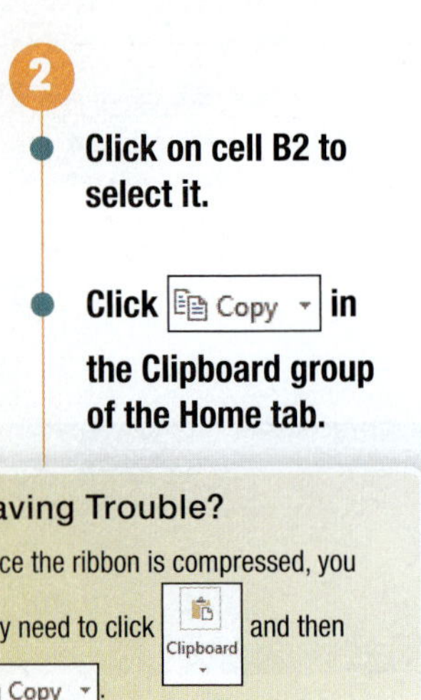

2

- Click on cell B2 to select it.
- Click Copy in the Clipboard group of the Home tab.

Having Trouble?

Since the ribbon is compressed, you may need to click Clipboard and then Copy.

- Make the PowerPoint window active.
- Right-click the title placeholder in the slide and choose Use Destination Styles from the Paste Options area of the shortcut menu.
- Click on the slide to deselect the placeholder.

Your screen should be similar to Figure 11

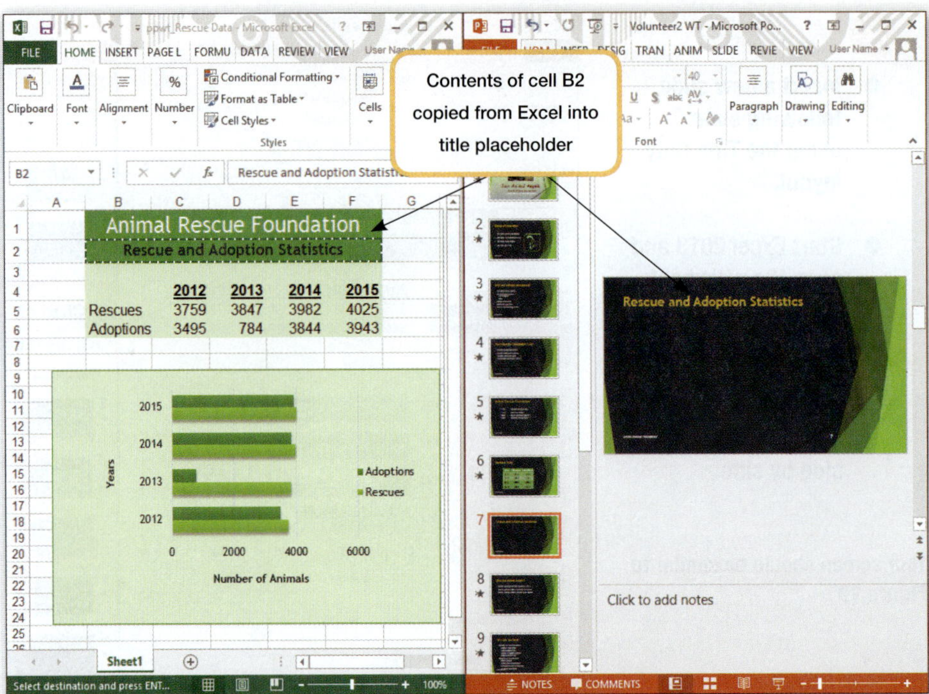

Figure 11

Now you are ready to copy the chart. By making the chart a linked object, it will be updated automatically if the source file is edited.

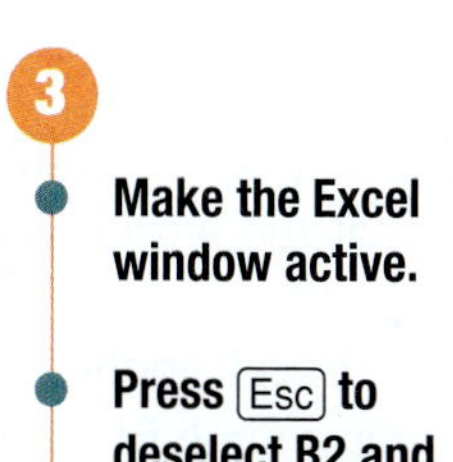

3

- Make the Excel window active.
- Press Esc to deselect B2 and then click on the chart object in the worksheet to select it.

Having Trouble?

Click on the chart to select it when the ScreenTip displays "Chart Area."

- Click Copy in the Clipboard group.
- Click on the slide.
- From the Home tab, open the Paste drop-down menu and choose Paste Special.

Your screen should be similar to Figure 12

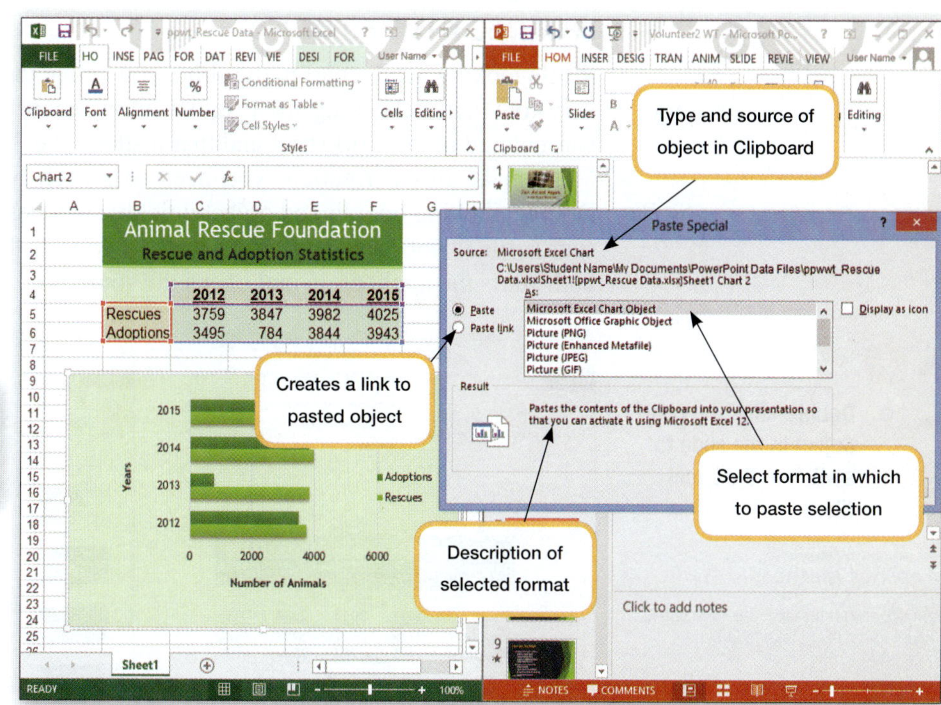

Figure 12

The Paste Special dialog box displays the type of object contained in the Clipboard and its location in the Source area. From the As list box, you select the type of format in which you want the object pasted into the destination file. The Result area describes the effect of your selections. In this case, you want to insert the chart as a linked object to Microsoft Excel.

4

- Choose Paste link.
- Click OK.
- Appropriately size and position the linked object on the slide.

Your screen should be similar to Figure 13

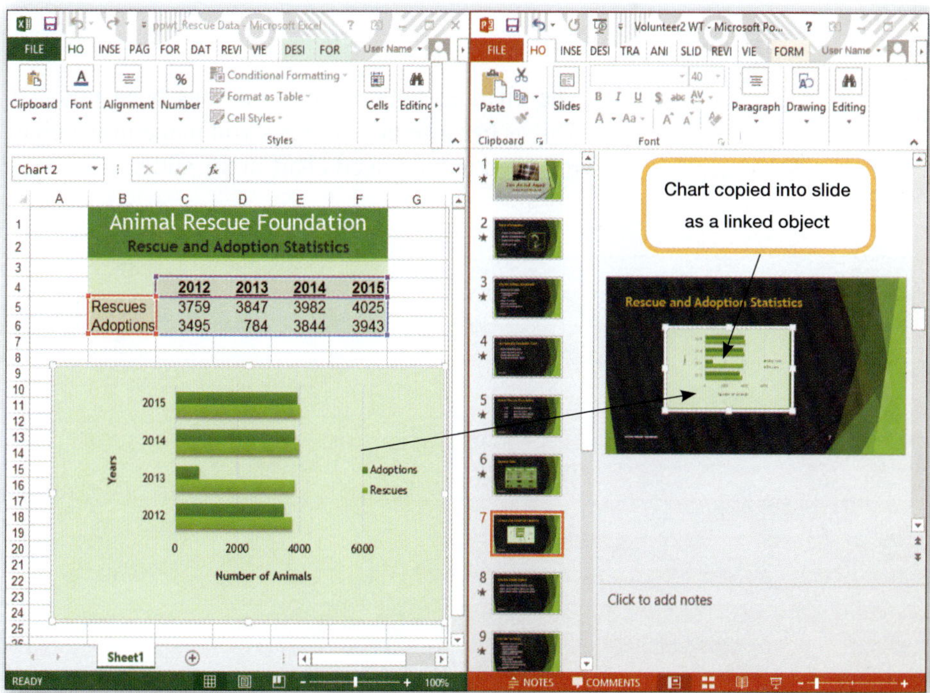

Figure 13

The chart object was inserted as a picture, and a link was created to the chart in the source file.

UPDATING A LINKED OBJECT

While looking at the chart in the slide, you notice the adoption data for 2013 looks very low. After checking the original information, you see that the wrong value was entered in the worksheet and that it should be 3784.

To make this correction, you need to switch back to the Excel application. Double-clicking on a linked object quickly switches to the open source file. If the source file is not open, it opens the file for you. If the application is not started, it both starts the application and opens the source file.

1

- **Double-click the chart object in the slide to switch to the Excel file.**

Another Method

You can also right-click the edge of the object and select Linked Worksheet Object/Edit.

- **Change the value in cell D6 to 3784 and press Enter.**

Your screen should be similar to Figure 14

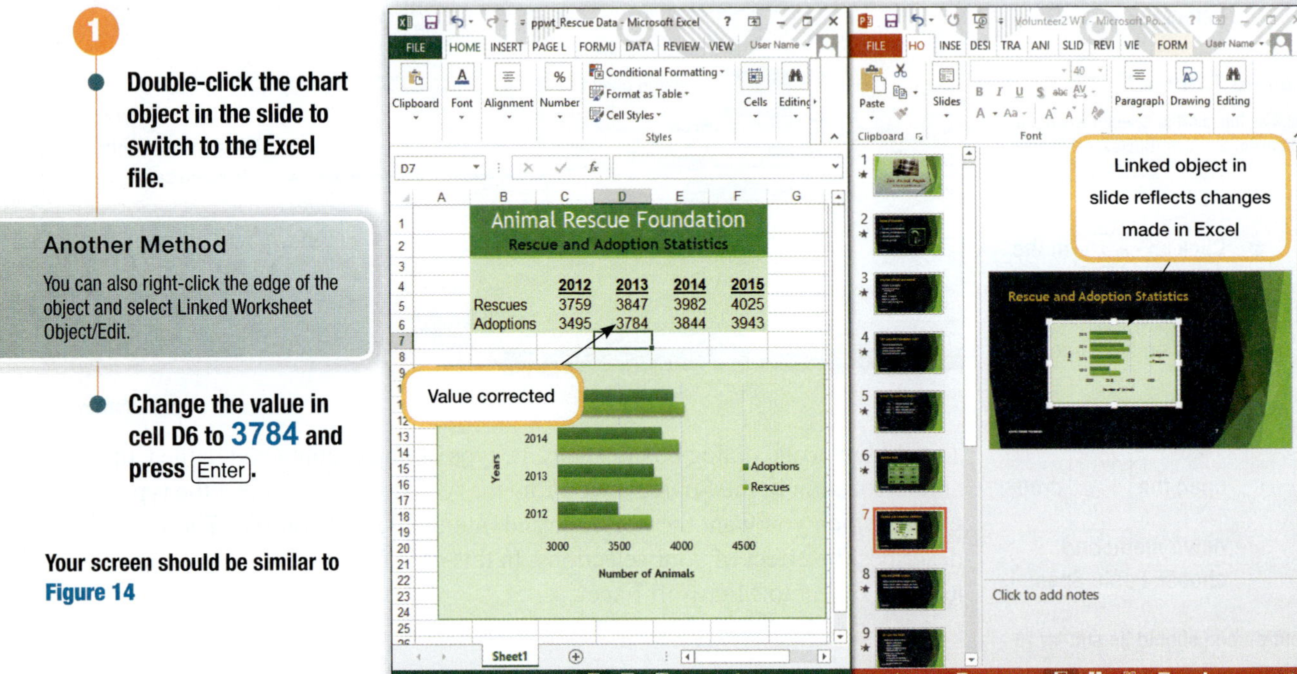

Figure 14

The chart in both applications has been updated to reflect the change in data. This is because any changes you make in the chart in Excel will be automatically reflected in the linked chart in the slide.

2

- **Undo the side-by-side window display.**
- **Save the revised Excel workbook as** Rescue Data Linked **to your solution file location.**
- **Exit Excel.**
- **If necessary, maximize the PowerPoint window.**

Linking documents is a very handy feature, particularly in documents whose information is updated frequently. If you include a linked object in a document, make sure the source file name and location do not change. Otherwise the link will not operate correctly.

Printing Selected Slides

Next, you will print the two new slides.

- **Open the File tab and choose Print.**
- **If necessary, select the printer.**
- **Enter 7,14 in the Slides text box to specify the slides to print.**
- **Specify Handouts (2 slides) as the type of output.**
- **Change the color setting to Grayscale.**
- **If necessary, click the Edit Header & Footer link and change the header to display your name.**

Your screen should be similar to Figure 15

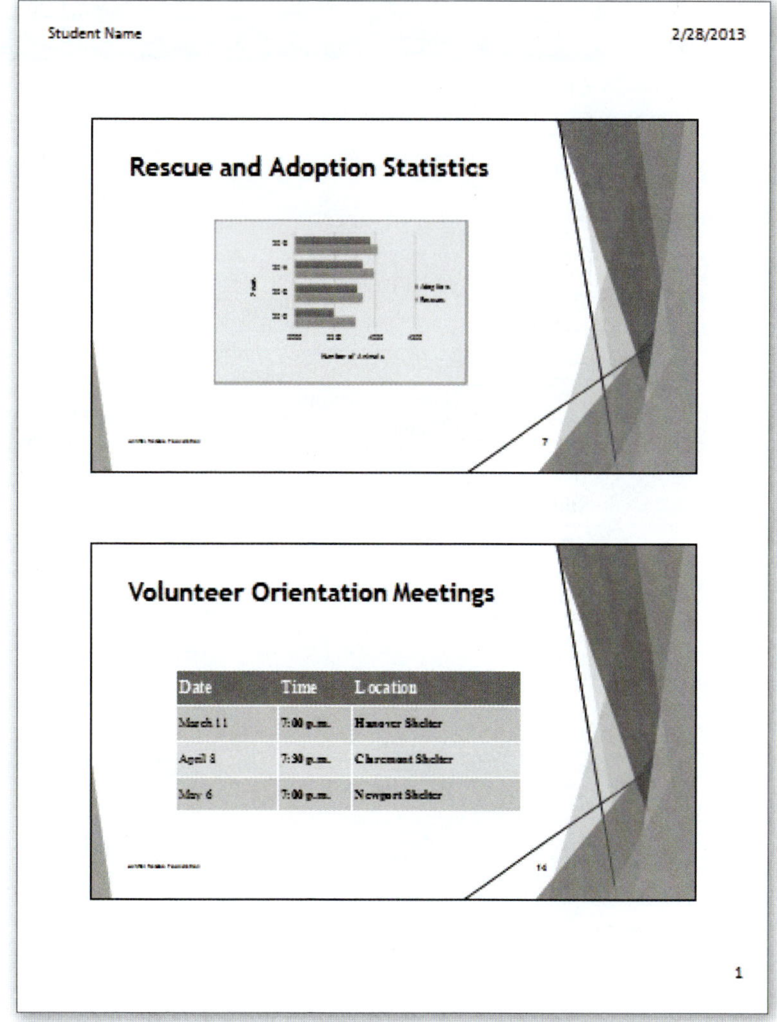

Figure 15

- **Print the page.**
- **Save the linked presentation as** Volunteer2 Linked **and exit PowerPoint.**

LAB REVIEW Working Together Copying, Embedding, and Linking between Applications

KEY TERMS

destination file PPWT.6
embed PPWT.6
linked object PPWT.12
live link PPWT.12
source file PPWT.6

COMMAND SUMMARY

Command	Shortcut	Action
Home tab		
Clipboard group		
Paste/ Embed		Embeds an object from another application
Paste/Paste Special/Paste Link		Inserts an object as a linked object
Paste/ Use Destination Theme		Uses formatting associated with presentation theme
Slides group		
Reset		Converts all the slides content to match the presentation's theme

LAB EXERCISES

Hands-On Exercises

RATING SYSTEM	
★	Easy
★★	Moderate
★★★	Difficult

STEP-BY-STEP

EMBEDDING A TABLE OF MASSAGE PRICES ★

1. At the Hollywood Spa and Fitness Center, you have been working on a presentation on massage therapy. Now that the presentation is almost complete, you just need to add some information to the presentation about prices for all massage services. Your manager has already given you this information in a Word document. You will copy and embed this information into a new slide. The completed slide is shown below.
   a. Start Word and open the file ppwt_Massage Prices.
   b. Start PowerPoint and open the ppwt_Massage Therapy2 presentation.
   c. Save the presentation as Massage Therapy.
   d. Add a new slide after slide 9 using the Title Only layout.
   e. Copy the title from the Word document into the slide title placeholder. Use the Keep Text Only option.
   f. Copy the table into the slide as an embedded object. Exit Word.
   g. Size and position the object on the slide appropriately.
   h. Edit the table to change the font color to an appropriate font color.
   i. Change the fill color of the table to match the slide design.
   j. If necessary, change the footer to display your name.
   k. Save the presentation.
   l. Print the new slide.

EMBEDDING A TABLE OF BLOWOUT INDICATORS ★★

CONTINUING EXERCISES

2. To complete this problem, you must have completed Step-by-Step Exercise 2 in Lab 2. The Blowouts section for the Department of Safety presentation is almost complete. You just need to add some information to the presentation about the indicators of a flat tire. This information is already in a Word document as a table. You will copy and embed it into a new slide. The completed slide is shown below.
   a. Start Word and open the ppwt_BlowoutSigns file.
   b. Start PowerPoint and open the Blowouts2 presentation. If this file is not available, you can use ppwt_Blowouts2 Widescreen.
   c. Save the presentation as Blowouts3 Widescreen.
   d. Add a new slide after slide 3 using the Title Only layout.
   e. Copy the title from the Word document into the slide title placeholder.
   f. Copy the table into the slide as an embedded object. Exit Word.
   g. Size and position the object on the slide appropriately.
   h. Change the design of the table to suit your presentation.
   i. Change the fonts and font sizes of the table headings.
   j. If necessary, change the footer to display your name.
   k. Save the presentation.
   l. Print the new slide.

Blowout Signs

Blowout	Effect
General	Loud noise Vehicle shakes
Front tire	Vehicle pulls to side of blowout
Back tire	Vehicle fishtails

STUDENT NAME 4

LINKING A WORKSHEET ON FOREST USE ★★★

3. To complete this problem, you must have completed Step-by-Step Exercise 4 in Lab 2. Kevin has found some interesting data on the increase in Americans hiking and wants to include this information in his lecture presentation. The completed slide is shown below.

   a. Start PowerPoint and open the Triple Crown Presentation2 file. If this file is not available, you can use ppwt_Triple Crown Presentation2. Save the presentation as Triple Crown Presentation3.
   b. Start Excel and open the ppwt_Forest Use worksheet. Save the worksheet as Forest Use Linked.
   c. Add a new slide after slide 6 using the Title Only layout.
   d. Copy the worksheet cell A1 and paste it in the title placeholder using the Keep Text Only.
   e. Copy the worksheet range A2 through B6 as a linked object into slide 7. Size and position it appropriately.
   f. Format the linked data so that it blends appropriately with the presentation.
   g. Add an appropriate Shape Outline to the linked object's container in the slide.
   h. You notice that the percentage for hiking seems low. After checking the original source, you see you entered the value incorrectly. In Excel, change the value in cell B5 to 42%.
   i. Copy the text in cell A8 and paste it into the Notes for slide 7.
   j. Save the worksheet and exit Excel.
   k. Change the look of the presentation by applying the Slice theme.
   l. Check each slide to resize and reposition objects as necessary.
   m. If necessary, change the footer to display your name.
   n. Save the presentation.
   o. Print the new slide.

Sightseeing	44%
Relaxation	36%
Viewing Wildlife	37%
Hiking	**42%**
Driving	24%

MOST POPULAR FOREST ACTIVITIES

7

POWERPOINT 2013 COMMAND SUMMARY

COMMAND	SHORTCUT	ACTION
Quick Access Toolbar		
Save	Ctrl + S	Saves presentation
Undo	Ctrl + Z	Reverses last action
File Tab		
Save	Ctrl + S	Saves presentation
Save As	F12	Saves presentation using new file name and/or location
Open	Ctrl + O	Opens existing presentation
Close		Closes presentation
Info		Document properties
New	Ctrl + N	Opens New Presentation dialog box
Print	Ctrl + P	Opens print settings and a preview pane
Home Tab		
Clipboard Group		
Paste	Ctrl + V	Pastes item from Clipboard
Paste / Embed		Embeds an object from another application
Paste/Paste		Inserts the copied text or object
Paste / Use Destination Theme		Uses formatting associated with presentation theme
Paste/Paste Special/Paste Link		Inserts an object as a linked object
Cut	Ctrl + X	Cuts selection to Clipboard
Copy	Ctrl + C	Copies selection to Clipboard
Slides Group		
New Slide	Ctrl + M	Inserts new slide with selected layout
Layout		Changes layout of a slide

POWERPOINT 2013 COMMAND SUMMARY

COMMAND	SHORTCUT	ACTION
Keep Text Only		Keeps the format associated with the destination format.
Reset Reset		Converts slide content to match the presentation's theme.
Use Destination Theme		Pastes text using presentation theme formatting
Font Group		
Bookman Old St Font		Changes font type
32 Size		Changes font size
Increase Font Size		Increases font size of selected text
Decrease font size		Decreases font size of selected text
Italicize text		Italicizes selected text
Underline text		Underlines selected text
Shadow		Applies shadow effect to selected text
Change font color		Modifies color of selected text
Paragraph Group		
Bullet list		Formats bulleted list
Numbered list		Formats numbered lists
Decrease List Level		Decreases the indent level
Increase List Level		Increases the indent level
Align Text		Sets vertical alignment of text
Align Left	Ctrl + L	Aligns text to the left
Align Center	Ctrl + E	Centers text
Align Right	Ctrl + R	Aligns text to the right
Justify	Ctrl + J	Aligns text to both the left and right margins

POWERPOINT 2013 COMMAND SUMMARY

COMMAND	SHORTCUT	ACTION
Drawing Group		
Shapes		Inserts selected shape
Shape Fill		Fills the selected shape with a solid color, gradient, picture or texture
Shape Effects		Applies a visual effect to the selected shape, such as shadow, glow, or reflection
Editing Group		
Find	Ctrl + F	Finds specified text
Replace	Ctrl + H	Replaces located text with replacement text
Select / Select All	Ctrl + A	Selects everything in the placeholder box
Insert Tab		
Images Group		
Pictures		Inserts picture from a file on your computer
Online Pictures		Finds and inserts pictures from a variety of online sources
Illustrations Group		
Shapes		Inserts a shape
Text Group		
Text Box		Inserts text box or adds text to selected shape
Header & Footer		Inserts a header and footer

POWERPOINT 2013 COMMAND SUMMARY

COMMAND	SHORTCUT	ACTION
Design Tab		
Themes Group		
More		Opens gallery of document themes
Variant Group		
More		Customizes the look of the current theme
Customize Group		
Slide Size		Selects Standard, Widescreen, or Custom slide size
Transitions Tab		
Preview Group		
Preview		Displays the transition effect
Transition to This Slide Group		
More		Opens a gallery of transition effects
Effect Options		Opens a gallery of effect options
Animations Tab		
Preview Group		
Preview		Displays the transition effect
Animation Group		
More		Opens a gallery of animation effects
Effect Options		Opens a gallery of effect options
Advanced Animation Group		
Add Animation		Adds an animation effect to an object
Animation Pane		Opens the Animation pane
Animation Painter		Copies animation effect to another object

POWERPOINT 2013 COMMAND SUMMARY

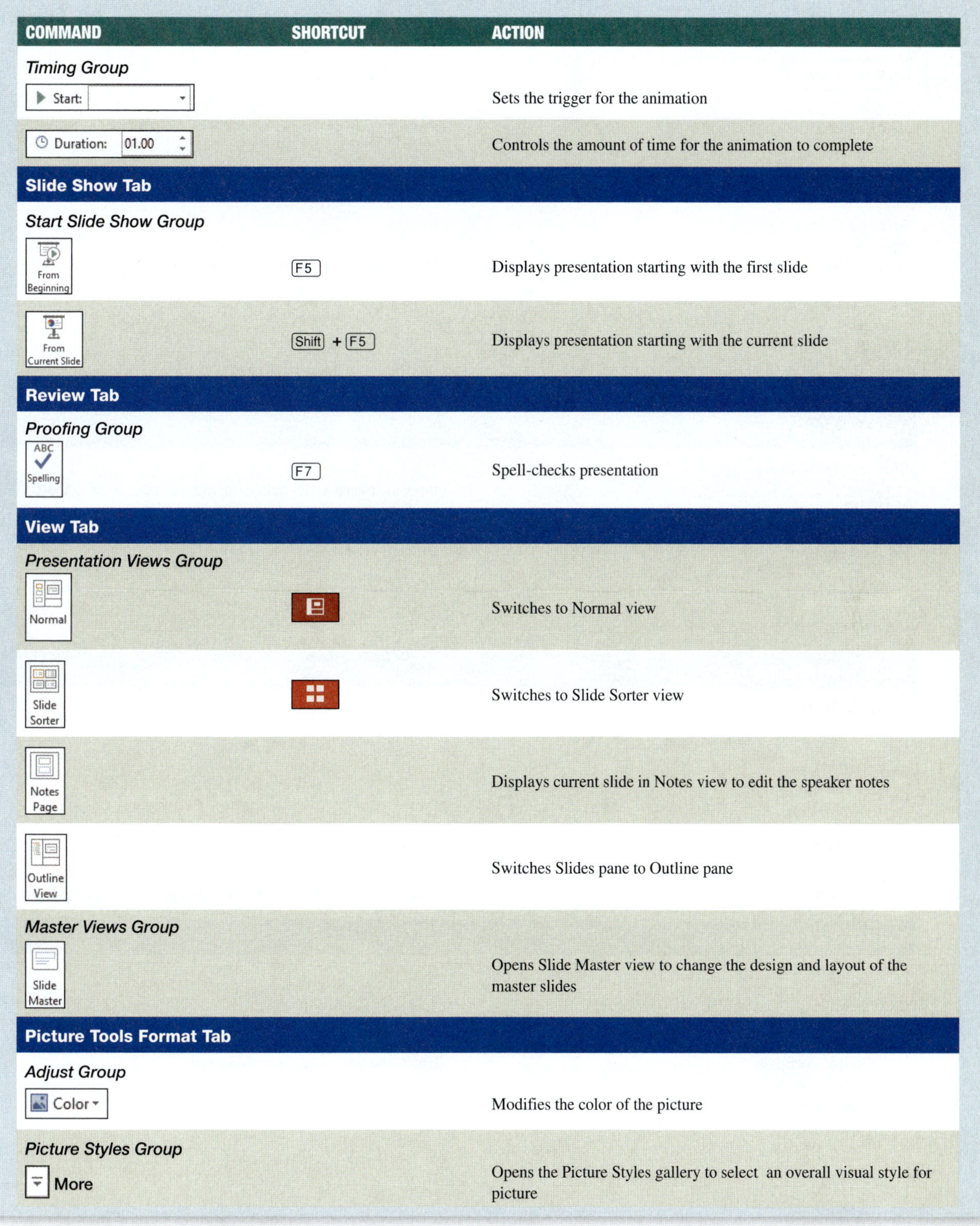

COMMAND	SHORTCUT	ACTION
Timing Group		
Start:		Sets the trigger for the animation
Duration: 01.00		Controls the amount of time for the animation to complete
Slide Show Tab		
Start Slide Show Group		
From Beginning	F5	Displays presentation starting with the first slide
From Current Slide	Shift + F5	Displays presentation starting with the current slide
Review Tab		
Proofing Group		
ABC Spelling	F7	Spell-checks presentation
View Tab		
Presentation Views Group		
Normal		Switches to Normal view
Slide Sorter		Switches to Slide Sorter view
Notes Page		Displays current slide in Notes view to edit the speaker notes
Outline View		Switches Slides pane to Outline pane
Master Views Group		
Slide Master		Opens Slide Master view to change the design and layout of the master slides
Picture Tools Format Tab		
Adjust Group		
Color		Modifies the color of the picture
Picture Styles Group		
More		Opens the Picture Styles gallery to select an overall visual style for picture

POWERPOINT 2013 COMMAND SUMMARY

COMMAND	SHORTCUT	ACTION
Picture Border		Applies a border style to picture
Picture Effects		Applies a visual effect to picture
Picture Layout		Changes layout of a drawing
Arrange Group Align Objects		Opens a gallery of alignment options
Size Group Crop		Removes unwanted section of a picture
Drawing Tools Format Tab		
Shapes Styles Group More		Opens the Shape Styles gallery to select a visual style to apply to a shape
Shape Effects		Applies a visual effect to a shape
Arrange Group		Rotates or flips the selected object
Table Tools Design Tab		
Table Styles Group More		Opens gallery of table designs
Shading		Colors background behind selected text or paragraph
Border		Applies a border style
Effects		Applies a visual effect to the table, such as shadows and reflections
Table Tools Layout Tab		
Alignment Group Center		Centers the text within a cell
Center Vertically		Centers the text vertically within a cell
Arrange Group Align		Opens a gallery of alignment options

Introduction to Microsoft Office Glossary

b

Backstage: Contains commands that allow you to work with your document, unlike the Ribbon that allows you to work in your document; contains commands that apply to the entire document.

Buttons: Graphical elements that perform the associated action when you click on them using the mouse.

c

Character effects: Enhancements such as bold, italic, and color that are applied to a selected text.

Clipboard: Where a selection is stored when it is cut or copied.

Cloud: Any application or service hosted and run on servers connected to the Internet.

Commands: Options that carry out a selected action.

Context menu: Also called a shortcut menu; opened by right-clicking on an item on the screen.

Contextual tabs: Also called on-demand tabs; tabs that are displayed only as needed. For example, when you are working with a picture, the Picture Tools tab appears.

Cursor: The blinking vertical bar that marks your location in the document and indicates where text you type will appear; also called the insertion point.

d

Database: A collection of related data.

Default: The standard options used by Office 2013.

Destination: The new location into which a selection that is moved from its original location is inserted.

Dialog box launcher: A button that is displayed in the lower-right corner of a tab group if more commands are available; clicking opens a dialog box or task pane of additional options.

Document window: The large center area of the program window where open application files are displayed.

e

Edit: To revise a document by changing the parts that need to be modified.

Enhanced ScreenTip: Displayed by pointing to a button in the Ribbon; shows the name of the button and the keyboard shortcut.

f

Field: The smallest unit of information about a record; a column in a table.

Font: Type style; also called typeface.

Font size: Size of typeface, given in points.

Format: The appearance of a document.

g

Groups: Part of a tab that contains related items.

h

Hyperlink: Connection to information located in a separate location, such as on a website.

i

Insertion point: Also called the cursor; the blinking vertical bar that marks your location in a document and indicates where text you type will appear.

k

Keyboard shortcut: A combination of keys that can be used to execute a command in place of clicking a button.

Keyword: A descriptive word that is associated with the file and can be used to locate a file using a search.

l

Live Preview: A feature that shows you how selected text in a document will appear if a formatting option is chosen.

m

Metadata: Details about the document that describe or identify it, such as title, author name, subject, and keywords; also called document properties.

Mini toolbar: Appears automatically when you select text; displays command buttons for often-used commands from the Font and Paragraph groups that are used to format a document.

o

Office Clipboard: Can store up to 24 items that have been cut or copied.

On-demand tabs: Also called contextual tabs; tabs that are displayed only as needed.

p

Paste Preview: Shows how a Paste Option will affect a selection.

Properties: Shown in a panel along the right side of the Info tab, divided into four groups; information such as author, keywords, document size, number of words, and number of pages.

q

Quick Access Toolbar: Located to the right of the Window button; provides quick access to frequently used commands such as Save, Undo, and Redo.

r

Records: The information about one person, thing, or place; contained in a row of a table.

Ribbon: Below the title bar; provides a centralized location of commands that are used to work in your document.

s

ScreenTip: Also called a tooltip; appears with the command name and the keyboard shortcut.

Scroll bar: Horizontal or vertical, it is used with a mouse to bring additional information into view in a window.

Selection cursor: Cursor that allows you to select an object.

Shortcut menu: A context-sensitive menu, meaning it displays only those commands relevant to the item or screen location; also called a context menu, it is opened by right-clicking on an item on the screen.

Slide: An individual page of a presentation.

Slide shows: Onscreen electronic presentations.

Source: The original location of a selection that is inserted in a new location.

Status bar: At the bottom of the application window; displays information about the open file and features that help you view the file.

t

Table: A database object consisting of columns and rows.

Tabs: Used to divide the Ribbon into major activity areas.

Tag: A descriptive word that is associated with the file and can be used to locate a file using a search; also called a keyword.

Task pane: A list of additional options opened by clicking the dialog box launcher; also called a dialog box.

Template: A professionally designed document that is used as the basis for a new document.

Text effects: Enhancements such as bold, italic, and color that are applied to selected text.

Tooltip: Also called a ScreenTip; appears displaying a command name and the keyboard shortcut.

Typeface: A set of characters with a specific design; also commonly referred to as a font.

u

User interface: A set of graphical elements that are designed to help you interact with the program and provide instructions for the actions you want to perform.

v

View buttons: Used to change how the information in the document window is displayed.

w

Worksheet: An electronic spreadsheet, or worksheet, that is used to organize, manipulate, and graph numeric data.

z

Zoom slider: Located at the far right end of the status bar; used to change the amount of information displayed in the document window by "zooming in" to get a close-up view or "zooming out" to see more of the document at a reduced view.

PowerPoint Glossary of Key Terms

a

Alignment: Controls the position of text entries within a space.

Animation: Special effects that add action to text and graphics so they move around on the screen during a slide show.

AutoCorrect: A feature that makes some basic assumptions about the text you are typing and, based on those assumptions, automatically corrects the entry.

b

Background styles: A set of theme colors and textures that you can apply to the background of your slides.

c

Cell: The intersection of a row and a column in a table.

Character formatting: Applies changes such as color and size to the selected characters only.

Clip art: Simple drawings; available in the Clip Organizer, a Microsoft Office tool that arranges and catalogs clip art and other media files stored on the computer's hard disk.

Color matching: Uses the eyedropper tool to copy a color from an object in the slide and apply it to a selected shape or object.

Cropping: Trimming or removing part of a graphic.

Current slide: The slide that will be affected by any changes you make.

Custom dictionary: The dictionary you can create to hold words you commonly use, such as proper names and technical terms, that are not included in the spelling checker's main dictionary.

d

Destination file: The file into which an object is embedded.

Document theme: A predefined set of formatting choices that can be applied to an entire document in one simple step.

Drawing layer: A separate layer from the placeholder.

Drawing object: A graphic consisting of shapes such as lines and boxes.

e

Embed: The process of inserting an object that was created in another program in a slide. An embedded object becomes part of the presentation file and can be opened and edited using the program in which it was created.

Eyedropper tool: Used to match a color on the slide and apply it to another shape or object.

f

Find and Replace: A feature used to find text in a presentation and replace it with other text.

Floating object: How graphics are inserted in a document.

g

Gradient: A gradual progression of colors and shades.

Graphic: A nontext element or object, such as a drawing or picture, that can be added to a slide.

k

Keyword: Descriptive words or phrases associated with a graphic or figure that give information about the properties of the object.

l

Layout: Defines the position and format for objects and text that will be added to a slide. A layout contains placeholders for the different items such as bulleted text, titles, charts, and so on.

Linked object: A way to insert information created in one application into a document created by another application. With a linked object, the actual data is stored in the source file.

Live link: Connection that allows changes made in the source file that affect the linked object to be automatically reflected in the destination file when it is opened.

m

Main dictionary: The dictionary that is supplied with the spelling checker program.

Master: A special slide or page that stores information about the formatting for all slides or pages in a presentation.

Metadata: Additional data saved by PowerPoint as part of the presentation, may include author's name and other personal information.

n

Notes pages: Pages that display notes below a small version of the slide they accompany.

Notes pane: View that includes space for you to enter notes that apply to the current slide.

o

Object: A drawing, picture or shape that can be added to a slide.

Object animations: Used to display each bullet point, text, paragraph, or graphic independently of the other text or objects on the slide.

Outline pane: Displays the text content of each slide in outline format.

p

Paragraph formatting: Formatting features that affect an entire paragraph.

Picture: An image such as a graphic illustration or a scanned photograph, created in another program.

Picture style: Effects added to a picture, such as borders and shadows.

Placeholder: Boxes with dotted borders that are used to contain content such as text, graphics and other objects.

Placeholder text: Messages inside placeholders that prompt you to enter text.

Presenter view: View that shows the full-screen slide show on one monitor for the audience and a "speaker view" on another monitor. Will show all information on one screen using a single monitor.

r

Rotate handle: Allows you to rotate the selected object to any degree in any direction.

s

Sans serif font: A font without a flair at the base of each letter, such as Arial or Helvetica.

Serif font: A font that has a flair at the base of each letter, such as Roman or Times New Roman.

Shape styles: Combinations of fill colors, outline colors, and effects used to enhance the appearance of a shape.

Sizing handles: The four circles and squares that appear at the corners and sides of a selected placeholder's border.

Slide: An individual "page" of your presentation.

Slide indicator: Identifies the number of the slide that is displayed in the workspace, along with the total number of slides in the presentation.

Slide show: Displays each slide full screen and in order.

Slide show control bar: Bar that displays icons for navigating, zooming and showing and hiding slides as well as tools to add freehand annotations during a presentation.

Slides pane: Displays a miniature version, or thumbnail, of each slide.

Slide window: Workspace area that displays the selected slide.

Source file: The original file used to create an embedded object.

Source program: The program in which an object was created.

Spelling checker: Locates all misspelled words, duplicate words, and capitalization irregularities as you create and edit a presentation, and proposes possible corrections.

Standard size: Slide size (4:3) designed to be displayed on traditional-size screens.

Style: A combination of formatting options that can be applied in one easy step.

t

Table: Used to organize information into an easy-to-read format of horizontal rows and vertical columns.

Table reference: A letter and number used to identify cells in a table. Columns are identified from left to right beginning with the letter A, and rows are numbered from top to bottom beginning with the number 1.

Table styles: Combinations of shading colors, borders, and visual effects such as shadows and reflections that can be applied to a table.

Template: A file containing predefined settings that can be used as a pattern to create many common types of presentations.

Text box: A container for text or graphics.

Text effects: Enhancements to the text such as color and shadow.

Theme: A predefined set of formatting choices that can be applied to an entire document.

Thumbnail: A miniature version of a slide, picture, or object.

Transition: Controls the way that the display changes as you move from one slide to the next during a presentation.

v

View: A way of looking at a presentation that provides the means to interact with the presentation.

w

Widescreen: Default slide size (16:9) intended to take advantage of new HD features and equipment.

Index

a

b

c

d

n

o

p

q

r

s

t

u

v

Credits

PP1.2 Blend Images/PunchStock

PP2.2 Thinkstock/PunchStock